Rodzinski, Halina
Our two lives

DATE DUE			
DEC 14 1979			
MAY 16 1980			

Our Two Lives

OUR TWO LIVES

Halina Rodzinski

CHARLES SCRIBNER'S SONS / NEW YORK

Library of Congress Cataloging in Publication Data

Rodzinski, Halina.
  Our two lives.

  Includes index.
  1. Rodzinski, Halina.   2. Rodzinski, Artur, 1894–
1958.   3. Musicians — Correspondence, reminiscences, etc.
I. Title.
ML422.R7R6   785'.092'4 [B]   75-37519
ISBN 0-684-14511-1

For Riki

Foreword

My husband was the orchestral conductor Artur Rodzinski.

For those who grew to musical maturity with the concert life of the United States in the 1930s and 1940s his name may still have an aura. For those who are younger, who have come to know musical personalities since Artur's death in November 1958, my husband is a dry reference in a musical encyclopedia or a name on a record cover in the cut-rate rack of a discount store.

But, then, it has ever been so with re-creative artists. Theirs is an ephemeral gesture, one that flourishes only to pass within its own moment. And even though we live in an era when almost everything is electronically documented or acoustically reproduced, the pressures of a constantly refined technology and the marketplace guarantee the traditional transience of the performer and his accomplishments. Ultimately, his memory is preserved not through sound but through the less universal, and most inappropriate, realm of language: the story of the life and times that compelled him to make music.

Few realize that how a woman performs as an artist's wife is an art, one unfortunately not taught at any university, academy, or conservatory. There is so much to know and to do, things for which one's entire life is a preparation and a continuous schooling.

On the surface, being the wife of a conductor appears glamorous: there are season openings to be attended in elegant gowns and viewed from the prestigious director's box; gala receptions; hobnobbing with The Great Ones (both actual and would-be); trips to the farthest reaches of the globe; large, numerous, and frequently-changed households to operate; correspondence to sustain (with and without secretaries); teas; intimate dinners for ten. But in short order this glamorous life develops a tedium of its own. There is so much of *it*, and so little time for one's own self. And paramount is the constant demand that one be a happy and loving wife when the husband one loves is himself capable of the most monstrous behavior because the pressures of this way of living are also depleting him, even killing him.

A woman learns to be either skillfully adept at this life or a compliant nonentity — sometimes she is both. In any case, the mortality rate of marriages to performing artists is understandably high.

The life has certain similarities to that of a drug addict. Somehow, once absorbed by its rigors and demands, it is quite difficult, if not impossible, to extricate oneself — especially when the person becomes tolerant of bigger and headier doses. Only the death of the partner can end the addiction definitively. And then begins the long painful withdrawal for the survivor.

When Artur died, I was utterly lost. For twenty-five years I had been at his side as he made music with the finest orchestras and soloists of this century. With his death, my life seemed to halt. There was not much purpose or focus to my being except for raising our son Richard. Everything else I had previously sensed or thought seemed to relate to Artur as shadow does to object. Whatever personhood I had I felt had derived from or was bound to his that was no more.

Eventually, after two years (and with no small surprise), I found that I was living an active and satisfying — even fulfilling — life of my own, independent of my husband, yet built on what our life together had been. Nothing had ended with his death. Rather, it was a new beginning, one of several I have known in my life. It was an experience to be assessed and developed — transcended, if you will.

In 1965 a group of friends in Cleveland who still cherished memories of Artur's artistry and of the ten years he had directed that city's orchestra asked me to share with them my recollections of those days. The little talk I prepared then set me on the course of personal exploration which has resulted in this book.

Initially, it had been my intention to write only of Rodzinski, but I lack both the patience of scholarship and the objectivity to be a biographer. The absence of these qualities was apparent to my family and to the few friends who read my first manuscripts. I had produced something like a film scenario about a bigger-than-plausible, terribly volcanic musical hero. While there was a heroine, her best scenes ended up on the cutting-room floor and as a person she was overwhelmed by an enormous mass of press notices. Not only was I almost entirely missing, but so was any rationale for my having entered into the kind of life I led with Artur. Why had I? Gradually, I came to believe that our marriage had been built upon an inexplicable and yet inevitable logic which contributed to our life's peculiar unity and sense of fulfillment, a logic rooted as much in my past as his.

I have reached a stage in life that others may envy: I have no future that must be protected by judicious concealment of my past. Put another way, I can freely speak my mind, a luxury this world affords only to the old. There are some tart opinions here about the mindless loss of much that was good from other days — good, not because it is part of a now-irretrievable past, but because there was once actually a system of ethical values most persons agreed with and adhered to.

H.R.

Acknowledgments

OVER the years I have worked on this book I have incurred many debts which I can repay only with the non-negotiable coin of my sincerest gratitude.

I am especially obliged to the numerous friends and members of my family in the United States and in Europe who were most generous with assistance and encouragement. Among these friends I count the players in the orchestras conducted by my husband, Artur Rodzinski, in many parts of the world. I must particularly name William Lincer, Carleton Cooley, Phil Kahgan, and Saul Goodman, for these men took time to write their reminiscences and estimates of Artur.

I owe a special debt to Mrs. James Lamy, a friend and neighbor in Lake Placid, who helped me to collect the material and worked with me for two years in preparing one of several drafts of this book.

Finally, though, my utmost gratitude goes to Peter Chrisafides, a brilliant writer and musician, who, after literally living many months with my husband's notes, correspondence, books, scores, and recordings, as well as my many chaotic drafts, finally made this book come to be. He deserves much credit for his hard work and genuine — indeed, loving — interest in and commitment and contributions to this, my story alone.

Spin love, spin love out of your heart
As from the worm the silk is wound,
As from the spring the waters start,
As flows the river underground,
Unroll love like those glittering sheets,
Papyrus-thin, and bright with glamor,
Which patiently the goldsmith beats
Out of an ingot with a hammer,
And blow love as the zephyr blows,
Upward and outward, far and wide. . . .

—— Adam Mickiewicz, from *The Lausanne Lyrics*,
translated by Kimball Flaccus *

* *Adam Mickiewicz: Selected Poems*, edited by Clark Mills, The Noonday Press, New York, 1956.

Our Two Lives

⮞ *PROLOGUE* ⮜

It all began again for me, my life, on what seemed then the most thankless of Thanksgiving Days, November 27, 1958.

At 4:00 P.M., an hour when most Boston families were seated at dinner enumerating their blessings, my husband, Artur Rodzinski, died of heart failure in Massachusetts General Hospital. It was, in a sense, fitting that his life ended on that day, for death must have been a thankful thing to him after years of heart attacks, heart failure, and the crushing pain of angina pectoris. He may even have welcomed the fingers that extricated his spirit from his body, because for years he had been literally working toward this end: with every concert he conducted, every climax he extorted from an orchestra, his heart wrung from the body that contained it its due in physical agony. The compensation of high fees, of applause and adulation, of accomplishing ever greater expressive heights had for a decade now come at a cost no human being could bear for long.

Yet it was not only Artur's heart that had pained him to the point of welcoming death. His inner tumult, not just the beleaguering doubts and dissatisfactions endemic to all artists, but that resulting from his quest for some spiritual focus, some almost tangible God, had exhausted his soul. The heart is complex both as an organ and as a concept — so its numerous entries in a dictionary testify. Suspended somewhere between the body and the mind is a heart that pumps the life blood of the spirit. This, too, can become sick and worn, as Artur's was.

The gods make mad those they wish to destroy. By pursuing artistic goals others thought impossible, Artur courted his own destruction by the gods and then used the madness they visited on him to achieve his own expressive ends. During the last years of his life, every spiritual torment that he suffered became, by some perverse alchemy, an even more incandescent moment on a concert platform or on an opera stage. The last *Tristan und Isolde* he conducted in Chicago, almost three weeks before his death, was the crucible in which he transmuted whatever dross his soul still contained into an evanescent gold that those who heard the performance will never forget. Only later came the realization that, in the process, he had burned himself out.

His will might have appeared indomitable to many, but in truth it was cruelly dominated by his willfulness and the guilt and remorse he

(3)

generated by his actions. He never forgave himself for the scandal he caused, whether justified or not, in resigning from the New York Philharmonic at the peak of his career a little more than a decade before his death. It was as though that flamboyant, even magnificent gesture, which had opened America's eyes to the corrupt practices of orchestral and artistic managements, a corruption less evident today thanks to his exposure of it, was a grain of sand that had passed into the shell of his soul. Although it yielded artistic pearls throughout his final decade, it tormented him nonetheless. The resignation was, because it had not succeeded as he had hoped, "a mistake" which affected the rest of his life.

Such thoughts jostled in my mind as I rode in a rented limousine, trailing the hearse that carried my husband's body from Boston to our home in Lake Placid, New York. With me was our only child, Richard (Riki), a son of our late years. He was thirteen. My youngest sister Marysia had been the same age when our mother died. Marysia also was in the car beside me, as were both her son, Karol Unilowski, a young man of twenty-two, and Artur's son by a previous marriage, Witold Rodzinski, then just forty, and a member of the United Nations delegation from People's Poland.

The day had started out crisp and clear, one of those New England autumn days that intoxicate by the cold brilliance of their air. Artur loved such days when we had a home in Stockbridge, Massachusetts, among the low, rolling hills of the Berkshires, and since that place was on our route, we stopped there to reminisce and to show Riki this home of which he had heard so much, a place where musicians and poets used to play at goat farming, and two queens-to-be once paid a call. Then, we rode on into New York State and through the Adirondacks. The sky took on an aluminum cast, and the soft fleece of the first snow began to fall, indolently, gently, consolingly. I thought that the carpet of snow spreading over the road that stretched before us was laid to muffle our progress, to surround Artur in the hearse ahead with a white silence to protect him from the irrelevant noise of traffic.

In the upholstered quiet of the limousine, a quiet faintly redolent of the vehicle's purpose, we talked in the dry, hushed, practical tones people employ when trying to be realistic in the face of glaringly unreal things. All five of us were hard put to it to understand anything real about the trip, that actually we were trailing a hearse. We spoke only of practical matters, fashioning a strange conversational mosaic of things to be done, people to be concerned about, financial arrangements to be made, lawyers and investment brokers to be seen. As if by mutual consent, we said nothing that might suddenly tap our immense reservoir of grief lest the dam give way and sweep us into the irrational void that had somehow got hold of Artur.

From where I sat I watched the back of Riki's head. I knew how greatly he felt the loss of his father, a father who, to him, was anything but the stern and overpowering person most people deferred to, even to the point of servility. Artur was Richard's confidant, his willing accomplice in any number of conspiracies. The two adored each other. They could sit for hours discussing worlds beyond our galaxy, or the worlds they jointly viewed through Riki's precision microscope.

Driving along, hearing the hiss of the big car's tires through the soft, wet snow, trying hard to keep a grip on those shreds of composure I needed to get through the remainder of the day, I found myself repeating Isolde's words from the *Liebestod*, *"Nur eine Stunde"* ("Only one hour"). The same words had echoed constantly in my mind while I was alone with Artur's body in that Boston hospital room.

As we approached Lake Placid, the snowfall turned heavy. Old Military Road, the road to our house, the long driveway barely protected by a windbreak of spruce and pine Artur had planted, all had been specially plowed by the township. The house itself stands at the crest of what had been called Chubb Hill before Artur and I had renamed it Riki Hill.

We settled into the house which Mrs. Eva Smith, an old friend and neighbor, had readied for us. Her son-in-law, Raymond Lincoln, without whom neither Artur nor I could ever have kept up the sprawling oiled-clapboard house and its hundred or so acres of meadow and woodlands, had dug a path across the front lawn from the driveway to the door of Artur's studio bedroom. It was through that waist-deep trench of pristine white that Artur's body would be carried the next day for a small service. When I saw Ray, my sense of loss became still greater. We embraced.

"Well," Ray began, his voice husky, "I guess we ought to be able to get Mr. Rodzinski into his room now all right."

Ray and Lera, his pretty wife, had been stunned when I called from Boston to tell them of Artur's death. The Lincolns did not know him as a celebrated musician, except by hearsay. Their Rodzinski was a man with occasionally "harebrained" ideas for planting the grounds, an unaffected man who liked to dig holes in the earth and set in saplings — the elm and the white lilac in front of my bedroom, the windbreak of evergreens along the driveway — a man with a joke and a smile for them on the dreariest of days, but someone not to be disturbed while he was sitting at his piano studying a score.

The next day we placed the casket, open, in the studio before the granite fireplace. Artur had designed its mantel in the manner of Polish crèches and roadside shrines. In the center stood a hand-carved statue of Christ the Shepherd, its blond fruitwood contrasting brightly with the weathered, gray barnsiding of the shelf. The statue, like so much about Riki Hill, reminded us of the days we spent in Zakopane, in the Tatra Mountains of Poland, where native artisans do such work.

The undertaker had dressed Artur in his best set of conducting tails, and he looked, to me, as though he might be gathering his thoughts before walking from the wings of a concert hall stage to the podium. I remembered that when I first knew Artur to be the man with whom I would share my life, he was also lying on his back, in a hospital in Krakow. It was as if the beginning had been the end, as if no time had elapsed.

His face was beautiful in death, delicate, with a look of serene satisfaction such as I had seldom seen in life. With Riki's help I placed in his lapel the red-and-white rosette of the Order of Polonia Restituta, once our native country's highest non-military decoration. In his clasped hands we put a black rosary (a gift from a Florentine friend of ours, Sister Ignacia) and a baton. His hands were so fine, so fragile. It seemed unreasonable that they could ever have drawn the massive sonorities from the air that they did when he conducted. It seemed even more unreasonable to Riki and to me that they would never do so again.

We also placed in his left inside pocket a photograph of Pius XII, the last of my husband's many spiritual mentors. These two men, dissimilar in most ways, were both made of the same stern material, and Artur, toward the end, had drawn a measure of strength from his contact with the Pontiff.

The lower part of the casket was covered with a blanket of red and white carnations, the colors of the Polish flag. On the floor were bouquets and wreaths from friends and musical organizations.

That afternoon, my sister Fela (Felicia) and her husband Kazik (Casimir) Krance, and another sister, Aniela Mieczyslawska, arrived. Many of our Lake Placid friends and neighbors came to join us for the prayer service and recitation of the rosary led by our parish priest at the time, Father Albert Salmon. Afterward, I spoke with Father Salmon to suggest a few things concerning the funeral mass the following morning, and it was decided that Kazik would play the organ.

The simple arrangements were my choice. My sister Aniela had urged that the funeral take place in New York City, with a solemn high requiem mass in St. Patrick's Cathedral and prominent musicians participating. Certainly, this could have been done easily. A few hours after news of Artur's death became public I began to be flooded with calls from performing artists who wanted to do something, anything. Leopold Stokowski, who had brought Artur to America to serve as his assistant, kindly put himself at my disposal. And Leonard Bernstein, who had been Artur's assistant when my husband was director of the New York Philharmonic, made a similar offer. As it developed, Lenny dedicated his next Philharmonic concert to Rodzinski's memory, and that same week our friend Bishop Fulton J. Sheen, then still Monsignor, celebrated a special mass in a chapel in St. Patrick's. That was all. And I knew it was all Artur would have wanted.

When the prayer service was over and the visitors left, our grief became a family affair. After dinner the others retired, leaving Riki and me with Artur. I could see how the boy suffered as we stood together. Finally, exhausted, he also went to bed, but I chose to remain at my husband's side where I had been throughout those last nine days of his illness.

Through that afternoon and evening in the studio we had listened to Artur's most recent recordings. Siegfried's Rhine Journey and Funeral March and the Prelude and Love-Death from *Tristan und Isolde* played again and again, music which I associated with Artur in life and which was a part of him as an artist in death.

When I felt certain that the others were asleep, that the music would not disturb them, I put on Artur's last recording, Richard Strauss's *Death and Transfiguration.* Then I knelt on a *prie-dieu* by the still-open casket, trying hard to pray, but my mind kept wandering. Artur's performance of Strauss's tone poem unfolded as if it were his autobiography. There is a restatement of the Transfiguration theme at the end which is said to describe the spirit's release from its earthly limits and its entry into heaven. It is a moment of music I had always found haunting in concert; but then, alone in the room with Artur, it was crushing. I found myself speaking to him. After all those years together there was no one else to whom I could turn or speak. Of what I said to him in that bizarre conversation — I use the word because I half expected a reply — I remember only one thing exactly, a Polish aphorism which summed up our life: *raz radosc, drugi raz smutek z tego dwojga zywot nasz upleciony* (one day joy, the next day sorrow, and of these two our life is braided). And I thanked him for all of it.

I also thanked Artur for our son, some part of his flesh to remain by me in what I could only imagine to be interminable years of loneliness ahead. It was a miracle that Richard had been born — my husband had not wanted children.

Then I lay down on Artur's couch close to his coffin and let my mind drift where it would, hopefully to sleep. But sleep did not come to me, instead my mind filled with fragments of the inconsequential stuff of which most of life is made, experiences I had known from girlhood that had been enriched or intensified in the years of my marriage. Again I experienced the expectant waiting for an opera house curtain to rise, the breathlessness that accompanies the hush when an orchestra's tuning ceases and a moment suspends itself until the conductor makes his way to the podium.

Artur and I had lived together for twenty-five years as one being shared by two, ego and alter ego being interchangeable. There had never been the possibility that it might have been otherwise. His simplest needs became my greatest wants, and even though there had been furious contests between us, trials of wills, these invariably were resolved with the victory being love's.

Artur was an intensely passionate man in everything he did, and everything he touched he possessed, even inhabited physically. Whatever he took hold of he invested with his love, a sweater worn and mended until almost a new garment; a score carved and molded by his red and

(7)

blue pencil markings into something even as beautiful as the composer's original notation; a dog-eared copy of Ouspensky or one of Schopenhauer's *Die Welt als Wille und Vorstellung* in which he had penned some lines from Goethe's *Faust;* the last sad color slides he made of autumn scenes around the house in Lake Placid, minute studies of a reed with a tearlike drop of rain glistening at its tip, or a lichen-encrusted rock formation.

"You have been pensioned off," Witold Gombrowicz, the novelist, later wrote to me. Retired, perhaps, from a life as the wife of a conductor and an amazing human being — but where was I as a human being myself? Unless kindly death would take me, too, my life would continue like an ornamental bottle long after its wine had been poured, a bottle that held only the air of regrets for the unfinished things of our lives, the unsaid apologies, the misunderstandings, all the things that a kiss and an embrace alone could wipe away.

Once before I had had similar feelings. Some thirty-three years earlier, I felt this deep sense of loss as I tried to live without my mother. While she had been as close to me as Artur, I discovered then that nothing in life really ends, that there are only beginnings anew, and that to those of faith, even death is one of these. Somehow, so long ago, I had found my way to start again, strengthened by my loss, supported by the reworkings of my previous life. I would have to find my way again, perhaps a more difficult one this time — there were many years of having surrendered my own will to our one life together to surmount or undo.

Chapter 1

I WAS born in Warsaw, Poland, on November 18, 1904. While nominally a subject of Tsar Nicholas II, I was as Polish at my birth as a Pole could be.

I was the second child born to Halina Wieniawska and Franciszek Lilpop, and had been something of a trial for my mother to bear. Concern that she might miscarry obliged her to pass most of her pregnancy flat on her back. This was not the case when she carried Antoni (Antek), a brother four years my senior, nor Andrzej (Jedrek), my brother two years junior, nor my three younger sisters, Felicja (Fela), Aniela, and Maria (Marysia), all of whom were born at two-year intervals thereafter until mother, father, and nature would have no more.

My delivery was unusual in two portentous respects: I emerged into the world with a caul, that cap of skin which folk widsom tells is a sign of an optimistic and cheerful disposition; and I stubbornly resisted taking my first breath until dunked in a pail of ice water. Cheerfulness and stubbornness, indeed, were to become dominant personality characteristics of mine.

My mother's family were those same Wieniawskis whose names are important in the history of nineteenth-century Polish music and letters. Mother's uncles, Henryk, the legendary violinist-composer, and Jozef, a pianist and composer of note, were younger brothers of my grandfather Juljan Wieniawski, who was once a very popular author of genteel comedies, novels, and memoirs. Grandfather was a romantic and highly-charged figure in my formative years, for in his youth he had been a leader in the ill-starred Polish Insurrection of 1863, one of the fortunate few to escape with his life. Through the talents of my granduncles Henryk and Jozef, grandfather was able to return to Warsaw from Parisian exile.

Henryk (or Henri, as he is often listed in musical reference books) and Jozef gave a recital for Tsar Alexander II. The autocrat was so pleased with their music-making he ordered one of the Grand Dukes to grant the brothers a favor. They asked permission for grandfather to return home, and this was granted. Once back in Poland, Juljan settled down to become a leading economist and successful agronomist, to marry a second time (he had been widowed), and to christen the daughter of this marriage Halina, after his new wife.

(9)

My mother's mother was the daughter of a popular Polish operatic figure, the basso profundo Wilhelm Troszel, who, among the numerous roles he created, sang the part of Stolnik in the Polish national opera, *Halka*, by Moniuszko. Since the premiere of that work almost coincided with the birth of my maternal grandmother, she was named Halina, of which "Halka" is an affectionate diminutive. Thus I am the third in direct succession to bear this Polish equivalent of Brünnhilde.

My father's family, the Lilpops, came to Poland from Austria in the eighteenth century to ply the crafts of silversmithing and watchmaking under the protection of the Polish Court. The family concern prospered, and Lilpops continued to operate the firm until World War II when most of the Lilpops were killed by the Nazis.

My branch of the family had turned to other things. Grandfather Lilpop was an architect as was my father. Indeed, the first home I can remember in Warsaw, an apartment building at No. 1 Zgoda Street, was designed by Grandfather Lilpop. Nearby was the Brothers Jablkowscy Department Store, the first modern emporium of its kind in Poland; it would be one of the few large structures to withstand the German bombing and fire-gutting of the Polish capital. *My* father designed that building.

As our family grew, Papa designed and built a new housing complex, with a much larger apartment for the Lilpops, at No. 10 Aleja Roz (Rose Street), a street some distance from what was then Downtown Warsaw. The neighborhood was suburban in feel and appearance, but still within the city's limits. Grandfather Lilpop at first did not like the idea. "You are too far out of the center of things, Franciszek," he gloomily warned, "No one will ever come to your office." Father was adamant, and he proved right. The apartment houses he built were never wanting for interesting tenants, and his architectural practice thrived. Number 10 Aleja Roz remained my family's home until well after I left Poland for good in 1934. I should add that those houses also withstood the Nazi occupation, perhaps because they served as housing for their forces. Today, still looking much the same, they are desirable residences for members of the People's Poland governing elite.

In our household life went along with clockwork regularity, perhaps a Lilpop legacy. Father was the source of authority to whom all members of the family deferred. But though I loved him very much, there was something austere and uncommunicative about him, especially when with his children. I worshiped Mama. She was, in the twenty years I knew her, my model in everything. If I have one continuing regret in a life that has been remarkably free of regrets, it is that I am not more like her.

Mama managed a large staff of nurses and governesses, maids, a cook, and various part-time help. Under her direction the Lilpop ménage ran according to a timetable that was very much to my father's liking. Meals were served at prescribed hours, and were guaranteed to include some delicacy which might please my fussy father who fancied himself a gourmet. The children were kept as far away from Papa as necessary, except for such preordained times as meals, or lining up for a goodnight kiss (no great pleasure because father had a scratchy goatee).

The first decade of my life was a golden age for me, untroubled, unhurried, and filled with love. Truthfully, there were some unpleasant moments when I earned the displeasure of my parents, and the normal run of difficulties with my brothers and sisters. My younger brother, Jedrek, I considered the bane of my young life. But as often as he tormented me, he in turn served as my victim. I used to take cruel advantage of his being a stammerer. I got on well with my older brother who, thanks to his extraordinary good looks, was the spoiled darling of our family. Toward my younger sisters I could be insufferably bossy, but time and our genuine closeness worked matters out so that we never bore each other any resentment.

My early schooling, like Antek's before me, was conducted at home, actually in a penthouse structure atop my family's Aleja Roz apartment. It was a cooperative arrangement among my parents and some friends. Their children joined us in the classroom to learn to read and write and figure sums, all preparatory to entering a private school when we were old enough. There was another reason for this at home instruction, too: we could learn our native language. In those days Tsarist rule over Poland was oppressive (there had been uprisings in the very year of my birth). A particularly harsh decree forbade the teaching of Polish in the schools. All texts were in Russian, a tongue detested by Poles because it belonged to our oppressors. Every Polish schoolchild had no choice but to learn some Russian. While I resented it then, the language proved helpful to me in later years, especially in communicating with Russian-speaking musical artists.

My Aleja Roz penthouse school's curriculum was suddenly revised by the events of the summer of 1914, at least as far as the need to know Russian was concerned. The Germans changed that by capturing Warsaw. Eventually they departed, but the Russians never returned.

When the Great War began, our family was vacationing at Kolacin, an estate belonging to my father's younger brother, Edward Lilpop. It was a magnificent place, with a large manor house designed by Grandfather Lilpop and thousands of acres under cultivation. Uncle Edward ran the farm with another brother, Uncle Boguslaw, who was a botanist. We summered there almost every year until Mother's death. Some of my loveliest memories are associated with the fields of poppies (raised for their seed), the farm animals, the flower beds (laid out by Uncle Boguslaw), and the harvest festivities which marked the end of our vacations. August 1914 was different. Papa made the three-hour trip from Warsaw, not for one of his usual fortnightly visits but to bundle us home before the German Army arrived. Indeed, we escaped with no time to spare. Kolacin soon became a battlefield.

My tenth year and the German occupation of Warsaw coincided. Neither fact disturbed the course of life in the Lilpop household. Well, not much. Good things came to our dinner table less frequently; and awful ones, like turnips, became commonplace. Food was scarce as was everything else, but Mother saw to it that her family fared as well as circumstances would allow. Her ingenuity must have been extraordinary.

About this time I realized my mother was deeply commited to the well-being of the less fortunate. An assembly hall near our house had been set up as an emergency shelter for some of the thousands upon thousands of refugees fleeing the Germans. They came there dressed in rags, their feet wrapped in felt or newspaper, and starving. Some of the children who died at the shelter were found to have sawdust in their stomachs.

Mother joined together with some of our aristocratic neighbors — many noble Polish families had villas and palaces near where we lived — to fund and operate a soup kitchen. Each household in turn undertook to provide and cook what food they could. That she still had her large copper kettles in which our cook could prepare huge quantities of soup also says something about Mother's resourcefulness. At one point in the occupation the Germans commandeered all metals that could be used in the production of munitions. The Lilpop household was stripped of its decorative brass and bronze doorknobs, drawerpulls, and hinges. But most of Mother's splendid copper cookingware survived, hidden in the basement beneath a heap of coal.

The war's privations really touched me very little, except where girls entering adolescence are likely to be sensitive: clothes. My wardrobe was a mess. All I had were made-over things or garments so darned and mended that the originals were barely recognizable. But in the autumn of 1918 I did get my first all-new dress in years, really a uniform, that of the Kowalczykowna-Jawurkowna School which I was to attend for five years, until 1923.

I felt uncomfortable in the disciplined hush of Kowalczykowna's corridors that first day. In this school, I had been told, silence was considered golden, and the classrooms and corridors were its bank vaults.

Among the few places where silence was not demanded were our cloakrooms. There we each were assigned a hook on the wall. We would hang up our outerwear, then sit on long wooden benches to take off our galoshes and high-button shoes and put on soft felt slippers. The slippers muffled the sounds of our feet to a dull, cottony whispering, also prevented scuff marks on the highly-waxed parquet floors, and had the added usefulness of keeping those floors buffed to a velvety sheen.

Deportment ranked high among the school's educational priorities, as well it might. Poles, perhaps more than many Europeans, and certainly most Americans, place a high value on social niceties. Even in the egalitarian society of People's Poland, a well-behaved man bows when he is introduced to a woman and kisses her hand. When I was young, a girl responded with a curtsy, though today a nod of the head will do. At our school, whenever we encountered a teacher or one of the two Headmistresses we made a curtsy. If a Headmistress extended a hand in greeting, we were expected to take it gently into ours, brush it lightly with our lips, and say "Good morning, Miss," never addressing them by last names.

Since the two ladies who oversaw our education bore the same baptismal name, the school was known among the students as The School of the Two Jadwigas. To distinguish them, we nicknamed them Jadwiga Black and Jadwiga White. Jadwiga White had blondish hair, Jadwiga Black's was the color of onyx. Their nicknames had nothing to do with their characters, however, which were sterling. It was generally agreed that Jadwiga Black had had either a blighted or barren romance with Mieczyslaw Karlowicz, a popular composer of songs and instrumental music, whose career was concluded summarily one day by an avalanche in the Tatra Mountains. It was a matter of accord, too, that no man had, or ever could have, set Jadwiga White's heart throbbing. Jadwiga Black wore severe, dark clothing, as though in life-long mourning, and was a bit too firm in her stride. Jadwiga White dressed in soft grays and beiges, and was the frail epitome of an Alfred de Musset heroine.

Several old friends, girls who had attended classes at our penthouse school, enrolled in the Two Jadwigas with me. We formed no cliques, but it was natural for those of us who had begun our educations together to retain a certain closeness. Moreover, our parents were involved with each other socially or in business.

I mention these things because they say something about the character of the student body. The girls came primarily from a middle-class or bourgeois elite, representing a wide variety of family interests and professions. The appeal of Two Jadwigas to my family and to my friends' parents, social status of the student body apart, was the school's excellent faculty and the thoroughness with which all subjects were taught.

Of subjects, there was no shortage. We learned history from the Cave to the Present. Our studies of the physical sciences ranged from the achievements of the Greeks, Arabs, and Chinese to the most advanced theories being speculated on then. We explored the principles of radio waves, and our mathematics studies began with the simple problems and reasoning of arithmetic and worked through to the dizzy heights of trigonometry.

Literature courses occupied a major portion of our time. They were meant to afford us insights into the complex world of feeling and sensation in which we would have to live. In this way the Two Jadwigas prepared us for a kind of nonacademic life that today seems unbelievably luxurious and leisurely — and no longer even exists.

Our readings extended from the Greeks and Romans to whatever respectable contemporaries were in print. We read the novels of Henryk

Sienkiewicz and W. S. Reymont, Poland's two Nobel Laureates, as well as excellent translations of foreign writers such as Galsworthy and Joseph Conrad (whom we did and did not consider a Polish author).

Books in our own tongue comprised the greater part of our readings. Poles have a language that, for good or ill, few people other than Poles can cope with. But for all its difficulties, our language has a rich and subtle music that has been used by great and thoughtful artists to create a literature second to none.

Of course, Adam Mickiewicz, our Romantic poet-patriot-philosopher, bulked large in our readings. We had to commit huge pieces of his homey epic, *Pan Tadeusz*, to memory. Juliusz Slowacki, his contemporary and rival, considered Poland's Shelley, was a favorite among us, not only for his exquisite use of our tongue but also for his delicate and refined sensibility. Another romantic we read avidly was Zygmunt Krasinski, the scion of a noble family who, in a masterpiece written when he was quite young, his "Undivine Comedy," foresaw the future class struggles of Europe in terms that the then (1833) adolescent Karl Marx would later develop.

Languages other than Polish weighed heavily in our curriculum, as one might expect in a nation that, though not by choice, was obliged to be polyglot. We studied German, French (of which I had a better-than-average grasp when I fell into the hands of Two Jadwigas), and Latin (simply because one was considered an illiterate without it, and the language conditioned the understanding of Polish grammar).

The Two Jadwigas held that the spiritual development of a child was as important as the intellectual. And, in keeping with their liberal, "Positivist" posture, they offered the girls courses of religious study, each according to her faith. The Roman Catholics were taught catechism and ethics. Separate and appropriate instructions, at the same hours each week, were available to the Protestant and Jewish girls. Many of my Jewish schoolmates were converted to Catholicism, perhaps because of the warm and rational approach our spiritual advisers took in teaching us our faith and guiding us in a Christian life. Perhaps for other reasons.

The genteel fripperies of a finishing school were also incorporated into the curriculum. There was art, in which I was already passingly proficient, and music. In the latter, from my child's view, I was deplorably deficient — especially regarding singing. There was a reason. When I was about two years old I suffered a serious throat infection which left my vocal chords damaged.

Students of Two Jadwigas were expected to work hard. The six-day, six-hour schedule of classes was matched by home preparations that often kept our noses in books or our fingers blackened with ink until bedtime. There were problems to solve, essays to be written, lengthy passages of Virgil to be translated or paraphrased. It was expected of us not only because we were understood to be bright or intelligent girls, but also because we were students of Kowalczykowna-Jawurkowna.

I learned many things under the tutelage of the Two Jadwigas. I have learned much more since, but I have done so only thanks to two lessons the Jadwigas taught all their students well: to think independently, and to base judgments on facts, not the timeworn fictions on which so many people build their lives. Perhaps I was meant to approach life in this way, perhaps it is in my nature. But I prefer to think that the school of these two gentle women, Jadwiga Black and Jadwiga White, made these characteristics a gift to me, and lovingly developed them along with other interests and talents.

Kowalczykowna-Jawurkowna School is no longer. It ended as an institution in the final days of World War II as the German Army systematically put Warsaw to the torch in their retreat from the on-coming Russians. When the moment came to destroy that block of Wiejska Street where the Two Jadwigas had cultivated the minds of young Warsaw ladies for forty years, the Misses Kowalczykowna and Jawurkowna were ordered to evacuate their premises. They moved to another place, and were either shot or allowed to perish in the flames that eventually also leveled that building.

Chapter 2

AT 11:00 on November 11, 1918, Miss G. interrupted her lecture on an obscure point of Polish Medieval History to inform her class that an Armistice had gone into effect. At this point in time, too, Poland was reconstituted as a free nation, after one hundred twenty-five years of Russian, German, and Austrian occupation. She spoke fervently to us of the event, what it had so long meant, what it could mean, and how we as students should work all the harder to be able to contribute to the strength of our fledgling, democratic state. Though we were, all of us, profoundly moved, that did not prevent the school from maintaining its daily routine.

The girls in my class were more alert than usual, especially to the cries of *"Dodatek nadzwyczajny"* ("Extra") from the newsboys in busy Wiejska Street just below the schoolroom windows. The special editions they were hawking spoke of the denouement of the historical tale all Poles of a few generations had hoped to live through: an independent Poland was one of the only terms under which the Western Allied Powers would consider making peace with Germany and Austria. It would

(15)

take but a few short months for workmen to begin converting the large building across from my school to house the Sejm, Free Poland's Parliament.

On my way home from school that afternoon, I saw Polish flags hanging from balconies or run up on standards. There were not many of them, but even one was more than I had ever seen publicly displayed in my first fourteen years. When I reached Aleja Roz, one or two houses displayed flags. Ours was not one of them, which gave me a twinge of shame. Within a few days, Mama and Papa found the cloth with which to have banners made, and then the Lilpop house, too, was resplendent with horizontally-divided fields of white and red.

I was so excited on that afternoon that I could only laugh or cry. Words could not express what I felt. And when I entered our apartment, I found all the members of the Lilpop household euphoric —even our current, phlegmatic governess and the two tiniest girls, Aniela and Marysia (who, of course, hadn't the dimmest understanding of the great happening). We had a particularly fine meal that day, the best that Mama and the cook could scrape together. I do not recall if toasts were drunk at the table, but if some were, they would have celebrated the health and long life of President Woodrow Wilson and Ignace Jan Paderewski.

Wilson's Fourteen Points set Polish independence as a requirement for an acceptable peace. Legend and history tell us that Paderewski convinced the American President to make this demand following a White House dinner at which the pianist, invited as a guest, performed Chopin. Actually, plans for an independent Poland had existed since November 1916 and already formed was a secret, *pro tem* governing body, the Rada Regencyjna (Regency Council), which operated clandestinely.

When the Kaiser's Army vanished from Warsaw, freedom came with a shock. Fortunately, the Rada had previously organized what behaved like a provisional government, and an effective one at that. It called for a free election, a constituent assembly, and for all Poles to unite and contribute their talents to the service of the new nation. The response was overwhelming.

From my viewpoint, it seemed as if all normal life had come to a jarring halt. Everyone had a social or economic program to put into effect, without which the infant nation would surely die. Everyone wanted to serve. Even my beloved, apolitical father burgeoned as an activist. He became the Police Chief of our district and wore a uniform of sorts. It consisted of a navy-blue woolen peasant's cap with a black leather visor, to which was attached a red-and-white ribbon. He also wore a red-and-white armband. In a few months Father brought the district's law enforcement to such a level of effectiveness and efficiency that he was able to turn his cap of office over to a professional with no loss of face. He was honored at a testimonial dinner given by a group of notables, and was presented with a golden police badge which bore the inscription: "To Franciszek Lilpop, from the grateful citizens of Warsaw."

The inflation, bad during the German occupation, became much worse after the Armistice. A piece of jewelry or a venerable Lilpop cream pitcher, in a pinch, could make the difference between food and clothing or nothing at all. Father's rental properties, of which there were a few, brought in a respectable amount of money. But Monday's paper marks, roubles, or zlotys frequently so depreciated that Tuesday's needs could not be met.

Ironically, Mother, who was accustomed to performing charitable serivces for others or giving whatever she could spare to the needy, found herself the cheerful and grateful recipient of American largess. The relief program which was organized and directed by the young engineer, Herbert Hoover, and which popularly bore his name, was a godsend to all Poles, even the well-to-do. With vouchers made out to our family, Mama was able to obtain what had become for us outright luxuries: bleached, white flour; an American soap that did not sandpaper one clean; granulated sugar; the creamy, thick, sweetened condensed milk we thought the greatest treat; and bolts of cloth with which to replace our worn-out dresses, blouses, and skirts. This Hoover cloth, as it came to be known, was a coarse-textured cotton fabric with alternating wide and narrow stripes of blue, much like mattress ticking. Clothing made of it became highly fashionable in the best Warsaw circles.

The Rada Regencyjna named Marshal Pilsudski Chief of State — on my birthday, incidentally — and head of the army which then consisted of remnants of his Polish Legion and volunteers from everywhere. The Rada moved to make peace among the Poles by bringing together representatives of the Austrian, German, and Russian parts of the reunified nation.

Pilsudski invited Paderewski to form a new government. Paderewski agreed. When he arrived in the capital to take office as Prime Minister, the welcome was tumultuous. Under the drab skies of a Warsaw January the city took on the coloring of a spring festival. Anyone who had a balcony draped it with bright-hued carpets. Polish flags flew everywhere. Children lined the streets along the path of his march. Everyone sported red-and-white ribbons. The sidewalks were clogged with masses of people. And people hung out of windows, climbed lamp posts, stood on roofs to catch a glimpse of the beloved pianist, whose once flaming-red mop of hair was now frosted over with white. As his horse-drawn coach advanced, the shouts of welcome rose like waves.

The affairs of the nation settled down for a while. Within a short time after Paderewski took office, members of the constitutional assembly were elected and a Constitution written. A provisional charter accorded extraordinary powers to Marshal Pilsudski as Chief of State until political stability could be achieved. The provisional constitution was in effect through nine different ministeries, of which Paderewski's was only the first, and not the longest-lived either. It was also in effect through yet another war — that against the Russian Red Army led by Leon Trotsky.

Poor Poland did not actually arrive at a government in which all the constitutional niceties so dear to Western democracies prevail until four years later. Only then did the first national assembly, Sejm, which convened itself in the building opposite my classroom windows, finally vote for the Constitution that established Poland as a Republic.

Chapter 3

ON a crisp, bright Sunday afternoon in the early winter of 1920, I rode on the Route Nine trolley car from the corner of Piekna (or Beautiful Street) and Aleje Ujazdowskie to Plac Teatralny. I was wearing my newest "best" dress, a navy-blue woolen affair with a white figure running through it. I sat with my hands shoved deep inside my overcoat pockets to keep them warm, a little disappointed that my coat concealed how elegantly I was gotten up. But everyone who cared to could see I was on an important trip; they had only to observe how the bows on my neat, tight braids matched the color of my hem.

The Route Nine rattled and lumbered straight into Saint Alexander's Square, which took its name from the handsome church in its center, then sped up through Nowy Swiat (New World Street) lined with shops. Resuming its usual sluggish speed, the trolley continued along Krakowskie Przedmiescie, past the Church of the Holy Cross, where Chopin's heart is entombed across the street from a famous statute of Copernicus seated, glowering, globe in hand. It meandered through the old University area, passed by a group of lovely baroque churches, including the Wizytki where my parents had been married, the Hotel Europejski with its wonderful restaurant (where my mother's brother, Uncle Antoni, once, for a treat, took me to dine), and the splendid palaces of aristocratic families like Count Krasinski's.

Then, abruptly swaying and metallically squealing, its conductor poles threatening to quit the electrical cables overhead, the Route Nine lurched to the left under the oblivious nose of poet Adam Mickiewicz's statute and into Trębacka (Trumpet Street).

When I clambered down the steps of the trolley, my feet landed in Plac Teatralny. In front of me stood the Teatr Wielki (Grand Theater), a superb building by Corazzi, an Italian master, which occupied the entire south side of the square. (Behind me, to the north, was the old City Hall, now gone.) The central portion of the Wielki housed the Opera. In the wing to the west was the Teatr Maly, a small playhouse where dramas used to be performed, and grand *salons* called Sale Redutowe, all on upper levels. On the ground floor was Semadeni, an excellent café notorious among the Lilpop children as the place which made *Babka Mascagni* (named after the composer of *Cavalleria Rusticana*), a dessert mother served guests whenever the family gave formal dinners. It was a light, airy cake, covered with ground chestnuts and iced over with buttery whipped cream. (We children always hoped fervently the guests would be too full of the other good things served to want much dessert beyond "a taste," and leave the rest for us to eat the following day.) There was also a restaurant called Pod Filarami (Under the Columns), since the wings of the Wielki had colonnaded walkways along the street. On the east side, running the length of the colonnaded wing, was the official residence of the director of the Opera (which is now a museum). That was where I was bound for.

There had been an unusual occurrence at Two Jadwigas in the fall of my second year. The Misses Kowalczykowna and Jawurkowna had admitted, without examinations *and* at midsemester, a new student — something completely unheard of. Such a privilege could only have been accorded the daughter of someone out of the ordinary who had to be an unusual child in her own right and stand out in a school that had a plentiful supply of the progeny of noted or famous artistic, professional, and ministerial families. The new girl's name was Alina Mlynarski.

Following the chaos of the war and the ups and downs of the peace (we were then at war with the Red Army), Warsaw, always proud of its cultural life, was determined to put its opera house in order, to organize it anew and make it equal to any in Eastern Europe. The new director was Emil Mlynarski, a Lithuanian-born violinist,* composer, and conductor. He was no stranger to the city. From 1897 to 1903, he had been an assistant conductor at the Opera. He had organized the Philharmonic Orchestra and conducted it until 1905, and had been in charge of the city's Conservatory of Music through 1909. Then he left, first to conduct in Scotland, and, when the war came, to continue his musical activities in Moscow.

Mr. Mlynarski apparently cast a spell over Miss Kowalczykowna. She considered herself a musical connoisseur and was already impressed by the man's reputation as well as his importance as director of the Teatr

---

* A student of Leopold Auer, incidentally, which made him a musical disciple of my Granduncle Henryk, who was Auer's master.

Wielki. And she was personally flattered by Mlynarski, who that first day brought his daughter to school himself and took a few moments to talk with Jadwiga Black of musical affairs. This served to entrench the new girl, Alina, as one of Miss K.'s favorites and a beneficiary of her special affection.

But anyone would have been attracted to Alina. She had bright, clear blue eyes, as big as silver zlotys, and pale blond hair, as straight and fine as drawn gold thread. Her manners and approach toward people were natural and warmly appealing. At the same time, she bore herself with an ease and social grace that gave her the air of a woman of the world, a rather impressive accomplishment for a girl not quite sixteen. The fact that she had come from Moscow, had seen the Revolution our parents talked about and dreaded would spread to Poland, gave her a certain aura among us. But there was also something, other than her good looks and her manners. Because school uniforms during the War were not mandatory, Alina appeared for classes that first day, and thereafter, wearing homespun suits of undyed wool that were made on her family's estate in Lithuania. Dressed so, she seemed to radiate neatness and cleanliness, two highly-prized characteristics in my particular scale of values. (She later told me she was drawn to these same points in my appearance.) In almost no time, Alina and I were fast friends. And it was this friendship, one of the first I cultivated independently and outside the circle of my family or its affiliations, that set my life on a direction I could hardly have anticipated.

I was excited and uneasy when I rang the doorbell of the Mlynarski apartment — excited, because I was visiting a now-cherished friend on her territory; uneasy, because of the awesome nature of that territory. Her pretty face as aglow as mine, Alina answered the door, index finger pressed to her lips. She emitted an intimidating "Ssshhh" as she ushered me in through the grand, formal living room, explaining in a whisper that "Tatka" (her father) was napping in an adjoining room. This information did little to diminish my discomfort. Beyond the living room was her room, and it was there, at a little table by a window that looked into Plac Teatralny, that we soon relaxed to chatter away in subdued voices about mutual acquaintances, the comparative virtues of teachers, and the tedium of Latin paraphrases.

We were joined after a while by Alina's brother Felek. I recall that I was rather attracted to him (as I was to almost any presentable boy in those years of blossoming womanhood), and he to me. He was tall and slender, and had the Mlynarskis' blue eyes and blond hair, although his was a shade or so darker than Alina's. He was, perhaps, two years older than we were then — just enough to put us in the silly-girl category. Yet he seemed to enjoy our company, and he talked at length about his service in the War against the Bolsheviks which then was drawing to its close. We in Warsaw had been in terror of the Red Army's advance. We had heard grim stories and were kept up nights by the artillery duels between the opposing armies.

Marshal Pilsudski's forces, with only nominal aid from our Western Allies, turned the tide against Leon Trotsky's far superior numbers and won a victory which is called "The Miracle on the Vistula River." This battle surely changed the flow of European history. With the ensuing rout of the Russians and the signing of the Treaty of March 1921, Poland secured nearly all of the ethnographic and historical boundaries of her pre-Partition days. Felek felt proud to have served in such a campaign.

The three of us were getting along famously when the door opened and Mr. Mlynarski entered. When I recall his face on the first encounter, how it melted all my apprehensions, I better understand how he had won over the indomitable heart of Jadwiga Black. A thin, blond moustache wreathed the warmest smile imaginable. Indeed, that smile and his full-pink cheeks come back to me now as more of a presence than his entire appearance. This I reconstruct from a photograph. He was not above average height, a little given to stoutness and, although only in his forties, almost completely bald. The hair that remained to him at the sides and the back of his head was blond, ever so slightly turning silver. And, of course, there were those huge blue eyes the family seemed to monopolize and which, in his case, were set beneath thick, bristling eyebrows. A dimple in his spade-shaped chin completes this picture of what I thought to be a most attractive man.

I had been, at bottom, frightened by the thought of meeting a famous *maestro*. Instead, I met a simple, affectionate man who had not the least pretension nor the assumed grandeur so characteristic of some celebrities I have since known. As I joined Tatka, who took my arm, and the others for tea and cakes, I knew I was genuinely welcome in that house and was delighted. In time it would become my second home.

My first visit ended with a tour of the apartment, breathlessly conducted by Alina. The director's official quarters could be described as one immense corridor, divided only by equally immense, floor-to-ceiling doors. One could open all these doors and, similar to an Italian Renaissance *palazzo*, have a clear view of the place from one end to the other. From most rooms tall French doors led out onto the balcony that overlooked Plac Teatralny.

Through a narrow hallway running parallel to the apartment one could enter several other rooms. This hallway was itself fascinating. It was a strange passageway (not dissimilar to one in a story by Edgar Allan Poe that I had just read) which led, by twists and turns, into ever darker, ever narrower extensions, lit only by an eerie glow from tiny windows set high in the wall, to end at a large, heavy metal door. Alina fetched up a big key from her pocket and opened the door. When I crossed that threshold for the first time, I felt much like Alice taking her first tentative steps through the Looking Glass into a magical world. I found myself in the Opera's backstage area. Never did I imagine on that first walk down the almost black passageway that most of my life would be spent in just such places, backstage Wonderlands of music.

(*21*)

Not many days after my first visit to the Mlynarskis, Felek invited me to attend a performance of *Carmen*. Dressed in my best party frock, I felt myself quite grand sitting in the first row of the *parterre* with the handsome young son of the Opera director. Felek and I shared an innocent friendship, I thought. Not until much later did I realize he had had a crush on me.

Felek, soon after we met, began to show the symptoms of an aggressive tuberculosis that he had contracted while in the army. Its effects would end his life all too soon, and with his death an important chapter in the life of my sister Aniela would end as well. Felek was sent to stay in Zakopane, in the Tatra Mountains, and we saw less and less of each other. By this time, my next to youngest sister had been absorbed into the Mlynarski household too. She met Felek there on his visits to the city, and they fell in love. Their engagement followed. But as God would have it for both lovers, Felek's condition rapidly worsened before a wedding could take place. He died in Aniela's arms. Many years were to pass before her heart recovered from the loss of that first real love.

That trolley ride on the old Route Nine from Aleje Ujazdowskie, with its precipitous lurch and turn under Mickiewicz's nose into Plac Teatralny, soon had no novelty for me. With increasing frequency I was a guest in the Mlynarski home. Before long I was familiar with everyone in the immediate family as well as with what seemed like a limitless number of cousins. (Since the Mlynarskis hailed from Lithuania, which was on the eastern borders of Poland, their house was always swarming with refugee relations.) I am no stranger to a large family, having dozens of cousins of my own. But the Mlynarskis could match the Wieniawskis and Lilpops twice over and still have some to spare.

On one of my first few Sunday afternoon visits, I met Bronek, Alina's oldest brother. He was in the army at the time, serving at the Military Academy just around the corner from Aleja Roz. More than the other children, he resembled the father, down to the charm of his smile and those pale blue eyes. I found myself much taken with him, but, understandably, he did not succumb to my amateurish attempts at flirtation. Not only did he think me too young, but at the time he was kept busy by ballet dancers and singers who succumbed to his charm.

Some months later, Wanda, Alina's older sister, arrived from Lithuania with little Nela in tow. Wanda had come on ahead of the others to complete preparations for her forthcoming marriage to the pianist Victor Labunski (brother of the composer, Felix). In a matter of days, Alina brought little Nela to school.

My first meeting with Nela was at the Two Jadwigas. Two big blue eyes, a pair of tight, curly blond pigtails, and a beige homespun woolen dress "skated" the length of the waxed corridor in a pair of felt slippers right into my arms. Alina had spoken so often and lovingly about her "baby sister" that I knew it must be she. Apparently, Alina also had talked of me to Nela. We embraced each other effusively, and from that moment on our friendship was sealed for life.

Nela, four years younger and just as attractive as Alina, had been accepted by the Two Jadwigas for the second grade. (Alina and I were in the fifth.) She was twelve then, but tiny for her age, and very, very graceful. Without any formal instruction, she had already begun to dance beautifully and had hopes of becoming a ballerina. Although my first vocational preference had been nursing, I was at this time aspiring to be either a portrait painter or an architect. Ironically, we both ended in the same line of work, and helped each other get our "jobs."

From the outset, Alina and I accepted Nela as one of our crowd. Her age made no difference to us, partly because she was so mature for her years. On May 31, the feast of Saint Aniela, Nela's patroness, I brought my sister Fela with me to the Mlynarskis, and that day in 1921 began another lifelong friendship.

After that visit, Mrs. Mlynarski, whom I met for the first time, relaxed her rules, and allowed her daughters to visit at my house. She even allowed them to come to our estate at Kolacin in summers. My mother instantly took to the Mlynarski girls and cheerfully increased her brood of four daughters to six.

Mrs. Mlynarski did not often stay in Warsaw. She was obliged to pass many months of each year in Lithuania, trying against all odds to manage and save a large estate. In her absences, Tatka was in charge of the girls. It often seemed, however, that the girls were in charge of him, functioning as his hostesses and watching over the complex details of an opera director's household.

Through the years, as I became more of a familiar in the Mlynarski household, my life and interests began to change. For one thing, I was now receiving an intensive education in opera. I regularly attended performances with Alina and Nela, going from their room, where we did homework together, down the dark passageway directly to the proscenium box to the left of the stage and jutting out over the pit.

From this vantage point, I learned the nuances of singing and acting and staging and scenics. When my ears did not tell me how effective a conductor was, I had merely to look at the faces of the musicians below to see how attentive they were. I soon came to appreciate, as do orchestral players, the clear, precise, and economical gestures that reveal a conductor's firm grasp of the work and the men he directs.

During those years, I aurally consumed a major portion of the standard repertoire (much larger and more encompassing in Poland than in the United States), along with a number of works that were then novelties and still remain so. Emil Mlynarski for the years he was in charge of the Teatr Wielki strove for a balance between the old and the new.

The greater part of my operatic education came, however, after the performance. We three girls would scamper back to the apartment along the passageway, bubbling with that enthusiasm and lightfootedness anyone who enjoys music experiences following a fine performance. At the after-theater suppers presided over by Alina and Nela, I was allowed to sit at the big dining-room table with whomever else was present from the family or from among their father's *confrères*.

Here, with a well-laid table to nibble from (I had in no way lost my appetite with adolescence), I would follow Mr. Mlynarski's careful critique of the evening's performance. Relaxed, warmed with something to drink and eat, he would go over all the details of the night, scene by scene, assuming that what was good was so, but pointing out all the things that went awry, mishaps so slight that only another professional or a well-schooled initiate in the audience might catch them. He would praise the sopranos Polinska-Lewicka or Zboinska-Ruszkowska, the tenors Dygas or Gruszczynski, the bassos Mossoczy and Michalowski, all of whom were first-rank artists. But while Tatka was praising these vocalists, one or another of his musically sophisticated children was likely to bring up some fault that he had overlooked. The Mlynarski children, it seemed to me, never missed a wrong note or some mismanaged bit of stage business.

Needless to say, I listened in fascination, a fascination that fortunately I never lost, because for years after, I listened to endless performance postmortems as part of my way of life.

Those were the golden years of Warsaw's Opera. Voices were superb, staging excellent, scenery imaginative, and guest appearances by internationally renowned artists frequent. One of the greatest baritones of any era, Mattia Battistini, enjoyed singing in Warsaw, and the city returned the feeling with outright adulation. Although he had been offered everything but the total wealth of New York City, he steadfastly refused to sing at the Metropolitan because of his fear of crossing the Atlantic. The Met's loss brought no tears to Warsaw's musical eyes.

At some time or another, many great artists were guests at that table, and I learned much from them and from overheard conversations. I remember on one evening, after a performance, Mr. Mlynarski spoke enthusiastically about a new young conductor he had "discovered." This fellow had had an unusual success in Lvov with his productions of Verdi's *Ernani* and a Polish novelty, Ludomir Rozycki's *Eros and Psyche*. The latter had been premiered to effect in Germany during the war, and, since the composer was from Warsaw, it seemed a good choice for the Teatr Wielki. The Director engaged his "find" to mount the piece for him.

Again over a late supper, I heard more of this conductor. He was apparently either a perfectionist or a fussbudget. He taught each singer his or her own vocal part, and rehearsed and rehearsed with piano, then orchestra up to the day of the dress rehearsal. So vigorous was his preparation everyone in the production was close to collapse. He once again rehearsed the morning of the "dress" and, after the dress rehearsal itself, asked Maestro for still a third rehearsal that night. The singers were in revolt. They complained — and with justification — that they would have no voices left for the premiere the following day. Mr. Mlynarski acceded to his conductor's wishes, however, and the opening performance was a sensation. The critics agreed that the name of Artur Rodzinski was one to be reckoned with.

The next season, Mr. Mlynarski engaged Rodzinski to conduct regularly at the Teatr Wielki. There was a shortage of apartments in Warsaw following the war. The city was bursting with refugees and Tatka, ever helpful and ever susceptible to someone else's troubles, gave his young discovery a room in his apartment, one of those smaller affairs on the other side of the corridor. Inevitably, I met Rodzinski one evening when we were seated at supper. He brusquely came in to ask Tatka a question about something, then bustled off. I doubt that he took much more note of me than I of him at that time.

I saw him often thereafter, but only from the angle afforded by the Mlynarskis' box. Alina and Nela had high regard for his conducting, but at that time I was not aware of his qualities. The only thing that impressed me about him, above and beyond other gentlemen in tails who occupied the same podium, was that he was more energetic, electric than they, seemingly more absorbed in what he was doing. Also, I wondered how he could see at all when his shock of bushy brown hair fell over his forehead as he nearsightedly leaned into his score. Not until the night of Jan Kiepura's Warsaw debut did I become aware of his musicianship. Rodzinski was in charge — the opera was *Faust* — and helped launch the Polish tenor on a career that soon led him to the world's great opera houses.

I became familiar with Kiepura's name over a plate of noodles and mushrooms. Director announced, "I have found a new tenor. He is a young University student and very sure of himself."

That, assuredly, was an understatement. When this latest find turned up one evening, white student's cap topping his handsome face and head, he behaved for all the world as if he had been already recognized as a star. His conceit and his undeniable talents soon conspired to make him one. When people referred to him as "the second Caruso," Jan would counter with, "No, the first Kiepura." Alas, for him, he built an international career on a musically-unsure base. He simply did not allow himself enough time to master his art.

He married Marta Eggerth, a Hungarian soprano with a lovely voice, though one too small for an opera house. Many years after World War II, Kiepura and his beautiful Marta appeared together in a production of *The Merry Widow* on Broadway. It had a long run, thanks to Marta's good looks and Jan's still-lovely voice. They made a fortune, which was among Jan's many-sided talents, a talent I often wished my husband had shared.

(*25*)

Most of the singers, stage directors, and conductors I met in those days are now merely names in musical reference books. Still, more than a few of the musicians who frequented the Mlynarskis' grand living room will be living memories for a number of readers.

It was not uncommon to see the short, dark, good-looking violinist Paul Kochanski draped over one of those magnificent (though imitation) Louis XVI chairs; Tatka had discovered Paul in Odessa and, being himself a fine violinist, undertook the young boy's training. As with anyone who was the recipient of the Mlynarski goodwill, Paul became a member of the family, with the status of a son, for Tatka had taken Paul under his wing at the age of seven.

Paul was witty and gay and had a unique talent for putting anyone at ease. He could also entertain an entire roomful of people without ever seeming to dominate them, an ability which his wife Zosia capitalized on. For years she "operated" a salon, with Paul as her greatest jewel. Paul and Zosia would become my friends until their deaths and were of invaluable help to me when I came to settle in the United States.

Paul's star was destined to rise high and burn bright. As he became famous so did his close friend and frequent recital partner, the composer Karol Szymanowski. Karol had the traditional pianist-composer's problems when writing for stringed instruments, and Paul gave him needed technical advice. His two violin concertos and such works as *Mythes* for violin and piano were dedicated to Paul. Karol was also a frequenter of the Mlynarski household, along with his sister Stanislawa, an excellent singer (with whom Karol often appeared in joint recitals).

Critics and music historians now rate Karol as Poland's most creative personality since Chopin. Unfortunately, the esteem in which he is now held was only hinted at during his lifetime. Most Warsaw music critics rejected his originality and technical brilliance and they were merciless when they reviewed Szymanowski's works.

There were all sorts of fringe types to be found around Mlynarski's Bechstein when Karol and Paul would play — among them Mateusz Glinski, the publisher of *Muzyka*, an influential musical review, and Ryszard Ordynski. Every generation and place has its Ordynski, the affable, attractive man who knows everyone, or will in time, and always seems to be where anything of interest is taking place. He had tried his hand at stage directing and films in New York and Hollywood, and had been an assistant to Max Reinhardt. In Poland he directed a production of *Journey's End*, a now-forgotten play by R. C. Sheriff about the Great War, and made a success. But then, as if to say, "I have established all of my credentials," he stopped directing.

There is a Polish proverb, *Gosc w dom, Bog w dom*, which translates, Guest in the house, God in the house. But there can be too many guests. Frequently, as Alina and Nela were growing up, they had neither the right atmosphere nor the time in which to study properly. Some cousin or other would be visiting, celebrities had to be entertained almost nightly. The girls hardly ever knew a moment's peace. Yet the Two Jadwigas demanded much of their students in the way of home preparation. To help them, my sister Fela and I, rather good students, would do our homework each evening and then telephone the answers to the Mlynarskis, according to a pre-arranged schedule.

As I have said, the girls, when I first met them, exhibited an attractive poise far beyond their years, no doubt a result of their association with the great and the musically mighty. Alina, who has grown her own way, one that differs from mine, became austere with passing years. Nela, however, has remained the bright, charming girl she always was — the girl with the pigtails and felt slippers, the little "sister" who confessed to me one night, a night I slept at the Mlynarskis after an opera performance and lessons, her passionate love for Artur Rubinstein. The pianist had already made a serious stir in the musical world and had captivated Warsaw, not to mention Nela's heart.

"He's a known ladies' man, Nela," I warned.

"I don't care," she answered. "I love him."

Chapter 4

ALTHOUGH I could caution Nela, I myself was not immune to the appeal of a handsome male. Quite the contrary. I was constantly "in love" from the time I was nine years old. As an adolescent I enjoyed flirtations, and collected the hearts of young boys about my age — a relatively harmless lot whose good behavior had much to do with our lack of privacy. Girls and boys did not meet without parental supervision. There was no "going steady" in my country then.

When I started attending balls, and there were many in Warsaw during the Carnival period between Christmas and Lent, Mother would always accompany me. As I passed near her while waltzing with my partner, we would smile at each other conspiratorially. I was immensely happy to have her approval of my popularity. I never missed a dance.

At parties in private houses we danced to small orchestras, sometimes even to the music of one blind pianist from the association of blind musicians for which my mother worked. Big official balls were held in the reception halls in the City Hall and in lovely ballrooms of the elegant clubs. I was constantly meeting new men. Once I was the cause of a duel in which an admirer had his cheek slashed with a rapier, leaving permanent scars on his otherwise handsome face.

Finally, at the age of nineteen, the inevitable happened. I fell madly in love. The man was Alexander (Olo) Lipinski, who was at that moment between wives. He was one of the best-looking men in Warsaw, and very much *en vogue*, thanks to his olive skin and jet-black mesmerizing eyes. I was taken not only with his dark handsomeness, but with his personality. He could make me laugh when often I would have cried. He could do charmingly innocent things, like crawling around on all fours in a game with my "baby" sister Marysia, or play dolls with her. And Mama, my other sisters, and Alina and Nela adored him for his thoughtfulness, his specially tender kindness to his ailing mother, his little gifts of perfume or chocolates, and his genuine concern with everything that concerned those near him.

But he was a "bluebird," as we say in Polish, a playboy. And even though we became formally engaged, there was something unsettling about our relationship; not especially to me, but to my parents.

In the fall of my twentieth year, Mama and Papa asked me into Papa's study. Mama sat deep in a green leather armchair. Opposite her was Papa, bulwarked behind his great mahogany desk. I sat off to the side, uneasy, not knowing what to expect.

Papa initiated the proceedings by clearing his throat of all the frogs that ever lived along the Vistula, then by giving his goatee several smoothing tugs. Suddenly he bolted out of his chair to pace the room, hands clutched behind his back. He was exhibiting all the signs that meant reluctance to carry out a "parental obligation."

"Halunia [as he called me], your Mama and I . . . ," he began, then halted to adjust the flaps on his coat pockets.

"We have only your best interests at heart," he continued.

"I know, I know."

"We, of course, are concerned about your future."

"Yes, Father," I murmured, thinking, "Well, at last they are going to set the date."

"And we know how close, how fond you are of . . . Mr. Lipinski, who is a . . . nice young man . . ."

"But, my dearest child," he warmly continued in his most professional paternal style, "neither your mother nor I believe that Mr. Lipinski is the man for you."

I had been struck by lightning. Mother knew how much this statement hurt. Though usually she left the unpleasant chores of disciplining the children solely to Father, this time she joined him in explaining how they had come to disapprove of my choice.

"Mr. Lipinski is a pleasant and appealing man," she began, "but not for you. He is unsettled in his life, he is reputed to have affairs with other women incessantly. He is not sensitive enough to know how easily things of this nature could hurt you."

My parents' carefully reasoned criticisms of Olo whirled about me, sucking away even the breath with which to offer a counter-argument. My eyes glazed with tears that would not fall. I knew they loved me. They had never consciously done me a hurt. My faith in them was so complete I had to defer to their judgment.

With my emotions finally in grip, a few days later, I wrote Olo a letter, to confess my love for him but my greater obligation to respect and obey my parents.

It was many years before I could divest my dreams of their vision of Olo and almost a decade before I could fall in love again.

Chapter 5

THE years of my early womanhood, with the exception of my unfortunate love for Olo Lipinski, were really untroubled in most respects. Indeed, matters in the Lilpop household moved with an organized calm and grace, a tribute to my mother. She could manage her home efficiently and, at the same time, keep constantly busy with numerous charitable involvements and musical associations. Partly because Grandfather Wieniawski had lost his sight, she was very active in work for the blind, and was one of the principals in the organization of Poland's equivalent to the American Lighthouse for the Blind. And coming from so rich a musical heritage Mother had a genuine love of music. She had a sweet *mezzo soprano* and accompanied herself on the piano. For pleasure, she belonged to a women's choir that gave concerts for good causes.

Matriculation at the University in Warsaw took some of my time, but did not prove to be what I had expected. My courses in art history barely held my attention. What thought I had ever given to becoming an architect had been squashed by my father: "No one would ever ask you to design a building — it's a man's field." In truth, nothing much interested me other than socializing with my friends, often in company with the Mlynarskis. I went to lots of parties and met many new, interesting people, but my heart still belonged to Olo.

In 1925 our entire family looked forward to my parents' silver wedding anniversary. That long-awaited day, April 21, began with a mass at the Wizytki Church where they had been married. It was followed by a splendid buffet in the evening for all the Lilpops, Wieniawskis, Troszels, and other relations who were available, plus numerous associates and friends. Two liveried footmen, called on for special events, glided about the apartment filling wine glasses. Eventually the guests warmed to the toasting that finishes off such evenings. One toast that my sisters and I particularly recall was made by an old school friend of my father: "Let us drink to Franio Lilpop's masterpieces, his buildings in concrete and steel and his most beautiful creations — his four daughters."

Soon after, my parents went on a trip to Paris and the Riviera. I was left in charge of the household. My university studies did not interfere — I was not attending to them seriously anyway. The visiting lecturers who fascinated me were invariably outside my discipline of fine arts. Mme. Marie Curie-Sklodowska was particularly captivating. She spoke of things that I barely comprehended, but I found her magnetism irresistible.

In addition to my work at the University I was studying painting at the private school of Professor Krzyzanowski. With me there was my cousin Irena Lilpop who had just married Stanislaw Krzywoszewski, a young lawyer. He was the son of Stefan Krzywoszewski who published *Swiat* (*The World*), a weekly magazine of news and opinion. Poland's finest writers contributed to its columns, and most of them could be met in the Krzywoszewskis' living room. Irena and her husband lived with his parents, and as I found myself their frequent guest, I soon became friendly with writers such as Boy-Zelenski, Ferdynand Goetel, Kornel Makuszynski, and many others.

When my parents returned from their anniversary trip, Mama was not feeling well. Something she had eaten while on the Riviera had poisoned her. The effects spoiled some of the trip, although she could still enjoy gaming at roulette at Monte Carlo, her pet indulgence. Yet, somehow, her energies were not quite what they had been before she left, and she did not take up her household routine with her usual vigor.

There were many things to be done. It was that time of year when the family set about packing for the summer's stay at Kolacin. However, Jedrek and Fela were both due for a nose and throat operation. Mama delegated to me the chore of taking the younger children to the country while she stayed in Warsaw with the "patients."

Our parting, even at the time, struck me as odd. It was on a fine fresh day at the beginning of June. Mama came to breakfast in a lovely pink silk dressing gown and a bonnet. After we had finished eating, and the others had gone about their preparations for our departure, Mama told me of a dream she had had a few days earlier.

"Grandmother Wieniawska spoke with me," Mama said in a sober, almost disembodied voice.

"She said that she is in a place of such beauty that there are no words in our language to describe it, no experiences or concepts that could parallel it."

Mama's telling of the dream did not, in itself, carry much significance. She often had such dreams. I do myself, even now. As one grows older, the people who populate one's dreams are more likely to be dead. And so Mama's dream did not perturb me, but what did prey on my mind, as Marysia, Aniela, and I drove away in the cab with our luggage, was the manner in which Mama had parted with us. Never before had I known her to press us so hard to her, to hold us so long, to kiss us with such warmth, almost passionately, desperately.

"Mama," I said, "for heaven's sake, we'll see each other in less than two weeks."

She made no reply. Her little half circle of a smile at the corner of her mouth arched even higher and more sweetly. Then, abruptly, she shooed the three of us off. As we drove down Aleja Roz, we saw Mama standing on the balcony, waving and blowing kisses, her smile as puzzling as ever.

Our trip to Kolacin was wonderful, the younger girls behaved like angels. And when we arrived our Uncles Edward and Boguslaw had all sorts of good-humored surprises for us. As the days passed, excitement built up over the imminence of Mama's arrival with Fela and Jedrek. Then, we received word that Jedrek had taken ill following his operation, that Mama would be delayed a while. On June 29, Marysia's thirteenth birthday, a telegram came. Jedrek was dead. Of scarlet fever.

Stunned, I rushed to the nearest telephone which was in the town of Rogow and placed a call home. Papa answered and told us that Mama was gravely ill. With scarlet fever. I was terrified. Fela was also sick. The doctor was not certain if she had the same infection. Apparently, the two children had contracted something as a direct result of the surgery they had undergone to correct a defect in their nasal passages.

The younger children could not understand how it was possible that their brother was dead. Then, twenty days later, another telegram arrived. Neither I nor my sisters were at all prepared. Our two uncles brought it. They were crying and could not bring themselves to tell us what it said. I tore the telegram from Uncle Edward's hand to read these words that I remember as well as the Pater Noster: *"Beloved Mama blessed you and bade you farewell. Thirteen hours unconscious, she fell asleep forever this morning. Father."*

It was as if I suddenly had been robbed of air, as if every fiber of my body had been anesthetized. For a moment I was not certain that my feet stood on grass or softly yielding snow. Then I became aware of the horrible wailing of our old nurse Mania, the cry of an animal possessed. My sisters and I took her into my bedroom, consoling her and ourselves in the process. We all knelt together by the side of Mother's bed in prayer. I do not recall how long we stayed there, but the sounds of the countryside at night were all about us when I started preparation for our journey back to Warsaw. The trip to the station, traveling for several hours in the sweltering heat of the train, our arrival in Warsaw: all of these things seemed parts of a dream. Even being met by Uncle Henryk, Papa's youngest brother, did not seem real, nor did the old house on Zgoda Street where we were obliged to stay with him and our aunt because the possibility of contagion in the Aleja Roz apartment was too great.

The experiences of the funeral were overwhelming for all of us. Strangely, we found that our grief, our sense of loss, was not a private or family matter. The church was filled to capacity not only with family and friends, but also with people we did not know or may have encountered only once or twice. A large crowd, with many blind persons among them, stood in the street outside. Many wept like members of the family. Yet who would not have been touched by the service. The music was performed by a band of blind musicians who had expressly taken upon themselves the prerogative.

I was especially moved by the playing of the Chopin Funeral March. How often had I heard that dirge from the B-flat Minor Piano Sonata over the years. During the Great War, it had sounded everywhere. And in the years which followed, while Poland fought against the Red Army and afterward, I heard it performed daily as bodies of soldiers were removed from the military hospital near my school building.

Chapter 6

THE two years following Mama's death were a desperate time for me.

At the start of this then-prescribed period of formal mourning my grief was genuine enough, but no person can remain both disconsolate and rational, particularly a young person. After the first year, I could think of my mother without crying; I could even smile when I thought of her foibles. Much more time had to pass before I could act without doubts and independently in those areas of my life where I usually relied on her help or counsel. Fela, Aniela, and Marysia reacted the same way. Papa was different. Mama's dying was the greatest, the sole dramatic event in his otherwise orderly life, and he seemed bound to relish it — or so my sisters and I sometimes felt. We rarely left the house the first year, and then only on Sundays to visit the grave in the Powazki Cemetery, to place flowers on the black granite vault where she lay buried among other Lilpops, and to water the blossoms with our tears.

I left the University and gave up my painting studies to become Mama's surrogate. While Papa had not asked this of me, it was apparent that it was expected, and very much to his liking. I ran the household exactly as Mama had done, and bore the additional burden of teaching Marysia her lessons. The child, at age thirteen, was too frail to be sent to school. Fela and Aniela, however, continued their studies at Two Jadwigas.

One of the first signs of an easing of Papa's mourning was his purchase of a new technological toy, a radio. Now in the evenings, he alternated between his favorite solitaire and his wireless. Papa would sit hunched by the large elaborate apparatus, twirling and twiddling the dials until he located a station. Sometimes he listened to a portion, never more, of a piece of music until the announcer identified the station, and then resumed the search for yet one more. On occasion, he lingered over broadcasts from Italy, even broadcasts of opera, because he had a fondness for the language.

While we were all together one winter evening, perhaps January or February of 1927, Papa adjusted a knob in the course of a transmission from Milan, looked up and announced that he had been giving some thought to his daughters' futures.

"It is time my girls saw something of the world. Halunia, Fela, what do you say to a trip to Italy?"

Fela was delighted, so was I. An Italian tour had been a favorite dream for years. We helped Papa gather up his Baedekers and old itineraries. In short order, he drew up a travel plan for the two of us that would have done Thomas Cook proud. For the next several weeks, Fela and I immersed ourselves in Italian irregular verbs with a tutor, while Papa prepared lists of cities, restaurants, pasta dishes, and *pensioni*, each relating to his happiest experiences traveling with Mama.

My sister, who was a student at the Academy of Fine Arts at the time, would be tour guide. Since I was the elder, and was effective in dealing with money, Papa designated me treasurer and overseer of all practical matters. By the time we left we were as well prepared as it was possible to be.

Our first stop was Venice, an enchanting city. Primarily because we had a photo of Mama doing the same thing, we hurried to Piazza San Marco to feed the pigeons under the haughty gaze of the Evangelist's gilded lion. We were struck dumb by the beauty of the Square. Never had we imagined the play of color, of formal caprice, and of space that we saw. When we entered the basilica itself, the sunlight passing through the big rose window, fell on the shimmering golds and bright red, blues, yellows, and greens of the mosaics. The effect was so stunning all we could do was sit in silence in the cool, magnificent church, awed by the works of human imagination in the adoration of God.

Delight and awe were to become familiar feelings during our frantic life as sightseers through Rome, Naples, Sicily, Florence. Everything fascinated and thrilled us. We walked miles of museums, visited hundreds of churches, tried our Italian on everybody. We even went especially one early morning to Rome's Borghese Gardens to see Mussolini riding his beautiful white horse on the Gallopatoio. He was then a virile, imposing figure — his people's darling who built new roads, made the trains run on time, and taught people not to swear.

Two weeks in Rome, which is what Papa had allowed us in our first Italian itinerary, were barely enough for a glance. Among the memories of that first visit I most treasure was the sight of St. Peter's Square as Bernini meant it to be seen. In the Twenties the Square could be reached only through two narrow and dark side streets which were alive with the physical smells that still pervade Rome on a damp day. The effect on entering the Square was an explosion of sunlight and of welcoming space. Words cannot convey adequately the emotions Fela and I experienced on entering the basilica, feelings that perhaps only Roman Catholics can share.

We went to a Papal Audience, an inevitable event for Polish Catholics in Rome. For us it had a special significance: Pius XI was the former Papal Nuncio to Poland, Achille Ratti. When the Pope passed near us we gave the traditional greeting in Polish, *"Niech bedzie pochwalony Jezus Chrystus."* It brought a happy smile to his face, and he replied warmly in our own tongue.

We left Rome and went on to Naples, a city as different from Venice or Rome as the toes on one's foot. Papa had told us that if there existed a point at which we could take Italy's blood pressure, it would certainly be Napoli. We found that where Italy was concerned, Papa always proved right.

Then came Florence. There is no better course to be had in the history of Renaissance art or the efflorescence of the human heart and mind in that period than a study of the Uffizi collections.

Although we were supposed to return to Poland after our two-week tour of Florence was completed, we stayed on because Fela contracted typhoid fever there. She was so desperately ill the doctor gave her up for dead, but miraculously she recovered. Two months passed before Fela was strong enough to make the journey home. In that period, once the crisis passed, we had the opportunity to learn Italian well, make friends with two young artists, Roberto and Augusto Passaglia, and feel completely at ease in this uniquely beautiful country where, decades later, I would live for several years.

Chapter 7

DURING the winter of 1927–28, I started to emerge from my cocoon, although the silken fibers of love for Mama's memory and Papa's helplessness clung to me still, holding me close to the household and its responsibilities.

I finally began to realize that my life had been at a standstill while great changes had occurred in the lives of my friends. Many had married, some scattered to far distant places.

The pianist Mieczyslaw Munz, whose dazzling technique drew raves from Paderewski, had come to Warsaw and swept Nela Mlynarska off her feet. After driving her to the altar in his big, shiny red "Caddy-Yak" (as we pronounced it in Poland in those days), Munz had taken her to the United States. There he was a professor of piano at the prestigious Curtis Institute of Music in Philadelphia, then directed by Josef Hofmann, the master pianist of the day and, of course, another Pole. Munz combined his teaching in Philadelphia with a rigorous schedule of appearances with major orchestras and recitals. Fortunately for Nela, she had her mother and father with her. Mr. Mlynarski's health was very delicate and deteriorating rapidly. He had an insidious form of arthritis for which in those days there was no relief. He could no longer sustain the demands of managing a major opera house. Thus, when offered the post of instructor in conducting in Philadelphia, and the direction of Curtis Institute's student orchestra and opera company, he accepted. The position would allow him to use his enormous knowledge and to pass on a great tradition to the developing artists of a musically-youthful United States.

Mr. Mlynarski's predecessor at Curtis had been another Pole, Tatka's former protégé, Artur Rodzinski, who at the same time had served as Leopold Stokowski's assistant with the Philadelphia Orchestra. When Rodzinski passed on his duties to Mr. Mlynarski, it was in order to take over direction of the Los Angeles Philharmonic.

There was something inbred about the Warsaw of my early womanhood, something that made a city of more than a million souls seem like a small town in which anyone who was anyone either knew or knew of everyone else. I was now a marriageable young woman and was flattered to be invited to many interesting parties. Our neighbors from the apartment below us, the Meyers, started asking me to their musical soirées. Zosia Meyer was a competent pianist. As children we would listen to her playing by lying down on our living-room carpet with ears pressed to the floor. In this way I was introduced to the artistry of Artur Rubinstein, their frequent guest. At the Meyers' parties I would meet the crème de la crème of musical Poland and, often, foreign musicians, many of whom I knew from the Mlynarski house.

My married relations and friends kept an eye out for a man for me, placing squadrons of handsome, well-connected young eligibles in my path. But all these "prospects" made me fussy. Perhaps in getting over my first love, Olo Lipinski, I had come to place less emphasis on appearance and more on what and how a man thought and spoke. Certainly, the dinner parties at my cousins, the Krzywoszewskis', home, followed by bridge, and conversation with the literati of Poland had confirmed me in what had been a long-developing intellectual snobbery. I cannot now, and could not then, abide a person who has only his social standing or his looks to recommend him. Mama had raised me to understand that true aristocracy is of the mind and soul, not in a time-encrusted title or the size of a fortune. To this day a person of intellect, talent, and imagination has a prior claim on my heart, as does any human being whose values are in harmony with himself and the world he moves in. Above all, I treasure those persons who bring the sincerity of their whole selves to their relationships.

As I moved about in an intellectual world, the new verse and fiction over which I enthused by day became dimensionally alive for me by night. The respectable literary world of Zeromski, Boy-Zelenski, and others of the older generation, attractive though it was in the household of the Krzywoszewskis, was too much filled with the aura of greatness to stir me. I was attracted more to the newer writers who spoke of foibles and follies that I understood, who could laugh or cry at themselves in terms I had experienced. And these I might chance to meet at Hania Lilpop-Iwaszkiewicz's country or city residences. Iwaszkiewicz was one of the leaders of Young Poland's literary renaissance. He was also one of the founders of the group called Skamander (which rates several pages in the *Columbia Dictionary of World Literature*), composed of innovative young poets seeking new modes of expression.

Associated with Iwaszkiewicz in Skamander were five men who were to become great friends, friends with whom I shared much personal happiness and no small amount of grief: Jan Lechon, Kazimierz Wierzynski, Juljan Tuwim, Antoni Slonimski, and Jozef Wittlin.

I cannot place exactly where I first came to know these men. It could have been at a dinner party, an "at-home," or at a cafe. Certainly, if I ever took myself to the Café Ziemianska, I would have found them sitting on "the mezzanine." The café (its name means "for landowners") catered to the ordinary crowd of coffee-house frequenters — plump, middle-class ladies who came to gossip over coffee and whipped cream, businessmen dropping in for a quick nip and a glance at a newspaper. Such souls sat at tables on the main floor of the Ziemianska. But on a small landing, between the ground and second floors, and big enough for one table only, gathered the literary giants of the younger generation. Lechon, Wierzynski, Tuwim, Slonimski, and Wittlin (when in town from his home in Lvov) would sit there several hours every day. They were the café's chief entertainment. Anyone with interests in literature would come to eavesdrop on their discussions, which were always *fortissimo*, and well worth the time spent over a coffee. An invitation to a young writer to join these men on "the mezzanine" in effect dubbed him a knight of the new Polish letters. When my future brother-in-law, Zbigniew Unilowski, was asked to sit among the Skamanderites, he felt it a great emotional experience. And when he drank *brüderschaft* with some of them, thereby using more personal forms of address, he behaved for days as if he had been tickled by God's finger. Unilowski, who with his first novel established himself as the first Polish writer in the then new tradition of Céline and Henry Miller, was a simple boy to whom such things might mean a lot. But his more intellectually acute friend, Witold Gombrowicz, reacted similarly when he, too, was asked to pull up a chair on "the mezzanine."

How these men became part of the life of No. 10 Aleja Roz, I hardly recall. Those days were hectic indeed. My sisters and I had begun to hold Sunday afternoons "at home." People usually dropped in, often at the invitation of someone else who had been invited. There was nothing formal about these gatherings — they might even have struck some as bohemian. People came and went until nightfall (and sometimes later), played bridge or a short-lived craze, Mah-Jongg, made music, conversed; in short, did what they pleased. There was always food and drink, and for those few who lingered late, a more substantial meal. In this informal setting the Skamanderites made themselves at home and we came to know one another.

Where Lechon cast a whimsically neurotic shadow over a group, Wierzynski came as sunshine to dispel it. As handsome as a sculpture of Phoebus Apollo, tall and athletic, Wierzynski was always bursting with that *joie de vivre* Lechon possessed only infrequently. His verse, from the first volume he published, sang wildly lyrical celebrations of anything in existence which might at the time enamor or intoxicate his muse. Spring green might fever his brain, or an athlete hurling a javelin, the sight of parched pears in his mother's cold-storage cellar: these were the substance of the songs he composed to life. In later years, living in exile, a sadder tone sounded in his poetry, but it was never the sadness of a man who was disillusioned or embittered. Wierzynski, and his wife — another Halina — drew very close to me, and to Artur, in the years of World War II.

Antoni Slonimski (a cousin of the Russian-American composer

Nicholas Slonimski) used to terrify me, but then I was not alone in being afraid of him. His cold and incisive wit could cut like a pathologist's knife. I never experienced it, which is why I could come to know him as a warm human being. His poetry reflected that analytic mind.

Where Wierzynski radiated a virile, rough-and-ready male beauty, Juljan Tuwim had an almost ascetic handsomeness. His features were delicate and fine, his eyes dreamy, and he had a "mouse" (a brownish mole) on his cheek, all of which caught whatever heart he sought. Tuwim was fun to be with, always full of jokes and puns and verbal games, things which also characterize his poetry, a sort of Joycean invention with words that defies translation.

The last in this list of my Skamander friends is Jozef Wittlin, Poland's "almost third" Nobel Laureate. He, too, I met about this time, but did not come to know well until the war brought him and his wife, yet another Halina, to America. He stood alone as a personality of huge gifts and intelligence, a one-of-a-kind. His novel, *Salt of the Earth*, was instantly acclaimed as a masterpiece. The precision of style, the nuance of language, and the mordant humor of the work come through even in its English translation (which is long overdue for a popular reprint).

In the Twenties, these men were literary figures of substance among a people more avid for books than most. In the Forties, scattered to the winds by German bombs, they were my friends in need of help. And being writers, their situation was doubly helpless, for they were cut off entirely from any audience. More than once Wierzynski told my husband how fortunate he was to be a musician, with a mode of communication intelligible in all parts of the world.

When all of us banded together in New York, despite differences in attitudes or personalities, we were merged into a family of sorts, all concerned for the fate of Poland caught once again between two giants, once again a battlefield. With their days of celebrity behind them, they had only tears to share with their fellow emigrés, for none of them came with fortunes other than their talents. The literate and cultivated Poles in America at the time could do little more than attend their readings or lectures, subscribe to the journals and books that they published, and try to provide an environment wherein these writers could express their Polish heritage. Those were sad times, but Chopin and Mickiewicz had known such times, and perhaps it was presumptuous of us to think that Poles would not again.

I don't remember exactly when Karol Stryjenski entered our orbit. He was in his early forties. To us, he seemed an old man. He had a passion for skiing and mountain climbing which he exercised in the Tatras, where protracted exposure to sun and wind had tinted and lined his face so that it resembled an oak leaf in autumn. I say he had a passion for these things. Actually, Karol had a passion for everything. Exuberance in any activity, intellectual or physical, was his hallmark. When he, in a sense, "discovered" Zakopane and the Gorals, the mountain people of the Tatras, he almost became one — speaking their dialect, singing their songs, and drinking as hard as the best of them. He greatly contributed to Polish awareness of the heritage of the mountaineers, deriving from their culture some of the style of his own work, and repaying his debt by developing local arts and crafts into a productive industry. Under his dynamic guidance, the Zakopane School of Arts and Crafts attained a national reputation.

Karol came from Krakow, in the Austrian-controlled province of Galicia. It was there that Pilsudski built and trained his Legion, many of whose officers had been boyhood friends of Karol. Consequently, when Pilsudski and his Legionnaires became the government of Poland, Karol had access to important people and he never hesitated to use them to aid the cause of Polish art.

Perhaps he had spent too much time among his beloved Gorals to tolerate for long the stuffy precincts of Warsaw's academic art world. They would have to change. Shortly after his appointment at the Warsaw Academy as professor of monumental sculpture he took on, almost single-handedly, the creation of IPS, the Institute of Arts, then the Capital's Museum of Modern Art.

To IPS, in it, and around it, Karol drew the finest of Poland's younger and more daring artists. The entire project was in his hands. Being an architect, he even designed the building. Then he chose the staff and organized the exhibits. Of course, the IPS building had to have a café — where else would artists ever gather? It was there, under witty and satiric murals by young Felix Topolski, that Free Poland's new painters and writers, including my Skamander friends, would often meet. The IPS café quickly became one of the places to frequent or to be seen frequenting. It housed for several seasons a literary cabaret of high caliber, while the big exhibit hall was used for special concerts, the first being devoted to the younger Polish composers. One of the soloists (playing Roman Maciejewski's compositions) was the pianist Casimir Krance, later Fela's husband.

Constantly involved in one set of projects or another, Karol had little or no time for anything but a change of shirts and a catnap. His life for the period I knew him, was very much that of a general conducting a forward campaign. Soon after he met Fela, who had studied with him, she became his aide-de-camp. On the face of it, his choice of Fela had much to do with her talents, her enviable stamina, and her organizational skill. But beneath the surface, I suspect there may have been a much muted love for my sister. Certainly, Fela and I thought of Karol as just this side of Papa. In any case, Karol came to live at Aleja Roz.

Karol took over the penthouse. In came his baggage as well as a string of charming painter friends. Among these were several of the group that called themselves "Kapists," after the initials "K" and "P" (*Komitet Paryski*), the society they formed to go to France, and under which auspices they exhibited in Western Europe to considerable acclaim. Their painting brought a new sense of color to Polish art, fresher and more vibrant than anything before. The arid, monumental historicism of an earlier age (when such things flourished in the name of national identity under Tsarist domination) vanished in an explosion of post-impressionist or expressionist freedom. When Stryjenski and his IPS gallery showed these works to Warsaw for the first time, the effect was sensational. The most talked about artist was the unusually gifted Zygmunt Waliszewski who, when struck with another bout of the dreaded Burger's disease (both of his legs had been amputated), found a temporary haven with our family.

Jozef Czapski, the founder of the K.P. group, together with his writer sister Marya, became habitués of No. 10 Aleja Roz which, under Stryjenski's guidance, was converted into a place where hungry, bored, or bridge-mad painters and writers could pass a Sunday afternoon.

Czapski, who writes as well as he paints, once said, in his book *Oko* (*Eye*): "The four Lilpop girls did more for Polish art than a dozen ministries of culture."

Another habitué of 10 Aleja Roz was one of Czapski's greatest friends, Jan Tarnowski. Unusually handsome, he was an extraordinary person and, although not an artist himself, certainly very much a part of artistic life in Paris as well as in Warsaw. In a short time he became Stryjenski's assistant.

Many times during these Sunday gatherings, the two Karols, Stryjenski and Szymanowski could be found near the piano where young Krance would be playing through a new piece of music for four hands by and with the bushy-headed, equally-youthful Maciejewski. Fela's attentiveness, perhaps, was for the music, but one could tell the pianist interested her no less. Stryjenski and Szymanowski, in conversation together, allowed their vast knowledge and experience to soar over every realm of the arts and life (which, for them, were inseparable), and music and bridge and snacks might all be forgotten as everyone gathered close by to hear these men talk.

But weeks have other days besides Sundays, and for these I lived just as much. Aside from the household and my work among the blind, the reading of a new book, supervising Marysia's lessons, and catering to Papa's finicky tastes, there was much to do. There were plays to see and films ("talkies" had come to Poland), ballet, Philharmonic concerts, and opera, and rounds of parties and balls in the Carnival season. Warsaw in those bustling days seemed to me a city that danced when it could spare time from politics, artistic cabals, and all the other heady things that contributed to the excitement of the new nation's capital.

Ryszard Ordynski, that amateur in everything except being socially well-connected, whom I had first met at the Mlynarskis' home in the Teatr Wielki, had invited me to an unforgettable evening. His parties were the talk of the town. Where or how he ever got the money for these affairs is a secret buried in the rubble of World War II since, surely, his sporadic ventures into the theater did not pay enough to maintain his life style. He offered the finest wines and food, and had them served by the most elegant footmen. His guest lists comprised an elite to make the most dedicated snob jealous, but an elite that was also fundamentally democratic. Shady characters bumped elbows with sterling aristocrats; people from the theater, Skamander poets, Kapist painters, composers, performing artists, and a sprinkling of marriageable maidens were all thrown into the same pot with colonels and cabinet ministers.

This entertainment at Ordynski's was a party given in honor of his house guest, Artur Rubinstein. Artur, still a bachelor, was in Warsaw for the first time in several years. His recital at the Philharmonic Hall had been sold out days in advance, and his reception was extremely enthusiastic.

I went to Ordynski's apartment in old Warsaw's Kanonia Street, behind the Cathedral, in the company of my neighbors and Rubinstein's friends, the Meyers. It was then very fashionable to live in these ancient dwellings (now reconstructed and modernized), with their twisting and narrow staircases. The place was furnished with many antiques, most of them genuine, a few just plain dissemblers, but all contributing to an elegant setting for Ordynski who ever appeared at his parties as a handsome, casual, beautifully-mannered penguin in a dinner jacket.

The early arrivals stood close to the buffet laden with the choicest delicacies, wines, and vodkas. This spot not only afforded the best view of those entering, but a chance to see them close up. Each new person who arrived was framed in Ordynski's doorway as if in a photograph for a society page gossip column, the captions being provided by those with a speculative turn of mind and a zest for gossip. It was a matter of great concern to see which actor arrived with which actress, suggesting a rupture in a much-discussed prior liaison, the female partner of which would later come in on the arm of a Pilsudski aide. A few writers might enter, engaged in serious and hushed conversation with some "power" in the Ministry of Culture.

When Rubinstein entered, there was a respectful hush, a parting of people like the waters of the Red Sea, then applause. The guest of honor was a garland of smiles and courtly manners to everyone. In moments he made his way to where the Meyers and I stood, and we met for the first time. He was amused when I mentioned his playing about ten years before at the Meyers' apartment at No. 10 Aleja Roz, and how we would listen to him through our living-room floor. By the end of the evening he asked me to join him the next night for dinner and dancing at a Warsaw nightclub, Oaza (the Oasis), along with the actress Marysia Modzelewska and our host, Ordynski.

I had known Marysia for some time. The reigning queen of Warsaw's theater was a much desired companion, with striking blond hair and the blue eyes and pert nose of a gamine. She had many broken hearts to her credit, and had already begun accumulating marriages. At the time of this "double date" she was between marital engagements.

The four of us enjoyed ourselves and each other's company that night. As anyone who has ever known Rubinstein in the role of a host will attest, he picked a superb menu and the best wines to go with it. After we finished dining, Artur invited me to dance. On the dance floor, where our feet slid through the aimless steps of a fox-trot, he announced that he had had "enough of the single life."

"And so?" I asked.

"And so I am looking for a wife, a Polish girl. The French, the Spanish, the Italians — they are all fickle. I want one heart, a faithful, loyal, Polish heart," he concluded.

Dimly, faintly, a conversation hoarded away in a back cupboard of memory echoed in my ears.

"I do know of a beautiful girl. She used to be very much in love with you."

"Could I have missed one? Who?"

"Nela Mlynarska."

"Ah. But she is married to Munz and is in America."

"Wrong," I came back at him. "She is divorcing Munz and presently lives in Germany where she studies dancing, under Mary Wigman, I believe."

Artur's pleasure was reflected in that electric and compelling smile of his.

Not long afterward he was on his way to Germany and the successful courtship of Nela.

I went home that night to find Papa, solitaire game laid out on his study table and eyes fixed blankly on some depressing chimera in space, the static of his radio hissing hypnotically. Papa was going into another of his depressive moods. Seeing him through them was one of the obligations I had come to accept in life.

Chapter 8

THE difficulty I had remembering dates when a student at Two Jadwigas still plagues me. Were it not for the log books and diaries I have kept most of my adult years, I would never recall all the important birthdays, namedays, anniversaries, historical events, and personal occasions that otherwise would simply pass like so many migrating geese.

June 2, 1932, however, is a date I do not have to research. Nela Mlynarska telephoned me that morning in high spirits. She was in the process of changing from the former Mrs. Munz to the present Mrs. Rubinstein, and wanted to share her happiness. I, on the other hand, had just been tapping Papa's psychological barometer, and had found that he was going into another slump, which put me out of sorts.

I was in no mood to take up her invitation to a party at the apartment of Mateusz Glinski, a music critic and sometime-conductor I had first met at her home when Tatka Mlynarski still directed the Warsaw Opera. I had only recently been to his place for dinner with Karol Szymanowski. Karol apart, the experience was one I did not care to repeat any too soon. Glinski for some while had struck me as an unctuously saccharine bore, one of those who always seem to be doing a kindness while actually taking advantage of you.

But Nela is a persuasive creature and I had to listen to her. The party was for a certain Olin Downes, the music editor of *The New York Times*, whatever that may have been. While in transit to the Soviet Union to hear what Russia's composers were up to, Downes had stopped in Warsaw to take in the Polish musical scene. Nela rattled away like a Gatling gun, shooting down every excuse I threw into the air: Papa's poor spirits, my lack of a suitable dress, my frank distaste for Glinski's company. Her most "telling" argument was laughable, really, the product of desperation.

"Halina, we need you because you speak English," she said.

"Nela, why don't you just tell me the reason — the *real* one!"

"Reason? What reason?" she parried. "It is always so nice to see you," she continued. And since we had visited together only a day or two before, and had talked about her forthcoming marriage, she set in motion a curiosity which broke the neck of my resistance. Perhaps something had gone wrong. The idea of helping a friend through a misfortune is always more alluring than facing one's own problems.

At any rate, I went to the party that afternoon, curious, but essentially in a nothing-better-to-do frame of mind. I could just as well be bored at Glinski's as at home playing *Garibaldka*, a card game, with Papa.

The Glinski apartment, a two-room affair, was not suited to the mass of people that filled it. It was drab, like its occupant, and heaped with journals, newspapers, and books, the stuff from which he assembled *Muzyka*, the influential review he published. The walls were covered with autographed photos of the famous musicians with whom he loved to rub shoulders.

The rooms were filled with familiar faces and old friends, including most of Poland's then current composers, men whose work has long since been eclipsed by the doings of Krzysztof Penderecki, Witold Lutoslawski, and others of the succeeding generation. Poor Olin Downes was seated in the midst of this sprightly, articulate group, reporter's notebook and pencil in hand, rapidly recording whatever he could understand. Nela was translating. She broke off in mid-sentence when I entered, to introduce me to this man who would become a good friend some years later, and I mumbled my pleasure at meeting him.

As soon as it was polite, I fled with Nela to Glinski's "other" room, where we plumped ourselves down on a lumpy daybed and began babbling away as we have been doing since the first day we met.

All at once something new was added. Through the connecting doorway we could see how the front room, active enough before, had taken on a new vigor, an air of dynamism, a point of focus, transformed as a stage is when the prima ballerina joins the corps. Through a fog of cigarette and cigar smoke I made out a figure I seemed to know.

"That wouldn't be Rodzinski?"

"So you remember him?" Nela asked archly.

"Of course, but where has he been?"

"In America, making a *fantastic* career for himself. You *do* know that Stokowski took him for an assistant in Philadelphia? Well, now he has an orchestra of his own, in Los Angeles, you know — where Hollywood is. . . ."

Rodzinski: that was a name which belonged seven trying, tempering years in the past, but the man had not changed much. His broad shoulders still sloped as I had remembered, he sported the same mass of thick, brown hair, only now growing appealingly grey at the temples. He was more near-sighted than I recalled, however, because from the other room he was squinting to see Nela and me, as if looking for one particular house from an airplane flying over a city.

The moment he was sure he saw us, he extricated himself from the musicians who had lost interest in Downes, and came to us like a shot. His greeting was in the Polish fashion — bow, hand kiss, and, his own contribution to the formality, the sweetest smile. Nela and I shifted across the daybed as though making space on a bench in a third-class coach, and Rodzinski sat next to me. Yes, of course he remembered me from those days in the Mlynarskis' apartment. How good of me to recollect his performance of this work or that, but especially *Rosenkavalier*.

And then, plop: I was dropped like a turnip into a soup kettle, while Nela and the young maestro talked around and through me as if I were a cloister grille. He told of his problems with his orchestra, how the financial situation of the arts in America had turned desperate since the Crash, the naiveté of American audiences where some kinds of music were concerned, and on and on.

Rodzinski spoke with authority, and with a rapidity that kept pace with Nela's, yet his tone or style was modest, even deferential; his voice low, raspy, yet intense. One eye twitched nervously behind thick lenses.

(*44*)

Although I had long been forgotten in the conversation, I could feel myself being scrutinized. But I, too, was giving him a good look, I admit. Indeed, few men escaped my discriminating eye. This was no clothes horse. His glen-plaid suit fitted him less than it surrounded him. I did not find him especially handsome. The smile had undeniable charm, but his physique — well, he was obviously not an athlete. Still, he had a fascination, the sort of mystique which makes a woman think again before marking a man down as not-her-type. And while these things were tripping over each other in my mind, a thought of my father at home intruded itself unpleasantly. What, I asked myself, *am* I doing looking at a man this way? Hadn't I resigned myself to taking care of Papa until my sisters were grown and settled, even halfheartedly accepted the notion of spinsterhood? That particular thought depressed me.

I excused myself, and moved to the front room to say my good-byes. As I was about to leave, my eye caught sight of Nela and Ro-dzinski silhouetted against the window in the other room, talking animatedly. My hand was turning the doorknob when Nela called, "Wait, Halina, let me take you home. I must get a cab anyway."

Driving to Aleja Roz, Nela blurted out — "Rodzinski wants to marry you."

"One of you is insane," I said, at first astonished out of my gloom, then amused, even intrigued.

"I am serious, Halusia. He knows all about you — as much as anybody else you would take up as a suitor," Nela continued. "When I last saw him in America two years ago, he was depressed by the way his marriage was going — he was near suicide."

"Nela, I am *not* interested," I said. Although I was flattered by Ro-dzinski's interest, the last thing I wanted from life was a married man, *and* a suicidal type.

"Halina, listen to me. He has been talking about divorcing his wife. Things have been bad between them for years — neither of them can take it any longer, but it is for their child's sake that Rodzinski and his wife have stayed together."

"And you *believe* that?"

"Halina, I know that men exaggerate, do everything they can to get sympathy or even pity, but believe me when I say that his marriage is a loveless mess. I know the woman. You even met her at Papa's."

"Yes, yes. I think I remember her — Ilse someone-or-other, a German name."

"My point is, dearest, I know this man, how warm, how genuinely loving he is, and I know the hell he has gone through with that woman. And I know you, and that you would be just the wife to suit him, his temperament. . . ."

"Nela, you know nothing of the sort."

"Darling, let me be blunt: you are not getting any younger, and I don't see how you can pass by a chance to live the life you would have with an artist, a great artist, one with a future as big as life itself. Of course, some marriages do not work, but that is no reason not to try it — at least once. Give Rodzinski a chance; you might be surprised by your feelings."

And on and on she went at about the tempo of "*Largo al factotum*," with few breaths and only implied punctuation. Her arguments won whatever they were supposed to. While her verbal barrage left me in shock, what she had said about giving Rodzinski "a chance" penetrated my defenses. More than once I had allowed myself to be courted by someone who did not interest me. I had nothing to lose by going along with her scheme. I agreed to join her the next day at dinner with Olin Downes, Rodzinski, and her brother Bronek at the home of her parents who were once again living in Warsaw.

I went to bed early and tired that night but not before checking to see if my pink chiffon print was fetching enough to do for the next day.

The Mlynarskis had set up housekeeping on their return from America in what was then a new section of Warsaw, near the airport. The days of Tatka's glory had, tragically, passed. Once so firm and bursting with a ripe sweetness, he now was frail, literally turning in on himself like a withering plant. His arthritis — the deforming variety — had been aggravated by the damp climate of Philadelphia, and his physician, in pursuit of one of the ephemeral theories of the day, had idiotically pulled out all of the poor man's teeth. At sixty-one, an age when most conductors are in their prime, Director Mlynarski was so crippled that he could barely hold or lift a spoon.

He was obviously put into good spirits by the company of his former assistant, Rodzinski, by Downes, and by memories of mealtimes past in the Teatr Wielki apartment brought back by the gay chatter of "Mamiti," Nela, Bronek, and me. But a tinge of sadness underlay the afternoon, one which still affected me long afterward. Time, which had seemed so plentiful when I first entered the Mlynarski orbit, now passed on a different plane, at another pace. Events, large and small, personal and public, had altered all of our lives irreversibly.

I could not help thinking as I looked at Maestro how much had changed since I was a girl of sixteen. Felek, the boy so proud of his soldiering, the near man with clear eyes like a cloudless summer sky, was dead. Alina was married and no longer the great good friend of schooldays. Wanda and her husband, Victor Labunski, had settled in the American South, Tennessee, with the help of Nela's now-divorced husband, Munz. All that seemed left to me with any feeling of continuity with the past was my friendship with Nela, Bronek's chronic gallantry, and the glittering eyes of Tatka which still signaled a sense of being welcome.

At dinner I sat next to Rodzinski, who from time to time would leave off his musical shoptalk to turn to me and smile in that sweet and shy way of his. Once, over the borshch, he looked at me in a way that made me feel embarrassed, and I realized I was vulnerable to the man. I smiled back, wondering if Rodzinski was truly serious, and if possibly I should have worn another dress, something blue. I had ample time for silly thoughts because Rodzinski, Tatka, Nela, and Downes were having an animated discussion about the American cultural situation. Downes held forth with what I later came to know as characteristic enthusiasm, and all of them spoke in an English too complicated and too rapid for me to understand.

When the meal ended, I, who had mostly only smiled at Rodzinski, spoken with him maybe no more than to agree about the subtle flavor of the food, discovered that I had accepted my impromptu suitor's invitation to join him, Nela, and Downes for a ride the next day in Bronek's new Chevrolet to see the Corpus Christi pageant at Lowicz, a colorful folk spectacle he knew would appeal to the American tourist.

The Chevrolet of those days was a utilitarian, far-from-commodious vehicle. The back seat was a tight fit for Nela, Downes, and me. And Rodzinski, who sat in front beside Bronek, performed amazing contortionist feats to twist around to keep an eye on me. I obviously interested him more than the landscape, and he was carrying off the role of the flirt with a style that I enjoyed immensely.

We returned to Warsaw at sunset, and for a special treat we took Downes to an outdoor restaurant on Aleje Ujazdowskie which at that time was filled with the perfume of the thick foliage of the flowering linden trees. Downes was exhilarated, excited about everything Polish — the folk costumes, the touching simplicity of the pageant (which years later he would recall time and again), the character of the countryside, Warsaw hospitality, and (paramount with him) the food. However honest he may have been in his other compliments, it was apparent from the way his round face shone as he ate that what he said of Polish cuisine was genuine. Dinner over, we went our several ways. Downes would head for Zakopane and a visit with Szymanowski that Rodzinski had arranged, then on to Russia. Nela was pointed toward London and her wonderful new marriage.

Rodzinski offered to walk me home, only a short distance, and I good-humoredly gave him my arm. He pressed it close to his side just a shade more strongly, even possessively, than our casual knowledge of each other justified. Dense, new leaves on the linden shrouded the street lamps which shed a vague, moonlike glow above our heads. The air was warm, caressingly moist as it sometimes wants to be on a spring night in Warsaw. The sensuality of the evening, coupled with Rodzinski's tight hold on my arm, made me edgy. We walked for a short eternity in silence; then, without prelude, he spoke.

"Would you like to come with me to America?"

The words came softly, hesitantly.

"What would your wife say," I returned, hoping to take him by surprise (he had not spoken of her to me), and thereby evade further talk along those lines.

"That could be arranged," he said calmly, not the least perturbed that I knew of the wife he had not bothered to mention. "What I want to know is, would you want to come with me?"

Another eon passed as we walked, neither of us speaking. How could I answer him? On the face of it, I felt like telling him he had made a mistake, that I was not interested in his "proposition." But he had stirred emotions inside me which were hard to ignore. I held my tongue. When we came to Aleja Roz and I indicated that this was where we turned, he halted. His hold on my arm tightened.

"I must know if you will come with me," he said. "I want very much to marry you. Will you come?"

"Perhaps," was my reply. The word escaped my lips before I even knew what I had said. Flustered, I sought to cover my traces with a smile and a wink, trying to make a joke of it and regretting not saying the "no" which reason called for.

Rodzinski missed both my humor and whatever had been vague or evasive in my answer. "That's all I wanted to hear," he said as we reached No. 10. Taking me completely by surprise, he folded me into his arms and kissed me on the mouth. It was so sudden that my response was clumsy. Indeed, I almost fell over backwards. His gentleness, the tender way he did it, had an undeniably strong effect on me. When the embrace was over my ears felt as if someone had crashed cymbals within inches of them, and my chest seemed like a sail when the wind drops off. Before I could even catch a breath, Rodzinski began walking briskly down our Street of Roses. After a few steps, and almost as an afterthought, he turned and said, "I'll see you tomorrow morning."

I let myself into the house wondering what kind of fool I had become involved with, and at the same time relishing the sensation of being sucked up by a whirlwind. It was incredible that he had fallen in love with me in so short a while, and yet — why not?

Through all the night, my thoughts gnawed at me like persistent mice, and I was more than a little physically unsettled. A quality in the man, something beyond identification, had destroyed my composure. His were not the first kiss and embrace I had experienced, but they were the only ones to thus tip over my psychological and physical equilibrium. Ironically, I was not attracted to him, although I could not deny that he fascinated me as a person, frightened me a bit. He seemed to possess a power, an ability to manipulate even to dictate my responses to him, and this after only three encounters.

Once more I reviewed my familial responsibilities, and, right or wrong, logically had to agree with Nela: I *had* done my duty toward my sisters and Papa. It was senseless at twenty-seven to entomb myself as warden and housekeeper to a depressive (and depressing) father. To have my own life called for the exercise of my own options. Ignoring them further meant merely existing. I *would* consider the proposal of this Rodzinski.

The focus of all my thoughts arrived early in the morning, just in time to witness the day's starting-up confusions. Papa, luckily, was out of the apartment, but my three sisters were very much in evidence. While curious to see the kind of man who might call at such an hour, they were much too busy with their own activities to interfere with our visit. Fela was at work with Karol Stryjenski on the project of the moment, surrounded with heaps of notes and sketches. Aniela, though still in love with the memory of Felek Mlynarski, was within days to become Mrs. Witold Mieczyslawska. Marysia was doing lessons with her tutor.

Rodzinski came armed with a huge box of chocolates, possibly to influence the dispositions of these girls whom he had undoubtedly heard about. I could see now how shy he was, and that pleased me, but he had nothing to fear from the girls: once they looked him over, he and his candy were taken for granted.

We talked about his immediate plans. He intended to join Downes in Zakopane for the meeting with Szymanowski, after which he had an appointment with a surgeon in Krakow for a hernia operation. He was a man in a frightful rush, one who had time only to do or say what was necessary, which included making me privy to all that his future wife should know. He was convinced that I was to be his, so much so that he did not bother to probe my interest in the matter. My "perhaps" the previous evening was enough.

During our conversation my role was simply to say "Yes" as frequently as he demanded agreement. Then, in a puff of time, he vanished, leaving me with my head still nodding assent. He said he would telegraph after his operation and somehow I had promised to visit him in Krakow. When the door closed behind him, my sisters, all gaily chewing on chocolate truffles or fruit liqueurs, agreed that Rodzinski was "a sweet man." His investment in the expensive candy had paid exactly the dividend he expected. What remained for me was an empty box, a table littered with fluted paper cups and almost as many uncertainties.

The next few days came and went like a summer storm, turbulent, exciting, swift moving.

Aniela, who years before had determined that one of her major accomplishments in life was to be the first Lilpop sister to marry, kept me distracted with last-minute preparations. Her husband-to-be, Mieczyslawski, was a diplomat, and my second sister had visions of receptions and balls and bemedaled Ambassadors and First, Second, and Third Secretaries coming to dine in palatial residences in exotic countries.

After my Italian sojourn, and other trips, I, too, had a taste for new environments and atmospheres. Often I found myself thinking about America, the land of Charlie Chaplin, Harold Lloyd, W. C. Fields, of skyscrapers, of Red Indians and Robber Barons, and, no matter how hard I tried to put him out of mind, of Artur Rodzinski and Los Angeles (the Angels), a pretty name, perhaps a pretty place, with palm trees and earthquakes like Naples and Messina. What a hash of notions and irresolutions simmered in my mind for three days and nights while that egotistic man, he who had insinuated himself into my life peremptorily and unbidden, kept me waiting for a telegram. And then it came, thank God.

Aniela and her husband were going to Zakopane for their honeymoon, and I went along with them as far as Krakow, which is on the same rail line. Some people must have snickered at "the old maid" traveling with them as a duenna. That suited me fine; it would do no good for Rodzinski and me to be gossiped about should the affair prove a flash-in-the-pan, for, honestly, my mind still was not made up — although on some far deeper level than I could reason with I knew that I had accepted him.

After checking into the Krakow hotel I went directly to the hospital and Rodzinski. Walking as if on egg shells, not really certain where any given step would lead, after an age I reached the door to his room. My heart was pounding. Half laughing to myself, I realized that on the verge of such a romantic encounter my mind was not filled with poetry and pretty sentiments, but with that primitive thought expressed by Isolde's first words:

> *Luft! Luft!*
> *Mir erstickt das Herz.*
> *Offne! Offne dort weit!*

"Air, air, or my heart will choke. Open, open there wide!"

And then I opened the door of that sickroom.

I looked at Rodzinski, ill, flat on his back, helpless as a child. In that moment I saw what I had been seeking for years, and in many men: a person stripped of all pretense, a person whose beautiful smile and arms outstretched to greet me said gratuitously, "I love you, love me." And from then on, I did — no matter how difficult it often proved to be.

Chapter 9

My "reintroduction" to Rodzinski by Nela Mlynarska in a drab Warsaw apartment affected my life like the kicking loose of a stone that initiates an avalanche. What in Warsaw only a few weeks before had begun in uncertainty and fear now moved with a terrible swiftness and inevitability toward a future I was more than ready to accept, although hardly able to foresee.

Throughout most of my life I have nurtured an inferiority complex; I was, in my eyes, neither bright enough nor beautiful enough to appeal to the kind of man I thought would fulfill my life. I, who had once cheated on a math final, and who still remembered Mama once saying that I had some of the characteristics of a pug dog, now found myself committed to a man whose stature, actual as well as imminent, was awesome. And he was drawn to me by qualities in myself that I was unaware of and so could not appreciate.

Even now, with Artur dead eighteen years, I sometimes still think of myself as one of the barely audible sound waves which lend an instrument its distinctive tone. I find it hard to see myself as having been anything more than an adjunct to the comforts of his private existence. Whenever I asked myself what it could possibly be that he saw in me, the answer was always ready at hand: it was me, just as surely as it was only by happenstance that the man I found myself so much in love with was a great musician.

Actually, considering how similar we both were, the two of us might have been brother and sister. Indeed, Artur's headstrong approach to all matters was not unlike that of my dead brother Jedrek, with whom I used to play a game of wills, which would fuel a mutual exasperation between us and lead to horrid fights that often threatened physical danger. Jedrek got a thrashing for his part in such games because he was, in Mama's and Papa's view, supposed to respect and obey his older sister.

In my relations with Artur I found the expectations reversed. The mores of the society which formed me decreed that a wife submit to her husband in respect and obedience. I quickly discovered that where there was a contest between our wills, I was the foreordained loser. The penalty or reward paid was the most exquisite kind: the fulfillment of our love. Artur hated hearing the word "No," and I, who cared for it no more than he, often found a joy in quietly saying "Yes." There were those occasions, however, when neither reason (of which I sometimes display precious little) nor the survival of my personality would permit my saying "Yes," and the rages that resulted could have shaken the Himalayas.

When situations so demand, I appear composed, seemingly rational. But this is the surface. Actually, I fend my way through life on instinct and intuition. Admittedly, this can lead to many disillusionments, but — as I felt when I was younger and still feel now — it also makes life more adventuresome and, ultimately, an act of faith.

I soon began to see in the ten days I spent in Krakow with Artur that he took life much the same way. On the surface, he showed discipline and determination toward his career, but underneath he lived the same kind of guileless life that I did. Like me, he too took people as his instincts found them, and presuming that all, or most, people are good, accepted them for what he presumed. This, at least, is the way he took me. And, in a sense, it was what made our love work. Accepting one another fully for what we were — a rare pleasure in any relationship — we owed each other a debt of loyalty and the honesty that goes with it to preserve the commitment of our mutual acceptance.

This all sounds terribly prosaic and thought through, and perhaps it is. Distance in time and his death have reduced our love to memories that ask to be figured out. But at that moment in Krakow when I knew I loved the man, it was romance of an embarrassingly sticky, old-fashioned variety. Though the setting was not redolent of the wilted violets and paper lace of my Grandfather Juljan's sentimental tales and plays, the feelings were the sort he fully appreciated. Some of the things I did because of my love for Rodzinski would not have found their way into Grandfather's plots, however, for real dilemmas, such as those his contemporary Ibsen traded in, never crossed his mind.

Before Artur went to Zakopane, then on to Krakow for his operation, I introduced him to Papa as my husband-to-be. My recollection of that encounter is vague, perhaps because I want it to be. I imagine, though, that Artur carried himself like an awkward suitor, and being modest (and somewhat in awe of Papa's family connections and importance as an architect) said as little about himself as he could, answering only the few questions that Papa would have asked. And Papa, who was in a low state, only spoke the comfortable minimum civility required. I am not even sure that the idea of marriage, or the subject of Artur already being married, ever came up, but they had would have had Mama been present, and that could have squelched the romance as in the case of Lipinski.

At some blurred moment before I left for Krakow Papa and I finally had a conversation about my interest in Artur. Not much of profundity or intensity had passed between us for a while, and this talk was no exception:

"He is rather old for you, isn't he?" Papa asked.

"Just less than thirteen years," I said.

"He looks older."

"He is prematurely grey, Papa, and please do remember that I, too, am getting on."

"Yes, yes. I suppose he is a reliable type."

"I would think so."

"Do you love him?"

"I will find out."

"Indeed," and he hardly blinked an eye when I told him of my plans to go to Artur. But I knew that he resented the whole affair: he hated losing his daughters to other men. Aware that my mind was in part determined to pursue what had been started to a conclusion, Papa said nothing further.

My three sisters saw nothing wrong in the course I chose. When I discussed the situation with Karol Stryjenski, told him of my doubts and how little I understood the emotions that Rodzinski had stirred in me, he simply said, "If you love him, you will marry him! *It won't be easy, but it will be worthwhile.*"

During those days that Artur was in the hospital, I spent my visiting hours fluffing up his pillows, pouring water, and generally bustling about playing nurse. Artur hugely enjoyed both my fussing and commiseration. A stifled moan of discomfort followed by a glittering but brave smile would stimulate in me a new wave of sympathy and concerned activity and he soon came to understand the connection. Like a sick child, his every wince and sigh was designed to extort an affectionate and reassuring response. And these I willingly gave. I had no idea it might be a psychological pattern, and I really did not care. What counted was that his illness and pain, which were geniune enough, let me demonstrate my love in practical ways.

My introduction to Artur's mother took place at his bedside. While we were very different, we found a common ground in our love for her son, and that made knowing her progressively easier. At first, she struck me as an uncommunicative and not especially pleasant or interesting in what she had to say. She was primarily concerned with simple things, keeping house well above all else. But she also was an attractive woman, with brilliantly alive eyes and a sweet and docile manner.

It soon became apparent to me that what appeared as limitations in her personality resulted from years of suppression by the "General," the family's nickname for her husband. He had been a medical officer in the Austrian Army, a colonel, and had transferred to the Polish Army after the war and the reunion of his native province of Galicia with Poland. On his retirement he had the rank of general. Artur's father had been a domineering, temperamental man who subjected his wife to quasi-military discipline. This suited Mrs. Rodzinska, who was really not interested in anything outside her kitchen and the doings of her children and other family. The "General," however, either did not carry over his military rigidity into his relations with his sons, or if he did, was inconsistent enough to turn them out as spoiled brats.

Artur's sickroom, when his mother was absent, was a gay place. But each time mother appeared, a subtle change in his mood came about. He became earnest about being ill. When I enquired about his somber tone, all he would say was, "I suppose it's because we are a doctor's wife and son."

A few weeks later, Mrs. Rodzinska provided a clue to understanding this anomalous behavior. At the outbreak of World War I, Artur, who was living with his mother while studying law and music in Vienna, had acute appendicitis. His condition, following the operation, became serious. The wound refused to heal properly, and for several months he lay completely helpless in a water bed, the incision suppurating. Mrs. Rodzinska's concerned and solicitous attendance helped bring him through the ordeal. Then and after, all hospital moments shared by mother and son were very serious indeed.

Shortly before Artur was to be discharged, one of his cousins showed up, camera in hand. Nothing would do but that Artur's "fiancée"-nurse have an appropriate costume for the role. I borrowed a starched white cap and uniform from one of the nurses I had become friendly with, and struck a pose a little in the manner of those comedies in which the toothsome nurse nabs the rich patient.

Once Artur was released from the hospital, we traveled in slow stages to Krynica, a Carpathian Spa where we would spend his recuperation. Because of Artur's discomfort we had to move cautiously, but his incision and disposition held up beautifully. And whatever it was that had happened between us was still going on, even more intensely.

He, Mrs. Rodzinska, and I stayed at the nicest hotel at the Spa. All three rooms were strung out like boxcars along the rear of the building and each had an exhilarating view of the mountains from its balcony. We helped Artur unpack and put things in order. Responsibility for my future husband's *necessaire*, a handsome leather case filled with bottles of everything from eyewash to aspirin, was delegated to me. My parents had taken such portable pharmacies along with them on their trips, and I had, too. But never before had I seen such a profusion of specifics to aid and console so wide a range of ailments. Sharing space with the pill and tonic bottles and shaving articles was a regiment of blue and red lead pencils, all with rapier points, and a sharpener.

"What are these for?" I asked.

"For you to keep sharp, and for me to mark scores," he said. That made sense, I thought to myself, and did it for many more than twenty years afterward.

The following morning I went to Artur's room to help him with breakfast and to have my own. I found him already awake in bed, propped up with pillows and cushions, a large conductor's score in his lap and a big grin on his face.

I sat on the side of his bed, gave him a good-morning kiss, and, with a thrust of my chin, raised a mute question about what he was studying. After popping a kiss on my cheek, he said "Strauss. *Zarathustra,*" which in those days was considered to be very modern.

"Don't you need a piano?" I asked.

"No," and another kiss. "I hear it all this way, like reading."

As I sat back I heard a crunching sound, like walnuts cracking. Artur laughed.

"You can start sharpening pencils now, if you like."

The score pages were marked all over, red and blue, with the most cryptic kinds of symbols, but with an ordered beauty that complemented the expanse of Strauss's engraved notes.

"I'll explain it some other time," he said.

We breakfasted together, and then Mrs. Rodzinska and I went to take the baths for which the Spa was famous, leaving Artur to study his scores, an activity that I came to associate with his mornings.

The love between us grew as the days of that summer lengthened and ripened. The golden air of the afternoons, the crimsons of the sunsets, and the black night skies iced with the crystal points of stars that can only be seen in that latitude created precisely the atmosphere and climate in which our kind of romance flourished. But as August's days began to shorten, and Artur had to leave, first for the tail end of the season at Salzburg, then California, a bit of tension developed between us.

One day, joking over all the medicines he carried about with him, Artur suddenly became very serious.

"Halusienko, I am no bargain, no great prize."

"Nor am I, darling," I said, a little nervous.

"Some people say I am crazy — well, difficult to live with."

"Is that your wife's opinion?" I asked.

"She's seen my temper, and it *is* awful. But I am not healthy. I have constant stomach trouble, headaches, bad eyes — I'm almost blind in one, and, who knows, the other might go. And," he continued, "I may be forced to stop conducting altogether. I have a piece of calcium in my shoulder joint which sometimes kills me when I move too violently."

"Artur, I am not worried," I said. I hesitated to tell him how something instinctive in me was aroused, even excited, by caring for sick people. It not only gave me pleasure but also satisfaction; there was for me a sense of fulfillment in nursing someone, a sense of the resurrection in every recovery.

Toward sunset that day we went for a walk among the cool, violet and dark-blue shadows of the pines and spruces that thickly crust those mountains, and it was then that he told me something of his musical preferences; and I spoke of my shortcomings in the same area.

"This countryside — any mountain woodland — always makes me think of Wagner. Of all composers, he is perhaps closest to my heart. Of course, I have an affair with whatever piece I am performing or studying at the moment. But Wagner — somehow, I disappear in his music; I am there conducting, watching every note as scrupulously as I can, but I am almost unconscious, almost like a medium. It's hard to explain."

"Artur," I said after a moment's pause, "I am certifiably unmusical. There is a waltz I can play on the piano, but I was forcibly excused from chorus by Mr. Majzner."

He had his arm looped about mine, as he did that night on Aleje Ujazdowskie, and he drew me tight to his side to whisper, "That's precisely why I love you."

"Ilse is a musician. . . ."

"Yes, an excellent one, the only woman I've ever known who could have been a first-rate conductor," he said quietly. "And I owe her very much. There was a time when I could never have grown without her help. But music and our son were the only things we ever really shared."

"They don't get on. That sometimes happens in marriages," was all Mrs. Rodzinska had to say about Artur and his wife. Whatever concern I might have had about mother-in-law problems disappeared in light of her candid, realistic attitude toward the mother of her grandson.

While she and I took our cure at the Spa, either at the baths or strolling among the invalids, hypochondriacs, and elderly leisured, Mrs. Rodzinska often spoke of her son, the only subject, aside from the "General," which could make her voluble.

"He was a pretty child — people used to congratulate me on my 'daughter,' " she said with a dry chuckle. "But he could be a demon. His brother Riki was so quiet, so easy. But Artur! We used to call him 'Turek' (little Turk). Halina, you have no idea the mischief that child caused, even from the moment of his birth. The 'General' and I had not intended to have any children after Ryszard. You know how it is, military man, a household here, another there. Children become baggage, and it is no way to raise them, simply not fair to move them around that way. Well, the 'General' was stationed in Dalmatia, at Split, and I became pregnant. I am sure you will think it dreadful of me to say I didn't want the child, certainly not the way I had wanted our first son, but I wasn't about to do anything wrong, either. Anyway, Christmas had come and gone, and I was still carrying the child — they say the second one is always easier — and for New Year's Day, I was frying up my *paczki* (doughnuts) when suddenly he gives a kick and, one-two-three, I had another son. The *paczki* were spoiled. The 'General' was a nervous wreck. (You'd think a medical man and Army officer would take such things in stride.) And despite all the misgivings I had had about having another one there he was in my arms, grinning and wriggling. Wait! Some day you'll have your turn.

"The 'General' was a very proper gentleman, you know, an officer down to his toenails, very ethical. But he perpetrated a forgery on Artur's birth certificate. It says 2 January 1892. You can be sure the correct

(56)

day was the 1st. This is how Artur managed to miss conscription! It made him one year younger for the first call-up, and then his appendicitis protected him for the duration. I'm not saying the 'General' had a vision of the Great War, mind you, but it was providence that may have made him cheat a little. Besides, the Emperor Franz Josef didn't need another Polish lawyer-conductor for his meatgrinder."

I still laugh when I recall her plumlike tone of voice, sweet yet with a tart aftertaste, when she spun off this tale. I'm amused, too, whenever I look in a music reference book, an old *Who's Who* or the *Encyclopaedia Britannica*: they all give Artur's birth as January 2, *1894*, a date inaccurate by one day and two years. The practice of playing loose with biographical data was carried 731 days further by the imaginative son. Vanity was probably the reason. Conductors as a breed and to a man are vain and like to preserve the fiction of youthful vitality as long as they can. It also helps professionally in another respect: if a man has not been named the director of a major orchestra by forty, he is considered a failure. If he can hang onto a post until sixty, he is a musical elder statesman who can get away with most things short of homicide — even mediocrity.

While we sat in bath chairs, wrapped in shapeless chenille robes and sipping at the nasty-tasting mineral waters, Mrs. Rodzinska poured out in dizzying profusion tales of Turek's youthful deviltry. While Artur was to me the romantic figure of our first encounters, through his mother's stories he emerged as thoroughly human. But there was also a side of him I was yet to see.

One day, at the dinner table in the hotel's grand dining room, I recognized a Warsaw acquaintance, no one I knew especially well, but well enough to nod a greeting. He came to our table and exchanged some pleasantries, was introduced to Artur and Mrs. Rodzinska, and then we said good-bye. I may have given him regards to some mutual acquaintance or even to his wife — I do not recall. Artur fell silent when the man left, and had only perfunctory things to say throughout the remainder of the meal. I asked him if he were not feeling well, and he replied that I might find him "poor company" that evening. We left for our respective rooms, and I read for a while. Suddenly, thinking that perhaps something was really seriously wrong, I put aside my book and went to his room.

"May I come in?"

"If you wish," he said coldly.

"How do you feel? Are you uncomfortable?"

"Uncomfortable? Me? I couldn't be better. But how's your . . . *friend?*"

"Friend? What *friend?*" I said, imitating his tone of voice to show that I understood something piqued him, but what, I could not fathom.

"The handsome fellow you went out of your way to talk to downstairs, in the dining room. Is that the *type* you prefer?"

There it was: jealousy, crude and naked. I told Artur I barely knew the man, that I wasn't sure he had a wife or not, that it was difficult even to remember his name to introduce him.

"Yes. I see. Well, it's late. I'm sleepy. Give your friend my regards. Goodnight." And with this little speech, he switched off a lamp at the side of his bed and rolled over. Unless I wanted to talk to his back and a huddle of pillows, the discussion was apparently over.

The following morning, when I went to join him for breakfast, and to sharpen pencils, it might have snowed overnight considering the chill in the room.

"I hope you had a pleasant night," he said, frost clinging to each syllable.

"Yes, I did."

"Thank you for the pencils."

"My pleasure," I said, and I went off to drink nasty mineral water with Mrs. Rodzinska.

"Artur can be jealous, you know," she told me.

"I can see that," I said, "but how long does it last?"

"It depends. Be patient."

It did not last long. That afternoon, by walking in the places where I knew he would not go, I avoided Artur. When my patience, curiosity, and love could hold out no longer, I took the paths he normally used until I saw him — deep in animated conversation with my acquaintance from Warsaw. The two of them got on famously until the day he left. That was my initial sample of the jealousy that would plague our marriage intermittently for years.

Our two-month interlude at the Spa was near an end. Artur was becoming restive. In a sense he was charging himself up for the ordeal of board meetings, conferences with managers, tours, personnel problems, patrons — burdens that the director of an orchestra must carry. His schedule, as he outlined it to me, seemed horrendously depleting. In addition, he had no great desire to go back to California, neither to his wife and their family situation nor to the place itself.

"Halusia, you cannot imagine how much I miss the snow that will fall on these mountains shortly," he said standing on the balcony of his room. "I miss the cycle of the seasons, the sense of time maturing, resting in its winter's old age, its revitalization in the first green of spring. You don't have these things in California."

"I feel cut off out there. I'm not in the center of things. There is no musical life. There is what I do, and not much else. It isn't like Vienna or New York where one drops in around the corner and hears a new artist or has a drink with a composer who is on to a new idea or sound."

"But you do go to New York, don't you?"

"Darling, it takes four days by train to get there from Los Angeles." I was appalled. I had never before fully realized the immensity of the United States. It was not just a nation, it was a continent.

"Of course," he continued, "my dream — the dream of any conductor over there — is a post in Chicago, Boston, Philadelphia, or New York. But if that ever comes it will be a long way in the future. For now, my hope is an orchestra in the heartlands: Cleveland. It's also a real possibility. The orchestra's director goes at the end of this coming season, and the board is looking for a new conductor."

"They'll hire you, you'll see," I said.

"Halusienko, they barely know how to pronounce my name, but they have invited me to do a pair of concerts around Christmas time. If I am a success, I might get the job. If not, I'll have to try harder to like sunshine all year round."

"You'll make a sensation, darling," I said.

"How can you be so sure?"

"You will do your best, and I will pray as hard as I can."

He laughed, then said, "For the time being I'll put my faith in what I can do, but don't let that stop your prayers — every bit helps. And I want Cleveland, not just because it moves me along the way to where I will go one day, but it will be the ideal thing for us — a place to start our lives among new people, no questions, no useless memories."

The following day, we entrained for Vienna, Artur, Mrs. Rodzinska, and I. The trip was tedious. Artur was edgy, Mrs. Rodzinska was in an uncommunicative reverie, perhaps happily off cooking in her mind's kitchen or pressing a dress tunic for the "General." I was preoccupied with the joyless things that I would resume at home and the loss of Artur. When we arrived in Vienna, the city was sweltering. He had dozens of phone calls to make, including one to an old flame, Fritzi. He wanted me to meet her, but, somehow, schedules could not be arranged.

"You will like her. She was my first real love, the first one I wanted to marry, anyway," he said.

"Don't you think I should be jealous?" I asked.

"I don't think it's in you," he replied. "You'd be hurt, but you'd hang on, a little like a pug dog," he said. Then, holding me close, he hesitantly asked, "If I get too lonely for you, darling, will you come visit me in California?"

"To the end of the world, Artur," I assured him, swallowing a mouthful of tears.

Our parting took place a few days later at the train station. In the last few minutes Mrs. Rodzinska, who had been at a news kiosk buying some magazines and papers for Artur, joined us. Just as the trainman began signaling the passengers to board, Artur took the magazines from his mother with one hand and kissed her on the cheek. With his other, he hugged me close for a kiss that seemed to last forever then he whispered in that soft, raspy tone of his, "Pray hard for Cleveland, and don't look at any boys, don't flirt. You know how jealous I can be." And he was gone.

Chapter 10

AFTER separating from Artur, I was overcome by emotional help-lessness — what was I to do with myself, and how. Other questions filled my mind. How would Artur's wife respond to the divorce proceed-ings which I assumed were about to be initiated? Would she resist the proposal and might not Artur weaken? After all, there was the son whom they both loved very much to consider.

My return to No. 10 Aleja Roz and my role as the mistress of Papa's household was no consolation. Indeed, this was the first time that I had passed through our beautifully proportioned arched doorway without a surging sense of homecoming.

In these ways I found that my love for Artur had changed me. I had emotionally become a part of him, incomplete in myself apart from him. For me the pivot of my existence suddenly ceased to be my family and its concerns. Rather, now, it was the well-being, the success, the fulfill-ment of another half a world away. I had begun to live for a future, barely tolerating the day-to-day aspects of a life that before had been a self-justifying satisfaction. To put the matter bluntly, I was desperately in love, and totally committed to a man whose telegram commanding me to appear at a hospital room had given me sleepless nights, first by the presumptuousness of the idea, then by the interminable waiting for it to be realized.

Within two days of my homecoming the postman became my new friend, his appearance almost as dear and attractive to me as Artur's. I had never noticed the fellow before, but all was changed after that first letter from Salzburg in which Artur told me that I held a mortgage on his heart, among other endearments. On the days when there were no letters for me with an Austrian, German, then later, American post-mark, I wondered if the postman beat his dog, brutalized his wife, or stole from poor boxes. If he handed over a letter that betrayed a flick of the carmine or green or blue of a foreign stamp, he appeared in my eyes as one from among the higher ranks of angels. This happened every three or four days.

Often, time permitted Artur only a few lines on a postcard. Finally, I received a letter which enclosed a review of the beginning of his season with the Los Angeles Philharmonic, a rave. From the little I could understand, it seemed that Los Angeles was more taken with Rodzinski than he was with them. His program included Strauss's *Death and Transfiguration* and Sibelius's First Symphony. The reviewer was impressed by Artur's "renewed vigor" and "increased authority" over his men, but he failed to speak of the ceaseless sun of southern California or the effects of a summer among the Carpathians; clearly, there were things I knew that the reviewer did not, and I was delighted.

I wrote daily, either adding a few lines to a long letter I would eventually mail or a short note in response to his constant demand to be reassured of my love. He was always enjoining me "not to flirt," and probably thought that if I spent all of my hours composing variations on the theme of "I love you," there would be no time for infidelities.

Actually, I had little free time. The household routine took care of that. Marysia, "the baby" for so long, was becoming a grown-up and was a great help in looking after things but the major responsibilities were mine. Fela concentrated on the design projects (the last one before she married handsome young pianist Kazik Krance was the residence for artists in Zakopane Karol Stryjenski had been working on at the time of his sudden death).

My routine revolved around our Sundays "at home," working for the blind, and dealing with Papa. The family's economic situation had very much deteriorated. When our domestic staff had to be reduced to one maid and a cook I thought the world was at an end, certainly the world as I had known it. We even talked seriously about moving from our apartment. It would bring sorely needed income. The family, now also short of Aniela, could move down to the ground floor after Papa's inactive *atelier* was converted into acceptable, if less spacious, living quarters. But these plans were only in the talking stage. Things would be ideal, I often thought, if I would get married — and *soon!* In this thought Papa concurred the few times we discussed it.

The spirit of Christmas 1932 made a perfunctory and noncommittal pass through the Lilpop apartment. It was without savor for me because my heart and mind were linked irrevocably now to a person outside the family orbit. I was fledged psychologically and spiritually. My first flight from the nest waited only for a destination and a date. These came shortly after Christmas. Artur cabled that his Cleveland concerts had been successful. The audiences were enthusiastic, the critics sympathetic. More importantly, he was engaged on the spot as musical director, beginning in September 1933. Along with this news came the request from half the world away to join him in Los Angeles, a request I had promised in Vienna to satisfy.

When I told Papa and my sisters of my intentions to join Artur, they thought an announcement should be made to the Wieniawskis, Troszels, and Lilpops at a formal family gathering. Accordingly, we invited all of my grandaunts, aunts, and female cousins, uncountable and often distant by several degrees, to a tea. The men would hear about my plans from their wives or sisters. Only my mother's half-sister, Aunt Maria Ejsmondowa, refused to come. She disapproved of my conduct so completely that she considered me a *demoiselle perdue*. I returned the compliment by not paying her a farewell call before my departure, and broke off relations completely. These were not renewed until the end of World War II when, like most Poles, I made every effort that I could to locate and help my surviving family.

My grandaunts, aunts, and cousins brought me a silver tea service, presuming that my marriage was imminent. I did not lie to them, but I glossed over the obstacles which still remained, and cherished the tea service nonetheless. Except for Aunt Maria, all the relatives gave my choice of man and decision their unqualified approbation, some expressing relief that the prospect of my becoming an old maid had vanished from their horizons and consciences.

Among the many farewell visits I made before leaving for America in late January 1933 was to see Director and Mrs. Mlynarski. Aside from their unconcealed pleasure in my choice and happiness, they gave me two other gifts. One was a beautiful laprobe "to keep warm on the trip," and the second was some sound advice. Tatka, never a cynical man to my knowledge, said, "You shall see how many new 'friends' you will quickly have. All the artists — singers, instrumentalists, and other conductors — will vie for your friendship. But do not trust everyone. You are to become a conductor's wife — not an agent." I put this into my luggage with the laprobe. The woolen gift long ago ended as a banquet for moths, but the verbal one still remains crisp and unfaded in my storage bin of useful things.

Toward the middle of January, after tearful good-byes with my sisters and a sort of uncomprehending surrender of me to my fate by Papa, I went to France by train and then sailed from Le Havre aboard the S.S. "Champlain" for what was an eight-day trip to New York.

The main attraction aboard ship was Auguste Piccard, the Swiss physicist, the first man to penetrate the stratosphere with his balloons. At that time he was preparing for a descent to the ocean's bottom in a bathyscape of his design. Today's astronauts, with all the national treasure, technological expertise, and truly incredible organization that supports them, are much less romantic than Piccard seemed in those days. Perhaps the reason was Piccard's independence, the assertion of his free curiosity and personal desire to explore what was "the unknown."

I myself made an important discovery in the dining room. I shared a table with a charming woman from Philadelphia, who, in every respect, was a well-bred lady. But she startled me by eating the table's floral centerpiece, a tall glass filled with the ridged stalks of a pretty, ivory-green, leafy plant. She took one of these plants from the glass, sprinkled salt on it, and began eating it with a noise that sounded like someone walking on a gravel path with heavy boots. "It's celery," she said. "Try some. It's tasty."

Usually, the dining room was empty. Few passengers had much stomach for both the ocean at that time of year and the huge array of rich French foods served in endless courses. Yet, I was able to indulge my own sometimes outrageous appetite without becoming sick during that rough winter crossing. Monstrous waves, walls of black, dense water, would rise above the mast or funnel to recede only as the ship shuddered and leaped forward and skyward, almost suspended above the ocean's surface at a forty-five degree angle. It was frightening, yet awesomely beautiful. My respect for Columbus and the same Champlain for whom the ship was named increased enormously when I thought of the frail, leaky wine barrels in which they had first gone to America. I also understood why old Battistini had refused to transport his glorious baritone to New York merely to sing for the Morgans, the Astors, and Vanderbilts.

And then came New York City's harbor, the Statute of Liberty, and the unreal skyline with its towering buildings, not at all unlike the expressionistic backcloths I was accustomed to seeing in productions of theater pieces with an American setting. As I walked down the gangplank the few English phrases I had memorized for the occasion fled me. Had I not seen Miecio Munz's tall figure and broad smile in the crowd I am sure I would have collapsed in a shuddering heap at the bottom of the gangplank. But Nela's former husband, alerted by Rodzinski to meet and guide me around New York, spared me all that.

What I have since come to see as beauty in New York's port was lost on me that first day. The docks appeared dreary and gloomy in comparison to those I had seen in Europe, and there was neither enchantment nor beauty in the streets through which our cab drove on the way to the St. Moritz Hotel, where Zosia Kochanska had reserved a room for me.

As we rode along 57th Street, Miecio pointed out Carnegie Hall. "It's in there that we go through our agonies," he said. It seemed enough of an agony to look at it from the outside, let alone enter it, I thought. But, then, the day was bleakly wintery, and coming from a place where a concert hall or opera house has to be an architectural event for the eye as well as the ear, it was understandable that I was not impressed. Today I would fight anyone to the death for proposing to raze that building.

At the hotel I found the elevator ride to what seemed the top of the world, as high as Piccard might ascend in his balloon, amazing. My ears popped as Miecio and I rode in the vehicle's dark walnut and brass interior. Certainly, I had been on much, much higher mountains, but never had I reached their peaks in so short a time. And then the view from the thirty-second floor! John Dos Passos, in a novel of his I had read recently, remarked that New York was "a standing city," whereas all the others in the world are lying flat, or at least sitting comfortably. Cars and trucks scurried like vermin on the streets below, and people were

(63)

mere dots of grey or occasionally red or yellow. And surrounding, rising up jaggedly, were the wonders of the world, the newly-built Empire State Building, the Chrysler Building with its graceful needle-like spire, the Waldorf Astoria, and the RCA Building, the first in the new Rockefeller Center complex.

"This is New York," Munz said, waving at the view like a sorcerer revealing a nightmare in his crystal. "Isn't it exciting?"

I quickly changed my dress and we left for lunch with the Kochanskis. The walk to their apartment at 74th Street and Lexington Avenue was a revelation straight from the pages of the Apocalypse. The sun had been permanently eclipsed. The prevailing architectural coloration was grey, and the sidewalks and streets were slush-slicked conduits for people and machines, all also equally colorless. The noise was dreadful, a mechanical Babel. At Park Avenue, Miecio pointed out the street as "the place where the rich people's rich people live, a most elegant address." "This dismal trench without trees," I said increduously.

Zosia and Paul had an apartment which, in its furnishings and taste, made me instantly feel at home. She had assembled lovely things with an eye for comfort when she put together the place. It had good carpets and paintings, and a few antiques to dispel the raw newness that, even after one-day's acquaintance, I saw permeating the city. Occupying a prominent position in the living-room was Paul's portrait, violin in hand, by Stanislaw Lenc, a noted Polish artist and a colleague of Papa's. It and the artist's familiar signature somehow made a link with that Warsaw which had begun to seem terribly, terribly distant.

Over a superb meal *à la Polonaise* Zosia and Paul told me of their lives in America. They were busy, frightfully so, it appeared. Zosia had a salon that attracted painters, writers, and (of course) musicians. It was some while since I last had seen her, and where before I had found her not especially attractive, I now felt the great charm Zosia possessed. Part of it, her ability to "listen well," was what elicited the affections of so many gifted, far more interesting persons. Paul, a born matinee idol of the violin, was as darkly handsome as ever, and still witty and warmhearted. Zosia socialized and entertained; Paul played to the greatest acclaim all over America. In addition, he was the jewel on the faculty of the then young Juilliard School of Music.

I had had the feeling that I was invited to lunch as a favor to Artur, but both Zosia and Paul made it clear they were glad to see me in their home for myself. And, as I was later to discover in my own social life in America, it was often sufficient excuse to entertain someone simply to exercise a Polish that tended to become rusted. We lingered at the table for hours while I refurbished my hosts' stock of current Warsaw gossip. I also had with me a letter from Karol Szymanowski telling his latest news about works in progress and his health (never better than so-so) and his pinched financial situation. The letter was eagerly devoured with our dessert, along with every bit of news I could give about

Emil Mlynarski who had done so much to develop Paul's gifts as a violinist. Unfortunately, there was little good that I could tell of Tatka's health.

To brighten the mood, Paul and Miecio decided on a plan for the evening: they would take me to Radio City Music Hall at Rockefeller Center to see the show. The place had just opened. It was immense, seating 6,000. There in addition to the talking picture, which would have been amusing enough, we were entertained by a "chorus line" and an orchestra and an organ.

Toward midnight the Kochanskis and Munz deposited a thoroughly exhausted me at the St. Moritz. Just as I entered my room a long-distance call came through from Artur.

"I can't wait to see you," he said. "You'll take the train in the morning."

"I can't wait to see *you*," I replied, "and I don't think I can take much more of New York. I'm dead tired."

"I can imagine," he said, "You saw the Kochanskis?"

"Yes, we lunched, then went out this evening," I replied. "They were very nice to me, although I really did not know them all *that* well at home."

"They've reason to be nice. . . . In 1925, they were among the first people I looked up after I arrived. Their reception was downright frigid. Imagine, they advised that I should have stuck with the Warsaw Opera instead of 'discovering America like a Polish Columbus' — I think that was the way Zosia put it. I was so hurt and disgusted, I walked out and swore never to see them again. I think I even spat on their doorstep. But, you know how it is, people forget these things and try to get along."

"Darling, it is very late, and though we could talk for hours I must have my rest if I am to be on that train," I said. And then I was given my first cross-continental kiss, and all the blessings and endearments that would make sleep at the top of the world possible.

Before sleep came, Artur's somewhat cryptic remark about the Kochanskis ("They've reason to be nice") suddenly made sense, particularly considering Tatka's advice about "everyone being a friend." Rodzinski had become an important name on the American musical scene. His debut in New York, with the Philadelphia Orchestra, had been a sensation. His success in Cleveland was news, and his appointment as director of the Cleveland Orchestra was probably making the circuit of musical gossips. I was to become Artur's wife. Ergo, the Kochanskis were "my friends." The cynicism of such a thought bothered me, but Tatka, never one to take a jaundiced view of things, had not given me a cynical piece of advice. Rather, he had told me of the realities of my new life.

As I lay in bed thinking about these things, I could see from the window the fairyland lighting of the skyline, the blinking neon, the running twinkling signs, the thousands of windows behind which lights turned on and off as the city, five times the size of Warsaw, went about its twenty-four hours of business. It was as though I were taking part in a deep sleep's dream. Far away and far below, a cab horn's *ouggha* or the disconsolate wailing of a siren sounded very much like the swarming of some kind of perverse winter insect. "This will be my home, this strange place," I said to myself, neither with conviction nor disbelief. My studies at Two Jadwigas had in no way prepared me for these things I had so far seen or was at that moment hearing. The America they taught me about in faraway Warsaw was Red Indians and Robber Barons, Columbus, and the invention of the telegraph.

Chapter 11

THAT next morning's excitement would have been unbearable had I seen on drawing the blinds glorious sunshine or some other omen favoring an important venture. What I beheld was the dismal grey of the day before, this time streaming from the sky to the streets below in semi-liquid form: it was sleeting. And instead of the bird songs that even in winter would greet me on awakening in Aleja Roz were those same niggling, nagging car, truck, and bus horns that had honked me to a restless sleep six hours before.

As I waited for breakfast, it seemed to me that Artur must be slightly mad: if there were a choice between the continuous grey that I saw through the window and continuous sunshine, the latter should be preferable. And when my breakfast came, the sun did too in a tall glass of freshly-squeezed sweet orange juice. At home we ate oranges, never drank them. They were too expensive to consume in the quantities needed to fill a glass. Here they flourished in semitropical Florida, and in that same California whose sunshine Artur cursed.

Shortly after breakfast Miecio Munz arrived. Within minutes we were in a cab to Grand Central Terminal. The place had a cavernous look inside, and it seemed that at each turning lurked another false direction or fateful destination, with one platform after another leading to someplace other than California. I was properly awed by Munz's ability to talk fluently with an information-desk clerk, and quietly followed him without question.

Since we found the right train in plenty of time, Miecio was able to see me aboard. He explained all the mechanical niceties of a sleeping car lower berth: how during the day my bed was a comfortable, green velour seat, and how at night, by virtue of a Pullman patent, it would turn into a bed-dressing space (room, I could hardly call it). The cars, very big by European standards, were not as elegant as the *wagon-lits* manufactured by Lilpop, Rau & Levenstein in Poland.

Munz also showed me where the dining car was, and introduced me to a porter, telling him of my need for "special attention," and unobtrusively guaranteeing the man's concern with a substantial *pourboire*. After that, we went to the observation car in the rear from which I would be able to see where I had been while on the way to where I was going. Then, with the harried ringing of a bell, and much chanting by blue-coated and capped conductors of "Awwwwwl-bord," Miecio took my hand, gallantly bowed, and disappeared like a good genie who had done all that he had been commanded. Our parting words were the last Polish I would hear for four days and three nights.

Throughout the journey I was excited by thoughts of what might await me at its end, fascinated by the sights and sounds of my fellow passengers, and overwhelmed by the panorama of this enormous nation passing outside my window. At Chicago, I changed trains — a frightening experience for someone somewhat helpless in English. The porter Munz had assigned to me in New York proved invaluable. I may have undertipped him for his kindness, but only because of my confusion over converting zlotys into dollars and in conceptualizing the American way of doing things. Tips in America, like everything else, I soon realized, come big. A raised eyebrow or a grimace of disgust told me as much as a statement in glib Polish would have, and my tips grew larger.

For years my sole and hardly reliable information about America had been Henryk Sienkiewicz's *Letters from America*, a collection of travel pictures published in the last quarter of the nineteenth century. Like Dickens' vignettes of his American tour, they concern themselves with the skin, not the heart, of the matter. Sienkiewicz had in no way prepared me for the world that the train passed through, one of vast plains, huge rivers, large (by the European standards of my youth) cities dropped helter skelter along the track, mountain ranges, and deserts.

When the train pulled into Santa Fe, I was startled to hear a porter shout my name. The message he handed me was from Artur reaffirming his love. All across Arizona that telegram was my chief occupation when I was not gazing with amazement at burning red buttes and the parched earth. I kept putting the little yellow oblong into my purse, retrieving it, unfolding it, reading it, refolding it.

When I arrived in Los Angeles, Artur was on the train platform, his face just visible behind a very large smile and bouquet of roses and orange blossoms. Somehow the flowers survived the crushing embrace and kiss we exchanged. As we stepped back to take a look at each other at arm's length we heard the sound of a throat being cleared. Only then did Artur remember to introduce me to his friend Vlady Drucker, the first trumpet player of the Los Angeles orchestra.

"Vlady will look after you when I can't be free," Artur explained, "so I thought you should become acquainted right at the beginning."

With Vlady's help we loaded my luggage into Artur's big Packard, and drove directly to the Montecito Apartments, where Artur had taken a two-room efficiency for me. It was on Franklin Avenue, and from the top floor, where my rooms were, I had a splendid view of Hollywood. When we entered the living room, a Filipino houseboy had just finished arranging flowers in various vases and was tidying up. This touch struck me as wonderfully exotic. Then, after amenities were exchanged with Vlady, who spoke Russian excellently, giving me a chance to put my creaky knowledge of that language to work since my English could not accomplish much, both he and the houseboy left me to Artur and a serious talk.

Artur had not yet been divorced from his wife, he had not even begun proceedings! Indeed, he had only recently broached the subject. I was disappointed, even hurt. But Artur had reason on his side as he pointed out. The filing of divorce papers would immediately be taken up by the press and the publicity could endanger his future position as director of the Cleveland Symphony Orchestra.

"Divorces are fine for movie stars," he said, "but proper Midwesterners expect their conductors to be above reproach, like Caesar's wife."

It was not easy to swallow this news. Yet I could understand just how delicate his position was. "You must be patient if you care for me," he said. After traveling eight days at sea and four days on a train to come to be with him I knew I cared for him, and I would find the patience required.

I saw Artur for a bit each day, and whenever he had an entirely free pair of days, we would go on an expedition. He was like a child excitedly pointing out anything of interest. The Los Angeles of those days was like a garden. Hollywood, Santa Monica, and Beverly Hills were quiet, even indolent little communities that had a definable shape and distinctive charm.

We would drive for miles without seeing anything but orange trees. There was so much natural beauty to admire on the way to Palm Springs, which had only one or two hotels and a handful of private villas, or to Pasadena, or to Santa Barbara with its exquisite, then pristine beaches. One sight Artur pointed out stands firmly impressed in mind, both as it was then and as it has handsomely come to be since. It was a grassy knoll surrounded by fruit groves and free of any noise save the rhythmical chatter of insects. It was there, Artur said, that the Los Angeles Philharmonic would have its home one day.

In February 1933 I passed, thoroughly shaken but unscathed, through my first earthquake. It was late at night, or very early morning, when the first tremor was felt. I was sitting up in bed, writing letters, when I was startled by a dense, muffled rumbling sound, something like a grand piano rolling across the roof of the Montecito Apartments.

Then, with the same noise, the entire room gave a shudder and seemed to twist at its corners much like a shoe box being crumpled for the trash. After that came an unnatural silence. No cars moved on Franklin Avenue below. There was no wind and none of the rain I assumed would follow the thunder-like rumblings. I looked out of the window, and seeing nothing unusual, returned to bed. Only then did I notice that the mirror above my dressing table and all the pictures in the room were askew.

The phone rang. It was Artur. "Just stay where you are," he warned.

The phone rang again. Vlady Drucker had the same advice. "Earthquakes aren't uncommon here," he added, "but I think this was a bad one."

The next day there were several more tremors of varying intensities. Now that I knew what they were, they gave me an insecure feeling. That evening's newspapers were filled with photographs of buildings sheared in half and of great, yawning fissures that had opened to swallow automobiles and people's front porches in the nearby towns. The following day my family cabled from Warsaw, no doubt having seen some of the same photographs (wirephoto services existed by this time). I quickly cabled back that I was alive, well, and still very much in love.

Although my social life was limited, I did go to parties with members of the orchestra. At one I had my first taste of illicit alcohol, not bathtub gin but "imported" liquor that was smuggled in from Mexico by motor launch and by men, who, if they carried fiddle cases, played in no local orchestra. Prohibition to me seemed to make no sense at all. The government had legislated against something everyone wanted, contradicting that "will of the people," which I obscurely understood to be at the heart of American democracy. The law helped make wealthy men out of criminals, and criminals out of the respectable people who bought their wares.

Much of my time was spent driving through the countryside. Vlady Drucker was my chauffeur if Artur could not be free. During the rides with Vlady I came to understand something of the role of a conductor's wife: she must be cordial with an orchestra's personnel, but never to the point of indiscretion. What happened between the instrumentalists and their director was a matter totally apart from their private lives. It was for this reason that Artur did not want me attending rehearsals, an obligation I had conceived would be mine and of which he disabused me: "It is unfair to me and the men to air our dirty laundry in public. What they do is not under performance conditions, and when I call down a player for something, it can be embarrassing if someone is present who doesn't understand our work," he said. "For us, it is a painstaking kind of job. We are striving to do something we each can be proud of. To get to that point sometimes involves playing or saying things that we would rather forget."

Vlady told me, "Artur is the boss. You might see us having a good time drinking in Tijuana after a San Diego date, but when we're up there on that platform, rehearsing or performing, there is no consideration for long-standing social intimacies."

Soon I attended my first concert. I cannot remember Artur's program that night. My attention was fixed on Rodzinski, the man on the podium, to whom I was being linked ever more inextricably, day by day. It had been so long since I watched him from the director's box in the Teatr Wielki that I did not recognize his special mannerisms — his hurried stride to the podium, head canted a little to the right, his jerky bow to the public and quick turn to the orchestra with arms outspread like a bird poised in flight before delivering his incisive downbeat. His gestures struck me as vigorous, yet graceful, especially in quieter passages, and overall, rather economical. Well-cut tails concealed the droop of his shoulders, and he looked, as does every man on a podium, bigger and closer to perfection than reality.

At the concert's end, he was given a genuine ovation, and this despite the fact that his Cleveland appointment had been made public. One might have expected some resentment at Rodzinski's leaving after only four seasons. But the people of Los Angeles had taken him to their hearts — so much so that they could forgive what would seem in another conductor a betrayal of trust.

Afterward there was a reception to attend given by Bessie and Cecil Frankel at the old Biltmore Hotel, then on the same square as the Auditorium. Frankel, one of Artur's friends, was a loyal supporter and admirer of his work. He was then president of the Equitable Life Assurance Society in California and at first I felt intimidated at meeting him. As it turned out, he was a gentle, soft-spoken person whose affection for Artur, which lasted throughout his life, completely won me over. And I also have much personal gratitude to him, for when Artur's small savings were wiped out by the Crash, Frankel steered him into life insurance among other investments. The basis for the income that I have now comes from those plans Frankel sagely advised Artur to make.

The party was memorable, too, because I met Ilse, Artur's wife, there.

Artur introduced us matter-of-factly. "Miss Lilpop, Mrs. Rodzinska," he said.

We both recognized each other.

"But of course," Ilse said. "We met at the Mlynarskis in Warsaw. Surely you remember, Artur." "Vaguely," was his reply.

"I gather you've taken up *nursing*," she said softly, but the emphasis on the word "nursing" had an inescapable sting. Artur must have sent home a copy of the photograph taken in his Krakow hospital room! I felt foolish, a little shabby, and betrayed. I must have blushed. Ilse was very civilized about the situation and indeed, she called me for tea the following day.

Artur drove me to his home in the Hollywood hills, a Spanish style villa, landscaped with orange trees, palms, and all sorts of flowering shrubs and plants. Ilse greeted me affably, and introduced Witold, her thirteen-year-old son. He was a tall, rangy boy whose features gave me an idea of what Artur must have looked like at that age. Then we made a grand tour of the household that missed not one marvel or convenience. When the house ceased to justify further conversation, Artur proposed that he and Witold go fly their kites on the slopes behind the rear garden.

Ilse and I had our tea while parrying light conversational thrusts. I was not good at this kind of small talk, and was certainly a novice at this kind of situation. Suddenly, and with a forthrightness I admired, she came to the issue between us.

"I simply don't understand why girls are anxious for marriage. I never had a really happy moment in all the years of mine," she said, neither sadly nor bitterly. "Possibly, I haven't quite the romantic perspective for such things," she added.

If I had had thoughts of the immorality of breaking up a marriage, she demolished them. "I imagine I was the first girl he knew who said 'No,' " she told me, "and that's why Artur wanted to marry me." I could see other reasons, however, for Ilse was quite beautiful in a cold, German way.

"He also regards you highly as a musician," I said, feebly trying to contribute something.

"Yes, I know," she said. "But he doesn't know how I feel about *him* as a musician," she continued. "I never praise him, only criticize. It's not very kind of me, but our marriage would have come apart at the seams had I told him what I really think of that side of him.

"Artur is self-made, you know. He had a protean grasp and feel for music, but these were acquired on his own. No teacher ever taught him — no teacher *could* have taught him what he understands with the ease that other people breathe. In his biographies the orchestra prints up for the papers, he is credited as studying with everyone on earth. As far as I know — and after all, I should, since we were students together in Vienna — he worked with no one but Professor Georg von Lalewicz at the piano, nothing more. The books say he studied conducting with Franz Schalk, composition with Franz Schreker, and did further work with Emil Sauer at the piano. Every bit of this is untrue. His first teacher, when he was a boy in Lvov, Willem Kurz, taught him most of what he can do at the keyboard, and he did not progress very far beyond that with Lalewicz. I think he signed up for a theory and harmony course under Professor Josef Marx, but I am sure he never handed in any exercises. And of the three years he worked with Lalewicz, he had to repeat one because his work was 'unsatisfactory.' That's when his father, the 'General,' was told by the professor that his son had no future."

"If this is all true, then how did he learn all that he knows?" I asked.

"Miss Lilpop," she replied, "no amount of training or certification will make a genius — only a qualified hack. Artur has a gift, God knows from where, that by discipline and hard work he developed, and will continue to develop. Where perfection is concerned, he is monomaniacal — and ruthless, at least with himself, But he will also drive players and singers to distraction searching for the right phrasing, the right dynamic level, rehearsing everyone to exhaustion. Were you old enough to hear his Warsaw performances of *Eros and Psyche* by Rozycki?"

"I heard about it," I said, catching the allusion to my age, and remembering how Artur had asked Tatka for rehearsals right up to the opening night curtain, how the singers were near revolt.

"Well, that was an instance of Artur's gift for making lead into gold. Somehow, he hears something in a piece of even the worst music and strives to make that something gleam. No conservatory certificate guarantees this, although Artur doesn't quite understand, inside, you know? He feels awfully insecure because he didn't serve as Mahler's assistant or some such thing."

"He worked with Stokowski," I said.

"The trouble with Artur is that he is as good as any of them, but in some secret place within himself a little voice says that he isn't. And that just may be what drives him further and further," she said.

The sun was low in the sky and Artur and Witold were returning from their kiting when Ilse stood up to end our talk. "Miss Lilpop, I hope you won't be a stranger during the remainder of your stay. You must come out and play tennis with Witold and me. Any afternoon. Artur or his friend Vlady could bring you."

The reference to Drucker made me aware of how little deception there was to my visit, or, if there was any, how inept it was.

"Certainly," I said.

"Any time. Good evening."

And with that, Witold and I shook hands, a little aloofly, and Artur, without a word, took my arm and led me to his car.

On the way to my apartment, he said, "I imagine she has told you all the family secrets. But it's better that they came from her than me."

And then he began to speak about their relationship. "I don't know why she married me," he began, "God only knows I've tried to puzzle it out. Her decision had not much to do with either love or attraction, although in the beginning I tried to make myself believe that I at least loved her. But we did get along, and we respected each other, and in many ways I didn't expect or even want much more.

"The last years of the war were chaotic. Vienna was a madhouse, Halusia. One day a senile old man who had ruled for as long as any living person remembered dropped dead. Then the weave of things began to unravel. Another person and maybe a job looked like enough to hang on to, to live for. We married and moved to Lvov. Then Witold came, the only part of the marriage that meant anything to her; she loves our son.

"In Lvov, I got hack jobs, playing the piano in cabarets for a handful of zlotys. There was an opening at the opera house for a rehearsal pianist, and I was taken on — I'm a good sight reader. Soon I became a vocal coach and sometimes rehearsed the chorus. One season, they decided to do Verdi's *Ernani* and since I had been working with both soloists and chorus, the director of the house told me to do the entire performance. I was scared to death. I knew the piece by heart, but I didn't know what to do in front of the orchestra. The concertmaster showed me some of the tricks. Then, I went home and worked with Ilse, she at the piano, me conducting her from the full score. Hour after hour of it. And sometimes my nerves gave out and I lost my temper. Then she would silence me by saying, 'Do you want to be a conductor? Well, work for it and hold your tongue!' And then we would start again.

"The strain between us grew worse, and we fought like two cats, but we worked together. I didn't depend on her any longer, but she was still there. In Warsaw she was only a rehearsal pianist and coach, yet she had the skills and the competence to do what I was doing. In a way, she threw over her own career for me."

The car was now stopped in front of the Montecito Apartments, and we sat quietly for a moment before Artur said softly, "You mustn't take the wrong idea, Halusia. I am grateful, very grateful to her for what she has done."

Then he kissed me and after promising to see me the following day, drove off.

I saw very little of Ilse and Witold while I was in Los Angeles, or any time thereafter. Years after Artur's death, we corresponded from time to time, and much of what is narrated here was freshened in my memory by her letters. Witold and I got on well, considering the plight in which so young a child found himself.

Toward the middle of April, I began to plan my departure. My situation in Los Angeles from the outset had been awkward, and with Artur's season coming to an end, there were many activities into which I would fit poorly. It was decided I should return to the East where Artur would meet me later.

In New York I was housed once more in the St. Moritz. I visited with the Kochanskis regularly, with Miecio Munz whenever he was free, and with my best American friend, Marjorie Oelrichs, who later married Eddy Duchin. I saw a museum or two, and heard some music, and generally found the city was really quite a livable place. Then Artur arrived with beautiful weather, and shortly thereafter we were aboard the S. S. "Rex," on our way to Italy together.

Chapter 12

OUR trip to Italy aboard the "Rex" was both uneventful and very roman-tic. If there were passengers of note traveling with us, we were unaware of them. The only people we saw or knew or had words for were each other. Ordinarily, at least for me, this would have been boring; but love has a way of making the repetitive and commonplace amusing, and both of us were quite helplessly in love.

Artur had made his breach with Ilse and had sent her and Witold back to Europe. Indeed, they would be in Firenze at about the same time as we, and perhaps also at Salzburg where Artur went every summer both for the music making and the proximity to his idol, Toscanini. Ilse we would avoid with ease, but not *Arturo Il Primo*. Part of our tightly scheduled travel plan included a stay in a little Umbrian town, Piazze, near Siena. There Artur intended to take a cure for his bursitis, that piece of calcium in his shoulder which he believed would eventually stop him from conducting. Toscanini would be in Piazze, too, taking treat-ment for the same ailment. It was Maestro, as every musician deferen-tially called him, who had found a certain Dottore Rinaldi, a peculiar physician with a remarkable course of injections and salves that could cure or alleviate the pain of this condition which is the bane of so many orchestral conductors. Somehow, I was more in awe of meeting Maestro than in fear of the possible embarrassment of an encounter with Ilse and Witold. Artur was convinced that his Arturo would like me and tried to assure me that my concerns were groundless.

When we were settled in Firenze, Artur rented a car, and I wrote, in Italian, a letter to Dottore Rinaldi, asking when we could come. Sev-eral days passed waiting for a reply which did not arrive. Artur was in-consolable. He had been told only the summer before by his surgeon brother in Krakow that the bursitis would have to be operated on, and he not only dreaded the surgery but also the gamble that he might lose the strength and mobility of his right arm and shoulder. The condition was so painful Artur had completed his final group of Los Angeles con-certs with his right arm in a sling, maintaining tempi with his left hand alone. Maestro Toscanini, who had lived with the same ailment for years, advised Artur against his brother's advice, and additionally had built up Artur's faith in this miracle worker who did not answer letters. Finally, when the tension became unbearable, I resolved the matter by placing a telephone call to Rinaldi's studio in Piazze. "He doesn't need any more sick people," the operator informed me. I discovered that Artur could no more accept a negative reply from a doctor than suffer a mistuned oboe. "We go there immediately," he said.

How we would get there and deal with Rinaldi was left to me. My Italian was certainly adequate, but my knowledge of the idiosyncrasies of the eccentric Italian physician was markedly deficient. I looked for assistance in familiar quarters, and called my old friends, the Passaglia brothers, Roberto, the half-hearted *fidanzato* of my sister Fela, and Augusto — or Zuzzi as he was known to friends. I remembered how helpful they had been when I had to deal with doctors and nurses while caring for Fela during her bout with typhus several years before.

It is odd how experiences shared in moments of crisis can build a camaraderie between people that bridges great lapses of time. When Zuzzi came alone to our hotel, for Roberto was away, the happenings of seven years earlier seemed like events of the previous weekend. We babbled away in several tongues about high fevers, water from Lourdes, the insufferable heat of that summer in Montecatini, and, of course, about this fabled Dottore Rinaldi.

The doctor was a cantankerous phenomenon, according to Zuzzi. Rinaldi even once refused to treat the Queen of Italy, writing to her that his last patient had died a horrid death and that in the best interests of the Italian throne she should seek care elsewhere. He was known to have seizures when new patients arrived at his door, not just ordinary temper fits, but ones that took their toll of furniture and medical apparatus. There was, however, no record of his doing violence to a supplicant, which heartened Artur to some extent. Among Rinaldi's eccentricities were a marked and very vocal detestation of Mussolini and a belief that poor and simple people deserved his treatment much more than the rich and influential. This did not mean that Artur should apply for Rinaldi's cure wearing sackcloth and ashes, but that a modest and long-suffering demeanor might be invaluable.

The next day, confident of Zuzzi's charm and Tuscan wiles, we packed ourselves into Artur's tiny rented car called Balilla and set off. Long-legged Zuzzi, folded up like a collapsed umbrella in the backseat along with our luggage, guided us to Umbria, through Siena, and into Piazze.

When we arrived in the early afternoon, we found ourselves in an indescribably primitive town that had not even a simple hotel. One could hardly miss Rinaldi's house, since it was surrounded by a horde of crumpled up, slow-moving people carrying a variety of canes and crutches. The other houses, of which there were not many, were the overcrowded homes of the local peasants. There was not a bathtub in the whole place, except, perhaps, at Rinaldi's, but there were no local stories of anyone ever having been invited in to use it. We were fortunate to find accommodations with three young sisters whose home had been

(75)

converted into a sort of *pensione*, a three-story affair with a sometimes workable toilet on each floor and washbasins in the bedrooms that could only be filled with a pitcher of cold water.

When we finished locating ourselves in various rooms throughout the house, the three of us set off for Rinaldi's villa. The place was walled around, but in the front there was a fence of tall iron palings, and beyond one could see a garden of a kind, its elegance being its unaffected and untended simplicity — random growths of nettles, crab grass, and rocks of all sizes. One scrawny pink rose was going bald on an almost leafless climbing bush. The entrance was imposing, however. There was a huge portal of fieldstone surmounted on either side by two cast-iron imperial eagles.

Round and about on the other side of the gate were a number of plain weathered plank benches for those who could sit. Displayed on these was an array of actual or would-be patients, exhibiting every conceivable form of arthritis and rheumatism. These victims, doubled up like jackknives or gnarled like old cypress roots, each had one or more walking sticks, most of chestnut, walnut, rosewood, one or two of ebony, several tipped or headed with silver ferrules.

We joined them and waited. There was little else to do. From time to time a sort of nurse or housemaid would peer out the front door at us. Finally, Zuzzi approached her in an unguarded moment, and through her gained access to Rinaldi. This caused quite a stir among the canes and creaking bones, a noise that sounded a bit like the *Danse Macabre* of Saint-Saëns, Artur thought. And the stir was even greater when Zuzzi came out, for the invalids were as curious as we to know what was the current mood in the Rinaldi establishment.

"*Dottore* lost his temper," he reported. "He said that he didn't want to know about any other ailing specimen of humanity, that he was not taking a census of such creatures, and that I and my Americans should go — away."

Artur flopped on a plank bench.

"I spoke up against the doctor's wishes, however," Zuzzi continued. "I told him about the disservice he was doing to music and to international relations, that here was a great American conductor who had humbly traveled half the world to seek his help, and more things that came into my head. I also cursed Mussolini for good measure, but I am afraid that it was all to no effect. When I wished God's blessings on him and a good day, he just snorted."

Disheartened, the three of us limped away for dinner at our pensione.

Somewhere between the *fettine di vitella* and the salad, a messenger from Rinaldi came to the house.

"*Il Dottore Rinaldi vorrebbe incontrarvi,*" stammered the poor fellow.

"So! The doctor will see *gli Americani*," Zuzzi trumpeted.

We returned quickly to Rinaldi's garden. The sun was going feeble in the sky, but the phalanx of patients on the inside of the iron palings remained steadfastly and rigidly where we had left them more than an hour before. Artur sat. I stood behind him, wringing my hands, a gesture that seemed to be the sole occupation of the other women standing behind their men. Zuzzi stretched out his ostrich legs and lit a cigarette, consoled in the knowledge that a Tuscan had once again conquered Umbria.

After a bit, Rinaldi appeared. He was short in everything — his hair, his arms, his fingers, his legs. He wore a surgeon's smock which came down to his shoes and which was spotted over with tomato stains and seeds and some brownish blotches that looked like either iodine or ancient gentian violet. He walked among the cripples brusquely, sizing them up, smiling at one or two and scowling at all the others. He finally circled around to where we were sitting.

Zuzzi shot up like a crossbow bolt, wished the doctor good evening, and introduced us.

My first impression of the man was of a diabolical creature with eyes of seething black. Then, suddenly, he smiled, and he was only a simple North Italian Doctor Jekyll. The heart that Zuzzi had conquered seemed to be of solid gold. Rinaldi led us on a circuit of his patients, by another route than his first, and into his studio. There he conducted a singularly uncomplicated examination. He asked Artur where his pain was located, how long he had had it, and then condescended to look at the X-ray pictures we had brought. These showed a chunk of calcium about the size of a pea. After a blood pressure reading, he told Artur that treatment would begin in the morning. We were dismissed.

Early the next day, Rinaldi's bleak garden was already filled with patients, many of whom we recognized. They were all rattling away about their aches and pains, asking and answering each other's questions as if they had been at it for months. Artur was in agony but it was difficult to say if the cause of his suffering was the bursitis — really inconsequential compared to the deformities around us — or despair about his future as a conductor and the efficacy of Rinaldi's treatment. Our fellow watchers in the doctor's outdoor waiting room were a cross-section of Italian society: factory workers, postal clerks, the obese wife of a landowner, the imposing widow of a former Cabinet Minister, a retired nurse, a cadaverous priest, and a most dignified man with a close-cropped beard, D'Annunzio style, to whom people made reference as "*Il Cavaliere*," and who carried an ivory-headed cane. Finally, toward noon, the doctor made a tour of his garden, sprinkling "*Come va?*" like grace, and accepting "*Bene, bene!*" for his fee. Truly, something miraculous was afoot: these people who moments before could speak of nothing but their wretched health now said they felt good in reply to questions about their conditions. We later discovered that if a patient did not report improvement the doctor would have one of his celebrated fits.

Since Artur had no fluency in Italian, I went with him to the doctor's studio as translator. I also found that the doctor enjoyed my presence, and having gotten this far with the celebrated man, I took advantage of his pleasure to endear myself with much batting of eyelashes and broad smiling. Fortunately, Artur was too occupied with his misery to notice.

"*Allora,*" Rinaldi said, wiping his hands on the same spotted smock he had worn the previous day, "*Cominciamo!*" He ordered Artur to lower his trousers and brace himself against the examining table. While Artur was doing this, the doctor took an immense syringe, the kind used by veterinarians on sick cows, perfunctorily dunked it into a bottle of alcohol and then proceeded to fill it with the arcane fluids he kept in drip-stained bottles on a dusty shelf. Fortunately, Artur was in no position to see the unsanitary conditions in which the doctor worked, nor the nature of the implement about to be used on him. The syringe's needle penetrated Artur's seat with difficulty, and whatever was in the syringe added nothing at all to the poor man's comfort. He did not yell, but I heard a few unpleasant Polish words strangle in his throat.

After the needle, the doctor ordered Artur to remove his shirt, and on the spot that was indicated, Rinaldi applied an ointment which stank awfully of decomposing fish and also burned — something as dark as iodine, but far, far stronger.

Poor Artur was now even more miserable. The bursitis was easy to live with compared to the cure. He could neither walk nor sit, and he felt as if his shoulder's skin had been seared away. He could only recline on his left side and mutter about what he had let himself in for.

Then, between treatments, Maestro Toscanini arrived with his friend and factotum, the conductor Bernardino Molinari.

Since Piazze offered no better housing facilities than the pensione that Artur and I lived in, it was here that Toscanini took up residence with Molinari. And it was at the *pensione's* dinner table that I first met Maestro.

For the event I dressed in my prettiest frock and took special care with my hair and face. I wanted to make a favorable impression on this great man as desperately as Artur wanted to be free of his calcium deposit. I was scared to death as I said a few words of Italian to him at our introduction. There was something intimidating about his blurry dark eyes. It was as though he were looking beyond or through, but not at, me. Later I discovered that he was terribly nearsighted, and too vain to wear eyeglasses. He immediately broke into a smile at hearing me use his tongue, a smile that thoroughly captivated me and removed the sting of his corrections: Maestro was no less a purist in his own language than in the musical languages of the composers he performed. He let no mistake go by, and every day in every conversation he would set right some grammatical construction. No woman ever had so august a tutor, I used to think, and yet he was so unassuming, when not in a rage, that it sometimes seemed silly to think of him as music's most commanding conductor since Mahler.

He had a raspy voice, even more so than my Artur, and a pitchless croak when he sang. He looked very proper and solemn in his black alpaca suits, butterfly cravats and black homburgs, a little like a rural politician. I can never recall seeing him in anything informal, save a dressing gown on a number of occasions. I was also surprised by his physical stature: he was about my height, which is short for a man. But he was well structured, muscular, and very forceful in his movements. In conversation he walked briskly about, clutching at the lapels of his jacket which he released only when there was a point to be made with some purposeful or descriptive gesture. When he was particularly excited, he would make waving motions as if conducting a Rossini *crescendo*.

Maestro took to me quickly, thank God, for life would have been insupportable had Artur's idol found me wanting. And, amusingly, one of those faults of mine, the one Artur had said Toscanini would appreciate, is what turned the trick.

"I love your face," he said, "because I love women with big mouths." Those teeth of mine, the subject of cruel teases by my brother Antek, had run the gamut from gross liability to invaluable asset. Accordingly, whenever Maestro and I were near each other I gleamed like a dentifrice advertisement. Another asset, of course, was my sex: Maestro had a wandering eye that, although myopic, ranged farther than broad smiles.

Our waits in Dottore Rinaldi's calciferous garden now became much more interesting. Molinari, Toscanini, and Artur would sit about, waiting their turns for Rinaldi's attention, discussing music, looking at scores, and gossiping, a favorite pastime of musicians. Toscanini was merciless in his remarks about other conductors. He never, or only rarely, had a good word for any of them. He was jealous and resentful of Koussevitzky, who returned the sentiments; and of Sir Thomas Beecham Maestro could only say that "he conducts like an amateur." Victor DeSabata was "*un pagliaccio*" (a big clown) because he moved too much on the podium, even danced a bit. And Stokowski was a "prostitute" because he threw away the integrity of a composition for an easy success with the public. In those years Maestro's evaluation had the resonance of truth, a truth that my Artur appreciated. But Stokowski, once the days of matinee glamour and spotlit hands and profile had passed into musical folklore, undoubtedly proved to be one of the few giants to stand on a podium in our era.

It was amusing to watch the two younger conductors dancing attendance on Maestro. Molinari was unashamedly obsequious. Indeed, there was no small, menial service that he would not perform for his friend and Maestro, including polishing his shoes. It was embarrassing to hear Toscanini say of Molinari, "Doesn't Bernardino do a good job?" while looking down at his gleaming footwear, and embarrassing to watch Molinari pick up these crumbs of demeaning praise with a spittled psychological finger and eat them whole. What Maestro had to say about Molinari as a musician, however, was hardly as complimentary as his appraisal of the man as a bootblack.

Artur, for the most part, sat basking in Maestro's presence, collecting whatever scrap of musical wisdom the older man would leave lying about. The discussion (mostly in English) in those morning and afternoon waits among the rocks and crutches of Rinaldi's garden were of tempi and dynamics, the real import of some problematic passage in a classical symphony, what modern compositions were worth playing and why. It was a liberal education for me, especially when I learned to divest Maestro's opinions or evaluations of their colored vocabulary. Words such as *cretino* and *imbecille*, among the politer ones, were used to describe not only other conductors, but most new composers, certain well-known orchestral players, a vast array of instrumental soloists, and a goodly number of singers.

Since Artur shared many of these views, he usually nodded whenever Maestro ranted critically. When he disagreed, his conscience forced him to look around for some particularly grotesque arthritic and point out the amazing improvements that Rinaldi's syringe and salve had worked. But when it came to expressing his own opinions, Artur would do so forthrightly, even though it might lead to a Toscanini tantrum.

One day Toscanini received a letter from Hitler inviting him to conduct once again at Bayreuth where, in the years before the Nazis came to power, Toscanini had given superlative readings of Wagner's operas. Maestro detested Hitler even more than he did Mussolini and would no more perform in Germany than in Italy. His feelings toward *Il Duce* went back to the latter's first foray into politics, shortly after World War I, when Mussolini persuaded Maestro to run for office on his ticket, then Socialist. Both men lost their respective contests, and Mussolini took his Fascist route. The venality of the Blackshirts, the castor oil and water tortures, the beatings, the anti-intellectualism, the imperial pomposities, all these things went against Toscanini's grain, and he would have nothing further to do with his former political crony. Some people said that he even became cold toward Puccini when the composer became one of Mussolini's Senators. In any case, even though Cosima Wagner herself pleaded with Toscanini to return, the presence of Hitler on German soil made it an unlikely place for Maestro ever to perform again.

Toscanini's knowledge of German consisted largely of phrases from opera librettos, primarily Wagner's, hardly adequate to translate Hitler's involuted prose style. Artur did the job, then aided Maestro in composing a negative reply. Although Hitler and the entire Wagner clan, including Cosima's son Siegfried and all the grandchildren, had offered unlimited rehearsals, choice of artists (except Jews, of course), and nearly the whole of the Rheingold for a fee, Toscanini refused with a dignified and temperate letter. While the language was suitable to a head of state, it was also a slap in Hitler's face. Artur later saw his letter in the Bayreuth museum in 1952.

Artur's cure lasted a bit more than a month, with as many as two daily injections of Rinaldi's fluids, and repeated paintings with his mal-odorous and blistering salve. Toscanini had shown definite improvement, and there were minor miracles taking place all about us. One involved a young man, no more than forty years of age, who had a deforming arthritis contracted in the trenches along the Austrian Front. He was as rigid as a bone when we first saw him, yet within two weeks he was able to move his neck slightly from right to left, and shortly thereafter he gave away his two canes.

Toscanini and Molinari had already gone on to Salzburg, and Zuzzi was back in Firenze at his easel by the time Artur and I were to leave Piazze. Before going, we paid a courtesy call on Dottore Rinaldi, for whom we had come to have genuine affection, and Artur, as was required, swore that he had never felt better in his life. This pleased the peculiar little man enormously, as did our promise to write and to come visit him again. But when we departed from Piazze, Artur continued to have severe pain, and was thoroughly disgusted with the entire escapade. Moreover, he faced the prospect of conducting his initial season with the Cleveland Orchestra handicapped by a crippled right arm. It was decided that we visit the orthopedic clinic of Professore Putti in Bologna. There, Artur would undergo surgery, in enough time, we hoped, to recuperate before the first concerts. It was already July and Artur's rehearsal schedule commenced in September. The outlook was bleak.

Professore Putti's establishment was world famous, and certainly much more scientific and efficient, outwardly anyway, than Rinaldi's. Artur felt confident that relief was at hand just by the odor of antiseptic that the place exuded. The white-haired orthopedist insisted on a new set of X-ray plates to determine exactly where to make his "cut." That word, since his youthful appendectomy, always made Artur blanch. He also dreaded the likelihood of a cast for a minimum of two months. Putti was amused when we told him of our stay with Rinaldi, but agreed that the man had achieved remarkable things. He talked as he wrote out a chart for Artur, scheduling the X-rays and an hour for surgery. We were consigned to the clinic's radiologist for a galleryfull of shoulder shots, and then went back to our hotel where Artur took some sedatives to help him sleep. His apprehension was very nearly uncontrollable.

The next morning, the phone awakened us. It was Putti's radiologist.

"*Professore* would like to see you as soon as possible," the man said.
"What about the operation?" Artur had me ask.
"*Professore* will discuss it when you arrive," and that was that.
Artur was dressed instantly. Panting, we were in Putti's presence in a matter of a quarter hour.
"Maestro," he said, "I will not have to perform this particular operation," Putti said.
Artur groaned. "What then, an amputation?" he asked.
Before I had a chance to translate this, Putti swept us over to an X-

ray viewer, and began to gesture at a plate of Artur's ailing bursa and bones.

"*Guarda qui, per favore? Non si vede nulla!*"

Artur looked incredulous.

In an English as fluent as Artur's Italian, Putti said, "You are the cured man, Maestro Rodzinski: Rinaldi has done the *miracoloso!*"

Where once had resided a bony pea on earlier X-rays now was nothing except what should have been there.

"But why do I still have pain?" Artur inquired.

"*Infiammazione,*" he answered, "and she soon go away."

Artur would have kissed and hugged Putti had not dignity prevented the former and his *infiammazione* stayed the latter.

Back at our hotel, we wrote to Rinaldi, thanking him from the bottom of our hearts, promising to come see him soon again. Unfortunately, before we had a chance to fulfill our promise, he was dead.

Whatever was the nature of Rinaldi's treatment, the world will never know: he never wrote it down. According to the doctors who knew him and his work, he had intended to publish his findings, but delayed too long. Everyone knew of Rinaldi's eccentricity: he charged fees from the rich commensurate to his cure, but he absolutely cursed banks as instruments of the devil. One night bandits broke into his house, and robbed and killed him. Some say that he was really murdered by *Fascisti* for his outspoken political stance, that they took the money as a cover. Whatever the truth of the matter, Rinaldi's secret was laid with his own bones to molder in the Piazze graveyard.

Before his death Dr. Rinaldi was able to help many of our musician friends who suffered the same ailment, notably the pianist-conductor Ossip Gabrilowitsch. Ossip's guide on the occasion of his own successful cure was the reliable Zuzzi, who by that time had developed quite a friendship with the strange but God-given Dottore Rinaldi.

Chapter 13

WITH a clean bill of health, Artur felt free to resume his summer's schedule, which included a trip to Rome for an appointment with Ottorino Respighi. Those were the years of the Italian master's greatest vogue, and Artur had hopes of coming away from the visit with a "first" to grace his coming Cleveland season. He certainly had prepared well for his visit with the composer of *The Pines of Rome*. Toscanini, while at Piazze, had written a letter of introduction.

Unfortunately, no Respighi premiere resulted, but the trip was not a total loss. Artur and I toured the city, cameras in hand. When we were not climbing over monuments and photographing each other photographing the same sights, we would take long and refreshing intermissions from the torrid heat in the city's smaller churches. It was during those hours of indoor touring that I discovered something about Artur's deep and personal spirituality.

Ordinarily, I went to mass by myself every Sunday. Artur would say, "Pray for me," but refuse to come along. I did not think this unusual, for most Polish men, unless in their later and repentant years, customarily leave church-going to their women. In the years after we were married he would attend mass on high holidays — Christmas, Easter Sunday, or the Feast of the Assumption. The reason, he said, was the "smell of incense." It was as if he feared an act of insincerity on his part to participate regularly in divine worship, and I never pressed the matter.

During our visits to those tiny churches that are among Rome's greater glories I found that, rather than wander from sculpture to altarpiece, Artur preferred to sit in an untrafficked corner, slouched over, head in hand. And he could remain like this for hours if I did not distract him. Once, as we left a church on Piazza del Popolo, I asked Artur what he had been thinking about. He replied, shyly, simply, "Him."

We left Rome and, following the lead of our whim, hopscotched the peninsula to find ourselves stopping, at the end of the vacation, in Montecatini for a two-week cure. Artur was still having pain in his shoulder, and had hopes of alleviating it with the hot baths and mud of the region. He also planned to visit there with two of his friends, Ossip Gabrilowitsch and the violinist Bronislaw Hubermann. Gabrilowitsch was ailing from arthritis, and Artur could hardly wait to sing praises of Rinaldi. Hubermann was suffering from some altogether unrelated ailment, possibly something muscular, but, he, too, would enjoy hearing Artur's tale of his Umbrian therapy.

I was beginning to learn something about performing artists that I previously had not even suspected. They were hypochondriacs, by and large. Even when they suffered real-enough pains, these often stemmed from psychosomatic sources. When at Krynica I unpacked Artur's *necessaire* and found enough pills, lotions, and tonics to stock an infirmary, my suspicions were first aroused. When later he told me he had a multitude of ailments which might make life with him hellish, I frankly disbelieved him. It was incomprehensible to me how a man in his early forties could possibly be so frail. I also hardly believed that the forceful human being I had come to know could seriously be reduced to a nervous wreck by the threat of an ailment or two which most people lived with in comparative sanity.

Gabrilowitsch was an artist whose gifts at the keyboard were already a legend by the time he had taken up the disciplines of conductor. He had literally been given the new Detroit Symphony Orchestra, with the blessings of the town's automobile rich, and had been having great successes. He was married to a daughter of Mark Twain, which made the Russian-born pianist almost as American as apple pie in his Detroit audience's mind. He was a charming man, tall, courtly, and a little self-consciously old-fashioned, wearing uncomfortable high starched collars and scarf-like cravats even in the swelter of Montecatini that summer. He also could be very funny, and that endeared him to me.

Hubermann was another kind of man. He was short, compact, a little like Oistrakh in physique, and very, very serious about most things. Gabrilowitsch, who could be no less serious, much preferred a joke, whereas Hubermann pursued a subject as determinedly and deeply as he played a Brahms Sonata. His interest in the Pan-European movement, in Theodore Herzl's dream of a resurrected Israel, and the founding of an orchestra in the embryonic nation were the sorts of things that flowed from him in conversations at the terrace cafés. He also politely recalled me from various encounters in the Aleja Roz apartment of the Meyers, or said as much. But to be honest, all I recalled was his face and a physical peculiarity that made talking with him embarrassing or difficult. Hubermann was walleyed, and far worse, one eye looked to the left while the other took in a view from the right. When he spoke to one directly it was hard to tell which eye was actually seeing you, for both seemed fixed on an indeterminate elsewhere.

The afternoons in the sun over coffee and musical gossip relieved the serious business of being ill at an expensive Spa. But when we would meet on our walks during the hours of treatment or examinations, the conversation was about the progress, or more pleasurably, the lack of improvement, in one's condition. Somehow, otherwise robust and vigorous persons at a Spa can be reduced to despairing invalids, musicians most notably. I had had enough to remember about sickness from my one previous visit to both Italy and Montecatini to last me a lifetime. I now wonder, having my past presently at hand, if I would have pursued my future quite so aggressively, had I known just how central Artur's health would be to it. For instance, when I look over the agendas and diaries that I kept over the decade when Artur, our son Riki, and I lived in Italy, they speak more to me of Italy as a place of sickness than the home of song, great art, and the healthy lusts that spawn them.

When our respective cures had ended — I, too, had bathed in the hot mineral springs and was packed in healthful muds — the four of us took different routes. Gabrilowitsch went off to give Rinaldi's bony garden a try, with Zuzzi as guide; Hubermann sought relief for his muscular aches somewhere else; I returned to Poland; and Artur had an appointment, alone, to visit the famous Bircher Benner sanitarium in Switzerland. Among Artur's many discomforts was hyperacidity, a product of his nervous tension, and while he had not quite developed an ulcer, one was on the way. At this particular Swiss Spa, the cure was vegetarianism: carrot bread, cauliflower pot roasts, corn puddings and ragouts of squash. Such a diet would ordinarily kill an ulcer patient, but the "cure" was held in esteem by those who had survived it.

Artur would also meet with his mother and brother Ryszard, then go to Salzburg to sit at the feet of Maestro and spend some time with his son while working out details of his divorce from Ilse. This part of Artur's summer commitments might not do his stomach any good, but it would give me time to catch my breath. This I did among friends at Zakopane before rejoining my family.

As soon as I returned to Warsaw I began readying myself for another trip to the United States. I could not wait to be away. My one prolonged solo flight from the family nest had made me realize that Aleja Roz could never again be home. My way of looking at things, my values, my sense of purpose, my aspirations for the years ahead — all were changed.

Papa had finally won out against the psychological malaise that had afflicted him since Mama's death, but the personality which survived the struggle was becoming crustier day by day. And where communication between us had always been difficult or detached, it was now very nearly nonexistent. We were pleased to see each other, after the manner of father and daughter, but there the matter ended.

The others in my family were also finding their ways to independent lives. Cursed by his beauty to be the spoiled linchpin of the nursery, ruined by his premature ripening as a man, and suffering from inflated estimates of himself that were impossible to equal in actuality, my surviving brother Antek had nevertheless somehow made for himself a workable life. He still gambled, he still had difficulty in finding suitable jobs, but he was no longer having breakdowns, and he had finally married a woman who understood his emotional mechanics and loved him. Fela's successes as a designer had brought her freedom and respect in the household, although she would not remain there much longer, for her attachment to the young pianist Kazik Krance was clearly pulling her toward the altar. And Marysia: the days of her rebelling against an older sister's authoritarian ways were over. In the time I had been gone Marysia had become a grown woman — attractive and sensible, too.

I had no difficulty in accepting these changes in my family. In fact, they helped me become aware that life was more than a routine bound up with family and thrice familiar duties: it was a splendidly evolving experience — for me all the more splendid because of my love for Artur.

Our main problem, at that time, was financial. The family's fiscal situation had deteriorated to the point where the proposal that Papa convert his atelier into living quarters had to be acted on: the Lilpops of Aleja Roz sorely needed the income that the spacious fifth-floor duplex would bring in.

This was rather how things were when I left Warsaw that autumn, more or less for good.

At Zakopane that summer, Szymanowski had been putting the finishing touches on a new Violin Concerto, his second, and Paul Kochanski was developing his interpretation with Karol's help. While the two men worked, Zosia and I socialized, and I found her full of encouragement for my forthcoming marriage. Paul, however, was more cautious, but was too busy to discuss at length what might have been reservations. Thus it was decided that we sail together for America. I remained in Warsaw long enough to hear the new concerto's premiere, then took the train for Le Havre, with a stopover in Paris for a reunion with Artur and Nela Rubinstein. Both had been busy, he concertizing in South America and she devoting herself to motherhood. Eva, their first child, had been born in Argentina; the next to arrive would be named Paul after Kochanski.

We had a fine time sightseeing, eating in restaurants which Rubinstein's educated palate had discovered, and socializing. We saw the poet Jan Lechon, recently assigned to the French capital as the Polish Embassy's cultural attaché, and Ryszard Ordynski, whose presence in the city was no more surprising than it ever was anywhere that he might turn up. Probably he had some celebrity to chase down, or some influential connection to make, I cannot recall. In any case, Ordynski was a good friend of Rubinstein's, and so he was part of the pleasant company of those few days.

A visit to the Rubinstein apartment gave me a chance to see Nela in her role as mother, and for the second time in our friendship I found cause to envy her. Watching Nela feed little Eva flooded me with equivocal feelings. I wanted children, but I wanted Artur more. He had made me agree that under no conditions were we to consider having children of our own. His difficulties with Ilse, to which Witold was witness, had hurt his son, and he had no wish to inflict any unpleasantness on another child, even one who was the product of a happier marriage. He further argued that the rootless nature of a performing artist's life would be unfair to a child. Yet, this kind of reasoning had not deterred the Rubinsteins, I thought to myself, selfishly wanting this part of my woman's role to be satisfied. While Artur was not explicit about it, he had another reason which was paramount with him: he wanted nothing less than my complete love and attention. A child would be a competitor.

My thoughts were interrupted when the Kochanskis arrived, providing the justification for another grand reunion at another marvelous restaurant. Rubinstein knew his way around the city's better kitchens as well as he did his Chopin and Brahms. We all ate too much and drank more than was good for us, all in the name of old times' sake, but the strength of the relationship between Kochanski and Rubinstein justified such excesses, or so we told ourselves.

Before parting that night, Nela and I had time for a quick heart-to-heart.

"You'll be happy, Halina, it will work," she said. "But have patience. These musicians — they're a crazy lot."

"But, Nela," I said, "there is still the divorce and so many other things that are unsettled. I feel as though I fly in a balloon that remains anchored."

"Patience, darling, patience," she said. "I know the man and what he is going through. You have waited this long, you can wait a while longer."

The next morning, bright and early, Rubinstein and Ordynski saw us off on the train while Nela stayed behind to nurse Eva. Paul looked dreadful. Zosia and I blamed it on the previous night's rich food and drink. I, for one, still felt a bit dyspeptic, to which the excitement of the trip added nothing good. Somehow I jostled Paul's funny bone, and once started he made jokes all the way to Le Havre.

We boarded the S.S. "Paris," one of the grand seagoing palaces of the day, and on shipboard we found two delightful companions, Vladimir and Odette Golschmann. "Vova," as Golschmann was playfully called, was of Russian parentage, but French to the heels of his dapper lizard-skin shoes. He had made a musical splash as the founder of the Concerts Golschmann just after the War, had conducted for Diaghilev's Ballet Russe, and the eccentric American *danseuse* Loie Fuller frequently commissioned him to keep order in the pit wherever she deigned to prance and posture. Golschmann was about to begin his third season as the conductor of the St. Louis Symphony Orchestra, in the same American heartland which seemed so incomprehensible to me, a place where divorces, at any rate, were distinctly no more acceptable than in Italy or Spain. Vova's pretty blond French wife was helpful in explaining the mores of the Midwest, but when I think back on what she had to say, her descriptions were more of a caricature than a true picture.

I do not think I ever told Odette how closely I watched her every action on that trip. She was living a part I was soon to assume, one I was thoroughly uncertain of. From her example I learned how the wife of a celebrated conductor should conduct herself. In Golschmann's company when others were about she was a gracious shadow, a silent, well-dressed tagalong; in private she was as alert and vivacious as only a Frenchwoman with a brain can be. This separation of her public and private selves I considered to be a key to her happy marriage, and a pattern for me to emulate.

Meantime, we had to endure a nasty crossing — the seas were wind-roughed, the skies a continuous drizzling grey. Zosia Kochanska was a poor sailor. Except when she issued from her cabin like some ashen apparition to stare, unaffected, at all the good things the French Line's master chefs concocted, she stayed abed most of the voyage. Paul and I spent many hours together making the rounds of our deck.

One day, perhaps our third at sea, Paul finally blurted out what seemed to be on his mind: "Rodzinski enjoys his little affairs, Halina. He's had his way with women for years. And I am honestly afraid that you might be, well, just another fling of his."

(*87*)

I argued with him, demonstrating point after point how Artur had never made a promise to me that he failed to keep. Yet, I could not deny that I, too, had some concern. At the very moment I was sailing to America to join Artur in Cleveland, I had no assurance that, indeed, a divorce was underway. I would have to face a highly compromising situation if one was not.

"What's really at issue, Paul," I said, "is that I love Artur enough to brazen the thing through if worse comes to worst."

"People talk, Halina, they say cruel, vicious things."

"So they do — and as much, I am sure, in Cleveland as they have been doing in Warsaw. But Artur once asked me which was more important: what people say or our relationship. He said that if my love wasn't strong enough to weather inevitable slights, then I should forget him. Well, I can't. He is my whole world."

"Then let's leave it at that," he said, looking uncomfortable.

"Let's," I replied, and we walked a bit more, not speaking. Suddenly, as if to delay introducing something else that was on his mind, he said, "Just remember that our home in New York is yours. And Zosia and I will help if you ever need us."

I thanked him, and should have said more, I suppose, because I was grateful for, and deeply touched by, his concern, but just then a tinkling silver steward's bell summoned us off deck to tea.

At table that night, Zosia joined us, but only for a few moments: an unexpected lurch of the great ship, mirrored in the shivering movement of a jellied consommé the waiter placed before her, sent Zosia, napkin to lips, scurrying back to her cabin. The Golschmanns, Paul and I laughed at the poor woman's miseries and went on eating. Paul, however, ate less than usual and with no gusto. Also he seemed uncomfortable.

"*Mal de mer?*" I asked.

"No," he quipped. "A little indigestion."

For the remaining days of the trip, Paul stopped making rounds of the deck, preferring to recline on a deck chair, bundled in trenchcoat under blankets, beret pulled down over his ears. He might pick himself up and join us for a quick pass, but he was clearly in discomfort. A day or so before we reached New York, when we were alone, he said, for the first time, "I feel awful."

"What's the trouble, still your stomach?" I asked.

"Nothing seems to sit right down there, and I have a stuffed sensation here that bothers me." He was pointing toward his lower right ribcage.

As a joke, I said, "Let me give a touch," and what I felt as I palpated his liver must have shown on my face.

"Something wrong?" he asked, like a boy caught in some wrong-doing.

"I'm only licensed as a make-pretend nurse, Paul," I said, trying to keep things light, "but I think you should see a real doctor."

By his silence and the way he turned distractedly to look eastward over the railing I knew that he, too, thought as I did, and was also both worried and frightened. Pressing his right abdomen was like pressing a rock or an inflated soccer ball.

My second arrival in New York City by sea had a slight feel of homecoming to it. The sights of the harbor were somewhat familiar and the weather was good. The Golschmanns left us after Customs with promises to keep in touch, and the Kochanskis went on to their Lexington Avenue apartment while I settled to roost on an upper floor of the St. Moritz again.

That evening, I dined with the Kochanskis, and Paul insisted that I come with him and Zosia to see their physician friend, Doctor A. L. Garbat, at his apartment. I demurred, but Paul said he wanted it that way. "Besides," he asked, "don't you want your diagnosis confirmed?"

While the doctor examined Paul in another part of the apartment, Mrs. Garbat entertained us, tactfully distracting Zosia by making her talk about herself and her summer.

When the two men rejoined us, it was Doctor Garbat who seemed ill. In all the years I was to know him, and often hear from him one kind of medical news or another, I cannot ever recall his looking so pale or quite so serious as when he returned to his living room with Paul.

"I'm fit for work," Paul said with a laugh. "Just a little liver trouble. I'll have to watch my diet, I guess. No more French cooking for a while."

Neither Zosia nor I was convinced.

Zosia alone saw me to the train the next day, Paul having gone to Juilliard to check his schedule and to meet new students. Although she tried to conceal her distress, she made a poor job of it.

There was nothing I could say under the circumstances. We hugged each other farewell, and as my sleeper to Cleveland pulled away from the platform, I saw Zosia standing dumbly, eddies of people swirling about her as she nervously shredded a handkerchief.

Chapter 14

I HAD spoken by telephone with Artur before leaving New York, and knew his schedule would not permit him to meet the train. In his stead was his assistant concertmaster, Felix Eyle. Felix proved to be a darling, his name appropriate to his disposition, and over the succeeding years he would become a brother to me. At the moment, however, his being a Pole, and, like Artur, from Lvov, was sufficient recommendation; the overnight trip and independent dealings with porters and dining-car stewards had exhausted my English, and anything but a cheerful smile and a word in my native tongue would have completely unstrung my nerves. I had fretted the entire journey — about the likelihood that Paul had a bad cirrhosis, or worse, and about the things he had said on shipboard concerning Artur and his "flings," none of which had been news, for Artur had told me of romantic involvements. Still, I arrived in Cleveland for the first time edgier than I cared to be.

Artur had arranged for me to stay at the Hotel Alcazar. The name might lead one to imagine something exotic, perhaps a replica of the Moorish King's castle in Seville. The only resemblance to the more famous structure was that it had a harem. Indeed, the entire place was a harem, and a gerontological horror to boot: it was filled with old ladies, either maidens or widows, who had taken residence there to finish their long lives in the tedium of each other's company. The building itself may have had a faintly Moorish cast to Midwestern eyes, but to mine the prevailing style was that of a gloomy, dreary stopover on the way to the graveyard.

The Alcazar had one virtue, however: it was close by Artur's apartment on Cedar Road where he had set up house with the help of a wonderful black couple. The wife kept the apartment and cooked, and her husband served as valet and driver.

Artur was in a superlative mood. He had conquered Cleveland. "The board is wonderful to me. The chairman, Mr. Severance, makes me feel like his son. The Orchestra gives me all I want. The audience and reviewers are appreciative and enthusiastic. And to top it all, I have my Halusia. It's almost too good to be true."

I was happy for him, happy to be near him once more, but not at all happy in my situation. For one thing, I was very nearly a state secret, kept under lock and seal, so to speak. The only persons who knew of my existence and the role I had in Artur's life were Eyle and another Polish friend of Artur's, Severyn Eisenberger, an excellent pianist who, along with Felix, taught at Cleveland's Settlement School of Music.

Artur was just as secretive about his divorce proceedings, which, finally, I found had been initiated. We both had only a primitive understanding of Midwestern puritanism, his at least based on some degree of experience, mine stemming from anecdotes and appraisals handed me by Odette Golschmann. In any case, neither Eyle, Eisenberger, nor Artur knew of a Cleveland parallel for our relationship, and so concluded, that if one existed, it was conducted as discreetly as negotiations between foreign powers.

When I was eventually allowed to appear from under the shrouds in which Artur wrapped me, I found that Clevelanders were like humanity anywhere else, that we had been excessively cautious. Cleveland friends would have been quite understanding of our situation had they known all the facts. I could agree with Artur, however, that gossip based on half-truths or less would have been disastrous at the outset of this new phase of his career, and so I took part in the conspiracy to be a nonexistent person. But I did not care for it, not one little bit. I was not accustomed to either conspiracies or a covert existence, neither is in my nature. Artur understood this, fortunately, but sometimes it was hard to draw consolation from his loving litany of "be-patient-darling" and "it-won't-be-long."

I was thrilled with the concerts. The Cleveland Symphony then seemed like a precision tool in contrast to the Warsaw Philharmonic which I had heard only a month earlier. All of the standard repertoire that Artur played with this fine new instrument of his had a rejuvenated quality. His Beethoven sounded like no one else's, nor did his Brahms, Schubert, or Tchaikovsky. He was coming to be his own man as an artist, and his players were inspiring him to grow, yielding subtleties in the score at each tick of Artur's fingers or baton in a way that could only make him probe the music more deeply, more intensely.

Artur had not exaggerated about the audiences. From all that had been said of Midwesterners, I anticipated polite applause to carry him back on stage for, perhaps, two bows. To the contrary, the Clevelanders deluged Artur in applause and bravos.

After a concert, I would take a cab to Artur's apartment (if he did not have a reception or party to attend) or to Eisenberger's place to await the new darling of the Cleveland's subscribers and board of directors. It was a frustrating state of affairs.

The Clevelanders and Artur went on tour that fall, and unless I were to travel with them in a harp case there was nothing for me to do but remain at the Alcazar among the antique biddies and walking dead, a prospect that enchanted me not at all. I had not traveled half the world to pass my days in a retirement convent. From this fate I was saved by an invitation from Zosia Kochanska to keep her company in New York while Paul was on tour.

When I arrived in New York, Zosia told me that Paul had called from Pittsburgh. The bad cold he caught there had developed into pneumonia, forcing him to cancel the remainder of his engagements. He returned shortly to recuperate in the Lexington Avenue apartment. Dr. Garbat, who saw him there, finally told us that Paul's liver condition was probably cancerous.

"I don't want to hear that word," Zosia said. She preferred "cirrhosis." It had no fatal ring to it, although neither was a consolation nor relief to Paul who continued to slip away from us day by day.

All the while Zosia maintained her salon, giving what seemed to be an interminable tea party, Paul wanted no visitors, and so had none, remaining in an uncomfortable somnolence in a back bedroom, distant enough from Zosia's overstuffed, incense-permeated living room that he heard none of the vast comings and goings and artistic small talk of his wife supervised from her tea pot and cookie trays. It was as if Zosia had a compulsive need to put people between herself and the ugly inevitability that was unfolding itself several rooms distant.

The company that filed through her apartment was as varied and cosmopolitan as Zosia's taste in decor, which ranged from turn-of-the-century upholstered elegance to Russian and Polish antiques, with a dab of chinoiserie and other Far Eastern exotica here and there. The journalist son of Richard Strauss's librettist Hofmannsthal and his pretty American wife might be found seated next to Jose Iturbi or Minnie Guggenheimer, the creator of the New York Stadium Concerts. The Damrosches were regulars, particularly the old conductor's daughter, Gretchen, and her husband, the diplomat Thomas Finletter. The singer Lucrezia Bori, the young composer George Gershwin, the violinist Albert Spalding, and the painter Pawel Tschelitcheff were also among the truly extraordinary company. Zosia manipulated all with a fantastic dexterity. To queries regarding Paul's health, she said sadly that "some days were better than others," then quickly moved on to another topic: repeal, the latest Hemingway novel, Picasso's newest phase. I went back to Cleveland and Artur as soon as grace and circumstance permitted.

Then, on January 12, 1934, I received a telegram telling of Paul's death. Artur bundled me aboard the next overnight train. "She's going to need people, Halusia," he said, and he was right.

Paul's body reposed in the living room of the Kochanski apartment in a mahogany coffin which was a gift from Irena Warden (now the Countess Cittadini), a Polish woman who had married a wealthy Main Line Philadelphian. Irena, who was widowed on her honeymoon, had been a friend of the Kochanskis for many years and shared Zosia's loss almost as if it were her own. She insisted on buying Paul's coffin because she wanted "to make one last present to him."

The room was filled with flowers, with barely a narrow path left for visitors to pass by the coffin. The viewing began early in the day and continued unceasingly until nightfall, and all the while Zosia stood in position near the open box to accept the condolences of this army of mourners, exchanging whatever sad banter was appropriate, shifting from French to Polish to Russian to English, replying to each expression of sadness with some personal and individual remark.

Funeral services were held the following day at the Juilliard School of Music. A number of famous musicians made eulogies, little of which I could understand, and there was music by a quartet of Paul's string-playing colleagues. The whole experience was very moving. The passing of Orpheus could not have been more sincerely grieved, nor have seemed quite as incomprehensible: for this great artist, the finest Polish violinist since Wieniawski, was dead at only forty-seven.

At home alone, Zosia and I opened hundreds of telegrams. Each one moved us to tears, and I began to understand how much it meant to Zosia that Paul had been loved, for it helped to reinforce her personal sense of tragedy. But I also began to understand, as the days of my stay became weeks, how little people care for the sadness of others. Perhaps Zosia overdisplayed her sorrow; for a fact, she remained the resolutely mournful widow at her tea parties for years afterward. No matter, she did not deserve the cut delivered in a note from one of her closest friends, someone whose absence was considerably noticed. The person wrote, "You must forgive me for not calling, but I can no longer take your sorrow."

Throughout that winter of 1934 I regularly commuted between Cleveland and New York. I wanted to be with Artur, but I had no desire to be closeted away, and the Alcazar distinctly was not a place where I could entertain myself. So New York saw more of me than Artur did.

Whenever Artur could break free from his Cleveland schedule, he would join me in New York where we could go about openly. We went to concerts, the opera, theatres, and, of course, visited Artur's old friends. One of these, the singer Sophie Braslau, was also to become close to me and to serve as my tutor. She had known Artur since his earliest Los Angeles days, both as musician and man.

With a fine operatic career behind her, Sophie lived in retirement, a wise woman, patient and generous in dispensing warmth and good advice. Her home on West 86th Street was a place where ruffled musical tempers could find solace in her understanding. To enter her apartment was to step into a Chekhov or Turgenev tale. The atmosphere, like Sophie, was immutably nineteenth-century Russian. The place was dimly lit by lamps with dark-colored fringed fabric lampshades. The floor was a profusion of thick, overlapping oriental carpets, and the walls were hung with a motley of fabrics and tapestries. Her tufted-velour chairs and sofas were hidden beneath heaps of cushions and colorful shawls. But the dominant color in the room was provided by Sophie herself: she invariably received guests wearing a wine-colored velvet hostess gown, lace trimmed at arms and neck, her brown, curly hair in calculated disarray.

For years Sophie had been an intimate of Arthur Judson who, I then learned, was *the* most powerful figure in American music. What Judson did not control could be more readily enumerated than the things that lay directly under his powerful thumb. Judson, I was to discover, was a tough-minded man in his dealings with artists, but in Sophie's hands was as compliant as a boy. She could soften his sometimes hard heart as no one else, and when artists had trouble with Judson and the innumerable agencies and artistic outlets he controlled, Sophie served as intermediary. Somehow, a disagreement with Judson could be resolved by a visit to Sophie, whose advice everyone, including Judson, followed.

Sophie taught me much about Artur as a personality, as an artist, and about the backstage intrigues of America's musical life. And she helped me understand the oftentimes trying relationship Artur had with Judson, extending back over years to his first days with Stokowski. Judson had Artur under his managerial control, as he had almost every other major artist active in America. Their artist-manager relationship had not always operated smoothly, or especially to the benefit of the artist.

Judson managed the Philadelphia Orchestra when Artur began his American career there, and had immediately pressed him into a personal contract. Since Judson also managed the New York Philharmonic and was manager in absentia of other orchestras, Artur had no choice but to sign. Judson, however, found few if any engagements for his young Polish conductor. Artur made his way on his own, picking and choosing opportunities as they presented themselves. Young Eugene Ormandy (who had come to America at about the same time as a violinist) and Artur were in the same boat casting about for a place to beach themselves and begin serious work. They both were offered the job as conductor of a theatre orchestra, but Artur refused the job as beneath him. Ormandy, who took it as a stopgap measure, then went on to Minneapolis and from there, under Judson's control, came to share the podium with Stokowski in Philadelphia. When Judson ultimately deposed the latter from the platform he had held for decades, Ormandy was the favored replacement.

Artur, however, had made his own destiny. When, after an appearance with the Philadelphia Orchestra in New York, Artur caught the attention of W. C. Clark, Jr., the financial backer of the Los Angeles Philharmonic Orchestra, it was none of Judson's doing. Indeed, had old Mr. Clark known that Artur was under Judson's management he would never have hired him to direct "his" orchestra. There was bad blood between Clark and Judson, and Artur, in his four-year tenure in Los Angeles, never once let slip that he was contracted to Judson's Columbia Artists' network. But all that while he regularly paid Judson his agent's fee. Even at Cleveland, another position Artur won on his own, and even though Judson had advised the Cleveland Board *against* hiring him, Artur still paid the contracted percentage. It was a bit like extortion or indentured servitude in Artur's mind, and he resented the whole business. Sophie, though, could calm him and willingly soothed Judson's temper on Artur's behalf. If she had not, Artur's situation would have been difficult.

Since Artur was obliged to be in Cleveland and I much preferred a public life in New York to a covert one in the Midwest, I quickly found myself Artur's intermediary with his mediator. It was a pleasurable duty in that it gave me an excuse to pass time with Sophie; but some of our conversations left me with ugly presentiments of future problems.

"The man you will marry," she said, "has a will of his own — and so has Judson."

On his various visits to New York, Artur took me to hear the

Philharmonic under Maestro Toscanini's direction at Carnegie Hall, that place which to my first glance had seemed an architecturally inadequate house for a great orchestra. My opinion changed: the simple door of the auditorium enchanted me, as did the acoustics, and the music making was truly incredible to one reared on the Warsaw Philharmonic. I had heard Beethoven's Eighth Symphony many times, but when I heard Maestro conduct it at that first concert Artur took me to, it seemed a new work. I could now appreciate Artur's idolization of the man in a setting more appropriately revealing than Dottore Rinaldi's garden.

At the end of the spring season in Cleveland Artur's bursitis had begun to misbehave once more, and following his last pair of concerts, which I attended, we drove to Washington, D.C. and on to New York. There we loaded Artur's car and ourselves aboard the S.S. "Carinthia." Among other ports of call on that summer's itinerary would be Professore Putti's clinic in Bologna.

Chapter 15

THE schedules I drew up for our time in Europe were very complicated. Artur was slated to visit Berlin for divorce hearings, to conduct concerts in Warsaw and at Leningrad's Borodin Festival, to travel to Moscow for mysterious negotiations about a "sensational" new opera by Dimitri Shostakovich, to be examined by Professore Putti in Bologna, and, eventually, to be married.

Although this last appeared almost as an afterthought on his agenda, I thought of and prayed for nothing else. Whether our wedding would or would not come to pass depended entirely on a judge in one of the new Reich's Courts, and neither of us would hazard a guess on what the Court's opinion might be. As I said, I prayed. Artur preferred to put his faith in an expensive attorney and the justice of his suit.

I went directly to Aleja Roz to await him and to plan for our wedding. The family was now settled in the ground floor apartment, and aside from recognizing some of the furniture, the place in no way seemed home: I felt like a guest.

Artur arrived from Berlin in early May, and stayed in Aleja Roz, using Fela's room. There was no news from the German court, an understandable state of affairs to Artur whose own doctorate of laws made him tolerant of the paper-shuffling and word-paring that comprise such proceedings. Despite his reiterated injunctions to "be patient," I was fast depleting my last reserves of that virtue. The suspense was killing.

We both found diversion, however, in Artur's performance with the Warsaw Philharmonic, his first in the city in nine years. By now his American successes were well-known, and he was greeted by the Warsaw players as an artist of international repute. The concert was sold out well in advance, with Lilpops and related families guaranteeing a major part of the house. It seemed as if everyone I knew was there, including, poor man, my unmusical Papa. I sat beside him throughout the concert, which was capped by Brahms's Fourth Symphony. His discomfort lasted right down to the last chord. Only when the enthusiastic applause began did his condition improve.

Artur then went on to Russia while I remained in Warsaw. My days were taken up with driving lessons, at Artur's insistence. I not only learned how to operate a vehicle but also what made it work, and why. These lessons in engineering presupposed miles of roadway with no service stations. Somehow, I passed the rigorous licensing examination, and working toward it helped pass the time.

From the few words Artur wrote, I gathered his Borodin Festival concerts had gone well. I also understood that he had fallen in love with a new opera by Shostakovich, *Lady Macbeth of Mzensk*. At its much-publicized premiere, he had met the composer who voiced his appreciation of Artur's performances at the Festival, and the two men discussed the likelihood of Artur giving its American premiere. As far as the twenty-nine-year-old Shostakovich was concerned, Rodzinski could have first rights to the work; but the decision ultimately rested with authorities in Moscow. It was not unknown to Russia's musical bureaucrats that Artur had taken Shostakovich's First Symphony as one of his warhorses, and that he had also done well by the dean of Soviet symphonists, Nikolai Miaskovski. Indeed, his New York debut with the Philadelphia Orchestra in 1926 included a city premiere of one of Miaskovski's dozens of murky symphonies.

Artur lingered on to hear every performance of the new opera. It had completely captured his imagination; this and the extravagant praise the international press heaped on the work decided the matter: despite the difficulties of wrestling for the rights, he would not be happy until *Lady Macbeth* was his own for Cleveland and the American debut.

In his generous contract with the Orchestra Board Artur was allowed a substantial budget for operatic productions. The Great Depression had eliminated Cleveland as a tour stop for the Metropolitan Opera, and the city was suddenly without serious musical theatre. The Board, aware of Artur's passion for opera, his early successes in Europe and later in Philadelphia and in Los Angeles, saw that the Orchestra could fill the gap left by the Met. In his first season Artur had done two operas: a *Tristan* and Wolf-Ferrari's *The Secret of Suzanne*. Both productions had been successful and on a level that even outdid the Met. Having an orchestra that he could rehearse far more than an opera house could afford, Artur had been able to give superior performances in that area where American opera would fall down — the pit. Also, the Cleveland's home, Severance Hall (named after the Orchestra's chief financial supporter, John L. Severance), had been designed to serve the dual, though not always compatible, purposes of concert hall and opera house. Luckily, it served both quite well, Artur discovered, and he was eager to do as many operas as his budget would permit. For the 1934–35 season he had already scheduled an *Otello* and a *Tosca*. If he could get her, *Lady Macbeth* might be a traveling companion for one of the Orchestra's visits to New York.

With recommendations to the right offices in Moscow in hand, Artur knocked on their doors, but with little immediate effect. Russian bureaucrats were as slow-moving and suspicious after the Revolution as they had been under the Tsar — perhaps more so, since Stalin's conservatism by now had set in. Fortunately for Artur, Stalin had not yet heard Shostakovich's brilliant score. That would happen — disastrously for the course of both Shostakovich's career and Russian music — a year later. Then, poorly placed in a box seat above the brass and percussion, Stalin would neither hear well nor be able to comprehend the doings on stage. But what he saw would strike him as scandalously un-Russian: the opera included several risqué scenes, innocent by today's standards, which were not the kind of thing the Soviet Union then wanted to promote as a cultural product of its great Revolution.

In his suit Artur was also aided by a happy coincidence: one day, in front of the Metropolitan Hotel on Teatralnyj Square, he met Vlady Drucker, his first trumpet player and friend from the Los Angeles Philharmonic. Both were astonished; neither had known of the other's plans to visit Moscow. Vlady, who was a Russian, became Artur's right hand in his negotiations, serving as translator and guide.

Artur found another ally in Artur Rubinstein, who also "just happened to be" in Moscow, concertizing there and in Leningrad that summer. The two Arturs had a good time together. Rubinstein made certain introductions that were valuable in clearing a path through the antechambers and minor functionaries of the Ministry of Culture to the doors of the Soviet Union's theatrical and operatic prime movers, the great Stanislavsky and Niemirovich-Danchenko, then directors of the Moscow Theater and Opera, respectively. With Vlady interpreting, Artur pleaded his case before them.

The discussions were tiresomely long, in the Russian manner, and called for all of Artur's forensic skills. They were further complicated by his old chief, Stokowski, who was at that moment firing off telegram after telegram to the same authorities, requesting the Shostakovich premiere for his Philadelphia opera. Stokowski had already produced Alban

Berg's *Wozzeck* to American acclaim, and he wanted nothing less than this Russian sensation to bolster his earlier success. When Artur got wind of Stokowski's interest in *Lady Macbeth,* he fought all the harder.

In the midst of this musical politicking Artur received word to appear before the divorce court in Berlin. Choosing between *Lady Macbeth* and me, he put his negotiations into abeyance for three days of travel to Berlin and the hearing. On June 9, I received a one-word telegram from Berlin: "Victory!" Then he went back to Russia to conclude the arrangements.

Whether it was Vlady's translations and appeals to the Russian sensibilities of Stanislavsky and Niemirovich-Danchenko or something unique in the character of Artur's argument, I do not know. But as history records Artur was given the production.

Obtaining exclusive rights to the American premiere was one thing; getting the score, parts, and various production materials out of Russia another. Artur was stopped at the border on the suspicion he had military secrets in his possession: the guards could not believe that the mysterious-looking papers showing footsteps on dotted lines plotted the movements of singers on a stage. Artur's explanations availed nothing. He contacted John Wiley, cultural attaché at the American Embassy in Moscow, and eventually through diplomatic channels got permission to take his treasure with him.

While Artur was arguing his way around the Byzantine minds of Russian bureaucrats, I was having my own complex dealings with the Church and the American Embassy.

Since Artur was divorced, the Catholic Church would not permit us to be married by a priest. The only alternative was a Protestant wedding, and with the help of some friends I found a Lutheran pastor who agreed to perform the service. The arrangement was highly irregular as far as the documents went. Artur, although baptized a Catholic, had been obliged to become a Lutheran in order to please his first wife's clergyman father. Thus, baptismal certificates, proofs of conversion, and wedding papers presented a confusion to the various church officials involved.

The decision for me to marry outside my faith was not too difficult to make. My father, prior to converting to Mama's faith in his latter years, had been a sometime Lutheran. I had also been brought up in the ecumenical spirit that all Christian churches were essentially one — even though some of us might believe the Roman Catholic Church to be the extraordinary expression of our common beliefs. While the exclusionary side of Church regulations made me a sinner, I did not think of myself as one, for I knew that Church Law was man-made. My conscience was clear. Over the years that followed, I regularly attended mass, but was saddened by the Church's prohibitions against my receiving both Absolution and Communion.

At the American Embassy, matters were a little less complicated,

(98)

yet difficult enough. It would take me two months to receive an immigration visa as the wife of a United States citizen. Artur had to sail by September 19, and if I were to leave with him, we could be married no later than July 19.

I told Artur of what had been arranged when he returned from Russia. He was in high spirits about his success in negotiating with the Russians, but when I informed him of our need to be married no later than that date in July, his spirits dropped rapidly.

"Can't I at least have a few months of feeling free?" he asked.

Artur particularly resented other people making decisions for him — and this was no exception. He stayed in bad humor until almost the day of the wedding. My humor was not much better. If I had second thoughts — and what first-time bride does not? — they came and went in time with Artur's moods.

Adding to Artur's premarital miseries was the nagging ache of his old bursitis, plus some soreness that remained from a fractured rib he had incurred two months earlier, thanks to a bear hug given by an overly affectionate basso profundo. Just before his concert with the Warsaw Philharmonic, Artur had looked in on a rehearsal at the Teatr Wielki and was treated to such a demonstration of love by his old friends, especially the bass Michalowski, that he was obliged to conduct his engagement swathed in adhesive tape. The rib he could live with, however, but not the bursitis and all the fears the continuing condition conjured up. It was mandatory that he see Professore Putti before the wedding.

Since there was no time to waste, Artur thought we should fly. The idea was a little terrifying in those days, to Artur no less than to me. But we did it anyway. In a single-engine, four-passenger aluminumized fabric craft we flew from Warsaw to Vienna, Vienna to Venice, not *above* all those mountains, but *between* them. The experience was thrilling, and the views were beautiful.

In Bologna, Professore Putti still saw nothing wrong with Artur's bursa, save the same *infiammazione* of the year before. There was certainly no need for surgery. Dottore Rinaldi, who was murdered that very summer, had indeed effected a cure.

To relieve Artur's ache, Professore Putti advised us to buy a *forno*, an immense ovenlike apparatus heated by a spirits lamp. Artur was told that if he sat baking his arm in this device, the pain would go away. He bought one on the spot. Because of the size of the thing, we were forced to take the train back to Warsaw.

From a meteorological point of view, Warsaw could not have had a better July 19, 1934. There was not so much as a cloud on the horizon. But in Aleja Roz that day there were many black looks and lightning flashes of short temper. The party that left for the city's Protestant Evangelical Church might have been on its way to an execution for all the good spirits shown.

The ceremony was simple. I wore an old navy dress. Our only witnesses were my sister Marysia and Bronek Mlynarski. Artur's wedding ring did not fit — I had ordered it by guess while he was in Russia — which gave him an excuse never to wear it. It seemed that both of us would experience the worse of the marriage compact sooner than the "better." When the Pastor said that the groom could kiss the bride, Artur made a face as if he had swallowed ipecac and gave me a peck that left my cheek frostbitten for hours.

One grim formality called for another, it seemed, and so we went on to the American Consulate to apply for an immigrant's visa. The witness to my signature was my only American friend in Warsaw, Maurice Pate, who years before had come as a Hoover Relief Adminis-trator, been enchanted by the city, and managed to remain assigned there. (Years later Maurice served as the first president of his brainchild, UNICEF.) From Artur's expression one would think that his passport was being taken away, not that his new wife was being given a travel permit.

All formalities concluded, Artur suggested I take advantage of "his absence" to pack our things that evening.

"And where will you be?" I asked.

"At the theater."

"Have a good time."

"I shall."

I later learned Ryszard Ordynski, of all people, ran into a thoroughly miserable looking Artur in the lobby of the Teatr Polski. Or-dynski apparently commented to him that the marriage was starting off nicely, with just the right touch of husbandly independence. Artur, it appears, merely groaned and walked out into the night.

I packed the little that remained of mine in Aleja Roz — a handful of clothes in a bag, and the memories of more than twenty-five years in my heart. Karol Stryjenski's piece of advice was a treasure I kept at hand for frequent use on my wedding night and during the trip to Zakopane for "our honeymoon." The part about the marriage "not being easy" I had already found to be true. The part about its being "worthwhile" I would have a lifetime to decide.

Chapter 16

THE bad humors of Warsaw gradually dissipated in the clear air of Zakopane where, on Antalowka, overlooking high Tatras, Artur had rented a villa for two months. Our honeymoon was anything but the idyllic isolation this suggests, however, for Artur's mother and his son Witold, whose custody Artur shared with his former wife, passed the entire summer with us, along with miscellaneous relatives.

I went ahead by train with our luggage, while Artur drove his pet Dodge from Warsaw, via Krakow, picking up a cousin en route, the same one whose photograph of me as a nurse had fallen into Ilse's hands in California.

In the first free moments we had after he arrived, Artur rather summarily laid out my role as his wife. "I come before everything and everyone else," he said.

It had never been my intention to dispute his primacy in our relationship, and the statement had a needlessly offensive ring to it. But as the days unfolded, I began to piece together the bits and snatches of his peculiar behavior and pointlessly harsh statements of the previous few weeks into a pattern that made some sort of sense. He had had enough of the stifling and inhibiting domination of a wife. For the time being, that was all he seemed to remember from his first marriage and he wanted to avoid the repetition. Now I understood his wish to "feel free" following his divorce, and his night on the town the day of our wedding. He also had been testing me, trying to see how completely, and under what circumstances, I would accept his dominance. The testing would continue for some time in ways that would often seem rude and insensitive. Our wedding night was only a sample of trials to come.

My prospects were not encouraging: Artur had given me much folderol about how greatly an artist needs emotional freedom; how jealousy and being hurt were his prerogatives, not mine; and how I should keep my eyes blinkered, if not altogether closed, in the presence of other men — even those I had known for years, even if they were married, and especially if they were at all attractive. Such talk told me much of how he had suffered in his previous attempt at marriage. It also told me that I had to roll up my sleeves and wade into the job of being Artur's wife because I had no other choice. That I loved him, I thought, would make it easier. That he loved me, I never doubted for a moment.

Fela and her handsome pianist boyfriend turned up for a visit. They passed most of that summer in and around Zakopane, Kazik basking in both the sun and the musical presence of Karol Szymanowski; that is, when the composer was not involved with Artur.

My husband and Karol spent many afternoons together, talking about and looking through new music. Artur shared his score of *Lady Macbeth*, only to find his enthusiasm for the new opera was not reciprocated. It intrigued Karol, but was not his cup of tea. The two men also looked over the score of Szymanowski's *Harnasie*, which Artur wanted for its American premiere. In the coming season, he had scheduled Karol's Second Violin Concerto, with Albert Spalding as soloist replacing Paul Kochanski. Zosia had given Albert Paul's own copy of the work, and he was to play its American premiere with Koussevitzky and the Boston Symphony in the coming December. The previous season Artur had given the *Symphonie Concertante* its first American performances, with his Cleveland friend, Severyn Eisenberger, as soloist.

Going over the Second Violin Concerto was saddening for the two men: so much of the relationship between Kochanski and Szymanowski had been stitched into the composition, a piece perfectly tailored to their dead friend's talents. Karol had me tell him of all that had happened in those last months of Paul's illness, but he was also very concerned about Zosia. "She has changed," he said sadly.

The villa Artur had rented came with a cook and a girl-of-all-work. Nonetheless, I was kept busy with household details. Artur's mother was quite fussy about the way food was prepared, and she was always on the watch to see how I performed as a wife. I survived her scrutiny unscathed, and we certainly got on well enough. That Witold was so much closer in age to a younger brother than a stepson made it relatively simple for me to develop an easy relationship with him. All of this pleased Artur.

The tensions of the first few weeks of married life relaxed. For our mutual pleasure, we had each other, and the dozens of guests that either stayed with us, just looked in, or were invited to dinner. Szymanowski came to dine without much persuasion; he only needed to know that a good red wine might be on the table and that I might have a new joke or two. I tried to oblige him with a sort that he especially enjoyed, not the kind often told in mixed company, but innocent and covert enough in their specialized off-color allusions that Mama Rodzinska never suspected a blush was in order.

Artur liked having guests around during the afternoons and evenings. His mornings were completely given over to work, which he usually began shortly after breakfast. This I brought to him in bed. If the morning were good, so was the coffee; if the morning were bad, the coffee was too — though it was made the same way throughout our marriage. Whether his mood was good, bad or indifferent, he had to have a ready supply of red and blue pencils, with points like hatpins, so that he could quickly set about marking the score of the moment. A good deal of that summer was spent on *Lady Macbeth*.

Every nuance of the new production was rehearsed in his head in those mornings atop Antalowka — the libretto, after a tale by Leskov, word for word in relation to the music; the movements of the soloists and chorus in relation to the stage size and tempi; and the timing of the numerous instrumental entr'actes Shostakovich provided, relative to the time it would take to change all the scenery. This required sustained intellectual effort and imaginative discipline, and when Artur finished his morning's labors he was hungry and exhausted. He wolfed down his food, which did his delicate stomach no good, and then napped. He might work again in the afternoon, or for a change of perspective distract himself with a walk, a book, or company. But the studying of scores, which was the most intense part of his summer's routine throughout his life, could resume at any hour of the day or night; for even though he laid aside the music physically, there was no guarantee that it did not continue to sound in that mysterious part of his brain where every last note played at an instant's recall.

Lady Macbeth was not the only opera to hold his attention that summer. In addition to the *Otello* and *Tosca* I knew about earlier, he on certain mornings could be found deep in the scores of Wagner's *Die Walküre*, with which he intended to open his Cleveland operatic season, and *Die Meistersinger*, with which he planned to close, and Rossini's *Il Barbiere* scheduled somewhere between. While these called for less effort, since he had conducted them many times before, in Lvov, Warsaw, or Philadelphia, he always reviewed the scores of a "standard" work, regardless of how often he performed it. Unlike a number of his surviving peers, Artur fought against learning a piece in some never-to-be-revised way. Each restudy of a composition uncovered some new detail, some further refinement to be achieved with his players, or an insight to the composer's intentions that could lead to a more cohesive performance.

Besides the works that he knew or had decided to learn for each new season, huge heaps and parcels of scores submitted for his consideration by publishers and composers blocked the view across his worktable or piano. Either he would look at every one of them or have an assistant winnow the ones worth his attention. When he returned a new score to a composer or publisher, he usually attached a comment that reflected his familiarity with the piece.

To accomplish as much as he did each summer called for great organization and concentration. From the outset of our life together I discovered that the strain of these intellectual efforts without a commensurate physical release made Artur incredibly irritable. Indeed, it was as if he energized a psychic battery during his vacations that would be expended in the electricity of performances when the season resumed. He certainly could not stay physically idle for long that first summer of our marriage. We had to take lengthy walks or a good stiff mountain climb every day to keep him even-tempered and the household peaceful. Soon I dreaded those days when it rained as much as I did Artur's temper displays, and often the two were inseparable.

The only home in Poland we were ever to share was that villa in Zakopane, and the time for turning its keys over to the rental agent came in the second week of September. Mama Rodzinska went back to her home in Lvov, and Witold, it was decided, would remain in Zakopane in the care of one of Artur's aunts, both for his health and to attend school. His education had by now a chaotically cosmopolitan character — private schools in Philadelphia suburbs, in Los Angeles and in Switzerland, with the sons of Quaker merchants, movie stars, and Arab sheiks for classmates. Artur thought it was high time that Witold study at a Polish state school. The experience was intended to give Witold an understanding of the egalitarian world he would have to live in. Little did his father realize, however, how much a champion of socio-economic equality Witold later would become as a result of his time at that school among the mountaineers' children.

We also had no idea that our farewell with Karol Szymanowski was to be the last. We parted sadly, not because of any presentiment of Karol's end, but because our honeymoon had finally been a happy one, and Karol's presence had been an important part of it. We each took away some part of him: Artur, the score of the Second Violin Concerto which they had studied together, and I, Karol's warmest regards for Zosia Kochanska.

We then drove in Artur's beige Dodge through Poland and Germany. I did not notice anything odd about Germany under Hitler, except for the replacement of the Weimar Republic's Eagle with the *hakenkreuz* (the limping cross of the Swastika). As we drove through Berlin, Artur observed how quiet the city seemed. Where not too long before discontented crowds had milled through the streets and riots were a commonplace, the capital now had an unnatural stillness to it.

At Hamburg we embarked on the S.S. "President Harding." If crossing the Atlantic had lost its novelty, being married had not, and we made a very romantic time of it. That lasted until we cleared customs in New York. Then life settled down to practical things.

The Rodzinskis paid a courtesy call on Maestro Toscanini and Donna Carla at their New York apartment in the old Astor Hotel. It was my first introduction to the great conductor's wife. She was an amazing person in her own right, I found, very strong and strong-willed, efficient, and with a nose for business. Among the numerous duties she performed for Toscanini was the investment of Maestro's considerable earnings, something Artur would never let me do. My husband believed that I had a pathogenic streak of generosity in me which ultimately would deliver him to the poorhouse door. In any case, Maestro had no idea of how much money *he* had, and seemed a happier man for his ignorance.

The visit was also to discuss matters concerning Artur's debut with the Philharmonic. It would be his first appearance in New York in eight years, and he wanted it to come off well. Maestro's invitation to Artur was a huge compliment: the only other guests that season, 1934–35, were Bruno Walter and Otto Klemperer, both considerably Artur's seniors in age and repute.

Another evening Artur introduced me to a New York friend, Alexander Siloti, the great and venerable Russian pianist and conductor. Old Siloti lived in the Ansonia Hotel, an odd rabbit warren of a place where celebrated musicians of all kinds had taken up residence. Siloti, though in retirement, still taught; and his aura as a living pupil and protégé of Tchaikovsky and of Anton Rubinstein made him much sought after by the students of Juilliard's piano department. It was also reputed that Siloti was Franz Liszt's bastard son. If this were so, the resemblance must have been startling to the Hungarian when he gave lessons to Siloti in Weimar in the 1880s. Siloti, especially in old age, was a replica of Liszt, with his hooked beak, long grey hair and identical number of warts in the same places.

I found Siloti a charming gentleman, courtly even regal in bearing, and the visits we made to him until his death were like a huge backward step into the history of manners and music.

New York was a pleasure, albeit a short one, before we went on to Cleveland. On the train I struggled to read through the current issue of *Musical America*. One article began:

"The eyes of the entire nation will be turned on Cleveland this fall and winter, when the Cleveland Orchestra under Artur Rodzinski, its dynamic new conductor, opens its seventeenth season. For the first time in its history the orchestra will present in combination two series of concerts and six staged grand operas on Thursday and Saturday evenings."

The Cleveland's "dynamic new conductor" was immersed in *Lady Macbeth* when I laid aside the magazine, and his luggage was filled with the other makings of that seventeenth season. My own bags contained some new dresses in which to make my first non-secret appearances in public, and my dowry, the tools of my new trade: a Polish cookbook, a metric scale, and a crock of dill that I had salted and preserved.

Chapter 17

My return to Cleveland as Artur's wife was marked by apprehensiveness on both our parts. Artur still doubted my suitability to be what the *Plain Dealer* called "Cleveland's first lady of music." His attitude did nothing to bolster my never great sense of adequacy. If I failed, I would have accepted the result as the inevitable product of my long list of imagined and real shortcomings, most of which Artur ceaselessly recounted throughout our marriage. Now I understand that these "deficiencies" in myself were actually Artur's chimeras and haunting insecurities transferred on to me. But in the autumn of 1934, I had no doubt these fears and uncertainties were mine.

Artur arranged for us to stay temporarily at the Wade-Park Manor, a residential hotel convenient to Severance Hall. As soon as our luggage was unpacked he telephoned the woman selected to be my first "public" friend in the city, arranging for us to meet the same day. Artur who wanted to begin work with the orchestra immediately, delayed long enough to introduce me to Mrs. Eleanor Painter Strong.

"Where is it?" Eleanor asked as soon as she came through the apartment entrance.

"What *it?*" Artur countered.

"The *piece of cheese* you *bought,*" she said.

Artur, who always spoke rapidly, and whose accent could be confusing over the poor telephone receivers of those days, cleared up the matter: "I called to tell you that I *brought Mrs. Rodzinski.*"

All the while, an embarrassed Eleanor was staring at me, and I was a complete blush from my hair to my toenails. Artur finally introduced us, and followed it with a nervous little speech about how much he hoped Eleanor would like me. I already had been told to like Eleanor, or pretend to, and above all to be on my best behavior. Moments after Artur packed up his scores and left for work, we both laughed. He wore his nerves as conspicuously as overshoes in summer, we agreed. Our stiffness disappeared and we found ourselves liking each other without reservation.

Eleanor had had a career as a singer — Artur had known her as a musician in Los Angeles — and had married well. Her husband, Charles S. Strong, was the owner of Taylor's, then a large department store in Cleveland. He was wealthy and much older than his pretty wife. The importance to Artur of my getting on with Eleanor was that she would be my entrée to various organizations supporting the orchestra, particularly the Women's Committee and the Musical Arts Association of which Mr. Strong was a mainstay.

My English proved adequate to our encounter as, apparently, everything else about me did, and Eleanor's favorable report soon brought invitations to teas and promises of courtesy calls from the doyennes of the city's society crowd. Before the social whirl began we had to have a home.

I made the rounds of available properties with a realtor of Artur's acquaintance, and rather sooner than expected found a nearly ideal place: a Tudor-style row house of fieldstone, with gables and crenellations and chimneys at odd angles, fully furnished. It was on what has since been renamed Fairmount Drive, in a parklike setting with a deep ravine behind which afforded us a sort of private mountain slope. There were two bedrooms, one smaller than the other, since Artur preferred close spaces, the little room became his. The living room was sunken, with several steps leading up into the dining room, the one relating to the other as parterre does to stage. This feature we later turned to good use for household theatrical parties.

Although altogether modest in dimensions, the house had many trees and shrubs surrounding, with the space and possibilities for a pretty garden. The street was quiet — a must for Artur — and nearby was a facility I felt sure he would make use of frequently, a riding academy with an indoor ring. Artur believed exercising horses was a marvelous way to maintain his own physical fitness.

The very day the lease was signed I moved in my cookbook, metric scale, crock of salted dill, and our clothes. A piano arrived at about the same time. All that was missing was a clock for the kitchen and a supply of household linens, and Eleanor helped me buy these.

The clock was purchased in what then seemed the most unlikely place, a Walgreen's drugstore. The clock's price was about two dollars, but the experience of touring an American pharmacy was worth at least ten. Never before had I seen a place where ice cream and club sandwiches were sold between corn plasters and cough syrup. It was all quite different and therefore exciting, but even more so as buying fleecy blankets, gleaming percale sheets, and fluffy towels at the city's better department stores with a charge account. Eleanor and I had a grand time spending, although when the bills came and Artur had to pay them, the thrill of American credit somewhat diminished. Artur detested that week which joins one month to another; when all the envelopes with tiny cellophane windows through which our name was visible had accumulated on his desk, his temper turned vile. Only when the bills were paid and he had found that we were not yet in the way of outright poverty would his temper sweeten. After that first spending spree he somehow faintly believed that a charge account in my hands was like a gun in the hands of a homicidal maniac.

Once settled in our new house, where I had Victoria, a Pole and an excellent cook, to help me, I began accepting the visits of Cleveland's society women. According to the customs of my homeland, it was my obligation to call on these ladies first, for they were all much my senior. But, it appeared, in America first visits were made to a newcomer whatever her age. If a newcomer passed inspection, then she was invited to call. Victoria and I made tea and cookies and prayed, and one by one the frighteningly wealthy and socially rigid grande dames of Cleveland came and left, each much less fearsome and more flexible than I had thought. With relief I realized the first of the several social obstacles I had feared was hurdled, handily.

But life with Artur, I regret to say, was becoming more and more difficult. From the beginning of our relationship, I had seen him only while vacationing or after a successful performance. Never before had I been privy to his immediate pre-season and pre-performance buildup of jitters. The result was that as the opening of Cleveland's seventeenth season drew closer, we had moments that made me wonder just whom and why I had married.

Artur preferred to lunch at home unless business required him to eat out. One afternoon, as we were leaving the table after a delicious meal, my husband exploded. Never in all my life had I heard such language, nor had I ever been spoken to in such a tone of voice. I thought he had gone mad. What possible justification did he have for his tirade: Was it my dress? The cooking? Something I said?

Perhaps it was all of these things. But I was certain the spark that had ignited his fiery tongue was something he never even spoke of: he simply did not love me. I took this foolish conclusion with me to my room for a good, long cry. Somewhere between my bouts of sobbing, Artur opened the door to my room and came to me wreathed in one of his most exquisite smiles. He had heard me crying, he said. When I caught enough breath to speak, I told him I was due an apology. For what reason? Since I was not about to repeat the monstrous things he had said, I merely replied, tearfully, "You know." To my utter amazement, he did not! As we talked it unfolded that he had no recall of *any* scene. Either I had married the world's most bald-faced dissimulator or a lunatic, but I was to find through further experiences of a similar nature that he was neither. Rather Artur was given to temper tantrums, like a willful, headstrong child, tantrums that came and went as suddenly as tempests; and one hardly expects a rational explanation about his behavior from a stammering, angered brat, or from a depleted thunderhead. The explanation for Artur's behavior lay in the imminence of the new season and his concern about that first concert, although any performance could also induce such flareups.

As the time for the first pair of concerts drew nearer, Artur instructed me in the various backstage duties which were to be mine; many of them came as a surprise. While I had seen and known many conductors from childhood, my knowledge of their work was sketchy and romanticized. I saw these men as oversized, glamorous beings who made music out of a void, who sculpted singing lines or craggy sonorities like a Michelangelo working in air rather than stone. Until I married Artur, I had no idea of the physical labor that went into a performance. A popular science magazine once noted that a conductor's performance exertions are equivalent to throwing a concert grand piano in the air to a height of three stories. True or not, I found that conductors perspired as if they did such things. For one of my numerous new jobs was to assist Artur with a change of shirts and tails at intermission. I was also taught to give him an alcohol rub and how to dry his thick hair with a brush and hot air dryer.

Artur wore his hair without a part and straight back from the brow, a legacy from Stokowski who, on Artur's first day at work for him in Philadelphia, "styled" his hair this way.

"That is how a conductor should look," Stokowski said, pointing Artur at a mirror in his dressing room in the Academy of Music. Artur accepted this Stokie touch without question for the rest of his life. But other things he acquired from Stokowski he did his best to eliminate. Once he told me his four years in Los Angeles were largely spent in divesting himself of what he considered Stokowski's bad musical habits and podium mannerisms — except for one: he always stood with his feet close together, never parting them even when his gestures became expansive to convey the shape and feel of music in climactic moments. On the podium he also stood erect, his naturally rounded shoulders concealed by the fine tailoring of his frock coats. Like Stokowski, he used a baton when it was appropriate — always in the pit of an opera house, otherwise according to the character of the music he might conduct in concert.

Artur was unfailingly grateful to Stokie throughout his life for what his senior had taught him in those Philadelphia days. But he was not uncritical of the man; Artur, like many Poles, doubted the tales of Stokowski's origin and the sincerity of his accent. Stokowski was undeniably a showman on stage, and something of an exhibitionist when off.

As Stokowski's assistant, Artur had to read through with the orchestra almost all of the new scores to be introduced. In those years the Philadelphians had become the leading American protagonist of new music. Audiences cared for it even less than today, but its programming vastly contributed to Stokowski's prestige. And working on this novel musical literature also served Artur well, giving him an uncanny ability to execute the densest pieces.

The circumstances under which these "readings" were done pained Artur, however. Stokie would sit in the gilded and red-plush emptiness of the Academy of Music while my husband took the orchestra through a Varese or Webern score. While watching the notes and players Artur was also obliged to keep an eye on a traffic-light arrangement rigged up on stage. When Stokowski wanted to stop, or have the orchestra play faster or softer, a red, green, yellow, or blue light on the podium would blink to cue Artur of his chief's intentions. It was exasperating and made Artur swear that he would always be kind to assistants (though, from time to time, given his temperament, he forgot this promise).

The matter of Stokowski's transcriptions, that famous series of orchestral works by the team of Bach and Stokie, is well-known. Any number of others did the work for the conductor, although Stokowski was quite capable of doing it himself. His principal arranger was the composer Lucien Caliet, at that period a member of the Philadelphia Orchestra. Stokowski later made adjustments in Caliet's instrumentations, bringing them more in line with the intentions he had given the orchestrator at the outset of a project. But since Artur, as well as others, had reservations about Stokie's "ear," the idea of making off with one of these frequently-played Bach-Stokowski transcriptions greatly appealed to him, the plan being to play the work under a variety of spurious attributions, Bach-This or Bach-That. Artur did just this, and for years Stokowski was none the wiser. It remained for the blind pianist-entertainer Alec Templeton to catch the fraud with his incredible ear and memory.

Artur's prestige in Philadelphia grew during his four-year stay. He

conducted both the student operatic and orchestral groups at Curtis Institute, then at its zenith under Josef Hofmann's guidance, and his work
with the student orchestra provided him with a corps of young musicians
who would play well under his baton in later years. Artur also conducted occasional performances of the Philadelphia Grand Opera Company to critical and popular acclaim. As a measure of how much he had
risen in the city's esteem, Artur's last season with the Philadelphia Orchestra had him billed as "guest conductor" rather than "assistant."

Those years were not without their emotionally trying moments as
well. Artur, no less "a personality" than Stokowski, would save his
temper until he returned home where he would stand before a mirror,
rumple his hair, and spit at his own face for having tolerated or withstood the irritations of the day. Alas, the emotional discipline he acquired then did not long survive his period of apprenticeship. And Artur's workload in his second season with the Cleveland Orchestra would
be his heaviest yet.

In Cleveland alone there were eighteen pairs of regular concerts, six
pairs of "pop" concerts, and six operas, each to be given two performances. Then there were tours with the orchestra to Oberlin, Akron,
Ann Arbor, Toledo, and many New England towns. Artur also had
guest engagements for two weeks with the New York Philharmonic
which Maestro had arranged.

Among the soloists to appear in Cleveland that season were our old
friends Severyn Eisenberger and Bronislaw Hubermann. Efrem Zimba-
list, Artur Schnabel, and the magnificent and incomparable Hofmann
were also to play. Artur's nervousness as the season began seemed understandable: he was a young man, who, though widely experienced,
found himself thrust among giants. But while there likely may have been
private moments of uncertainty about himself or his abilities, publicly he
radiated self-assurance.

In his opening program there were only two compositions scheduled — Beethoven's *Eroica* and Richard Strauss's *Ein Heldenleben*.
Whether through hubris or some inner sense of personal destiny, Artur
had selected works which aggrandized his position and dominion over
his new situation.

As we drove to Severance Hall Artur was tense. I had kept my own
wits together by concentrating on my assigned tasks before leaving the
house: helping him dress, laying out and packing intermission changes
plus scores, thermos of tea, rubbing alcohol, comb and hairbrush, hair
dryer, face powder, and a few good-luck tokens — the most important of
which was a loaded revolver.

The gun Artur carried was old and rusted by long residence in his
right rear pocket over the many years he had conducted. He had purchased it, while yet an adolescent, to murder the husband of a woman he
passionately loved. Since he loved every woman he met in those days
with an equal intensity, a new love fortunately came along before the re-

volver was put to its original purpose and he soon found another for it. When he made his debut at the Lvov Opera, and for a reason I never quite understood, he placed that gun in his pocket. The debut was a success, and because performing artists are a superstitious lot, Artur thereafter refused to conduct unless that particular charm was in the seat of his pants.

Besides the valiseful of oddities I took to the concert hall for Artur, I brought my own tote bag filled with a disorganized tangle of fear and elation. I desperately wanted a success for Artur. I also wished success for my own debut, as much for my sake as Artur's. Artistically, he was accepted. Whether I would be the proper social complement to his glamorous life, and thus consolidate his position, was still a question. Gossip had it that some Cleveland women resented my arrival, that they had enjoyed their new conductor's gifts and not just in the auditorium. I had more than a social role cut out for myself. In the argot of the race track, I had a lot running on myself. To be fair to Artur, I should add that he had generously contributed to the preparations for my debut. While in Paris, he selected and bought for me a stunning gown, a white crepe affair, an original that did wonders for my morale.

At the hall, its namesake, old Mr. Severance himself, was waiting in Artur's dressing room. I was to sit with him in his box, and as my escort he brought me a white orchid corsage, which completed my ensemble and further boosted my spirits. Satisfactorily gotten up, a woman can brazen any social situation, and accompanied by the right man, she is invincible. John L. Severance was such a man. A courtly gentleman of a uniquely American mold — and a nineteenth-century one at that — Mr. Severance brought with him all the confidence I required. He was of medium height and build, but always seemed to me larger. He wore his silver hair, moustache, and beard trimmed in the fashion of King Edward VII, and though anything but a young man (his father had been one of John D. Rockefeller, Sr.'s oil partners), his pink, sleek cheeks gave off the healthy glow of a baby's. I was put at my ease by his greeting. And I could understand, when he wished Artur good luck, why my husband had so strong a filial affection for the man. His voice resonated confidence and warmth. I could not have been a more fortunate or prouder human being than when I entered Box Number One, in the very center of the house, on Mr. Severance's arm.

Once seated and sufficiently in control of myself to appear only *casually* to view the surroundings, my eyes were dazzled. The brightly lit auditorium was filled to capacity with elegantly gowned and bejeweled women and with men dapper in tails or dinner jackets. Still untouched by the nation's fiscal collapse, Cleveland's social elite turned out in force. Their demand for seats had been so great that two extra aisles had been set up. Herbert Elwell, the composer who served as the *Plain Dealer*'s critic, wrote of those assembled, "any one of Cleveland's most distinguished citizens could have been paged at a moment's notice."

The lights dimmed, the house fell silent.

Then, when Artur entered from stage left and the orchestra rose to greet him to the enthusiastic applause of the audience, I could barely see: my eyes had filled with tears. I was numb throughout the whole of the familiar *Eroica*. Only when the audience loudly expressed its pleasure did my reverie end. The clapping and the bows Artur shared with the orchestra were my signal to go backstage. When I arrived at my husband's dressing room, he was seated in an armchair, perspiration pouring down his cheeks.

"How did the Beethoven go?" were the first words out of his mouth.

"Splendidly," I said, though I had hardly heard a note. "And the applause, certainly, that tells you how much everyone liked it."

But what he wanted to hear had nothing to do with my critical responses or reactions (ever suspect to him in those years), nor with applause.

"Did you hear any comments? Did my new tails wrinkle in the back when I raised my arms? Were my movements too exaggerated in the Scherzo or the Finale?" Such were the questions he wanted answered while I dried his hair and he sipped some hot tea.

After a bit, he stood up, took off his shirt, and cupped his hands so that I could pour alcohol into them. He rubbed his chest and arms while I massaged his back. He then put on a fresh change of linen and a second full dress suit because the first was drenched. His heavy hair was brushed so that not one strand stood out of place. As this last bit of costuming went on the orchestra manager, Carl Vosburgh, came in to report the glowing things he heard "out front." This encouraging chitchat braced Artur to face the concert's second half.

Before ever setting foot on stage for a performance, Artur went through an entire course of rituals, the superstitious accumulations of years. For one, he would pat his trousers to be sure he had changed the pistol with his pants. Then he would kiss his father's photo and give me a kiss, which I returned with one on the forehead and a blessing. These done, George Higgins, Severance Hall's stage manager throughout those years, would lead Artur to the stage, then give his left arm a wrenching pinch which, like an injection of adrenalin, sharpened Artur's senses, though it kept his arm mottled with bruises all season long. Following the pinch came the adjustment of a ring he wore, not our wedding band, but a Chinese curio with a frog. I have no idea of the symbolism of that tiny gold amphibian, nor its particular meaning for Artur; but the creature had to face him in a certain way when he raised his hand or otherwise its mysterious powers would be inoperative.

Ein Heldenleben was already off to its soaring start, its impetuous, triadic Hero's theme swaggering through the Cleveland's low strings, by the time I returned to my seat. Somehow, the conceit of Strauss, the occasion, and Artur's mood were all in perfect accord. I was later to hear

(*112*)

him conduct the work many times when its details were better articulated, and with orchestras that yielded richer sounds, but his flair that night was so extraordinary he could possibly have drawn the music from a stone. This is not to say the orchestra did not play its best: indeed, quoting Elwell again, "The orchestra . . . never sounded better." The wind passages in the section where the "Hero" does battle with his critics raised the hair of one's neck, according to another reviewer. After all that happens in the work, the expansive nature of its overall tone and striking variety of rich color, Strauss could only have concluded the piece as he did — quietly, subtly, pensively. But these are characteristics which, as conclusions to big compositions at the close of a concert, can easily fail in their effect; that is, unless a conductor creates a tension that will sustain his tired audience's attentions. Artur accomplished this that night, and the glittering Clevelanders went mad. Artur was called back to the stage fourteen times.

Winding through the backstage areas of Severance Hall, so much better lit and less arcane-seeming than the passageways of the Teatr Wielki to which my school friend had introduced me an age before, I had an overwhelming sense of déjà vu. Tears welled in my eyes and had it not been for the people swarming about I might have found relief in a good cry. People clogged the corridors to Artur's room, and even the room itself. There were introductions and greetings and kisses and embraces, and more than anything else, a steady chant of congratulations and compliments which Artur sopped up like a sponge. In time, I came to understand how greatly he, like all performing artists, needed such contacts.

That evening there was a reception at the home of Dudley S. Blossom, a wealthy businessman, who, along with Mr. Severance and John D. Rockefeller, Jr., had contributed to the construction of Severance Hall. Mr. Blossom, like Mr. Severance, was also one of Artur's admiring supporters. I had no real reason to be unsure of myself, but on that drive through the countryside to the Blossoms' estate, I was nervous. The Blossoms' guests were all people in Cleveland who counted, who, as Cleveland's *Social Register* showed, were to the manner born, the American equivalent of our native Poland's gentry or minor aristocracy. I never gave thought to such things in Warsaw where it seemed to me one could move through various social strata with impunity. But here, in democratic America, there existed obstacles. Of course, some of these were of Artur's contrivance; on that ride he practiced with me in detail just what and how I was to speak to a host of people. And to add to the ordeal was my still awkward English. I could express myself, but with neither fluency nor the relaxed sense that I was above some tactless or tasteless barbarism.

The spacious living room of the Blossoms' home was entered from a raised foyer, and as Artur and I appeared, and then took several steps down into the room, it seemed that every eye was taking my measure.

My legs wobbled, and I clung to Artur's arm more for physical support than out of social grace. My husband was greeted with applause and cries of "Bravo!" which flustered him. He blurted a perfunctory introduction of me to our host, and then was off, quickly, nervously, kissing ladies' hands and making small talk with friends and acquaintances.

Mr. Blossom introduced me to his guests. Except for Eleanor and Charles Strong, there was no one I knew, though several faces seemed uncertainly familiar. It was an interesting gathering. Most of Cleveland's prominent citizens were there, including the entire board of directors of the Musical Arts Association, personalities such as Mr. and Mrs. Newton D. Baker (he had been Secretary of War in the Wilson Administration); Senator and Mrs. Robert Bulkley; Congressman Chester Bolton and his wife Frances (who on her husband's death succeeded him in the House of Representatives); the composer Arthur Shepherd and his wife; the Alfred Brewsters; the Frank Ginns; and Mrs. Adela Prentiss Hughes. The last three names were inextricable from the doings of the orchestra, and Mrs. Hughes had been the driving force behind the Cleveland's organization sixteen years before.

At the end of the night I felt that I had carried off my part rather well, and was euphoric when Artur said, on the long drive home: "Halusia, I am so happy. You have won everyone's heart. Now I can concentrate on my work while you take care of all the social nonsense that goes with the job."

The following day Elwell, in the *Plain Dealer*, after discussing the quality (improved) of the orchestra's sound, wrote: "the evening belonged primarily to Rodzinski. . . . He has achieved a degree of perfection in ensemble that puts our orchestra in the front rank. Other cities might sit up and take notice — *Cleveland has a great conductor.*"

Chapter 18

ARTUR had set the signature of the hero triumphant to the beginning of his second Cleveland season. Concert after concert revealed his increasing command of himself, his men, and the music they performed. The rapport between conductor and instrumentalists grew and consolidated itself. Artur's operatic venture, moreover, though costly in time and dollars, gave the Cleveland Orchestra's board an increasing sense of civic pride. Not just the board and the Musical Arts Association but the audiences were enthralled. Where the New York Philharmonic under Maestro Toscanini and the Met with its glittering roster of stars blushed at rows of empty seats and tiers of vacant boxes, Artur played to full houses, for symphonic concerts and operatic performances alike.

Maestro had selected Artur to lead two weeks of concerts with the New York Philharmonic in November. The invitation in itself was quite flattering; it also expressed Toscanini's confidence that Artur could meet the challenge of the Philharmonic and its players with ease.

The New York orchestra was, and still is, notoriously hard on guest conductors. Then, as now, if the Philharmonic's virtuosi could find no respect for a guest's musicianship, or thought him to be disagreeable in other ways, he would get scant cooperation from them. Their subtle ways of scuttling a new conductor were well known to my husband, and frankly he approached the great ensemble in fear, although each first encounter with an ensemble terrified him a little.

For what small consolation it offered, I attended Artur's first Philharmonic rehearsal. From the moment he appeared on the podium the men were with him. This did much to give him confidence, but nothing to eliminate the tension of opening night in Carnegie Hall. He was as edgy as he had been in Cleveland. The concert could make or break him nationally. In Cleveland, and in little more than a year, Artur had developed a devoted audience, a reliable board, and had found a certain sense of security. New York was different, however: a "market," as he put it, a place where musicians came "to peddle their wares," and, as far as guest conductors went, it was distinctly a buyer's market. On the way to the hall, he said, "One comes, shows his goods, hopes for a few sales, then gracefully disappears to wherever he belongs."

The "goods" Artur offered on his debut were made by contemporary Soviet composers. Though audiences cared little enough for new music then, Artur and his program charmed the house. Even the not-especially-modest Philharmonic players joined the audience in giving Artur an ovation. Francis Perkins of the *Herald-Tribune* wrote: "He is, without a doubt, a conductor who knows his business."

For his second program, Artur played *Ein Heldenleben*, this time less as a hallmark for the season than as a test piece, for it was a score that New Yorkers had heard under dozens of batons, including the composer's. Artur's reading stood up against these precedents, and the press paid tribute to his "extraordinary technique" and ability to project a "firmly-knit performance" of so big (and loose) a structure with an unfamiliar orchestra and few rehearsals.

For myself, there was much to enjoy during the visit besides Artur's successes. I saw good friends — Zosia Kochanska, Sophie Braslau, old Siloti, Miecio Munz, and others — and had a chance to compare Cleveland and New York. While the latter, by far, seemed more exhilarating, Cleveland was distinctly homier and less impersonal. The effects of the Depression were more apparent in New York.

Artur's New York schedule was a carefully laid mosaic of time in which rehearsals and performances with the Philharmonic were only the obvious part of the design. Every free moment of his was spent at work with the soloists and chorus for the forthcoming Cleveland premiere of *Lady Macbeth*. The singers belonged to an emigré group called Art of Musical Russia, Inc. The members of this organization, many of whom had been trained in the Moscow Art Theater or for the Chauve-Souris, were all "Whites" and might have been expected to rebel against representing musical Russia to Americans through the work of so adamant a "Red" as Shostakovich. Rather, they shared Artur's enthusiasm for the opera as a piece of great theater, as much in the Russian tradition as anything they might perform.

Artur worked many long and grueling hours with the Russians, sharing with them his enthusiasm for the opera and being re-enthused by their sensitive, exuberant response. When voices failed to find a pitch in the novel harmonic texture demanded by the young composer and repeated passages began to fray tempers, one singer or another would pull a characteristically Russian prank or joke to ease the tension. The work was exhausting. I cannot find the total number of hours Artur spent in preparing the chorus and soloists, but the job took every free hour he had from the beginning of the New York Philharmonic season until the Cleveland premiere in January.

The advance publicity based on reports from Russia piqued the interest of musicians and laymen equally. Everyone expected something sensational, but in just what sense only the performance would show. There was talk of the opera being a Marxist-Leninist tract, that its music was composed by dialectics, and that it exhibited such things as had never before been seen on stage. Of course, this was nonsense. The libretto by the composer and an associate was based on the Leskov tale precisely because it included every device to be found in dozens of successful operas — though, admittedly, the others rely on only one of these devices apiece. Heaven knows where opera would be without poisonings, illicit loves, pictures of the mores of a rejected regime, and spoofs on the church. Shostakovich, in his youthful brashness, had wished a *schlager* in which to set his stamp on these operatic situations once and for all. And with one work at that.

Bolstered by his Philharmonic debut, Artur threw himself into the rest of the season, especially *Lady Macbeth*, with an obsessive drive. He and Severyn Eisenberger checked through the score to catch all sorts of errors. These involved recopying of orchestral parts to the tune of more than 150 hours. The stage director, Wilhelm von Wymetal, Jr., on loan, so to say, from the Met, conferred with Artur on every movement of singers and chorus. Shostakovich's patterns and tempi would be followed to the letter with only one innovation, Scene VII, the second scene of Act Three, which takes place in a police station. Artur had the idea of turning the Russian constables into Keystone Kops. The stage set, which had to afford quick scene shifts (there were nine in four acts in Shostako-vich's first score), covered by a minimum of between-scene music, was designed to Artur's satisfaction by Richard Rychtarik. It conveyed the milieu of Russia circa 1840, but was spare and modern, and most impor-tantly, functioned like an integral piece of a mechanism.

Yet with all the time demanded by *Lady Macbeth*, for her first non-Soviet appearance, Artur produced an *Otello* and a *Tosca*. Among other new works prepared for the orchestra's audiences was the Cleveland premiere of Strauss's *Also Sprach Zarathustra*. These efforts, plus nu-merous trips to New York, seemed not to tire but rather to energize him.

I was only too glad to stay put in Cleveland, serving tea and cakes to the dowagers. Though Artur now considered such affairs my job, it was not like work in any sense. As a matter of fact, I loved every minute of it. I had been raised in an era and ambience in which genteel socializing was not nearly the bore it seems today.

On January 12, I accompanied Artur to New York for the last re-hearsals with the singers, and to meetings with Mrs. Claire Reis, then chairman of the League of Composers' executive board. The League, alas, long since defunct, was one of the glories of the American musical scene in the years that saw native music come into its own. Serving with Claire were two of the country's most outstanding talents, Aaron Cop-land and Roger Sessions, along with Marion Bauer, Frederick Jacobi, Lazare Saminsky, Minna Lederman, and the conductor Alexander Smal-lens. The group promoted not simply the works of American contempo-raries, but also those of whatever stimulating new talents might be emerging anywhere. The League did this by sponsoring concerts and operas and through its publication *Modern Music, A Quarterly Review*, for whose pages wrote America's most intelligent and literate critics.

Lady Macbeth had attracted the League's interest. When Stokowski sued for her rights, it was not merely as one more *coup de théâtre*, but in his capacity as the League's director of stage productions among which had been works by Schoenberg, De Falla, Stravinsky, and Prokofiev. Mrs. Reis decided to take Artur's production for mounting under the League's auspices at the Metropolitan, February 5, as a benefit for the Composers' Fund. It was on this basis alone that Toscanini's old friend Giulio Gatti-Casazza, the Met's director, would consider leasing the house on Broadway and 39th Street to the League.

Artur decided that a rest was in order before returning to Cleveland for the premiere, and one was taken at Atlantic City. I was enchanted by the place, the great length of boardwalk with its smart shops and restau-rants and hotels, not yet the honky-tonk strip brought about by the Depression. Our visit to the seaside resort was Artur's sole break in that season; after eight months of planning and work, dreaming and hoping, came that brief time of repose. The vacation was not without event, however. One grey morning, we ran across Bruno Walter, broad-brim hat, coat with wide fur collar, lap robe and all, in a rolling chair on the boardwalk, much like an apparition of the Flying Dutchman. There was musical talk, and I felt a twinge of homesickness when Walter reminded us how bad the Warsaw Philharmonic had become under Fitelberg. Artur smiled, but inwardly winced.

Back in Cleveland, the Russians had invaded Severance Hall for the first stage rehearsals. Every performer was ideally cast. Anna Leskaya as Katerina was a beautiful woman with a wonderful voice and a great personality. Ivan Ivantzoff, her lover, could have been younger, but he was such a good actor and singer that it scarcely mattered. Artur was thrilled with the scene in which Dora Boshoer, who played Katerina's maid, Aksinia, was rolled in a barrel by drunken peasants, yet still could watch his beat and sing a rather difficult part in tune while upside down.

The premiere on January 31 was the most publicized and awaited theatrical event of the year among musicians. It was also the first time that Cleveland had had such national and international notice. The daily press had created a demand for tickets that far exceeded seating for the two performances in Cleveland. Requests came daily to the box office from Chicago, Detroit, New York. Even Californians were willing to make a three-day trek by train just to pass several hours with *Lady Macbeth*.

Ordinarily on concert days Artur ate only a light but nourishing lunch and no dinner before conducting. That day he lunched on a thick T-bone steak, boiled potatoes, and stewed fruit. As was his habit, he then went to bed for a long, deep sleep.

He woke up after 5:00 P.M. with rosy cheeks and a happy smile. The maid brought some strong tea with crackers and I started to prepare his evening clothes. I took out four extra shirts, a change after each act. Since he would not be seen in the orchestra pit during the operatic performance, he could wear soft shirts instead of the stiff formal ones. When the bag was packed I went to my room to dress, and Artur, still in bed, took up his score for a last look.

Usually Artur left for the concerts at the last possible moment, but that day he rose much earlier to dress much faster. He couldn't wait to be in Severance Hall. I knew by now that it was best for me to be quiet while I helped him with his clothes and on the way to the theater.

Backstage was a beehive of singers, stagehands, managers, electricians, orchestra men. Vosburgh, very agitated, was checking to see if everyone was in place. The singers began to vocalize, creating pandemonium.

Artur adored this kind of excitement. He made me give him a double portion of granulated Cola Astier (a stimulant made from cola nuts) which he took for extra pep. Von Wymetal and Rychtarik came for last minute instructions. Eight o'clock was approaching.

I kissed and blessed Artur and ran to the box where I was to sit with friends from Chicago: Claire Dux, the great singer who had married Charles Swift, the head of Swift & Co., the composer John Alden

Carpenter and his wife Ellen, and the Detroit Symphony's Ossip Gabrilowitsch. In other boxes I noticed important guests. Among them were George Gershwin, Grace Moore, and Fray and Bragiotti (the brother of authoress Gloria), the well-known duo piano team.

From the first note a current flowing from Artur to the singers and orchestra seemed to touch the audience. Applause burst out many times during the performance. The scene at the police station where the policemen moved in silent-film motion drew roars of laughter.

The only slightly communistic touch was the gay, dancelike music played at the entrance of a Russian priest who prayed over the body of the poisoned father-in-law.

"Shocked, Amused, Gasping Audience Roars Acclaim to Rodzinski at Soviet Opera," the *Plain Dealer* headlined its front page article next day. Elwell wrote:

> Surely nothing quite like it has been heard here. . . . But as to the reaction of the audience which packed the house to the door, there can be no doubt. Its members were shocked and stimulated simultaneously. They tittered and gasped. They recalled principals time after time, and when Rodzinski appeared at the beginning of the third act, applause broke into deafening roar.

Time, which sent its principal critic, described the opera as follows:

> In the respectable quiet of East Side Cleveland . . . an old man ate poisoned mushrooms, died in wriggling agony. A merchant was smothered with a bed pillow, and his corpse dragged into the cellar. A prostitute let out a blood-chilling scream as she was pushed to her death in an ice black lake. Yet as the heroine of Dmitri Shostakovich's Lady Macbeth of Mzensk, the woman responsible for these three atrocious murders was really a gentle soul whom only the sternist moralist would blame for her crimes.

> Conductor Artur Rodzinski called it "one of the most important contributions to music brought out in the last 20 years." The ardor of his performance proved that he meant what he said.

We left for New York right after the second performance, our spirits buoyed by reports that the Metropolitan already was completely sold out. It was the first time in years that this had happened, because the Met was then at its lowest ebb — though later that season the discovery of a great new star, Kirsten Flagstad, once again brought the public back to the opera house.

The third performance of *Lady Macbeth* was given on a cold, dreary day of mixed snow and rain. Artur awoke with a bad case of Slavic pessimism: "The house will probably be empty . . . I hope the singers won't have sore throats . . . my head hurts, my stomach is upset. . . ." I poured Anacin into him for the one, and Alka-Seltzer for the other, and told him that the weather would be an excuse for the wealthy to wear their furs, and that the singers would consider the day a sunny one by Russian standards. Surely, not one would dare have a sore throat. It was amazing how such trivial talk could soothe him. We remained in our hotel the whole day while Artur studied the score. A nap followed lunch. Refreshed, certain that the notes were all in place in his head, he was ready for the evening.

We arrived at the artists' entrance on 39th Street to find a line of people that stretched around the block, all waiting to buy standing-room tickets. Robert Lawrence, the conductor and expert on French opera, told me years later that he, as a young man, was the last on line to reach the box office, one too late to buy the last ticket.

A surprise awaited Artur in the dressing room. On his table, next to a sheaf of telegrams, lay a package. The telegrams would say predictable things, but the box was a mystery, so it was opened first. From numerous swathes of tissue paper appeared a small ivory carving, an elephant. Accompanying it was a typewritten message, unsigned. It read: "This little elephant will bring you good luck on this great occasion. When you have received seven of them you will be on top of the world."

"What a nice thought," Artur said. "It must have been you, Halusia. Tell the truth — you sent it."

I could deny the act with impunity, although I did share the gift giver's belief in Artur's future. The anonymous gesture sent Artur's spirits soaring as he left for the pit.

I do not know of another musical event that ever was honored by such a distinguished audience. Everybody was there — Toscanini, Bruno Walter, Stokowski, Damrosch, Koussevitzky, Reiner, Klemperer, Bodansky, Smallens, Sokoloff, Stravinsky, Heifetz, Siloti, Ernest Hutchinson, John Erskine, Carl Friedberg, Olga Samaroff-Stokowski, Albert Spalding, George Gershwin (again), Artur Schnabel, Lawrence Tibbett, Mischa Elman, and many others whom I did not know or do not remember. There were theatrical people, painters, sculptors, singers, composers, and over 3,000 more enthusiastic listeners.

The social crowd included Mr. and Mrs. John D. Rockefeller, Mrs. August Belmont, Paul Cravath (then chairman of the Opera board), Mrs. Vincent Astor (now Mrs. Lytle Hull), Marshall Field, Mrs. Cornelius Vanderbilt, Mrs. Myron Taylor, Mrs. Theodore Steinway, Mr. and Mrs. William Breed, Mrs. Henry Alexander, Ganna Walska, Prince Serge Obolensky, Mr. and Mrs. Sidney Howard, Mr. and Mrs. Thomas Finletter, Mr. and Mrs. Herbert Witherspoon, and of course, Mr. and Mrs. Reis and Mr. and Mrs. Herman Irion. Mrs. Irion, the former Yolanda Mero, a pianist of some note, was president of the Art of Musical Russia, Inc.

From the first sombre notes of the score, depicting the gloom of Katerina's situation and state of mind, the audience was captivated. Applause punctuated various scenes, a unique response to the performance of a new, and then rather modern opera. An entr'acte from Act Two brought a call for an encore — again something unheard of, and not just for a contemporary opera.

The reaction was even more extraordinary when one considers the audience. America's wealthiest public, at the height of the Great Depression, was applauding a Communist's damnation of the way of life and political pieties of a capitalistic society and governmental form only recently overthrown in Russia. Perhaps some in the house appreciated the irony, and the parallel to the Parisian premiere of Beaumarchais's *Le Mariage du Figaro*, when the audience that laughed at itself comprised the beneficiaries of a regime soon to be labeled *ancien*. Small wonder that the opera by Mozart using *Figaro* as a libretto initially was kept off the Viennese stage by the Austrian Emperor.

As *Lady Macbeth* continued, it evoked more and more applause for the singers. When the opera ended and Artur joined the principals in front of the curtain, the applause reached its peak. Alone for a bow on stage, he drowned in it, smiling happily. Artur Rodzinski had conquered New York.

Toscanini stood in his box, heartily clapping long after the public started to leave. Then he came backstage to congratulate Artur: *"Bravo, bravo, Rodzinski, magnifico lavoro, bravo, bravo,"* he kept repeating.

Maestro found the opera musically fascinating. He especially liked the beautiful chorus in the last act, sung by convicts on their way to Siberia. Toscanini's compliments meant the most to Artur, though he was also happy to accept praise from Walter Damrosch and other musicians crowding his room.

Next day the reviews were divided:

An extraordinary thing was witnessed last night at the Metropolitan Opera House when Shostakovich's *Lady Macbeth* was performed magnificently for the first time in New York. On this occasion an opera with a musical score flimsily put together . . . with almost no originality or creative quality . . . had an immense success. . . . Gales of applause swept through the house . . . cheers for the opera, the conductor and the artists.

—— Olin Downes

. . . the production was an undeniable triumph with Artur Rodzinski proving himself an operatic conductor of prodigious power and eloquence.

—— Leonard Liebling

Shostakovich's talent as a broad musical satirist is beyond question . . . it will be long before I forget the extraordinary characterizations of the principals and the incredible identification of the chorus down to its last member. . . .

—— Samuel Chotzinoff

Whether *Lady Macbeth* will find a place in the world's operatic repertoire is a matter for doubtful conjecture. It is difficult to think of it without an all-Russian cast in which every member has a real feeling for an earthy Russian village.

—— *Time* Magazine

For me it is the most important new work for the lyric stage in several decades . . . [the] Shostakovich score is a gigantic one, calling for the greatest

technical mastery on the part of the conductor. Mr. Rodzinski possesses
that. . . .

——— Walter Kramer
Musical America

I thought the critical reaction stupendous, but Artur was disappointed that Downes didn't appreciate the music enough. At the time Olin was still fiercely anti-Communist. As a matter of fact, Virgil Thomson observed, "The New York audience loved it. The New York critics hedged. In fact, the degree of approval expressed by them was in pretty close proportion to the political leftness of the respective newspapers for which they work." At any rate, Artur was an overnight celebrity in New York and across the country.

Ironically, Stalin had by then gotten around to hearing the work under the unfavorable circumstances I described earlier, and the work had just been damned. The reason: insufficient promotion of Marxist ideology. The effect: an era of Socialist Realism that crippled Soviet music until Stalin's death. At the time, such matters were of no importance to Downes, for him a little bit of Communism, even in music, was more than enough. Yet later Downes was to find in Shostakovich a symphonist worthy of sitting alongside his idol Sibelius, thanks to the cordiality of the "United Front" détente of the war years.

Twenty-two years later, in 1957, Artur and I passed a morning in a hotel suite in Rome with Shostakovich, then a much older man, if not a particularly politically wiser one. We had come together because Artur had heard of the composer's intended revisions of *Lady Macbeth* and he was determined to have the rights to a La Scala premiere. Despite the early hour, Shostakovich served us vodka and a mountainous heap of the very best caviar in nearly-Tsarist surroundings of sumptuousness. While I enjoyed my caviar and a crisp roll with butter, the two musicians, after liberally toasting each other and praising the cooperation that had wrought successes with premieres of other works in addition to *Lady Macbeth*, talked over the revisions. The redone piece would be called *Katerina Ismailova*.

"I hope to finish work soon," Shostakovich said, "but I am a lazy sort by nature. It is difficult to promise when I will set the last note in place. But I promise that you will have the premiere outside Russia."

Maestro Francesco Siciliani, then artistic director of La Scala, scheduled the opera for 1958–59, and bombarded Shostakovich with letters and telegrams urging completion. Artur was less concerned with the delivery of the score than approximating a cast that had brought him such success in 1935. Only Russians, with a feel for their own stagecraft and culture could make *Katerina* live on stage, and they were then in short supply. There were no more youthful, vigorous "White" Russians to be found to put Shostakovich's characters through their paces. The opera's topicality was about as apt as the Great Depression, then as much forgotten as remembered. And Artur, who had initiated his own time of national and international celebrity with the opera, was a man in partial eclipse. By the time Shostakovich completed his work, Artur had finished his life.

Chapter 19

ARTUR's annual tour with the Cleveland Orchestra began the day after *Lady Macbeth*'s New York premiere. The orchestra looked forward to it, but Artur did not. To him, tours were the worst part of each season's schedule.

They meant hours of train travel through relentlessly ugly industrial landscapes, concerts after hurried meals and changes of clothes, the ordeal of sleep in an unfamiliar bed. He usually required several hours to relax after a performance, and while on tour it always seemed that he had only just said good night to the orchestra's manager when, suddenly, Vosburgh hovered over his bed saying "Maestro, the train leaves in an hour."

The players, on the other hand, enjoyed themselves away from the monotony of their ordinary routine. There were no rehearsals, no teaching schedules, only card games, drinking, and jokes, both dirty and practical. Artur was often the butt of their pranks, which he usually took with reasonable grace, and sometimes repaid in kind.

The orchestra returned to Cleveland and it was business as usual. Artur and his men were encouraged by the reception they received at their next public concert. As the pride of the city's cultural scene the orchestra was given an ovation, and Artur was presented with an outsized laurel wreath inscribed "Cleveland Proudly Welcomes You."

The high spots in what remained of the season were appearances by Josef Hofmann in a Chopin Concerto and Artur Schnabel playing Beethoven's Fourth Concerto. Two more operas rounded off that part of the season: Rossini's *Barbiere*, with Warsaw's Eva Bandrowska imported to sing Rosina, and Wagner's *Meistersinger*, featuring the Met's incomparable Fritz Schorr.

Somehow, despite the work involved in these concerts and opera productions, Artur still found time to lead ten special radio concerts for NBC. He did not mind the additional work these extra performances meant. Rather, the chance to affect the tastes and attitudes of a larger audience stimulated him. He loved the letters that came in, appreciative and cranky ones alike, and found time to dictate answers to any that called for more than formal acknowledgment.

By the end of February, Artur had begun to think of vacationing. He wanted a complete change, to forget music altogether. All invitations to guest conduct were refused, even though such engagements would have been a logical follow-up to his new celebrity. Where could we go that would be distant enough from music and musicians? A trip to Poland was out. Artur resented my large family and friends, and he felt uncomfortable in that social whirl.

I laid hands on every travel brochure that came my way, but none of the exotic, musicless places I suggested excited his interest. Then, one night at a dinner party in Cleveland, Lou Rorimer and his wife, our new friends, told us of a trip they had made to Morocco. Lou, a member of the orchestra's board, was an antique dealer, and had a sensitive eye for interesting sights, a gift that he passed on to his son James who would become a director of New York's Metropolitan Museum of Art and create the Cloisters.

At home that night, Artur asked "Why don't we go to Africa?"

Once again, I answered "Why not?"

With the Rorimers' help, I plotted an intinerary that took us by car across France, through Spain, and to Morocco and Algeria from Gibraltar.

The season's last concert was on April 18, an all-request program which began with a transcription by Respighi of Bach's great organ *Passacaglia*, and ended with Stravinsky's *Petrouchka Suite*, an infallible audience-pleaser. Elwell's review was headlined "Audience Cheers in Wild Tribute," and his *Plain Dealer* copy ended on a hyperbolic note: "It was the termination . . . of the most triumphal year in the orchestra's history." Perhaps the first of Artur's anonymously-given elephants had worked its magic.

That same day we left for New York where there was pleasurable court to be paid to Maestro and Donna Carla, and also business to attend to — auditioning new players for the orchestra and singers for forthcoming opera productions. Claire Reis was pleased with the hit *Lady Macbeth* scored for the League of Composers and anxious for Artur to do another operatic premiere, hopefully of as fine a work, this time one by an American. George Gershwin seemed the likeliest candidate since talk had it George was writing a serious stage piece.

We were invited to lunch with Gershwin through the good offices of a Cleveland friend, Kay Halle, a professional people collector who had had President Roosevelt and Winston Churchill among her prizes long before they were world figures, and who at one time had been engaged to Winston's son Randolph.

Kay met us at Gershwin's apartment and showed us about his living room. Alongside paintings by modern masters were hung many by Gershwin whose work was more than that of an amateur. Gershwin enjoyed hearing such compliments.

This was my first meeting with George, and I was captivated from the outset. He was good-looking, brilliantly witty but in a natural, unaffected way, and utterly unspoiled by his huge public and financial success. Although he lived elegantly — lunch was served by a butler — there was nothing extravagant about him. Conversation at table was primarily about music and theater. *Lady Macbeth* took up a good part of the talk. Inevitably, Artur mentioned the opera which George was rushing to complete against the deadline set by the group which commissioned the work.

Artur asked to see the score, and we all moved off to a room where work sheets were laid out on a large, high stand of Gershwin's own invention. He was proud of his work table — even more so, it seemed, than the score he unassumingly showed Artur. As he turned its pages his mounting enthusiasm showed.

"*Porgy and Bess* will be a fantastic hit, George," Artur said. "You are creating a true American folk opera!" George was delighted.

"Give it to me for a Cleveland premiere, then New York. We'll create a sensation every bit as great as *Lady Macbeth* did," Artur said.

Gershwin had admired Artur since his days in Los Angeles, and was sincere when he said that he would like to have Artur conduct all his works. But he doubted whether those who had commissioned it would relinquish the score for a purely operatic premiere. "I'll try my best," he promised.

Unfortunately, George's best was not enough with the businessmen who had invested in a Broadway hit, and so *Porgy and Bess* entered the annals of American musical theater as a musical comedy. But when we sailed for Europe, there was still hope that *Porgy* might crown Cleveland's coming season.

The moment we disembarked at Le Havre my husband was a new man. Each time he set foot on European soil he was transformed. It was always a homecoming for him, and the things that would exasperate him in Cleveland or New York were tolerated in Europe with equanimity.

We packed our things into the Pontiac we had taken along with us and drove to Paris. It amused Artur to drive at a relative snail's pace behind a herd of cows or a horse and wagon on the narrow, winding roads. (A traffic jam in downtown Cleveland could put him in a rage.) In Paris, we picked up my sister Fela and her husband Kazik Krance. Together we traveled through the Château country of the Loire, on south through Provence, over the Pyrenees, and into Spain for two weeks before sailing for North Africa.

Artur's temper stayed contained for the better part of the trip. He entertained himself with his penchants for driving his big car furiously over terrifying roads, or taking pictures. These two passions of his life rated only slightly lower than music.

Richard Wagner's *Parsifal* was my husband's most favored opera, admired even more than his adored *Tristan*, and the composer had been inspired to compose the piece after a visit to Monserrat, near Barcelona.

Artur would not rest until he had visited this famous monastery which sits perched atop a mountain that rises suddenly from the arid plain. We drove to the base of the mountain and from there rode a funicular to the holy place. Since women were not allowed to enter, Fela and I waited in the square outside while the men attended the early morning service.

Artur returned an hour or so later, deeply moved by the superb singing of the monks' and boys' choir, renowned throughout Europe for its musicianship. Boys who were accepted had to have perfect pitch as well as purity of voice. Without difficulty they could sing the most elaborate polyphonic music at sight.

"What an ideal place for a performance of *Parsifal*," Artur said, as we rode back to our hotel. "It would be inspiring, with this extraordinary chorus and in this setting. How I would adore to do it here. It could become an annual event."

His mind already had established a festival. He hurried to Madrid to see the Minister of Culture and sold him on the project. They corresponded throughout the next winter and it appeared that Artur's dream might materialize. Then came the Spanish Civil War and the plans were abandoned.

Wherever we traveled, Artur looked at everything in terms of what would make a good photo. The Krances and I never had a choice about what we would like to see because Artur centered the whole trip around his interests. Most of the time that meant following at his heels while he photographed: steep, winding streets in Toledo and the house of El Greco; donkeys in the traffic of Madrid; the game of pelota; the King's palaces; old Moorish castles; cathedrals of Cordoba, Sevilla, and Granada; gypsies, beggars, cattle fair and, most exciting, a bullfight with the leading matador of the day, Ortega.

Before he came to Spain, Artur associated the bullfight solely with the opera *Carmen*. Now he was eager to see what always takes place off stage in the opera. Off to the bullfight we all had to go. He enjoyed the crowd, so agitated, its sense of anticipation heightened by the wretched, off-tune playing of a band. Women were banked like lovely flowers up the sloping sides of the arena, some in colorful dresses and shawls, others wearing mantillas of black lace that swayed delicately in the breeze. Everything seemed designed to add to the tension until the deafening roar when the bull trotted testily into the sandy ring.

What followed thereafter was shocking. All of us were appalled by the bloody doings of the picadors as they wounded the splendid animal with lances and darts. Yet when the great Ortega appeared, Fela, Kazik, and I shed our disgust for amazement. He moved as gracefully as a dancer, performing his half and full veronicas as though choreographed. Though the name of the pass a torero makes with his cape has Christian significance, its origins spring from some barbaric and pagan ritual. Surely there is something paganly sensuous in the torero's elegant posturings before a murderous bull, a courtship with suicide that is supposed to, but does not always, end in the slaying of the bull. Along with my sister and brother-in-law, I responded to the spectacle, and followed the ritualized butchery breathlessly to its end when Ortega, with one perfect plunge of his sword, severed the animal's cerebral cortex to enter its heart. The public rose to all but a man to applaud both the bull-fighter's skill and give vent to some deeper primal feeling. Artur, however, had become morose. He sat glumly as people around him clapped and shouted, throwing hats and flowers into the bloodied pit below. He was disgusted.

As luck would have it, *Carmen* was performed at the opera that night, and it seemed an ideal close to the day. Artur brightened at the idea, but the performance was nothing but provincial trash which left everyone out of sorts.

For the rest of the trip Artur seemed to take subtle revenge on all of us for our "bloodthirstiness" at the bullfight. He had understandably enjoyed the winding roads that took us through villages and farm lands for a view of Spanish life. Suddenly, he changed our route to include as many mountains as possible. Perhaps I do him a disservice: it may be that coincidentally we came to the high Sierras just then. But there was no doubting his intention to stand our hair on end with his "civilized" negotiation of hairpin turns 7,000 feet above the earth. The views were breathtaking, though not half so much as the driving.

From Gibraltar we crossed to North Africa where we drove through Tetuan, Rabat, and Casablanca to Marrakesh, returning via Fez to Algiers. The Arabs distracted Artur from his impatience with us. Devout Moslems do not take kindly to photography, and Artur enjoyed fooling them, shooting frame after frame through a prism device which permitted him to point his camera in one direction while photographing in another. In this way he was able to capture natural poses of men in white burnooses seated in tiny patches of shade sipping mint tea, and of women, wrapped in cloth up to their smouldering black eyes, filling water jars at a well, and of merchants seated crosslegged on mats in their cagelike shops, surrounded by stocks of pots and baskets.

Artur could have illustrated an encyclopedia with the shots he took, and I wonder if he saw much of the place except through his viewfinder.

The remainder of the trip was increasingly tense, with Artur as eager for a fight as he was to find his "ideal shot": an Arab saying his sunset prayers with a camel and a palm tree in the background. One evening, shortly before our return to Europe, the three subjects came into his viewfinder and he snapped the shutter. At that very instant the sun went down, and the picture never came out we discovered later in our Cleveland darkroom when we developed hundreds of photographs of the trip, printing them and reliving the better part of the journey. He reached the French Riviera where the Krances went their way and Artur and I headed for Italy.

Our plan was to look for a place in the mountains where Artur could study scores for the coming season, a house with sufficient space for us and his mother and son Witold. But first we paid a call on Toscanini at his summer home, Isolino San Giovanni on Lago Maggiore. An invitation had been extended by Maestro and Donna Carla when we last saw them in New York.

We arrived on a warmish Sunday afternoon in mid-June to find the entire family still at table having coffee. Maestro's children, with their families, were all talking noisily, animatedly, very much in the tradition of an Italian household. Walter was present with his wife Cia and son Walfredo, as was Walli, her husband Conte Castelbarco, and their daughter Emanuela. Toscanini's youngest daughter, Wanda, sat dandling Maestro's favorite grandchild, little Sonia Horowitz, while Vladimir stood around shy and out of place in the midst of such Latinate family doings.

The two daughters were haranguing Maestro for not demanding greater royalties for his recordings, and generally ignoring anything he had to say in reply. This was the conversation the moment we were announced. There was an intermission while introductions were made, then it resumed with all the fervor of a Toscanini performance.

Artur was genuinely shocked. He had placed Maestro on so high a pedestal that he thought the man far above such family scenes, and one with a subject that impinged on his rights as an artist. Royalties and fees were subjects that Artur never discussed with me.

Finally the family went off for its siesta, leaving Maestro to Artur and me for what was an unforgettable afternoon.

Maestro loved his little island. It made him feel detached from the currents of the world, especially at night when peace permeated its shores like some sweet opiate. Yet the drug of those quiet nights was not quite sufficient to ease the ache that tormented his bursitis, helped so frequently by Dottore Rinaldi, but since that strange medical man's death, not relieved by a single other physician.

Mention of Rinaldi's death immediately produced a venomous harangue against the *Fascisti*. Maestro firmly believed that the Blackshirts had done in his friend and alleviator of his pain. Then, Maestro dropped into a solemn mood.

Artur left us for a moment and I spoke frankly with Maestro about something that had bothered me. By this time I felt that I could be free in his company. He listened sympathetically while I expressed my concern over Artur's continuing discontent with his work despite his success.

"*Cara*," Toscanini said, "in all my artistic life I have never had one moment of complete satisfaction." I was thunderstruck. "I cannot believe you, Maestro," I told him bluntly. Here, before me, was the most beloved and famous conductor in the world, a man whose fame and talents were admired by men who had known or worked under Mahler, von

Bülow, and Richter. It seemed utterly unbelievable so great a man had not had "one moment of complete satisfaction" in his long musical life.

"*Cara*," he replied, "the people who love and make a conductor famous are a crowd, and crowds know nothing. No true musician can be satisfied with his performance, even though an audience is driven to a frenzy. A performance can always be better. We never reach that perfection we strive for. Sometimes I even hate my performances, though the crowd may be clapping in ecstasy."

He fell quiet as he looked away toward the shoreline where the sun was beginning to set the sky ablaze with scarlet above the Alpine peaks. Artur returned just then to hear Maestro say "I am tired, and soon I will stop conducting."

"Maestro," Artur broke in, "you cannot be serious. You still have tens of years to make music."

"No, Rodzinski," he murmured, "I am tired, and I have already done enough. *Sono stufo, e sono stanco!*"

These were sad words to hear, and we refused to accept them, arguing that he was depressed by the pains of his bursitis, that when he felt better the mood would pass. But he said "No" once again, that already he had it in mind to resign as director of the New York Philharmonic. We parted with hope that his depression would pass by the time we saw him again later that summer in Salzburg.

We headed north, stopping en route to visit Schnabel's place at Tremezzo which the pianist described to us so glowingly when he had played with Artur in Cleveland that winter. After searching the area, Artur found no house which appealed to him. Farther to the north we saw many places of great appeal, including a few that seemed ideal, but each house that took Artur's fancy was either rented or promised to someone. The situation predictably made my husband short-tempered, a state of mind hardly suited to what we faced the day we left Bormio for Cortina.

On the map, the route through Stelvio Pass looked short and simple; there was no indication of the altitude, however. We left in the afternoon, wearing only light clothes since the day was hot and sunny. Soon, the road became extremely winding and steep and our poor Pontiac began to boil. Every few turns we had to stop for water from a mountain stream. Before us lay only other high mountains, with no sign of a pass. There wasn't a soul on the road to ask how much farther we had to climb. The air quickly became cold. On one of the stops to cool the motor we unpacked our sweaters, and then with stubborn perseverance drove up and up.

Twilight found us at 2,500 meters altitude (about 8,000 feet), and it was getting dark when we arrived at the Italian border hut where a lone guard stood talking to a couple of workers who had been plowing snow in the pass.

"The road is closed; there is still plenty of snow," they said. "We hope to open it for cars in about two days."

"What do we do until then?" Artur asked. There was no place to stay overnight.

"You can return to Bormio and take a longer way to Bolzano and Cortina," was the answer, "or you can go down here over a mountain road to Santa Maria in Switzerland and from there to Merano and Bolzano."

"How is the road?" Artur asked.

"Well, we opened it today. There's no snow, but it isn't paved and it can be slippery."

This meant nothing to Artur, who set off downhill jauntily. The road we traveled was intended for mules or donkeys, not cars. Barely wide enough for both wheels, it had no wall or protection at the outer edge. We could look straight below for several thousand feet. The water from melted snow on the slope made the roadbed, such as it was, disastrously slippery. At almost every curve Artur had to stop facing the precipice, back up, then turn sharply again to follow the road.

I was certain that this was our last hour on earth. Artur whistled for courage. That scared me still more, and I prayed with all my heart. My eyes closed and heart stopped every time he made a turn.

The trip seemed endless in the dark and cold. Finally, after hours of this agony, we arrived at the Swiss border station. The guards couldn't believe that we had driven that road in a huge American car. As we were asking them directions to Merano, one of the men noticed that one of our front tires was flat. We dared not even speculate on what might have happened had the tire blown while we were coming down the mountainside.

I don't know when we enjoyed a night's sleep more than the one in the Schweizerhof at Santa Maria that night. We were very grateful to be alive. After becoming accustomed to that once more, we could appreciate the beautifully cool night so unlike the period of terrific heat in Italy. We fell in love with Santa Maria's green fields and pine forests surrounded by snow-covered mountains, and thought it an ideal place to stay, but we also knew it would be rather boring for Artur's mother and Witold, lacking all attractions except scenery.

We continued our search through the valley of the Inn River and into Austria. One place where Artur would have delighted to stay on was the Itel Castle, near Linz. Liszt and Wagner had been that family's friends, and we were shown the gold piano on which they both played when they visited. Artur felt that this would be an inspiring place to study but, again, what would Mother and Witold do here. We sat in the sun in the large courtyard where medieval tournaments once had been held and discussed with our hosts the problem of finding a spot that would satisfy the entire family. They suggested that we try Zell am See.

The last available place there was a primitive house across the lake from the village, which at least had the benefit of privacy. It was not what we really wanted, but by this time we were too desperate to be fussy. One of the inconveniences Artur would have to live with was sharing the same bedroom with me. An old icehouse nearby could serve as a study. At first we had trouble finding the piano Artur needed, and this, logically, was all my fault. Then, after a scolding and a sleepless night, my prayers and Artur's wishes were answered: we found a small upright, and as soon as it was installed in his icehouse he began to work and I could breathe again.

The location proved to be ideal — far enough from Salzburg so that we wouldn't be tempted to spend too much time at the music festival, yet not so far that we could not attend Toscanini's performances. The Festival was then near the peak of its prewar success, drawing people from all over Europe and the United States.

We went one afternoon to visit Maestro at his villa at Liefering and found him in a bleak humor. His arm was bothering him and he cursed his decision to conduct at Salzburg. At his invitation we accompanied him to a rehearsal of *Falstaff*. As soon as he began to work, Maestro forgot his pain and conducted with terrific fervor, croaking the whole score and flying into rages whenever the orchestra did not give its best.

There were only a few singers on stage since the big stars hadn't arrived yet. Filling in was a young man who ran about singing most of the parts from memory. When Artur asked who the fellow was, someone from the theater management said, "He is assisting Maestro as coach and prompter. His name is Erich Leinsdorf."

"Brilliant boy," said Artur, and turned back to admire Maestro shaping Verdi's comic masterpiece.

His rehearsals were unique experiences. Toscanini, wearing his famous black cassock, taught each singer not only how to shape every phrase and where to put an accent on each word, but also how to move. He would leap from the orchestra pit to the stage to demonstrate even the smallest gesture. He adored *Falstaff* and conducted it superbly with wit, life, and humor. Herbert Graf, who was the official stage director, told me that Maestro actually decided every detail of the production.

On the day of the full rehearsal of the second scene of the second act, everything seemed to be ready, the curtain went up, and with the swiftness of a lightning flash, Maestro launched into one of his finest tantrums.

"What color is this dreadful scenery? It looks as if someone drank red wine and vomited! It's horrible! What idiot did this? Everyone here is an idiot, from first to last! *Tutti cretini, tutti idioti!*"

He then slammed his score closed and ran from the orchestra pit, leaving everybody speechless. Backstage they pleaded with Maestro to return, but he would not do so until the scenery was repainted. Of course it was done, and the next day's rehearsal went off as though nothing had happened.

(*131*)

The performance that followed was superb. "I will never dare to conduct *Falstaff* after having heard such perfection," Artur said, and he remained true to his word.

Walter and Cia Toscanini wanted to spend a month in the vicinity of Salzburg. At Donna Carla's request, I found a little apartment for them next door to us. The weather was exceptionally nice, and we were able to stay most of the time on the lake shore basking in the sun, swimming, and rowing. Little Walfredo, or Dede as everyone called him, won Artur's heart. They played together as if they were the same age. Dede could do anything with Artur, whom he called affectionately "Prosciutto," after his favorite food. If Artur was irritable, little Walfredo could change him completely.

I asked one day, "If you so love this child, why do you object to having our own?"

"If I could be guaranteed that our child would be as wonderful as Dede, then of course I would not object. But how could we be sure?" he answered. The memories of the trials he had with his first son who was a difficult boy raised by constantly quarreling parents still blocked his mind on the subject, and he would not be persuaded.

Artur took lots of pictures of his little friend which he later framed in a montage as a birthday gift for Maestro, who adored his only grandson. Maestro was so pleased with the gift that he wrote by hand a long, warm letter of thanks which became one of Artur's treasures.

During the two months we passed at Zell am See, Artur's own son Witold and Mama Rodzinska came and went, with nothing remarkable to record about their visits except that Witold was quietly maturing to a serious young manhood, and Mama could still placate Artur better than I when he was out of sorts with himself or his surroundings.

When Artur's enormous physical and psychological energies demanded some sort of release and none was at hand, he vented his anger. For him, the word *rest* had none of the meaning intended by others. He interpreted it as a time of repose in which he found the peace to study new scores, relearn old ones, and to fill the remaining hours with activities that were otherwise prohibited by his work schedule. Certainly it did not mean long catnaps in the sun, though there were enough of those after the midday meal and his morning studies; but it included satisfaction of his various whims or capricious inclinations — an automobile excursion, for example.

On August 5, 1935, the newly-built Grossglockner Pass into Italy was to be opened with auto races. Artur, with his passion for cars, could not miss the event even though the road and his Pontiac were not especially suited to each other. We had tried this long climb once before the road was officially opened, and had had terrible trouble: the motor boiled over five times, and five times we had to stop at length to cool the engine block and add to whatever water had not gone up in steam. Since that fiasco, Artur was determined to make the trip without a stop.

His solution was to keep adding measured amounts of cool water to the radiator while moving, which made sense enough; the application was something else. It called for special supplies: a large bucket of cold water, a long piece of thin rubber hose connected to a funnel, a pitcher, and an arm. All of this was in readiness when we set out the morning of the races in order to be at the top before the event began. I should add the weather was anything but ideal — cold, grey, with rain more often than not.

Artur had somehow obtained a press card which he displayed behind the windscreen. This got us passed through all the barriers at the base of the mountain, and we were very proud and confident as we set off on the ascent. Artur had inserted the rubber hose in the radiator and had me hold the end with the funnel in my hand. Every now and then, I would pour some water into the thing, then hold my arm out of the window as high as I could for the water to gurgle its way to the radiator. This method was neither easy nor pleasant, and after about a half mile of sitting in that position the muscles of my arm had become rigid and the cold had turned my skin a ghastly blue. But there was no stopping: without this awkward method of satisfying the Pontiac's thirst, we never would reach the top.

Artur's "invention" worked. We made the ascent in an hour without the engine once overheating, to the envy of all the motorists we passed along the way whose fatigued engines noisily blew geysers of steam by the roadside. Artur was quite satisfied with himself and his ingenuity when we stopped to explain his amazing gadgetry to interested and applauding motorists. That my arm remained nearly frozen rigid in the position of a Fascist salute for a short while thereafter had hardly occurred to him as part of the price for his efficiencies.

The summer was coming to a close at about this time, and Artur left Zell am See for Munich where he attended performances of Wagner's *Parsifal* and Strauss's *Der Rosenkavalier*. These were works he intended to produce in Cleveland during the coming season. Aside from assigning me the job of closing up the house and preparing for the return journey, he commissioned me to speak with Maestro — of course to cheer him up if his depressions of the previous months continued, but particularly to put in a good word for Artur. My husband appreciated that something special and cordial had blossomed between Toscanini and me, and thought that it would not be awkward for me to ask what Artur was too shy to request.

Maestro and I did have a chat, a sad sort of conversation in which he bemoaned the political deterioration of Central Europe. "Some of us may be driven from our homes, *cara*," he said, "and many of us may never live to return." Feeling a bit embarrassed, I mentioned Artur's interest in appearing at Salzburg. His reply was to the point: "I will see to it." The following summer Artur was engaged.

On our way to France to embark for New York Artur and I made a "must" stop in Switzerland: a visit to Morges and Paderewski's home, Riond-Bosson. It had been many years since the great pianist had been in office as Prime Minister of Poland, and he considered himself living in exile, for he had no love for the Pilsudski regime. Everything about his residence maintained the formal airs appropriate to the old man's former status. Put another way, the Rodzinskis simply could not drop in for tea. Through his secretary, an old friend of mine named Sylvin Strakacz, we were extended an invitation to dinner two days following our arrival. I need hardly say that I was flustered by the prospect of passing an evening in the company of one of Poland's historical treasures, both political and musical.

We arrived at the home of the great pianist at 8:30 P.M., prompt to the second. Mrs. and Mrs. Strakacz greeted us at the door to lead us into a large living room where Mme. Wilkonska, Paderewski's sister, presided as the hostess for Monsieur, *Le Président du Conseil*, a role she assumed after the death of her sister-in-law. There were about ten guests, mostly Poles and musicians.

Either because of business or whim suited to his station in life, the great man made us wait awhile before putting in his appearance. This was just as well with me, for I faced the evening terrified of doing or saying the wrong thing. Somehow, I had, at least in my mind, reverted to the days and sensibilities of that schoolgirl at Two Jadwigas who had missed Paderewski's triumphal entry into Warsaw.

Suddenly a pair of tall, wide doors at the opposite end of the room from where we sat opened and on their threshold stood Ignacy Jan Paderewski. His once fiercely red hair was now a silvery white, and the rest of him was clad to match — suit, shoes, shirt and necktie. He stood in the doorway like an archangel or a Parsifal Knight. He eyed each of us, sensing the effect he made, yet taking care not to overdo it. Then he moved forward, not an instant too soon, to greet us with an affable handshake and smile. When he took my hand and greeted me in Polish, I shivered a bit.

His most remarkable characteristic was his overwhelming dignity, calculated to the last gesture. That same sense of effect which marked his concert performances had been transposed to his political life.

At dinner I sat at the right of *Monsieur le Président* and set myself the task of making interesting conversation. He had known my mother's family, the Wieniawskis, and had frequented my Aunt Maria's Warsaw salon, but that was good for only limited mileage. Rather than helping me to relax, this talk put me on edge lest I say something to the disservice of the Wieniawskis' good name. Paderewski understood my discomfort and enjoyed it.

In the midst of some careful statement of mine, he suddenly began tapping his forehead with the index finger of his right hand. I felt the blood rush to my face. In Poland and among my friends that gesture meant that someone was either crazy or talking nonsense. I could have sunk under the table to die, but instead I choked out a question: "Did I say something wrong?"

With a mischievous grin he told me that my fault was in nothing I had spoken. "But you do wrinkle your forehead, young lady. You shouldn't do that. It will make lines. Do try to stop it."

The conversation finally came around to music and the people who make it, and I was able discreetly to describe Artur's extreme nervousness before each performance and to ask if it was characteristic of musicians. He assured me that it was, saying that in his own experience it even increased rather than diminished with age. He confessed to agonies before every appearance, and said he was only too glad to be done with the concert platform and living in retirement. All the while this bit of conversation went on at our end of the table, Paderewski eyed Artur who was seated at the right of Mme. Wilkonska at the other end. Artur had not touched his wine, and Paderewski, who was a textbook host, thought that it possibly did not meet with Artur's approval.

"Perhaps this vintage does not suit your palate, Mr. Rodzinski," he suggested, "possibly another. . . ."

Artur did not want to say that he suffered from acidity whenever he drank red wines, and so drank some that had already been poured for him, praising it enthusiastically and paying for his politeness with a night of heartburn and pain.

After dinner, our host asked us to play bridge, a custom of the household and one of Paderewski's favorite pastimes. Artur never played cards. I played a passable game, but in Warsaw had never been ranked as a player people went out of their way to have as a partner. I tried to excuse myself, saying that my game was not good enough.

"Nonsense," he replied. "You'll be my partner, and I will help you."

There was no way out, especially since we were guests of honor. "Go ahead," Artur urged, "there's nothing to be afraid of," although he was frightened witless.

Fortune was with me. I had excellent hands throughout the night, and there was never a moment's difficulty with bidding. Paderewski and I won the game easily.

"Why did you say that you are not a good player?" Paderewski demanded to know. He interrupted my protestations by certificating my skills with the remark "You are an excellent player!"

That was the pinnacle and end of my career as a bridge player, for from that moment thereafter I never again played the game. Next morning we dropped in to say good-bye and to take a few photographs.

The visit to Riond-Bosson capped our summer's adventures. Our vacations were now becoming so much of a pattern of celebrities, relaxed moments together that were impossible during the working months, and tours of out-of-the-way parts of the continent. At that time Artur and I still considered Europe more our home than the continental sprawl of America.

On our way to meet the "Champlain" at Le Havre, we stopped off in Paris for some shopping and a visit with the Rubinsteins and their two children, Eva and Paul.

I will never forget one of our conversations as we all sat having lunch on the terrace of a restaurant in Montmartre. My Artur was insisting that Rubinstein should come again to America for concerts, but Artur and Nela were more than reluctant.

"Never again," said Rubinstein.

"Musical life in the United States is developing wonderfully," my husband insisted. "You won't recognize the country since your first visit. I guarantee that you'll be a tremendous success."

But Rubinstein did not seem persuaded. At that time America had the greatest pianists anywhere concertizing every season. Rachmaninoff was at his peak. Horowitz was making a phenomenal career. Hofmann was adored.

"Remember," said Artur as we parted, "if you ever decide to come to the United States, your first orchestral concert must be with me."

Chapter 20

WE arrived home in Cleveland on September 26, 1935, a date of no special significance except that it was the day after the championship bout between Joe Louis and Max Baer. That event had taken Artur's imagination — so much so, that he wired from the "Champlain" for tickets and insisted on a New York layover to see the match. The *Plain Dealer* noted Artur's interest as if musicians were a breed apart from other forms of humanity: "You don't think of a symphony conductor enjoying prize fights," a columnist wrote, adding that the reader would be "equally surprised to learn that after the fight Dr. Rodzinski was seen having refreshments with Primo Carnera."

Soon the new season, the orchestra's eighteenth, began. The program for the opening night included the Fourth Symphony of Brahms and the city premiere of Paul Hindemith's *Mathis der Mahler*. The occasion was no less glittering than the previous season's first night, but far easier for me to take in stride. I no longer had concern about my position as Artur's wife or as the city's "first lady of music." Those persons who were disposed to like and accept me had done so unreservedly. This bolstered my self-assurance as did my increased facility at making small talk in English.

One person I was glad to be with once more on opening night was Mr. Severance. He had again asked me to sit in his box, and when Artur and I met him waiting in my husband's dressing room it was like being reunited with a member of our family. We both felt ourselves to be good friends with this remarkable man.

Mr. Severance had a unique attitude toward artists not often shared by those Americans who were, at least, his fiscal peers. He thought a gifted person had sensitivities and needs that deserved special considerations and tolerances, that the gifts of artists were to be repaid with respect and the sort of appreciation that fostered the sense of security and approbation on which artists thrive. Although he may have had no technical yardstick by which to measure them, Mr. Severance thought Artur's talents large, and viewed them humbly. Other men in his position would have thought themselves equal to an artist by virtue of their dollars and felt as though they had the right to dictate or argue matters of taste and aesthetics on a par. Mr Severance knew his limitations, however, and in precisely that same sense an artist worth the designation knows his. Thus a relationship based on sympathetic mutual esteem grew between the two men. Mr. Severance provided Artur the appreciation on which he thrived and guaranteed him the freedom to pursue his work as a sensitive craftsman. Artur's part of the compact was to work as best he could.

At bottom, such an arrangement is built on a core of love, and so it was that when Mr. Severance died Artur suffered more than the loss of a sympathetic employer. Although my husband later worked with chairmen he respected as human beings, he never fully attained a working relationship with any of them that equaled his unique arrangements with John Severance. More than once in later years he, indeed, served as musical director of orchestras under men who thought their dollars and status as business men in their communities merited them positions in the musical world superior to a mere artist. Many conductors in America know the odious nature of this sort of situation, but they speak of it only in private.

In Artur's third season with the Cleveland Orchestra, he held audiences as if by magnetism. There seemed to be little if anything the orchestra's members would not give Artur in rehearsal and performance. And, in turn, Artur gave totally of himself. His immersion in his work at times involved every cell of his being, leaving him limp and depleted after performances. There were times when he came off-stage after a performance unaware of my presence or even of what was happening around him.

Artur's great week in the season of 1935–36 was the preparation and performance of Strauss's *Der Rosenkavalier*. He had an unreserved love of the composer's music in any form, but was especially fond of this work because of its Viennese milieu. The score brought back memories of his student years in the Austrian capital at the time of World War I. Its libretto by Hugo von Hofmannsthal, brimming with the sensuality and poetry of love in youth and age, and even of foolishness, had parallels in Artur's experiences. He had premiered the work in Warsaw shortly after having been invited to conduct there, and had known the pleasure of teaching it to a cast and orchestra that had never heard a note of it.

In Cleveland, Artur's players had it well in hand by the time his singers arrived. The cast was headed by Lotte Lehmann who was to sing the Marschallin, a role that Strauss himself had taught her. She was, by far, the greatest Marschallin of our time.

The critics raved about the performance — the singers, Rychtarik's designs, and Artur's coordination of the whole from stage to pit. But perhaps more important than any press notice was Mme. Lehmann's opinion. During the second act, when Marschallin has nothing to do but repair her makeup and change costumes, Mme. Lehmann stayed in the wings listening to the orchestra. She told Artur that she had never heard the music played so beautifully — a rare compliment, considering that she knew the score as well as most conductors and had often sung it under the composer's own skilled baton.

My own enjoyment of *Der Rosenkavalier* was tarnished because while staging it Artur had a flirtation. Then, and for the first time, I learned how much and how outrageously I was expected to tolerate his behavior as a "different" sort of person, one for whom standard behavior was no measurement.

Artur had warned me that conquering women was something of a sport for him, that his ego frankly and crudely fed on women throwing themselves at him. He went so far as to say that for an artist an occasional affair was stimulating, even necessary. While I had been told these things before our wedding, I had discounted them, in part, as the talk of a man who was reluctant "to lose his freedom" a second time. Moreover, Artur had said I could take for granted that he married me because he loved me more than any other woman in the world. Little did I then appreciate how *everything* he spoke had been the truth.

Rosenkavalier had always been associated with romance in Artur's mind. He attended his first performance in the company of a Viennese girl he wished to marry at the time, his beloved Fritzi. When he premiered it in Warsaw, he fell madly in love with an innocent young thing who sang the part of Sophie. This time in Cleveland, the composition still had its aphrodisiac effect: he became infatuated with the production's Octavian.

I knew it immediately. He could never deceive me — he was too poor a liar. Though it galled him time and again, I could invariably gauge his thoughts before he ever spoke them.

It was painful to watch him conducting himself like a fool in the woman's company. And, fearing the damage gossip might do to Artur's reputation, I did not dare unburden my feelings of jealousy and disgust to anyone. I was left throughout the time to the tearful solitude of my bedroom, and the words from an aria in a Polish opera, Moniuszko's *The Countess:*

> To play with, to laugh with, people abound;
> To cry with, there is no one to be found. . . .

Hard as this particular lesson was to learn, I was its master in a short time. Arthur's affairs, I discovered, rarely lasted long. The moment a woman began chasing him, his interest waned. This one began demurely enough, but ended up aggressively insisting that Artur divorce me and marry her. I was not good enough for him. I could not have given my adversary better advice on what to do to wreck her designs. Painful experience had taught me that Artur could and would say anything he wished about me, such was his exclusive right. But let no one else ever dare criticize me to his face.

As the years passed, Artur broke many hearts, not the least among which should be numbered my own. Yet each time his ardor for a smile or well-turned ankle cooled, he would fan the smoldering coals of my love into blazing anew. He would approach me timidly, guilt and contrition smudging his face like the evidence of the jampot. Bit by bit, he would become more tenderly aggressive, never presuming that because I was his wife I must necessarily yield to his advances. Indeed, it was as if he presumed nothing, that a restoration of the status quo ante was to be effected solely by the degree of loving gentleness and sincerity he showed.

In short, he courted me afresh each time, pleading and wheedling his case with all the cunning and art he could muster. And in a day or two, I succumbed, for it was nearly impossible for me to resist him. It seemed that once I had committed myself to him my love would support almost any degree of hurt. And the warm intensity of our making up often was in proportion to the hurt I had felt; more frequently than not, it obliterated that hurt. Despite his occasional deviations from the marital straight and narrow, Artur, I found, truly loved me and strived to be a good husband, if not always a conventional one.

In addition to having a weakness for women, Artur was shy, something few people could understand. Many thought that because he was an artist who laid his soul bare on the concert platform, he was at least an exhibitionist if not an egoist. In truth, he was afraid of people — of orchestras, of audiences, of his artistic seniors, and of people who were "successful" by conventional standards of money, political power or social station. While he appreciated his own talents and always saw them in a balanced way, he rarely saw them as putting him on an equal footing with "important people." Of course, he intellectually knew this to be nonsense, but he could not readily surmount that onrush of shyness which sometimes crippled him in his day-to-day exchanges with persons who were important to his work, yet did not share his understanding of music.

I soon realized how great a problem this was for Artur, and early on in Cleveland tried to do what I could to humanize and personalize his contacts with members of the orchestra's board and of the Musical Arts Association. Dinner parties were hardly the way: Artur detested them. He could not bear being trapped at table after a meal was eaten (he usually bolted his food anyway), and he particularly was pained by having to converse exclusively with those poor souls seated to his right and left. But my husband did enjoy social situations that were fluid, situations in which he and others could be at their ease, could be as free and zany as they pleased (and it must be noted that Artur had a wonderful sense of fun and horseplay). So it was that I planned a special kind of entertainment.

We decided, in concert with Artur's stage designer of the moment, Rychtarik, and with Boris Goldovsky, whom Artur had brought that season from Philadelphia as his assistant for choral works and operatic performances, to stage a parody of *all* the operas given in Cleveland under my husband's baton. As I mentioned earlier, our dining room related to the living room as stage does to parterre, and there was a heavy curtain that divided the two. Goldovsky was especially full of ideas for the "production" and eventually was the one who wrote the story, liberally and irreverently mixing and twisting together parts of all the operas. The travesty, announced to more than a hundred invited guests on flyers like theater placards designed by Rychtarik, was titled *The Secret of Lady Carmen. . . . The Tragic Adventure of La Tosca and Barber Tristan, The Mastersinger of Nuremberg, with The Silver Rose.* The "promotional copy" promised a "World Famous Cast and Bloodcurdling Effects." The tickets: "Priceless."

The rehearsals for this "opera" were pandemonium. The bulk of the work was to be done by special "guest" stars and the cast of a production of *Carmen* which Artur was giving the same week. Everybody laughed so much that it was impossible to organize the performance. On the day of the party, December 1, 1935, I was laid up in bed with a migraine, something I rarely ever have. Perhaps the tension and the complexity of the doings were more than I could take.

While I stayed in my darkened room with hot compresses over my eyes and forehead, Victoria, our housekeeper, arranged furniture, and cleaned up after and around Rychtarik's crew of scenery builders. I was certain that I would pass the evening in my room, that everything would turn into a fiasco because Artur would become flustered and say or do all the wrong things. Fortunately by late afternoon my headache subsided. By 8:00 P.M. I felt well enough to put on my costume — a red hunting coat, white breeches, silk top hat, and long whip. I was to be the Ringmaster, a role derived from Alban Berg's *Lulu*. At 8:30 sharp the show went on, with a nervous, husky-voiced accent that somehow emanated from my own throat to announce the presentation by "my Barnstorming Company."

The performance was a sensation, but the success of the evening belonged to Mr. Severance — dressed in the full hoop skirts of the Marschallin, his white hair hidden by the towering silvered assemblage of curls of the Fürstin von Werdenberg's traditional wig, his own goatee disguised by a pink scarf. With a fine sense of the appropriate and an appreciation of how ludicrous his part was, Mr. Severance laughed so heartily that with the rise and fall of his belly, the poor Rosenkavalier could hardly keep her head balanced in his lap. She could not sing her burlesque of Octavian's music, breaking up into roulades and trills of mezzo-soprano laughter instead. None of this mattered, although Goldovsky at the piano may have wished for a bit more composure from his cast. The comedy so delighted our audience of Cleveland's more awesome and sedate socialites that they roared and guffawed and slapped their thighs until everyone swore he could laugh no more.

People who had always regarded Artur as a bit of a terror or someone too olympian to be approached discovered how essentially simple, outgoing, and hospitable he was. Our guests left that night each liking Artur as a person, a result that gave me much satisfaction. My seemingly childish idea for a party had somehow accomplished in one stroke all that I had previously wanted and not been able to manage for Artur — the demonstration of that indefinably lovable side of him which I cherished and I knew others would appreciate if only they saw it.

Another benefit of the party was the effect it had on Mr. Severance. Long-time friends of his said they had not seen the old gentleman so sprightly or gay since the death of his wife some years before. People said he seemed rejuvenated.

Mr. Severance, who was planning to leave for a California winter vacation the following month, offered us the use of his home, Deerwood, on the upper Saranac Lake, in New York's Adirondacks for Artur's forthcoming mid-season break. This was the first time Artur and I had ever heard of that part of the country, and we gladly accepted Mr. Severance's offer. We both instantly fell in love with the region, its lush wilderness of evergreen and birch forests, and its ancient, friendly mountains reminding us of our familiar Tatras and the area around Zakopane.

When we returned to Cleveland, we found Mr. Severance still in the city, in bed with what did not seem to be a serious illness. Our visit to him was very cheerful, full of dry jokes about the possibility of his appearing in a production the coming season, perhaps as Wotan or the Commendatore, roles that would be in keeping with his stature and beard.

But on January 16, 1936, a Thursday, and at the hour a concert was to have begun in Severance Hall, he died at the age of 72.

The entire city mourned. His funeral was held at Longwood, his magnificent residence at the corner of Mayfield and Taylor Roads. The Cleveland Orchestra, under a morose and tearful Rodzinski, played the Funeral March from Beethoven's *Eroica*. Artur later conducted a special free concert to honor his lamented friend and benefactor in that same Severance Hall that had been meant to be a monument to Mrs. Severance.

The *Plain Dealer*, in announcing the concert, spoke of Mr. Severance's long-standing interest in music: "It was an integral part of his life," the article said. "It was during his visits to California that he first heard and enjoyed the conducting of Rodzinski. . . . In a thousand ways Cleveland music will inevitably feel the loss of this American Esterhazy, who, as devoted to the arts as any European aristocrat, was as democratic and friendly a man as any of us has ever known." Surely, no one felt the loss more severely than Artur. "I have once again lost my father," he said.

Soon afterward we left on the orchestra's annual tour. The schedule had been expanded to three weeks on the road, thanks to a demand stemming from Artur's new-found celebrity and national reputation. Between concerts, we were able to pass a day in New York where we had two rather important encounters.

We lunched at the Russian Tea Room down the street from Carnegie Hall. Also there was the impresario Sol Hurok, who in those days had a table reserved on the left side, close by the entrance. Hurok did much of his work there since the restaurant was the meeting place for musicians and managers.

"Mr. Hurok," Artur said, adopting a domineering tone of voice he would use to arrest attention of those he felt sure might not listen closely, "when are you going to take my advice and bring Artur Rubinstein to America?" Hurok, looking impassive, listened as Artur went on: "It is crazy that one of the world's greatest pianists is sitting in Paris, while you, one of the world's greatest managers, sit here over *blini* and tea. If the two of you would get together, you would take America by storm. You like sensations, you like quality: why pass up a chance to have both?"

Hurok, poker-faced as a Russian diplomat in the United Nations who does not mean to give away the nature of his vote, said tersely: "Rubinstein doesn't like America, not after his first visit. He won't come again."

"And have you lost those powers of persuasion you are so proud of? Try! Talk to him," Artur flattered and cajoled. "And when you get his okay, let me know. I want that man to play with me in Cleveland. I want to be the first to have him."

Hurok grunted, shuffled some papers, and made clouds of cigar smoke.

We took our leave, Artur not especially convinced he had made a dent in the impresario, to pay a call on Maestro and Donna Carla. Part of the reason for the visit was to thank Toscanini for getting Artur an invitation to conduct at Salzburg. The commitment had already been contractually set.

Again, as at Isolino San Giovanni, Maestro was depressed.

"Rodzinski, *mio caro*," he said, "I am resigning from the Philharmonic."

After a pause in which to gasp, Artur, shocked to his toes, said, "You cannot do it, you cannot stop now!"

"No, it is decided," he said. "You will read it in the papers in a few days. *Sono stanco, sono stufo da morire.* . . . I will be sixty-nine years next month. You — you have youth, energy, you can't understand. Me — I have conducted such a long time, nearly a half century. I must finish and rest before the work finishes me."

Artur attempted to dissuade him, gently, forcefully, pleading with reason or playing to his ego, but no form or course of argument could move him. His mind was set. Suddenly, Toscanini broke off the discussion by saying that he had heard Artur's last radio program, which had included Beethoven's Seventh Symphony. He grabbed up a copy of the score and asked why Artur had taken a certain passage at a faster tempo than the metronome indication allowed. He quickly strode to his piano, set the metronome at the given marking and began playing the passage.

"This is the way," he said. But soon enough the spirit and drive of the wildly galloping last movement began gathering momentum, and Maestro was a fraction and some ahead of the tocks and ticks. Maestro noticed the discrepancy and stopped playing. He struck his right hand with his left. He threw an embarrassed glance at my husband (who was suppressing a smile), and as his face flushed, shouted: "But I have blood in my veins!"

Artur, at a loss as to how to save Maestro from his embarrassment, picked up a book at hand. It was on conductors, with a chapter that sang Toscanini's praises glowingly, even ecstatically. "A fine book, Maestro?" Artur asked.

"Fine!" he rasped. Incredible as it seemed, lightning was about to strike. Toscanini picked up the book, nearly tearing the pages from their spine as he searched for the approbrious reference.

"*Ecco! Guardi qui!* You read? You see how 'fine' the book is? Weingartner!" Maestro raged.

Artur read the offending passage: it cited the German conductor as Beethoven's finest exponent. Artur blushed. Maestro took the book back. Before anything worse could happen, Donna Carla with her little dog under her arm bustled noisily into the room to ask about our plans for the coming summer at Salzburg.

When we left, Donna Carla accompanied us to the elevator. She wanted to tell us, out of Maestro's hearing, that Toscanini was going to suggest that the Philharmonic board engage Artur and Furtwängler to share the coming season.

The news was as unexpected as Maestro's retirement. The idea pleased Artur; he was flattered by his idol's confidence in his ability to do well by the assignment. But he dared not believe the board would entertain the suggestion seriously. They had far too many older, more experienced, and better-known artists to choose from.

Maestro's resignation was announced in the press on Saint Valentine's Day. Almost instantly began the speculations on who would be Toscanini's successor. The more established conductors were mentioned with frequency, but Artur, despite his youth, was talked of.

Two months later, and just as Donna Carla had said, Artur received from the Philharmonic's management an invitation to conduct the second half of the forthcoming season. The first half would be under the baton of Furtwängler.

The news struck Cleveland with tornado swiftness. Our telephone rang incessantly. Letters and telegrams of congratulations arrived in thick packets several times a day, and many of the correspondents spoke of Artur as Toscanini's likely successor. The directors of the Cleveland Orchestra generously granted Artur a leave of absence and replaced him with the guest conductors whom Artur suggested.

Our life, far from dull before, became even more exciting. Indeed, there was turmoil and bustle enough for a dozen seasons, or so it seemed to me. But where all of the new activity, anticipation, and sense of great promises to be fulfilled left me breathless and near exhaustion, Artur found in it a feverish drive to work. He began rehearsals for a production of Wagner's *Parsifal*, the climax to his 1935–36 Cleveland season, with the intensity of someone reborn. On April 9, the first of three sold-out performances was given. (Vosburgh told us that people from forty different cities and towns around the country attended them.)

The cast was extraordinary for the day. The basso who sang Gurnemanz was Ludwig Hofmann, an artist who had done the role many times at Bayreuth where the quasi-sacramental character and tradition of Wagner's last opera had been established and so carefully preserved. Hofmann said that he had never felt so inspired. Singers, in my experience, are given to saying things like that, but in truth one often knew he had difficulty in singing those three nights as tears choked his voice. Gertrude Kappel, the Kundry, also gave an exquisite and poetic performance. As for Artur, he was in one of his trances. Almost every time he conducted Wagner's music, and the music of *Parsifal* more than any other, he was usually overwhelmed.

I sat with Dudley Blossom and his wife; Dudley had succeeded Mr. Severance as chairman of the orchestra's board. He was not a demonstrative man, yet several times during each act I caught him dabbing his eyes with a handkerchief. I saw others unabashedly weeping, many of them people I thought incapable of such emotion.

The day of the performance was Holy Thursday. Following the old Bayreuth tradition, and in consideration of the day's liturgical significance, no applause was permitted, and as the audience filed out of Severance Hall one heard only that hushed murmur familiar to church vestibules. Although the less religious among my Cleveland friends would not have said as much, they, along with me, behaved as if they had shared in a deeply moving ritual.

Following the season's closing program, Artur and I left the city, stopping in New York on our way to Europe, but this time with very important matters to set in order. Artur wanted to discuss his Philharmonic programs with Arthur Judson, the New York orchestra's all-powerful manager. I had heard enough about the man from our mutual friend, Sophie Braslau, and not just a little from Artur. None of what I had been told was calculated to put me at ease when I accompanied Artur to Judson's office for the discussions.

Judson made Artur ever so uneasy; me, no less so. There was something very cold, very aloof about him, something emotionally formal and formidable. He smoked cigars, alternately wielding them like truncheons, batons, or fairy wands. I thought him handsome after a fashion. Yet when I try in my imagination to picture his face with its regular features, the image is blurred by a blue haze of smoke. I do remember clearly his impeccable grooming and his decorous manners, both very like the style of a sleek businessman.

That he knew something of music was evident from his talk, although I later discovered that his degree of musical savvy was a hash of cliches and stereotyped views. His own musical background, which was a bit broader than most orchestra managers of the day, included a stint as a fiddler in an Atlantic City hotel orchestra.

Judson, unquestionably, was the most powerful man in American music. He seemed disposed to make or establish that point with my husband not through any reasoned discussion but rather by an elaborate process of negation. Every time Artur proposed a composition, Judson said "No," forcing my husband to defend his choice or posture. Considering that Artur programmed with a great care for contrast, for an audience's ability to sustain attention, and all within his own aesthetic criteria of what was good music, the quashing of a particular work on any given program would make great problems for him. Often, it meant scrapping a program altogether because a single comparable piece did not exist in the literature to replace the "undesirable" (from Judson's purview) composition. Artur, throughout the talks, was near exasperation. Then Richard Strauss's *Elektra* was mentioned. Artur wanted to do it in concert form. Judson protested, this time with vehemence. Although it is not much longer than the average concert in length, Judson said that the audience would not be able to take it.

"Who," Judson asked in his final attempt to demolish the idea, "wants an opera without the action?" Then, with all the conviction of a man either ignorant of the music or without the least sense of aesthetic and artistic integrity, he said, "It could never be a success!"

"I might agree," Artur said, "if it were any other opera. But, Mr.

Judson," Artur added slyly, "the orchestra, *as you know*, carries all of *Elektra*'s action. Nothing happens on stage. Even the blood and gore takes place in the wings." It then became evident, without a word having to be said by Judson, that the most powerful manager in American music most likely did not know the Strauss work. After much more discussion in which cost then became the major issue, Judson conceded — but in such a way that he might have cursed the performance to failure.

There were other matters on Judson's mind when we saw him that day. The Furtwängler invitation had met with a very bad public response. The German, though never sympathetic to the Nazis, had been criticized for failing to resign his position as director of the Berlin Philharmonic after Hitler came to power. When Jewish musicians were purged from the orchestra's ranks, Furtwängler still clung to the post, though it is said he aided his Jewish players to flee Germany. In any case, Furtwängler was pressured to refuse the invitation to conduct in New York, and Judson was for a long time hard put to find a replacement. Then one came along in the heretofore unfamiliar shape of the young Englishman John Barbirolli. Judson was a happy man — not merely because Barbirolli had made a good impression on some Philharmonic board members who recommended him highly, but also because he was well-mannered, timid, and compliant.

The day before we sailed for Europe Artur and I lunched at the Russian Tea Room. Sol Hurok came to our table.

"Dr. Rodzinski," he said, "I gave your suggestion some thought, and have decided to bring Rubinstein for the 1937–38 season."

My husband was as gleeful as a little boy.

"Then you will also remember," Artur said, "that I suggested Rubinstein's first appearance with an orchestra be with me in Cleveland."

With a nod, Hurok went off in a puff of smoke, and soon thereafter Artur and I were on an Italian Line steamer bound for Naples and a summer at Sorrento.

Chapter 21

OUR vacation of the summer before, we agreed, had been more taxing for Artur than an entire season's work. So we decided to pass the leisure part of 1936 in some quiet, relatively untraveled roost where he could study and rest without distraction until it was time to head for Salzburg.

We chose Italy because, next to Poland, it was the closest to both our hearts. Poland was out of the question because Artur still resented my friends, social connections, and my family, and he fretted over what influence they might have on me.

After disembarking in Naples, Artur and I drove to Sorrento where we would meet Mama Rodzinska. She had been invited to stay with us at the Villa Cocumella. A hotel remodeled from an old convent, it had a maze of long, cool, dark corridors from which sprouted numerous and rather small rooms. And the lovely large garden, lushly planted with musky roses, wisteria, and mimosa, offered a superb view of the Bay of Naples and Vesuvius.

During that summer of 1936, almost as an omen, Vesuvius was continually erupting. Each night we could see the orange or wine-red jelly of lava slowly, stickily, sliding its way down the mountainside toward the water. From time to time, day or night, there would be rumblings or thunderous explosions.

Next to the main building of the Villa Cocumella was the former convent's chapel, and this was given by the hotel management to Artur for his use as a studio. He had much peace and quiet there, disturbed only by Vesuvius or a Neopolitan Fascist singing "*La Facetta Nera.*"

Sorrento was beautiful; the *Napolitani* were incorrigibly and adorably Neapolitan; the perfume of the roses, the gold of the sunsets over the bay, and the volcanic pyrotechnics of Vesuvius were sensual and intoxicating. A Fascist or two could be tolerated, at least enough for us to seriously consider buying a house there. When Artur — after score studying, reading, correspondence, program planning, meals, and naps — found himself needing an excursion to work off his energies, we went house hunting.

Then the weather swiftly changed. It became unbearably hot: the torrid winds of the sirocco began to blow. Artur always suffered from heat, like most true northerners, and the dry, scorching winds from North Africa debilitated him. We fled.

On our way to Austria, we stopped over in Rome to visit the famous tailor, Caraceni, who cut Artur's full dress suits, also those worn by Toscanini, Douglas Fairbanks, Gary Cooper, and half of the world's nattier diplomats. His tailoring was so perfect that the backs of Artur's frock coats never wrinkled and the shoulders never bunched up when he conducted. Given Artur's peculiar physique, Caraceni's dress suits were more like works of art than needlework.

For Mama and me, the journey was a joy, especially when the parched reds and ochres of the Italian south gave way to the dusty grey-greens of the north, and the greener greens of the Alpine zones. For Artur, it was a time of tension and of preparation. Conducting at Salzburg was not just a matter of Toscanini's having arranged an invitation with the festival's officials. The other conductors to appear that season were, aside from Maestro, that redoubtable duo of German orchestral music, Bruno Walter and Maestro's loathed rival Felix Weingartner. Both men were in their sixties, each more than twenty years older in age and experience than Artur. That Maestro believed Artur capable of holding his own in such company was flattering. But would the orchestra share the Italian master's convictions?

The Salzburg Festival orchestra is actually the Vienna Philharmonic, an ensemble Artur knew from student days, and an orchestra which still included players who had worked under Mahler, Richter, and Schalk. Standing before these men, to Artur, was a bit like having a congress of quantum physicists check one's arithmetic homework. Also, they were known, like most virtuoso orchestras, to enjoy playing new or unknown conductors for fools. Artur ordinarily was apprehensive each time he came before a new ensemble. But in this instance he was a little more than ordinarily fearful: he had selected a program of contemporary music which was unknown to the musicians. No matter what, he would breathe the fresh air of youthfulness and the twentieth century into the precincts of the Salzburg Mozarteum.

The musicians were already beginning to come on stage to rosin their bows or tootle and scrape scales when Artur and I arrived. In the artist's room the manager greeted my husband respectfully, and told him whatever he might need to know about the rehearsal schedule, all in German which then I barely understood. I helped Artur into his rehearsal coat and then went into the hall where the players were by now fully assembled. When Artur appeared, everyone fell silent, except for the clearing of a throat or the shuffling of feet and adjusting of chairs.

Once on the podium, Artur bowed a respectful greeting to his players, then announced *"Meinen Herren, die Erste Symphonie von Shostakovich."* Nothing else. Then he raised his hands in anticipation, darted his weak eyes about to catch the attention of the semicircle of one hundred or so players ranged before him. His firm downbeat should have produced that crackling whiplash trumpet figure which opens the Symphony, but it did not. The solo lacked both incisiveness and accuracy. Artur stopped, tersely pointed out what had gone wrong, then began anew. The clarinet which replies to the trumpet with a skittering little motif was all wrong. Once more Artur dropped his hands and, sotto voce, pointed out the false tones. A bit later, still within the first ten or so bars, yet one more "mistake" occurred. With a craftsman-like coolness and objectivity, Artur continued to point out the errors, note for note to each of the responsible players.

I knew that Artur was under immense strain. But he kept his composure and his respectful corrections had effect: that special current of approbation passed through the various stands of players. They understood this Rodzinski knew what he was about. This young foreigner, this Pole, American — whatever his nationality — was the paramount musical craftsman, a man with an ear, a technique and, unquestionably, a determination not to be flustered by the orchestra's tricksters. From that point on, the orchestra cooperated wholeheartedly.

The following day Maestro came to the work session not without some curiosity. He wanted to see how his protégé stood up to the strain of working with these instrumental prima donnas, and also to hear the Shostakovich, having now an interest in the young Russian's work since the premiere of *Lady Macbeth*. So fascinated was he with both the score and Artur's working methods, which were always a model of efficiency, that he attended all subsequent rehearsals.

The performance proved to be a great success. The vibrant, boyish impetuosity of the score, when played with maximum polish and the élan Artur always brought to it, was a surefire applause winner. And the distinguished audience, usually discomposed by anything but heavy-handed readings of Beethoven, Brahms, Mozart and Haydn, gave Artur a standing ovation. Maestro, enthused by the score and Artur's performance, hurried around to the stage to stand behind the players applauding and croaking out innumerable "Bravo, Rodzinski's," thus publicly setting his seal of approval on his young colleague's work. Rarely could a conductor claim so impressive an *applauditore* or leader of a claque!

Afterward, in the artist's room, when members of the orchestra came to congratulate Artur, Maestro, like a proud old eagle, hovered about saying to the musicians, *"Non avete piu bisogna di me — c'e lui!"* ("You don't need me any longer — you have him!")

Before leaving Salzburg we went one morning to see *Arturo Il Primo*. We found him with his family relaxing in the sun.

"Maestro, may I have a few minutes of your time?" asked Artur shyly. "I would like you to show me some tempi in Verdi's *Requiem*. I am going to conduct it this season in Cleveland."

"Of course, *mio caro*," said Maestro, *"Andiamo* — to the piano."

"You come, too," Artur called to me, and so I sat in a corner of the room and witnessed a unique scene.

Instead of just marking the score, Toscanini sat at the piano and played the whole *Requiem*, singing in his croaking voice the parts of each singer. I had Artur's camera on my lap, and I decided to try to take a picture of these two men, so completely immersed in music, heads close together. I had no idea how to use the complicated Leica, but set it on "time" and took a few photographs. They came out well and for Christmas I gave them to Artur as a surprise.

That Christmas would be spent in our new home, a stupendous house compared with our first Cleveland residence. When we returned to the city in the fall, I promptly set about moving in. It was large, fully furnished, and, best of all, situated on a golf course which was like a semiprivate park. Victoria, our housekeeper, and I had plenty to do organizing things to Artur's tastes and convenience, including the arrangement of a darkroom, with adequate space for all of the equipment he had acquired, where his photographic pastimes could be indulged.

Once back in Cleveland, however, Artur had little time for much else than work, or the social obligations that went with his position. Before the season began on October 15, the Mayor of Cleveland, Harold

Burton, gave a reception "in tribute to Rodzinksi's musical triumph" (in part also to blow the city's own cultural horn) where Cleveland's leading citizens lavished praise on my husband.

The new season, so carefully planned in Sorrento, featured Jascha Heifetz, young Eugene List, Nathan Milstein, and Myra Hess. Josef Hofmann and Gregor Piatigorsky, by now old friends as well as collaborators, were to appear, along with Vladimir Horowitz. Joseph Fuchs, the concertmaster, was to do a Prokofiev concerto (on a program that included a long composition by Cleveland's Arthur Shepherd, *Horizons, Four Western Pieces*). The orchestra's principal violist, Carleton Cooley, played a work by Ernest Bloch, who had been influential in the city's musical life at one time, having taught at and directed the Cleveland Institute of Music (1920–25). Also appearing that season to premiere his own Concerto in C Major was the then present director of the Institute, pianist-composer Beryl Rubinstein (no relation to Artur). The new work, when published, was dedicated to my husband.

Guest conductors included Vladimir Golschmann and a pair of composers: Igor Stravinsky and Georges Enesco. Stravinsky had Samuel Dushkin along with him to perform his new Violin Concerto in D.

A cornerstone to the season was the "Manzoni" *Requiem* of Verdi, featuring Rose Bampton, with Helen Traubel's luxuriant soprano crowning the vocal quartet. There were also two operas: Wagner's *Tannhäuser*, and Strauss's *Elektra*. The number of operas had to be reduced from the preceding season for lack of funds. The Depression had become a way of life, and those with money had begun to hold onto it, at least as far as music went.

Tannhäuser featured Paul Althouse in the title part, Grete Stueckgold as Elisabeth, and Richard Bonelli as Wolfram. Wymetal controlled the doings on the stage designed by Rychtarik, and Boris Goldovsky prepared the chorus (as he did for the Verdi and Beethoven pieces). Boris, like every chorus master before and since, had trouble with the procession of monks in the last act — they simply could not make their entrance from offstage singing on pitch. Goldovsky did all he could think of, but Artur finally arrived at an ingenious solution: one of the orchestra's clarinetists dressed in a cowled habit that concealed the instrument in its folds would cue the singers, the color of his instrument blending almost unnoticed with the male voices.

By now Cleveland's opera productions had become so highly regarded that critics came from around the country to cover them. Downes of *The New York Times* found the performance "exhilarating . . . full-blooded and dramatic . . . welded and energized by Mr. Rodzinski's temperament, orchestral mastery and feeling for the stage." That sort of praise Artur came to expect, but what pleased my husband more than anything else was Olin's appraisal of the Clevelanders: the orchestra was "the best in the Middle West."

The first short tour with the orchestra took us to, among other places, Chicago for Artur's debut in that city, which had been his dream ever since coming to America. Artur felt that with its musically well-trained public and a demonstrated love for opera Chicago had great artistic possibilities. The conductor of the Chicago orchestra, Frederick Stock, was very much loved, but he was old and tired after thirty years in the position. The devotion which the Chicago public had consistently shown Stock, plus the large number of Poles living there, made Artur feel that this might be the secure, permanent post he had always sought. He had a vision of creating a great musical center there.

The Chicago concert, therefore, was an important step for him and, as it turned out, a successful one. From that day the Chicago people took him to their hearts, and they remained faithful until the end.

The short tour over, Artur resumed work in Cleveland with renewed zest. There was always something invigorating to him in new audiences, even if he complained about the miseries of touring. But also boosting his spirits was the realization that artistically he was coming into his own. Artur felt that, if his luck held, the New York Philharmonic could be his. Both the Los Angeles and Cleveland orchestras had engaged him as musical director at times when his appearances as a guest conductor coincided with their search for a permanent conductor. So Artur expected much to come of his eight-week engagement with the Philharmonic, especially now Furtwängler was out of the contest.

Thus imagine Artur's shock and disappointment when he read in the press that the most prestigious orchestra in the United States, against Maestro's advice, had signed a contract with John Barbirolli — who was as unknown to Artur as to the general public. In a sense, it was an affront to Toscanini and to the audiences that had come to expect the highest level of technical and artistic excellence from the Philharmonic. As far as anyone knew, and few in truth did, Barbirolli had a limited repertoire and experience on the podium. In reply to the criticism that appeared in the press, the Philharmonic management said that Barbirolli would "grow and develop artistically" while working with the orchestra. One can hardly deny that Barbirolli learned much in the three years he spent with the Philharmonic, but, then, few conductors in their conservatory years ever had so fine an orchestra to teach them their craft. While the Philharmonic learned several pieces by Elgar from him, Barbirolli learned to conduct from them.

As one wag of the day put it, most of the pomp surrounding Barbirolli's appointment was in its circumstances. No one doubted his talent (which grew in maturity to merit the knighthood bestowed on him), but he was not at all ready to assume the helm of an orchestra of the importance and cultural responsibility of the Philharmonic. He was well-mannered, however, and in the jaws of such an opportunity, inclined to be deferential — especially to Arthur Judson. The power-loving manager had gnawed his lip and chewed his cigar through an eleven-year Toscanini reign. With Maestro gone, Judson saw his chance to take control.

(*151*)

Barbirolli would program according to the manager's tastes, invite the right soloists and conductors (all from the Columbia Artists' stable), and generally behave himself. Judson knew that in Rodzinski he would have another strong-willed, musically-independent artist of the Toscanini and Stokowski stripe, a man who would take no orders, program as he pleased, and invite soloists of his own choosing. With Barbirolli, Judson could consolidate his power over America's musical life. (At that time Judson managed the New York and Philadelphia orchestras, had his private network of artists' representatives, and even owned a share of the Columbia Radio and Gramophone Corporation, predecessor of the Columbia Broadcasting System.)

Artur immediately responded to Barbirolli's appointment with an angered cry of "Plot!" He not only saw the naming of the new conductor as an insult, "a slap in the face," but also saw an intrigue against him by Judson. For a fact, Judson had not helped Artur to a single post, and any guest engagements he got were usually through his own efforts. Artur had never forgiven Judson for advising the Cleveland Orchestra's board against him. Nonetheless, he was under personal contract to the man and regularly paid Judson his percentage, a sum that seemed and felt more and more like payments to an extortionist than to someone contracted to assist him in his career. Although Artur had had his eye on the Chicago orchestra, the possibility of an appointment to New York opened new vistas. Certainly, it was any musician's goal to aspire to an orchestra that Toscanini had directed.

Initially, Artur wanted to cancel his concerts with the Philharmonic. "I will not suffer this quietly," he said. But when his wrath burned down, he became depressed, and for that reason as well did not feel that he should appear in New York. When Artur was enraged I could do little but hear him out in silence. His depressions were different. I could usually reason with him then. When the doldrums set in I urged him to go to New York, arguing that "now more than ever you must show what you can do. This is your big chance; you may have a long wait before conducting for that audience again."

Perhaps what really convinced him to go were the radio broadcasts of the Philharmonic transmitted by CBS to its own stations and a network of affiliates. Reaching new, ever-widening audiences was something Artur could never resist. Recall that this was the age when the long-play record had barely been imagined, wire and tape recordings had not yet been developed, and recorded music was heard only on acoustically inadequate machines with breaks every four-and-a-half minutes when a cumbrous, if fragile, record had to be changed manually or else automatically with a continuity-shattering clatter. Listening to an extended composition without interruption outside a concert hall was a rare treat, and the only music that most Americans could then hear was on the phonograph or the radio. A generation of musically aware Americans was developing. Toscanini's live CBS Sunday afternoon broadcasts had found an audience for serious music that was growing geometrically and, as technology expanded, was to provide a continuously widening market for recordings.

Artur relented and he kept his Philharmonic engagement. But at the end of that season, he canceled his personal contract with Judson.

The threadbare cliché that artists grow on sufferings is a dismally true one. Although few Clevelanders understood to what extent Artur was pained by the decisions made in the New York Philharmonic's offices, they all knew that their Rodzinski was better than ever. Artur buried his anguish in furious work, particularly concentrating on Strauss's *Elektra*. The soprano Gertrude Kappel sang the principal role. When the performance ended, she and my husband shared one of the greatest ovations ever extended by Cleveland concert-goers. Watching Artur bobbing his head in his peculiar, shy bow into that evening's sea of applause, I thought back to my first year in Cleveland and words spoken to me by Mrs. Frank Ginn, wife of one of the orchestra's board members: "The Cleveland public may not seem demonstrative to you," she said. "We adore the concerts, but we don't know how to show our emotions." With a bad pun, she referred to the trait as "Western Reserve." The Clevelanders were not reserved that night nor at most of Artur's concerts.

Our social life continued apace, with many delayed invitations to be repaid now that we had moved into our new home and had the space. One idea I had paid off in an unexpected service to my native land.

I thought to serve a Polish meal, featuring *bigos*, a dish traditional to hunting parties where it was heated in enormous kettles over campfires in the woods. The basic ingredients of this "hunter's stew" are sweet and sour cabbage combined with different meats, Polish sausages, wine, mushrooms, onions, tomatoes, apples, dried prunes, and a variety of spices. The stew requires days of simmerings and coolings to bring to just the right consistency and to blend all the disparate flavors. Also a huge collection of pots and pans are necessary when preparing it for as large a number of guests as we had invited. Artur was worried about the effect of such food on the steak-and-potatoes stomachs of our Cleveland friends. In truth, I was concerned myself, for I had never seen cuisine laid on American tables which used such a combination of flavors and textures.

When our guests filed past the buffet, a few sniffed in wonderment, but all filled their plates and went away to try it. They were back in short order, and soon enough my immense kettle was emptied. I heard only compliments, along with requests for the recipe.

At just about that time Polish ham was making headway in the American market and, pressured by United States farmers, a move was afoot in Congress to impose a heavy duty on the product. After reading of this in the newspapers, I wrote to one of our dinner guests, Ohio's Senator Robert Bulkley, saying that I probably could not afford to invite him for *bigos* again, that it was Polish ham which gave the dish its unique taste. The Senate rejected the heavy tariff first proposed, then substituted a much, much lower one.

Artur was so pleased by that dinner party's success that he praised me. Ordinarily, he was stingy with compliments. My husband expected everyone, including himself, to do his best as a matter of course. I could live without his fine words because I loved him, but they were nice to hear. To others, they were hugely important. Felix Eyle, the orchestra's assistant concertmaster and a friend from my first stay in Cleveland, would often chide Artur about this trait.

"Why don't you say something pleasant to the orchestra for a change?" Felix once asked. Artur, who enjoyed sharing with the violinist old memories of Lvov where they had both grown up, stared at him in mute amazement. Felix continued, "We only hear your criticism and your grumbling, and think we never satisfy you. If we do meet with your approval, why not show us a pretty smile now and then?" At this point, Artur broke into a grin like dawn itself, something he would do periodically thereafter at rehearsals or during a well-executed phrase in a performance.

I tell this anecdote not to show how dour Artur was, but to point out how he could be so by mere inadvertence. Actually, he was quick to respond to humor and kind to anyone needing encouragement. But work was a deadly serious matter to him, and smiles were something he had not yet incorporated in his work methods.

Artur had generosity in abundance when it came to fostering new talents. His taking up of Shostakovich's *Lady Macbeth* was a gamble. It could have been a fiasco, in spite of its quality, and a failure that would have been costly in time and money. But, when Artur believed in the gifts of a "new" composer, nothing would be spared to bring his work before the public in as sympathetic and faithful a manner as possible.

That particular season's dinner parties brought us together with two talents for whom Artur had the highest regards, plus a beloved and very special friend. Samuel Barber and Gian-Carlo Menotti were invited to dine with their patron, Mrs. Mary Louise Curtis Bok, the sponsor of Curtis Institute, as were we. The occasion was the Cleveland premiere of Sam's *Symphony in One Movement*, a work that had its debut in Rome with the Santa Cecilia orchestra under Bernardino Molinari. Sam, the winner of a Prix de Rome, made his home in Italy at the time. Artur's performance, later followed by Bruno Walter's, were among his first major American hearings.

Gian-Carlo also was coming to the fore that same season. Fritz Reiner, then directing Curtis's orchestral and operatic activities as had Artur less than a decade before, produced two of Menotti's first stage pieces, *Amelia Goes to the Ball*, and that delicious little curtain-raiser, *The Telephone*. The success of the two pieces led to a later New York theater presentation and Gian-Carlo's career as America's most active composer-librettist was launched.

Mrs. Bok was ever *Pani* Mary to Artur. He had much affection for that adorable human whose sweet smile, slight, delicate figure, and snowy hair betokened a seemingly-shy person. Instead, she was a woman of great strength and character who knew exactly what she wanted and how to accomplish it. Her appointment of Josef Hofmann as director of Curtis Institute showed that she would spare no expense to develop the talents that "her" school attracted. Some of America's finest composers come from "her" Curtis. Her purse had no bottom when she believed in someone, and Sam and Gian-Carlo were special beneficiaries of her largess. They became her children in the sense that they meant more to her than protégés. Artur was an ex-officio protégé and her "Prodigal Son" — she always addressed him so, once inscribing to him a volume of Wagner's letters with that sobriquet in a way which implies she could have forgiven Artur anything. Artur, for his part, would do anything that *Pani* Mary asked, including taking an interest in her other protégés. To do so, however, was in no way onerous, for *Pani* Mary could discern real from false talent. Sam Barber was the genuine article.

Our dinner party with Sam and Gian-Carlo, both as handsome as matinee idols, and *Pani* Mary, looking like a chic Rossetti "Blessed Damsel," turned into a memorable evening. Several of the other guests had also worked or studied at Curtis Institute, making the gathering a sort of school reunion. The spirit of reunion was carried into the intermission of the concert when Artur assembled those members of the orchestra who had been graduated from Curtis. *Pani* Mary remembered each of them and had a kind, personal word or reminiscence to share. It was a joy for all concerned.

Sam's Symphony was so well received that Artur asked him to remain in the United States for several weeks to hear it with the Philharmonic. Artur also intended to premiere it at Salzburg the coming summer as the first composition by an American to be heard in the city that gave the world Mozart.

While Artur was still rankled by Judson's hiring of Barbirolli, his resentments were less acute. "If *Pani* Mary can forgive her 'Prodigal' anything, I at least can bear with Judson's insult," Artur reasoned, and he readied himself once more to take his "wares" to New York.

Chapter 22

ARTUR'S rehearsals commenced the day we arrived in New York. The men of the Philharmonic were glad to see him back and gave him perfect collaboration. More than once Artur flashed his smile in genuine pleasure at his and his players' achievements. He had surmounted his anger and hurt at the appointment of Barbirolli and felt free of all the constraint that being in line for the post would have imposed. Indeed, he performed with brilliant abandon. That first performance brought him more than the usual sheaf of telegrams of good wishes, also once again a little elephant swathed in ounces of tissue paper. The message that came with it congratulated Artur on having taken the second major step in his career.

Artur's programs were nicely balanced between standard literature and the latest contributions to the contemporary repertoire. Among the latter were Aaron Copland's *Dance Symphony*, Arthur Honegger's *Le Roi David*, and Sam Barber's *Symphony in One Movement*. The German composer Paul Hindemith, who had been among the first of his country's leading creative personalities to flee from the Third Reich, made his first appearance before the American public as the soloist in his own concerto for viola and orchestra, *Der Schwanendreher*, under Artur's baton.

On Easter Sunday, 1937, Artur presented the whole of the last act of *Parsifal*. On March 31, Myra Hess played Brahms's Second Piano Concerto. The same program included the New York premiere of Karol Szymanowski's *Harnasie*. Artur had given the work its first American performance two months earlier in Cleveland, and the reviews had been excellent. We had sent them along to Karol who was living under the strictest medical supervision in the south of France. Both Karol and Artur looked forward to its reception by New York's more sophisticated audiences, especially with the vocal parts sung in Polish by members of the Art of Musical Russia (those same singers who had done so well by the score of *Lady Macbeth*).

Harnasie with its tale of life among the people of Poland's mountain borders met with the acclaim Artur had anticipated. The public resoundingly applauded the work and critics poured praise over it, but Karol was to know none of this. He died two days before the concert. Accordingly, the performance was dedicated as a memorial to him.

Karol's death had taken a dear friend from us. It was more than a personal loss, however, for Szymanowski had at last found his own musical voice as a composer, one unique and Polish in our century, and just as it had begun to sing its own songs it was stilled forever. All Poland mourned. As Karol had once bitterly predicted, the Polish nation gave him a state funeral fit for a king. In true Polish fashion, those who wept most copiously at the interment included many musicians who, while he lived, denied he possessed the least shred of talent.

Artur's notable achievement with the Philharmonic that season, and one of the high marks of his career, was the *Elektra* in concert form. Even Judson was obliged to concede that it was "a fine success." Yet, preparations for it got off to an uncertain start.

Soon after we arrived in New York, word came from Germany that Gertrude Kappel, the Cleveland Elektra, had canceled because of illness. Artur was upset. He had relied on working with an artist who knew his concept of the composition, but he wasted no time in contacting an alternate. The soprano Rosa Pauly was reached by cable in Vienna, and this artist (whose Elektras were known to Artur only through press reports) agreed to take the fastest boat for America.

Pauly's interpretation greatly stirred Artur at their first rehearsal. "She was born for the part," he said. "She is utterly fantastic!"

The performance bore out Artur's appraisal. Everyone on stage was excellent, but Pauly was nothing less than phenomenal. For that matter, Artur, whose *Elektra* in Cleveland I had thought impossible to top, completely transcended himself. The public went wild with enthusiasm. To a man, from parterre to galleries, the audience in Carnegie Hall stood and shouted and applauded for a full twenty-five minutes. I had not seen an ovation like this before, neither for Artur nor anyone else. My husband was sublimely happy as, time after time, he led Mme. Pauly and other members of the cast back on stage with him for bow after bow. Raising the orchestra to share the applause with him drove the audience to noisier, prolonged acclamations. It seemed as though they would never stop.

When we returned to our hotel suite Artur sat down on his bed and burst into sobs. I was shocked. Instead of the ebullience that should have followed such a triumph came deep, deep dejection. Over and over he said, "I am finished, I will never conduct again, I gave everything I had, I am empty." I tried to tell him that he was simply tired, that it was natural to feel low after so draining an emotional ordeal.

"No, Halusia," he said, "I am nothing. It was all noise and appeal to public hysteria. You will see. The critics tomorrow will murder me. They'll see through it. Maybe they'll have good words for Pauly, but me they will flay. You'll see."

He was exhausted, psychologically, physically. He had worked most of that summer in Sorrento on the score, had performed it three times in Cleveland, nearly to his complete satisfaction, but that first

New York performance was the climax of all his efforts, a refinement on refinements that would be a pattern for all the rest of his opera performances, even till the end of his life. Strauss's tortured music, Pauly's immense artistry, the tensions of the preceding months caused by Barbirolli's appointment, his sense of a Judson cabal aginst him — all of these had strained him to the breaking point.

I held him in my arms for a long time trying to console him as I might a terribly hurt child. It was very late before I could help him undress and go to bed.

I, for my part, could not sleep. I kept looking at my watch, then at the New York skyline through my window, waiting for the first glow of spring sun, all to tell me that it was time to be up, and down to the lobby for the papers. I remember my hands trembling as I took a dollar from my handbag to pay for copies of the *Times*, *Tribune*, and other major morning papers. I sat in an overstuffed chair in the lobby, one hidden behind a column out of sight of the bellhops and guests.

What Downes had to say I read first. Although he had been a friend, dating back to the day that Artur had begun seriously to think of me as his wife, Olin for that very reason went out of his way to be hard. The sting of his critical pen dug deepest into those artists who knew him best as a friend. What I read produced in me a flood of tears much like Artur had shed the night before — though for another reason.

Downes wrote:

> One of the most thrilling and dramatic performances that this writer has been privileged to hear in thirteen years of music in New York. . . . The audience was beside itself with enthusiasm . . . applause and cheers must have continued for twenty-five minutes, and no wonder. No wonder in the first place because of the mighty power and majesty of Strauss' peroration: because of Mr. Rodzinski's superb reading of the score, compact of dramatic fire and a master's control of the situation. . . .

When Artur first stirred, and with good coffee to hand him, I showed him the *Times*. As he read his smile slowly, almost surreptitiously, emerged as if from behind a cloud. Then I handed him the *Herald-Tribune* in which Lawrence Gilman, all of the musician that Downes was not, stated:

> It was a daring enterprise on the part of Mr. Artur Rodzinski, present conductor of the Philharmonic Symphony. . . . I have seldom heard a more stirring disclosure of the music of *Elektra* or one which more movingly expressed its dramatic implications. Mr. Rodzinski's interpretation of the music was one of complete and impressive mastery.

The man who was "empty," who would "never conduct again," glittered and twinkled like all of Times Square's neon and incandescent lights. But if he felt any vindication, both of himself as an artist and in the rightness of his view that *Elektra* would work in concert, it was when he read the *World-Telegram*'s Pitts Sanborn:

Put it down as the most stupendous evening a Philharmonic audience has known since the departure of Toscanini.

The evening press said more of the same, repeating the superlatives sufficiently rehearsed in the morning sheets. Gilman of the *Tribune* would do an unprecedented second review after attending the performance the following Sunday, his praise even more lavish:

> The repetition of a concert already heard and discussed would ordinarily call for only brief notice. But it is impossible to let so extraordinary and unprecedented an achievement as this unique realization of *Elektra* pass without an added word of tribute to those who accomplished it — especially since it aroused an enthralled and agitated audience to demonstrations of excited enthusiasm which are not common these days at Carnegie Hall.

> Not until Mr. Rodzinski had repeatedly led forth the exhausted Mme. Pauly — who had danced herself to death — and the other artists, and had bade his orchestra rise to its feet, did the audience begin reluctantly to disperse, dazed and undone.

> Mr. Rodzinski's musical direction and the Philharmonic Orchestra's playing were consummate — it would be hard to imagine a more potent and magnificent evocation of all that Strauss has enclosed in the instrumental fabric of his score.

Toscanini made headlines too that season. After refusing to accept any American engagement, Maestro changed his mind and took an offer from the National Broadcasting Company to lead a new, specially-created orchestra for a series of radio concerts. He was enraged at the Philharmonic's board and at Judson for having hired Barbirolli over his advice. Thus, in accepting an offer from NBC, Judson's and the Philharmonic's Columbia Network competitor, Maestro could show his pique. His point: if the Philharmonic had no faith in Rodzinski's talents, let that august body see what Rodzinski can do by making an orchestra that will satisfy Toscanini. Nothing could have given Artur a sweeter taste of artistic revenge.

At about the same time that the news broke, I received a letter from Cia Toscanini, Walter's wife, in which she wrote:

> We have been thinking so much about you both these past days because everybody in the Toscanini house took very much to heart this unkind thing that was done to dear Maestro [referring to my husband] by those people of the Philharmonic. And I have to tell you that if Toscanini agreed to return to America it was because he wants to give a lesson to the Philharmonic. He likes your husband very much. . . .

When Artur was contracted for the job of putting together the new orchestra, he quickly learned that NBC intended merely to augment its existing radio group, perhaps picking up a few good new men who would only play Toscanini's concerts. As soon as Artur understood that this was NBC's thinking, he sat down and wrote a long memorandum to

(*159*)

David Sarnoff, president of Radio Corporation of America, NBC's parent company. In it he carefully detailed all the reasons why an orchestra so composed would never satisfy Toscanini. Such a conductor should not be asked "to perform with a second-rate fiddle," Artur reasoned, and NBC's management agreed, but only after long detailed conversations was my husband given the carte blanche he required to fashion a first-rate instrument for his beloved Maestro.

Sarnoff himself authorized Artur to build a new ensemble that would work on a permanent, year-round basis. He told my husband, finally, to engage the best musicians he could find anywhere, to offer whatever was wanted to tempt them to leave their permanent positions. Not much temptation was often required, however, since most players were then not only anxious to live in New York but also willing to play under Toscanini's direction even at going rates of pay.

Artur was, of course, in his element. Probably due to a strain inherited from his father, Artur was a born Chief of Staff, a methodical organizer. In no time at all he was auditioning. Since he had led most of the orchestras in the United States, he knew precisely where to look. Also, Hitler had put a number of first-class players at Artur's disposal. In a matter of weeks he had heard everyone worth hearing and had begun to make his final selections.

Artur had an uncanny feel for musicians. He once said that he could tell if a player was an artist by the very way he entered a room. (To my recall, he was never wrong.) For days he did nothing but talk about how this person or that other one would or would not suit Maestro's purposes.

One afternoon Artur was especially happy. "I found a genius, Halusia, a real cellist," he bubbled. The "genius," alas, was only seventeen, a student at Curtis Institute, and *Pani* Mary was not about to let young Leonard Rose go until he had completed his studies that year. The following season, 1938–39, Lenny joined the NBC. Two years later, without even another hearing, Artur engaged him to serve as the Cleveland Orchestra's principal cellist, and six years after took him in the same position to the Philharmonic. When Artur resigned, Lenny did, too, taking up his career as one of the finest cello soloists to have been trained in an American conservatory.

The bustle of those days was fierce. Artur was busy with four concerts a week, for which there were rehearsals. There were the unceasing auditions for the NBC Symphony Orchestra. In addition, there was a social calendar stacked, slotted, and juggled with engagements.

Our circle had widened vastly. If there was no dinner to attend, there was a theater party or a movie. But — and this I saw to — there was always time to be found for old friends such as Sophie Braslau (who did not have much longer to live). Another old friend, one of the few Americans I knew from Warsaw, was Marjorie Oelrichs. She had once had a passionate romance with a Polish friend, Jan Tarnowski, which came to little in the end but a broken heart. She managed, however, to mend it somehow, and was at this time happily married to a young jazz pianist, Eddy Duchin. Marjorie was very proud of her husband and had much faith in his talents. Indeed, Rachmaninoff himself had told Duchin he had a great future as a serious musician, and Marjorie wanted to test the composer-pianist's opinion against Artur's.

One evening Artur and I went to a movie theater on Broadway where Eddy was playing between showings of the feature film. Eddy had taken up ornamenting pieces from the classics, particularly Chopin, and the freshness of his style was not only in its novelty (and the shock of hearing a revered chestnut roasted in jazz), but also in its complete and glittering musicality. Artur was impressed, as Rachmaninoff had been, but it was evident that Eddy was not eager for a new venture. His career as a piano "stylist" was well established. He was crazily in love with Marjorie, and a baby was on the way. Everything, from Eddy's view, was perfect.

While Artur and Eddy fell into musical conversation of the sort that left Marjorie and me to talk of pregnancy (not anywhere visible on my horizon), layettes, and the virtues of girls over boys and vice versa. That was our last visit together. Marjorie had her son, Peter, that summer, and died soon thereafter. Although Eddy was left with something of his adored wife in their son, Marjorie's first great passion was celebrated in the boy's name: it had been the name of Jan Tarnowski's pet monkey.

Inserted almost as a footnote to one week's New York agenda that season was an important event. The Polish government, in recognition of his talents, his furtherance of the cause of Polish music and musicians, awarded Artur its highest civil decoration, the Order of Polonia Restituta. Count George Potocki, Poland's Ambassador to the United States, came from Washington to the Ritz Carlton Hotel to present the medal and citation. About fifty people had been invited for cocktails and to witness the Ambassador pin the amaranth-and-white ribbon on Artur's lapel. Count Potocki, in his speech, referred to my husband as "the greatest Polish musician in the United States since Paderewski." I am afraid that tears spoiled my makeup, although Artur's eyes looked no less misted over, for he was much moved by the entire ceremony.

The indignation over Barbirolli's appointment was immense. He was hired after only a two-week display of his fragile "wares," and whatever approval his naming met with in some circles was destroyed by his further performances. Some people were furious because Artur had not been given a chance, or had not even been considered seriously.

Among the persons most disgruntled by the situation was Claire Reis of the League of Composers. Claire gave a luncheon for me to which she invited all of the important women active with the Philharmonic's board and various committees. But the luncheon was to serve a purpose beyond honoring a visiting conductor's wife. Once a bisque, aspic, and fruit salad had been done in, I was asked point-blank why Rodzinski had refused to become the director of the Philharmonic.

Had I been shot, I doubt that I could have been more startled. *"Refused?"* The word stuck to my teeth like a piece of caramel. *"Refused?"*

Yes, that was the word, I was informed. The board had been told by Judson that "Rodzinski would not be interested in coming to New York as permanent conductor because he had just bought a house in Cleveland." Indeed! Moreover, I heard that Judson had told the Philharmonic's board that "Rodzinski is so happy in Cleveland that he would never leave that town." I had all I could do to retain my composure. Artur was ever so right about Judson's ability to be Machiavellian in his malice. His instinct had sensed out the impresario's fine, Scarpia-like touch in Barbirolli's appointment. There was no paranoia behind Artur's outrage. There was no peremptory folly in Artur severing his contractual connections with Judson as of the end of that season. My husband had seen and tangled with a real adversary, not one of his imaginings, an adversary who would even lie to further his power-seeking designs.

When asked if there was any truth to Judson's statements, my answer was as short as my temper: "Of course not!"

I later learned that my words caused Judson no small amount of trouble with his board. Judson's shabby handling of the situation, especially since he was Artur's "personal manager," became known to all. That poor Barbirolli was driven very close to a nervous collapse over the next few seasons, thanks to prematurely assuming a burden beyond his capacity, seems in retrospect another proof of Judson's callousness.

When I told Artur my news, he barely reacted. This was a time of satisfaction. He had had his triumphs, excellent press, and public response to his artistry, and he had capped everything by showing himself as an orchestra builder: the NBC Symphony Orchestra was being readied for Maestro's baton and torrid temper the coming season. How little a Judson weighed in the balance of such accomplishments!

I wanted to make the most of Artur's run of luck, and suggested that we give a large party before leaving town. We held the party at the Colonnades in the Essex House. More than a hundred people came, including Mrs. August Belmont; Mrs. John Pratt; Mrs. Charles Guggenheimer; Mrs. Otto Kahn; Mrs. Myron Taylor; Mrs. Henry Alexander and her sister, Countess Mercati; Mr. and Mrs. Gerry Chadwick; the Charles Marshalls; Paul Cravath; Mr. and Mrs. Richard Aldrich; the Samuel Barlows, Chotzinoffs, and Sam Dushkins; Leopold Godovsky; Mr. and Mrs. Jascha Heifetz; the Damrosches; *Pani* Mary Bok; the Sarnoffs; Myra Hess; Pavel Tchelitcheff; Mr. and Mrs. Chester Burden; Mr. and Mrs. Olin Downes; the Duchins; the Reises; Mrs. Frederick Steinway, and others.

There was then current a blues song that Sophie Tucker had made her own. Its refrain was "Nobody loves you when you're down and out." How dreadfully true. But Artur was up and coming, and that party in the Colonnades was attended by people who could not wait to deliver best wishes to the musical hero of the moment. The party was a gay, happy event for everyone, and particularly the Rodzinskis.

Two days later, Sunday, April 18, when Artur conducted the last of his concerts with the Philharmonic, "The orchestra greeted him standing up and the audience applauded him loud and long. And well they might," wrote Samuel Chotzinoff in the *Evening Post*, "for of all the conductors that have wooed the Philharmonic patrons he is perhaps the only one who really knows his business."

Chapter 23

"May 4, 1937. We sail for Europe today aboard the S.S. 'Paris.' Glamorous deckmates. . . ."

The deckmates noted in my diary entry were even more than glamorous. On board were Serge Koussevitzky and his first wife Natalie; her niece, Olga Naumova, later to become the conductor's second wife; Mme. Nadia Boulanger, from whose musical bakeshop so many American composers of the mid-century had come; violinist Sam Dushkin and his Cleveland-born wife, Louise; and Igor Stravinsky.

Stravinsky invited no intimacy, speaking little and usually of himself. There was a hard edge of arrogance to him that occasionally softened when he soaked in the admiration of others. The Boswell and guiding genius of the composer's latter years, Robert Craft, somewhere in his voluminous writings has said that Stravinsky was a shy man. That is as good an excuse as any to justify the behavior I noted at the time. But, then, I too am shy, and perhaps my discomfort in his presence was my own self-consciousness and sense of inadequacy. Dushkin and Boulanger got along famously with him. Artur was always correctly polite.

When we all sat together for after-dinner coffee, Boulanger would keep an eye fixed on Stravinsky's immobile face. If she caught the flick or tic of some muscle indicating the composer might speak, she silenced the rest of us with a minatory glance.

Boulanger herself was no less severe looking than Stravinsky, although a far more sympathetic person. She reminded me of those schoolmistresses of my youth, what with her hair tightly knotted at the back of her head, and a pince-nez dangling from a black cord as the only ornament on a high-necked, long black dress. If she smiled, I cannot remember the event, although I do recollect her enthusiasm as she recommended a new composer, a student of the moment who excited her, a boy named Olivier Messiaen. "Remember his name," she told Artur like an Old Testament sage underlining a Prophecy, "He will be great."

Koussevitzky was Stravinsky's opposite: he had a fine, if somewhat childish sense of humor, and was friendly almost to garrulity. He dressed in the latest sports clothing (knickerbockers, shooting coat and golf cap) for his morning strolls around the deck, even though he strode with the solemnity of a Russian Grand Duke in an Easter Procession. Natalie and Olga attended to him as if he were the Tsar himself. I thought it all very funny, but only because I recognized myself doubled in them, for I waited on Artur just as obsequiously. "Koussie" passed the time talking to Artur about the Berkshire Festival, which he had just begun in Lenox, Massachusetts.

Artur had begun to pay physically for the emotional strain of the past season. Our friend Dr. Abraham Garbat, the New York physician who had discovered Paul Kochanski's cancer, told Artur that his problem was nervous hyperacidity. In those pre-Maalox days the prescription was to keep one's stomach filled with food that absorbed the excess acid. This meant I had to stock my handbag like a portable delicatessen with crackers and small chunks of mild cheese. At the first wince signaling heartburn, I was ready to serve my husband a snack.

We landed at Le Havre and then, in the new Buick we had shipped over with us, drove to Budapest in three days. Artur had accepted a few summer engagements, the first being in the Hungarian capital. We were guests of one of the Esterhazys, a gentleman we had met at Salzburg the year before. He attempted, on a much-reduced scale, to maintain the traditions of connoisseur and patron so admired of Haydn's celebrated Prince Nicholas. It may have been through Esterhazy that we spent a wonderful evening with the composer Zoltan Kodaly, ranked then much higher in Hungarian esteem than his friend and colleague Bela Bartok.

Artur was fond of Kodaly's work, especially the *Hary Janos* excerpts and "Galanta" Dances, music whose bright, splashing orchestral colors belied the composer's personality. He proved to be a retiring, humble man, possessed nonetheless of a strength of character that glowed through the passive beauty of his Christ-like face. Mrs. Kodaly (the first) was much older than her husband and a warm-hearted, hospitable lady. She served us some exquisite Hungarian cakes which she had made, and while the two men talked music — Artur had hopes of getting a score to premiere — Mrs. Kodaly showered me with presents for "my new house," Hungarian folk artifacts of every description. One I still cherish as a wall-hanging is a colorfully-embroidered man's apron of black silk and velvet.

A few days later, we were in Vienna for Artur's debut with the

Vienna Philharmonic. After the concert, Mme. Alma Mahler, then married to novelist Franz Werfel, came to Artur's dressing room in an ecstatic mood. "You have conquered Vienna!" she exclaimed. Coming from the great conductor's widow, the words carried much weight with Artur who ever wished to see himself in the light of the Austrian capital's traditions. It was the city that had trained him as a musician, had provided him with some of his earliest musical experiences — and any number of love affairs.

Mme. Mahler-Werfel invited us to a party at which she and her husband had assembled in their house the intellectual elite of the city. Unfortunately, my German was not up to the tone of the conversations; Artur, however, was quite at ease among that brilliant crowd. The beautiful Mme. Mahler-Werfel knew everyone in those days. Arnold Schoenberg and the painter Oskar Kokoschka, even before Mahler's death, had been among her passionate admirers. And soon after she was first widowed, she married the architect Walter Gropius, by whom she had a lovely daughter (whose premature death was memorialized in Alban Berg's poetic Violin Concerto). This gifted (she was a composer *manqué*), vibrant, and independent woman became legendary not only because of her composer-conductor first husband; with her keen intelligence and refined tastes she unerringly found and kept about her the most original creative figures of the day. Even the formidable Dr. Freud, somewhat awed by her, had her as one of his very first "psychiatric" patients. She had feared that her love for Mahler was inappropriate because her husband was old enough to have been her father. Dr. Freud asked Mme. Mahler what was the wrong in that, whereupon she went back to being the composer's loving wife until his death from a heart ailment.

At that party, some officials from the Austrian Ministry of Culture approached Artur with the idea that he become permanent conductor of the Vienna Philharmonic. Artur was not interested, he had greater freedom in Cleveland than any artist could have had in the acrimonious musical world of between-wars Vienna. Yet, he was flattered, the offer appealed to the sentimental side of him. The realistic side, however, understood how readily the situation could be insufferable, that Vienna was still the city that drove Mahler to distraction. Moreover, the political situation was increasingly less stable. Where once in Artur's youth the streets were bright with the dress tunics of Franz Josef's officers, they now were drab with brown shirts.

These thoughts saddened our stay, as did the illness of Artur's brother Riki. We passed many hours at his bedside in the clinic where he was being treated for a severe heart condition. Riki looked nothing like the fellow I first had met years before in Artur's Kracow hospital room. He was suffering dreadfully from edema of the legs; being a physician, he knew how serious his condition was. Both brothers were depressed. When they parted, Artur knew that it was for the last time.

Artur was shortly to make his Paris debut. He had been invited by

Paderewski to represent Poland at the International Music Festival that was part of the World's Fair held in the summer of 1937. Europe had recovered from the Great Depression and was anxious to put on a show of prosperity.

As we drove to France through Switzerland, a trip Artur thought would divert him from thoughts of his dying brother, I found myself constantly foraging in my handbag for crackers and cheese. The prospect of confronting the men of another new orchestra was no solace either.

At the festival Artur was to conduct Straram's Orchestra. Supported by Ganna Walska, a wealthy Polish-American, the ensemble was comprised of Paris's best free-lance players. They were a fussy, virtuoso group, strong-willed and resentful of a new conductor. Adding to Artur's concerns was his complete lack of French. Fortunately, my brother-in-law Kazik Krance volunteered to act as Artur's private secretary and translator. Being a musician, Kazik could express the nuances of Artur's musical intentions in a French he commanded as well as his keyboard. He never left Artur's side for a moment during the rehearsals.

The Polish contribution to the festival concert was Karol Szymanowski's Violin Concerto No. 1, with Eugenia Uminska as soloist. Against everyone's advice Artur also intended to do Brahms's Fourth Symphony. Paris and Brahms had never gotten on from the first, and over the years the French capital's public had even developed an outright animosity toward the German. As a sop, however, Artur planned to conclude his concert with Ravel's *Daphnis et Chloe*, the first orchestral suite. When they rehearsed this work, the players, cigarettes dangling from their lips, to a man said, "We don't need to go through it — we know it by heart."

"Let's try anyway," Artur urged, and set about cleaning up note after note, changing sloppy habits and notions, all to the annoyance of the players. But this, only at first; the rehearsal over, the men rose to shout "Bravo, maestro!"

The final rehearsal was to be held on the morning of the concert itself. The manager of the Théâtre des Champs-Elysées offered Artur two starting times: 8:00 or 10:30 A.M. The theater had also to accommodate a Viennese orchestra's rehearsals under Bruno Walter for a concert to be given the next day. Artur, though he slept best in the early morning, relinquished the 10:30 A.M. time out of respect for his senior. Unfortunately, the courtesy was not reciprocated.

Artur went through the Szymanowski with Uminska, then the Brahms. He had just begun to work quickly through trouble spots in the Ravel when suddenly a backstage door opened to show Bruno Walter waving his hands to indicate Artur's time was up. Without dropping a beat, Artur lifted his left hand toward Walter, his fingers outspread, meaning he would need five more minutes.

In less than that time, Artur stepped off the podium, his work done.

On his way backstage someone from management told him that an impatient and angry Walter had ordered his trombonists to warm up in the wings —*fortissimo*. They had refused, to Walter's discomfiture. Artur just smiled sadly and left the hall.

At the concert that night Szymanowski's work was warmly received, and Brahms's Fourth was most enthusiastically applauded by a public that supposedly detested the composer's music. The triumph, though, was *Daphnis et Chloe*. To have played that score in Paris was like carrying musical coals to Newcastle. Audiences knew it inside and out, having seen it regularly on stage since its premiere, and heard it under every conductor's baton, including Ravel's inept one. The storm of "Bravo's" and applause that followed was thus a great compliment.

Artur's dressing room was crowded with musicians telling Artur that they had not known previously how to play Ravel. Composers Florent Schmitt and Albert Roussel came, full of enthusiasm. Roussel asked, "How could you achieve such precision with a French orchestra?" Artur laughed as Roussel said, "You even made me love Brahms."

Artur and Roussel visited the day after the concert. It resulted in Artur receiving a gift of scores — and a lasting interest in Roussel's music. More than once he was to play the French composer's Third Symphony, Symphony for Strings, and the first suite from his ballet *Bacchus et Arianne*.

We drove a meandering route from Paris through Switzerland, where we stopped to give Paderewski a report of the concert, then went on to Austria and Salzburg.

Artur's premiere of Barber's *Symphony in One Movement* launched Sam as an American composer in the minds of the German public. Sam was delighted and bubbled over with appreciation as the three of us rode around the Austrian countryside. Artur told Sam that his growth as a composer would be ample repayment, that it was a pleasure to play his music, and suggested Sam write a piece for Toscanini. "Maestro really liked your Symphony," he said. "Why not do something for him and his new orchestra?" In this way the justly celebrated *Adagio for Strings* was born, to be premiered by Toscanini and the NBC as later was his *First Essay for Orchestra*.

When we were not driving over the mountain passes around Salzburg, Artur liked to relax with *Kaffee mit Schlag* on the veranda of the town's Café Bazar. This was a meeting place for musicians attending or participating in the Festival's activities, and a must for those musical tourists who had to gawk at the great and near-great. One afternoon, a handsome, military erect young Austrian approached Artur, introducing himself as a conductor "just making his way." They had talked a while, when the youthful Maestro asked Artur for help in solving some problems in a new score. The two men got together for several hours another day, and Artur was impressed by his new colleague's musicianship and seriousness of purpose. It was no surprise to him that Herbert von Karajan's fame thereafter grew in Germany, in no way hampered by the Nazi regime.

While in Salzburg, we passed as much time as possible with Maestro Toscanini and Donna Carla. Maestro was delighted that Artur's work with the NBC had gone as far as it had. He approved all the players Artur had hired, and actually began to anticipate his return to the United States. His year of rest had restored him; the words *"stanco e stuffo"* temporarily were retired from his vocabulary. Toscanini was quite evidently not retired considering the work he undertook at Salzburg that season: Beethoven's *Fidelio* and Wagner's *Meistersinger* were scheduled besides various concerts.

Maestro was pleased that time had been scheduled for him to relax before taking over the NBC's podium. Pierre Monteux had been engaged to conduct those concerts which Artur could not lead. Both men felt he was a good, "pure" musician who would not undo the things being built for *Arturo Il Primo*.

Artur's concert at Salzburg was successful enough, winning him yet other engagements for the coming season. But all the successes in the world could do little to relieve his concerns about his brother's deteriorating health — and about his own. His stomach continued to bother him. The doctors suspected an ulcer that X-rays failed to reveal. Artur had begun to dwell on the possibility of stomach cancer and soon had himself near death. No food would stay down; even Cream of Wheat caused discomfort. I was eager for Dr. Garbat to examine him. But despite his constant aches, burps, and fears, Artur worked on new scores and planned programs for the coming season, now not for the Cleveland Orchestra alone, but the NBC as well.

When the Festival ended, we remained behind, as did Toscanini, to rest. Maestro came to us one day for lunch at our hotel in Hof Gastein. It was the first time we had had him to ourselves in a very long time. We took our meal on a veranda overlooking the mountains and the town.

"I am glad I go to America soon, *cara*," he said while Artur was getting a score he wanted Maestro to see. "Mussolini is mad, Hitler is crazier — *tutti sono pazzi*," he said. Then he sat with Artur against a backdrop of mountains that Mozart had known to examine the score of Bartok's *Music for Strings, Percussion and Celesta*. My husband was just then learning it.

He looked, first squintingly, at the score held an inch or two from his nose, then questioningly at Artur, repeating the process a number of times. Finally, he raised his shoulders in a shrug of doubt and said, "If *that* is music, I leave it to you, the younger generation. *Non mi dice nulla*," he said. "It says nothing to me."

Artur was amazed. The two men had always agreed on most musical matters. Maestro's pronounced verdict on Bartok's masterpiece was almost the demarcation of eras, Toscanini's/Rodzinski's. Artur never thought such a time would come, though his turn too came: in his last years, when confronted with the pointillistic score of *Agon* by Stravinsky, Artur opined that such "bloops and blip-blip-blips" were not music.

We drove our Buick to Berlin, then flew to Warsaw for a short visit. Artur could not help but let me become the Godmother of my sister Marysia's new son by her husband of little more than a year, Zbigniew Unilowski. Karol was named for Szymanowski who had been Zbigniew's protector and promotor. The Unilowskis seemed very happy. They were living with Papa on the ground floor of Aleja Roz. Zbigniew was a hugely popular author by now, with two novels to his credit. Marysia had grown into a handsome young mother who appeared to have her jovial husband and our father in hand. Although Papa had been reduced to a shadow of his former self, he still had something of a twinkle to his eye when he looked over the tops of his eyeglasses approvingly at me and my husband.

Returning to Berlin we found ourselves in the midst of maneuvers. Our Buick's headlights had to be covered with heavy black paper for night driving, leaving only a tiny slit through which a weak ray illuminated the roadbed inches before us. Our entire trip to Hamburg had to be taken at a crawl, with many stops to permit military vehicles to pass. I thought we would never arrive on time, but fortunately a young soldier on leave hitched a ride with us; he knew every meter of that road and guided us the rest of the way.

We sailed for home aboard the S. S. "Manhattan," a poorly designed ship that rolled with every ripple and had both of us violently seasick for the first time in our lives.

Chapter 24

WHEN we landed in New York, Artur's demise from abdominal cancer seemed imminent. He had a waxy pallor not unlike the blocks of Emmenthaler I still carried in my handbags (which had begun to reek like a delicatessen basement).

We immediately went to see Doctor Garbat, who was shocked by Artur's looks and distressed by his hypochondriacal terrors. Instead of sympathizing, which might have been disastrous, he gave Artur a slap on his cheek, light enough to be playful, hard enough to make him listen.

"You're crazy, Artur!" Doctor Garbat said. "How could you let yourself get into this state? There's nothing wrong with you a little rational living won't cure." And he prescribed gastric lavage, a procedure which involved running a rubber tube down the throat to the stomach and pouring a neutralizing solution through a funnel at the external end. Naturally, the whole mess would have to come out — neutralized acid, cheese, and whatever else. (I thought back to our drive over a certain Alpine pass when I cooled off the engine block by a similar if less messy procedure.) We did exactly what the doctor ordered. The treatment gave Artur such great relief that he insisted on a gastric lavage before every concert, which added one more chore to that nerve-wracking hour of pre-performance preparation.

When we returned to Cleveland, Artur was greeted with a union problem. There was a protest against the importation of five new solo players from other cities. The Cleveland Orchestra's union representative insisted the instrumentalists come from the ranks of the city's unemployed musicians. Union insistence kept the new men from playing the 1937–38 season's first concert. After a week's negotiation, however, the union had to agree it was impossible to find equivalent instrumentalists locally, and Artur had a new trombonist, French hornist, tympanist, flautist and bassoonist for his second concert.

Thanksgiving week of 1937 Artur Rubinstein made his American orchestral debut playing the Brahms Second Concerto with my Artur and the Cleveland's men.

Rubinstein conquered. Whatever misgivings about American audiences he had from previous encounters on his first tours toward the turn of the century were forgotten. The audiences loved him.

The choice of concerto was a wise one: The Brahms Second is among the very few in the repertoire in which piano and orchestra are equals. Both men could thus exhibit their talents cooperatively. Arthur Loesser, himself a pianist, wrote: "The inspired, masterful conducting of Rodzinski and the pianistic brilliance of Artur Rubinstein combined to elicit an almost unparalleled storm of enthusiasm. . . ."

Nela and Artur were our guests for the week, and for the four of us it was a non-stop round of sentimental reminiscing. Nela and I once again skated Two Jadwigas' hallways in the felt slippers of our memory. We recooked and redigested all the suppers we had eaten after opera performances at the Wielki, basking in Tatka Mlynarski's warm smile or lingering on his words as he critiqued each singer's contribution to the night. My Artur reminisced of his first years under Mlynarski's guidance and teased Nela about the fine time he and her Artur had had in Russia three years earlier, just before our marriage. We also spoke of the good and ill in matchmaking, more or less having each other to thank for our respective marital arrangements. It was that sort of Thanksgiving which can only be had with friends whose ties and roots extend unbroken back to childhood. And with Nela and Artur in America, and his success well launched, we knew that they would frequently be with us in years to come.

That season's autumn half was furiously busy. Artur conducted two concerts in Cleveland, then entrained for New York to spend Sundays and Mondays whipping the new NBC into shape. Although he was working with two entirely different kinds of orchestras simultaneously, with tiring travel in between, my husband's health was none the worse. Indeed, his stomach thrived. Neither Dr. Garbat nor I needed further proof that Artur's botherments were psychosomatic.

A long article in the *Herald Tribune*, under the title "Tuning Up the Band," described Artur's five weeks of training the new NBC orchestra:

> Eagerly awaiting the arrival of Maestro Arturo Toscanini, ninety-two musicians have turned the largest studio in Radio City into a beehive of activity as they rehearse under the baton of drill master Artur Rodzinski. The assignment of organizing the orchestra . . . is to Mr. Rodzinski "the answer to a conductor's dream . . . to me this commission brought nothing but pleasure. It is the answer to a life-long dream." During the five weeks' intensive rehearsal, Mr. Rodzinski will put the musicians through their musical paces, molding the distinguished individual talent into a unit he hopes will become recognized as one of the finest symphonic bodies of its kind.

> The orchestra is unique in this respect, the conductor added, in so far as it came into being in full bloom, rather than through the process of various stages of growth that usually mark the development of many other symphonic groups.

> "I am more than elated with the progress up to now. When I heard the strings after the first rehearsal, I wept for pure joy."

Artur occasionally took me along to New York. While he made music I shopped or took in some theater. One trip was highlighted by a dinner party at the Sarnoffs.

General Sarnoff was *terribly* interested, or so he said, in Artur's progress with the new orchestra. NBC's founding father and guiding business genius had somehow forgotten the shabby initiation of the project, how he and his associates had intended only to add "a few good men" to their standing radio ensemble — and "only for Toscanini's appearances." Now, the corporate giant was touting itself in its Educational Bulletin for having "spared no time, effort or expense to bring together a symphonic organization worthy to take the same high place among the orchestras of the world that Toscanini has long occupied among conductors." One thing must be said of American businessmen: once they have been urged, against all their baser fiscal instincts, to do something really fine, they will spend any amount of money — especially if they smell a profit in the wind. I would like to think that General Sarnoff was different, an American corporate Esterhazy, but the thought must remain in the conditional mode. Sarnoff saw money in heaps to be reaped from sponsors of the forthcoming broadcasts, from sales of phonograph records (to be played on RCA gramophones), and, ultimately, from television broadcasts.

Sarnoff's rise from the heroic young telegrapher who kept to his post during the entire saga of the "Titanic" sinking, to the most powerful magnate in a fledgling communications industry was, to say the least, impressive. But as he talked over dinner of the work Artur was doing with the new orchestra, I sensed that in Sarnoff's practical view aspects of the job other than its art were important. In fact, Sarnoff was interested in changing the subject and leaving the table for his study where he could show us the latest electronic marvel: television.

The picture on the experimental set was poor. We saw shadowy figures moving through a violent blizzard in which each flake was the size of a snowball. Voices emerged through the storm with clarity but the storm was unceasing. No matter — Artur and I were as excited as children by it.

Artur's annual Cleveland tour, unfortunately, came at the time the NBC was to begin its own season, and he was unable to conduct the new ensemble's inaugural concert. Pierre Monteux officially gave the orchestra Artur had created its first public downbeat. The historic program included Respighi's transcription of the Bach C Minor *Passacaglia*, a Mozart Symphony, César Franck's *Psyche et Eros*, and Debussy's *Iberia*. I listened to the premiere alone in Cleveland at 9:00 P.M. Saturday, November 13, 1937. Artur was on the road. In spite of the poor reception, the orchestra sounded magnificent, clear and crisp in the Mozart, and glowing in the French works which Monteux could do so exquisitely.

Maestro was to take over the podium in December, for a Christmas Eve concert. Beforehand, however, Artur would lead three broadcast concerts as well as a number of public rehearsals. When Artur began to work on the rehearsals for his three concerts, he panicked. There were "imperfections" in one of the orchestra's sections, and my husband was in despair. He asked Sarnoff to postpone Toscanini's arrival.

"I will need a few more months' work with the orchestra," he told the NBC hierarchy; it was his Warsaw Opera perfectionism all over again, except with no sympathetic Emil Mlynarski to say "yes" to the extra rehearsals.

NBC was in turmoil: broadcast schedules had been announced, promotional materials distributed, programs printed, and a huge radio public was sitting by its Atwater Kent, not to mention RCA, cathedrals. The critic Samuel Chotzinoff, as artistic advisor to NBC, tried to tell Artur that he exaggerated. But Artur remained unconvinced. He had told the *Herald-Tribune* he would hand over to Toscanini an instrument so perfect that it "would leave Maestro breathless after the first broadcast."

It was Sarnoff who finally pacified Artur. He began by telling him how much everyone appreciated his work and how well everyone *else* thought the ensemble sounded. He said these obvious things with just the right measure of warmth and sympathy, and calmed Artur's nerves. The storm clouds dissipated, Artur quieted down, and the rehearsals that followed went along perfectly. At the first concert, Artur walked on stage knowing the package delivered to his dressing room contained yet one more elephant to trumpet still another highpoint in his career. Artur's program included that same Beethoven Symphony which Toscanini eventually made his own with the NBC, the Fifth. There were also works by Handel, Debussy, and Albéniz. The second program gave the radio public Stravinsky's *Petrouchka* suite, plus Shostakovich's Symphony Number One, and pieces by Smetana and Tchaikovsky. His last program, before Maestro assumed the helm, featured Haydn's "Military" Symphony and Brahms's Fourth.

After the second concert, the *Tribune* said of *Petrouchka:* "The NBC Orchestra played this tricky and fascinating music with a clarity, color and dazzling brilliance which surpasses any of the achievements so far of its brief career." Toscanini heard that concert shipboard en route to New York and sent a cable of congratulations.

The third evening, when Artur conducted the Brahms Fourth, Maestro listened in Studio 8-H. Afterward he was full of praise: *"Bravo, bravo, Rodzinski! Orchestra magnifica e magnifico concerto . . . che bel lavoro!"*

Toscanini's first broadcast on Christmas Day, 1937, made American history. His program consisted of works by Vivaldi and Mozart, crowned by Brahms's First Symphony. We listened to that concert in Cleveland with Artur's son Witold, who was then a student at Williams College and spending his holiday vacation with us. Artur's ears were alert to the sound of each instrument in order to reassure himself that the radio pick-up and transmission were perfect. I felt that he was satisfied and maybe even proud of his achievement.

That season, for all its triumphs for Artur, was a sad time for me. As the year drew to its end, so did Papa's days. He died quietly in Warsaw October 20, 1937. The eulogies in the press and the reports of his funeral were as grand as anything I had ever read. Franciszek Lilpop had meant a great deal to many people. He was interred alongside Mama in the Powaski Cemetery with all the pomp and official mourning Warsaw could give a leading citizen.

No less painful was the death three weeks later of my brother-in-law, Zbigniew Unilowski, widowing Marysia and leaving little Karol at only one year of age without a father. He was twenty-eight when struck down by a disease contracted while traveling the Amazon to do a journalistic piece on Poles in Brazil. He left behind two fine novels and the reputation of one from whom much was expected. I mourned his death more than Papa's in a way, regretting all that he had left unsaid, undone. And I mourned for Marysia who bore the loss of both men alone, for the Lilpop sisters were scattered. Our brother Antek was about, but in one of his more irresponsible phases.

Then, news came that Artur's brother was dead. Artur was in a stupor. We heard the announcement of Riki's death on the day of a concert when Artur was to conduct Anton Bruckner's Seventh Symphony, followed by Roy Harris's Chorale for Strings, Opus 3, and Ernst von Dohnanyi's Suite for Orchestra, Opus 10.

For the first time since our marriage, I could not attend his concert. A severe back ailment, perhaps a psychosomatic malady of my own, confined me to bed. All I could do was pray nothing bad would happen because, to Artur, my presence was as much of a superstition as his revolver, photograph of the "General," ring with the toad, and all the rest.

The symphony was conducted beautifully, Felix Eyle told me. The men and Artur played as one to find and reveal all the poetic magic so frequently lost in Bruckner's scores by those who play them without sympathy. But after conducting the piece, Artur fainted in his dressing room. He was revived and went on to lead the second half of the program. Afterward, he was brought home exhausted. The doctor said that the sorrow and strain had been more than Artur could bear.

Time and a weak heart had taken Riki, and this Artur could understand. But that Hitler had taken Austria (almost simultaneously) was incomprehensible. He would never go there as long as Hitler was Chancellor of his Third Reich, of which Austria was now an integral part. The Salzburg Festival was lost to Artur. It was now also lost to Toscanini. Bruno Walter was automatically *persona non grata*, and he, along with Franz and Alma Werfel, was already en route to America. Artur cabled to the Festival's management, cancelling his engagements.

Chapter 25

MY backache proved to have a more substantial cause than psychological stress. An infected tooth had spread its poisons along the nerve paths of my spine to settle in the lombar region. There were days when I was so paralyzed that I could barely wiggle a toe, and I was unable to accompany my husband and the orchestra on their extended spring tour. Artur, alone on the road, was constantly depressed although the concerts were well received and he had the possibility of a new triumph to look forward to.

Artur had slated the American premiere of Shostakovich's Fifth Symphony for April 9, 1938, at one of three broadcast concerts he gave to end his year with the NBC orchestra. Everyone was eager to hear the piece, Artur particularly, since the Fourth Symphony had been withdrawn from rehearsal as a result of Stalin's disapprobation, and the Fifth was heralded as the young man's *apologia pro sua vita*, a recantation of his "bourgeois-formalist" ways.

Many conductors wanted the Fifth for its premiere outside Russia, but Artur, thanks to his good connections with the composer, was awarded the prize. NBC's John Royal, through the American ambassador in Moscow, made the arrangements — at a huge price. The Soviet government demanded the then unheard of sum of $5,000 for the premiere. Since introducing the piece would be as much of a coup for the radio network as for Artur, NBC's management did not object to the cost.

After all the expense and effort in acquiring the score and parts, Artur was a bit concerned the piece might not be all that was expected of it. His reactions when he first examined it were far from favorable. There was a coarseness to the sound of the scoring. The piece seemed overlong. Indeed, Artur was not altogether sure he cared for it. In discussion with NBC, it was decided to perform the work just as it had been delivered — without cuts, without reservations. If the critics did not care for it, no one could blame Rodzinski.

Gradually, in rehearsals, the work began to take Artur's imagination, and soon enough he even was in love with it. The piece entered his repertoire and became one of his specialties. The recording he later made with the New York Philarmonic for Columbia was a mainstay of that company's catalog for years. Twenty years after the premiere, Westminster asked Artur to re-record it, and that performance still holds up well against its competitors.

The closing concert in Cleveland was of Bach's great *Passion According to Saint Matthew*, given as a memorial to our good friend Ossip Gabrilowitsch, who had died after a long illness. The music was performed in a version made by Ossip, a fitting tribute to the fine musician that ne was. Although Artur had intended only to honor the memory of the founder of the Detroit Symphony Orchestra, the Bach also served to commemorate all that had happened during the season. Severance Hall's audiences, refraining from applause at Artur's request, ended the Cleveland concert year with a solemn sense of occasion.

A special benefit concert with the NBC in Carnegie Hall (for the Austrian Relief Fund, an organization of prominent citizens under the chairmanship of journalist Dorothy Thompson) concluded Artur's work year. Jascha Heifetz appeared as soloist in concertos by Max Bruch and Mozart. Artur performed Richard Strauss's *Also Sprach Zarathustra*, and to celebrate happier, bygone days of the Austrian capital, Johann Strauss's *Tales from the Vienna Woods*. The artists donated their services in the cause of "arousing the conscience of the whole free world," to use the words of the publicity Miss Thompson released. The public responded

(*175*)

generously and the concert earned somewhat more than $10,000 to aid a flood of refugees.

Thousands of musicians, writers and painters, doctors, lawyers and scientists had already escaped from the Nazis. But there were thousands and thousands more waiting for help, either in cash or through political influence. Artur personally sent affidavits and guarantees for friends who were desperate to reach freedom; yet there were limits to what a handful of concerned individuals could do. The Carnegie Hall concert with the NBC and Heifetz, broadcast by the orchestra's parent, elicited a mass concern. An intermission plea for funds brought in to Miss Thompson's office a trickle of cash that steadily mounted.

For some while Artur had wanted a permanent hideaway, a home away from home with privacy for study and relaxation. So while he rehearsed his last NBC concerts, I made a list of real estate agents and likely properties in New York and New England. We had several cramping criteria, however: a house in reasonably good condition on *at least* twenty-five acres of woodland (preferably pine), near a stream, distant from traffic noise, yet close by a shopping district—and all of this for between $10,000 and $15,000.

Our hopes high, we set out from the Essex House Hotel in Artur's smart new grey LaSalle coupe, our little dog Haile Selassie (Lassie for short) sitting in my lap as Artur drove. We felt deliciously free and prey to fantasies of a home in which each stick of wood and butterknife was to be ours forever. No more gypsy wanderings for us, no more leases which itemized all the things that were to be returned as we had found them. If Artur wished to smash an entire tea service in a tantrum, it would be *his*. Every day we visited with the agents I had contacted, then saw their listings. The properties were incredible. Artur's desired woodlands usually turned out to be a handful of scraggly ailanthus trees or a scrub pine or two. His requisite nearby stream was either a malarial swamp or a muddied ditch that flooded with the first thaw. And as for the houses, dilapidated is too genteel a description.

We learned quickly to tell from an agent's sales pitch what kind of property he was likely to show us. Sometimes we were fooled into expecting something better, but not often. By the second week we only rarely left the LaSalle to look. I had no objections to the search.

Moreover, I had the distraction of learning the geography of New York's Hudson River area, also most of Connecticut, and a good piece of Massachusetts. My assigned task was to check the maps, frequently drawing in uncharted roads and names of villages previously unknown to the oil company's cartographers. No apple orchard, onion or dairy farm, or truck garden in the tri-state area seemed too remote for us in our quest. Although some of them may never have been assessed for tax purposes, they were all usually priced at more than $15,000, a considerable sum in the late 1930s.

When finally we landed in Great Barrington, Massachusetts, Artur's temper had begun to fray. Lassie had taken to sitting in the back seat, and I was seriously considering how it would feel to ride in the trunk, drawn and quartered, if the agent we were to see had nothing decent to offer. He had nothing, and I was in despair. Before Artur could explode, I telephoned Gretchen Damrosch Finletter's sister, Polly. I had met Polly and her playwright husband Sidney Howard at a party Gretchen gave after the Austrian Relief Fund concert. Sidney had said not to buy anything until we looked over the Berkshires, and since we were in the neighborhood, the Pulitzer prizewinner came to our rescue. He drove over from his Tyrringham Valley farm in time to forestall an acrimonious outburst from Artur. At dinner in our hotel, and calmed with a cocktail, Artur cried on Howard's shoulder.

"Sidney, I have no more strength for this househunting," he complained. "Imagine, we have looked at 137 shacks — most of them with crescent moons cut into their front doors. . . ."

"Courage, Artur," Sidney said. "I know an agent here in town who is bound to have something."

"No. We go back to Cleveland," Artur said, his eyes halfclosed in exhaustion, but Sidney was already away from the table and at a pay phone in the lobby. When he returned, he announced that a Mr. Lord would call in the morning to show us property in Stockbridge. Sidney left for Tyrringham Valley, and we went to bed too tired to dream even of what good the new day might bring.

Mr. Lord took us to a place about a mile off the main highway along a country road. We turned in a gate in a stone wall that had paralleled most of the road and up a long driveway to the most attractive house I had seen in a month. It was of field stone, beautifully cut and fit. We entered through a solid oak door, a good three inches thick, hung on and mounted with beautiful hand-wrought iron fixtures. The house was immense, cool, quiet, and furnished in exquisite taste. The view from every window was superb. There were, on three sides, woods of pine and birch that, along with the gently sloping hills, instantly reminded us of southern Poland. Below the main house we saw two cottages, two large barns, a fourcar garage and two chicken coops.

"Why in heaven did you bring us here?" Artur started to fulminate. "You know this place is out of my range. . . ." Then, after a moment's pause, Artur sheepishly said, "Just out of curiosity, how much *is* it?"

Mr. Lord, shyly working loose a small stone in front of one of the barns, whispered the figure, "$150,000."

"Ah! You are all mad, you real estate people. I've had enough. Halina, we go back to Cleveland."

I shrugged, my face beet red, and wistfully looked around.

Driving back with us to our hotel, Mr. Lord kept urging Artur not to lose hope. "I have other properties, Dr. Rodzinski, and I'll show them to you tomorrow. But what *did* you think of that place? Nice, eh?"

"Nice? Of course it's nice. What do you think orchestral conductors earn? As *much* as movie stars?"

Mr. Lord winced, but made Artur promise to stay one more day to see what else he had. That night, we went to see a film to forget our troubles. It was *The Wizard of Oz*, with a little girl named Judy Garland, and it cheered us both immensely.

Soon after dawn, the telephone rang. I answered. It was Mr. Lord: "Ask Dr. Rodzinski if he would consider paying $20,000 for the house we saw yesterday."

I passed the question on to Artur in Polish. In Polish he told me to ask the man if he were crazy. Then, not sure I would translate his meaning gracefully enough, he took the phone from my hand and asked, "Are you joking?"

"No, Dr. Rodzinski, I'm serious. The owner is coming up this afternoon to sign the deed over to you if you don't object to the price."

"Is *he* crazy?" Artur asked, half laughing, half serious.

"No, sir. His wife left him, the place has too many unhappy memories, he's been trying to sell it for close to three years. When he heard that *you* liked the place, he told me to sell it for whatever you can pay."

"Who is he?" Artur asked, incredulous.

"John P. Argenti." The agent seemed to think we would recognize the name, but we did not.

We drove out to the farm with Mr. Lord to take another look around. Mr. Argenti, whom we were anxious to meet, would arrive within the hour.

While Artur talked to Mr. Lord, I made a little run with Lassie over the weedless expanses of lawn, a sea of close-clipped velvety grass that flowed down from the front of the house. The drive of white granite and marble aggregate that circled the house to meet with the main road at the bottom of the hill had been raked only that morning. Even Lassie was cautious about disturbing its manicured surface, slowing his run to a suspicious trot as he approached the elegant path.

Watching us was a towering old pine, a noble lady who stood in the center of the great front lawn. It was as if I had been whisked to Kolacin, the Lilpop family estate where now I summered only in my dreams. I shivered slightly in the cool moist air that blew from the nearby Housatonic River, almost hearing the echoing laughter of my younger sisters, our old nurse Mania calling us to breakfast. Then Lassie, who had been rolling in the dew-laced grass, rubbed his wet coat against my calf. And I was off on a search for clovers, a pastime from my childhood. Down by the handsome dairy barns I saw clumps of it that had escaped the mowers. Clustered around sweet smelling purple blossoms grew dozens of quatrefoils, even cinquefoils. I gathered a handful to show my superstitious husband.

"One alone is an omen, Artur," I said, "but see how many fours and fives there are!" His eyes opened wide and the corners of his mouth flickered into a grin as he tightly pressed my hands and the clovers into his.

Mr. Lord, who tried not to seem embarrassed by our intimacy, cleared his throat. "Mr. Argenti," he said, "is a nice enough person, but he was not exactly the sort the neighbors took to."

Mr. Argenti drove up then. He was of medium height, dark skinned, with a sad pair of eyes. There was something very sweet and gentle to his expression, something wistful, like a boy too proud to tell of his disappointments. He spoke with Artur of his admiration for his work, having attended concerts Artur conducted in New York. A music lover, he especially enjoyed opera, so much so that the sad man had named his only child, a son, Tristan.

As we walked through the house and over the grounds in the company of their proprietor, he enumerated the virtues of the place: new plumbing and wiring in the house, entirely new furniture, all manner of new, useful farm machinery, and some good livestock — two sleek, strong-shouldered horses, four fine, fat dairy cows, and a number of hardy laying hens and their husband. Artur could have it all, he said, plus a station wagon and a truck for $5,000 more than Mr. Lord had originally quoted — $25,000 in total.

Artur took a moment to collect enough breath to say "Yes," then the men headed into the house where, on the magnificent Spanish oak dining-room table, Artur wrote out a check in down payment, boldly dating it May 20, 1938. When Artur handed the pale blue oblong to Mr. Argenti, the man's face brightened. "You are now the owners of Greystone Farm," he said, sighing like a man who had just laid down a heavy burden, or a bundle of sorrows. Mr. Lord handed us the keys and departed with Mr. Argenti. The necessary papers would be drawn up the next day. (The title and deeds were to be a miniature history of Colonial America: the first recorded owner was an Indian with a name that filled an entire line.)

We moved in, so to say, that very moment. The house, which had been built of stone taken from a fort once used in the Indian Wars, was warm enough for us to sleep comfortably under our overcoats. We awakened the next morning as two of the happiest people in the world. I remember how I came into what was to be "Artur's room" to find him looking through a window at the beautiful garden below, planted with bright perennials and rare shrubs, and at the ranks of silver and yellow birches, their pale first foliage blending with the dark blues and greens of pines and spruces beyond, all leading the eye upward to the rows of mountains still further beyond. It was like the views sometimes seen through the arcaded balconies of certain Renaissance Annunciation scenes.

Artur held me close by his side, pressing my head to his shoulder. "I am afraid to believe that this is all truly ours, Halusia," he kept murmuring. "Nothing *so* good has ever happened to me before."

(*179*)

That day we went into Pittsfield to buy bed linens, blankets, and some food. Artur, who still remembered my reckless expenditures for such things in Cleveland soon after we were married, was now oblivious to my extravagances. The fine sheets and pillow slips, the downy double-ply blankets of pure wool were for *our* home.

I stopped at a drugstore to use the pay phone to call our precious Victoria in Cleveland. She was overjoyed to hear that we found a house which pleased Artur, and we prepared a list of all that she would have to bring by train. She could hardly believe that the kitchen was already fully equipped, with even an entire English Spode china service for twenty-four, from soup frogs and tureens to tea things. Victoria arrived two days later with our clothing, and instantly moved into the kitchen as if it had been her hereditary demesne and cooked Polish delicacies as if the stove and kettles had known no other cuisine.

True to his word, Mr. Lord had the deed and title transfer papers prepared almost immediately. We were, in fact, the sole and true owners of the 250 acres off Ice Glen Road in Stockbridge, Massachusetts. When, on May 22, we lunched with Sidney and Polly Howard, along with Papa and Mrs. Damrosch, we had the papers in hand to show everyone.

Once word got about, neighbors came to see the new owners of Greystone Farm. First there were the Percy Morgans who had the adjacent farm, then the Owen Johnsons, the Leslie Buells, the Adolphe Berles, and Dr. and Mrs. Ira Dixon. We soon discovered that among our closer neighbors were Albert Spalding, the violinist, and his wife Mary.

Our new possession absorbed us almost totally, but we did make a day trip to Tanglewood and Koussevitzky's festival site. The two conductors were delighted to be neighbors, promising to visit whenever time allowed, though neither had much to spare. Koussie's hours were filled with the affairs of Tanglewood, Artur's with a cram course in the ways of gentleman farming. Mr. Argenti had had two gardeners to keep up the grounds, an expense Artur did not wish to sustain — at least not while he could do half the work. He let one man go. From the other he was learning how to trim shrubs, prune trees, dress vines, and tidily rake the driveway's gravel. It was an ideal situation: in those periods when Artur was not studying scores or planning programs, he could work off his surplus energies constructively, caring for living things that were his own.

I had some ideas of my own about the place. Having a farming heritage from both sides of my family, I firmly held that possession of land carried the obligations of dominion. Mother Earth, I thought, had to pay her way. A farm which produced no income was not to be tolerated. That this one didn't, was made apparent by the set of well-kept books Mr. Argenti turned over to us. The money that went out nowhere matched the few dollars that came in. There was a salary for the gardener-farmer, taxes, insurance, feed for two horses and four cows (whose amours also had to be paid for, since we had no bull), electricity, water, fertilizer, and an endless number of little things. The return on this outlay was a few dollars for milk sold to neighbors.

"This is impossible," Artur decided, visions of the poorhourse looming before his nearsighted eyes. "We will plow it up and make things grow. But what?"

It was not long before we found our answer — goats!

Artur's stomach, though improved, still depended on gastric lavages, Emmenthaler, and crackers. He had been told by Dr. Garbat to drink milk periodically, but the stuff that came from cows only added to his hyperacidity. (Indeed, I now believe he was allergic to it.) We had heard, however, that goat's milk was easier to digest. One day, pondering our future cash crop, someone mentioned that a priest who lived close by had a milking nanny for sale. Victoria, a farm girl in upbringing, rode with me in our new station wagon to fetch a goat we bought for only $5.

Artur looked at the skinny creature's swollen udders when Victoria and I chained her in the barn. "When can I have some to drink?" he asked. "She must get used to her new home before she'll give," I lied.

The following day at 11:00 A.M. I brought Artur his milk and crackers, just as I had in the past. He made an ugly face, chewed the crackers, gulped the milk and continued at his scores. He downed this snack several times a day for several days, continuously asking when the "damned goat" was going to feel enough at home to do her job. "Soon, darling," I said.

"I don't think I'll need her milk," he said. "I've had no acidity for the last few days. Cow's milk is good enough."

"Oh?" I said, while Victoria burst into laughter.

"What's so funny?" Artur asked, a little put out.

"But you *have* been drinking goat's milk," Victoria told him.

"That cannot be so," Artur said, miffed. "I had goat's milk in Spain, and it tasted dreadful — not to mention the stink."

"That was because Spanish goats are not clean, Mr. Rodzinski," Victoria explained.

The next morning Artur was aglow. He had had an acid-free night's rest. "We shall raise goats," Artur proclaimed. "We shall make money bringing relief to the upset stomachs of America. We can keep the farm going and do humanity a service." Chattering to himself about the marvelous "cure" for hyperacidity he had "discovered," Artur went off to the barn to visit his benefactress.

In practical ways we then began to investigate the feasibility of goat farming. We found a showplace near Albany, beautifully and smoothly operated by a couple whose baby daughter had been saved by goat's milk when she could digest none other. The people were as enthusiastic about the genus *Capra Bovidae* as Artur, and gladly opened their hearts as well as their books to the neophyte cultist. They gave us a fairly accurate estimate of the costs involved to start up an operation, the sorts of animals to acquire, and so on. After this visit, we were committed to the Great Goat Caper, lock, stock, and milking pails. I even had the costume — a genuine Tyrolean *dirndl* (full skirt, apron, cap and blouse) picked up in Salzburg the year before.

Since no great coup is prepared for in public, the Rodzinski goat venture was initiated with the secrecy that befits a price-setting cabal between international oil producers. "Someone might steal the idea," Artur reasoned. Yet, even the Stockbridge Village Idiot could see something was afoot. Artur plowed and seeded the fields for hay, of which we would need enormous amounts. To do this, of course, Artur had to buy a tractor and seed. Our horse-drawn vehicle was not adequate for the work so Artur, after no small amount of research, acquired a big Cletrac Caterpillar tractor.

The tractor's arrival transported Artur to ethereal heights never before known to him. The ominous looking piece of machinery bespoke power and utility, two things Artur mightily enjoyed. Moreover, it was his, and his alone, to play with. Our hired farmer could only look at it if he promised to keep his hands in his pockets. It was Artur's to disassemble, grease, reassemble and drive about, all according to the thick operator's manual he had memorized. Needless to say he required a costume, and so bought himself a broad-brimmed hat and several pairs of baggy bib-and-suspender coveralls. What a splendidly rural figure he cut coming to lunch, drenched in his own sweat, his hands larded over with rank, gritty axle grease. This was the picture that greeted Dr. Garbat and his wife when they came for a weekend visit that summer.

"Artur," the physician said, "you've added ten years to your life. This farm and the work are better medicines than anything I could ever prescribe."

We planted potatoes and seeded a vegetable garden, fertilizing it with manure amply provided by our two horses, now turned into permanent houseguests, and the four cows who in time would be sent to a butcher. The vegetable plot was my chore: Artur could not bear to think of anyone idle — not while he was plowing up the countryside, fixing machinery and studying reams of pamphlets, newsletters, and bulletins that came in the mail from the county, state and federal agricultural authorities.

One thing that did not come in the post, however, was a reply to Artur's insistent letters requesting confirmation of his engagement with the NBC orchestra. Artur, when not studying goat lore and scores, was planning his coming season's schedule, and his own management in Cleveland wanted to know which concerts to reserve for guest conductors. Finally Artur could wait no longer and called NBC's John Royal.

"What are my dates?" Artur asked.

"We have you penciled in for four . . . ," Royal began.

"And the remaining six?" Artur queried.

"There are only four, Dr. Rodzinski," Royal replied.

"But the contract I signed called for fourteen engagements. I gave four concerts, you owe me ten."

"*You* signed the contract, Dr. Rodzinski," Royal said. "We did not."

Artur was dumbstruck. He recalled having put his signature on the papers in company with an NBC executive to whom he had even handed his own pen. There were photographers to be grinned at as flashbulbs popped, hands to be shaken. Artur had not noticed that the gentleman from NBC returned his pen unused. That was in March 1937. We sailed for Europe soon thereafter. Artur had assumed that copies of the contract would be forwarded. None ever came, and each time he had asked after one he was treated to some piece of corporate evasion. The four engagements with the NBC in the coming season were a handout, in effect. After they had been announced by NBC, Artur was reluctant to do what his instincts urged him to do, to tell everyone to go to hell. He was losing $10,500 in fees, and had been played for a fool at that.

We consulted an attorney in Pittsfield, a former judge. It was his opinion that Artur forget the matter. "You would never be able to win a suit against so large a corporation," he said. "They are too rich, too powerful, and they would spend ten times more than what they owe you *not* to make settlement. It's a matter of principle with them."

"Yes," Artur said, grinding his teeth, "just a matter of principle." He laid the thing to rest.

But I was not about to take the affair supinely. I went to see David Sarnoff myself, unable to believe so wealthy and mighty a man would behave in so small a way, or that he would allow subordinates to do so in his name.

My reception was friendly enough, and Sarnoff and I spoke courteously, but he said he was unable to rectify the "mistake," that Artur ought "to be more careful" about his affairs. As we concluded our talk, Sarnoff asked after the farm and said our new home would not be complete without a combination radio-phonograph, of course, an RCA set. The equipment was sent, along with several boxes of records, as a gift — Artur's sole payment, aside from the fees for his four concerts, for hundreds of exhausting hours spent auditioning, organizing, and rehearsing the NBC Symphony Orchestra. In later years, when Samuel Chotzinoff was to write his book about Toscanini and the NBC, the "critic" turned corporate executive hardly mentioned Artur's work on behalf of Maestro.

Artur was crushed by the affair. He told me that even his tractor was no consolation, that he brooded while plowing up his acres, often wishing one of the furrows would swallow him. Part of his bad mood, of course, was that he saw his own stupid complicity in the matter, that he had behaved with the naive open-heartedness of a peasant. Such behavior suited the man gashing the rich black soil of the farm but not the man who carried a doctorate in law from one of Poland's finest universities.

On June 14 of that year Artur acquired his second degree, a doctorate of music, *in causa honoris,* from Oberlin College. Since the farm demanded my every waking moment, I was unable to attend the ceremony.

As the summer wore on, Artur began to be bored with his plowing and seeding and study of goatly ways. Enough was invariably enough. Appearances with the Chicago Symphony Orchestra at its summer home in Ravinia came at just the right psychological moment. He led the Chicagoans in their opening concert and for two weeks more, then entrained for Los Angeles and a series of Hollywood Bowl appearances with his first orchestra. I was along for the trip, and, thanks to goat's milk, could leave Emmenthaler, crackers and the grim equipment for gastric lavages behind.

In Los Angeles I saw some old friends, including Artur's trumpet player, Vlady Drucker, and the Cecil Frankels, with whom we stayed at their Santa Monica home. I also made some new acquaintances, among them the actor Edward G. Robinson, who invited us to see his magnificent collection of paintings.

Later, we traveled through Washington and Oregon, where Artur led concerts in Seattle and Portland. But we also had an eye out for our business venture. Artur had read in the *Goat Breeders Journal* of several model farms in the Portland area, and when members of the press came for interviews, Artur wanted only to question the reporters about goats, to everyone's amusement. One of the writers drove us to see a farm he knew of which also had breeding stock for sale. From a herd of pure-bred Saanens, lovely white creatures, we purchased fifteen nannies and arranged for their escort by train to Albany. They cost $200 apiece, but we calculated they would pay for themselves in no time at all. Each would give five quarts a day. A quart sold for 45 cents. That would be $33.75 daily return from the herd.

Back in Stockbridge, we had the machinery shed rebuilt to house the expanded herd, and then waited impatiently for the goats to arrive.

When Railway Express notified us that there were fifteen swollen, baa-ing ladies awaiting us on a train platform in Albany, Artur and I set off to meet them in our new truck. After some difficulty loading — a photographer for one of the state capital's dailies photographed Artur pushing a recalcitrant nanny's nether parts onto the truck — we started back. The trip home was a tiring if riotous affair: the ladies jostled and butted and baa-ed the whole way. I was often afraid that at an intersection one of them might go straight through the side of the truck, the others following. Once settled in their new stalls, however, they were quite well behaved.

How proud we were to see them in their newly-enameled quarters! We felt like lords, and they must have felt indeed like ladies when led into the gleaming white milking room where their udders were washed with disinfectant before they mounted a special elevated platform for the work at hand. Artur once or twice squirted himself in the face until he got the hang of it. I had already learned the knack from practicing on our first nanny. Soon, everyone about the place was expert, at least in getting milk out of udders. Other kinds of expertise took a bit longer to acquire.

One problem we had was keeping the bacteria count at the lowest possible level, for Rodzinski's milk had to be the best. Although goat's milk is purer than cow's milk, bacterial growth commences the moment the warm fluid leaves the animal. The problem was one of instant cooling. The samples we took to the Pittsfield Milk Exchange were good enough for the milk to be sold, but there were still enough bacteria left to perturb Artur's finicky sense of quality.

One morning, as I was making some cereal in a double boiler for breakfast, he ordered me to clean the pot and give it to him with ice in the bottom part. After eating the cereal, we took his invention out to the milking room and milked one of the nannies. Rushed to the Exchange, the milk showed the lowest count on record. Artur was overjoyed, and ordered stainless steel double-boiler type milk pails made to serve our purposes. They cost a fortune, as did the refrigeration units we required, but at least they assured the world that Rodzinski was giving it the purest product.

And therein lay the second problem: having the most bacteria-free goat's milk on earth will not necessarily sell it. We advertised in the *Berkshire Eagle*, but with little response, presumably because ulcerated stomachs were rare in the region. We then rewrote our copy, stressing the benefits to babies. Still nothing happened, though our farmer, Victoria, Artur, and I waxed prosperous, not with cash but by drinking goat's milk rather than water, for my husband would not see a drop wasted.

Artur then one day had the idea of inviting the county medical association's members to a Sunday afternoon cocktail party. Fifty physicians accepted, and when they were gathered Artur led them on a tour of the gleaming barn and shed, the spotless milking room. Back in the house, each man was given a tiny cup of cow's milk and one of goat's milk and told to guess which was which. No one could taste the difference, proving Artur's point. The doctors, however, were far more interested in the cocktails which we served as promised. As far as I know not a quart of goat's milk was ever sold thereafter on prescription — at least not Rodzinski's goat's milk. Indeed, we continued to be our own best customers through that summer.

And what a spectacular end that summer had! On September 21, 1938, there was a hurricane. The storm devastated Long Island and parts of Connecticut. By the time it reached us it was only a fierce storm, but the heavy downpour caused dams to burst and brought on flooding; the lovely, lazy Housatonic turned into a raging monster that overflowed its banks. Our fields were inundated, and the only road to town was under three feet of water. Our house and farm buildings were built on high ground by a foresighted farmer who had little faith in the Army Corps of

Engineers. The electricity was out, but we had plenty of candles and oil lamps. The telephone did not work, but that bothered no one. We were cosily and romantically situated on an island, with all the goat's milk anyone could want. Our glorious isolation was spoiled by a neighbor who canoed over to check on us and take word of our well-being (and a shopping list) back to the mainland, wherever that might have been. The next day the grocer rowed out with bread and a few other things, and two days later the waters receded sufficiently for us to return to Cleveland, two people sick to death of goat's milk, but sad to part with house and herd and the beautiful Berkshire countryside.

Chapter 26

THE 1938–39 season in Cleveland was to be a brilliant one. Invited to play with the orchestra were violin soloists Erica Morini, Georges Enesco, Nathan Milstein, Joseph Szigeti, Adolf Busch, Jascha Heifetz, and Artur's concertmaster, Josef Fuchs. Pianists to appear included Artur Schnabel, Rubinstein, Ruth Slenczynski, and the one-armed Austrian virtuoso, Paul Wittgenstein, who was to play the work he had commissioned from Ravel, the Piano Concerto for Left Hand. The season was to end with a performance of Beethoven's Ninth, and there was also to be a special all-Wagner program with Kirsten Flagstad.

The glitter of the opening concert was dulled by another death, that of Dudley Blossom, Artur's president since 1936. To honor him the program began with a memorial reading of Wagner's "Good Friday Spell," from *Parsifal*. The rest of the concert was "new music," in a sense. Arnold Schoenberg's arrangement of Brahms's Piano Quartet in G Minor, Opus 25, was the major piece. The composer, who had taken up residence in Los Angeles, had just finished it when Artur visited him the previous summer. The work was introduced to the public first in Los Angeles under Otto Klemperer, although Artur had wanted the privilege. He believed that Schoenberg, who recast the Brahms composition in much more than orchestral garb, had actually wrought the Hamburg master's Fifth Symphony. Artur had asked Chotzinoff at NBC to allow him to do it for the radio public, but the rental and royalty fees ($45) were held to be too high by the "critic"-executive. Actually, the money was not at issue, considering the $5,000 paid for a Shostakovich work. Schoenberg's name was poison, and Chotzinoff, despite all assurances to the contrary, had the impression the new piece was a twelve-tone horror. The concluding half of the concert consisted of Delius's *Paris* and a set of Waltzes from *Der Rosenkavalier*.

Artur's sixth season in Cleveland began a new era. In former years he had worked with a board comprised of men of broad culture who understood the requirements of making fine music, men like John L. Severance, Frank Ginn, and Dudley Blossom. Whenever my husband had hopes of performing an opera or oratorio, works that required costly soloists and additional orchestral players for proper effect, Artur was welcome at board meetings to present his proposals. These men had usually acceded to my husband's wishes — all, save one: the enlargement of the Cleveland's strings by a few stands.

On more than one occasion, Artur was forced to wits' end by the lack of sufficient strings. He could not produce a rich or warm enough sound in certain works without resort to doublings of instruments to express a composer's intentions. Artur hated this sort of thing, saying it was cheap and vulgar, though his beloved Maestro was not above such tinkering, despite Toscanini's much-touted fidelity to an *ur-text*.

To the Cleveland's board, the cost of the extra players became a niggling difference by which, in denying Artur's repeated requests, they could show their conductor "who was in charge."

To my husband's way of thinking, the extra players were what the orchestra wanted to finish what for six years he had been building. "All I need for Cleveland to be the equal of NBC or the Philharmonic is that damned handful of strings," he would say disgruntledly. "They would be the orchestra's soul."

The board members, however, were pleased by what they heard in Severance Hall without comparisons to other orchestras and budgetary increments. Indeed, they were constantly tightening up on costs. Artur, hoping to gain his extra men, foreswore all future operatic productions (even though the audiences loved them) and held large choral works to a minimum. But when he made these concessions to men of a lesser calibre and understanding than a Severance, Ginn, or Blossom, Artur found that he had played into the hands of cost accountants. His new president, Thomas Sidlo, and the board were tougher and less sensitive to artistry than my husband had expected, and one frustration after another came out of their meetings.

Goat farming diverted Artur from these concerns to the limited extent that it could at long distance. But its demands led to separations depressing to both of us. I had to spend many weeks alone at Stockbridge trying against great odds to change the milk-drinking habits of our corner of Massachusetts. Being alone in that great stone house on bleak winter mornings was anything but pleasant. I could feel myself rattling around in it. For company, I had only my dog, Lassie, our uncommunicative farmer, and the drifting snows which the winds sculpted into weird and fantastic shapes. One morning on my way to the barn a drift, perhaps no more than four feet deep, tripped me, plunging me into its cold white depths, seemingly bottomless. I thought I would suffocate as I fell deeper and deeper with nothing to grab hold of but more of the cold, yielding snow that stopped my ears and nose. Our farmer, thinking I was a strayed goat, pulled me out.

I was able to rejoin Artur in New York for his appearances with the NBC, the four concerts which the radio company's management had thrown to Artur like a bone. Maestro Toscanini was away on his winter vacation.

The NBC concerts were attracting greater public and critical attention that season. Young Barbirolli and the Philharmonic were now under severe attack from the musical press. People from the Philharmonic's board realized their mistake in following Arthur Judson's advice rather than Toscanini's. Sibelius and Elgar had had their hearings, but the public had found them wanting. People from the Philharmonic were regularly entertaining us, sounding Artur out about the likelihood of coming East. Their covert offers flattered him, and he worked all the harder with the NBC, almost as if to prove his qualifications for that post Maestro himself had designated Rodzinski's. Artur's reviews were excellent, and the warm admiration of New York's fickle public also gave him hope that eventually the city would be his.

Walking back to the Essex House from NBC's Studio 8-H one day, Artur said, "I feel my future is here, you'll see."

These words made me happy. His disgruntlement with Cleveland's board over the extra stands of string players was brewing into a confrontation. His ordinarily alternating cheeriness or flurries of rage had settled into a sort of even pessimism. Toscanini had taken to calling him "*un uomo ombroso*," a gloomy man. But within was a volcanic force expecting to burst its bounds, hopefully in some constructive way. Thus when he said, "Some day this city will be mine," I could take heart.

Since the prospects of accomplishing what he wanted to with Cleveland were diminishing, Artur began seriously to think of a change. His greatest satisfaction would have been to share the honors with Toscanini, his hope from the moment he began developing the NBC Symphony Orchestra. But the puzzling behavior of NBC's officials, including the contractual chicanery of the top management, seemed to preclude that. We tried to explain the odd ways of John Royal, Chotzinoff, and others as reactions to Artur's erratic handling of the Shostakovitch Symphony, and his momentary dissatisfaction with the NBC orchestra's sound before delivering the ensemble to Maestro. But both of these incidents occurred *after* the hoodwinkery of the contract.

In any case Artur began to extend his connections with the Philharmonic board. He had heard that Marshall Field, the Chicago millionaire and newspaper publisher (*PM* was then his New York project) who served as the Philharmonic's chairman, was a patient of the brilliant Russian psychoanalyst Dr. Gregory Zilboorg. We did not know Field, but through some friends we met Zilboorg. From their first encounter, Artur and Gregory became good friends. They shared many personality traits, including impulsiveness, and an enthusiasm for photography.

Initially, Artur was frightened by the idea of psychiatry. In his opinion it had aspects of a dangerous fraud. Still, when after talking about it casually, Zilboorg proposed that Artur and he have some therapeutic sessions, my husband relented. He agreed because Gregory had approached the idea as a friend and human being rather than as a technologist of the emotions.

I long knew that Artur needed some kind of help. His suspicions concerning certain happenings in his career verged on the paranoid. "You are too ready to find enemies, Artur," Zilboorg said, allowing that even paranoiacs have real enemies, however. "But we must learn how to live with them without destroying ourselves with fear."

This, for a while, made sense to Artur. He had several sessions with Gregory, and it seemed to me that Artur was better able to control his suspicions whenever the oddities of the NBC matter were broached, or Arthur Judson's name came up. Unfortunately, the sessions stopped after we passed a Sunday afternoon with Zilboorg and his family at their country home. On the drive back into New York City, Artur declared, "That man can't help me — why, he is as crazy as I am, and certainly just as mean to his wife!!"

"*Just* as mean?" I asked, incredulously.

"Well, you saw how he spoke to her."

Artur and I celebrated Christmas in New York in 1938. He led NBC in its Christmas Eve program that year, the anniversary of Maestro taking over his new ensemble. And where Toscanini had presented the Brahms First Symphony, Artur set Schoenberg's Brahms G Minor Quartet arrangement as his concert's climax, having prevailed at last against Chotzinoff's cost objections.

Our Christmas dinner was taken with the Damrosch clan, Papa, Mrs. Damrosch and their children and children's families. Polly and Sidney Howard were there, and the playwright and conductor discussed the virtues of goats over cows, and the brute power of a Cletrac Caterpillar Tractor. Artur almost had sold Sidney on buying one of those huge machines.

Papa Damrosch was a special person for Artur: the older man, while active as director of the New York Symphony (before its merger with the Philharmonic Society of New York), had invited Stokowski's "assistant" to conduct in 1928. The critics had said then that Rodzinski was "likely to make a name for himself." A decade later, Papa Damrosch was able to lift his glass at the dinner table to toast "the young man who fulfilled his promise."

New Year's Eve was not as pleasant as it should have been. The final concert of Artur's last four NBC engagements was on the last day of 1938. The featured work was Alexander Scriabin's *Divine Poem*, a composition which requires an augmented orchestra. In rehearsal Artur did not find the additional trombone players at their stands. He was furious. Phil Spitalny, the orchestra's manager, told him that "No money was available for the men . . . be satisfied with what you have, maestro!" Artur took the matter "upstairs" to John Royal, and to Samuel Chotzinoff who, at least as a musician and "critic," should have been able to understand Artur's insistence on the extra men. Both executive and "critic" replied alike: "This orchestra is too expensive. NBC can afford additional money only for Toscanini." Artur was affronted and frustrated. He would have gladly changed the program had he known the amplified orchestra would be "too expensive"; but he did not hear of this until long after the program had been announced nationally. Therefore, and reluctantly, he had no option but to play, in Toscanini's presence, the Scriabin with the men at his command.

Despite a thinner sound, Artur managed to be as faithful to the intent of the *Divine Poem* as he could. The orcherstra played brilliantly and the public in Studio 8-H gave Artur a great ovation. Few people missed the handful of brass.

After the concert, David and Mrs. Sarnoff gave a reception to welcome the New Year and friends to their new home. All the guests greeted Artur admiringly, complimenting him on his Scriabin performance. Artur was elated and happily proceeded to the table where Maestro Toscanini was seated to pay him his respects and extend season's wishes.

Maestro, in reply to our affectionate greetings, merely tilted his chin upward and wheeled about on the base of his spine to face in the other direction.

We were shocked. Artur looked as foolish and pained as one of those characters in a Twenties film who had to clear pie from his eyes to see. The party became a nightmare. We could not leave though every fibre in our bodies urged us to fly out into the night.

When we were able to escape back to the Essex House it was only to face our pain in private. Neither could sleep. And neither understood how so many years of friendship could end in such abrupt rejection. "What had I done?" Artur asked. "I will write to Maestro and ask him to explain. No! I will go to see him."

At noon, Donna Carla called us from the lobby. Could she visit for a few moments? Artur was greatly cheered: "She is bringing an apology."

On the contrary, she brought us the worst imaginable news: the breach was for the time being irreparable. "You must understand, *caro* Rodzinski, that Toscanini is just that way," she said. "He suddenly turns against his best friend and no power on earth can make him change his mind. Sometimes he does it without any reason, sometimes he makes up one. Either way, don't try to see him, to write to him. He will only become angrier. *Lasciate stare!* Some day, maybe he will forget, and be your friend again. For now, promise that you will not see him. It will be best for everyone."

"But Donna Carla," Artur asked, "what did I do?"

"*Non so*" (I don't know), was her reply; that and a shrug. Either she did not know or did not wish to say.

Toscanini's behavior continued to mystify us long afterward. One day, commiserating with Chotzinoff who had also by then fallen from Maestro's grace, the "critic" told us he considered it to have been a great compliment: "He only does it to intimates. I'm frankly flattered."

Although I kept my counsel, I was of the opinion that Toscanini had not liked the ovation Artur received for the Scriabin, that the older man resented the successes of his brilliant junior. The truth was actually rather remote from my view of the matter; indeed, it was even built on a lie. After Artur's death I discovered that Toscanini had asked Spitalny, the orchestra's personnel manager, of the whereabouts of Rodzinski's extra brass. "He never asked for it, Maestro," was Spitalny's reply. Toscanini, the perfectionist, is said to have become infuriated.

Artur and Maestro never fully made it up. This continued to pain Artur, though by the time Maestro died in the year before Artur's own death the hurt had become a mere dull ache. Although Maestro could, as I saw, be coldly cruel, he was not an insensitive man, and he must have had twinges of regret for his actions whenever he faced the Rodzinski-trained players of the NBC orchestra. Directly under his nose, at the first viola stand, sat Artur's own principal and close friend, Carlton Cooley, sacrificed from the ranks of Cleveland that Toscanini might have the very best.

Back in Cleveland, Artur realized a long-standing dream: the inauguration of the Public Auditorium concerts. He had persuaded his otherwise hardheaded board to offer a series of special performances at popular prices to a mass audience. Big "name" stars would draw the people who could not or would not attend the regular concerts. Of course, it was an immense undertaking, since the hall, which ordinarily housed wrestling and boxing matches, held 10,000 seats.

Flagstad, who had been making history for four years as the greatest Wagnerian soprano then on the stage, was Artur's "name" for the opening concert, January 4, 1939. Despite the board's fears, the event drew an unprecedented 9,000 ticket buyers.

Later in 1939, Artur gave a speech in which he said, essentially, that music was not just entertainment but spiritual nourishment, "as necessary for the well-being of people as food for their bodies." He thought that by failing to offer the liberating devices of the arts to its people America was diminishing their freedom; that if the United States was to have an egalitarian society in the best sense, opera and concerts, along with other forms of artistic expression and thought, should be more than the purview of the rich.

On May 3, 1939, a Polish national holiday then, Artur gave a concert in Carnegie Hall to launch the opening of the Polish Pavilion of the New York World's Fair. He played works by Szymanowski and Moniuszko, among others, and the soloists included our old friend Jan Kiepura, his days of student caps and braggadocio behind him, although he still remained the handsome fellow I first met in the Mlynarskis' home. For Poles the occasion of the concert was a very patriotic one. It celebrated the first twenty years in this century of political freedom and cultural achievement for our native land, though the signs were out for all to see that these two decades might not reach into a third.

We left for Stockbridge and White Goat Farm, as we had renamed it, directly after the May 3 concert. Awaiting us was not only a great deal of work, but also a host of friends and neighbors. No sooner were we unpacked than Polly and Sidney Howard came by with their new baby. Once again, a friend's baby made me regret my own childless state — but that had been part of my marriage compact with Artur.

Artur and Sidney spent their free time together, talking alfalfa over timothy and which would yield more milk from Sidney's cows and Artur's goats. They also talked tractors for days on end. Finally, after seeing the fun Artur had with his Cletrac Caterpillar, Sidney decided he would buy himself the same machine. When Howard's came there was a christening party of sorts at one of their regular Sunday luncheons, as Sidney rode the tractor around for all his guests to see — neighbors, New York theater people, and his in-laws, the Damrosches, who came up for a visit that spring.

A favorite topic at our get-togethers was the Rodzinski goat venture. No one dared yet to joke with us openly about our business, but sly grins and knowing nods accompanied every narrative flight that Artur made about goat's milk. The fact was, for all the nutritive and digestive value in the milk, we had not found a means of selling it, at least not in the Berkshires. Soon, however, Artur began to explore the New York possibilities.

"It can sell," he said triumphantly after reviewing the data. "But there's a problem. We'll have to pasteurize the stuff."

"Good God, Artur," I said, "you don't realize what you're getting into!"

Shortly, he did, toting up huge bills for a beautiful plant with a stainless steel pasteurizer, cooler, and bottling machine. The new equipment made a wonderful impression on us, no less than on the stream of people who responded to the sign Artur posted by the road announcing that all were "Welcome." It was my husband's fond hope that an open-door policy might encourage sales. There were days when I could barely eat an uninterrupted meal. My role as the official guide came first. I was the one who could enthuse over the virtues of goat's milk while exhibiting the imperturbable herd, their gleaming living quarters, the spotless milking room, and the model pasteurization and bottling facilities. Every visitor became a fascinated listener. Some even tasted the milk which they agreed was delicious and without a detectable difference from the cow specie. But not many of them bought it.

When the summer turned hot, and I would most have enjoyed the cool of the Berkshires, Artur sent me to New York to peddle milk. I visited doctors, soliciting testimonials from pediatricians and obstetricians as well as internists. Artur's name opened an amazing number of doors, and the medical gentlemen showed at least some interest. But, in the end, only one or two ever recommended our milk.

The Board of Health granted us a license to deliver our product in New York City, thanks to its almost nonexistent bacterial count. But that sought-after permission only produced still one more problem: how to ship the stuff? Artur's ingenuity found an answer: specially built balsa wood boxes, tin-covered for strength, and packed with dry ice. The milk was not marketed in bottles — they would have been too costly — but in new cone-shaped cartons just put into use for soft drinks. This necessitated another expensive machine, but the cost was nothing compared to what already had been spent. We had hopes that the design and slogan we worked out would convince people to try the stuff. I drew a baby goat on a blue circle, under which was printed Artur's slogan: "Drink goat's milk . . . Your health rebuilt."

We now required extra help. Besides our farmer-gardener, we hired one man to work the fields and pasture the animals, and another to milk, pasteurize, and deliver the packaged product to the rail depot. Expenses mounted alarmingly. Artur was horrified. Then, with the abandon of the drunkard who cures a hangover with another drink, Artur decided to expand the herd to thirty milking nannies. "If we can get around to selling the stuff, we'll have $67.50 a day in income. Terrific!" Or so he reasoned, not having, as I realized, much of a head for business. Just when our hollow-horned ruminants were digesting us out of our savings, a few checks began to come in from a New York goat milk distributor, and these grew larger every month. By autumn, it had become fashionable for musicians to drink goat's milk with their luncheons at the Carnegie Hall drugstore where its owner, Mr. Fisher, cleverly promoted it.

We now had need for more pasturage and hay. Artur plowed up an entire slope above the house, one so steep that I feared the huge Cletrac would tip over. He seeded the virgin soil, and in weeks we had a five-foot high growth of alfalfa. The county agent could hardly believe his eyes. Artur had called the man in for advice on drying the crop. The agent did not know exactly what to say other than he had heard how northern Europeans dried hay on wire fences. What kind of fences he did not say, but nothing daunted Artur. The man who had intuitively solved the problem of cooling, shipping, and now marketing goat's milk could figure out anything around a farm. Artur ordered poles and wire to string a fence. The freshly cut hay was heaped on to dry, and the fences promptly collapsed. More poles were ordered cut to brace the fallen uprights. That did the trick, and soon the hay was dried and safely stored.

The Berkshire Festival lasted only two weeks in those days. The Koussevitzkys — Serge, Natalie, and her niece Olga — just then had no home of their own in the region, and when Artur went on the road that summer to earn money to feed the goats, Koussie and his two ladies came to stay with us. I remember that visit well, since it brought me closer to those people I so enjoyed. I particularly relished conversations with Koussie. He had a way of making a lady feel naughty but good all the same. One day, on his way to a rehearsal after breakfast, he said, "I have the same feeling of anticipation as if I were going to a rendezvous with a gorgeous woman."

He accompanied me to Tanglewood that summer to hear a young soprano who was said to have an exceptional voice. A petite black girl modestly walked on stage and stood in the bow of the piano. I do not recall what it was she sang, but I cannot forget the impression she made on everyone. Many members of the Boston Symphony Orchestra were present, along with the Koussevitzky clan and a few friends. Everyone I knew was in tears, as was I. Koussie exclaimed, "That is a voice from heaven, the most beautiful I have ever heard!" He was also captivated by her impeccable musicianship, and set about helping her establish a career. Later, when Dorothy Maynor became a treasured friend, that first encounter still remained strongly imprinted in my memory.

While staying at our house, the Koussevitzkys went hunting for a place of their own. Madame Koussevitzky was able to find, at a reasonable price, a large mansion on a hill just above Tanglewood with a superb view of the lake. They moved in later that summer, and we gained a new permanent neighbor.

We also lost one: Sidney Howard was killed in a grotesque accident. He had been working on a filmscript and had little if any time for his farm. Those chores which needed the big Cletrac Caterpillar were performed by the farmer who worked for him when Sidney could not leave his desk. Unlike Sidney and Artur, the farmer had only a passing knowledge of the tractor's mechanics, and after he finished for the day, put the machine away in the barn with the motor still in gear. Not knowing this, Sidney, the following morning, cranked the starter. The Caterpillar lunged forward, crushing him against the wall. He was killed instantly.

Artur heard the news on the radio returning from tour. He arrived just in time for the funeral, absolutely miserable. He felt responsible for Sidney's death. "If only I had not urged him to buy that damned thing," he kept saying time and again, and he could not look Polly in the eye without choking back tears for weeks after. Our own barn door remained closed over the snout of Artur's Cletrac.

The day before Sidney's funeral, August 24, Hitler and Stalin signed their infamous pact. On September 1, 1939, the German mo-

(*194*)

torized cavalry and Panzer corps wheeled across the Polish plains. Via shortwave all we heard from Poland was patriotic music and pleas for help.

"I cannot sit here like a helpless child." Artur said. "There must be *something* I can do." He would go to Washington.

Before he left he sought out our Stockbridge neighbor, Raymond Buell, the president of the Foreign Policy Association. In Washington he saw another summer neighbor, Adolf Berle, Jr., then an Assistant Secretary of State. Both men were pessimistic.

"Is America going to come into the fight?" Artur asked. It was too soon to say, was the only reply our friends could give. "If we do, I want to volunteer," Artur said. A citizen of the United States since 1933, he was as proud of that fact as he was in pain over the likely fate of Poland. His offer was politely noted, but as both Berle and Buell told him, there was nothing anyone could do as yet.

On his way back to Stockbridge, Artur stopped in New York to visit with Dorothy Thompson. The journalist, among the very first to warn of the Nazi menace, was a friend of Poland. She had influential connections in Washington, and Artur, in whose debt she was for the Austrian Relief Concert, asked her to get him some sort of work to do. "Dr. Rodzinski," Miss Thompson told him, "go home and make music. In these times we will need as much of it as we can get. The Germans can squash a land, but not a people's spirit. Play music and keep that spirit alive!" But Miss Thompson's pep talk did little to relieve Artur's frustration and concern.

As September wore on, and the air turned crisp under greying skies, Kanarek began a portrait of Artur. The two men had to do something to keep from going mad. While Artur sat the radio buzzed and crackled out awful reports of constant German advances against the Polish Army. The fate of the Republic was suddenly set on September 17: as part of Stalin's agreement with Hitler the Soviet Union advanced from the east, acquiring a buffer zone against the Germans and reoccupying territory Stalin still considered Russian.

Artur's mother in Lvov was in the area controlled by the Russians. On October 1, my sister Marysia and her little son Karol found themselves German captives along with all the others in my family who were in Warsaw when Poland finally capitulated.

Chapter 27

I TOOK a great step on February 2, 1940: I became an American citizen. I was about as fluent in English by then as I am today and knew by heart the Constitution. Having passed the test, I was administered the oath of allegiance to my new country under the marmoreal paternal chin of a statue of George Washington in Cleveland's Federal Building. The occasion was photographed by the press and wound up on the front pages of newspapers in Cleveland. This brought me a temporary celebrity which I put to use.

The Paderewski Fund for Polish Relief was at that time just organized, with headquarters in New York, and I had been asked to develop a Cleveland committee. At my invitation a group of Cleveland's wealthiest citizens gathered for a meeting where I spoke to them about the tragedy of Poland, stressing the need for financial aid. My first speech in English concluded, not with any burst of fiery, patriotic rhetoric, but when my ordinarily hoarse voice choked with the tears that came when the words I had so carefully mastered and rehearsed failed me. I felt ashamed of myself, being publicly emotional before persons who had always seemed to me glacial where their feelings were concerned. But my reaction was foolish. I had misread the humanity of my Cleveland friends and acquaintances. They, too, were greatly moved, and instantly pledged assistance. Mrs. Francis F. Prentiss, Mr. Severance's sister, to name but one, wrote out a check for $1,000.

Although as a child I had been taught the ideals and techniques of charitable committee work by my mother and, following her death, had taken up some of her responsibilities in working for the blind, I had never yet organized or directed such activities on my own. Artur helped me marshall my thoughts into sensible plans. He aided me in writing newspaper articles, speeches, appeals to be made over the radio.

Somehow, money came in, but not nearly enough in proportion to the need. So it was, with Artur's encouragement, I planned a giant fund-raising concert, in the 10,000-seat Public Auditorium. I had hoped to have the orchestra's services, but the union wages were more than my budget would allow. Instead, we invited a group of great artists to contribute their talents for the benefit. Our committee was lucky, or else the cause was worthy and Artur's name weighed heavily, but everyone I asked volunteered: the pianist Josef Hofmann and the tenor Jan Kiepura, who as Poles could hardly have said no, and the Russian-born violinist Nathan Milstein. Jan, at the last minute, was unable to appear. Anna Leskaya, the Russian soprano who had been Artur's Katerina in *Lady Macbeth*, gladly substituted.

Selling 10,000 tickets took all of my time (of which I had precious little, given the demands Artur made), and all my reserves of strength. I attended meetings of every Polish organization and civic club for miles around. I called on stores, banks, private offices. I attended ladies' club and business luncheons until I could not bear the sight of peas and creamed chicken. I spoke in English, Polish, or whatever language would sell seats. I even went from door to door, often approaching people who had not the least idea what a "concert" was. From mid-February through the end of March, I rarely was at home on time for meals, and when I did arrive, it was to face an irritable husband. His enthusiasm for my activities had cooled, and he said so angrily at every turn.

I begged for the few days of patience I would need until the event came off. "*You* wouldn't quit just because at the first reading the orchestra couldn't get all the notes straight, would you?" I argued. Artur acquiesced, but only to the extent that he snorted more than he snarled. The Saturday before the concert made him more cheerful with me. I had sold, with not much aid, all of the tickets, and, all costs figured, the princely sum of $10,000 was in a bank. When we arrived at the Auditorium, he was euphoric. The place was packed — and on an Easter Sunday afternoon at that!

The program, in a sense, was a family affair. Artur (seen for the first time in profile in Cleveland) accompanied Leskaya in an aria from Moniuszko's *Halka*, from which derives my name; and Milstein played music by great-uncle Henryk Wieniawski. And then there were Hofmann's performances of Chopin!

Hofmann was in his prime then. There was nothing that his hands could not accomplish — a separate *tempo rubato* in each line, a delicacy of touch, a thunderous strength. Those later years, when he had begun to drink and his playing became erratic, are unfortunately better remembered by many people. But to me, the thought of Chopin invariably resurrects memories of an Easter Sunday concert and Hofmann's spirit.

When the Public Auditorium benefit ended in success, Artur was delighted. He boasted of his wife's "fantastic" achievements, crediting me with the capacity for hard work, tenacity, and other attributes that ordinarily he assigned, by way of negative comparisons, to others. I was terribly happy. His praise boosted my negligible self-confidence, reminding me that I, too, was a person in my own right. Nevertheless, that one concert was my last venture as long as Artur lived. My attentions reverted to him, never again to be divided until our son was born.

In the spring of 1940 I received a cablegram from my sister Fela who was still living in France; her husband Kazik was directing the affairs of a family metalworking business important to French armaments. Fela said that Marysia and her son Karol were alive in Warsaw, and that our other sister Aniela and her diplomat husband Mieczyslawski had escaped to Roumania. Of Artur's mother, no word could be had. The Soviet sector of Poland had been sealed.

Artur was gladdened by the news of Marysia, not only because it eased my worries but also because he had a genuine fondness and respect for her. She was one of the few whose advice he would accept, even solicit, on such taboo topics as his behavior and music. Unprompted, Artur set to work to obtain an American visa for Marysia. I was overwhelmed, particularly since he also wanted my sister and her son to live with us.

Daily, Artur and I had letters from writers, painters, musicians, scholars, friends and strangers, who were in transit or landed somewhere in Europe, South America, or the United States. Everyone needed help: cash, an affidavit, information. We did what we could, which often was little enough.

When Paris fell on June 9, 1940, Fela, who with Kazik and her young son Karol (named after Stryjenski) were en route to the south of France, wired that Marysia and three-year-old Karol had embarked for New York aboard the S.S. "Washington." After France capitulated on June 16, we lost touch with the Krances, but soon thereafter Marysia arrived.

Marysia and Karol had been on the last ship from France to get through, nearly having been torpedoed. The passengers were kept in lifeboats for hours until the Germans were certain the vessel was not a camouflaged military ship.

At the pier I could barely recognize Marysia: she, who had always been slight, was wasted away to a frail twig, too frightened even to tremble. Karol, long and stringy for his years, clung to his mother in terror. The processing of Marysia's papers dragged on and on, consuming time my fatigued sister could ill afford. Something had to be done. I recalled meeting Francis Biddle, then President Roosevelt's Attorney General, at one of Artur's concerts. He had offered us his services should there ever be need for them. In desperation I called him in Washington. I found him in and quite willing to help. No sooner had I hung up the phone than he was on another line to the chief inspector at the dock. Within a few minutes, Marysia and Karol were cleared.

We took the tired travelers directly to White Goat Farm. On the way, Marysia told us what had happened to her. Somehow, the most delicate of the Lilpop children had grown into a tough-minded woman who survived the near leveling of Warsaw by enemy planes, the street fighting, the casual slaughter of family, friends, and neighbors by the Occupation troops. She brought the news that Antek Wieniawski, our cousin, had died as the first wave of Polish horse cavalry met the invading German tanks. Numerous Lilpops had been shot or arrested for no other reason than that they were Poles. There had been no food in the city from very soon after the attack began, but Marysia had somehow managed. She learned to cook a soup out of three potatoes and a gram or two of fat, the limits of the available rations or the extent of a gift that someone could make. She also had somehow found ways to house friends of the Lilpop family or of Unilowski: artists, politicians, professionals, Jews. Marysia had lived in constant fear of her life, and little Karol had contracted the fear like a disease.

When we arrived at White Goat Farm, my sister broke down. "It can't be really over, Halina," she said, sitting on her bed, looking out the window at one of those Renaissance vistas, Karol clinging to her knees. Karol was afraid of everything for weeks, even a walk in the garden to see the flowers or to the barn when the gentle nannies all came home to be milked. If Marysia was not in the corner of his eye, the boy would shake uncontrollably, then cry. On the Fourth of July, when the Stockbridge Village band could be heard in the distance playing a medley of patriotic airs, Karol screamed "Mama, Mama, the Germans are coming back!"

Artur had a grand time getting to know the boy, and was genuinely pleased to have Marysia about. When once the reality of her changed situation sank in, her spirits revived, and she became an amusing and constant cohort of Artur's free moments. Of these, he had not many. Music and the business of the farm took the greater part of each day. Our milk was selling well; checks came every first-of-the-month in increasing amounts. One for $450 seemed a stunning vindication of all our efforts — until we had to pay the bills, for costs kept step with income. And our herd flourished mightily and splendidly. From one ratty $5 nanny gotten from a priest neighbor, White Goat Farm's ruminant population had expanded to fifty registered animals, each valued at more than $200, costing about half that amount to keep.

The county agent, poor fellow, tried to figure a way for us to turn a profit, but the facts and the figures stood in the way of a paying proposition. Gentleman farming is really a hole in a purse at best, but the Rodzinski venture had the appearances of a fiscal sieve. For one thing, we did not have enough tillable land, which meant the rental of fields from two neighbors on which to raise more hay to keep the feed bills down. But at bottom the problem with the goat-milk business was the sexual behavior of the goats themselves. For a nanny to flow, she must have a kid. Considering the reputation goats have as incorrigible rutters, one would think that a nanny would keep a goat farmer's production regular. This, unfortunately, is not the case. The ladies prefer to satisfy this particular appetite only in the fall. Then, there is the matter of their husband. A billy goat may, with his handsome horns, tuft of chin whiskers, and propensity to pose commandingly on every hillock or high place, be a wonderful sight in the eyes of nanny goats. But a billy goat is also a thorough stinker.

(199)

Our farm's billy was housed as far away from the house as possible. When the wind blew from where he lived, the house stank something horrid. Poor Artur, whose fussy and sensitive nose could not bear the smell of garlic cooking, or even of burned toast! But our herd of snow white ladies loved the smell. How charmingly they scamped up the hillside for their assignations.

The goats' milking days ended after their visits to Billy and then the goat business turned good: the ladies dried up for the winter to drop their kids by early spring — adorable little things that usually came in twos and threes. Since the goats' milk was too valuable to waste on their kids, we bottle fed them with the cow variety. By the beginning of summer, we could bring relief to any gastric sufferer in New York with the sense to want it; but, dismally, when our production peaked in midsummer most of our customers, like the Rodzinskis, had fled the heat of the city. Result: more goat's milk on hand than customers. Clearly, the undertaking was a fiasco, though Artur only admitted the truth when he paid the bills from his private account.

Relentlessly, he sought, and found, a way out of this self-imposed catastrophe: "Since we can't throw the milk away, why don't we make it into cheese?" He first told me what a great delicacy goat cheese was, and then what he had in mind: "Of course, Halusia, you will learn how to make a good cheese, won't you."

I did. The thermometer outside may have stood at eighty degrees, but that did not deter my husband's "Halusia" from standing over a stove, her arms elbow deep in gooey curd, stirring and evenly spreading the golden mess in large flat pans. Soon, our cellar was full of ripening yellow cheeses, the smell of which pleasantly countered in part the billy stink when September came round.

We ate goat cheese until we were sick of the stuff while Artur figured out a way to market it. The price he finally set was outrageous: $1 a pound. "I admit that it is high," Artur said, "but it *is* a special cheese. Homemade, even." Incredibly enough, the cheese sold.

The farm did thus flourish, if only with a subsidy from Artur's personal accounts. I might have conceded that it was worth it had I enough time away from the stove and the cheese to enjoy the Berkshires. I talked with Artur about the enormous amount of work and money the place demanded. The work did not bother Artur much. He hated to see anyone, particularly me, idle. But the money did. Then, one day, he discovered tax deductions. "I can save money by losing money," he crowed. "We really can afford to keep the place going."

My parents, Halina
and Franciszek Lilpop.

Lower left: Our house, built by my father.

Right: Mrs. Lilpop with her six children. Jedrek, Aniela, and Fela are in front.
My mother is holding Marysia, and Antek and I are in back.

Jadwiga Black.

Emil Mlynarski.

Warsaw, Plac Teatralny (before 1939).

Artur (*on the left*) at age four with his parents and his brother, Ryszard, in 1896.

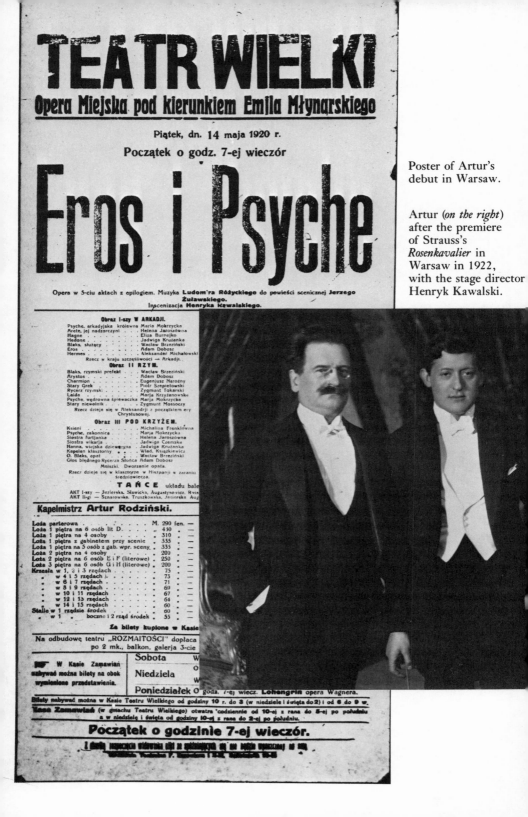

TEATR WIELKI

Opera Miejska pod kierunkiem Emila Młynarskiego

Piątek, dn. 14 maja 1920 r.

Początek o godz. 7-ej wieczór

Eros i Psyche

Opera w 5-ciu aktach z epilogiem. Muzyka **Ludom'ra Różyckiego** do powieści scenicznej **Jerzego Żuławskiego**.
Inscenizacja **Henryka Kawalskiego**.

Obraz I-szy W ARKADJI.

Psyche, arkadyjska królewna	Marja Mokrzycka
Arete, jej nadzorczyni	Helena Jaroszówna
Hagne	Eliza Burnejko
Hedone	Jadwiga Kruzanka
Blaks, służący	Wacław Brzeziński
Eros	Adam Dobosz
Hermes	Aleksander Michałowski

Rzecz w kraju szczęśliwości — Arkadji.

Obraz II RZYM.

Blaks, rzymski prefekt	Wacław Brzeziński
Arystos	Adam Dobosz
Charmion	Eugenjusz Narożny
Stary Grek	Piotr Szepietowski
Rycerz rzymski	Zygmunt Tokarski
Laida	Marja Krzyżanowska
Psyche, wędrowna śpiewaczka	Marja Mokrzycka
Stary niewolnik	Zygmunt Mossoczy

Rzecz dzieje się w Aleksandrji z początkiem ery
Chrystusowej.

Obraz III POD KRZYŻEM.

Ksieni	Michalina Frenklówna
Psyche, zakonnica	Marja Mokrzycka
Siostra furtjanka	Helena Jaroszówna
Siostra wikarja	Jadwiga Cremska
Hanna, wiejska dziewczyna	Jadwiga Kruzanka
Kapelan klasztorny	Wład. Książkiewicz
O. Blaks, opat	Wacław Brzeziński
Głos błędnego Rycerza Słońca	Adam Dobosz

Mniszki. Dworzanie opata.
Rzecz dzieje się w klasztorze w Hiszpanji w zaraniu
średniowiecza.

TAŃCE układu bale

AKT I-szy — Jezierska, Sławicka, Augustynowicz, Ross
AKT II-gi — Sznarowska, Truszkowska, Jezierska Aug

Kapelmistrz **Artur Rodziński**.

	M. 290 fen.
Loża parterowa	M. 290 fen.
Loża 1 piętra na 6 osób lit D.	„ 450 —
Loża 1 piętra na 4 osoby	310 —
Loża 1 piętra z gabinetem przy scenie	335 —
Loża 1 piętra na 5 osób z gab. wpr. sceny	335 —
Loża 2 piętra na 4 osoby	200 —
Loża 2 piętra na 6 osób E i F (literowe)	250 —
Loża 3 piętra na 6 osób G i H (literowe)	200 —
Krzesła w 1, 2 i 3 rzędach	75 —
„ w 4 i 5 rzędach	73 —
„ w 6 i 7 rzędach	71 —
„ 8 i 9 rzędach	69 —
„ w 10 i 11 rzędach	67 —
„ 12 i 13 rzędach	64 —
„ 14 i 15 rzędach	60 —
Stalle w 1 rzędzie środek	60 —
„ w 1	boczne i 2 rząd środek	55 —

Za bilety kupione w Kasie

Na odbudowę teatru „ROZMAITOŚCI" dopłaca
po 2 mk., balkon, galerja 3-cie

W Kasie Zamawiań nabywać można bilety na obok wymienione przedstawienia.	Sobota	
	Niedziela	o
	Poniedziałek O	godz. 7-ej wiecz. **Lohengrin** opera Wagnera.

Bilety nabywać można w Kasie Teatru Wielkiego od godziny 10 r. do 3 (w niedzielę i święta do 2) i od 6 do 9 w.
Kasa Zamawiań (w gmachu Teatru Wielkiego) otwarta codziennie od 10-ej z rana do 5-ej po południu
a w niedzielę i święta od godziny 10-ej z rana do 2-ej po południu.

Początek o godzinie 7-ej wieczór.

Poster of Artur's debut in Warsaw.

Artur (*on the right*) after the premiere of Strauss's *Rosenkavalier* in Warsaw in 1922, with the stage director Henryk Kawalski.

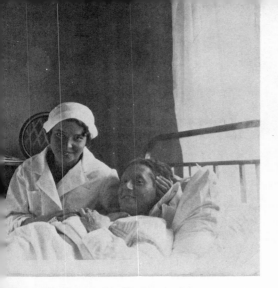

Above: The hospital in Krakow, with "nurse" Halina.

Above right: Leaving Poland for good. My father is very sad.

Below: My visit to California during our engagement.

Right: Our trip on the S.S. "Rex" to Italy when we went to see Doctor Rinaldi.

The famous Dr. Rinaldi with Toscanini, Rodzinski, and Molinari.

Artur with Szymanowski and Olin Downes (June 1932).

Artur with Eugene Ormandy at Salzburg, 1932.

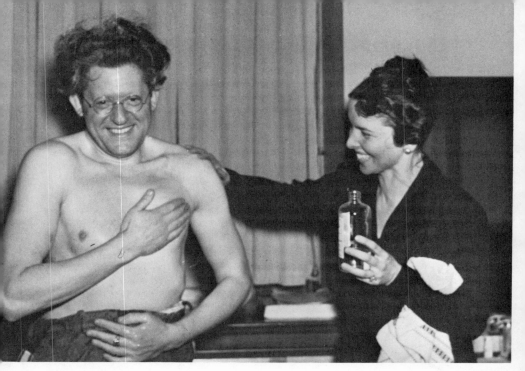

My job.

Artur's three helpers negotiating in Russia for *Lady Macbeth of Mzensk:* Prokofiev, Rubinstein, and Vlady Drucker (1934).

Artur with his talismans before a concert. The picture on the bureau is of his father.

The Cleveland Symphony Board of Directors: Alfred Brewster, Artur, Dudley Blossom (*standing*), and John L. Severance.

The dress rehearsal for *Lady Macbeth of Mzensk:* Ivan Ivantzoff, Anna Leskaya, Dora Boshoer.

Artur studying his scores in bed.

Right: Resting for a few days in Atlantic City we met Bruno Walter.

Artur Schnabel with Artur after
a concert in Cleveland.

Josef Hofmann and Artur.

On this visit Maestro told us he was
resigning from the Philharmonic.

Artur and Paderewski. Our visit in Riond Bosson.

The premiere of *Der Rosenkavalier* with Lotte Lehmann and Grete Stuekgold.

The invitation.

The party. Boris Goldovsky is fourth from the left in the second row. Richard Rychtarik first left in the top row. Mr. Severance, as the Marschallin in the middle, can't be missed. I'm the Ringmaster in the first row and Artur is in back of the Marschallin.

FIRST & LAST TIME IN CLEVELAND IN AMERICA IN THE WORLD!

SENSATIONAL & UNSURPASSED

HALINA RODZINSKI presents
THE BARNSTORMING GRAND OPERA Co
OF BUCKEYE STATE
IN

THE SECRET OF
LADY CARMEN
OF SEVILLE OR
»THE TRAGIC ADVENTURE OF LA TOSCA
AND BARBER TRISTAN, THE MASTERSINGER
OF NUREMBERG, WITH THE SILVER ROSE«
WITH WORLDFAMOUS CAST AND BLOODCURDLING EFFECTS
SUNDAY, DECEMBER FIRST AT 8.30 P.M. SHARP.
AT RODZINSKI'S THEATRE R.S.V.P. TICKETS: PRICELESS.

Artur with the Bayreuth singer
bass Ludwig Hofmann who sang
Gurnemanz in the *Parsifal*.

Artur being decorated by the
Polish Ambassador, Count Potocki,
with the Polonia Restituta, 1936.

Below: Salzburg, 1936. Artur's
conducting debut there.

Our dinner for Sam Barber (*in the lower left corner*) and Gian-Carlo Menotti (*singing, on the left, with Boris Goldovsky*). Mrs. Curtis Bok has her hand on Barber's shoulder.

Drinking *brüderschaft* with Jascha Heifetz.

A party for Jascha Heifetz at Eleanor Strong's: duo piano with Beryl Rubinstein and Arthur Loesser.

Sam Barber, Mary Louise Curtis Bok, and Artur.

Our glamorous trip to Europe in Spring 1937. Olga Naumova, now Mrs. Koussevitzky, is on the far left, the Dushkins are next to Artur, then Natalie Koussevitzky, Stravinsky, Koussevitzky, and myself.

Nadia Boulanger, Stravinsky, Samuel
and Louise Dushkin, and Artur.

With Kodaly.

Artur showing Toscanini a Bartok score, *Music for Strings, Percussion and Celesta.*

Artur created and trained the NBC orchestra at the request of Toscanini.

The NBC SYMPHONY ORCHESTRA

PIERRE MONTEUX
3 Concerts: Nov. 13-20-27

ARTURO TOSCANINI
10 Concerts: Dec. 25-Feb. 26 incl.

ARTUR RODZINSKI
3 Concerts: Dec. 4-11-18

The Rubinsteins came just before the war. A party at Eleanor Strong's: me, Mrs. Rubinstein, Mrs. Strong, Arthur Rubinstein.

Lenox R. Lohr, president of NBC, signing the contract with Artur to conduct the NBC Symphony in a series of ten concerts.

The goats at home in Stockbridge.

The house at Stockbridge.

When the war started, Artur rode his scooter or used the horse and buggy.

Rodzinski the farmer.

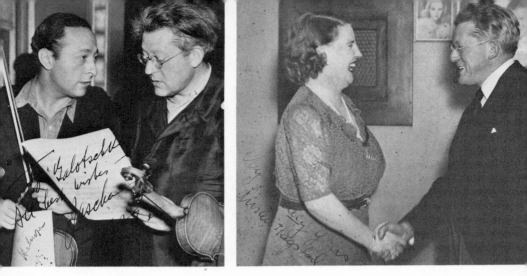

Above left: Artur was very happy with the good soloists who came to brighten Cleveland: in 1939, Jascha Heifetz, for the premiere of William Walton's Violin Concerto.

Above right: Kirsten Flagstad.

A rehearsal for the Polish Relief Concert on Easter Sunday, 1940: Josef Hofmann, Anna Leskaya, Arthur Balsam, Nathan Milstein, Leon Machan (pianist of the orchestra), and Artur.

Judson, Rodzinski, my nephew,
Mrs. Judson's niece, and
Mrs. Judson visiting us in
Stockbridge.

Zdzislaw Czermanski, the Polish
artist and caricaturist, and
his wife, Janina, arrived in
America with the Wierzynskis
in 1941.

Kazimierz Wierzynski, the Polish poet,
and his wife, Halina.

Polish refugees: the poet Juljan Tuwim,
Ela and Alexander Brailowsky, the famous pianist,
and Mrs. Tuwim with Artur.

Me, Frank Buchman, and Artur.

Artur at Stockbridge smiling happily over
his appointment to the New York Philharmonic.

Artur's fiftieth birthday (he was really
fifty-two): Bruno Zirato and the manager
of Marshall Field's herd present a
pure-bred cow named Tulip.

The four Lilpop sisters: Marysia, me, Aniela, and Fela.

The new assistant, Lenny Bernstein.

Ambassador Jan Ciechanowski, his wife, and Rodzinski.

Conducting the Philharmonic.

The day of the serenade, February 8, 1945. Seated, left to right: Ignace Strasvogel, me, Artur, and Leonard Rose.

With Riki.

After the rehearsal of Rachmaninoff's Third Piano Concerto with Vladimir Horowitz and Mrs. Rachmaninoff, standing.

With José Iturbi: the first
picture Artur sent me from Milan.

Maestro Francesco Siciliani,
Tatiana Pavlova, and Artur.

Naples, a symphony concert.

Recording in London for Westminster.

La Scala, Milan.

Happy days in Rome.

Florence, 1957: *Tristan und Isolde*. From left: Gustav Neidlinger (Kurwenal), Wolfgang Windgassen (Tristan), Grace Hoffman (Brangäne), Otto von Rohr (King Marke), Rodzinski, and Birgit Nilsson (Isolde).

The Papal concert.

August 1958 in Cortina d'Ampezzo.

Artur's last happy evening, on the boat.

Artur with his two sons, Witold and Riki.

Arriving in Chicago.

Chapter 28

THE fall, winter, and spring of the 1940–41 season were miserably gloomy in Cleveland. One grey day of rain, sleet, or snow followed another. The weather seemed to parallel the world's condition and corresponded to the mood of the Rodzinski household. Marysia and Karol now lived with us, and both were the source of what joy we knew. My sister's energetic bustle in the house, and her wry, sometimes bitter sense of humor livened things up a bit. Little Karol's charm and uncanny maturity wheedled their way into Artur's heart. He had begun to think of the child as a son, and Marysia and I had all we could do to keep Karol from calling Artur "Papa."

Then, Aniela, my second younger sister, came, leaving her husband Mieczyslawski in London to continue his work for the Polish Government in exile. Though at the time we did not realize it, their separation would end in divorce. Aniela, who always had a practical side and a head for business matters, at Artur's insistence went to a school to improve her English and to learn typing and shorthand. Since our increased ménage with its diverse activities called for more space, Artur rented a house on Lake Shore Drive, one large enough for four adults and a child, and with a spare room where we shared our new joint passion: the assembling and wrapping of relief packages. Pleas for help were unceasing. We heard from every corner of the world, even Siberia where some of our Polish family and friends were interned.

The opening concert of the season was a gala affair, yet it had an overlay of the events of the day. In tribute to the British whose coexistence with daily Luftwaffe bombardments had begun, Artur programmed Ralph Vaughan Williams's *London Symphony*, Richard Strauss's *Tod und Verklärung*, and one of Elgar's *Pomp and Circumstance* marches. The selections were each intended to point up a facet of life in Great Britain, past, present, and via the Elgar piece, forever after. The Elgar march was one of those jauntier things that somehow catches the panache and indomitable character of the English winning out over adversity.

The presidential elections that fall found me scrutinizing the candidates from the angle of a prospective voter. We followed the speeches of Franklin D. Roosevelt and Wendell Willkie closely, with intense interest. Roosevelt finally won our hearts with his solemn promise to free all occupied lands. Naively, Artur and I took the promise to include Poland.

The second All-Star Concert in Cleveland's Public Auditorium was jammed to the rafters with people who paid between fifty cents and $1.50. They had come to hear Sergei Rachmaninoff, who had a fine success. On stage he was superb, but off stage he had caused me some embarrassment.

Before the performance, José Iturbi had asked me for an introduction to the sombre Russian. We found Rachmaninoff in the artist's room, stolidly plumped into a big armchair, his head bowed as if in sleep, deep thought, or unutterable sadness, his hands encased in heavy, furlined gloves reposing motionlessly in his lap. The Russian looked up at me with that solemnly expressionless face of his when I introduced the short, cheery Spaniard. Then, without so much as a snort, he lowered his head. I dared not look at Iturbi's face, as we both swiftly exited. I had heard that Rachmaninoff was a snob, and not always pleasant to his colleagues, but I had never expected anything quite like this.

During the season, Artur began to make recordings for Columbia. It was for him an exciting venture: at last he would be able to reach those massive audiences who relied solely on radio and records for music. Moreover, Artur was challenged to develop a new way of looking at his scores. The line of a piece had now to be broken into three-, four-, and four-and-a-half-minute segments (all that could fit on a shellac disk's side) without destroying the shape of the composition. The problems were ticklish, but Artur enjoyed solving them. Also, he found an associate with whom he could work, a young composer named Goddard Lieberson who combined efficiency as a recording assistant with a fine musical instinct. Goddard's wit won Artur's heart from the start, and they were soon fast friends. Goddard was one of the few people Artur never quarreled with. That is saying much, considering the nature of the record business itself and the number of years Artur and Goddard worked together in Cleveland and New York. His personal and professional qualities were such that it came as no surprise when Goddard Lieberson's name finally appeared on the door of the Columbia Recording Company's executive suite as "president."

Once, after a recording session at Severance Hall, the two men passed a street display of publications put out by the notorious Father Coughlin. As they walked close to the display stand, Artur without warning sent its racks of pamphlets flying with a well-aimed kick. The Coughlinites stood about in the same disarray as their publications while Artur, arm in arm with Goddard, walked slowly away.

The news (and lack of it) drove Artur to distraction. He was often terribly depressed over the lost contact with his mother in the Russian sector, and he was infuriated with a radio that never told him of a German defeat.

Artur's work circumstances did little to cheer him either. The board still refused him his extra strings which fed his dissatisfaction. He felt stifled in Cleveland, particularly since this was the first season he was unable to conduct the Philharmonic or the NBC. He had had no invitations from these ensembles, both of which he held to be the finest in America. The only fresh air to relieve his artistic suffocation was in work with a guest artist of Rachmaninoff's calibre, or the chance to premiere a new score. Accordingly in 1940–41 he introduced more new music than in any earlier season.

Bela Bartok, who had come to America's shores a sick man, destitute, and with no public, appeared as soloist with Artur in a performance of his splendid Second Piano Concerto. Even now a difficult work for audiences, its rendition by Artur and Bartok brought critical respect. Cleveland's critics knew that they had been in the presence of a great musical personality, but, for all they grasped of it, his music had to wait for another generation to be appreciated. Theirs was an opinion the audience seconded, and, alas, the evaluation was only too true. In death Bartok found recognition and that was long after leukemia, penury, and the thought of leaving so much great music unwritten had caused him so much suffering. Many musicians had quietly contributed to the man's support. Koussevitzky, at Artur's suggestion, commissioned the *Concerto for Orchestra*, little realizing that a modern masterpiece, deceptively witty and charming and bursting with vitality, could come from a dying man's pen.

After the relatively stiff dose of Bartok, Artur unkindly treated his audience to a still more difficult composition — Alban Berg's Violin Concerto in a performance by Louis Krasner who had commissioned the piece. The composition, dedicated to "the memory of an angel" (the daughter Alma Mahler had by Walter Gropius), completely perplexed the critics, who showed a singular immunity to the work's limpid, poetic opening or its poignantly delicate concluding chorale variations. All they knew was that the concerto had been composed by way of Schoenberg's serial methods. That the work was also unambiguously tonal (in an old-fashioned sense) failed to be perceived by their ears. Herbert Elwell, who as a composer ought to have known better, wrote that the "soloist appeared as the true hero in the service of what . . . is already a lost cause." Elwell's, as history proves, was the lost cause. I cannot recall hearing a piece by him since leaving Cleveland and the Berg concerto is played today by ranking violinists. Artur, over much protest, insisted on recording the work for Columbia. Almost instantly it became a "hit."

In the spring Artur premiered Paul Hindemith's Violin Concerto, with Felix Eyle in his debut as soloist with the Cleveland. Then came two premieres of American masterpieces: Walter Piston's *Incredible Flutist* and Roy Harris's Third Symphony.

I had often wondered just what it was that Artur sought when he examined new compositions for performance. Roy Harris provided me with something of an answer. He said that Artur liked his Third Symphony "because it is passionate, self-generating; it does not start and stop. It is like a tree growing." Roy also told me he was never anxious when Artur performed his music: "He conducted simply, directly, without any false motions; he was not trying to be a dancer. He just played what the composer wrote. He was also tremendously concentrated."

Roy recalled an incident at one of the first rehearsals of his Third: "In the middle the strings have a rough time of it. The counterpoint becomes dense in a double inverted canon. Everything went well in the first reading — up to the canon. Then it all fell apart. Artur told the players, 'You didn't practice. I gave you the parts two weeks ago. Practice now.' He sent the winds and brass out for coffee, and, while the strings worked, he sat on his high stool, smoking cigarettes and watching. At the end of the hour, everyone came together to produce an exciting performance."

Although the Harris, Piston, Bartok, and Berg works, along with many other compositions Artur introduced that year, have since entered the repertoires of American orchestras, they could not penetrate the barricades of tradition erected in the minds of the Cleveland Orchestra's subscribers. And the press did little to pave the way for a change in taste. Nasty mail followed each concert, and the audience's rebellion forced Artur to give the remainder of the season over to the old favorites. Artur did not mind much. It meant less work, and relieved him of one of his newer complaints, headaches.

With not much urging, Artur went to see Dr. George Crile who directed the Cleveland Clinic. The physician gave my husband a battery of tests, none of which showed a thing. "Then why these awful headaches, Doctor!" Artur asked. "The answer is all that music you play, Maestro," was the physician's reply. And he was right: when Artur stopped reading through new scores his headaches stopped. The blur of thousands of barely distinguishable manuscript notes in dense orchestral textures had taxed his weak eyes.

As soon as the season was over, and we could depart from Cleveland for White Goat Farm, Artur felt much better physically. He bought himself a new Cadillac coupe, and drove alone to Stockbridge. I traveled there with my sisters and Karol in the old car by another, leisurely route which included a stop at Niagara Falls.

But when we arrived a day or so after Artur, we found him in a listless state. His old enthusiasm for the place was gone. There were no new grandiose projects, no innovations in goat farming, not even a desire to do any of the physical work he had formerly enjoyed. Oh, for a fact, he rode his tractor to plow and mow, but duties such as the ongoing combat against the dandelion which he used to relish were relegated to the three former Lilpop girls and little Karol. The expanse of lawn was, in spite of Artur's prior exertions, dotted with yellow blossoms when he arrived, and he assigned each of us a quadrant to pluck clean. With

Artur looking on, we crawled about on all fours. When finally cheese making freed me from the garden, Artur shepherded my sisters and nephew in another exercise. I could not say a word, however; he had to realize what he was doing on his own. When he did, he relented; but not much. He found other chores to occupy us, and the only free time we ever had that spring was the hour or so when Artur napped after lunch.

I was distressed that Artur had no interest in the goat business which had been so costly in time and money. Somehow, I was able to broach the matter tactfully, and he admitted that perhaps he had made a mistake, that possibly he had been over-enthusiastic. "But Artur," I said, "if you don't want to be a goat farmer, who then will handle affairs? I certainly am not up to it alone." Whereupon he said, "We'll sell the goats and equipment."

We had no trouble at all going out of business. Our herd had become almost as famous as Carl Sandburg's goats. Though I was not glad to see the goats go that summer and fall (I really had grown fond of them), I was relieved to be quit of milk peddling and cheese making, along with the attendant agonies of Artur's temper when the time to make up the deficit came round each month. I also thought that the end of the goat business marked the beginning of a quiet time, but in this I was much mistaken. For Artur there could rarely be a period without some all-absorbing, extra-musical interest.

White Goat Farm that summer began its career as a haven for Polish refugees. Friends of ours arrived each week, people I had known when I still lived in Aleja Roz, people Artur knew from schooldays, or musicians with whom he once had worked. Kazimierz Wierzynski and his pretty second wife, another Halina, came that summer; then Jan Lechon, Juljan Tuwim and his wife, and Rafal Malczewski, and Zdzislaw Czermanski the caricaturist, with Janka his wife. Capping everything off was the arrival of my sister Fela, her husband Kazik, and her little Karol. The four Lilpop sisters again were united under one roof.

It was at about the time that Wierzynski arrived that Artur took to reading on bees. He had found Maurice Maeterlinck's book on these insects and was fascinated by the behavior which the Belgian poet so sensitively and philosophically described. Soon there were other books about bees littering the table in Artur's room, followed by an experimental hive made of glass and fitted in his window so that he could recreate some of Maeterlinck's experiments. His new interest gave Artur something other than the persistence of dandelions or his aches and pains to talk about. One of his ailments persisted annoyingly, both as topic and a fact — a backache which successfully eluded diagnosis and treatment.

His back had bothered him more or less throughout the previous season. While in Chicago to do a benefit performance of *Salome*, he had complained of it to the singer Claire Swift. She, in turn, persuaded Artur finally to see a Boston orthopedist of her acquaintance. I say "finally" because Claire had been urging the man on my husband for years;

why, I could never be sure until after Artur actually met Dr. Loring Swaim.

One morning, Artur had me call the physician for an appointment. "I'll drive over to Boston myself," he said. "It will be good for my nerves." Marvelous, I thought, since I had just about had my fill of his nerves, and did not relish the idea of driving with him even those few miles.

When he returned rather late that evening, he was not the man I had said good-bye to after breakfast. He was calm, gentle — so very much changed. A drive alone did him good, but not *that* much good. Something had happened. All Artur said, however, was: "I met an angel . . . the most wonderful human being. No one ever spoke to me the way he did today."

His tone was dreamy. Perhaps he was sedated. "Did Dr. Swaim give you something?" I asked.

"For my back, Halusia? Oh, no. He said eighty percent of such rheumatic pains are nerves." Then, after a vague pause, he said, "You must come with me to meet him next week."

I certainly would. Still, my curiosity would not hold for a week, so I asked what the doctor had done.

"He asked me if I believe in God, and I told him what you already know — that I think of God as little as I have to. He told me that there was the source of my trouble. He said, 'If you have no faith in a power greater than yourself, you have yourself as the center of the universe, and expect everything to obey your will.' "

True, I thought, that was exactly how Artur often approached life.

"The doctor also said that, and these are his words, Halusia, that 'since the world will not submit to your will, you suffer frustrations and their unhappiness. When you accept a power infinitely superior to yours, a spirit that alone has the power to change your situations, to change the hearts and minds of those you deal with, then your aches and pains will go away along with your frustrations and unhappiness.' "

"You will understand when you meet Dr. Swaim," he said as he gently folded me into his arms.

When we went to see Dr. Swaim in Boston, I half expected a fraud; my Roman Catholic formalism made me skeptical of people who spoke of God as Loring Swaim supposedly had. Thus it was no little surprise to find the doctor and his wife to be charming, warmhearted people, and extremely intelligent. During dinner, conversation never once touched on spiritual life, and there was, indeed, no need for such talk. The Swaims lived by whatever it was they believed, harmoniously and in peace with themselves and others. I was impressed both by the Swaims and their amazing effect on Artur. When we left it was with a promise to meet soon again, at Tallwood, a sort of camp where the Swaims would vacation, on Maranacook Lake in Maine. Before then, however, there was a less pleasurable obligation to meet.

Ignace Jan Paderewski had died on June 30, 1941, in a suite in the Hotel Buckingham, down the street from the Steinway Building where the offices of the New York Philharmonic were located. The patriot was eighty. The pianist had passed away many years earlier. His death should not have been a shock, all considered, but it nonetheless was to those of us who remembered his days of pianistic glory, and how, even after many, many years of self-exile in Switzerland, he had continued to represent the spirit of Free Poland.

The funeral was at St. Patrick's Cathedral in New York City. The church was packed while Fifth Avenue was jammed with thousands more, Poles and non-Poles alike. A Solemn High Requiem was sung by Archbishop Francis Spellman who, in his eulogy, said that Paderewski, before his Maker, would be told, "Well done, my son!" Artur leaned toward me to whisper, "I'm sure He won't say that to me!"

In August we went to Tallwood, the Maine camp where the Swaims were vacationing. Artur was overwhelmed by what he saw and encountered there. Regardless of class, education, occupation, or sex, a large group of people lived content within themselves and those around them. Among them there was a spirit of goodwill almost as insistent as Artur's dandelions. It came effortlessly, or so it seemed, and was even contagious. Artur's exchanges with the people he met, were, for him, unique. No one was impressed by his name or celebrity half so much as by Artur being one more good soul among others. Dr. Swaim and his wife made no attempt to put us at our ease. They allowed the spirit of good intentions to capture us. Artur was easier with himself than I recalled seeing him in years.

Dr. Swaim and Artur talked, but not especially of God. Rather, the essentials of the group gathered at Tallwood were discussed. They were all members of an organization loosely called MRA (Moral Rearmament). In England, where the movement had started, it was called the Oxford Group. Often in conflict with the British Government, members were variously accused, among other things, of being pacifists, Fascists, and subversives.

On our last day at Tallwood, over bowls of blueberries and milk, we met Frank Buchman, the man who inspired the Oxford Group through the loose thesis he called Moral Rearmament. Seated at a trestle table opposite him, we saw a short, pudgy person, bald, with a moon face interrupted only by a beak atop which were perched thick glasses that lent him an owlish look when he stared. The name Frank suited him, for he was as candid as the word implies, and had, additionally, something of the simplicity of the Francis who once set Europe ablaze with a renewed and forthright Christian spirit in the Middle Ages. It was significant that we met Frank Buchman alfresco, with birds twittering morning songs and cajoling their fledglings to quit the nests.

Buchman, who surely had been told of Artur as a prospective "convert," recounted the experiences which led him to believe in God, and how to "tune in on His Word." His message held a sense of complete realization and he communicated it with the intense conviction of a True Believer. It was this sense of truth in faith that Buchman emanated and to which Artur responded. Already a man in rapid transformation, he listened as Frank spoke. The vertical crease in Artur's brow, characteristic of him in close attention, relaxed as Buchman's high-pitched voice revealed an unadorned message of living in love with one's fellows instead of in fear, and following the advice of God which was free for the asking, if one would only listen to it.

We left Tallwood with regret. We had come to like the kindly people clustered about Buchman. And we both had come to have a feeling for the man himself, even though we knew him for so short a while. The MRA group was to visit us when they passed through Pittsfield later in the fall, and when they arrived they took over our house for one of the most joyous and delightful times we were to know at White Goat Farm.

On our way home from Tallwood, we stopped to visit Arthur Judson's Canadian camp at Lake Temagami. It was at the impresario-manager's request. Fortunately, Artur had been primed with love enough for all men on earth, and the encounter with Judson was far from the horrid event it might have been the month before. Truth is, they got on splendidly. Arthur noted how "human" Artur had become, and Artur, seeing Judson puttering in his garden, observed that Arthur had qualities unfortunately concealed by the crush of business. Neither, as fate had it, saw the other very clearly. However, at just that moment, a détente was setting in like a thaw in an endless winter, and to everyone's mutual convenience.

Barbirolli's contract with the Philharmonic had two more dreary years to run. The young man had overreached himself enormously, and the critics were unflagging in their zeal to bring him down. The orchestra had begun to sound ragged; personnel discipline was at its lowest ebb. The Philharmonic's directors, with the orchestra's centennial rapidly approaching, had to sleep with the nightmare of an ensemble that sounded barely born. The solution they set on, and which Judson had invited Artur to Temagami to discuss, was the hiring of several guest conductors to fill the remainder of Barbirolli's term. It was hoped the ensemble's discipline would thus improve, and a more varied literature be performed.

That Rodzinski was a name to conjure with in New York, not even Judson could deny. My husband had opened that summer's Lewisohn Stadium concerts with Rubinstein in an all-Tchaikovsky program. The two Arturs drew 20,000, a monstrous crowd in those days. Though neither Judson nor my husband said as much, it was understood that a mistake had once been made, and that Rodzinski would figure importantly in the Philharmonic's future plans. We parted cordially, and truly a new era had begun in my life, Artur's, and surely in that of the Philharmonic and its management.

A new period also began in Artur's relationships with the world at large. On our return to Stockbridge, Artur was an angel toward my sisters and me. Our dandelion ordeal was at an end. Artur had the farmer do the weeding when he could not, for he once more took to physical work, since he had no backaches, stomachaches, or headaches to disable him. Somehow — and I do not mean this humorously — God, by the simple fiat of Artur accepting Him, had in a marvelous way eliminated much of our unnecessary suffering.

Despite all this change taking place, the hosts of refugees and MRA people who took over the farm, and a number of guest engagements, Artur still found time to study, plan programs, and attend Koussevitzky's concerts or rehearsals at Tanglewood. Actually, his was a mandated attendance, for if Artur was not present, Koussie wanted to know "Whyyyy?"

It was thanks to Koussevitzsky and Tanglewood that another of the many rewards of that summer came to us. Dorothy Maynor, the young singer whose audition had so moved me the year before, was to appear there with the Boston Symphony Orchestra. Knowing the trouble she would have with the area's hotels, we invited her to stay with us. Dorothy took to our madhouse life, and what had started as admiration on my part grew into a life-long friendship. During her career there were many slights and open insults Dorothy had to bear silently. Her suffering and her talent fused together into the superlative artistry still richly alive on a handful of recordings. It is evident, too, in the Harlem School of the Arts, which Dorothy's determination saw grow in New York as a means for black youths and adults to express themselves in the languages of music, theater and painting.

That same summer, MRA decided that Artur would be a good convert to add to their rolls. Our friends around Stockbridge, Adolph Berle and his wife in particular, did not like what they saw the day the Tallwood people came to White Goat Farm. "You will see, Halina," they told me, "they merely want to use Artur's name and reputation." I could not see that at the time, nor could Artur. What we both saw and understood was that some amazing changes were worked in his personality. Artur had found greater peace with himself than he had ever known.

Among the MRA group was young Tony Austin, the famous English tennis player who had retired from the sport after meeting with Buchman. He was selected to be, so to say, Artur's novice master. When the others left Stockbridge, Tony remained behind to work with Artur. My husband spoke to him about all his resentments, fears, and indecisions, his apprehensions and jealousies, none of which he could ever control, or ever much tried to. Tony then would find a Biblical quotation which addressed itself to the matter and after an explication of the text, the two men prayed. Tony was a sensitive, kindly boy who felt with Artur his inner turbulence and desire for a solution. Whether the solution was truly to be found in God or self-discipline was an issue never fully resolved, as time would show. In either case, Tony's patient and loving efforts with Artur yielded fruit.

One morning the two men sat for the longest while in absolute silence, meditating and praying. Afterward, Artur came to me with out-spread arms, an utterly beatific expression on his face: "I had a great experience, Halusia," he said. "I had the feeling that Christ reached His hands to me, and asked if I would follow him. I now begin a new life, a wonderful life in which you will help me."

From that day forward, the forces set in motion by Artur's first meeting with Dr. Swaim came to a point of repose. My husband's enlightenment, such as it was, led to one of the most completely happy periods in our two lives. Our relationship, give or take the periods of pain that is the cost and measure of love, never before had such consonance or compatibility. That was true as long as Artur remained in the throes of Moral Rearmament.

More than a few of my readers, regardless of their religious convictions or spiritual predilections, may find some of this laughable. In almost every sense I can agree with them. All, save one: that the dynamics of a God-centered life, its mode of attainment or outward appearance notwithstanding, lead to an inner sobriety or balance that is its own reward. If Artur had a problem with his new-found spiritual life, it was that it was not very sober. Indeed, with the zeal of the convert, and my husband's propensity to overdo everything, Artur promptly set about carrying the message to the world at large, disposed to hear him or not. Having tasted the happiness of MRA, and walking in the light of his spiritually renovated motivating demon, Artur set out for Cleveland like one of his beloved Saint Francis's original followers, determined to sermonize even stones into loving harmony with the divine intent.

One of the first things he did was bring sweetness and light to his annual Women's Committee pep talk, hoping to inspire them to fulfill their subscription campaign goals in a spirit of love. I was still in Stockbridge and did not hear the talk, but he must have been amazing. Our good friend, Eleanor Strong, wrote:

Artur Dear —
You can't have any idea of the reaction to your speech the other day! It is simply overwheleming. Staid and primly conservative old dears have hauled out from their dusty vocabulary words they haven't used for years! They are positively belligerent toward this narrow world that has misunderstood you these many years. You are "adorable," and "human," and so "warm" and "witty" and "wise," and "brilliant." Truly — what you did was more than make a speech. You performed a psychological miracle — within yourself and within that hall. From the mere shifting of your own mental attitude — a shift that threw off the shackles of your own disbeliefs (for you know you never quite believed that all you had to do with people to win their undying love and loyalty was to give out a little of your own self first!) People have only been in awe of you before. Now they are in love with you . . . you can accomplish anything you wish here, I swear — if you will live up to what you have started. It is terrific. I embrace you and Halina with joy. Come and take over your domain as the loving and beloved Ruler you are.

Chapter 29

THE changes wrought in Artur's behavior were manifest to everyone. His president, Thomas Sidlo, and one of his tougher directors, Grover Higgins, said he was much easier to work with. Felix Eyle reported that Artur had never been so relaxed with the men in the orchestra as now. He found subtle ways to encourage the players, a compliment here, a bit of patience there. Accordingly, the men played better than ever — even if Artur's morally-rearmed ears still told him that the Cleveland Orchestra would be much improved by more strings. His insecurities about his nominally negligible musical background, though never too far away, were no longer a driving force in his perfectionist's quest. He did things well because he could do them so — not, thank heavens, merely to compensate for the lack of a Mahler or a Richter as his teachers. He now did things for the joy of doing them, not just to impress people, or to make a *coup de théâtre* to the advantage of his career.

When Artur went to New York for the four-week Philharmonic guest engagement Arthur Judson had arranged in the new spirit of friendship which existed between the two men, the Cleveland players gave him a farewell party in Severance Hall after their last concert.

Even the players with the Philharmonic caught the new spirit of Rodzinski. This thoroughbred among virtuoso ensembles, somewhat demoralized by Barbirolli's tenure, was infused under Artur's direction with a new vitality and discipline. And, to underline the changed character of his approach to music making for New York's intelligentsia, Artur's first Philharmonic program opened with Jerome Kern's "Scenario for Orchestra on the Themes from *Show Boat*," a composition Kern wrote at Artur's suggestion. My husband thought the original musical a classic as deserving of a hearing in concert as the works of Johann Strauss or Jacques Offenbach. Flattered, Kern composed the piece as Artur asked, and it was successfully premiered in Cleveland. In New York it was a smash. Olin Downes was so impressed with the notion of taking American light music seriously that he devoted an entire *Times* Sunday column to the subject.

The second program of that 1941–42 guest stint was played on the fateful Sunday December 7. The concert began at 3:00 P.M. to accommodate the radio broadcasts over the Columbia Network. Both Shostakovich's First Symphony and, with Artur Rubinstein as soloist, the Brahms Second Concerto were stunningly performed, and the audience time and again called soloist and conductor back on stage. At the end the announcer, Warren Sweeney, instead of describing over his microphone the action on stage and listing the program of the coming week's broadcast, walked on stage. He signaled to Artur, and asked him to read an announcement. Artur looked at the paper Sweeney's trembling hand held, then blanched and shook his head "no." This much I saw from my seat. Later, Artur told me that he was too upset to utter the words he had read, that he had no heart to tell the public such unspeakable things, let alone the voice with which to say them. Thus Sweeney read the awful words which a large part of America would hear for the first time. "Ladies and gentlemen," he began tremulously, "the President of the United States has just announced. . . ."

The audience gasped. A few people wept. No one moved, except Artur and the orchestra. The Philharmonic, on its feet, struck up the national anthem. Part of the great wave of emotion caused by the news that the nation was at war spent itself in the singing.

Momentarily we were all shocked, frightened, and confused by the rush of events. America became a different place that Sunday. Personal problems paled into insignificance as we became a nation with a unity of purpose and a sense of mission.

But while we were all "pulling together," as the slogan of the day had it, we still had our private lives to lead. We returned to Cleveland with Artur's even temper intact and we were to find Rachmaninoff's sour disposition sweetened. The Russian loved honey, and when he and his wife came for lunch one day while the composer-pianist was in Cleveland to play again with Artur and the orchestra, I discovered this fact. Initially, I had expected that same cold taciturnity I met with when once I tried to introduce Iturbi to him. On this second encounter, relaxed by a few vodkas and talk of bees, Rachmaninoff smiled. He spoke of his youth in Russia, of the golden age of Rimsky-Korsakov, of Tchaikovsky, of Anton Rubinstein, each of whom he had known intimately. He was fourteen when Borodin died, he recalled, and eight when Moussorgsky drank himself to death. His reminiscences were like fairy tales.

Tours had always been trying for Artur. But after his mellowing, my husband joined in the hijinks all touring musicians indulge in to relieve the tedium of train and bus rides. Usually each ensemble has its official jester, and the Cleveland's clown in those years was the second cellist, Charlie McBride. He knew how, and, most importantly, when to make my husband laugh.

One trip took us to Kalamazoo, a place name which amused Artur. It always seemed to him so remote, the epitome of nowhere, and the word itself was funny to his ear. Whenever a player misplaced a note or missed a cue, Artur would urge the guilty party "to get a job in Kalamazoo!" When we settled into our hotel in that town, Artur went down to buy a newspaper to see what was happening with the war. The papers on the newsstand brought him up short. A banner headline stared at him in big, black letters: "Rodzinski Signed by Kalamazoo Orchestra." Artur was flabbergasted. Just as he was catching his breath he heard a burst of familiar laughter and turned to see Charlie doubled up by his own joke. The cellist explained how he arranged for the dummy papers to be printed in Cleveland, then bribed the news dealer to put them on his stand. Artur laughed, too, and thereafter was respectful of Kalamazoo, especially once he found its citizens to be cultured and musically well-informed. He had no idea then that in the same city was a very young boy who was someday to become an excellent conductor himself — Thomas Schippers.

Artur liked to play at Smith College each year, nominally because college students were receptive listeners. The fact that it was a school for young ladies was not wasted on him, however, nor on the orchestra men either, for they took advantage of an all-girl audience and the Smith auditorium to play a deliciously wicked joke.

The acoustically good hall had a balcony that extended over the stage. Anyone there could even follow the conductor's score when they chose to. That night one of the pieces was Piston's *Incredible Flutist*. Artur, as usual, conducted through the first section from memory, then turned a batch of pages until he found some given place to conduct from the score for a while thereafter. He came to the customary place, then nearly broke an arm turning the big pages rapidly to conceal what had been clearly visible to the decorous Smith misses in the balcony. "Who did it!" he said in a stage whisper. "I'll kill him!" he hissed — and all without dropping a beat. What Artur and the girls had seen was a full-length nude "girlie" picture clipped to the page.

Artur now took such jokes in stride, but the Smith incident deserved a bit of vengeance, not the murder he had promised. The same composition was played in Schenectady the next night. At one point in the score, there is an extended bassoon solo. Artur's routine was to cue the player, then let him go ahead on his own. On this occasion, Artur, after giving the cue, put down his baton and reached into his pocket to pull out half a lemon which he sucked on while the poor bassoonist tried to keep his lips pursed and his cheeks puffed out.

As soon as the season in Cleveland was at an end, we took ourselves directly to White Goat Farm and Artur's new money-making scheme: beekeeping.

Maeterlinck's poetic treatise on bees had been superseded in the winter of 1941–42 by more pragmatic texts, plus bulletins from the Department of Agriculture. By spring, we had an apiary with twelve hives at the bottom of our vegetable garden. This was safely distant from the house, although it made work in the garden a bit hazardous.

When Artur worked around the bees, he was adequately costumed for the task. He wore a costume straight out of the Buck Rogers space fantasies of the day: a set of heavy white coveralls and coat, heavy gauntlets (also white), a broad-brimmed hat with netting secured beneath his collar, and clumsy shoes. How he loved to root out the surplus queens and do them in. This forestalled unwanted swarming, wars, and hive divisions that would have taken some of his worker bees off to the woods where he could never find them or their priceless caches of honey.

The honey itself might have been considered overpriced by anyone who bought it. Artur had set the retail value at one dollar a quart. In those days, it was a ridiculous figure. But the flavor *was* exceptional, derived from the nectars of our fields' clover and the wildflowers in the meadows and woods around the house. Moreover, the labels, hand drawn and written by me, bore the legend Rodzinski's Honey.

Our costs, however, were minimal, nothing like those of a quart of goat's milk. The greatest expense was in labor — our own. It goes without saying that Artur made me his helper. I can certify that beekeepers earn every cent they make. The effort it takes to smoke hives (and eyes and lungs), lift out the heavy frames filled with the wax and honey of the combs, all in the midday heat (when the workers are out gathering what they will), while wearing those outlandish and heavy protective suits, is beyond price.

Marysia, when not at her radishes and beans, worked with us. She operated the honey-extracting centrifuge which had replaced the pasteurizing machine in the barns. When Artur and I lifted the heavy, gooey combs out of their frames into the machine, Marysia cranked until all the sweets had been emptied. Later the frames were again placed in the hives for refilling by the workers.

Artur was enormously pleased that summer by the reduced expenses at White Goat Farm. The bees paid their own way. But they failed him in one respect: they did not provide sufficient outlet for his surplus energies. Not surprisingly, he took on another project.

Although the Housatonic was not far from our property, we had no purling brook by which Artur could sit and contemplate the delights of his pastoral life. We did have lots of mosquito-infested swampland, however, and on the county agent's not too sage advice, Artur bought dynamite to blast himself some drainage ditches that might, if a source could be found, be made to flow. Unfortunately, the land at the swampy places was level and would not drain at the rate of a purling brook. But the swamp ditches did begin to throw up a verdant carpet of watercress, and in this Artur saw a new source of income. Victoria and I were ordered to gather and bunch the tangy greens and sell them in the local market. I often wondered if the peasant women who sometimes brought such things to my mother's kitchen in Aleja Roz ever became immune to the mosquitoes, ticks, and poison ivy that bedeviled Victoria and me, and all for a few miserable cents which barely paid for our trips to the Stockbridge market or for calamine lotion to ease our itching. Fortunately, the cress flowered and was no longer good to eat.

Artur then got the idea of building a swimming pool where the ground was not swampy. He hired a bulldozer to dig a very large hole, and, knowing nothing of engineering, and with only the help of a carpenter, built a wooden dam to hold the water. To his great joy, the hole filled with water within a short time, and we had a swimming pool.

That was not the end. He then decided to fill the pool with thousands of trout, delivered by the government. The dam held up very well for two seasons but during the second winter a heavy frost broke it, and all the trout swam to the Housatonic River.

At the Berkshire Festival that summer, Koussevitzky was to give Shostakovich's Seventh Symphony its American concert premiere. He was peeved when he discovered that the Russians had assigned the actual "first" first to Toscanini and the NBC, and that Maestro would broadcast the new, much-anticipated war symphony two weeks before his own concert. He was really put out, and yet not: this very long composition for a huge orchestra arrived in manuscript on microfilm and it took time to have it photographically enlarged. Koussie always had trouble learning new works in score, much less in such condition. (He would have a pianist play each work he studied until he was its master.) Thus Maestro's radio premiere was a mixed blessing. Koussie would be able to hear the composition and follow it with the score. But a dreadful electric storm came up that Sunday afternoon, and the transmission from New York was interrupted by static and thunder claps.

The telephone rang: "Artur, can you hear anything?" Serge asked.

"Nothing," my husband replied. Artur suspected that the old man was happy with the storm. At least no one local had followed the performance, and his would indeed seem the premiere. On the other hand, however, Koussie gained no knowledge of the score.

In a few days a flat package came in the mail. Artur took it from the postman and told me to call Serge. "Ask him to come over immediately," he said, "and bring his score of the Shostakovich."

In minutes, a black chauffeur-driven limousine pulled up to our front door. "Artur, what happened?" Koussie asked breathlessly.

"Nothing special. I just received a recording of the symphony — Toscanini's performance."

The two men closeted themselves in Artur's room to listen. They emerged, tremendously impressed by the work. "But how did you get it," Serge asked. "Never mind — but the recording is yours. Take it home."

Koussevitzky was stunned. "Nobody did such a thing for me, ever," he said. "Aaartooooor, you are my best *freund*," he added, near tears. He was able to learn the score in time for his performance.

My husband often did such things, but his reward was the act itself, for few of his colleagues reciprocated. For a fact, Koussie, in spite of his promises of engagements at Tanglewood and other proffered courtesies, never repaid Artur's many kindnesses. He once did get around directly to inviting Artur to lead a summer concert, but the program he offered was not to my husband's liking, and he knew it would not have enough effect on the audiences. Serge did not much care for other conductors as conductors. When he would have bouts of insomnia, the first Madame Koussevitzky told me, she gave her husband valerian drops, rubbed his brow and wrists, and told him what a terrible musician Toscanini was. Then he would quietly fall asleep. He would often say, "If I am tired and don't feel like making programs, I use Rodzinski's — they don't fail."

That summer at Stockbridge was one of the most idyllic I had known in years. Our Polish emigré friends came to spend a few days at a time, each batch recreating some piece of our happy and now so distant pasts. The disconcerting presence of the war had brought us all together once again, a presence whose reality we could hardly escape. Indeed, it came home to us in the form of a khaki-clad Witold. He had enlisted in the Air Force after having finished his studies at Columbia University (where he had transferred from Williams College). Artur was concerned for his son's safety, although proud of him. On one furlough visit, Wit brought home a young wife, Jenny, later to become the mother of his two daughters.

Princess Juliana of the Netherlands — Wilhelmina still ruled then — and her children, Princesses Beatrix and Irene, were living in Ottawa during the war, but for the summer they rented an estate in Lee, close by our farm. Discovering that we had such noble neighbors, and with children, Artur got the bright idea of sending them two young billy goats for pets. "We'll send them as gifts from our Karol," he said.

We still kept a few goats at this late date for their milk and Artur's stomach. The progeny that kept our nannies swollen were surplus ordinarily given to friends and neighbors to supplement their meat rations. We once sent a kid to the Toscaninis, with whom relations had improved somewhat, as an Easter gift, goat being a great Italian delicacy.

We packed the kids for the Princesses in a large carton, colored with the red, white, and blue of the Dutch flag, and trimmed the animals with ribbons of the same colors. Attached was a note from young Master Karol Unilowski, "From a Polish refugee to their Refugee Highnesses Beatrix and Irene." Soon after the box was delivered, we had a call from Juliana's secretary, inviting Marysia, Karol, and me to tea. Of course, we felt honored to the point of prostration, and dressed accordingly — with hats and gloves which no one in her right mind would wear in such weather. Imagine our surprise on arriving in Lee to be greeted by a Princess in a cotton smock with sandals on bare feet. I, for one, felt a bit silly, but Juliana immediately put us at ease. The Princess Royal and Karol needed no waiving of formality to get on. While the future Queen was introducing us to her mother, the heroic Wilhelmina (who had come for a short visit), the children had gone off to give a seesaw some exercise.

Juliana dispensed with the impersonal address. "Not 'Your Highness,' " she said, "simply 'you.' " So much for protocol, at least among the members of the Netherlands' monarchy, I thought, but I restrained myself from giving Queen Wilhelmina my garden hat when she admired it. We had our tea in the sweltering heat like visiting neighbors, while our children — girls, a boy, and two goats — pranced over the lawns.

We asked the women of the House of Orange to visit the Rodzinski demesne soon, and a few days later all save Wilhelmina who had flown back to London, came. Juliana, her children, and her secretary-companion, Martine Roëll, called at the appointed hour little knowing of the chaos and work that preceded their arrival.

Polly Howard and her two little girls, and Mrs. Robert Casadesus and her children, were also invited, and they helped Marysia, Jenny, and me to prepare the party. Artur, never one to do things by halves or simply, was determined that we make paper dolls in Dutch costumes for the girls, and that the lawn be decorated with red, white, and blue cut flowers spelling the Dutch word for welcome. These things, and the food, took days to ready. But shortly before the three Princesses (and royal companion) materialized, four secret service agents went over White Goat Farm in Artur's company, looking for spies, saboteurs, assassins, and whatever random Nazis might lurk beneath the hedges.

Artur could overcome stage fright but was too frightened by the prospect of the royal visit. The security check gave him an excuse to hide, and since our farmer was busily haying against an expected rain, my husband even had an excuse to be elsewhere. I was heartsick. No supplication could move him from tractor and drying fences. Rather, it aggravated him. "Hay is more important than Princesses," he said, legs spread in the bellicose stance of a stubborn boy. To make matters worse, he had on his farm clothes — baggy coveralls, denim shirt, and a floppy straw hat.

When I embarrassedly explained Artur's absence to Juliana, she laughed and agreed with Artur — haying *was* more important than a gaggle of noble ladies. She was impressed that Artur was so good a farmer, and also so democratic he even worked with the men himself. I could not tell her that he was really hiding, democracy apart. Witold's wife, too, refused to meet our royal guests.

Juliana insisted on visiting Artur at his work. Holland being an agricultural country, the fragrances of barns and hay were nothing new to her. No one could be sure how Artur might behave, but I bravely took the future Queen down the hill to my husband, anyway. She disarmed him totally, first by her simplicity, then with her interest in his work. He, of course, was as courtly as a Gentleman of the Royal Bedchamber, kissing her hand in greeting and reciting a little speech he had prepared as a contingency measure. Having been paid the tribute which all artists since Beethoven have demanded, Artur returned to the house with us, chatting amiably of farms and farming as if he and the Princess knew nothing else. He even got his motion-picture camera out to film the children playing tag and King-of-the-Mountain around a big rock on the lawn. The film turned out to be lovely. Several minutes of footage show Juliana, then pregnant with Princess Margariet, sitting on the grass, as three-year-old Princess Irene falls down, loses her drawers, then runs with tears of royal mortification to Mama for consolation.

We all became friends that summer, occasionally exchanging letters and courtesies, and often met Juliana at Tanglewood where she attended the concerts outside the tent, spread *à la Watteau* on a blanket in the grass, knitting booties and baby sweaters in time with Koussie's beat.

Chapter 30

ARTUR's tenth year in Cleveland and his ensemble's twenty-fifth anniversary coincided with the 1942–43 season. And as the war continued, Artur finally found a way to be of service. Our friend, Secretary of the Treasury Henry Morgenthau, who had been supportive in Polish relief ventures, told him, "We need music to build morale, and music to sell bonds." Artur promptly offered to conduct a free concert for bond buyers. As he led the orchestra at the first rehearsal Artur could deeply feel the need to do his part: nineteen of his young men had been drafted and their places were filled by elderly musicians.

The second week's pair of concerts brought Artur's premiere in Cleveland of Shostakovich's Seventh, the so-called *Leningrad Symphony* which Toscanini had introduced by radio and which Koussevitzky had debuted at Tanglewood. Artur rehearsed this sprawling, coarse-grained score six times, he and the men becoming more and more emotionally enmeshed in its structure. The symphony's power and sweep are undeniable, and it was this which Artur, admittedly under the mood of the moment, was able to capture and project with a conviction he shared with Cleveland's players.

The new symphony's performance was a popular, critical, and artistic triumph. People came from great distances to hear what was expected to be an authoritative reading. The press was impressed by the fact that Rodzinski led the long piece from memory. But what really bowled everyone over was that indefinable electricity Artur generated. What was musically coarse or bombastic glinted with sparks as he unfolded the piece to ears still unaccustomed to such music. Where in lesser hands it could have sprawled unconscionably, Artur contained the work's power like a battery case. But, then, he also deeply felt and understood the experiences Shostakovich was trying to capture, the sense of a great nation and people in a valiant struggle.

The applause and cheers after each concert, ever music to my husband's ears, were now received in that spirit of sobriety which characterized his life under Moral Rearmament. He truly was content with himself.

And then his composure was blasted by news from Chicago of Frederick Stock's death. The old conductor had stood on that city's podium for thirty-five years. The orchestra's board immediately sought a successor, and Artur knew he was a candidate.

At the same moment, matters with the Philharmonic were looking up. When we arrived in New York that November for Artur's guest stint, the situation was very bright indeed. Our stay at the Essex House was a delight. Management gave us one of its nicest suites, one on the twenty-eighth floor, with a southward view of the city's skyline, full of clear autumn sunlight by day, a bit drab by night what with blackouts and other wartime austerities.

Before Artur's first concert, another prophetic little box was delivered to his dressing room. Even unopened, Artur knew that it would contain one more elephant and a message forecasting future triumphs. But though the omen predicted change in direction, Artur hardly knew if the turning was east or northwest of Cleveland.

The day after his first Philharmonic concert, Artur and the New Yorkers went to Camp Kilmer in New Jersey. There they played the same concert for soldiers who were to embark for Europe the next day. The program was full of symbolic touches: Rossini's *William Tell* Overture, Beethoven's Fifth, whose motif had come to signify the Morse Code "V" for Victory in the popular imagination, and Morton Gould's *Spirituals for Orchestra*. The audience was as appreciative as any I ever saw, and it got an encore — Sousa's "Stars and Stripes Forever."

The concert over, Artur mingled with "the boys," as we called them in those days. Exhausted and swimming in his own sweat — he did not even take time to change his shirt — he shook every hand he could grasp.

The Kilmer concert helped Artur cement his rapport with the orchestra. The New York Philharmonic players gave him all that he asked, so that each performance showed an improvement in ensemble. Arthur Judson was much more than courteous when he complimented Artur on improvements in "The Dead End Kids." And there were tidbits I gleaned from talking with the ladies who oversaw the Philharmonic's affairs. Something was in the works.

But whether that "something" was a contract in New York or in Chicago tormentingly eluded Artur. For a fact, New York was as acceptable as Chicago, but the latter post seemed more secure: hadn't old Stock been there for longer than anyone could remember? New York, on the other hand, kept no conductor more than a few years. Maestro had the post for over a decade, but that was Toscanini, a man whose contract one renewed without question.

Artur's performances of the Shostakovich Seventh in his third week with the Philharmonic created a stir, partly through the piece's novelty, partly because of the brilliant playing, a technical élan that Carnegie Hall had not heard for at least three years. The critics wrote lavish praise, and the radio audience deluged the Philharmonic's offices in the Steinway Building with enthusiastic letters. If the wind of change was blowing in any pronounced direction, it was from New York.

Then, suddenly a gust came in from Chicago. Edward Ryerson, the steel magnate who headed the Chicago Symphony's board of directors, invited Artur and me to join him and his wife at the St. Regis "for a drink." The Ryersons had attended the Friday reading of the Shostakovich and were, frankly, quite moved.

All the way to their hotel, Artur agonized over his old dream of making Chicago the nation's musical hub: "Perhaps Ryerson is going to offer a contract. If he does, I'll accept on the spot. No! I'll be diplomatic, and 'think it over' for a day or two." As it turned out, Ryerson was the diplomat, the very essense of politic evasiveness. The board chairman questioned my husband about his interests, but the only information he divulged was that Rodzinski was a popular name in Chicago and the orchestra's directors had not yet decided on Stock's successor.

Such deliberateness in decision making was not in Artur. He always acted peremptorily, and hardly understood people who did not. I tried to explain to him that while impulsiveness might be a good quality in an artist, it was not likely to be admired in businessmen. Artur was content with this thought momentarily, but not happy with it.

The Philharmonic celebrated its centenary on Sunday, December 6. No special events were connected with the observation except that Artur included two works from the program of that first concert in 1842: Weber's *Oberon* Overture and Beethoven's Fifth. The next day, the anniversary of Pearl Harbor, he played a USO concert aboard the U.S.S. "Prairie States," an old warship anchored in the Hudson at 135th Street where it was used to train future naval officers.

For his final concerts with the Philharmonic, Artur performed Berlioz's *Damnation of Faust*, a great piece that had long been gathering dust. The revival was a great success, helped in no small measure by Jarmila Novotna as Marguerite and Ezio Pinza as a handsome and sonorous Mephistopheles. The work and performance were critically held to be the high spot of the season, Artur being praised for rescuing a masterwork from oblivion and doing it the justice it deserved.

With only one or two more *Damnations* to go, Minnie Guggenheimer came to lunch with us at the Essex House. Minnie wanted to talk with Artur about some Lewisohn Stadium concerts in the forthcoming summer, among other matters. She was in an impish mood.

"If you promise never to tell anyone I told you, I will tell you a secret," Minnie extorted.

"I promise," Artur solemnly replied, hand over heart.

"Judson soon will invite you to be the Philharmonic's permanent director," Minnie said.

Artur blushed like a girl, genuinely embarrassed, and considering his talk with Ryerson, not a little confused. "Are you *sure*, Minnie?" he asked.

"Positive. It's all decided — so much so that you might not want to conduct this summer," adding that this was why she gave away the "secret."

"I don't know what to say, Minnie," was all that he indeed could say.

That night, however, he was a man beset. He prayed as never before, seeking God's guidance in the spirit of MRA with a vengeance. Chicago? New York?

The next day, Arthur Judson phoned to ask if he could come by. We made a date for that evening. Pre-MRA, Artur would have fidgeted more than when encountering a new orchestra. That day, however, Artur was as calm as could be, and genuinely so. When Judson arrived at our suite, my husband greeted his onetime enemy with an affability that, not surprisingly, was returned. The manager was serious, but his handsome face wore its friendly drapery. Ringed in halos of bluish cigar smoke, sipping a preparatory Scotch and soda, Judson eased himself deep in the sofa's cushions and then complimented Artur on the response to his concerts, in the hall, in the press, but above all, at the box office. Finally, Judson got around to his goal: "The board wants me to offer you a permanent contract."

"I don't know, A.J.," Artur said. "You are aware of Chicago's interests . . ."

"Yes, yes, I know all about that. But they haven't offered a contract yet."

Artur twisted his mouth in a quizzical way.

"Look, Rodzinski, they have had plenty of time to make up their minds. It's up to you to decide. Which do you want — Chicago or the most important musical post in the land?"

Studying his glass, Artur said, "Yes, you're right, the decision's mine. Chicago has had enough time."

Judson's cigar smoke billowed in short bursts, many of them.

"Of course I've never been one to turn heel on a challenge," Artur continued. "I rather like them . . . I'll take New York, A.J."

Through the smoke one could sense Judson's satisfaction. When A.J. took his cigar from his lips, there was even a broad smile.

The two men then discussed the difficulties. Artur outlined all that had gone sour in the ensemble since Toscanini's departure some four years before. "There is deadwood and dry rot throughout," Artur said, "and the morale of the orchestra is low, very low. The critics don't call them 'The Dead End Kids' without reason."

"That's precisely why we want you, Rodzinski," Judson encouraged. "We know you're an orchestra builder. Well, make the Philharmonic the great orchestra it used to be."

"That is more easily said than done," Artur cautioned. "There will be rough times ahead."

"Think it through when you return to Cleveland. You'll have the board's and my cooperation in everything. When you come back, we can talk details." As he walked with Artur to the door, Judson's step had a spring to it which suggested high spirits.

"And please say nothing when you get home. The board would like to break the news."

The two vigorously pumped hands as they parted, the manager-impresario looking like a man who had accomplished his end and my husband flushed with exhilaration.

Before bed that night, we talked about the differences between Chicago and New York. Artur had wanted the post old Stock had held because it offered the possibility of once more doing opera in conjunction with the regular work of the season. Opera in New York was nearly out of the question. Still, Chicago had not made any offer as yet, and Judson had. As to the difficulty of working with A.J. again, Artur seemed to see no great or immediate collision. My husband's fears had been moderated by MRA, and Judson had responded to Artur's new and positive behavior. Had there been any deep concern over a possible confrontation with the manager-impresario, it was minimized by two things for which Artur had hungered for some time now: challenge and change.

Back in Cleveland, Artur found it hard not to speak about his impending move. He loved the orchestra which he had so carefully built up. He also knew that many players remained in the city solely to work with their conductor. In a sense he thought he would betray the men if he left. Yet he would betray himself if he remained. Still, as his successors discovered, no one could make further headway with the ensemble without additional stands of strings, and the present board, for which Artur had little affection, was as obdurate as ever on the subject of "Rodzinski's handful of strings."

Then, on December 29, 1942, the Philharmonic's press release went out. New York and our hometown papers carried the story on their front pages, along with editorial comments praising and congratulating Rodzinski. The congratulations of our friends were somewhat reserved. Many Clevelanders thought they had a proprietary claim to my husband and his talents. Perhaps the most regretful good wishes came from Ryerson in Chicago.

"We rather hoped to have you in Chicago next season," he said on the telephone.

"And I had hoped to be with you," Artur replied, "but three months passed since Stock's death. It didn't seem you were all that interested."

"We only recently made our decision," Ryerson said.

"I'm sorry about the matter, too," Artur sincerely returned, "but New York acted sooner, and I was obliged to answer on the spot."

Truth was, the line for the Philharmonic post was a long one. Toscanini himself might have quit the NBC and returned for a large enough fee. Koussevitzky was restive in Boston, and difficulties with the American Federation of Musicians' *capo*, James Caesar Petrillo, were not helping much. Sir Thomas Beecham was looking for a permanent post as was Bruno Walter. One of the reasons for the board bypassing these men in favor of Artur was age. Maestro was seventy-five at the time, the others in their late sixties. Artur was a needed infusion of youth. Another young conductor under consideration was Dimitri Mitropoulos. *Time* thought him more brilliant, if less tough, than Artur, but Henry Luce's critic knew the Greek only from a few guest conductor appearances away from his Minneapolis Symphony home. It is ironic that when Mitropoulos finally did take over the Philharmonic, his brilliance quickly dulled and his lack of discipline nearly wrecked the orchestra. It is also ironic that Artur's one-time assistant, Leonard Bernstein, was later heralded by the critics as the only man who could pull the ensemble together again.

Soon Artur was busy planning New York programs and working to finish his last Cleveland season with the flair and dash it deserved.

The Cleveland had excellent solosits in 1942–43. Artur introduced the Chilean pianist Claudio Arrau. Alexander Brailowsky made a return engagement with a Chopin concerto. Leonard Rose, who had joined the orchestra as Artur's first cellist, gave a superb performance of the Dvorak concerto. Tossy Spivakovsky, the new concertmaster, introduced the Bartok Violin Concerto. And Artur Rubinstein, as a tribute to Rachmaninoff who had died in Hollywood in March 1943, played the plush C Minor Concerto. Two All-Star Concerts in the Public Auditorium featured Marian Anderson and Fritz Kreisler.

Artur especially loved this great man and great artist. At the rehearsal for this concert Kreisler took off his jacket and stood in his shirtsleeves and suspenders next to Artur who was ready to start. Suddenly Kreisler turned to him. "You know this Concerto. I know it, too. Let's go home." And, of course, the Concerto went perfectly well.

As for American music that season, Artur introduced new works by Copland (his *Billy the Kid*), Paul Creston, Cleveland's own Herbert Elwell, Gershwin, and Edward MacDowell's *Suite from Childhood*. The audience was developing a taste for homegrown products possibly because the war had made musical chauvinism rather fashionable. Whatever the reason, people took unfamiliar music more in stride than in earlier seasons, and they enthusiastically applauded Artur with a tinge of justifiable pride. He was not just Cleveland's possession, but the nation's: the Philharmonic post was at the top of the American musical mountain.

As the time to leave for New York drew nearer, the meaning of the move became clearer to Cleveland. Thomas Sidlo, the board chairman, began to realize how much he had been able to take for granted during Artur's tenure. For one thing, he now had to find another conductor, and solicited (and rejected) my husband's advice. Artur proposed George Szell, Alfred Wallenstein, Vladimir Golschmann and Fritz Reiner as successors. Sidlo wrote down the names, then forgot where he put the list. A contract was signed with young Erich Leinsdorf, the gifted conductor Artur had first encountered at Salzburg working as Maestro's assistant. Leinsdorf, who had become an assistant to Artur Bodanzky at the Metropolitan Opera, was, unfortunately, not much more experienced, nor had he a larger repertoire, when he came to Cleveland, than was poor Barbirolli when the latter was signed for the Philharmonic. That both men grew enormously in later years one would hardly dispute.

There were a few Clevelanders who, rather than take pride in their city having been home to a great conductor, took offense at Artur's wish to leave. Most, however, graciously shared in his achievement. The *Plain Dealer* editorialized:

> No higher honor could be bestowed on a musician than that which comes to Artur Rodzinski in his appointment as musical director and conductor of the famed New York Philharmonic Symphony Orchestra. Dr. Rodzinski is a world figure, but his ten years at Severance Hall have made him a Clevelander, and the community is justly proud of him. We wish him unbounded success.

Chapter 31

ARTUR's tenure with the New York Philharmonic began on January 13, 1943. It ended exactly to the day five years later. He began his direction of the orchestra with a scandal of his own making that was rehearsed in the press. He ended it the identical way.

When Artur, while still under contract to the Cleveland's board, took up the affairs of the Philharmonic, there were a number of distasteful things to be done. According to the terms of his New York contract, he was to review and make decisions concerning the orchestra's personnel and its ability to contribute to the new director's vision of an improved ensemble. This meant assessing each player. And such assessments would have to be made apart from those sentimental and human considerations to which Artur, no less than the players, would be prone: longevity in the Philharmonic's ranks, age, family, personal problems. To refuse to renew a man's contract in a city such as New York can be or seem to be a heartless move. To have been refused continued membership in the exclusive club that is the Philharmonic is anything but a professional credit, especially when in middle life a player will find a queue of skilled youngsters already forming in his shadow.

Marshall Field, the Philharmonic's cultured chairman, and Arthur Judson had both backed my husband in whatever actions he felt would be necessary to bring the orchestra up to standard. Indeed, he was contractually mandated by them to hire and fire as exigency demanded. But Artur was aware of the hardships that could come from letting go the "deadwood" and "dry rot" which he knew weakened the various sections of the orchestra. He was personally deeply pained by the prospect. There was more than one sleepless night in which I went to his bed to find him restive, or sitting up, his face a mask barely illuminated by his cigarette. "I have known these men for years, how can I do it to them," he would ask again and again.

Having worked with the orchestra so often and with such care for so many seasons as a guest, Artur knew which men played well, which ones worked with or without enthusiasm, who faked his part. He also knew of the personal life of a number of them through his first-hand contact with the men — and, often, through the observations of Maurice Van Praag, the orchestra's personnel manager and Arthur Judson's man. Having come from the orchestra's ranks himself (with a brother then still among the players), Van Praag had many old scores to settle, and knew well enough the mode of intrigue that was the Philharmonic's uniquely.

Judson had handed Van Praag to Artur with the idea that the man "would help work things out." Artur, not trusting much either to Van Praag's judgment or style, scouted the orchestra himself. I was asked along to attend a concert with him, more as a good luck piece than for my expertise.

We sat on the left side of the house, on the third tier overlooking the stage. Fritz Reiner was on the podium. Artur made a list of anyone who sawed, blew, or banged listlessly, sat slouched, without any sign of tension or involvement. In almost all instances, the men's superficial attitudes related closely to Artur's evaluation of their musicianship and skill. The several exceptions were based on considerations only Artur understood.

The following day, Artur sat down with Van Praag and went over his list. Van Praag, in turn, had one of his own. Of course, Artur's took precedence, but Van Praag knew which men were up for contract renewal. According to the American Federation of Musicians, these men were to be notified of severance six weeks before the date for signing a new contract. Artur and Van Praag worked out fourteen "must" instances where player contracts were not to be renewed. The slate was a horror to my husband, because heading the list was none other than a longtime personal friend, a truly fine soloist, the orchestra's concertmaster Mishel Piastro.

Artur was disconsolate the afternoon he returned to the Essex House. Without removing his coat, he handed me the list which he and Van Praag had made, then stared numbly at the view of Central Park and a wintry sky as I read, in shock, Piastro's name.

"What am I going to do, Halina? He is one of the best violinists and musicians around, but he is no more interested in being an ensemble player and leader than . . ." He ended with a sigh, then turned to go out. "I have to talk this over with Maestro," he said, and left.

He went directly to NBC's Studio 8-H to see Toscanini, who was then rehearsing. Relations with the Toscaninis had never really ruptured. Donna Carla and the children and their husbands and wives had remained our friends. Only Maestro continued to be somewhat distant, although much, much less so. Our gift of a kid to Donna Carla for an Easter *festa* had taken the animosity out of the old man, but we no longer shared the intimacy of former days. Still, he remained the faithful musician who would talk over an artistic problem with someone he basically respected, and willingly sat down with Artur to study the problem.

"I agree, Rodzinski, that these are necessary changes," Maestro said, carefully scrutinizing the names. Then, looking Artur in the eye, Maestro asked, "Must you do it all at once?"

"It has to be done sometime."

"Agreed; but I would not go so fast. *Poco a poco,* a bit this season, a bit next year."

"If it must be done, why not now and all together?"

"It will come as a shock. But it is your responsibility. You are their maestro, now. Do what you feel you must." Artur explained to Maestro that the board, Marshall Field and Judson wanted action. "Then act," Maestro said.

Artur went to the management offices of the orchestra in the Steinway Building down the street from Carnegie Hall, and handed his list over to A.J. "I'll see to it, Rodzinski," the manager said.

While Judson relieved Artur of personally having to speak to each player, he also did an awful thing. The list of musicians "not re-engaged by the Philharmonic" appeared in *The New York Times* first. Artur was scandalized. So was nearly everyone else, especially the players who, in effect, were publicly blacklisted. Had they been released quietly they could have put whatever good face they wished on their separation from the orchestra, say anything they pleased to those whose curiosity might affect their professional future.

A storm broke loose. Jimmy Petrillo, the head of the American Federation of Musicians, forbade the entire orchestra to sign contracts for the coming season. Petrillo even threatened to cancel Artur's union card and standing; the grounds were "defamation of character and jeopardizing the livelihood of brother musicians."

Before long it seemed as if everyone had become engaged in the fray. As a Philadelphia paper put it, "A cacophonous welter of charges and countercharges, fanfaronades, alarums and excursions . . . developed as the dispute [went] from one crescendo to the next."

Artur's personal mail had become a nightmare. Everyone we knew wrote letters, taking one side of the issue or the other. Even Eleanor Roosevelt wrote to ask if something could not be done to reinstate the discharged men.

Publicly, Artur held firm. He repeated his view that the changes were vital to the orchestra's well-being and health. Privately, however, he was spitting mad. "Only Judson could pull a trick like that, and I have to take the blame for it," he raged. Perhaps Judson was just insensitive to the matter, I argued. "No, Halina, he did it to put me on the spot."

Then, just before we were to leave for Cleveland, Olin Downes, in his Sunday column in the *Times*, described the situation in a way that clarified both sides' cases. Olin noted that Artur was obliged by contract to do what he did, that the infamous list's appearance in the paper had been meant to allay wild rumors that had been rampant for days, and that "It is hard to see how the matter could have been handled differently." Olin also pointed out that the incident was not without precedent: Koussevitzky had, at the end of his first season in Boston, "dismissed not fourteen but seventeen players." Such actions were necessary, Downes observed, if the Philharmonic was "to survive and justify its tradition and fulfill the wishes of its public."

The union eventually backed away from its stand against Artur, with the hope that the discontent and ill will the incident bred would be punishment enough. When Artur actually took over the orchestra, he had his work cut out to win back the faith and esteem of the men.

In Cleveland, for those who felt Artur had betrayed the orchestra which had served him for a decade, the scandal took on a new dimension when those players who did not care to remain with the orchestra without Rodzinski resigned. Thomas Sidlo came to Severance Hall to discuss the subject with Artur, all but accusing him of being a pirate. I was witness to what was anything but a friendly conversation. My husband was accused of not caring about the fate of the Cleveland. Artur was near tears of anger and genuine hurt when he said this was untrue. But he could convince no one, least of all Sidlo, that indeed he cared a great deal about the orchestra, that he had nothing to do with the resignations of certain players. Of course, he would take them to New York if they met his standards, but he could no more tell them what to do than could the orchestra's executive. "They are not wage slaves, Mr. Sidlo," he said firmly. "They are artists."

And artists they were and are. They played with whatever

greatness was in them for Artur's farewell concert, a repeat of the program with which he had made his debut in the city more than ten years earlier, the program which led to my husband being signed on the spot. At the end of the intermission, Sidlo staggered on stage to present a gift to the departing conductor. It was a huge silver tray, the weight of which would make anyone falter slightly. But Sidlo was also downright drunk, which became apparent as soon as he began a speech of presentation and farewell.

On Saturday, April 17, the very last performance, the orchestra players entertained us, and made us a personal gift of a beautiful clock in a handsome walnut case which plays the Westminster chime sequence. Its tiny silver plate is inscribed to me as well as to Artur. Today the clock occupies a prominent place in my Lake Placid home and those men and women still hold a special place in my heart.

The following day, April 18, we left Cleveland, going directly to our Stockbridge farm. We were joined there by Marysia and Karol, who even at age six threatened to top six feet. He was a pleasure for Artur to have around, having just that mixture of childishness and seriousness to attract and entertain any adult, let alone one who was himself often only a grave boy grown old. We were able to have a quiet, family Easter together before the spring and summer flow of guests and part-time farm workers.

Artur had some union and other personnel-related issues that demanded his attention even in Stockbridge. The musician's union had softened its stance toward Artur's decision, but something had to be done to save Petrillo's face and, with my husband's participation, to restore peace among the Philharmonic's players. The fact that the infamous "list" had actually been circulated to the press by some of the players who were on it helped moderate Jimmy Petrillo's position; and Artur's willingness to make the union chief's role appear one of authoritative cooperation led to the temporary reinstatement of five of the released players. These men eventually would resign on their own, this being the graceful solution to their embarrassment. Had Artur not left the affair to Van Praag and Judson, this would have been the way things were worked out at the start.

With these problems resolved, Artur settled down to the work of shaping programs that would excite and challenge the players and audiences alike; selecting soloists and guest conductors; and, probably his most difficult job, finding suitable players to replace the ones released and engaging a gifted assistant conductor. Certain players would come from Cleveland in time, but in the interim my husband had to rely on available musicians working around New York. It was not a generous supply, since the better, younger men were rapidly being drafted. Artur also had to find replacements for several Philharmonic players who had already been called up. Somehow he found men who satisfied his criteria, but he still had no assistant conductor.

(228)

His guest conductors were Howard Barlow, the composer-director of the Columbia Broadcasting System's orchestra, and Bruno Walter. Artur was delighted when he heard that Walter was available, and to show he had no resentment against his senior for the business of rehearsals and trombones in Paris years before, went to the man's residence to extend the invitation in person. Walter, I suspect, had forgotten the incident, or pretended he had, and wrote to my husband a touching letter of confirmation. Walter also spoke highly to Judson's people of Artur's amiable respect in waiving the agents, correspondence, and the telephone calls which are so much a part of the hauteur of musicians in places of authority. Artur also allowed Walter his own head in programming, which meant that my husband had to sacrifice works he wanted to perform so as not to throw out of kilter a carefully considered balance.

Programming that summer was a bigger headache than usual because the Philharmonic's Lewisohn Stadium concerts were to be broadcast under the sponsorship of the U.S. Rubber Company. Although Artur would not conduct these performances — A.J. was against the idea — he had to select the pieces to be aired to avoid duplicating items which would be performed when he began his season in October.

By this time, Artur's program-making had evolved a technique of its own. At the foot of his bed was hung a large bulletin board divided into twenty-eight sections representing the weeks of the season. The pieces he, or someone else, would play were written on slips of heavy paper and pinned in place under the weeks where they seemed to fit best. Artur ordinarily began with the dates soloists appeared, then moved to the major works he or a guest would lead at each concert. When he sat in bed, he studied the board, shifting compositions as if trying shapes in a jigsaw puzzle. Sometimes a composition moved into a final position from the lower left corner to the upper right; why, I never fully understood. Somehow, Artur saw a design to each program which eventually locked into a pattern. There was much shifting of a trial-and-error sort before the right configuration emerged. But until that magic moment, a glance at the board through sleep-clogged eyes over the first cup of coffee could send him off to switch four or five of the slips of paper on which he had written the title of the composition, its composer, length, and other pertinent information.

Complicating the entire procedure was the fact that radio concerts had to come to an unalterable (and inflexible) total of minutes. Of course, this has much to do with "time sales" by broadcasters, something that Europeans have sagely avoided, assuming as they do that both time and the airwaves are every man's possessions and not subject to commercialism.

A uniquely American cliché in the days of which I write, and now mercifully changed, held that the only good conductors were imports. This irritated Artur no end, though he surely was a beneficiary of the

(229)

notion. Even so, he found it hard to believe youthful, native talent did not exist. If he had looked among the ranks of assistant conductors with major American orchestras, he would have lost the case he wished to make. Most "assistants" were greybearded, bespectacled has-beens or never-weres, all with impeccable European credentials and accents. The fault may have been laid at the feet of their *chefs*, since few conductors in those days cared to risk the vigorous competition which marks the present American musical scene.

At any rate, Artur wanted a young, native-born assistant, someone to whom he could offer both experience and opportunity, just as Emil Mlynarski had done with him. Artur understood very well from his days in Lvov how, without practice with an orchestra, even the most gifted musician is at a loss. He understood, too, how a chance to advance a career can result from a *chef*'s head cold or an accident. Artur's own successful New York debut, premiering a Miaskovsky symphony with the Philadelphia Orchestra as a stand-in for Stokowski, led directly to his appointment as director of the Los Angeles Philharmonic.

Artur's search for the right aspirant — one with knowledge, musicianship, and flair — led him to write to all the best music schools. Nothing promising resulted from the effort, and he was becoming a bit uneasy as fall drew closer. Finally, during the Tanglewood season, Koussevitzky introduced Artur to a talented student he had had in his conducting seminars, a shy, medium-sized, rather good-looking young man. The young man's name was, of course, Leonard Bernstein, and Artur definitely was interested in him. My husband invited the blossoming maestro to spend a few days at White Goat Farm so they could get to know each other.

I am sorry to recall that I spoiled that visit for Lenny. The guest room I put him in was the one where Femcia, our little cat, usually napped. His first night's sleep brought Lenny to breakfast with what seemed to be a bad head cold, tears streaming down puffy cheeks, eyes inflamed beneath almost closed lids. Too late we discovered his allergy to cats.

Lenny's discomforts, however, in no way dampened his enthusiastic talks with Artur in which the new assistant's duties were outlined. Possibly, Lenny was even grateful that the incident had occurred, since Artur and I then knew how he suffered from his allergy and could appreciate that his draft board had classified him 4-F for good reason. Everyone was defensive about such things in those days, and an otherwise healthy young man had a bad time of it explaining why he was not in uniform.

In the evenings after dinner Artur would slump into his leather chair facing the fireplace, while Lenny would sprawl on a fur (not cat) carpet opposite. The two talked for hours, with Artur prodding information from Lenny about his background, his family, his education. Artur felt bad that so gifted a young man should be earning his living copying manuscript, perhaps recalling unhappily the days he supported his first wife and Witold thumping *mazurs* and *obereks* in Lvov cabarets. It was during these talks that Artur opened Lenny's future for him. His job would be to sit in on all rehearsals and know each score sufficiently to step in for Artur or any guest conductor at a moment's notice. He was also to sift through the new scores that came in and select those really worth consideration. I do not think Lenny at the time foresaw how many hours of boredom and bother this part of his assignment would entail. But everything he had to do must have seemed a snap in consideration of one other job: conducting one week of concerts during the second part of the season.

Eyebrows lifted when Artur announced his "revolutionary" decision to engage twenty-five-year-old Bernstein as his assistant conductor. For a fact, no one in the Philharmonic establishment was much enthused. A New York critic wrote that "it must have taken considerable courage on the part of . . . Rodzinski to make this choice. For there are doubtless a dozen more experienced men available and anxious for the appointment. They may be expected to feel hurt, and some of them to raise their voices in sharp criticism." The man's appraisal was correct, for even Mishel Piastro, the retiring concertmaster of the Philharmonic, had the conducting virus, and later made his fame and fortune leading radio's Longines Symphoniette. Such things apart, Artur was not about to change his mind. He had faith in his "apprentice" and would stick by the decision.

Among our other house guests that summer was Bronislaw Hubermann. This superb violinist was very much concerned with the settlement of Jewish refugee musicians in Palestine and had, among other projects, hopes of developing an orchestra there. It was a pleasure to see the man, not only because of our long-standing acquaintance, but for his very marked Polishness. Hubermann, like Lechon, Tuwim, Wierzynski, and other Polish intellectuals of that generation, enjoyed sharing a common mother tongue and memories of an epoch which was irretrievable. Hubermann was also a great humanitarian, a man with whom Artur talked for hours about the deeper meaning of what had torn our world to tatters. Though the violinist felt that he and others who shared his concerns had failed Europe and mankind in the between-wars period, and here I refer to Hubermann's Pan-European projects at which he had worked with the elder Masaryk and Hermann Hesse, he had great hopes for the postwar world. It gladdened us to see such faith, and also to see him enjoy the warmth of our family life. He had been rather lonely since his wife left him some years before to marry the pianist-composer Erno von Dohnanyi.

One invited guest could not keep his date that summer — Sam Barber. His Uncle Sam had given him a new wardrobe and job. But his army activities did not stop his composition. In May Sam had written to Artur inquiring if he would be interested in the premiere of his *A Stop-*

watch and an Ordnance Map, a setting of a text by Stephen Spender for male chorus and tympani. Like most conductors, Artur liked to introduce new works. Sam wrote that he could not come to Stockbridge because he did not have "any pull in this organization." Artur played the piece anyway.

Maintaining a correspondence with performing artists and composers had always been an important part of Artur's year-round work routine, one that grew in volume and importance with his appointment to the Philharmonic. In his more exposed situation in New York he would have great need for soloists, guest conductors, and composers of interest and value, especially in consideration of the city's insatiable demand for novelty and quality.

The promotional side of his position also involved a certain friendliness and accessibility. Many artists of rank and personal stature are frankly too busy to be interviewed with the frequency that would please the musical and general press, and their séances with reporters often are granted more like imperial favors than the mutually serviceable gestures which they truly are. A reporter needs copy to justify his salary; and an intelligent, well-placed story can only add to the public's interest in an artist. Artur, at least, thought so, but it must also be said that he behaved outrageously when giving interviews. Perhaps the fault stemmed from his early exposure to fame and the press, first via Stokowski, then through the publicity-stunt mentality of Los Angeles. He had a penchant for mugging and flamboyant balderdash, some of which made him appear foolish or irresponsible. But he also had a notion of what made "good copy," and make it he would. Luckily, his eccentric interests, such as goats or bees, were effective story material which did not impinge on his standing as an artist.

The person who exerted a subtle rein and check on Artur's relations with the press while he was at the Philharmonic was Dorle Jarmel, now Mrs. Dario Soria. She devised the ideas or schemes about which she thought Artur might safely talk, then set up the interviews and photographic sessions. That summer when Dorle and Artur began working together, there were interviews for *Harper's Magazine, Harper's Bazaar, Cue,* and *The New York Times Magazine.* The last assigned Olin Downes to the job.

Olin and his beautiful wife Irene often came to Stockbridge for the Tanglewood concerts, using White Goat Farm as their base of operations. The reasons, apart from a long-standing acquaintance which had grown into a close friendship, included the culinary skills of our cook Victoria and Olin's passion for minor agriculture. He was one of those city folk who are thrilled when clods of earth respond to their digging and seeding by producing carrots and beets. He once dug our vegetable garden, then claimed, like a sharecropper, a part of the yield for his efforts. Olin was also an ardent fisherman, and infected young Karol with a fever for the sport. The man and boy would spend hours catching grasshoppers for bait, then loll on the edge of a pond feeding the fish.

Artur's interests in insects were limited to bees, and whatever spare time he had was invested in his hives. Neither Olin nor Goddard Lieberson, another weekend farmer, shared Artur's interest in bees. While Olin dug and seeded furrows and Artur smoked bees, Goddard, who really visited to discuss recording repertoire, would barber our front lawn to a putting-green velvet with a power mower we had acquired. Lieberson's ascent up Columbia's corporate mountainside had been spectacular, but the air at the top was not so rare that Goddard could not still laugh — and the nicknames he and Artur improvised for each other were screamingly funny, but, unfortunately, not especially printable.

For that matter, Artur that year was himself a bit of a joke. Since gas rationing had immobilized our cars and truck for all but essential use, he bought a horse and buggy. Although our farmer looked on the horse as another mouth to feed, my husband loved it. Both horse and artist shared many a happy hour, the one hauling the other while exploring the back roads en route to Stockbridge. Artur's enjoyment usually peaked when he made his way through the town, dressed like a Grant Wood model, with his anachronistic transport. His only competition for attention was the old mailman who had delivered the post that way for years. The summer people had a good laugh at the sight of a celebrity going about in such a rig and get-up. The villagers just added it to a growing list of peculiar doings by the fellow at the old Argenti place.

The summer slipped by quickly that year, the suddenness of the change in our fortunes and our complete happiness making the time pass all the faster. There were no ups, no downs by which to mark off days or weeks. Artur had established an emotional equilibrium for himself, thanks to MRA and its pseudo-Messiah, Frank Buchman, who was also among the summer's many visitors. The two men had a fine relationship, one that was directly beneficial to Artur. At the time, however, all I saw, and certainly appreciated, was the good effect of MRA on my husband and our marriage, which had never been so filled with fine moments.

When the last honey was gathered, the hives readied for winter, and the air around Stockbridge nipped through sweaters, it was time for all of us to return to work. Artur had scores to discuss with his principals, Marysia had to get Karol ready for his first year at school, and I had once again to set up house in a city I knew well enough but had never lived in except as a guest.

Chapter 32

ARTHUR Judson's right hand and man of all work was Bruno Zirato. He was also the world's visible access to Judson and, as associate manager of the Philharmonic, my husband's route to A.J. in ordinary matters. Zirato had a courtly way about him that could make the most distasteful circumstance seem gracefully bearable and a flair for subtle intrigue.

It was Zirato who communicated with Artur about his contracts with Judson and his contracts with the Philharmonic, which amounted to the same thing, for A.J. tolerated only a few artists not under his Columbia management and only to the extent that appearances had to be kept up. Zirato's letters to Artur on the touchy issue of an artist's contract with the orchestra *and* Judson are models of verbal decorum and tact. The letter in which he suggested that Artur, who had severed his artist-manager connection with Judson years before, rejoin the Columbia fold was a masterpiece of diplomatic prose.

His skill with words was a legacy from his pre-American years when he plied, with no special success, the trade of *giornalista* in Naples. Somewhere along the irregular line his youthful life traveled, he met Enrico Caruso who engaged him as a factotum. He dealt with the singer's correspondence, but it was in his capacity as Caruso's assistant that he acquired those skills which Judson came to prize: whom to admit (or not) to an exalted presence, and how to make it seem a favor when it might have been a right. At Caruso's death, Zirato's connections and skills were for hire, and Judson employed them to his advantage. For more than one reason, and language not the least, A.J. had difficulty in dealing with Toscanini when Maestro was the Philharmonic's director. Toscanini at best was a difficult man, determined, inflexible, and autocratic in all matters musical. Even reasonable concessions to management were hard for Judson to gain: Maestro, if he wished, could dissolve any discussion in a bath of acid Italian invectives and a chilly claim of incomprehension. With Zirato as A.J.'s velvet-tongued intermediary, however, Maestro's croaked *"Non capisco nulla!"* carried neither threat nor finality. Bruno's personal warmth, seasoned with just the right dash of servility, could take the sting out of Toscanini's menacing tirades, and could buy time for Judson until Maestro's temper cooled or the source of a friction was forgotten.

It also must be said that Bruno's presence in the Steinway Building offices of the Philharmonic added a touch of humanity to the place, for he was, at heart, a typical southern Italian, able to sympathize with the widow and orphans of the man he had helped to finish off.

I begin here with Zirato at such length because it was he who greeted a nervous Artur at the stage entrance of Carnegie Hall the day of his first rehearsal as the "permanent" director. And it was Bruno's warmth which comforted Artur enough to face what he knew would be a hostile band. Before he left our new apartment, Artur and I prayed, and with the moral reinforcements of various MRA friends, he girded himself in an armor of love and goodwill. He would disarm his "enemies" with the kindness and variably-turned cheeks of the Christian. Bruno's deferential greeting and expressions of good fortune somehow helped Artur to do a difficult and unaccustomed thing — make a speech to the orchestra before beginning to work. Artur did not believe in too much talking at rehearsals. "They know their job, I know mine," he would say. He thought conductors who explained the philosophy of a composition, or the emotional intent of a passage, ridiculous at best. "If I can't generate the emotion musically, no words will help me," he reasoned.

Tremulously, perhaps with stage fright greater than he suffered before a critical performance, Artur addressed the men in very simple, forthright terms. If they were to produce great music, he said, they must "work together as a team." He needed them as much as they needed him, and only mutual trust and understanding would produce the results expected from each other. "I give my heart to all of you," he said, "and I hope that in time you will give me yours."

The players listened, but, as one musician later reported, without being overly impressed. The cynics said it was all talk; the skeptics said they would wait and see. If the speech made no immediate mark on the men, it served Artur's purpose very well indeed. The ice was broken, and he, at least, by being candid could no longer be accused of bad faith. The rehearsal went off to everyone's satisfaction, and that night, dining at Zirato's house, Artur appeared genuinely happy.

Rides to concert halls are a part of my past that I can live without happily. They were always tense, expectant moments, rather like those one has in an earthquake belt when every rattle of plates implies something worse to come. Marysia was with us that night, October 7, 1943, as we rode in silence down Fifth Avenue and through Central Park to 56th Street, to enter the drab rear entrance of Carnegie Hall with our satchels full of extra shirts, tails, fetishes, hair dryer, brushes, stimulants, and scores. Very little was said in Artur's dressing room. His table was littered with the usual stacks of letters and telegrams from wellwishers and friends, except that now as director of the Philharmonic the litter was greater. Amid the familiar heap stood another recognizable element, one of those prophetic little packages. Ignoring the rest, Artur opened the box, his seventh. This time, the elephant was of gold, and much larger than its brothers. The anonymous typewritten message that accompanied the figurine said, "This is your last elephant. You are on top now. Stay there." Artur's smile was as gleaming and golden as the elephant's finish when he laid aside the note to stroke with a finger the line of the upthrust trunk. No other wish from friends and colleagues pleased him half as much as this from a faithful and still unknown admirer. Artur never learned who this mysterious person was.

A.J. appeared briefly to offer his best as Zirato prepared to lead Artur down to the door leading onto the stage, there to administer the jolting pinch. Marysia and I raced to my box, Number 61, which was filled with my other sisters, my brother-in-law Kazik, Zosia Kochanska, and the Polish Ambassador, Jan Ciechanowski, and his wife.

From the opening notes of Beethoven's *Leonore* Overture No. 3, I was overwhelmed with that same combination of fear, elation, and pride I had felt when I had first heard Artur conduct in Cleveland, and that mixture stayed with me throughout the Brahms Second. The audience was generously receptive, calling Artur out several times. Each time he shared the applause with the ensemble.

During intermission, while helping him change, dry, comb, and brush his hair into place, he mumbled his usual questions, "Did it go well?" "Did I overdo my movements in the Brahms?" "Did you hear any comments?"

The second half began with a private scherzo: Edward Elgar's symphonic study, *Falstaff*, partly as a backward glance toward the Barbirolli era, partly to show how well it could be done, and partly because it is a well-written work. To conclude, Artur had scheduled one of his surefire favorites, the second *Daphnis et Chloe* Suite. That night it was a model of musically intelligent orchestral showmanship, and the audience loved it.

I used the shortcut backstage to reach Artur's room before the handshakers, autograph seekers, and old friends appeared. When I entered his room he was soaked to the skin and exhausted. But he was smiling with satisfaction as he asked the invariable rhetorical question, "It was terrible wasn't it?"

His success was absolute, and he knew it. The enthusiasm in the auditorium, backstage, on the street, and later at a Columbia Recording Company party hosted by CBS president William S. Paley was as sweet as fresh cream. Goddard Lieberson almost developed a tic in one eye from winking at Artur each time someone asked where Rodzinski had been all those years past. Marshall Field, the board chairman and president, and Mrs. Lytle Hull and Mrs. John T. Pratt, the two vice-presidents, were proprietary toward "their Rodzinski." One might have thought they invented him. The guests, especially the ladies, took special delight in Lenny Bernstein when Artur introduced him around. People did not mind a bit of youth in the Philharmonic family, not if it was guaranteed to come in such handsome and charming packaging. Everyone enjoyed himself immensely — as the photographs the press took show — including Judson and Zirato.

Our living pattern varied little from the Cleveland model, except in magnitude. There were more rehearsals, more concerts, more interviews, more photographers, more invitations to dinners and parties, more invitations to be returned, more demands from composers, soloists, and conductors, more telephone calls. There were days when, with all the whirl, the fatigues of my chronic anemia would land on me like a bomb. Not so, Artur. Never had his health or his spirits been so good or so high. And the more that "more" was demanded of him, the greater seemed his stamina. With his demon in spiritual harness, Artur knew few limits to what he could do. His working hours now regularly spilled over into our household time.

Artur never cared to go before an orchestra with a soloist unless he had fully in mind the details of an artist's interpretation. "It wastes too much time," he used to explain. Sessions with this violinist or that cellist and Artur at the piano at home often held up dinner while some knotty problem was worked out and noted in their scores. Artur had become so fussy in his quest for the perfect that he made Tossy Spivakovsky, who was to appear as soloist in the Bartok Violin Concerto, go over the work several times, even though the Cleveland's young concertmaster had introduced it with Artur only the year before.

Artur's punctiliousness was combined with an irritating stinginess of words. I said that Artur did not like to "bore" his artists with speeches, the long talks, aesthetic chit-chat and "funny" stories that some conductors use to communicate and relax with orchestras. Artur's players complained he was so quick that they barely had time to turn the page when he called another rehearsal number or letter in a score before his hands were raised to deliver the beat.

William Lincer, who had worked under Artur as first violist in Cleveland, then later in the same chair with the Philharmonic, told me that Artur was "an incomparable master at rehearsals — economical in time." According to Bill, Artur took each section alone, sometimes each stand, and, if necessary, individual players. The men did not care for the first rehearsal of each week. "Black Tuesdays" they were called. Each man could be called to play difficult passages by himself, and this brought on "panic, fear, or terror," depending on the case, as Bill remembered. "One would find instrumentalists in different corners of the hall practicing. . . . When the passages were 'clean,' he combined the individual players into sections again, blending the sound until it was like one instrument." First, he worked on the strings until they were balanced to his satisfaction, then the woodwinds, the brass, and, last, the percussion. "By the second rehearsal, the technical problems were solved," Bill recalled, but next came "the musical structure of the work to be played, the building up of each section harmonically, contrapuntally, rhythmically, and expressively." In the violist's view, the outstanding characteristic of Artur's technique was the speed with which this rehearsing was done. Finally, before a performance, Artur would read through an entire piece so that both the men and he had a sense of the flow and line.

Lincer knew Artur as well as any man who played with him, and his evaluation of my husband's moods rings true to me, for when, around our home, Artur was nice, he was very nice, indeed. But God spare humankind when Artur had a case of the "glums." Lincer: "his personality always seemed to work in his favor. If he was kindly disposed toward the orchestra one morning, the orchestra worked well. If he came in looking at each man as if he were an enemy, the players, with trepidation, tried even harder to please him. Some players loved the man, others hated him. They all, however, had respect for him — and worked hard."

And the harder the players and Artur worked, the more enthusiastic the reviewers became. The improvement in the orchestra was there for all to hear. In his review of Artur's second week of concerts, Olin Downes addressed himself to "further gratifying evidence of the manner in which the orchestra is improving in technical and tonal ways, almost hourly." The program was all-Tchaikovsky, *Romeo and Juliet*, the Violin Concerto (with Zino Francescatti as soloist), and the Symphony No. 4, hardly a collection to warm the hearts of the brainy critics. Even so, the acutely knowledgeable Virgil Thomson could write in the *Tribune:* "It was a distinguished rendering of familiar masterpieces . . . [which] gave the most remarkable evidence yet furnished of the new musical standards and higher intellectual tone that have been adopted this season. . . ." It is interesting that both critics — one no musician, the other a musician *par excellence* — chose to use the word "evidence," so suggestive of skepticism, not to say a trial. But after poor Barbirolli's stay, musicians and audience alike doubted anything much could be done with the Philharmonic, and it was, indeed, up to Artur to prove that they were wrong and that the Philharmonic's board had not misplaced its faith in him.

The third concert in October commemorated two events: the twenty-fifth anniversary of the Czechoslovakian Republic's founding, and the obliteration of the little town of Lidice by the Nazis as a reprisal for Czech resistance. Sponsored by an ad hoc organization called the American Friends of Czechoslovakia, the program of works by Smetana, Dvorak, and a premiere of a specially composed piece by Bohuslav Martinu, brought together two old friends, the soprano Jarmila Novotna and the pianist Rudolph Firkusny. Artur and Firkusny were also able to share a sentimental tribute to their common piano teacher: Firkusny played Wilhelm Kurz's version of the Dvorak G Minor Concerto. Martinu's *Memorial to Lidice* was commissioned by the League of Composers as a result of a suggestion to Claire Reis. Artur had met Martinu and liked the man as much as his music. Mrs. Reis had initiated a series of commissions to leave behind an artistic expression and record of the war, and to Artur it was only natural that Czechoslovakia's most prominent composer since the death of Leos Janacek write a piece for the series. He also gave the New York premiere of Martinu's Second Symphony later that same season.

Artur that season commenced a short-lived series of "reading rehearsals" at which compositions sent to him by composers, publishers and agents were given a hearing. The pieces were selected by Lenny Bernstein. From the mountains of scores that came to the office Lenny was able to winnow a number of worthwhile compositions. Wherever feasible, the works were rehearsed before an invited audience of musicians, critics, and publishers. The composer, of course, was in attendance, and if he felt up to it, Artur let him conduct. The activity was judged to be an important one, but though it was a stimulation to all concerned, it was more than my husband's schedule or that of the Philharmonic could sustain, and soon dwindled to an irregular or sometime event.

New York's work schedule was much more tiring than Cleveland's. Although out-of-town engagements were less frequent, the number of at-home concerts was greater. Thursday nights were the most demanding: the press, board of directors, and more important subscribers attended then. After a Thursday performance, Artur was too tense to fall asleep. He might have slept later on Fridays had it not been for the concerts at 2:30 in the afternoon. At the matinee performance, he was far too tired to give his best, though he strained to generate what excitement he could. But for an audience of elegant ladies, many quite advanced in age, it was truly an ordeal. Artur could dredge up quantities of energy when he sensed enthusiasm in his public. Those Friday afternoon ladies, however, never took off their beautiful suede gloves, and their applause, even when expressing the greatest satisfaction, always sounded like someone jumping up and down overhead in soft bedroom slippers. That exasperated my husband, along with the ladies' habit of leaving before the concert ended in order to catch a train or be on time for a tea. The creaks of their chairs as they rose to go, and the squeaks of the long aisles' floor boards as they tip-toed to the lobby afflicted Artur's sensitive ears like a volley of arrows shot at a musical St. Sebastian. To compensate for the martyrdoms of those afternoons, Friday nights were set aside for visiting friends.

Saturday night concerts were not "regular." These were "student" concerts, and the tickets were less expensive. The Saturday public did not hear the Thursday or Friday program if a famous soloist had been part of the earlier concerts. Most name artists then, as now, cost too much for popular prices. But Saturday's audience from Artur's viewpoint was very stimulating, since he could try out unfamiliar music and young artists.

(239)

The last concert of each week was Sunday's at 3:00 P.M. It was every bit as demanding as Thursday's, but in a different way. All of musically interested and frequently highly knowledgeable America with radio sets could hear it broadcast nationwide over the CBS network. Also, Artur had to make sure that each note fell into its precise time slot to accommodate the commercials. U.S. Rubber Company, the sponsor then, paid my husband and the players an extra fee for these performances, and the Philharmonic-Symphony Society also banked a tidy sum, one which covered the orchestra's entire deficit. While Artur was at the orchestra's head, red ink was seen rarely on its ledger sheets.

My husband knew how his work would tax him, and so he built into his schedule a two-week rest period following each four weeks of conducting. A guest maestro slaved while Artur and I lazed at White Goat Farm. Bruno Walter was on the podium our first midseason vacation. On Saturday night of the second week, Artur had a worried phone call from Bruno Zirato.

"You've got to come back, Artur," he said. "Walter is ill and doesn't think he'll be able to conduct the radio concert."

"Call Bernstein," was Artur's immediate reply. "That's why we hired him. This is his chance — I won't rob him of it. You've got to let him conduct."

"You're the boss," Zirato said, using an expression that Artur thoroughly enjoyed.

We drove back to New York the next afternoon, and missed the radio broadcast. Artur was as nervous as an expectant father all the way. He was happy for Lenny, but justifiably concerned. The program was Schumann's *Manfred* Overture; a piece by Miklos Rosza; Strauss's *Don Quixote*, and Wagner's *Die Meistersinger* Prelude. Most of the music was easy for someone with Lenny's gifts, but the Strauss composition called for experience in addition to talent. "There are a lot of tricks and problems," Artur worried, not the slightest being those of two soloists in addition to the composer's giant orchestra. But Lenny had the tricks and solutions well in hand; and the orchestra and soloists — violist Bill Lincer, cellist Joseph Schuster — did their utmost "to give the kid a boost up," as one player put it.

The public heartily welcomed Lenny. The critics, notified of the substitution, came, heard, and were conquered by the young man's ability. Olin Downes's review was so great a rave that the *Times* ran it on its front page. The Bernstein star was in the ascendent. Some people say he took on the role of renaissance universalist prematurely, and that he has squandered his creative gift for serious composition by writing too much and indifferent popular music. His work as a popularizer brought a generation of Americans into the concert hall. His "musical comedies" refurbished a stagnant, indeed, moribund genre. When Lenny skyrocketed to the top, Artur lost an "apprentice," certainly a "musical son."

Prior to his chance success, Bernstein exhibited an irritating capacity for self-insinuation. When people crowded into the Green Room to congratulate the artists after a performance, Lenny would edge himself into the situation, either by accepting a compliment for a distracted soloist or conductor, or by letting no one misunderstand precisely who he was. This irritated Artur. In time, Artur had Zirato forbid Lenny to enter the Green Room. Artur's quasi-military upbringing precluded pushy behavior.

There were a few incidents during Bernstein's first stay with the Philharmonic that received unfortunate publicity, both from the press and through Lenny's own, somewhat colored accounts. One in particular, the episode of the "sick assistant" and a haircut, received more attention than it was worth. If Lenny remembers the letter he wrote to my husband in apology for a supposed physical assault on his person, he would more than obligingly revise his version of the incident, bruises, death rattles, *et al.* That is, unless the letter was not sincere, but merely a piece of hysterical obsequiousness. After that incident and the letter which was meant to wipe the slate clean, Lenny's father asked Artur how he ever managed his son. He wanted to know because, as he said, "I never could."

One of Artur's ways of "managing" Mr. Bernstein's gifted son was by deflation. He asked his assistant to start a rehearsal of Beethoven's Fifth. The first two measures are devilishly tricky: though they sound easy enough, they demand an incisive beat and absolute control of the orchestra's attention. Lenny waved his hand to suffer the fate of the Sorcerer's Apprentice. The thing fell apart. Amusingly enough, in some of the published essays extracted from his television concert-lectures on conducting, Lenny pointedly uses this same Beethoven example to show the difficulty and art in a well-delivered beat. Lenny may not remember learning much from Rodzinski, but he can hardly deny that his first *chef* made him acutely aware of the need to couple his talent with a secure technique.

Another youthful Leonard appeared as a new star that November — Pfc. Pennario was the first soloist to perform a Liszt Concerto while in khaki. That same weekend, a chubby-cheeked winner of the prized Leventritt Award for that season, pianist Eugene Istomin, made his Philharmonic debut in the Brahms Second.

On a trip to Princeton for a concert in the McCarter Theatre, I had a chance to meet Albert Einstein during an intermission and receive a compliment as the second Mrs. Rodzinski: *"Selten kommt etwas besser nach,"* he said with a sweet smile, "a better thing seldom follows a bad one." Einstein ardently loved Tchaikovsky's Fourth, but against his better instincts stayed to hear John Alden Carpenter's *The Anxious Bugler*, another of those special war commemoratives commissioned by Claire Reis. Einstein was not keen on trends in contemporary music.

Through either fate or coincidence 1943 in New York began for the Rodzinskis in the hands of one Italian and ended in the hands of another:

Mayor Fiorello LaGuardia. Artur, at the Mayor's invitation, conducted the concert, on December 11, inaugurating the City Center of Music and Drama. The evening opened with the Metropolitan's Lawrence Tibbett singing the national anthem, then a speech by the "Little Flower." His short, rumpled, rubicund figure was greeted with thunderous applause. The man who had read the comic strips to children over the radio during a newspaper strike spoke of how much that evening meant to him, how it was "the fulfillment of a great dream." It was LaGuardia's and New-bold Morris's vision that had turned the old Masonic Temple on 55th Street into a cultural treasure. The enterprise would make the perform-ing arts available to all at moderate prices, underwritten by the city and civic-minded citizens.

That evening's meeting with LaGuardia identified for me the little, black-suited man who, after the first measure of a concert, would enter darkened Carnegie Hall to scurry to a seat in the fifth or sixth row of the parterre's far-right aisle, then would hurry out before the concert's end. He was a Thursday night regular and — he told me then — his discreet entrances and exits were to avoid crowds of constituents to whom he could never turn a deaf ear.

Chapter 33

ARTUR's birthday in January 1944 fell on a Sunday when he was to conduct a radio concert. He asked his sponsor and CBS to allow him two minutes airtime for a speech which he had prepared, and they agreed. We had written it together. I should say, rather, Artur did draft after draft, trying them out on me for style, forthrightness, simplicity. No other piece of writing had previously cost him so much effort and pain. And understandably: he would be speaking to millions of radio listeners, presumptuously outlining for them in two minutes what he and Moral Rearmament believed to be the *only* plan for world peace.

While Robert Casadesus was acknowledging the applause of the Carnegie Hall audience for a performance of Beethoven's *Emperor* Piano Concerto, Artur raced backstage to the announcer's booth. After a brief introduction, which gave him time to catch his breath and seat himself Artur read these words:

> In our orchestra we have many nationalities, creeds, types, and tempera ments. We have learned to forget our individual likes and dislikes, and ou differences of temperament for the sake of the music to which we have dedi cated our lives.

I often wonder why we could not solve the world's problems on a basis of harmony. Think what a single individual in a symphony orchestra accomplishes by forgetting himself and giving up his individual traits and ambitions in the service of music! Why could not every individual and every nation in the world learn the same secret in the service of world harmony?

We hear nowadays so much about secret weapons of destruction, but we forget the existence of a seemingly old-fashioned secret weapon — love. The secret is easy to learn. It is simple. It is practical. . . . some might call it co-operation, mutual understanding, teamwork, but it all springs from the same source of an all-embracing love for the whole of mankind, and for your neighbor in particular.

The simple secret of loving and caring makes sound and happy homes, harmonious and prosperous communities, and peace-loving nations.

A great spiritual awakening is arising from the depths of human misery. It calls for a different way of life. It calls for a changed life for everyone. Only when every one of us and every nation learns the secret of love for all mankind, will the world become a great orchestra, following the beat of the Greatest Conductor of all!

The utter lack of sophistication in the statement was too disarming to suffer with a composed face, especially among the members of the Philharmonic and its management. But the little talk brought an incredible mail and telegraph response. People congratulated my husband for saying something that "should have been said sooner." They wrote of how he had given them "something to think about." One man went so far as to write that Artur "should be at the peace conference when the war is over."

That January Sunday night Artur invited all 110 players to his birthday party. There was not space enough in our apartment at 1158 Fifth Avenue for the wives, and these I invited to a tea ten days later. When the men arrived it was apparent that many came under some sort of self-conceived duress. I heard one fellow say, "What kind of guy is this? He scares us to death at rehearsals, then expects us to eat his goulash and wish him a happy birthday!" A reasonable confusion, I must say. But had any of them chosen to pass up the goulash (catered) it would not have mattered in the least, not to Artur, at any rate. He was aware of this attitude among the men, and if they came to celebrate his birthday because they feared a glower or a piece of criticism at rehearsals, they would soon discover the contrary. Music making was a thing apart.

Behind the disgruntlement of the men who did not care to be at Rodzinski's party was an old, well-cultivated Philharmonic conviction that all music directors are inhuman brutes, and that each Philharmonic player knows more than his maestro. The men then, as now (and they will resent me for saying so), had no regard for themselves as a collective unit, and a high estimate of themselves for being among the few individuals to have made it to the top.

What it all came down to, actually, was that no conductor before had ever shown the men any personal interest — and I offer here a piece of advice to young conductors, including those to whom I have said these things directly. No maestro will lose respect, dilute his authority, or otherwise encourage disaster by acknowledging that his instrumentalists have human needs and wants identical to his own. When Artur's birthday party was over, a few more players were won over by such acknowledgment, and did their work all the better for it. The few words Artur shared with each man softened some hearts that night.

The tea with the wives went much better. I was shocked to find that although many of their husbands had played together for twenty years, the wives had never met. This prompted me to say that we all ought to become friends, that we might be able to help each other. "After all," I reasoned, "we have one thing in common — slightly crazy husbands." And on this understated view of our husbands, a bond was made, and the Philharmonic Women's Club came into being. Its main purpose was the improvement of relations between the men, the stifling of gossip, the rooting out of jealousies, and the placation of animosities. We wanted to make the orchestra "one big family." I cannot say that we succeeded, piranha fish are not likely to be made vegetarians; but we did reduce petty squabbles and personnel tensions substantially. One of our devices was a buffet luncheon on days when there were two rehearsal calls. In what used to be Carnegie Hall's picture gallery, now the bar, we would feed our men sandwiches, coffee, and — to keep liquid whatever ice had already melted — some beer. Because we genuinely enjoyed each other's company, we extended our activities to volunteer war work.

One of the Philharmonic's vice-presidents, Mrs. Lytle Hull, complimented me, saying that I was "the best conductor's wife" the orchestra ever had. I doubt that was the case; it was just my good fortune to have a husband who, at the time, thought that what I wanted to do fitted nicely into his scheme of things. Other conductors' wives could do as much.

Artur's birthday plea for universal harmony was not so all-encompassing that it extended to all types of music and musicians. That winter, after a USO concert given at Camp Kilmer, my husband addressed himself to the "pop" genre and its leading exponents in an interview he gave to a reporter for the camp's news sheet. The young man asked Artur what he thought of jive. My husband responded with the rather hoary opinion that "the style of boogie woogie which appeals to hep cats is a great cause of delinquency among American youth today."

Artur, alas, rarely thought much when answering "off the top of his head." Truth is, his head was rarely involved in such statements, and once started, he was likely to continue with inexorable consistency. In this instance the army reporter was told furthermore that "devotees of Frank Sinatra are pitiful cases. I can't understand why thirteen- and fourteen-year-old children go wild over him."

The story appeared in the Camp Kilmer paper and was carried overnight across the nation by the wire services. The same teleprinters in the morning carried Sinatra's reply: "Bunk!" The King of Swoon, his domain under attack, was more reasonable than my husband in his interviews. "Why do these longhairs always knock the popular field?" he asked. "We never knock them, even though I've heard some pretty awful classical stuff in my time. . . . I don't know exactly what the causes of juvenile delinquency are, but I don't think any one can prove that popular music is one of them."

The matter ought to have rested there, but it did not. People in movie houses, nightclubs, and on street corners were asked for opinions, and these clearly amounted to picking up the gauntlet Rodzinski so mindlessly had flung. Even Stokowski wedged himself into the act, for fun, and like Artur, because he could rarely miss a chance to say something outrageous to a reporter. "Some foreigners," said Stokowski, "do not understand how rich the United States is in folk music and how important it is to the culture of America." Stokie should have known that popular music and folk music are two different beasts. And Artur had absolutely nothing against pop music; he was often in trouble for espousing the causes of Jerome Kern and Gershwin as artists equal to Offenbach and the lesser Strausses. He liked the music of Richard Rodgers and Cole Porter. He enjoyed good jazz, and praised it. Lenny Bernstein's ingenious boogie improvisations delighted him.

Artur relished the farrago, since it made good copy. Dorle Jarmel wondered. Sinatra had no objections. And an army of jumpers and pushers were at hand to leap on a bandwagon noisily set in motion. The papers carried letters variously suggesting that "classics are dead," that Artur could "be up to date for once" in his life, that Sinatra was "doing more for the morale of the girls whose fellows [were] at war," and more. On the other side, some moral stuffed-shirt opined that he was "glad" my husband had "courage to speak out on this abominable source of disintegration of character" respresented by "Frankie." The silliest, and saddest, letter came from a prematurely old boy, one with a great career ahead of himself as a long-suffering priggish parent: "I am fourteen years old," he began, as if to give authority to his statement. "I am very glad," he continued, "that someone in this country finally had the guts to stand up and say something about this terrible music and those good-for-nothing singers that everybody is going crazy about. I hope that through your efforts something will be done about this plague to our democracy."

As these things sometimes end, Artur and Sinatra met, and neither found the other half so terrible as either's statements made him out. Indeed, Sinatra had an ear for "longhair" music, and even attended a performance as my guest in Box 61. In later years when Sinatra had matured as a man and artist, Artur could not help but admire the man's phrasing, expressive control of a phrase, and good taste in materials.

Quality in contemporary music was what Artur sought, and it was not often or easily come by. Many items he programmed in the Philharmonic's 1943–44 season unfortunately were in the category of "new music." Some remained in the repertoire, if only on a part-time basis. Only two became "classics" or standard fare: Paul Hindemith's *Symphonic Metamorphosis on Themes of C. M. von Weber*, which Artur played for the first time anywhere, and Bartok's Violin Concerto, which he introduced to New York audiences. Lenny Bernstein premiered his own symphony, *Jeremiah*, a piece which deserves a better fate than the neglect it since has experienced. Sam Barber's *Symphony in One Movement* was revived by Bruno Walter, and could be said to number among those pieces treated fairly by posterity, taken out for an airing every now and then. But, with the possible exception of William Schuman's *William Billings* Overture, all the other pieces introduced that season promptly fell into a desuetude which they probably merited. Among them were occasional pieces for Claire Reis's League of Composers commissioning series by Carpenter, Roy Harris, Bernard Herrmann, Martinu, Milhaud, Bernard Rogers, and William Grant Still, the only black composer anyone performed in those days. Works by Nicolai Berezowsky, Deems Taylor, Camargo Guarnieri, Paul Creston, Vladimir Dukelsky (songwriter Vernon Duke), Alexandre Tansman, Miklos Rosza, and Karol Rathaus never had another Philharmonic hearing as far as I can discover, although the Creston piece, a Concerto for Saxophone and Orchestra, must be played somewhere, considering the paucity of material for the instrument. The best to be said of all these pieces is that they were well made.

At least one work drew great advance attention and continued to hold interest as long as the war continued and the plight of Russia could move Americans: that was Shostakovich's Eighth Symphony. Artur received rights to its first radio performance in the United States (the concert premiere went to Koussevitzky), again for a huge advance: $10,000. That sum was paid by U.S. Rubber, the sponsor. In a sense, the truly regal royalty demanded by the Soviet Union was just, for the radio transmission could reach fifteen million CBS listeners, and it was also relayed throughout the Americas and to the Armed Forces in Europe, Africa, and Asia.

Although the extra-musical hoopla of the Philharmonic's and CBS's publicity made the new work out to be a masterpiece, the critics did not seem to share the opinion. Ernest Newman, writing in the *London Times*, said Russia's latest symphonic opus was "for the most part barely third rate." It certainly did not have the brute driving force of the Seventh, which was composed by Shostakovich between stints as an air-raid warden in Leningrad. Henry Simon, *PM*'s critic, called it an "anticlimax after the mighty Seventh." Olin Downes thought that the composer "writes too fast and too long," to which Virgil Thomson's observation should be added as seal: "Matter ordinarily sufficient for a twenty-minute piece has been stretched out to last an hour." Oddly enough, when Artur, then Koussevitzky, first played it, neither *Pravda* nor *Izvestia* had yet seen fit to commit themselves to a review.

But even if some bad or uninteresting music took up space on the orchestra's programs that season, they drew far better audiences than had been seen for years. Ticket sales improved to where the *Sold Out* sign was no stranger at the Carnegie Hall box office wicket. Also, one of Artur's ideas, that of admitting free all servicemen and women in uniform when seats were at hand, eliminated another once-chronic Philharmonic problem — that of certain sections looking disturbingly empty.

The improved ticket sales were generated by more than interesting programs and soloists. Artur's MRA-inspired behavior had brought about a new spirit within the orchestra that reflected itself in a quality that was above and beyond what hard work and stricter discipline could accomplish.

At first one player, then another unburdened himself to Artur about personal problems. Artur listened sympathetically to all of them and offered advice or help when it was wanted or possible. The men appreciated Artur's concern and went away from the encounter willing to give more to their maestro. Matters were so much improved that a player who had led the opposition to Artur's releasing of deadwood called on me one day when he knew my husband would be away. "I know that you will be happy to hear that things are better with us," he said. "Relationships are not just a hundred, but a thousand percent better." Considering that the base figure was zero, the increase was not so impressive; still, once thinly-concealed resentments and open hatreds among the instrumentalists had been effectively moderated.

Maestro Toscanini was among those to notice the change. "How do you get those men to play as they never did for me?" Artur explained, but his techniques were not for Maestro, whose essential tool with his NBC men was terror: "I often pretend that I am so mad they get scared and play better." I was told by Maestro's principal violist, Carlton Cooley, that Toscanini ordered his men to listen to the Philharmonic: "Play as well for me," he recommended.

There remained some recalcitrants in the Philharmonic who were embarrassed by Artur's religiosity. No one could deny that at times my husband was laughable, for his enthusiasms in all things other than music invariably blurred the boundary separating the reasonable from the excessive. I could understand their unfavorable reactions to Artur when he was on the crest of his religious high. He had "experiences" out of William James — apparitions and presences of the Divine even in the alley behind Carnegie Hall.

One night Artur came back to our apartment after rehearsing Mahler's *Resurrection* (the Second Symphony) and reported he had found waiting for him at the stage door a striking human being, a very tall, handsome, blind man with a long beard, dressed in a brown cape like a Franciscan's habit. "He looked like a Christ," said Artur. "I was even afraid for a moment. But he introduced himself to me, and asked if he could attend a rehearsal of the Mahler. Of course, I told him to come whenever he liked."

Since Artur did not approve of outsiders at rehearsals, including me, I knew that he had been truly moved by this person whose name was Louis Hardin. Louis and Artur eventually became friends. And Artur, whose new religious concerns had not erased his superstitiousness, believed that Louis brought him good luck.

When we found that Louis lived in a cold loft somewhere, we tried to help him out with some warm clothes. Artur, who never parted with so much as an old slipper, gave Louis one of his suits and a heavy wintercoat, which Louis sold. Louis was also averse to shoes, and frostbitten feet he knew well enough. He had nothing against seeing again, however, and gladly went with me to visit a well-known eye specialist, Dr. Milton Berliner. I vaguely had a notion that the new art of corneal transplantation could salvage some vision for Louis. The verdict was negative. Both eyes were too hopelessly damaged for surgery, having been destroyed by an explosion when, as a child, Louis played with dynamite.

Louis Hardin used to be a familiar sight on the streets. His usual haunt was the Avenue of the Americas where, unless he has died or moved elsewhere, he probably still pads around in sandals, horse-blanket cape, and now a headdress that looks as if cadged from an old production of *Die Walküre*. For a coin, he will tootle a pretty song on his recorder, and give all the conversation one wants for nothing. Most people know him as Moondog. His fortunes, such as they ever were, improved when Goddard Lieberson recorded some of his mournful compositions for Columbia. One of them, a song made out of a borrowing from a Dvorak chamber piece, even became the jukebox hit "Nature Boy."

The Mahler Second which brought Louis Hardin into our lives, was given several beautiful performances and was a hit with both public and critics. The Westminster Choir appeared with soloists Enid Szantho and Astrid Varnay. Mahler was then not at all popular. People blanched at the thought of a concert-length symphony. After the Thursday reading, Carnegie Hall was packed. My box had people sitting on the low partitions and standing. Seated beside me — and it made the moment a proud one — were Alma Mahler and her last husband, Franz Werfel. Mme. Mahler later wrote to Artur of her appreciation of the performance, telling him that his rendition was like a reincarnation of Mahler's own. This touched Artur greatly, for one of his life-long regrets was that Mahler died before he ever had a chance to hear him conduct anything, let alone his own music.

At about the time the scheduling of guest conductors for 1944–45 was on Artur's mind, our Los Angeles friend, Cecil Frankel, came to New York with his wife, and I visited them at their hotel while Artur rehearsed. We were having a delightful time when an unexpected pair of guests arrived, Mr. and Mrs. George Szell. I later mentioned meeting the Szells to Artur and suggested the Czech as a guest conductor. Rather than bite off my nose, Artur said, "That's a good idea." Until then, Szell was unknown in New York, except for some Met performances. With the wartime glut of emigré conductors, many fine talents had no chance to perform, or to show their versatility. When Artur suggested Szell to A.J. his response was tepid. "He's an operatic conductor," Judson said. All proposals to Judson were initially answered with a "No," and I sometimes wondered if where artists were concerned the reason was their not being under contract to A.J. Whatever the case, Artur challenged Judson and won. Szell was invited for the coming season, along with Pierre Monteux, whom my husband always respected and admired, and Lenny Bernstein. Lenny was advanced from "assistant conductor" status to that of "guest." Artur was anxious to get Thor Johnson, but the Army would not discharge him. Ignace Strasvogel then became the assistant, now that Lenny had engagements everywhere, and commitments as a composer.

Toward the end of the 1943–44 season, on a tour concert to Hartford, Connecticut, Lenny and I shared a compartment; Artur had one to himself in order to nap before the performance. While I read or counted the telephone poles leaping past, I noticed Lenny take a pad of staved paper from his briefcase, then draw notes. I pretended not to watch, but was amazed at the speed with which he covered sheet after sheet, rarely pausing or making an erasure. He looked up for a moment, smiled handsomely as he caught my peeping eye, and said, "You have no idea how exciting it is to hear in one's head the music that comes out in these black dots." The stuff those arcane dots coded was the delicious jaunty, jazzy score to Bernstein's ballet *Fancy Free*.

The last concert of the season came soon after that trip, and to celebrate it the Philharmonic Women's Club held a party at the Horizon Club. We staged a parody of our husbands at work. The board and officers, and, of course, management, were invited to hear what we thought an hilarious text, prepared by several of the women. I portrayed Artur in rehearsal, imitating his accent and gestures. Everyone laughed, including Artur and A.J.

"If Rodzinski continues to work as he did this year," Judson told me in what I took to be a friendly aside, "there is no reason why he couldn't remain with us for as long as he lives."

The manager-impresario was particularly happy with the changed attitudes among the players, especially as evidenced at that party. On the face of it, Artur had welded 110 men into one happy family, a prime objective of that season. His others were beautifully stated by Virgil Thomson in an end-of-season appraisal for the *Sunday Tribune*.

No longer need one speak of the Philharmonic's improvement. Real quality has already been arrived at. Not an ugly sound, not a faulty balance, not a forced blast or screaming tutti marred yesterday's readings. The orchestra made music all the time, just as Philadelphia and Boston do, and Dr. Rodzinski gave constantly, to the phraseology of it, all clarity and all appropriate emphasis. The Brahms Symphony opened the doors of his eloquence without his losing any care for the amenities. Everything was clear and beautiful in sound, gracious, consecutive, meaningful. . . . I doubt if I ever have heard it so convincingly, so quite without lushness or painting, so coherently as to sweetness and strength. . . .

We now have an orchestra that is a joy to the ear . . . and we owe it all to Artur Rodzinski.

Chapter 34

ARTUR was exhausted at the end of his first Philharmonic season. As we drove to the farm that spring with Marysia and Karol, he made it clear he wanted to do nothing but tend his bees, mow his acres, and study scores for the coming year. He had booked only one concert, a radio broadcast for U.S. Rubber. My activities, other than bees and entertaining house guests, were to be unexpectedly and altogether pleasurably varied.

The year before, I had spoken with Helen Wishard, one of our Buchmanite friends, of all the good things that had come my way since Artur had joined the spiritual ranks of Moral Rearmament.

"We have a life together now that is very nearly perfect," I said. "Artur has never been so personally fulfilled, so close to his artistic goals."

"And your own fulfillment, Halina?" Helen asked.

I could not easily answer her. She and her husband Sciff, one of Artur's closer MRA associates, had long known how much I wanted a child. But the satisfaction of that urge and need of woman and wife, as Helen and I talked, was as unattainable for me as the peaks of the Himalayas. I could see them in imagination, and be content that they were there, at least for others. For me, they would soon be impossible. I was thirty-nine. I would be forty in November 1944.

"Artur wants me all to himself," I finally replied. "He's a possessive creature, and though he no longer shows it much, he still resents even the feelings I have for my sisters. A child is simply not in Artur's scheme of things."

"Artur cannot decide the matter, Halina," Helen insisted. "If God means you to have one, you will. Trust Him."

"I've never doubted Him, darling," I replied.

"Believe, Halina," she said, "and leave Artur to God." That was as easily said as done, since there was no other way.

In May 1944 there began those usual signs of something unusual taking place. After several weeks of them, I was certain. I could not be sure just how my husband would take the information, and I rather wished the announcement could be made by some one other than myself.

I went to his room the afternoon of May 22, right after his nap. He was sitting in his big armchair, reading a score by the golden light that poured through the window. He looked up when he heard me enter, smiling the way he did when his mind was clear and relaxed.

"Dearest," I began, "we have almost all that we have ever dreamed about. . . ."

Artur creased his brow slightly, cocked his head to one side, smiling still, but curious to know what could have gotten into me. "Yes, of course."

"We are the happiest people we know."

"Yes."

"And now, along with all the other happy things God has seen fit to give us, I think there will be a child." Although I had buried the crucial word under so many others, I still could not help separating it by a sigh and a lowering of my voice.

An awful silence in the room contrasted with the sounds outside — Karol laughing as he chased our barking dog and both stirring up distress cries from the nesting birds in the trees just outside the window. Though the light came from over Artur's shoulders, I could see him flush a deep, deep red. His blushing was often an embarrassment to him and could make him testy, but there was no bad temper in him at that moment. He was stunned. And his movements, the closing of his score, then laying it aside as he rose, came slowly, deliberately, as if to fill time until words could shape themselves in his mind.

He took my hands in his, but looked away through the window as he spoke. "Aren't we too . . . old, darling? And is this a time to bring a child into the world?"

I wanted to shout "no" to these commonplace questions, but held my peace and said, "I may be wrong. I will see a physician in Pittsfield tomorrow to be certain."

Artur then took me under his arm, brushing some hair from my brow with his free hand to make a space to kiss.

That night, after dinner, he played the piano for several hours, Chopin waltzes and polonaises, and told Karol a very long and complicated fairy tale at bedtime. Artur had taken the news far better than I had expected.

My visit to the doctor, in Marysia's company, confirmed the pregnancy, but it was a mixed blessing. I called Artur from Pittsfield to report that the gynecologist had confirmed my condition but had found something wrong. An exploratory operation was necessary. "He says that if everything is all right, he'll sew me up and I'll have the baby," I told him.

"He'll do nothing of the kind," Artur roared. "Hurry yourself home — we're going to New York!"

In the time it took Marysia and me to drive from Pittsfield, Artur had called our friend Dr. Abraham Garbat and had arranged with him to meet us with an obstetrician, Dr. Mortimer Rodgers, at New York's Lenox Hill Hospital that evening.

The trip, ordinarily about four hours, was made in just under three. We barely spoke the whole way. Artur was tense, and I had presentiments I was reluctant to voice, not the least of which was that the new life I carried might be the cause of my death.

The doctors confirmed the pregnancy, but also located a tumor which could force me to abort. "She is not young, Dr. Rodzinski," Dr. Rodgers said, "and since you aren't keen on having the child, we could legally operate, remove the tumor — and everything else." When Artur told me, I was stunned.

"I want a consultation with another specialist," Artur said. "If the other fellow corroborates their findings, they will operate tomorrow." The consultant, a Professor of Obstetrics at Columbia, agreed with his colleagues, and I was admitted to the hospital to be prepared for surgery.

That night I could not sleep, despite the sedative the night nurse brought. I prayed, rehearsing with God the gamut of emotions and hopes that I harbored, arguing my case in the knowledge that not one but two lives depended on His decision. I had dreamed of having a child since my own childhood, of experiencing that mysterious process I had seen my mother undergo so often. I, too, wanted the joy of sensing beneath my own heart's beat the echo of another's. It did not seem to me that God had initiated the fulfillment of this great, long-standing desire of mine simply as a trial or temptation.

It was a thwarting debate with One who would not answer in any words but my own. And yet even these became a source of consolation as I worked my line of reasoning around to the inevitable: the matter was in God's beneficent hands, and He would do what was meant to be done. I drowsed toward daybreak, at peace with myself and Him, and somehow convinced that all would go well for me and the barely-formed being in my womb. If ever I had felt the presence of God, it was in those moments when I was comfortable in the sudden, irrational assurance that the outcome of what was taking place would be good.

My eyes had been closed for barely a few minutes, it seemed, when a nurse came with the pre-operative sedation. I refused the pill of Nembutal, saying I would do very well without it. The nurse insisted and prevailed. In moments I began to feel myself being sucked into a velvety blackness that I knew I must avoid. With my fingers I held the lids of my eyes apart, gripping them as if they were the rims of that void down into which I was being drawn. I had to keep my head above that dark place — at least until I could see Artur. Then, through a blur, and with no more strength to hold on, I saw his face, his smile, and heard, as if distantly, his voice say everything would be all right, that there would be no surgery. I then let go and slid away, feeling his hand on my forehead, and knew, really knew how good God is.

When I awoke from a dreamless sleep, I saw Artur handing a monstrous basket of gladioli and ferns to a nurse half its size. My husband's face was radiant as he told me what had happened overnight and in the morning. He had been with Sciff Wishard, whose face I vaguely remembered seeing before that deep, deep sleep, and the two men had sat up discussing the impending operation, "seeking guidance" in MRA parlance. When they finished their prayers, even as I had concluded my debate with God, they went together to see Dr. Rodgers. He was already preparing himself for surgery when they asked what would happen if the operation were not performed.

"We don't know what course nature takes," Dr. Rodgers told them. "She might lose the child by the fifth month, and then the tumor would have to be removed. She might even carry through the ninth and have a normal delivery. We just can't say."

"If there is no medical danger, then let's leave the outcome to God," Artur told the obstetrician. Dr. Rodgers is said to have had tears in his eyes when he took off his white smock and cap, explaining to Sciff and my husband that he always hated doing such work.

The tumor, that aberration of living cells, had saved my child's life. There was something circular in the logic of the matter, wonderful in its roundness like a child's ball or a tiny bird's egg, something even divine. It was coincidence, one might say, that tumor and child appeared together, coincidence that as I prayed, Artur prayed, too. Perhaps Artur would have insisted on an abortion had everything been normal. There *were* ways of doing such things in those days. But the surgical dangers presented by pregnancy *and* tumor conspired to make Artur listen to a voice other than his own.

Sciff's friendly, patient talk with Artur did much to make him discuss the case again with Dr. Rodgers, who was, in any case, reluctant to perform the operation. I like to think that God gave me the tumor so that He might also give me a child.

From that day forward, Artur was as anxious about becoming a father as I was for motherhood. He was the soul of consideration, putting himself to the chores which ordinarily were mine, even the shopping and nuisance errands which are every wife's lot.

For my part, I gladly accepted such attention. Not only were they novel, but also they showed me aspects of the man which made him still more lovable. While I crocheted or knitted little wardrobes in pink, blue, and yellow against all contingencies, and lived in dreams of perambulators, nursery wallpapers, and a future far beyond, Artur kept to his scores and errands.

The fact of my pregnancy was a secret, thanks to Artur's superstitiousness. But while my condition was not discussed with the hordes of guests we entertained that summer, only the imperceptive or casual friend could miss the signs. For one thing, I had peculiar appetites: hard-boiled eggs, tomato juice, and Dubonnet. For another, those elliptical parts of my anatomy, both fore and aft, became decidedly rounder. Yet where nature took no pains to hide what a quick eye could see, I suffered concealing my happiness from those with whom I thought I should share it. Artur would not permit me to speak, however, until it was certain that all was well.

While I bit my tongue, Artur, more darling than ever, became a marvelous host, at least with old musician friends who visited. Olga Samaroff-Stokowski was a frequent guest that summer, along with her most talented student, William Kapell. Mme. Samaroff and Artur had been close since my husband's days in Philadelphia, and he respected her enormously. A successful pianist herself, she was also a brilliant teacher and an intelligent and sensitive person. Artur used to say Stokowski divorced her because she had an irritating capacity for always being right. She was surely so in staking all on Willy Kapell's abilities, who even at this point was accomplished enough to have severed their student-teacher relationship. But, like a thorough teacher, she continued as Willy's mentor, helping him face the problems of human growth without which no amount of digital facility nor musical intellect will make an artist.

Also summering in the Berkshires that year were Alexander Brailowsky, the Russian pianist, and his Polish wife Ela. The Wierzynskis visited, Halina and Kazimir. Kazio, as ever, played the farmer, deriving some odd relish from hog-slopping or protracted conversations with a calf, to whom he fed the most delicate morsels of hand-cut grass. Poets are not very practical farmers, but they enjoy themselves at the work, especially the costuming. It was Kazio's pleasure to wear Artur's coveralls while doing his self-arrogated chores.

There were quiet moments, though, when the house was free of guests, when Marysia and Karol were off visiting neighbors, or together in mother-son tête-à-têtes. On one such an occasion, Artur listened to a Lewisohn Stadium concert over the radio. Fabien Sevitzky had been scheduled to conduct, and the program included one of Artur's trade-marked pieces, Shostakovich's Fifth. My husband called me to join him by the radio, General Sarnoff's gift console.

"Listèn, how wonderfully that man conducts! I never thought Sevitzky had it in him!" As the piece progressed, Artur kept interjecting remarks like "How well he sustains the line," or "Hear that balance!" He was agog that the conductor of the Indianapolis Symphony Orchestra had such control over the ensemble and such musicianship. "I think he must have studied my recording," Artur observed. "His tempi are almost like mine."

Bit by bit, Artur blushed. "I have been ungenerous to that man," he said. "I never believed he had any talent, and I must make it up to him. He is a *great* conductor."

When the performance ended, we expected a thunderous ovation; the reading deserved one. But there was no applause, just a moment or so of dead air, then an announcement that the Stadium event had been rained out and in place of Sevitzky's performance the network had played Shostakovich's Fifth as recorded by Artur Rodzinski.

As the summer advanced, so did my pregnancy. Claire and Charlie Swift came from Chicago, and Helen and Lytle Hull of the Philharmonic family stopped by, and were let in on the matter. They were the only ones to know of my condition before it became physically impossible to hide it any longer. Artur also invited them to be the child's godparents, but on the condition they not tell the secret to others.

By the time the 1944–45 Philharmonic season opened there was no more secret. My appearance at that concert, the night of October 5, was a public announcement. One can hardly hide a mountain under chiffon and sequins, merely obscure it. John and Ellen Carpenter were in Box 61 to hear John's *Sea Drift*, and required no more confirmation of my condition than a nod of assent to their question: "Halina, you're *not?*"

The news got about and made something of a sensation. Artur was a national figure, and not a young one. And I was almost as grey as he. Part of the sensation, I found, was the totally American notion that such things as childbearing and all that leads to it ceased when the hairdresser's dye bottles became a part of a weekly schedule. Indeed, many felt there was something less than respectable and slightly amazing in having children after thirty. Would not my mother have laughed, or Papa's mother with her immense brood!

With the coming of a child, we needed a larger home; and that fall, before the work of a move would become impossible, I located one with the help of Judson's secretary, Nora Shea. It was a large, luxuriously furnished house at 7 East 84th Street. When we looked at the place, Nora said, "This is how a Philharmonic conductor should live!" She might also have said the same about a Prince or a Balkan King in exile. There was a huge living room joined to a large dining room by a wide hall, perfect for parties. Artur, at first sight, feared the rent would be outrageous, though he had never earned nor saved as much before in his career. After some calculations he decided that we could afford it, and chose as his room the third-floor library whose sun-drenched spaces were more than enough for a grand piano and all his other musical necessities. My room, with a bed the size of a boxing ring, was on the same floor. Above us, we fitted out an apartment for Marysia and Karol, and adjoining them were two rooms with a bath which we prepared as a nursery. Still one more floor remained, the fifth, which had once been used for servants. The rooms up there were set aside for itinerant Poles and visiting MRA-ers. Thank heaven the place had an elevator!

Since the house lent itself to entertainment, we did a lot of it that season. Frank Buchman suggested we give a dinner for Dr. Carl Joachim Hambro, president of the Norwegian Parliament for thirty years, and also president of the newly convened United Nations.

(255)

I was a bit upset at the thought of making conversation with Dr. Hambro, as I had always been nervous with such imposing men. Frank Buchman laid my fears to rest with some advice: "You don't need to talk. Just smile, listen, and ask questions. People love to talk about themselves when they have good listeners. Remember that every person actually is afraid of everybody else and that, when you meet someone, the other person probably is as scared of you as you are of him. You can help him by showing that you are interested in him."

Frank's sliver of advice helped me through that night and ever since. Buchmanite principles also worked to improve our Philharmonic family affairs. Indeed, things were so cheerful inside Carnegie Hall — and generally cordial outside, thanks to the Women's Club's activities — that we all decided to have Thanksgiving Day together at 84th Street. The ladies each prepared her favorite and best dish, salads, pastries, and five turkeys, all to feed our 110 men and their conductor. The table looked like a gourmet freighter.

Appetites and spirits were near their peak when I announced the day also celebrated my fortieth year. That news, coupled with the event anticipated for January, made our celebration a particularly festive occasion. Those who had no hangovers or indigestion the next day were in a very abstemious minority. It was truly the happiest Thanksgiving Day I had ever known.

As far as January went, things moved smoothly. My monthly visit with Dr. Rodgers — who was, by the way, the composer Richard's brother — revealed nothing unusual, although he did suggest that Artur and I forgo our mid-winter vacation at the farm. He thought it best to be near a major medical facility. So Christmas saw us holidaying at, of all places, Asbury Park, New Jersey. I rode no ferris wheels nor merry-go-rounds, but the long walks on the beach and the deep sleeps that followed were restful.

Expectant fathers, even reluctant ones, are all the same, and Artur, as the days ticked past, was curious about our constant but unseen companion. "What if it is terribly ugly," he wondered. "Can such a crazy father produce a normal child?" Mama Rodzinska had often said Artur had been a beautiful infant, so on that score I had no fear. As to the sanity of the child, I relied on my line's blood to dilute Artur's in reasonable measure. Names gave us no trouble. A girl would be Halina, the fourth in succession to bear the name. A boy would memorialize Artur's late brother Richard, or Riki. "It's the same name in every language," Artur observed.

We also discussed the likely attributes or gifts of our child and I rather succumbed to some old tales I had soaked up from the various wet nurses about the Lilpop household when I was a child. For one thing, I rarely missed a concert, in hopes my baby would be a musician like its father. I was certain the little creature heard through all the fat, muscle, and water that surrounded it, particularly in that it kicked most violently and in tempo when music played, but napped when there was quiet. It was not comfortable, however, for a very big mother-to-be who often made trips to the ladies' room. I went so often that season that the attendant and I got to know each other, and when the baby finally came she sent a card of congratulations.

On January 13, only ten days before delivery day, Toscanini conducted a Pension Fund Benefit. He was nostalgic that night, and pleased to see me when I went backstage. The image of Maestro's smile on noting my condition is even now before my eyes. He placed a hand gently on my abdomen, said not a word, then patted it gently. It was like receiving a blessing.

I saw Dr. Rodgers on January 22. "Everything is just fine," he said. "We'll operate tomorrow."

"Can't we wait a day," I asked. "Artur has a concert in Newark tonight, and the news would upset him."

"Your house guest doesn't want to wait," he said. "When Dr. Rodzinski goes to New Jersey, leave a message for him that you are at the hospital."

I did not care to deceive Artur, but did as the doctor advised. I also concealed from my husband that there would be a cesarean section, since the tumor had to be removed with the child.

I packed Artur for his Newark date, making sure his gun, his photos, a few elephants, his music, and some brandy were in among the changes of clothes and other paraphernalia. When Artur left, I dined with Marysia and Karol, and what the doctor had told me should be a light meal became a demonstration of voracity, for in addition to everything else I polished off almost an entire cheese cake. Marysia, who, after all, did have some experience to pass on, warned I would regret my piggishness. But my sister rarely took my advice, and I saw no reason to follow hers. The regrets came the next day.

I went into Lenox Hill Hospital, and while Marysia unpacked my things, I readied myself for bed, then fell into a deep sleep. The operation, at which Dr. Garbat would assist, was the next afternoon.

Marysia met Artur when he returned. He became very excited when my sister told him I was in labor. He would hear nothing about "going to bed and letting things take their course." He put on his coat, scoured New York for a florist's shop, eventually buying a big bouquet at Pennsylvania Station. He was disappointed to find me asleep, but awakened me anyway. "Where is it?" he wanted to know.

"Where it has been for nine months. Go home and get some sleep, darling," I urged. "The pains have stopped."

He did, but was back early in the morning. He sniffed a rat. "Nothing yet?"

As luck has it in such cases, Dr. Rodgers came at that moment and made a clean breast of everything. I thought my husband would faint, and his color hardly improved when the doctor made light of the procedures as run-of-the-mill.

In a mild panic, Artur left the hospital to wander the city, killing time. He stopped in at a movie house somewhere on Broadway, then left, and went to a bar to have a stiff drink. That did not work, since his nervous stomach and the whiskey combined to make him violently sick. Then another movie, still another bar. When four o'clock came round, Artur was glassy-eyed. I saw him for a few minutes as they put me on the cart to take to surgery. His face was so desolate, so hurt, with big tears bulging in the corners of his puffed eyes.

In the operating room, before the anesthetic was administered, I prayed. Then, as I began to fall into those velvety black depths of dreamless, drugged sleep I looked up at Dr. Rodgers and Dr. Garbat. Not at all strangely, they seemed a pair of kindly angels in their white smocks and caps.

I awoke to Artur's voice softly, hoarsely, asking if it was "all right that she is so pale?" Seeing me move, he bent over and kissed me as gently as a feather, whispering over and over again, "You have given us a son, a beautiful boy." I made a try at smiling, but it did not work; the muscles reacted as if they were of plaster or hardened wax. And the rest of me, somewhere lost below the sheets, was not much more responsive to my will to move. But something in my head and heart leaped up at Artur's words, *"Masz slicznego syna,"* so silken in Polish, as musical in English, "a beautiful boy."

I remained under heavy sedation for the next few days, dangerously ill. I was allergic to the anesthetic, it seemed, and peristalsis had refused to return. That my intestines were clogged with rich cheesecake only worsened things.

I understood how ill I was, but suspected something was wrong in the nurses' story that I could not see Riki because "all cesarean babies must stay in the incubator until they are strong." Drugged as I was, I could do no less than accept their authority. On the second day, a nurse admitted my sisters, but they were too morose to be good company. Fela was especially glum. "Aren't you happy about the baby?" I asked. "Of course, that's why I'm crying," she replied. Since that was not Fela's way, I really began to worry, yet only as much as one does in the dreamy, blurred reality of sedation.

Artur visited several times a day. The birth and his rest period coincided, but my husband looked far from rested. There was still as much anxiety on his face as when the doctor had told of the cesarean.

On the fourth day, a priest came to see me, a man from St. John the Baptist, at Lexington Avenue and 76th Street. I remember his praying over me, but I could not be sure that what he was about was Extreme Unction, now more appropriately called a healing rite. I say appropriately, because that night I began to feel better, more conscious of myself and my surroundings. And, the next day, I saw my son.

I know of no greater exaltation than that which I felt when first I saw the living being that only days before had been a part of my flesh. Despite the drugs, my heart felt a pain as if it were literally being burst by joy. Artur had spoken the truth. Riki was beautiful. His well-shaped head was covered with fine dark-blond hair, and his skin was almost transparent, the bluish white of thinly scraped ivory. There was something puzzling, however: on one side of his head a small part was shaved, and there was a tiny patch of adhesive plaster. I asked why, and the nurse who knew so much of incubators and cesarean births said a test had been performed. How easy it is in happiness to accept such tales.

Gradually, I was allowed more visitors, and all the flowers the room would hold. Of those, there were enough to make my husband a regular churchgoer, taking the overflow every afternoon around the corner to St. John's. The mail and telegrams arrived in little bundles. Since the news was on the wire services, and *Time* had carried an announcement, we received congratulations from hundreds of people I had never heard of. I can imagine what it must be like to give birth to a Crown Prince: the expensive gifts, the silver spoons, the porcelain dishes with warmers, the blankets, booties, and caps the colors of the spectrum. Richard went home in a blue bunting sent by Mrs. Theodore Steinway which had come with a card that read "To wrap your little miracle in."

It was the day before I took my infant son home that I understood what Mrs. Steinway meant in calling Riki a "miracle," and what sort of "test" had led to his temple being shaved. The pediatrician, Dr. Carl Smith, who had assisted Drs. Rodgers and Garbat in the delivery, told me all.

Richard was born at 4:00 P.M. January 23 (a date easy to remember. because it can be written 1/23/45), weighing in at a hefty nine pounds. The tumor, luckily, had not grown commensurately. But while I slept under sedation, ten hours after the child was delivered, neither Artur nor Dr. Garbat was able to catch a wink. Around two o'clock in the morning, my restless husband decided to see if everything was as it should be. He had a premonition of something wrong. At the exact same hour, Dr. Garbat woke up; as if ordered to do so, he dressed and came to the hospital. Ordinarily, the physician would have stopped by my room. But this time, he went straight to the nursery to check Riki, and thought he seemed unusually motionless. He entered the room for a closer look, and when he lowered the thin blanket that covered the child, saw a pool of blood: the infant's navel had burst and he was hemorrhaging to death. He had stopped breathing altogether. The doctor ordered a coagulant administered and quickly called Dr. Smith, Dr. Rodgers, and a transfusion specialist. Dr. Garbat knew little of babies except that their stamina and life force are phenomenal. Banking on that, physicians and technician worked on Richard under an oxygen tent for four hours, giving him blood, drop by drop, through the only vessel that had not collapsed, the slender blue passage above his left temple.

While the doctors worked, Artur, who had no idea of the gravity of the situation, sat by my bed or paced the corridors. He prayed as never before. When the doctors told him they could not guarantee survival,

Artur calmly, and to the physicians' amazement, replied, "He will live because God wanted him here."

Mrs. Garbat later reported that her exhausted husband said more or less the same thing: "It had to be God's doing, because it simply wasn't humanly possible."

Although nurses had made me walk for some while, Dr. Garbat, at Artur's insistence, ordered me to spend my first day at home in bed. I was whisked to the third floor in the elevator, bypassing the rest of the house, and sent to nap. Suddenly, I heard glorious music and called to Artur, asking when he had gotten the superb new radio. "We still have the same radio," he said, "but put on a robe and come keep me company downstairs."

I reminded him of Dr. Garbat's orders, but he slyly grinned and said he had special permission for me to get up. And I did, to walk arm in arm with him down the flight of stairs, into a dream as wonderful as an Alice in Wonderland ever had, for there in our living room was our orchestra playing the "Siegfried Idyll" composed by Wagner to celebrate the birth of his son seventy-five years earlier.

I am a sentimental woman. Or perhaps I am simply moved by honest emotions. But when Artur sat me in a chair facing those men to hear their exquisite music, I cried waterfalls. I could not look up at them until after they had finished playing, and when I did I saw tears in their eyes, too. In Artur's face was a radiance I saw only seldom, and if it is possible to reveal gratitude in a smile he showed that to me as well as to all of them. These busy men had dropped their extra engagements to give us this greatest proof of their affection.

Chapter 35

RIKI was continual discovery for Artur. One day it was an odd facial expression, a smile of recognition; the next, a growth in appetite or the grasping of a finger. If the man who was once ill-disposed to a child had any complaint, it was that his son slept when Papa wished to play. But Artur did not hold the child's lack of consideration against him. Rather, he would tiptoe into the boy's nursery to stand by the crib like a guardian angel, smiling until his cheek muscles ached. He made me a lovely present one day after a few minutes' watch by the sleeping infant: "It was stupid and selfish of me not to have wanted a child," he said, patiently tolerating the blush that accompanied his words.

Once, while feeding Riki, I expressed sadness that he had suffered so at birth. Artur consoled me, and surely himself, with a Polish saying: "A bad beginning brings good tidings in tow." The words proved prophetic. As the child prospered and grew, his initial hardships tempered into a sunny disposition, yet marked with a lack of aggressiveness that made him a pleasure to rear. He was a born peacemaker; his motto was, from his earliest years, if others will fight, that's their business, but making things up is the better part.

Artur rollicked in fatherhood. When he returned to the podium on February 8, 1945, he led the Philharmonic in Haydn's *Toy Symphony*, a silly piece but fun when played by virtuosi. The audience loved it, and the players gave a little more because the reading was for their maestro's new boy. Riki also received some other dedications, pieces composed by friends or admirers of his father. Sam Barber sent a lovely little lullaby, handsomely copied out in a wreath of hand-tinted flowers. Roy Harris wrote some variations. Igor Stravinsky, who conducted as guest that season, wrote an autograph of something that could be either a puzzle canon or blandly shapeless melody. Arnold Schoenberg wrote a delightful, complex, canonic setting of a text which talks of diaper changings and the composer's George songs. Stravinsky's biographing factotum, Robert Craft, recorded this piece, along with several other Schoenberg *a capella* canons, for Columbia.

Schoenberg was one of the five composers given world premieres on Artur's programs that season. The score was *The Ode to Napoleon Bonaparte*, Opus 41-B. Although the facts are not easy to ascertain, it generally appears that Artur had seen the composition in its original version for piano quintet and narrator. Wanting it for performance, he is supposed to have suggested Schoenberg arrange the work for string orchestra, and in this form it was introduced with Mack Harrell reciting the ticklish and prosodically-Germanic setting of Lord Byron's pompous, if rousing poem. Eduard Steuermann, a student, colleague, and friend of Schoenberg essayed the difficult piano part. The Philharmonic audiences first heard the piece on November 23, 1944, and it was later repeated on a Sunday afternoon broadcast, at which time the composer heard it. Schoenberg had been ill and unable to travel. Just as well, one should add, for the audiences failed to comprehend what the great man had done. The performance had been carefully prepared, which fact Schoenberg remarked to Artur in a letter appraising the broadcast, and was dramatically effective. But the Philharmonic's subscribers could find no tunes in the piece, and few could even detect that the "Ode" was, within Schoenberg's serial method, tonal (E-flat). Had the program notes not pointed out that Schoenberg cited Beethoven's Fifth Symphony frequently, that detail would have gone unobserved. All anyone, myself included, could grasp was a wild, passionate statement by a man whose reputation was greater than any public familiarity with his music. George Szell, whose musical intelligence was unquestionable, leaned over the ledge separating his box from mine to whisper to Zosia Kochanska, "I don't understand a thing!" But what Szell failed to understand the radio audience did not even attempt. The mailbag after the broadcast performance brought, aside from Schoenberg's letter, a host of insults. Schoenberg's day, like Mahler's, was yet to come.

Other world firsts that season included *The Prairie*, a cantata by Lukas Foss; Paul Creston's Second Symphony; Walter Piston's *Fugue on a Victory Tune*, and Virgil Thomson's masterful *Symphony on a Hymn Tune*, the only composition, other than Schoenberg's, to enter the permanent repertoire.

An all-English program, a salute to British gallantry, debuted for Philharmonic audiences Ralph Vaughan Williams's thrilling Fifth Symphony, William Walton's durable *Belshazzar's Feast* and a work with a peculiar story behind it. The previous season, a young Englishman, Wing Commander John Wooldridge, of the Royal Air Force, attended a concert while in New York on a special mission. He introduced himself, and Artur found out the "fly boy" was a composer. They struck a bargain: if Wooldridge shot down five German planes, Artur would perform one of the man's works. By the end of November, Wooldridge had far exceeded the quota, and Artur played the flyer's *Solemn Hymn for Victory*, with the composer present by special arrangement.

Other Philharmonic firsts included works by Hector Villa-Lobos, Ernest Bloch (his *Israel Symphony*), and young William Schuman (his Symphony Number Three). The Schuman Symphony received the Music Critic's Circle award as the finest American composition heard in New York that season. Composers leading their own works, where they had the competence, was a novel idea of Artur's, and that season he shared the podium with Thomson (who conducted his own Symphony's premiere) and Villa-Lobos. Stravinsky appeared alone.

Soloists who made their debuts that season were violinist Isaac Stern and Lenny Rose, Artur's new principal cellist. Others to appear included Menuhin, Piatigorsky, Alexander Brailowsky, Heifetz, Todd Duncan, and a trio of Poles, Wanda Landowska, Josef Hofmann, and Artur Rubinstein.

Mme. Landowska was to play Mozart and Haydn Concertos, and, according to Artur's inflexible rule, the two were to have a work session alone before the orchestral rehearsal. The rule was bent slightly, however; the work would be done at Mme. Landowska's apartment on Central Park West. I went along, partly from curiosity, partly as a courtesy. Ultimately, it was for laughs.

Mme. Landowska was a creation. When Artur and I arrived, the door was opened by one of the musician's two live-in assistants. We were led by her into a music room suggestive of a Pleyel showroom or funeral parlor. It was stuffed with the black, coffinlike cases of several harpsichords, and a piano. Soon the other assistant came to greet us, then the two assistants opened the door for "Mamusia" (Little Mother), as they called her, who made an entrance almost as spectacular as Paderewski's so long before at his Swiss residence. Mme. Landowska stood, effectively backlit, in the doorway, transfixed like some gorgeous, huge, wine-red butterfly, its velvet wings lightly shedding dust motes. It was a shock when she actually moved forward to greet us, quite effusively I should add, and extended a hand for Artur to kiss.

After a short discussion about the Mozart specifics, Mme. Landowska moved toward her piano to play for Artur. Her assistants preceded like acolytes, to open the piano case and keyboard with great ceremony, place her music on the rack, then drape on the floor the folds of her dress. Raising her handsome head, its raven hair parted down the middle to a knot at the nape of her neck, she stared into space. Then her long graceful hands darted out of her cavernous sleeves to play the Mozart. From time to time she abruptly stopped to explain how or why she executed a certain passage, then continued her reading, which, if taped, could have been spliced into consecutive sense, so thoroughly did she pick up a dynamic level or an ictus.

When she moved to a harpsichord for the Haydn Concerto, the same little procession and ritual ensued. I was fascinated by the show of it all, without which she could never have brought the harpsichord and its literature into vogue again. People who entered the Landowska cult for whimsy came away musically enriched. But her eccentricities were also a large part of the whole thing, though some of them were rather private.

The night of her first Philharmonic appearance, I looked in on her dressing room which adjoined Artur's. She and her assistants had recreated the Landowska environs, yellow roses in a vase atop a piano, clothes (mostly velours) spilling from open suitcases, and, of all things, a chamber pot. Wanda scorned public facilities, perhaps for sanitary considerations, but undoubtedly through a sense of her worth. In either case, it was among the duties of the two assistants to minister to her thunder mug, and even this they did with grace and smiles, so loyal and dedicated a pair they were.

Her appearance on stage was electrifying: she glided on like a classic Roman matron. Her performance was a thing of great exquisiteness, and Artur strove to give her the cleanest, most sympathetic accompaniment he could; but, unknown to him, he made a faux pas — awful, but not irreparable. After the orchestral tutti before the first movement cadenza in the Mozart, Artur rested his left hand on the piano case. Landowska rose up in an explosion of velvet and stood back as if bitten or stung. She walked over to Artur, lifted his hand from the lid, then executed the pyrotechnics. Later, Artur said he was so startled he almost forgot to cue the orchestra for the coda. But he accepted her peculiarities as the price of her artistry. And it was art that made her move his hand. "It affects the sound of the piano," she explained.

Her post-performance reception of homage — there is no other way to describe it — was a performance itself. She sat in an armchair while the assistants knelt before her, changing her slippers, draping her long dress, and all but singing Sapphic odes to a lyre. Admirers were admitted and perforce had to bow to the seated virtuoso. Men received a white-gloved hand to press lightly to their lips, but, heaven forbid, never to shake or squeeze.

There are hundreds of funny things to retail about Landowska, but perhaps the funniest is that of her china. She bought it in Paris at a bargain sale of Wagon-Lit's. It was handsome enough stuff, but her prime concern was that it bore her monogram. There is also one about visits to Count Leo Tolstoy's estate at Jasnaia Poliana where she would play for him to prove that music was not the devil's invention, and when the little house concerts were done, the novelist would roll on the floor laughing at Wanda's and her husband's jokes. Her husband was not Mr. Landowska, but a Polish writer named Henryk Lew, a fellow people once thought brilliant and clever. It was he who persuaded Wanda to abandon the piano for the harpsichord, and encouraged her to develop her gifts along such unique lines. The salon the two of them held in Paris was frequented by everyone: Moritz Moszkowski, Enrique Granados, Francis Poulenc (who wrote a harpsichord concerto for her). Rodin, it is said, enjoyed lunching from her Wagon-Lit service.

Josef Hofmann had been engaged to perform Chopin's Second Concerto with the Philharmonic in February 1945. Although the pianist's appearances had become less frequent through the Thirties, and he had, in a sense, "retired" with his resignation from the directorship of the Curtis Institute (in 1938), he was still king of virtuosi. In the late Thirties and early Forties, however, reports of Hofmann's performances were colored slightly by legends of past greatness, for at sixty-nine he had already passed his prime. For several years he had been falling apart. Drinking and the physical coordination demanded of a virtuoso pianist make for a wretched match.

The week Hofmann was to play, a week Artur looked forward to with eagerness and concern, the pianist came to our home under the steady wing of a Mr. Greinert of Steinway. Our old friend looked awful. His face was puffy, the color of parchment, and he was unsure of his feet and would have stumbled without Greinert's support.

When the man before whom Rachmaninoff behaved deferentially, from whom Godowsky solicited criticism, sat at the grand in Artur's studio, his hand trembled as if he had stage fright, and he fumbled one phrase after another, starting and stopping, repeating simple (for Hofmann) figurations like a mere student at his practice. At one point he grabbed two fistfuls of notes, then threw his shaking hands up on the rack and, staring at the useless things, told Artur, "Don't worry, things will be all right tomorrow."

My husband then came across the hall with Greinert into my room. Artur's forehead wore a pair of vertical creases and he gnawed his lower lip. Greinert kept lifting his eyebrows and shoulders and sighing. "He has his good days and bad," Greinert finally said.

"He is in no shape to rehearse tomorrow, much less play Thursday," Artur said. "It would be best if he canceled," he added, firmly.

"Dr. Rodzinski, it will kill him!"

"It will be a merciful death compared to what those lions in Carnegie Hall would do; could he survive the orchestra's sniggers? The gasps from the audience? The giggling? What if he can't finish and just gets up and walks off stage?" Artur turned away from Greinert. "It would be a sadder end, a tragedy, if we let this great man appear in this state."

"You're right," Greinert said, with a shrug and the sigh of a man hoisting a huge burden. "I'll take care of him."

The two went back to the studio. I trailed behind them as far as the door. Hofmann had been practicing intermittently. He stopped when Greinert touched his shoulder. "Josef," he said, "we have both thought it over, and you really aren't . . . in form . . . today. It would be much better to postpone the concert until a later date."

Hofmann's short, thick-set torso, so powerful-seeming in performance, suddenly appeared shapeless and frail. Lethargically, he pivoted himself on the piano bench to look up at the two standing men, showing them a face of total desolation and abandonment. "I know," he said gently. "This is the end. I will never play again." His back to the piano, he reached along the keyboard to finger a slow trill with his right hand, while his left rested on Greinert's arm. After he left, Artur came to my room. "How sad to see so supreme an artist finish this way," was all he could say.

The Thursday and Friday concerts went on without a soloist. Artur substituted two orchestral pieces for the Chopin Concerto, and the program carried a printed slip which explained the changes as "owing to the sudden indisposition of Josef Hofmann. . . ."

But there had been nothing sudden about it. His drinking had become increasingly heavy as the years passed. Indeed, in those last few years he could always be found amiably relaxing before and after rehearsals and performances at any number of bars in the vicinity of Carnegie Hall. And on the afternoon of that Thursday's performance which mercifully never took place, he was found in a Seventh Avenue bar — drunk, numb, and nearly senseless — by the faithful Greinert who bundled him into a cab.

At the April 5th and April 6th pair of concerts, Artur played Bruckner's Seventh Symphony, his first reading of it in the seven years which had elapsed since his brother Richard died in the week of the Anschluss. He could perform the piece without collapsing now, for at home in his nursery was another Riki, and the brother lived no less in the nephew. Artur's soloist for that pair of concerts was one of the most brilliant of his generation's pianists, a man who himself has a son to be counted among an even more amazing breed of keyboard artists. The father, Rudolph Serkin, played Beethoven's Third Piano Concerto. If Artur admired the man's modesty, warmth, and pure and honest musicianship, how he would have loved Peter Serkin for those same qualities, long hair, dashiki, and all.

Artur's agenda for Friday, April 13, 1945, had unsuperstitiously pencilled in the activities of a father christening his son and a musician conducting his season's last concert. The program was Strauss's *Ein Heldenleben* and the Brahms Second. But Artur did not have to concern himself with straining for a good reading for a Friday afternoon audience after depleting himself on the preceding Thursday night. The Thursday concert was canceled.

President Roosevelt had died: Friday's concert would be a memorial.

Artur wanted to dedicate the Strauss to F.D.R., a piece about a hero to honor a man whose life and death had been heroic. Judson and others in management agreed it would be a fine idea. Later, however, Bruno Zirato phoned to say Olin Downes of the *Times* objected vehemently.

"Strauss is a no-good-Nazi-son-of-a-bitch," Olin charged, and neither management nor Artur could afford to disregard the powerful critic's opinion. Artur was upset, nevertheless. He only understood good music and bad, and never could understand how a tone poem, much less a symphony or concerto, conveyed a political message or ideology. In deference to Olin's sensibilities, and what would seem to have been others', Artur played the second movement of Beethoven's Seventh and Mozart's 40th Symphony in G Minor. He reserved Brahms's Second Symphony as the vehicle to express his sadness. I missed the performance, being busy with preparations for the christening.

Artur rejected the idea of Brahms's D Major score as one "of idyllic pastoral moods," "a light-hearted symphony." "I feel great tragedy in this music," he said, "and I conduct it so." He based his view on the fact the work was written during Brahms's most unhappy period, that time when Robert Schumann's widow, the pianist Clara Wieck, refused her dead husband's friend and protégé.

When Artur read Virgil Thomson's review of the performance, he said to me, "This man is the first person to understand what I mean when I conduct this symphony." Virgil wrote:

> It was the first time this season that your reviewer had had occasion to hear the orchestra play under its own conductor a program of this kind. At any other time, indeed, such a program would have seemed to him over-conventional and consequently not newsworthy. In the present circumstances it was most welcome, however, and the beauty of the concert's execution added warmth to the seriousness of it all. . . ."

Coherence is always difficult to achieve in the longer works of Brahms. Their meditations are so inward and their eloquence is so outward that the adoption of a mood capable of expressing both presents problems of rhythm and phraseology for which there is no standard solution. So much dreaminess and so many straightforward emphases are hard to hold together in one piece.

Well, Rodzinski did it; and I don't know how he did it. He simply opened his heart to the music, I suppose, without losing his head. And if anybody thinks that is an easy or common manoeuvre in the handling of Brahms, I can only wish him the hearing, one after another, that a reviewer has in any season, of all the conductors great and small in their mostly unsuccessful comings to grips with the problem.

Riki's christening took place as planned. We got permission from the church to have a Polish priest perform the ceremony at home. There was a hitch, however: Charlie Swift could not come from Chicago, and we had a great problem finding a new godfather at the last moment. Helen Hull was to be the godmother, and Artur decided to have a Polish-American combination. We didn't want to hurt any of our friends by choosing one and not another, and so we asked Jan Karski, a person whom we hardly knew. A hero of the Polish Resistance, Karski had recently escaped and had published a book called *The Secret State*. For us he was a symbol of fighting Poland.

More than a hundred guests came, many of them directly from Carnegie Hall and raving about the Brahms. Most were staunch Republicans, disliked Roosevelt violently, and were relieved rather than saddened by his death. "Papa" Damrosch came and brought a fancy sculpted baton for Riki with blessings "from the oldest conductor to the future one." Donna Carla Toscanini, who was very shortsighted and wore thick, heavy glasses, bent close over Riki to get a better view. He began screaming and never stopped throughout the ceremony. Helen tried without success to pacify him, and Karski also failed. Goddard Lieberson observed that Riki already resented being upstaged.

When we arrived at Stockbridge in the last week of May, the weather was hellishly hot, and Artur's moods somewhat less than completely angelic. Once again he began to lose interest in the farm, although he did keep after his bees. The work with the Philharmonic in the second season had taken more out of him than he appreciated, and called for more extra-seasonal work than he had anticipated.

Artur's relaxations and pleasures were few, and almost solely derived from hours passed with his infant son. Of course, his inability to sleep through the hot summer nights did not help his moods, but I should have foreseen that in his restiveness might have been the seeds of some future difficulties. And when I speak of restiveness I refer to his continuous talk that summer of selling the farm to take a place farther north, one cooler and away from the Berkshire Festival and the casual visits of musicians. Certainly, there were symptoms of an inner uneasiness in wanting to be away from colleagues and friends, a withdrawal inconsistent with his Moral Rearmament stance. But I didn't recognize them when I heard him frequently complain: "I can never find any privacy or peace around here!"

Chapter 36

I WAS not distressed by the seams and cracks which Artur's MRA facade showed during the summer. Truth is, I was too happily occupied with my son and role of mother to notice or attend to much else.

On the face of it, Artur was at his zenith when the Philharmonic's 104th season began in October 1945. Concerts were sold out. The critics had rarely been so complimentary. The Sunday broadcasts were a success with all concerned — the home audiences, U.S. Rubber, and the board of directors, whose annual deficit was made up by the sponsor's payments. And the players and Artur received a generous extra income from growing sales of Columbia recordings, demand for which was encouraged by the radio performances.

Olin Downes, on one of his summer visits, interviewed Artur on his new season's plans. They were ambitious. New composers should be heard and stimulated to produce, he told Olin; audiences should be kept vitally in touch with contemporaneous tendencies in an art constantly renewed by fresh creative ideas.

To reinforce these statements which appeared in the *Times*, Artur opened his season with Aaron Copland's *Appalachian Spring*, the first concert performance of the suite derived from the ballet composed for Martha Graham. The work won the Pulitzer Prize and the Music Critics' Circle Award.

The second week brought the premiere of Dmitri Kabalevsky's Piano Concerto and a pleasant reunion with soloist Nadia Reisenberg. When Artur made his debut with the Warsaw Philharmonic some twenty years earlier, Nadia was also at the beginning of her own career.

It was during a break in rehearsals for this performance that Artur pulled one of his crazier stunts. While he sat in his room checking the Kabalevsky score, someone told him of a crowd of sailors gathering outside Carnegie Hall for a Navy parade. In the few minutes left to the rehearsal break, Artur assembled the whole Philharmonic on the corner of 56th Street and Seventh Avenue. With a cue, they sailed into "Anchors Aweigh." The sailors roared approval, which led to Sousa's rousing "Stars and Stripes Forever." Then a military band joined in down the street. Though the war was over, the crowds lining Seventh Avenue cheered and applauded.

Artur later told a reporter, "This was the first time the Philharmonic's members had turned street musicians." Dorle Jarmel, slaving at her typewriter to get off a weekly press release, could only applaud such undignified stunts!

Such spontaneously outgoing gestures could be credited to MRA's influence, the principles of which Artur apparently still subscribed to. He seemed as happy as I ever knew him. The pattern of our life together hadn't changed. When he drank that crucial first cup of coffee in bed, he was a thorough jewel, snuggly, cuddly, and loving. Then we would have what we called our "quiet time," a period when we read aloud passages from Scripture to one another, and thought on them a while. After that, the concerns of the day could be faced.

Artur's relations with the Philharmonic players, though sometimes set on edge by the connivances of the personnel manager, Maurice Van Praag, generally had never been better. When smiles and praise were due, both flowed like syrup. But work was work, and as Artur gave of himself in rehearsals and performances, he expected payment in kind from the men. Some continued to mistrust my husband, fearing him in a way he understood. They felt insecure in their present situations and worried about the future. Artur controlled their destinies, and had even courted disaster to clear away "dead wood" and "dry rot," something any of them might some day be considered.

They did not know as I did, however, that Artur had great feeling for each man as a human being. Nor did they know how Artur, too, had long lived with similar fears, that someone in management or on a board of directors held a whip that one day just might be cracked. Unpleasant experiences with his last board chairman in Cleveland had taught Artur a thing or two about the real power of musical directors of American orchestras. His prior experiences with Arthur Judson certainly had shown him something of the awful strengths that resided in a business office. Still, with his growing spiritual convictions, my husband managed to find a point for cooperation with nearly everyone during his first three Philharmonic seasons, including A. J.

Stage fright, a big fear all artists must conquer, was even eased for Artur at this time. And, to the advantage of his performances, he was able to pass his sense of assurance on to his soloists, which resulted in some remarkable collaborations. His years in an opera house had taught Artur the great need for support each soloist has, and he himself had always drawn security from carrying them musically in his arms, leading them through the difficulties and tensions of making music come alive.

I remember an instance with Willy Kapell in that season's fourth week. He was to play Rachmaninoff's Rhapsody, a work which held no technical terrors for someone with his technique. Yet as the time to go on stage drew near, Willy was paralyzed with fear. Artur, whose room was adjacent, knowing the pianist's state of mind, went to him, with only minutes to spare before the two were to be on stage. They spoke quietly for a few moments. Then Artur put his hands on Willy's shoulders, lowered his head, and prayed. Both men soon left the room jauntily to walk on stage together. Willy seated himself at the keyboard as Artur stepped on the podium. They shot each other an encouraging grin, and all went well — splendidly well.

The skein of Artur's good relations extended from home to orchestra to guest soloists and even to board chairmen and managers. Charles Triller, who followed Marshall Field as chairman, was pleased as punch with my husband. The Philharmonic made money and news, and attracted newer and larger audiences. As Triller wrote in a letter regarding Artur's new contract, "the orchestra gives every evidence of marked improvement under your inspiring leadership." The contract was arranged to satisfy one of my husband's new desires: instead of taking a two-week break after every month of concerts, he wanted a two-month leave in January and February in order to conduct abroad. Europe was returning to something like normal, and requests for guest appearances came to Artur from every capital and major musical center on the continent. Such work would be a burden, but he was in excellent physical form, and the travel and chance to play with different orchestras would be a stimulus. And, indeed, that restiveness which first reared up the previous summer was prodding him. He needed new experiences, he said.

Since New York appeared to be our home, more or less for good, we decided to find a place of our own. The house on 84th Street which we rented was offered to us at a price of $40,000. In 1945 that seemed a monstrous sum (although when the place last changed hands, it was for a quarter of a million dollars). Artur thought about buying it, but there were problems with the plumbing, and in those days of scarcity, especially of copper pipes and tubing, my husband decided against the purchase.

Artur, in turning down the house on 84th Street, in a sense revealed his unspoken, underlying uncertainty of what the future held for him. His psychological need for a home of his own, which eight years earlier led us to buy the farm, was now no more. It was as if stability of residence and mind mirrored one another. But all this is quite after the fact. At that moment, we had to find an apartment in a time of housing shortages. We managed to locate one finally, with the help of Floyd Blair, a Philharmonic board member. The place was at 1160 Park Avenue, that same street which seemed so misnamed when, an age earlier, Miecio Munz had first showed it to me.

We called on another friend, Treasury Secretary Henry Morgenthau, for help in getting a telephone (which in those immediate post-war days, was a priority item, and required application to the War Department). To furnish the place, we cannibalized our Stockbridge home for choicer items, including Mr. Argenti's handsome Spanish oak dining-room suite. Everything was close to perfection, and perfection itself was attained with the coming of Susie Taylor.

Susie was a black woman Marysia regularly met and talked to while on shopping trips. Completely charmed by Susie's style of forthrightness, Marysia urged us to hire her. We had lost Victoria to a husband some time before, and the procession of housekeepers and cooks we subsequently had left much wanting. "Susie will fit like a glove," Marysia said. "Engage her." I did, and our family grew by one more soul.

Susie was striking, with silver-white hair and a velvety, dark olive complexion. She was an excellent cook and excelled at any other task she set herself. Her eye for clothes and what looked appropriate was fabulous. When I wore something new or different, I fretted over Susie's reactions, for she could damn an expensive frock with a glance, and make me feel the fool for buying the thing. "Mama, you just don't look like Mrs. Rodzinski in that," she would say. But if the dress was approved, she would beam, give a low whistle, and say, "Now *that's* okay, Mama."

Artur was "The Boss," and she passed on his appearances, too, inspecting him from head to toe before a concert, giving his winged collar and white bow an adjusting twist, or brushing off whatever lint dared settle on The Boss's frock coat. Part of Artur's pre-performance superstitions now included Susie's last-minute attentions, plus her funny good-luck wishes: "Jive 'em with that Beethoven tonight, Mr. R." Or "Boss, curl them longhairs for Susie, you hear." Artur laughed, usually only barely comprehending her slang. If Artur was in a pet, and my temper on the rise, Susie stood as buffer. "Mama," she would say, "this is The Boss's day. 'Patience' is the word. Let's make him laugh."

Artur was a hospitable man; he loved drop-in visitors, though later he might grouse about his lack of peace and privacy. Someone who stopped by in the afternoon was, a priori, expected to stay to dinner, regardless of the quantity of food available. This never flapped Susie. Unlike most cooks, she took such things in stride, and made sure that her meals could do what she called the Six-Way Stretch. She also stocked the refrigerator accordingly.

Social obligations, as any conductor's wife can confirm, easily get out of hand. One of my few ways of meeting them was with an invitation to a concert. Box 61, however, was meant to seat eight; but often there were as many as twelve for which the ushers had to find extra chairs. Jerry, the backstage usher, often let my friends in without tickets: all they had to say was "Box 61" or "Mrs. Rodzinski." Things were different then, vastly different. A visiting musician without a ticket could easily enter and be seated somewhere. Always, after a concert, familiar faces would smile through the doorway to Artur's dressing room, or step in to make a comment on a performance. The people in his room were a hash of celebrities, of nearly-so's, of has-beens, eccentrics, favor-seekers, sincere or begrudging admirers, composers with scores, conductors without podiums, pianists, violinists, and cellists by the gross with time for an audition anywhere. There were also florists' boys, Western Union messengers, and myriad nameless people who ran other people's errands, the anonymous boys and old men who brought memos and mail from Judson's Steinway Building offices to Artur's in Carnegie Hall.

One messenger, whom Artur never saw, delivered a letter from an unknown U.S. Air Force officer and a slip of paper written in a cherished hand: "Am alive. Would love to see you. Mother."

Artur was beside himself. He phoned me at home to read a letter that accompanied his mother's scrap of paper. An American plane had landed at Lvov in the winter of 1945. The city, occupied by Soviet troops, became sharply alive to news of the American presence, and Artur's mother sent a girl with her note to look for the fliers. The girl found them in a restaurant, and informed them in a species of English that the note was for the conductor of the Cleveland Symphony Orchestra. One of the officers knew Artur had been with the Philharmonic for three seasons, and took it on himself to forward the message.

From that moment on, Artur's free time was given over to bringing Mama Rodzinska to America. He wrote reams of letters, made hundreds of phone calls, and several trips to Washington. Surely someone from among our influential friends could do something, he reasoned. But, alas, this was not the case. Our friends and acquaintances could sympathize but little else.

Then a bit of good chance came our way. The new United Nations had been meeting in New York for the first time, and the sessions were tense. Artur proposed that the Philharmonic board invite all the UN delegations to a special performance of Beethoven's Ninth. "Who would fail to be moved by the fraternal aspirations of the composer and Schiller?" Artur asked. Few directors believed the choral ode's words about brotherly love would move many hearts, but it did seem worth a try. "We'll plant the seeds of liberty and cooperation in their hearts," Artur said, naively, but the concert was given nonetheless.

The event was instantly oversubscribed. Goddard Lieberson asked me to let Frank Sinatra attend in my box. "He's such a nice boy," Goddard said. That he was, and a very moved one. He must have whispered "Gee whiz!" several dozen times. The audience generally was moved by a performance which Louis Biancolli described in the *World-Telegram* as "a sermon in world understanding." The UN delegates also got the point, and there was a cordial atmosphere in the Hall's old Picture Gallery where a special reception was held.

Among the many diplomats to speak with Artur was Andrei Gromyko. He was especially complimentary, and clearly touched by the music. He said that it came to him as a gift which he could never return.

"But perhaps you can," Artur said. "Perhaps you could do me personal favor."

"My privilege," Gromyko replied. "Come and see me at my office."

That night at home Artur unfolded his plan. "Do you remember the story you once told me of your Grandfather Wieniawski: how he was allowed to return from exile?" "Of course," I said. "Granduncle Henryk had played for the Tsar and one of the Grand Dukes had been told to grant a favor." "That's it," said Artur, "and we are going to do the same thing."

The very next morning, Artur made me phone the Russian Consulate for an appointment that afternoon. I was awfully nervous when we arrived at what had once been the town house of Mrs. John Pratt. My legs actually trembled when we entered the foyer. There were four men in leather jackets, their hands thrust deep in their pockets, immovably seated like compass points in the lobby's four corners. They followed our every step with a sort of humorless, professional impersonality.

A young receptionist ushered us into an elevator, which whisked us up to the top floor where Gromyko greeted us with an affability that put the starch back into my knees. Most Americans remember only the stony face of the harried diplomat of the years before "détente" became a fashionable word. But in those early days he still had a youthful handsomeness, and nice manners.

As we chatted on the way to his own office, in English — Gromyko's was fluent — the diplomat once again praised Artur's performance. Then, when we were seated, he became all business. "What is it I can do for you," he asked.

"It is for my mother," Artur said. "After all these years, I have had word that she is alive in Lvov, alone, without food, heat. I have tried to bring her here, but with no success."

"I see," Gromyko said, making notes.

"She is old, Mr. Ambassador, and I could make her last years comfortable. She is not . . . political."

Gromyko stood up, the meeting over. As he came from behind his desk, he said, "I will do my best." Then, once more, he talked of music, of Beethoven's Ninth, and returned us to the receptionist who took us back to the lobby.

Two weeks later, the Soviet Consulate informed us Mama Rodzinska received a package of warm clothing, a case of tinned food, and a supply of scarce, scarce coal. Artur felt absolutely certain that things would slowly progress toward her release.

Early in April Goddard Lieberson was married to the beautiful and talented dancer-actress Vera Zorina, and the party given by Andre Kostelanetz and Lily Pons, then his wife, was for me the social event of the year. I always have had a weakness for marriages of friends, and this one meant a lot. Vera was not only getting a husband destined for marvelous things, but also one who would make her laugh whenever things were far from wonderful. The Kostelanetzes' guests included all of the staff and artists of Columbia Recording Company, opera stars, conductors, pianists, and violinists. And Vera's theatrical friends were well represented. Judson, who had a finger in everything that bore the Columbia label, came to smile and wave his Havana cigar.

Throughout that winter Artur had spoken about disposing of the farm. "I'm a musician," he reasoned, "not an agronomist. All we need is a summer place." This kind of talk made me uneasy, unhappy. I had become selfishly attached to our house, our neighbors, and the whole feel and setting of the Berkshires. The farm was our only real American home, the place where I had first been able to have a sense of rootedness. The thought of selling the farm also upset Marysia and Karol. The place was theirs, too. "You know how variable Artur's moods can be," I said, trying to placate them as much as myself. "He's bound to have a change of mind." But the fact is, since MRA, Artur had not been all that variable in his ways. Subtly, almost imperceptibly, he and I were sliding into former patterns of behavior.

That summer's heat wave did not help my cause much. Artur never could tolerate heat, and the spring and summer temperatures were the worst in local memory. Moreover, the roads were clogged with Tanglewood folks, audiences, students, and musicians. Artur could no longer drive his horse and buggy, his scooter, or his car without being a tourist attraction. And he also for some time, and perhaps not unreasonably, had found onerous the obligation to attend Koussevitzky's rehearsals and concerts. "I used to feel free around here," he said. "Now I don't."

I fought Artur's arguments with a plentiful helping of Susie's "patience," but it was a losing struggle. Artur just invented new arguments, and an obsession or two to buttress them, the greatest of these being an atomic war in which New York would be a target, and Stockbridge would receive the fallout. Thinking of Riki's welfare, he argued that we should have a place as far removed from New York as possible. I might have bought his thinking were it not for two flaws: we lived in New York most of the year, and we had absolutely no guarantee an atomic war would be conducted in summer, let alone formally declared. Still, when Artur insisted on his way, it would have been easier to lift neighboring Greylock Mountain with a finger than force an alternative.

Artur had his way: that summer was spent at Lake Placid, New York. We rented a large house with a garden and fine view of the Adirondacks, and looked for property. The area was one we had often heard about and knew slightly from a skiing trip on the Upper Saranac many years before. Our friends Percy Eckhart, president of the Ravinia Festival, and Dr. Martin Buchband, an ear, nose, and throat specialist who had often treated my husband, had both raved of its beauty and climate.

While I scouted for a house or a piece of ground on which to build one, Artur studied the score of Arthur Honegger's *Jeanne d'Arc au Bucher*, the handsome setting of Paul Claudel's mystery play for speaker, soloists, choruses, and large orchestra. Artur hoped to premiere it the following season, with Goddard Lieberson's wife in the speaking title role.

"Vera will be perfect in the part," Artur said. It calls for an actress with a sense for the music (that Artur and Goddard both could drill into her).

Finally, my husband and I found the land we had dreamed of. It was an old golf course, surrounded by forests of pines, birches, and beeches, covering more than two hundred acres. The only buildings on it were an old shack and a sort of club house. Like a pair of romantic fools we bought it. The terrain looked Polish, and was blessed with an extraordinary view of the Adirondacks.

At just about this time, Arthur Percival and his wife, a pair of Tanglewood friends to whom we had rented White Goat Farm, said they wanted to buy the property. Still hoping to discourage the sale, I set what I thought was a preposterous price. It gave them not a moment's pause, alas! The Percivals came from Stockbridge to Lake Placid for the closing, but no sooner were the bill of sale and deeds signed over to them than Artur had second thoughts. He began to realize that building a house on the piece of ground we had bought near Lake Placid would be a herculean task, and it was.

The large plot, divided by a winding, graveled lane called Old Military Road, was atop what the maps called Chubb Hill. (We redubbed the topography to suit our tastes, giving it the name of our son: Riki Hill.) Water and power would have to be run a great distance to the meadow where Artur had decided the house should sit. In 1946 one had to be either a national emergency or very well connected to get pipes and wire. My husband understood himself to be both, and wrote to authorities and business associates with a truly caesar-like sense of self-importance. Strangely enough, he got all the building supplies that for years had been on the shortages lists.

The architect we hired, William Distin of Saranac Lake, was extremely pleased with the commission. A house on the scale we wanted had not been constructed in that locality for years. There were to be eight rooms, plus three full baths, a powder room, and a kitchen where Susie Taylor would stand guard. Artur would have a studio at the other end of the house. The whole thing would be done in the style of mountaineer homes in Zakopane. Folk motifs abound in the finished oiled-cedar woodwork, traditional patterns of cutouts and appliqued surfaces. The nucleus of the structure was to be the former golf course's club-house, and this, since Artur never did things by halves or simply, was moved several hundred yards away from the road, involving many man hours and the reconstruction of a magnificent stone fireplace.

Artur, when he laid his scores aside to play at real estate developer, made everyone work. And our regular summer guests, the Wierzynskis, were pressed into my husband's forced labor gang. Kazimierz had no objections. When he wasn't writing he liked physical things — the clearing of brush, sawing up of trees, and whatever other work was needed. It was a relaxation for both men, actually. We two Halinas stayed out of their way.

During that summer at Lake Placid, Wierzynski was feeling particularly out of sorts with his lack of a readership ("Who but Poles read Polish?" he would say). It was then that Artur hit upon an idea. The one-hundredth anniversary of Chopin's death was to be celebrated in two years (1948), and my husband suggested that Kazio was the man to write a centennial biography. "There's not a good book on him," Artur said.

Wierzynski argued that he could not write professionally about music, that he knew very little about biography, and that prose was a beast apart from verse. "You can do it," Artur encouraged, and Wierzynski began to consider the project.

The clincher came when Percival and his wife arrived with the White Goat Farm papers for Artur to sign. Percival met Kazio and the two men got on quite well. Seeing this, Artur explained the poet's problems to Percival, who offered to finance Wierzynski if he wrote the Chopin book. Additionally, he offered Halina and Kazio one of the cottages at the Stockbridge farm for the two years needed to complete the manuscript. It was settled. (Wierzynski produced the most sensitive nontechnical book on Chopin ever published in English. Artur Rubinstein wrote a preface, the reviewers generally treated *The Life and Death of Chopin* very nicely, and in time the book was translated in many languages.)

On August 4, 1946, just four months after the meeting with Gromyko, a cablegram arrived from a cousin of Artur's in Katowice. Mama Rodzinska had come from Lvov by train in the company of a Russian nurse, and she was en route to Stockholm.

We were deliriously happy. Artur arranged to meet his mother in Sweden. But like the best laid plans of mice, those of anxious and loving sons are also capable of being scotched. At the last moment, Artur was invited to conduct the Philharmonic in a Hollywood film, *Carnegie Hall*, a piece of cinematic kitsch which my husband could not resist. He wired his mother that an American diplomat would meet her in Sweden, which he arranged, and that he would greet her in New York.

The reunion was a deeply emotional experience, and as with most of these in life, it was compounded of equal parts of joy and sadness. Mama Rodzinska, once so plump and shyly self-assured, was a withered old woman who leaned on the arm of a nurse as she exited from the plane. What little flame was left after seven years of war's privations under two occupations flickered cautiously into a smile when she saw her "Turek." Her heavy oddments of clothing contrasted harshly with her son's tailored summer suit as the two embraced. There were more tears than words exchanged.

We took her back to Lake Placid where she was introduced to her grandson. It was a touching moment for her. Her first Riki was no more but here was another.

Mama Rodzinska's luggage contained a number of antique Polish tapestries and carpets, between which had been carefully laid a collection of deer horns mounted on lozenges of black lacquered wood, each marked with the date and place the animal had been shot by Richard. They were treasures to us. When our house on Riki Hill was finally built, the horns were hung to decorate the dining room.

Susie and Mama Rodzinska got on quite well, considering that neither could understand the other. Their common bond was Riki, who was beginning to walk and talk. We had tried, with little luck, to raise our son bilingually, but since he heard English spoken more frequently than Polish, he had resisted his parents' native language. Soon, however, he realized his grandmother could only speak those funny sounds; Riki and Grandma soon became inseparable and necessity made the child fluent.

Artur was so delighted to have his mother around that he showered her with little attentions, a number of which were received as nuisances. Breakfast in bed was one. When he brought her a tray that first morning, she was annoyed. She did not like to be waited on and told Artur she could get to the table on her own.

Mama Rodzinska had a rather unfortunate manner in one respect. While she was a loving person, she did not know how to show affection, and accordingly did a poor job of accepting any expression of it. When she tried, the results were invariably unhappy for her and everyone else, except Riki.

Whatever the joys and problems with his mother, Artur had a house to build. He was delighted when his letters to friends, acquaintances, and total strangers broke through the bureaucratic web that had made pipes and wire premium items. The president of General Electric, whom Artur had never met, was pleased to send him the heavy duty cable needed to carry electricity to the building site. The favor, he wrote, was in gratitude for the hours of pleasure he had from Philharmonic broadcasts. And so it went. Arthur Percival put us in touch with makers of nails (scarcer than hens' teeth), with purveyors of bathtubs and toilets and even of priceless steel tiles for the bathroom walls. Percy Eckhart, through his seat on Montgomery Ward's board, helped scrounge up the metal-frame windows our architect wanted.

With supplies arriving daily at the Lake Placid freight station, Mr. Distin began work with the hand-digging of a trench a half-mile long, through rock and mud for our water. By the time we went back to New York to our apartment on Park Avenue, the little clubhouse was slowly moving on log rollers from one part of the field to another.

Chapter 37

THE start of Artur's fourth Philharmonic season marked the end of his MRA days. Living in absolute honesty, purity, unselfishness, and love began to weigh on him. One morning, in a rage, he threw his Bible to the floor and shouted. "Toscanini and Koussevitzky live without Moral Rearmament, and look where *they* are now!"

From that moment Artur preferred to follow his own path rather than one prescribed by someone else. When friends from the Group came to visit, to offer aid to a confrere in spiritual trouble, Artur became irritable. He was coming to see that he had idealized quite ordinary folk as saints. The magnificent structure he built for himself of MRA materials crumbled altogether to dust. Frank Buchman's precepts had lent Artur's life an aura of sobriety, of equilibrium, but only an aura. Yet the effects of his renunciation of them would soon become apparent.

Contractually, my husband was obliged to review and approve the program of guest conductors. Each one understandably selected compositions which assured success with the public and critics. Sometimes they chose the same works, often by coincidence. For instance, in 1946–47, Stokowski and Szell each wanted Beethoven's *Pastorale*, Brahms's First, Tchaikovsky's *Pathétique*, and the Second Symphonies of Sibelius and Schumann. Charles Munch and Stokie both wanted Ravel's *Daphnis et Chloe* and Debussy's *La Mer*. Many of these same pieces, however, my husband had intended for his own programs. They were proved audience fetchers, effective capstones to programs, and the sugar coating which could make a less familiar, if equally valid, composition or some bitter novelty easier to swallow. Ordinarily, and even before my husband's MRA intermezzo, Artur would distribute the "plums" unselfishly.

The trouble began with a contemporary piece, Arthur Honegger's Symphony for Strings and Trumpet. Munch wanted this piece. The Frenchman was making his Philharmonic debut, and he sequestered for himself all the effective music of his compatriots. As far as Artur was concerned, Munch could have the Ravel and Debussy pieces which the guest requested, and works by Franck and Berlioz to boot. But Artur wanted the American premiere of Honegger's Symphony. The composer's wartime works were much anticipated, and Honegger was said to have produced a gem in this particular piece. Artur refused it to Munch. In a letter he told Bruno Zirato that the forthcoming performance of *Jeanne d'Arc au Bucher* would be detracted from by dividing publicity with the Symphony premiere of the same composer. "We cannot take away from [*Jeanne d'Arc*] all the attention it should have," he wrote. After mentioning that "you thanked me for my generous attitude toward Munch for relinquishing so many numbers to him," Artur concluded with an ominous reminder to Zirato that "as musical director responsible for planning, I am against letting Munch introduce the new instrumental work."

Zirato, with whom my husband's relations had never completely cooled (though by this time there was frost on his dealings with Judson), tried to persuade Artur to yield. Artur would not budge. I begged Artur not to be obstinate, but nothing I said helped. Following the exchange of a few more memoranda, Zirato gave in to Artur. But the genial, warm-hearted Italian's disposition was moderated by his maestro's uncooperativeness. Indeed, Zirato, either on his own, or at Judson's suggestion, informed the board of Rodzinski's "difficult behavior."

The contest between Artur and Zirato over Munch and the Honegger Symphony was the first round in a psychological boxing match between Artur and Judson that was to run the course of the season. It was also what sportswriters call a "grudge fight." The friction was a historic one, which had begun with Artur's first Columbia Concerts contract. Artur felt that the percentage Judson claimed on each of his fees was unwarranted, simply because he performed no service to merit compensation. Judson might argue he promoted his artists' careers, but to this Artur could reply with concrete evidence to contradict him. His appointment as director of the Los Angeles Philharmonic had been gotten through the commendation of Stokowski (another man who had little liking for Judson), and finally on his own abilities. When William C. Clark in Los Angeles chose Artur to lead the ensemble he supported, Artur even concealed his affiliation with Columbia, of which Judson was president, though paying the agent's fee all the while. When John Severance heard Artur in Los Angeles and invited him to Cleveland, there once again was an initiative taken by an individual with no connection to Columbia Concerts. And there was every proof that Judson had even argued with the Cleveland's directors and managers *against* hiring Artur. Still my husband paid Judson's percentage. When, over the recommendation of Toscanini, Judson brought John Barbirolli to the directorship of the New York Philharmonic, Artur could bear the situation no longer and severed his contract. This was the second time he had done so. The first time — shortly after he discovered the adverse opinions Judson circulated to the Cleveland's manager, Mrs. Adela Hughes — was soon followed by Artur's capitulation. He signed again because the stranglehold Judson had on American orchestras was such that he could not take many guest appearances without Columbia Concerts' participation.

While the first rebellion by Artur was short-lived, the second was longer. It lasted until his MRA interlude, and his being considered for the New York Philharmonic somehow coincided.

Again contracted to Columbia, Artur maintained a cordial relationship with Judson during his first season with the Philharmonic. Their friendliness dissipated over the matter of ticket sales. Artur wanted the subscription plan enlarged. Judson did not. My husband preferred the programming freedom that came from a guaranteed audience. Judson wanted to use the box office as a "test" of interest in soloists, conductors, and program content. In Artur's view value judgments of performers and compositions should be made in musical terms, not cash flows or popularity contests. A piece by Schoenberg which has stood well in time's opinion, or a Bruno Walter, who in those days did not sell out Carnegie Hall, were considered failures by Judson's criteria.

Artur complained of these things to certain members of the Philharmonic "family." The ticket-sales issue was raised at a Philharmonic board meeting, and Judson was angered. He believed Rodzinski had gone over his head as well as behind his back. A.J. cooled toward Artur. And, with the impersonality of an autocrat, battled to protect his empire.

I saw Judson at work at a meeting of the Ladies' Auxiliary Board. He was masterful. His argument was that full subscription sales would result in a "stale audience," the notion being, I suppose, that people who listened to music were like so many loaves of bread. True or not, the ladies were enchanted, perhaps not so much with the ludicrous reference as with Judson's good looks and his air of authority.

Characteristically, Judson the businessman did not care for innovation. My husband did. New music, new artists, and new kinds of programming concepts were for A.J. a pointless flight in the face of "a good thing." Moreover, Judson did not care to engage artists who were not under his personal contract. What else, then, would be the sense of Columbia Concerts' interlocking relationship with the Philharmonic and other orchestras?

My husband was spoiled by his decade in Cleveland. There he had been allowed at will to present his thoughts at board meetings. In New York he had to request "permission." Otherwise, my husband's ideas were enunciated and elucidated to the directors by Judson. When it came to the production of a big, expensive work, an operatic or choral work, my husband correctly understood that Judson argued at cross purposes with him. To Judson money saved on an expensive oratorio, say *Jeanne d'Arc au Bucher*, could be put into fees for a soloist, from which, in turn, a commission could be extracted. During Artur's tenure, at least, costs which contributed to an operating deficit could not have been an issue. The Philharmonic broke even when it did not show a surplus — and this for the first and only time that I know of.

Further cooling relations with Judson was Artur's suggestion that

(280)

the Philharmonic engage Stokowski for the 1946–47 season. Stokie was Judson's mortal enemy. It was Judson, who while manager of the Philadelphia Orchestra (in addition to the Philharmonic), had undermined Artur's former *chef*'s position with his board, eventually introducing another of his clients, Eugene Ormandy, as co-conductor. It was a bad situation which could only end with the worse part going to Stokie, as indeed it did, and he left. Many years passed after that 1940–41 season before Stokowski, at Ormandy's invitation, reappeared in Philadelphia's Academy of Music.

When Artur proposed his old patron lead the Philharmonic, the board was enthusiastic about the idea, if Judson was not. With the white-maned celebrity contracted to someone else, the agent's percentage would be paid to a Judson competitor and Stokie's fees were high. Judson, however, was only another employee of the Philharmonic, and he was obliged to acquiesce.

Stokowski was delighted with the invitation. It was a vindication of sorts, and, besides, he no longer wanted to fight. He came to our home to express his gratitude directly to Artur, and to introduce us to his new bride, the young Gloria Vanderbilt. Artur, in his turn, was delighted to do something for the man who had once helped him by bringing him to the United States, and also to put their mutual "enemy" in his place.

My husband next saw Stokowski at the Lotus Club, that haunt of the New York music crowd, lunching with Judson. Artur later discovered that Judson made it up with Stokie, and had gone my husband one better in publicly rehabilitating the older musician — he was planning a European trip for the Philharmonic with Stokowski as conductor.

This was a terrible blow for Artur. His dream was to take his New York orchestra on tour in Europe. But there was no money for the trip. (The United States government had yet to see the propaganda value in such ventures.) Financing had to be private, and Stokie assumed responsibility for raising the funds. As things turned out, the venture never materialized. Artur bore Stokie a slight grudge thereafter, but slight compared to his resentment of Judson.

All of this is prelude to the actual season, which opened October 3, 1946. The novelty on that first program was a William Schuman composition with a symbolic title, *Undertow*, a ballet score the just-appointed head of Juilliard had written for Martha Graham's dance company. Artur's mother attended. Her white hair had been attractively done by my hairdresser and was strikingly set off by a long black gown. White orchids completed the effect. She once more looked every inch the General's widow.

Schuman's dance composition was one of a long list of contemporary pieces Artur offered to the Philharmonic's audiences that season. Unfortunately, the mortality rate for them was appallingly high. Manuel Rosenthal's *Musique de Table* is characteristic. Well-wrought, engagingly tuneful, and orchestrated with the élan of a man who knows the orchestra as a conductor, the piece, one might have thought, would surely enter the repertoire. Rosenthal is best known for *Gaité Parisienne*, the ballet he arranged from Offenbach items. At the time Artur introduced Rosenthal's *Musique de Table*, the composer had completed the monumental task of reorganizing Radiodiffusion Française, and had conducted numerous broadcast concerts which showed his countrymen that despite the years of Nazi domination, French composers and their music had thrived and grown.

Rosenthal informed Artur that he would be in North America, and offered to conduct one of his own works should my husband be interested. Artur was, and invited Rosenthal to lead several concerts, and he did so without consulting Judson. This was resented, perhaps justifiably. But Judson's resentment took a vicious route that is impossible to justify: he refused to pay the composer-conductor a fee. This was communicated to Rosenthal without my husband's knowledge. Indeed, Artur learned of the manager's actions by way of a letter from someone in the French cultural ministry. The gist of the letter was that rich America was taking cruel advantage of a Frenchman pauperized by the war. A niggardly fee of $500 was finally arranged, an honorarium in a sense. And Artur received a memo from Judson's office "informing" him that his paycheck would be docked for half the amount. The money meant nothing, but the high-handed and arrogant way it was extracted irritated Artur terribly, and soured him on his work.

Mama Rodzinska noticed this, and shook her head. "I never thought I'd live to see my son lose enthusiasm for his work," she said gloomily.

It was with something less than enthusiasm that Artur led a concert with selections from Debussy's *Pelléas et Mélisande*, sung by the British soprano Maggie Teyte, who had studied the role with the composer, and who was making her American debut. By the time the premiere of David Diamond's *Rounds for Strings* fell due, my husband's spirits picked up. And when the score to the last of Shostakovich's "war symphonies," the Ninth, was introduced, he was rather back to normal. The Russian's new symphony had been a disaster in the U.S.S.R. It was criticized for "ideological weaknesses," and "failure to reflect the true spirit of the Soviet people." Artur replied to American criticism of the composition by saying, "History alone can sit in final judgment on any artistic effort." History apparently sat. One seldom hears the piece these days.

There was a pleasant interlude in the course of the season's bustle. Zoltan Kodaly made his first visit to America that fall, and heard his *Hary Janos* Suite conducted by my husband. The hospitality which Kodaly and his wife had shown us in the Thirties when we first met in Hungary we returned at a dinner party. Olin and Irene Downes were among the guests, and Kodaly told us of the years of the Nazi Occupation. Olin later reported one of the composer's accounts in a *Times* article:

Accused of [sheltering Jewish fugitives] by the Gestapo, [Kodaly] coolly confirmed the charge and added that he would not under any circumstances reveal the places where he had hidden the fugitives or make any promise that he would desist from such practices in the future. It says much for his position as a patriot and an artist beloved by his countrymen that apparently the Nazis did not dare to prosecute him.

Social life — intimate evenings with artistic friends or big and noisily gay parties — distracted Artur from the day-to-day clashes which were occurring with increasing frequency. Now he even sought out social diversions. He really tried to keep distinct the border between preoccupation and obsession, and fought the resentments and fears that followed the painful exchanges with A.J. Perhaps Artur was no longer as successful in his efforts as when Moral Rearmament's precepts had served him, but he remained committed to a straightforward, if qualified, exercise of the Golden Rule. He would do good to those who could do him no harm.

My brother-in-law Kazik Krance, my sister Fela, and a group of émigré Poles had organized an American Committee to Aid the Institute for the Blind at Laski, Poland. The school educated blind and otherwise handicapped children, of which Poland had more than her share after the war. The Polish government had little help to give. The American Committee's hope was to fund a rebuilding and training program.

Helen Keller agreed to assist in the Committee's first fund-raising efforts. At a public meeting this extraordinary blind-deaf-mute communicated her life's story through a companion who understood her "language" of touch. Miss Keller's own speech, though she had mastered it quite well, was difficult to understand. The audience responded when she pleaded that each handicapped person be given a chance to find an independent life, that the most advanced training techniques be made available to them.

Artur was so affected by her talk that he offered an initial gift of a thousand dollars to the Committee's fund. His contribution was matched by Stanton Griffis, who had just returned from Warsaw where he had served as the first U.S. Ambassador after the war. Other sums were rapidly collected or pledged before the meeting closed, and the Committee, of which I have had the honor of being chairman since 1959, was on its way. Miss Keller, when we were formally introduced at a reception following the meeting, said she "listened" to my husband's Philharmonic broadcasts every Sunday by holding her outspread palms to her radio's speakers and feeling the vibrations. "You are giving me the greatest joy of my life," she told Artur. To him it was a revelation that music could be truly "felt" this way.

Soon thereafter a celebration of Artur's twenty-fifth anniversary as conductor provided my husband with another important diversion from his day-to-day irritations. There were press releases to work on with

Dorle Jarmel; also, since the anniversary would figure in the publicity for the season's second half, a *Time* magazine cover story to help work up. When the cover story would finally appear, it would celebrate an incident of another sort.

For quite some while, Artur's lawyer, Allen Dulles, had been discussing Artur's contract renewal with Ralph Colin of the Philharmonic board. Colin, the board's counsel and also counsel to Judson's enterprises, was drawing the negotiations out pointlessly, or so it seemed. Dulles, the brother of John Foster and the head of the Central Intelligence Agency, was an astute bargainer. He urged Artur to bide his time. But Artur believed the delays in formalizing the agreement were tied to an increasing flow of nasty memos from the Steinway Building. He suspected that Judson wanted to be rid of him. Certainly, the file folders I have bear out the need for such concern. Judson's hostility toward Artur was now only thinly concealed. Each powder-blue half-sheet memo that arrived on Artur's desk produced a new tremor of concern. He would personally talk over the matters they treated with Zirato, who would then send him a pale green half-sheet memo which took an entirely different tack from the one discussed face to face. Artur smelled jeopardy everywhere, and in fact it was there.

Van Praag, the personnel manager, was Judson's Carnegie Hall agent-informer. If my husband became impatient at a rehearsal, the phone rang in Judson's office down the street. Judson would then fire off another powder-blue half sheet, addressed variously to "My dear Rodzinski," "Artur Rodzinski," "Dr. Rodzinski," "Mr. Rodzinski," "A.R." and even sometimes "Artur," the mode of address previewing the tone of the memo. Artur then reacted instantly, especially when he could trace a "leak" from Carnegie Hall directly to Van Praag.

Behind Artur's back Van Praag even said that "it was a mistake to make Rodzinski Musical Director." Of course, there was something personal in the personnel manager's opinion. When Van Praag had put together *his* list of the men who should not be reengaged at the start of my husband's first season, Artur uncovered — and put a stop to — another bit of private enterprise in the Philharmonic set-up. Van Praag had collected a tribute. Those who had not paid it had, to a man, found themselves on Van Praag's "little list," a list, I must add, much longer than Artur's.

Van Praag also brought Artur before the Musicians' Union that season to answer "grave charges." Artur was accused of "swearing at the men in Polish," a language none of them understood. The whole thing had been engineered by Van Praag as a humiliation. Artur repeated his "objectionable language" in translation, the "vile things" he had uttered sotto voce, for example: "Where the hell did I put that pencil?" To a player encouraged to fret by Van Praag and concerned, perhaps, about his own insufficiencies, phrases such as this must have been terrifying. The "grave charges" were dropped.

Artur was angry and he let his baton speak for him during a concert toward the end of November. On the same program which included the world premiere of Darius Milhaud's Concerto for Cello and Orchestra, with Edmund Kurtz as soloist, Artur led the Philharmonic in Stravinsky's *Le Sacre du Printemps,* a work he had first introduced to Los Angeles, then Cleveland. The performance that night was one of my husband's finest. He unleashed all his pent-up rage through the medium of Stravinsky's calculated primitivisms, the slashing dissonances, the screaming orchestral tuttis. The effect in the hall was hair-raising, and brought an ovation on Thursday night. At Friday afternoon's concert, it brought a powder-blue half-sheet memo from Judson, delivered by Zirato: "I do not like *Sacre du Printemps* as a concert piece, but you certainly did a swell job! Congratulations. A.J." Mumbling something under his breath, Artur turned from Zirato with a shrug as his reply, and Bruno carried the shrug back to the Steinway Building.

That was the last concert my husband conducted before his projected European tour, the date for which was coming near.

We had hired by this time an excellent nurse-governess in whose hands we could leave Riki safely. Mama Rodzinska was to remain at home with Susie, so Riki would not want for concerned attentions. Also, my three sisters lived at that time in New York. But Artur now suddenly was concerned about leaving our son while we toured. Previously he had upbraided me for the very same thing. "I just can't go," he said, and talked of canceling two months' engagements. Nora Shea, Judson's secretary and an administrative assistant to the manager (one of whose agencies had contracted the tour, perhaps the first real work the Columbia group had ever done for Artur), tried to dissuade him. "Artur, you'll be blacklisted by every orchestra and manager in Europe," she warned as a friend. Ignoring this advice, Artur spoke even louder about canceling, thereby, and only incidentally, threatening to cut Judson out of some hefty percentages on my husband's fees.

I cannot say with certainty that it was unwise on Artur's part to consider staying in America. His intuition told him that much dirty work could be done while he was away. Allen Dulles and Ralph Colin had made no progress on the new contract. Indeed, the talks had hung fire so long that Artur resolved to handle the matter himself. In the second week in December, he went before the Philharmonic board to say that he was unhappy with a year-to-year renewal, and that in order to effectively plan, he needed a long-range agreement. He pleaded his case well, as a legally-trained musician might, and the board members gave him a unanimous vote of confidence. They voted Artur a five-year guarantee with "no strings attached," and wrote a letter confirming this.

Despite Judson's marked coolness to my husband's board-room performance, Artur was elated when it was over. He seemed to have all the directors behind him, he told his mother and me as he described their reactions in minute detail. He had so convinced himself of a triumph by

(*285*)

the time he finished his narrative that he wrote a personal thank-you to each member of the board. He expressed gratitude for the "lovely Christmas gift you voted me" and promised for the New Year a fine gift in return: "my paramount goal will be to make [the Philharmonic] the best orchestra in the world."

But Artur's troubles were far from over. He now took over the negotiations for his contract from Dulles and got absolutely nowhere. Each time Artur tried to make contact with Ralph Colin, Judson's and the Philharmonic's attorney was busy. A.J. and Zirato were invariably burdened with "previous engagements" when Artur tried to catch them for lunch. It looked as if they wanted to delay, at least until Artur went away on tour. It looked suspicious. And then one of his oldest, and long-suppressed fears boiled to the surface: "They're waiting until I'm out of the country to fire me."

On that note of horror, he definitely canceled the European tour. "I couldn't go with this ax over my head," he said. "We'll go to Lake Placid where I can keep in touch with what's happening — and we'll build our house." So I dutifully unpacked all the finery purchased for Europe and refilled the bags with ski clothes, mittens, scarves, and furs for the snow and cold of the Adirondacks.

Chapter 38

ARTUR spent the winter building a house — and also programming for the rest of the season, studying new scores, remembering what it was to be a father and a son, and negotiating, secretly, for a new future, should his strategy come to nothing.

Jeanne d'Arc au Bucher held his imagination that winter, along with the Third Symphony of young Peter Mennin, whose concert overture he had introduced earlier. He thought highly of Mennin, and while studying his new orchestral piece, kept marveling over his fluency and sense of organization. "He's talented," Artur said, not one of his frequent comments about young composers. That Mennin's "organizational sense" would lead to success as director of Juilliard School of Music's complex operations was something no one could foresee in those days, however.

While Susie Taylor, Riki, Mama Rodzinska (or "Babcia" as her grandson had learned to call her), and I tried to make home of a rented cottage, Artur passed his free time away from his scores and program charts at the site of the house taking shape off Old Military Road. For several hours each day, he alternately helped or hindered carpenters, plumbers, and electricians. A project he had set for himself was paneling our living room and dining room with some barnsiding we found. Artur sorted the rough, random-width boards so that the living room, with its large stone fireplace, would be lined with silvery weathered surfaces. The dining-room's wood would have the golden warmth of what had once been stalls. Artur became engrossed in working with wood, even to the extent of designing and building some clever fixtures for indirect lighting.

The work took his mind off his problems, or else gave him the leisure to brood on them — which, would be hard to say. Indeed, his smiles that winter were few, mostly rewards for Riki's antics. He frequently talked about the regrets that gnawed at him, the cancellation of his concert tour, and the outcome of the contest he had entered with Judson for control of the Philharmonic.

Soon after Christmas, Edward Ryerson telephoned from Chicago. The conversation lasted a long while, with Artur saying very little at his end. My husband turned to me as he hung up the receiver, rather subdued, to say: "He offered me the Orchestra. What do I do *now?*"

There was no ready answer. On the face of it, accepting the proposal was an easy way out of a complex tangle. The situation with Judson, I now see, was even at that moment untenable. The manager had once, years before, described his relations with my husband as "both distasteful and unprofitable," and was now again of that opinion. Both men, so strong willed and with so much at stake, were locked in a contest and neither was likely to compromise.

Ryerson had asked Artur to meet him in New York for more discussion, and he had agreed. My husband took the sleeper the next day, saw Ryerson, then immediately returned.

Although the talks went well, Artur was still undecided. The Chicago's board chairman had proposed a five-year contract, which New York's board had also promised (if only verbally), along with the same salary and vacation considerations Artur had requested. Most importantly, however, Ryerson had said that Artur could produce operas as part of his season's activities. This, all considered, was an immense temptation.

The conductor Chicago hired in 1943–44 when Rodzinski was not to be had was Désiré Defauw, and the poor fellow was in over his head. Whatever his talents, they did not appeal to Claudia Cassidy, the critic for the *Chicago Tribune*. She, with her sharp pen, was dealing the conductor one slashing review after another. The public was drifting away. As Ryerson saw it, Artur was the only man who could help the situation, especially since Claudia Cassidy was enthusiastic about him.

The decision was hard to make in the face of common sense and Artur's long-standing interest in a Chicago base. He knew the city took great pride in its orchestra, certainly more than New Yorkers in theirs, and remembering old Stock's thirty-five years with the ensemble, he viewed the post as a secure one. Aside from the fickleness of New York's audiences, the critics there could easily run against him if he failed to come up with some novelty, some sensation to applaud in their reviews. "You're only as good as your last concert," Artur would say.

New York, though, was far more prestigious, a greater source of publicity, and prospectively more lucrative, thanks to recordings and radio broadcasts.

The next several weeks were agony. Ordinarily, Artur would make up his mind intuitively, and act. That had been his way for most of the years I had known him, dating from the day he told Nela Mlynarska I was to be his bride. Now, like a tightrope walker, he measured his steps carefully, cautiously. We sat up night after night, watching the snow fall, rehearsing over and over again each "pro" and its relative "con." As soon as I would back the soundness of one view or the other, he would argue its opposite. To opt for Chicago would swing him back to New York.

He was constantly talking with Floyd Blair in New York. "Artur, you've got to be crazy," Blair, a friend and member of the Philharmonic board, must have said a hundred times. "You have the best position in the world, and the best arrangement — all the vacation you want, a bigger salary, less work. And we're all behind you to a man." But when my husband would raise the subject of Judson and the machinations of the Steinway Building offices, Blair would reply, "Your fears are groundless, absolutely groundless." Without any basis in fact? "None whatever," Blair would repeat. Artur, of course, knew otherwise, though not to what extent.

Then a call would come from Ryerson: "Anything you want, Dr. Rodzinski," and Artur would repeat, or modify, his conditions for accepting the post. "Yes, I agree," Ryerson said to each, but the Chicago board chairman could no more pin my husband down than Blair. Then once again, until two and three in the morning, Artur went over the same arguments and counter-arguments. (This, in the long run, was why an artist usually had a manager, I thought to myself.)

I admit that I also still thought that Artur's fears of A.J. were largely self-conceived, and that my husband's lapse into the clutch of some negative force was the result of booting MRA and God from his thoughts. I could not give credence to Artur's conviction that Judson was working against him, and that the board would eventually side with Judson. He would tell me time and again: "They're *all* businessmen, they understand each other. Me? I'm a musician, and not to be listened to seriously — as if anyone listens to me. Judson gets to them first. He goes to meetings. I'm told of the decisions, without a chance to explain myself."

Two months of this, and I was exhausted. I could no longer take the torment of his indecision. And Artur's sudden flights from a fear I could not perceive but which pervaded our rented house like a cold winter draft were even affecting Riki and Babcia unpleasantly. Everyone's nerves were on edge, and no matter how many times Susie urged "patience" I found myself always on the verge of tears. I have never been sure if Artur had a nervous breakdown during those weeks, but I am certain that I was close to one.

We returned to New York on February 2 and the next day Artur appeared at a session of the executive board to discuss his new five-year contract. The meeting was at 3:30 in the afternoon. A few hours before, Artur received a copy of the agreement and pored over it with an intensity that left him drained. I could understand why when I read it myself. "Isn't this incredible? Can you still tell me I make up things? That Judson isn't working against me?" His hand shook with rage as he took the papers back from me.

"No," I said, "you have been right all along."

He left for the meeting in an extremely agitated state. I had no notion how things would turn out when the door closed behind him but that a battle royal was about to begin I did not doubt for an instant.

I was later told that Artur entered the board room in command of himself, the directors greeted him amiably, and one of them handed him a copy of the new contract to sign. Artur is said to have darted a quick glance in the direction of Zirato and Judson before tossing the papers on the table.

"This isn't the agreement I expected after December's vote of confidence," he said. "You promised me a contract without strings. Instead you hand me one with chains!"

He then took some notes from his pocket, or so I imagine, to be better able to itemize his grievances. I found such sheets on his desk that night, and on them I find he charged the board was intending to limit his powers in selecting guest conductors and soloists, and in deciding their programs. Thereafter, as Artur understood the proposed contract, Judson and the board would decide who was to conduct and what. Thus, Artur would lose control over the concert year's planning which alone made possible the kind of musical balance which he felt to be necessary. Matters of aesthetics apart, however, Artur would cease to be musical director as he understood the function.

After blasting the contract, he blasted Judson, calling him "a dictator who made musical progress impossible." He pointed out that in the quarter century of Judson's tenure as Philharmonic manager there were "twelve major conductors who had marched in a ghostly parade before the audiences," and that all of them, with the exception of Toscanini, sooner or later evaporated, never to be heard from again. "Only Mr. Judson remains," he said, "a situation without parallel anywhere in the world."

Then Artur said the unsayable. "As manager of many soloists and conductors, Judson engages as many of his own clients as appearances will allow. He uses the Philharmonic as a testing ground for unproved performers. He uses it to give them publicity. And, of course, he doesn't run from the profits he reaps."

The accusations became bolder, and the nakedness of the language made Artur's words just that much crueler. A few men tried to interrupt, but Artur talked over them. Ralph Colin periodically was heard to interject: "This can't be true." But the picture that Artur drew bore a repulsively close resemblance to what everyone understood, had quietly accepted, tolerated, or had chosen to ignore. Judson is said to have sat there, slumped in his chair, visibly disturbed, pale, too distracted to even relight his cigar. Zirato was stupefied.

Finally, Artur had no more words. He fell silent, and after this, his most crucial performance to date, and one with vast consequences for the health of American music and musicians generally, there was not so much as a whisper. Artur said most of those present merely sat looking at the board table's dark wood, not daring to look at one another, much less at him or Judson. Triller was the first to break the silence.

"What, then, Mr. Rodzinski, is your decision," he asked. "*Will* you sign this contract, or not?*"

"I want twenty-four hours to think it over," Artur said, and the meeting, such as it was, came to a close. Everyone left in an awful gloom, all save Artur. He returned home happy.

"I told everything," he said. "All the dirty linen's been aired. It's up to the board now: they clean up the mess, or do business as usual — Judson's kind of business. Whatever happens, though, the next musical director may have an easier time."

But that was not the end of the affair. As Artur saw it, the board could do no less than take Judson's part. Sensing this, and already too deeply committed to his grand strategy, Artur felt obliged to get the jump on what would inevitably be the board's and Judson's next move — so, he would quit before being fired, and he would do it publicly. Together we wrote a press release which I phoned to all the city's newspapers and *Time* and *Newsweek* magazines.

Artur then sent a telegram which would arrive at the board meeting at the hour Judson, Zirato, and the others sitting around the conference table were sharing their embarrassment over the public furor. The telegram, addressed to Triller, read:

> I am deeply touched with your appreciation of my work which found expression in offering me a long term contract as conductor of the Philharmonic Orchestra. It has been my goal to make this great orchestra the greatest in the world. It is already on its way but the job is not finished yet. Unfortunately the existing circumstances and the organizational shortcomings make the attainment of this goal impossible. Therefore, with great regret I would appreciate your releasing me from all conductorial duties as per October 1947.

"Now Judson can't give it out that I was released," Artur said as he sank down in his red leather chair and sighed. "I am free," he said. "I'm going to Chicago."

When the city's eight newspapers hit the streets pandemonium engulfed our block of Park Avenue. The phone and door bells jangled. Western Union boys came and went. Reporters swarmed like bees. Various friends added to the welter of noise and confusion. Poor Susie was driven to distraction. Many friends were stupefied, puzzled, appalled, all by turns. It was difficult to make clear just how much Artur was in his element. He loved and encouraged the hubbub, and in his sessions with the reporters prodded the facts behind his actions to the brink of plausibility. Rodzinski would not fail to make good copy. All the years such impulses had been subverted by MRA now were being compensated for at once.

Soon, the young assistant to the manager of the Philharmonic arrived with a letter from Triller. Artur opened it with a certain smug, self-confidence, expecting nothing more than an acceptance of his resignation. He had not anticipated reading that "under the circumstances, it is in the interests of the Society to terminate [Artur's] services immediately, rather than in October."

The board *had* counterattacked. That was not considered in my husband's strategy. Still, what did it matter? He had achieved his major objective, and had a sanctuary awaiting him in Chicago.

Later that afternoon Floyd Blair called at the apartment, wearing an unhappy face. He had come to discuss the financial settlement, he said. The decision to sever relations was taken because of Judson. The board thought, and rightly, that relations between the manager and musical director were too damaged for effective work. Judson's feelings were "deeply hurt," Blair informed us. Artur's, apparently, were not considered.

If Artur entertained some hurt because Judson had been retained in preference to him, the notion was eased out of mind by the congratulations which poured in from every branch of the musical world. He was lauded quite to intoxication for his "courage in exposing Judson's Mafia." More than one letter or wire came from some poor soul whose musical destiny had been darkened by Judson's business doings. "That man actually retards the development of musical life in America," one prominent performer wrote.

There were others whose words of encouragement were notably unvoiced — those whom Judson still managed. These silent conductors and soloists still had to grovel before him for whatever crumbs he might throw them. And a few conductors stood to benefit from their silence. After all, someone had to replace Rodzinski.

My husband's actions, though they brought him no end of pain in the years to follow, were eventually vindicated by time. It was ever so with him: his irritations in Cleveland over a "handful of strings" made it possible for George Szell, after Erich Leinsdorf's brief tenure, to insist effectively where Artur had failed. When Leonard Bernstein succeeded Dimitri Mitropoulos, it was as a conductor unhampered by a Judson and with a board much chastened by the happenings of intervening years. My husband's musical accomplishments may have been forgotten, but the changes his bold actions wrought in the realm of orchestral management and administration survive as a monument to him.

At the time, the *Herald Tribune*'s Virgil Thomson was the only member of the musical press to confront the issues raised by Arthur's actions. Olin Downes did little more than equivocate. Poor Olin, friend though he was, felt it his responsibility to see both sides of a story that assuredly had only one. But Virgil wrote:

> Artur Rodzinski has gone and done it. For years the knowledge has been a secret scandal in music circles. Now he has said it out loud. That the trouble with the Philharmonic is nothing more than an unbalance of power. Management has usurped, according to him, certain functions of the musical direction without which no musical director can produce a first-class and durable artistic result. He has implied that no conductor, under present conditions, can keep the orchestra a musical instrument comparable to those of Boston and Philadelphia. He points to Arthur Judson, a powerful business executive who manages the orchestra as a side line, as the person chiefly interested in weakening the musical director's authority. He is right, he is perfectly right; he could not be more right. An orchestra can use one star performer and one only. And such a star's place is the podium, not the executive offices. . . .

> The Philharmonic case is simple. Arthur Judson is unsuited by the nature and magnitude of his business interests to manage with the necessary self-effacement a major intellectual institution doing business with his other interests. He is also a man of far too great personal force to serve effectively as a mediator between a proud musician and the equally proud trustees. That is probably why no conductor ever stays long enough with the Philharmonic to accomplish the job that everybody knows should be done, namely, to put the orchestra permanently on an artistic equality with the other American orchestras of comparable financial resources.

> Artur Rodzinski has done more for the orchestra in that respect than any other conductor in our century has done. Mahler and Toscanini were greater interpreters, were not such great builders. If Stokowski and Munch, also great interpreters, have been able this winter, as guests, to play upon the orchestra in full freedom and to produce from it sonorous and expressive beauties of the highest quality, that achievement has been made possible by Rodzinski's personnel replacement and his careful training. Such an achievement on the part of guest conductors has not heretofore been possible. Today the Philharmonic, for the first time in this writer's memory, is the equal of the Boston and Philadelphia orchestras and possibly their superior.

Time Magazine, in its February 17, 1947, issue, elevated Artur to the minor nobility by making him its cover man of the week. That, I suppose, was recompense for the subtly uncomplimentary feature article. Artur came in for laughs at the expense of his MRA convictions, while Judson garnered adjectives such as "handsome" and "leonine." Integrity and convictions were words that failed to appear.

Chapter 39

On February 5, 1947, the day after my husband's Philharmonic breach made national headlines, Artur and I quietly boarded a sleeper for Chicago after dodging reporters and leaving a trail of false leads to our whereabouts. We were whisked from the train station outside Chicago directly to Ryerson's country home, and it was there that we met with the Chicago orchestra's executive board at a dinner that evening. Artur's "great future" was toasted with champagne served in the finest crystal. In reply to a round of clicked goblets, he said, "My dream has at last come true. I will accomplish here what I have long hoped — to make this city the musical hub of America." Applause, and another splash of champagne. Somehow, a genuine aspiration on the part of the artist had fortuitously coincided with the rhetoric of the Chicago Chamber of Commerce.

The next day Ryerson, Artur, and I worked to draw up plans for the forthcoming season in a general way. When we finished, Ryerson smiled, and asked, offhandedly, if he and Artur ought not draw up a contract.

My husband, also smiling, stretched a hand to the industrialist, and said, "You never had a contract with Stock in thirty-five years. I don't need one either. A handshake with you is a contract for me!" They pumped each other's arms as if working a dry well.

When the press announced that Rodzinski had been engaged in Chicago, the news brought another furor in its wake. Reporters led to our doors a horde that included composers, singers, and instrumentalists by the dozens. Friends who had been shocked before were now delighted. Goddard Lieberson came to congratulate Artur, to discuss the possibilities for recordings, and to see what chances there might be for doing *Jeanne d'Arc* in Chicago. Artur was deeply committed to the work, and if he had any immediate regret about throwing the Philharmonic to the winds, it was giving up the premiere of the Honegger oratorio. Vera Zorina, Goddard's wife, was no less disappointed. She had worked long and hard to master a complex and demanding role for which, suddenly, there was no performance prospect.

When this second, though less draining, burst of activity ground to a halt, it left Artur in need of a rest. He decided Florida would be an interesting change, and he drove down. Riki, the nurse, and I followed by train the next day. As usual Artur was able to gather up his thoughts behind a wheel and he relaxed in the sense of unimpeded speed that one still could find on highways in the Forties. He drove day and night and actually arrived at Fort Myers, where we were renting a cottage by the beach, several hours before our train did.

Artur had letters to write, answers to congratulations, and a careful defining of plans to do for Ryerson and his fellow board members. While there were also programs to be planned and some study, he had already accomplished much of his work in preparing for the Philharmonic's coming season. Too soon Artur ran out of things to do aside from his routine of long walks along the beach, collecting seashells, and swimming several times a day. With nothing really able to engage his mind and with no substantial outlet for his physical energies, he began to brood.

Fortunately we had Lake Placid to go to after Florida, and there my husband distracted himself with the ongoing work on our home. He spent hours designing decorative metal work — hinges, latches, hasps — for use throughout the house. I had not known previously how sensitive and sensible about such things Artur could be, or how talented he was mechanically until he installed a complete power workshop in a shed near the house. The biggest surprise, however, came in his flair for interior decor. He instinctively knew the right place for a splash of color, against which wall to hang one of Babcia's antique Polish carpets, in which little niche to secrete a piece of pottery to subtle advantage. But as much as he enjoyed these things, so he relished the little tagalong Riki had become, a son who admired each bit of his father's handiwork, and sometimes shared in it. And while Babcia sunned herself on our front porch with its view of the Adirondacks, Susie and I made tasty things to feed to a steady stream of musician guests. To all of them Artur told how happy he was to be rid of Judson.

Our friend Percy Eckhart stopped by, and the two men talked over the Chicago situation. In a sense, Percy was responsible for Artur's popularity in the city, for it was Eckhart, through the Ravinia summer concerts that he sponsored, who had first offered Artur's talents to the Chicago public.

But all was not happy in their talk. Percy said, "I'm afraid you won't have it easy."

"Why so?" asked Artur.

"Ryerson is as stubborn as a mule . . . and he doesn't know a damned thing about music. In fact, I'm not sure he even likes it."

When Percy's car pulled out onto Old Military Road, Artur was left to mull over the prospect that Ryerson might be Judson's mirror image. He told himself there were substantive differences. Ryerson had no need for plots and nefarious dealings. He was a successful man whose fortune

(*294*)

and position should place him far above the petty double dealings of a Judson. Moreover, the relationship of Ryerson to the Chicago orchestra was disinterested in comparison with the parasitic Philharmonic connections of Judson. Artur was determined to make a success of his Chicago situation. It was a chance to bring to life a great city's musical potentials with unfamiliar music and programming, new standards of excellence, and great opera. Still, these two observations about Ryerson affected Artur.

Our move to Chicago was without the same clearly articulated sense of purposeful design and fulfillment which marked our departure from Cleveland when Artur took over the New York Philharmonic. Then, also, the sense of triumph and vindication had been strong. Now, rather, there was only a feeble show of elation for public consumption, beneath which lay unresolved resentments and regrets, and more than a tinge of worry.

Our close friends in Chicago knew nothing of Artur's state of mind, so well did he conceal it, initially at least. Ellen and John Alden Carpenter, who located a furnished apartment for us in their building on North Lake Shore Drive, discerned no change. Claire and Charlie Swift, who were neighbors in a house close by, were unaware of any difference in him. I mention this because it seemed incomprehensible that not one of them could pick up what to me was so glaring. But it was just as well, for both John Carpenter and Charlie Swift were members of the Chicago's board, and it would not have been good for them to think that Artur was assuming his new post with uncertainties and suspicions.

On October 9, 1947, nearly ten years after his introduction to Chicago's audiences at Ravinia, Artur opened his season with the Chicago Symphony Orchestra. The house was sold out, and the public warmly received its new maestro. The press, especially the *Chicago Tribune*'s Claudia Cassidy, was laudatory. Indeed, the critics dusted off those superlatives that had lain neglected during poor Defauw's years.

The printed program promised the audience the brightest musical future: Artur's straight symphonic programs would be intermingled with "concert versions of operas . . . *Elektra*, by Richard Strauss in December; a portion of Wagner's *Parsifal* for Holy Week; and the Chicago premiere of Honegger's *Jeanne d'Arc* in April. Additionally, Rodzinski would give . . . *Tristan und Isolde* in full scale in the Civic Opera House for the benefit of the Orchestra Pension Fund."

Not too long after the opening concert, Ryerson gave a grand dinner party for us, to which were invited the orchestra's major benefactors. Everything was cordial. Ryerson, pince-nez clipped to his thin-bridged nose, made a speech, the general purport of which was that Rodzinski was "the best thing that had happened to Chicago." He said that Rodzinski "has won everyone's admiration . . . his name is to be heard everywhere."

When Walter Paepcke, one of the orchestra's trustees, struck up a conversation with Artur, Ryerson edged close to eavesdrop. Paepcke, a man of broad culture with commitment to the intellectual life, had begun to form his Aspen Institute which was to incorporate a summer music festival. He was asking Artur to consider the possibility of bringing the orchestra out to the old Colorado mining town where the scenery alone made the site a competitor to Koussevitzky's Tanglewood. Artur was intrigued by the idea, but as he began to warm to it, Ryerson joined the men and casually intruded a change of subject.

But there was really little time for thoughts of summer festivals. Chicago's work schedule was too demanding. It was much more strenuous than Artur had been led to believe. There were regular concerts on Tuesday, Thursday, and Friday; frequent appearances in Milwaukee; a number of short and long tours; and a regular, hour-long radio concert sponsored by the Chicago Title and Trust Company, given at the Eighth Street Theatre before an invited audience.

Rehearsals involved more than learning new works and shaping standards. Artur had to do a lot of cleaning up: there were weaknesses in every section of the ensemble, the same deadwood and dry rot which had had to be surgically removed in New York. If Artur learned anything from his Philharmonic experience, it was not to remedy an orchestra's deficiencies with a scalpel. He neither needed nor wanted a fight with the American Federation of Musicians and James Petrillo, now one of the most powerful union leaders in the nation. Still, personnel changes would immediately and vastly improve the sound. Artur tried to solve part of the problem by shifting a player from one stand to another less-exposed position, replacing the fellow with a finer instrumentalist. (Demotion of a player is a dangerous proceeding today.)

Before the next day's rehearsal, Artur had a phone call from Ryerson: "Dr. Rodzinski, that man is a friend of ours. I'd appreciate it if you left him where he was."

Ryerson's polite phrasing did not conceal his meaning. Artur had been given a command that was not based on musical considerations. He did as he was told, but he felt this countermanding of his decision weakened his authority. There was also something Judsonesque about the approach.

Soon thereafter, another change had to be made. A certain string player was not up to the work he was assigned. When Artur made it known the fellow ought to be moved, Ryerson once again intruded: "You leave him where he is. He plays string quartets with the wife of one of our board members." Once again Artur held his tongue, and wondered if perhaps Judson had told Inland Steel's boss something of the behind-the-scenes doings at the Philharmonic. Such personnel changes were completely within the purview of a musical director. Artur was on edge. The Chicago Symphony Orchestra in the late Forties was not the gleaming precision instrument that Fritz Reiner was later able to create (with big-salaried new men in the first chairs and the elimination of poor players) and to leave behind for Sir Georg Solti. Indeed, there were works in the standard repertoire which simply could not be brought to concert quality without extensive rehearsals. And for lack of them, thanks to the orchestra's heavy schedule, Artur was obliged to make a change in an already announced program. Needless to say, Ryerson made a big issue of it, imperiously. My husband was appalled. Belatedly he was discovering that Edward Ryerson considered the orchestra his private property. Percy Eckhart's words echoed in Artur's ears.

"If this is the way things will be, I won't get any work done," Artur told John and Ellen Carpenter. John understood. He had had dealings with Ryerson. "You'll have to live with it," John told my husband.

The Carpenters, whom we saw daily, were privy to another point of conflict between my husband and Ryerson. Inadvertently, they even helped raise it. On the orchestra's first short tour to Ann Arbor and Toledo, Artur noted a striking difference in the quality of the Chicago players' tone. The acoustics in out-of-town halls were superior to Orchestra Hall. "I discovered sounds that I never heard here," he later told John and Ellen.

"Oh, the Hall has *awful* acoustics. Everyone knows that. It was a mistake to give up the old Auditorium," Ellen said.

"Where is that?" Artur asked, and the same day we drove out to see the building, then part of the Roosevelt College campus. It looked dreadfully neglected and forlorn, but it had a handsomeness that only a blind man could miss. "All the opera performances used to take place here," Ellen explained as we entered the house.

"The place was designed by Louis Sullivan," Ellen continued. The interior seemed like a dream, with its gentle arc-like proscenium, and visual echoes of that form throughout, both in structure and in each lovely decorative detail. Artur was enchanted and wandered about the moldering place. Ellen and I stood on the stage, talking of productions she had seen there, while Artur walked at his peril to the topmost seats. Suddenly, like a clarion blast from heaven, his voice reached us: "I can hear every word you say down there — and I'm talking to you from up here at only a conversational tone!" He was euphoric when he rejoined us. "This is the place for our concerts," he enthused. "We've got to find a way to move them here."

"That," said Ellen, "is not likely to happen. The trustees built Orchestra Hall as the Chicago's home. I doubt Ryerson and his cronies will want to pay rent here. And just look at the place — it would cost a fortune to renovate."

Artur soon found that Ellen's observations were right. The merest mention of using the Auditorium in preference to Orchestra Hall of which Ryerson and his friends were so proud was enough to produce indignant objections. (When, many years later, the architectural make-it-new mania had subsided in Chicago and with it the lunacy of demolishing beautiful old buildings, the Auditorium was, in the early Seventies, revamped at a cost of many millions. It had been rescued from collapsing altogether by Harry Weese an enterprising architect with a respect for America's traditions. When it reopened and music was heard there once again, Artur's opinion of 1947 was seconded by everyone. Acoustically it was superior to Orchestra Hall.)

Nevertheless, at the time, Artur said what he had to say. And Ryerson's score of black marks against my husband grew by one more tick.

By this point, my husband had already started to lobby for his views and opinions, sometimes indiscreetly. It was safe to mention his preference for the Auditorium at a luncheon given by Ellen Carpenter at which we met her son-in-law, Adlai Stevenson, then engaged in his first campaign as Governor of Illinois; safe, because everyone agreed, including Adlai. This man, who was so immediately likable, spoke sensitively about music and the arts generally. But he also talked of politics and the chores of politicking. Just that day he had attended a meeting at which he had shaken the hands of hundreds of Poles. I liked Adlai, and I cherished his friendship.

The great Norwegian soprano, Kirsten Flagstad, had been branded in the American press as a collaborator for her return to Norway during the war to be at the side of her "Quisling" husband who was dying of cancer. Thereafter, New York's Metropolitan refused to hire her. One would think that by November 1947, almost two years after the war, passions against the greatest Isolde might have died down. But they had not. The Pole Rodzinski, with as much right and reason as any musician to bear a grudge against anything Nazi, took it on himself to engage her for the projected *Tristan*. Ryerson was in a rage. Artur would not lose this round, however. "You want a great performance? You need an artist who can give one. There is no other Isolde on any stage!"

When Flagstad's engagement was given to the papers the reaction was generally mixed.

Artur worked harder on that *Tristan* production than his body and mind could bear. Usually a good sleeper, he began now to wrestle with insomnia and was in a state of exhaustion. The day before the crucial dress rehearsal, he had given an afternoon concert and had had an evening run-through of the opera with singers and orchestra. That night he was at the point of fatigue where sleep becomes impossible.

"If I don't get some rest tonight, I'll fall apart tomorrow," he said. "I must have a sleeping pill to relax me." He took a Seconal. It had no effect. After tossing and turning, he left his bed to take a Nembutal. That did nothing either. Then he tried a second Seconal and finally fell into a deep sleep.

When I came to him with his coffee the next morning it was impossible to rouse him. I called to him, shook him. Nothing. I sprinkled him with ice water, and that made him at least blink his eyes. He stayed in this stupor for almost an hour, then he opened his eyes and asked me to

(*298*)

help him out of bed. Once on his feet he revived enough to walk to the bathroom, where he was violently ill. When he returned, he could barely stand upright. His muscles were like putty, he said. Black coffee had no effect. It just made him ill all over again. He was thoroughly drugged, even poisoned.

The dress rehearsal was at 11:00 that morning, and the hour was approaching. I was in despair, and when I phoned George Kuyper, the orchestra's manager, to see if the time could be rolled back, he was, understandably, furious. The logistical problems and expense would be immense, but he would see what could be done. After consultations with Ryerson and everyone directly concerned, Kuyper called to say that the cast and orchestra would be ready at three in the afternoon. I breathed with relief, drew the blinds and draperies in my husband's room, and sent Riki and his nurse out of the house so that Artur might sleep it off. But, though he tried, he could do no more than doze; finally giving the whole thing up as a lost cause, he nibbled some lunch and looked over the score.

When it was time for him to leave, his legs were like rubber. I had to help him dress and lead him like an invalid to the car. He was glassy-eyed all the way to the Opera House, and so dizzy as he made his way to the pit that he had to be supported to keep from stumbling over his own feet. Anxiety was on every face.

But the moment he began to conduct, everything went well. The concentration and physical exertions detoxified him, and the rehearsal came off even to Artur's satisfaction. As the curtain descended, a burst of applause went up from everyone present. A success was in the wind.

The curtain rose again that following Sunday afternoon, November 16, on one of the greatest triumphs of Chicago's musical history, and, assuredly, my husband's. The *Chicago Tribune*'s Claudia Cassidy wrote:

. . . unforgettable performance . . . As wonderful as the singers were, the top honors of the day went to Artur Rodzinski . . . superb interpreter of Wagner's music drama. . . . The audience sat transfixed . . . and hovered between tears and cheers as the just tribute to the blazing incandescence of a magnificent *Tristan and Isolde* presented by Artur Rodzinski. . . .

Newsweek's reviewer wrote:

It was a historic performance which no member of the packed house will ever forget. Rodzinski and his symphony were magnificent and, for a Flagstad Isolde grown greater with time and trouble, the audience didn't bother with cheers — it yelled. The Met's caution was Chicago's triumph.

The audience needed no reviewer's views to guide its response. The place broke into pandemonium, an unremitting thunder of foot stamping and applause as thousands of voices howled "Bravo! Brava!" It was the kind of ovation every artist dreams about and thinks only someone else will ever have. It lasted a full half-hour, with thirty-seven curtain calls. When the acclamation finally dwindled to the rhythmic clapping of a handful of diehards, with the house emptying, Ryerson turned to me. Poker-faced, he said, "Without question, the greatest performance we have ever heard." He polished his pince-nez, then clipped it to his nose to add, "but we shouldn't have done it. It was far too expensive." With that, he left the box.

Perhaps Ryerson thought the *Tristan* cost the orchestra too much in cash. Alas, there was no dollar measurement for the production's cost to Artur, for it taxed his physique and mind cruelly, coming as it did in addition to his regular concerts and social involvements. He immediately developed a bronchial infection which skirted pneumonia to settle down as pleurisy. The schedule for the next week was handed to my husband's assistant, a young Finn, Tauno Hannikainen. The week after, however, Artur returned to the podium, his pain notwithstanding.

Claire Swift, who always rode to the Friday afternoon concerts with us, thought Artur mad to conduct in his condition. "That pleurisy will not clear up without rest," she said. "You'll never be able to sustain *Elektra* in your condition. But my husband was banking on time healing the inflammation. When nearly a month later, December 11, the concert *Elektra* was due, there had been no improvement in his health. The doctor insisted that Artur cancel, but he would not even discuss the matter and asked that his affected side be strapped.

Considering who his Elektra would be, Artur's discomfort was a secondary matter. The soprano was Marjorie Lawrence — the courageous woman who, after being crippled by polio seven years before, had gradually retrieved her career, and intended to sing in a standing position for the first time since her comeback. She performed the grueling part, among the most taxing in all operatic literature, supported by a specially-constructed steel apparatus on wheels.

This concert added more reviewers' superlatives to those which accumulated deservedly in Artur's scrapbooks. It had been a long while since Chicago's ears had heard its orchestra sound as good. Old Frederick Stock, a worn and bored man at the end, had allowed the orchestra he inherited from Theodore Thomas to deteriorate. His successor, Defauw, was no stickler for precision, nor for the balances that distinguish first- from second-rate ensembles. That critical terror of every conductor in Chicago, Claudia Cassidy, though not a musician, responded sensitively to the changes Artur had worked: "It's a pleasure again to spend Thursday nights in Orchestra Hall," she wrote.

From Artur's vantage point, much more remained to be done. And he was anxious to get on with the work. He wished to achieve in one season what took him nearly three to do in New York. But there was a reason. He wanted to make progress, for its own sake, of course, but also to show the Judsons and Trillers in the East what Rodzinski in the Midwest could effect. In rushing things, though, Artur worked against himself. He became anxiety-ridden, openly irritable, and, often in frustration, uncooperative with the people who formed the top of the orchestra's power pyramid.

Artur refused all advice, both from old friends as well as from people who, while annoyed with his quirks, appreciated what he had done, and would do in the future. Claire Swift often tried to give constructive suggestions about the board, and especially Ryerson. But Artur would hear none of them. Then, once, inadvertently, Claire set his nerves completely on edge by raising the issue of contracts, vis-à-vis old Stock. The German who had survived for a record thirty-five seasons had clung to his podium by being compliant. He had been a "good employee," albeit always insecure, never ruffling the feathers of the board. More than a generation of such docile accommodation had clearly left a wretched legacy for a musician of Artur's temperament. His ideas for unique programming concepts and drive at this point to produce opera, his first conductorial love, caused conflicts with Ryerson. Change for its own sake, to Ryerson, was a sort of intellectual anarchy, and my husband's operatic schemes appeared insanely impractical. Understandably so: the board's notion of "supporting the arts" meant making them "pay their way."

Toward the end of December 1947, discussions were initiated among Artur, manager George Kuyper, and Ryerson about the 1948–49 programs. The talks then moved to the executive-committee level, at which point Artur reminded Ryerson before his peers of the five-year contract he had originally offered him. Because of what Claire Swift said of Stock never having a signed agreement, Artur, in that meeting, began to press for one. He now would feel secure about making long-range plans only with something more substantial than a handshake in his pocket. The executive committee was surprised by the talk, almost as if Ryerson had never told its members on what basis he had negotiated with and hired my husband. Soon surprise turned to reluctance to discuss the matter further. Artur insisted, however, and the meeting ended on a tense note.

Artur's birthday in 1948 fell on the same day as a Friday concert, and I invited Ryerson and his wife, along with several others, to a party following the performance. Piatigorsky, that week's soloist, also came. He and Artur were praised to the heavens for their afternoon's work. Everything seemed smoothed over with Ryerson; I think that his wife's presence helped somewhat. She cowed him, I suspect. As the Ryersons were leaving, Artur said the two men ought to get together the following week for a heart-to-heart talk. Ryerson agreed.

When they met, one thing led to another, and with no clear resolution in sight, Artur candidly brought the conversation to the central point: "You are a wonderful businessman. Stick to your business, collecting money for the orchestra. Leave the artistic side of the operation to me. You're green in musical and artistic matters."

On Tuesday, January 6, Artur had a discussion with three men who had been delegated the task of working out a contract with Ryerson's outspoken "employee." The negotiations, if that is the word, were difficult. Indeed, when Artur told me of what occurred, it seemed he had been handed a dictum à la Judson. "It's New York all over again," he said bitterly. Accordingly, my husband reacted resentfully.

I tried to pacify him. "Darling, nothing will come of another fight. Listen to them," I pleaded, "try and bend a little. Both you and what you want to do are new to them." Instead of listening to me, he bolted from his chair and telephoned to George Kuyper. What he said to the manager could not have been uttered by a man in control of himself. It was a tirade against Ryerson, the steel executive's lack of musicality, and his inability to understand my husband as either man or artist.

That same week's Thursday concert was one of the few I did not attend. Artur refused to let me go. He was angry, brutally so. When he left I was beside myself with fear dreading what might occur.

On his return he was quieter, a normal enough thing, and he wanted to talk; but he was depressed, something unusual after a performance.

"I have a pain in my left arm," he said.

I thought it was a remnant of the pleurisy.

"Maybe," he said, "but it goes all the way up to my chest."

I turned to stone at his words. We massaged the arm, applied heat, but nothing helped. I gave him a tranquilizer and put him to bed. Only after a long while did the pain ease enough for him to sleep.

He conducted the next day's matinee concert, which I attended. He was weak and listless when I went to his dressing room. "I think we should see Barborka," he said.

Dr. Clifford Barborka attended Artur whenever we were in Chicago. The physician, an amateur musician, was temperamentally able to understand my husband. An appointment was made for the following Monday. He, too, thought the ache stemmed from the pleurisy. "Artur overdoes things, you know."

Dr. Barborka went over Artur, front and back, with his stethoscope, then made an electrocardiogram. He tore off the strip of graph paper with its pattern of india-ink waves and went to a window to study it. I walked over while Artur was putting on his shirt and tie. The doctor ran an index finger along the line, pointing out an anomaly, sighing. "I don't like the looks of this," he said softly. I could hardly see the green and white markings, the jagged black line after Dr. Barborka spoke.

"Well, it's to bed with you for a few days," Dr. Barborka said when Artur joined us near the window.

"What's wrong?" he asked.

"Nothing that complete rest won't cure," was the physician's answer. He had no wish to upset his patient.

I called Kuyper from home to report that Artur could neither rehearse nor conduct Tuesday's concert. Kuyper was angry, and snapped at me rudely.

The next day, Artur had me call Kuyper again. My husband would conduct the Shostakovich Fifth, but Hannikainen could do the rest of the concert. Artur was afraid his assistant was not up to the symphony. Kuyper, who as manager ought to have been able to give an answer one way or the other on his own, took up the matter with the trustees — *all* of them, convening a meeting which Ryerson chaired. The answer that came back was an emphatic "No!"

The night after the concert, which Artur did not conduct, the Chicago Symphony Orchestra's board issued a statement to the press, announcing that Artur Rodzinski would not be reengaged for the coming season. The news was justified by a long series of charges which followed, a list that read like an indictment.

A copy of the "indictment," signed by Cyrus Adams as the orchestra's vice president, was delivered to us the following day. Ryerson's signature was not affixed to the bill of charges because he had departed for Manila, a convenient enough place for a brave man to be at such a moment. The letter simply withdrew any proposal for Artur's further services.

Then came the newspapers. The *Tribune* carried a large front-page story. The *Daily News*, ran a large page-one headline which read "Chicago Symphony to Drop A.R." All the papers printed the "indictment."

It accused my husband of making program changes. He had actually committed this "crime" on two occasions only, because the orchestra's ridiculously heavy performance schedule left too little rehearsal time, and the crime was preferable to criminally bad performances. They said he was guilty of wanting a written three-year contract, instead of an oral year-to-year arrangement. "Guilty," I plead for my husband — except that he had had an oral understanding for a *five-year contract* with Ryerson when they talked in New York, and had been given to understand that that was what he would get at the meeting with Ryerson in February 1946. The three-year arrangement was a concession on Artur's part at a later point. But the crime my husband committed was simply in now wanting an assurance of employment. Surely Ryerson did not sell his steel plate, piping, and cable without guarantees, yet for some perverse reason the businessman found it incomprehensible that an artist's services and product should in turn be guaranteed.

Among the other charges were the "outrageous" costs of Artur's operatic productions (which made money, if only by building an audience), and his insistence on the superiority of the Auditorium over Orchestra Hall.

Artur had always feared being "fired" from a post, and now that bogey lurking in his mind since his first years as a conductor in America became real.

Close friends, the Swifts and Carpenters, tried to ease the hurt. But if there would be any restorative for Artur's morale, it would come from a wholly unexpected quarter. Some reporters asked if Artur wanted to "give his side of the story." Quietly, he said, "I will let music speak for me," and with that got out of bed, against Dr. Barborka's orders, to conduct the radio concert at the Eighth Street Theatre.

When he stepped on stage the house gave him a standing ovation. Artur was very moved, and conducted with a special intensity.

Afterward, in his dressing room there was a stream of people, and in the crowded corridors there was angry talk. But not one malign word passed Artur's lips. He would no longer play their game.

Artur had never been at a lower ebb. The strains of the feuding in New York had worn him down tremendously, so much so that he had no real energy to face the tragedy in Chicago. Though still in his early fifties, he was aged in body and heart more than either of us fully understood.

Chapter 40

THE furor that came fast on the heels of the Chicago board's refusal to rehire Artur for the 1948–49 season, and its disavowal of the terms agreed upon before my husband even considered the job, was thoroughly enjoyed by the city's press. Each week of the four months left to the season brought some other choice bit of feuding to public notice. The music critics and reporters generally were on Artur's side; and this, in turn, produced a popular sympathy for my husband's cause, aside from his intrinsic attractiveness to the city's audiences. But Artur, with a sagacity born of exhaustion and a realization that any more dealing in dirt could only damage him further, held his peace. Ryerson and his clique remained silent. Fascinatingly, my husband's own silence only added to his popularity. Ryerson's closed mouth only exacerbated the public animus against the board.

Some concerned citizens supporting Artur took action, slight at first, but gradually more brazen. Initially, it was limited to letters to editors signed by prominent citizens; these outweighed covertly-sent letters from other "important" persons who inveighed against the near unanimous support of the publishers for Artur's position. Indeed, Claudi

Cassidy had offered to resign her *Chicago Tribune* post, thanks to the nasty letters. But Colonel McCormick, who had no special brief for Artur, simply doubled Claudia's salary, told her to file her typewriter to a rapier point, and hang the rest. He had no special brief for Ryerson, either, and probably relished the ruckus.

Then, on January 30, 1948, the papers reported that Samuel Laderman, general manager of the International Chemical Workers Union, had taken up the issue with Chicago's mayor. Laderman acted on behalf of union members who annually subscribed to a fifty-ticket bloc. Soon after the papers spoke of attorney Walter B. Wolf leading a group which demanded Rodzinski's retention. Wolf told reporters that he had received many letters offering vocal and financial support. This ad hoc organization was followed by the formation of others.

At about this same time, Witold wrote his father a letter telling him he had decided, with his wife, to live in Poland. This upset Artur greatly. Communism was, in Artur's mind, inseparable from Stalin's brutalism. And Communism in Poland could only mean a reversion to that state of affairs he and I had grown up with and were taught to loathe: foreign domination. The merits of Socialism were an issue between Artur and his son, from whom he was, as of Witold's letter, now physically as well as ideologically separated.

Dr. Barborka understood my husband's need for respite from anxiety, and prescribed tranquilizers and sleeping pills. But Artur, not one to do things by halves, developed a dependency on the sedatives of which the doctor knew nothing. He wanted Artur to marshal all his strength against some greater strain on a heart that had made an irregular black line on the cardiogram, indicating a mild coronary strain. In fact, Dr. Barborka advised Artur just to rest altogether and not to take the Chicago orchestra on tour. But this advice Artur could not follow. It would have angered Ryerson and his directors and give them a justification to finish off the Rodzinski affair once and for all. So Artur toured with the orchestra, covering hundreds and hundreds of miles by bus or train, day and night, giving concerts that for him were followed by sleepless or drugged nights in strange hotels and Pullman cars.

The Ryerson board provoked Artur as far as they could to quit. Knowing how much he wanted to do Honegger's *Jeanne d'Arc au Bucher*, the board cancelled the scheduled performances. The reason given was a $30,000 deficit which had been caused by "Rodzinski's expensive operas." If a board's function is not to raise money to cover deficits, one is hard pressed to know precisely just what it is. But Artur so yearned to have "his" *Jeanne d'Arc* brought to an audience's ears that he even offered to conduct gratis a special concert series after the regular season.

Artur tried to outline for the board his plan for the special performances and some other projects. He believed that once face to face with these men who once toasted him with Chamber of Commerce effusions and champagne he could change their opinions. He did not exactly intend to grovel before them but he had some strange illusion that whatever had gone wrong could be made right by a flood of goodwill, personal charm, and persuasion. But if it was Moral Rearmament's "free admission of error" Artur had in mind, I cannot say.

My husband toured alone that spring: Riki, Babcia, and I were sent to the Southwest for a vacation. Artur said he would relax better without me. Since his quarrel was mainly with himself, I would have been only a supernumerary scapegoat. Thus we three made our way to Arizona where, in two weeks, Artur was to join us. Rather than a vacation, it was a time of anxiety. I knew Artur would be in the hands of Kuyper, whom by now Artur ferociously resented. That resentment would be one of the subjects of his phone calls from Baton Rouge, Little Creek, Des Moines, Wichita, Tulsa and Dallas. His anxieties reached such a pitch that one day he reproached me for letting him make the tour alone.

Artur caught up with us in Phoenix, feeling very tired. "He looks as white as rice," his mother observed, and she encouraged him to stay in the sun, to eat, and relax completely for his five-week vacation. Artur would not listen. He stayed only long enough for Riki, now four years old, to recover from chicken pox, and then we drove to Santa Monica to spend some time with insurance executive Cecil Frankel and his wife. But Artur also wanted to visit with Frank Buchman in Los Angeles. Although my husband's break with MRA had been complete from the moment he threw his Bible to the floor and decided that his destiny was his own affair, he still had genuine feeling for Buchman as a person. There existed from that first encounter over a plank table and bowls of fresh berries nearly seven years earlier a very strong affection between the two. I suspect Artur envied Frank's straightforward, simple beliefs, and even half thought that this goodly, if sometimes foolish man could lift his weight of problems by a simple laying-on of hands. But Frank was no faith healer. MRA, as Buchman outlined it, was a do-it-yourself ethic, and my husband thought he had outgrown such stuff. The visits with Frank had an easing effect, however, and we drove back to Phoenix in good spirits. Phoenix was then a small, quiet place, urban enough to offer some diversion, but with none of the hurly-burly of today. There was some Spanish architecture to be seen, much sun, and a few people.

We received an invitation to dine with Frank Lloyd Wright and his family and the students who clustered around him in what Wright called "the fellowship." Wright greeted us at the entrance to Taliesin West, the quasi-mythic name he gave to his extraordinary home and atelier, and showed us around. The pink and grey live rock of the very site had been used in such a way that site and house appeared as one, concealed from all but the shrewdest eye like a lizard whose coloring and habitat are nature's own.

The first words Wright spoke were contratulations on Artur's Chicago problems. "I'm happy for you," he said. "Genius thrives on suffering." We had not looked at the problem quite that way, but we respected the statement. It came from a man who knew Chicago as well as anyone. He had been Louis Sullivan's greatest disciple, and had been called all the nasty and ridiculous things that once were reserved for his master.

Artur and Wright talked a bit about Sullivan's Auditorium and much more about the crassness of men who would dispose of such a jewel in favor of the newer, acoustically-flawed Orchestra Hall. "Did you know that Sullivan was called in to fix the Hall?" Wright asked. "When they asked him what it would cost to correct the failures, Sullivan said, 'Not much — the price of six sticks of dynamite.' "

We had a good laugh at that, parting friends, determined to keep in touch. When Wright and his family came to Chicago later that year they attended Artur's concerts as our guests.

We also visited with Koussevitzky and his second wife while in Phoenix. Natalie had died, and Serge had married her niece, Olga. They kept a small house there for Koussie's winter vacations. Indeed, Koussie first came out to Arizona at Artur's suggestion, fell in love with the climate and landscape, so totally unlike anything a Russian would ever have known, and decided to make Phoenix the antipodes to Tanglewood.

The conductors talked over the New York and Chicago blow-ups, and Serge was sympathetically indignant, as any conductor might well have been. On his way home, Koussie was interviewed at the Chicago airport by Claudia Cassidy. A friend mailed us a copy of Serge's supportive statement:

If you ask me what is to be done I can see one outcome only. Let those who brought about this issue have the courage to apologize to Rodzinski and ask him to continue his wonderful work and musical directorship of the Chicago Symphony Orchestra.

In all large institutions, the position and functions of every member or group are distinctly understood and outlined. Thus in the realm of musical art, the responsibilities of a symphony orchestra are shared by the board of trustees, the conductor, and the manager.

Yet what happened in Chicago? One has the impression that the *trustees* of the Chicago Symphony Orchestra *exercise a dictatorial power and act as though the orchestra belonged to them rather than to their city and community at large.* Their action with regard to Artur Rodzinski is shocking and unethical. It is of course within the power and rights of the trustees not to renew a contract with the conductor. But to announce in the newspapers in mid-season that the conductor had been dismissed — that is, that his engagement would "terminate" at the end of current season — is brutal and a great injustice because it is detrimental to the conductor and may affect his future life and career.

Rodzinski is a conductor of the first rank and his success in Chicago is a proof that the public as well as the orchestra not only accepted him but also admired him.

I quote the statement in its entirety, not only because of the generosity of spirit shown — something rare among the conducting kind —

but also because it was Serge who, in saying these things, explained the Chicago problem more clearly than even we had earlier understood it. The words emphasized above went to the heart of the matter.

Meanwhile the issue of private versus community ownership of the orchestra was being joined in the city itself. Throughout that vacation Artur kept up a lively correspondence with several Chicago attorneys who had organized yet one more group, the Friends of the Chicago Symphony, which lobbied for Artur's reinstatement. A Mr. Ellis filled us in on what was happening in the Windy City:

> Ryerson's complete silence in his talk with Laderman [the Union leader] regarding the libelous and unfounded charges brought against you in the Orchestral release grows more and more astonishing. Apparently he has found it necessary to abandon his charges that you malingered, that you changed programs at the last minute, that you ran the Association into a deficit, and that you ran the same programs Tuesday, Thursday, Friday and Saturday without the consent of the Association. If he has abandoned the charges, he ought to tell the public that he has abandoned them and that they are untrue, and thus put you in the proper light in your profession. A silly present contention that you tried to sell Orchestra Hall is really an abandonment of the position taken in the Association's release regarding the Auditorium imbroglio.

Artur came back to Chicago suntanned and took over the orchestra for the season's last six weeks. The press hailed the event. "RODZINSKI RETURNS IN TRIUMPH," one front page trumpeted. According to the story beneath, "Rodzinski was greeted with a heartwarming, sustained ovation when he strode to the podium. There were cheers from the gallery, and there was an exciting note of revolution, of angry loyalty in the air."

The Friends group distributed leaflets at the entrance of Orchestra Hall, reproducing the correspondence between Artur and the directors to show that there never had been a serious problem or difference between my husband and the Ryerson-led group. What did show was the sheer whim and caprice of the board's actions. The Friends also regularly published appeals for public support in the press.

On the board itself, Charlie Swift, John Carpenter, and Chauncey McCormick tried to influence Ryerson and the others to listen to the public who bought the seats and subscriptions to the Symphony which then was completely subscribed for the whole season. The Ryerson group remained intractable. Even public statements by leading members of the city's musical world availed nothing. Published interviews with two singers — Rosa Raisa and Edith Mason Ragland — who were once the operatic darlings of the city, might have intimidated lesser souls, but not Ryerson.

As the end of the season drew closer, the frustrated audience became more raucous. His silence, Artur felt, had perhaps made things worse. Having had his fill of the controversy, Artur was ready to take the cue that Frank Buchman had signaled when we visited him in California: he went to see Ryerson face to face and sincerely offered to appear with him in a gesture of amity on the stage of Orchestra Hall. Innocently, I rather thought that this might work, remembering how such goodwill had changed things for Artur in the past. It did not.

During this period Artur's only outlet was his music. He lost himself in the music he conducted, submerging his personality in the scores and minds of the composers he recreated. And in this he grew artistically, but at a fearful cost. Each concert's end for him meant a more dismal return to the reality of a world with Ryersons and Judsons.

The last Thursday concert of the season was given on April 29. Orchestra Hall swarmed with uniformed policemen. The main entrance was cordoned off.

"What is this all about? What happened?" Artur asked one young officer.

"I don't know, sir," he replied. "We were just told that there might be some fighting."

I could not believe it had come to that, but apparently Ryerson did. Two policemen stood guard over the door to his box throughout the performance.

The program included two pieces identified with Artur: Strauss's *Ein Heldenleben* and Brahms's Fourth Symphony. The concert concluded with Sousa's "Stars and Stripes Forever," done for whatever reason justifies such things on a request program.

Claudia Cassidy wrote glowingly of the performance, of the extraordinary circumstances under which it was played, and of the marvel that Artur had stood up to the season's strains. She reported that after the Sousa ". . . the audience began to shout its anger," and that the policemen "might have come in handy, except that Mr. Rodzinski, who had given a superb performance, [could] control a situation, too, [holding] up a quieting hand. He said that they were within the sacred walls of a temple of music and that it must be elsewhere that he, who has said nothing, will discuss a situation without parallel in the history of music. . . ."

The following Sunday's papers carried the interview Artur finally gave. Too depleted to speak with any bitterness, Artur told the reporters the simple replies Ryerson's "indictment" deserved. He had been "arbitrarily cashiered without hearing or notice." Defamatory things had been said, that he had feigned illness: "In truth I conducted when in great physical pain, and against the advice of my physicians." It was "charged" that he created deficits: "In truth, I had nothing to do with expenditures." After answering all the other untrue things of which he had been accused, Artur said that at bottom was a "misinformed president, acting under the suggestion of an incompetent manager disloyal to the president, the trustees, and to himself."

We packed up and left Chicago soon thereafter, without Artur ever having a chance to answer in person to the board the charges made against him. The only official notice taken of our departure was a resolution passed by the City Council on May 11, "expressing the appreciation of the people of Chicago of your inspired direction of the Chicago Symphony Orchestra during the past season, and extending best wishes for your success and happiness in the future."

Chapter 41

As far as I can tell, my husband never studied the Sixth Symphony of Gustav Mahler, or if he knew the work, left no traces of such knowledge. There is no score of it in his library, which proves nothing, since there also are no scores of this composer's Seventh and Ninth Symphonies. Yet these last two compositions, along with the others for which study scores exist, were listed by Artur with his timings in a catalogue of works he had performed, or intended to. Although in the final decade of his life the book was not scrupulously maintained, the absence of this particular Mahler Symphony has a special significance.

Throughout Artur's career, certain compositions in his repertoire served him as psychological hallmarks — symbols, if you will. Beethoven's *Eroica* and Strauss's *Ein Heldenleben* reliably echoed my husband's moods: they alternately crowed his sense of triumph or stressed the mood of tribulation he might endure. Assuredly, the selection, even on a request program, of *A Hero's Life* for his last program in Chicago was the conscious manipulation of a musical symbol.

The last two operas Artur wished to conduct, and it would be in Chicago that he intended to give them, were Moussorgsky's *Boris Godunov* and Wagner's *Tristan und Isolde*, works in which Artur felt close to the male protagonist: Boris, the powerful, willful forger and follower of his own destiny; Tristan, the lover. The one is destroyed in pursuit of his inwardly-directed demon. The sad knight dies in pursuit of his "other."

At some points of his life Artur strongly identified with Mahler. Although the composer-conductor had been dead for several years when my husband left Lvov to study in Vienna, that city was still permeated with Mahler's traditions; and any aspirant to a podium could not avoid wishing to emulate his titanic figure in all things. Indeed, Mahler's difficulties with most of his posts had direct correlations in Artur's career. Mahler had dramatic blowups with management at the Vienna State

(*310*)

Opera, with the Metropolitan in New York City, and even with the New York Philharmonic. He also developed a coronary condition which finally caused his death.

The Sixth Symphony, in a sense, was Mahler's forecast of his own end, even more so than *Das Lied von Der Erde*, for the "program" which the composer devised for the composition deals with a heroic figure who is thrice struck down, symbolized by three terrifying percussive thuds in the score's last movement, the final blow leading to an epiphany. What three blows Mahler experienced or actually foresaw will keep biographers busy for decades more to come. Whatever the case, Artur had a premonition of an impending, perhaps catastrophic, blow to follow the two severe ones he had experienced in New York and Chicago. It could be argued that any reasonable man might sense as much in my husband's circumstances. But Artur Rodzinski was not exactly what one calls a "reasonable man." Indeed, he was the very plaything of irrationality in most of his personal affairs. Intuition, whim, a sudden shift in humors, all stuff that would make an empiricist blanch, were the grist of my husband's decision-making will. And it could only have been an unreasoning fear of a shadowy but foreseeable and inevitable happening — a premonition, in short — that sent Artur flying back to Los Angeles and into the arms of God's own emissary (as my husband thought of him), Frank Buchman. The breach with MRA was not being categorically closed because Artur had, on a deeper plane, seen the "errors of his willful ways."

Although he once again accepted the MRA concept of God's Will, Artur had had his fill of trustees, directors, managers, agents, women's committees and the labors of rebuilding orchestras. None of this, he decided, would be his lot if his career were given to guest engagements. He had not the strength for more. He was a tired man.

When Artur let it be known he would take guest appearances, offers came in from everywhere, even Australia and Japan. He immediately accepted engagements for the 1948 season at three major festivals: London's Royal Festival, the Biennale di Venezia, and Salzburg, which was to start that year for the first time after the war.

Artur, Riki and I sailed on the S.S. "Batory" for England on June 18, leaving Babcia in the care of Susie.

Buchman had arranged for us to be put up at MRA's London headquarters. It was a lovely old building at 45 Berkeley Square, the former residence of Lord Clive of India, who had donated it to Buchman and his cause. London itself was a city of rubble and shards. Food was scarce, and everything was rationed, though the rations had "improved," we were told. Yet even three years after the war's end, Britons were still sustaining themselves on a meager diet. What I had been able to buy in New York on one week's ration stamps throughout the war would have sufficed an English family for a month.

But at 45 Berkeley Square we were fed like royalty. Artur had a special diet of the best available foods, and all of it he wanted. The Oxford Groupers set aside the large house's finest rooms for us, the best going to my husband, whom they particularly coddled. Those terrible and trying days before a first rehearsal with a new orchestra were eased by our Group friends' morale boosting. Artur faced the concerts themselves with vigor and confidence, and the reinforcement now of some heartfelt prayers.

After Artur's debut appearance in London, one of the day's most influential concert managers in Europe, Harold Holt, said to me, "I had heard Rodzinski is a great conductor, but I had no idea he could be *this* great!" The London public's and Holt's enthusiasm led the manager to outline grand plans. Artur listened eagerly — and began to see an entire new, much better life in Europe spreading before him. "If Holt does half of what he says he can, things will be easier than New York or Chicago," Artur said.

Buchman, before we left America, had urged that after London we summer in Switzerland at Caux sur Montreux where an old hotel had been converted into an MRA resort. He promised to join us there, and I, for one, liked the prospect. In the past Frank's presence always had been salutary for Artur, and I hoped my husband might once again succumb to all the positive aspects of MRA and its way of life.

We arrived at Caux before Buchman or any of the MRA people we knew. On the sincerity of those gentle folk whom we found there I pass no judgment, but I understood how Artur could have been bothered by their unceasing good cheer and smiles. That was not precisely the kind of mood Artur was in.

Dr. Barborka had warned in Chicago that Artur was on the verge of a breakdown, a nervous or physical collapse, whichever might come first. And while we were at Caux I walked on eggshells and cautioned Riki to follow my lead.

Suddenly and unexpectedly Artur left Caux and went to the Valmont Sanitarium which Koussevitzky had once mentioned as a cure for people suffering nervous strain. Unfortunately, the Sanitarium did nothing for my husband. He remained depressed, inverting that anger with himself which at Caux he had covertly targeted against members of the Group. At the base of it were the inevitable self-recriminations, followed, and just as inevitably, by accusations against or anger toward me.

During one of his sleepless and uncomfortable nights, he wrote me a long letter in which, in great detail, he blamed me for having ruined his life, and saying that the whole affair of New York, then Chicago, had been my fault. Artur was not able to put things in logical sequences just then. It was as if he had written a lunatic divorce brief; that, at least, is how it read to me. I thought he had lost his balance altogether and was grateful he was in a sanitarium. I called Valmont to check with his physician and was informed Artur had signed himself out. He had vanished, and no one at Valmont knew where he was headed. I was too numb to worry. Frank Buchman, who by that time was in Caux, prayed.

Then, a small package arrived for me, but with no return address or message, except for the words "Always — Artur" inscribed on the gold cross the box contained. "He'll be back, you'll see," Frank encouraged, "he's finding his way back to the Lord." This my husband never did, but he did find his way back to Caux, arriving just as abruptly as he had left.

"I tried to run as far away from you as I could," he said, "but I kept running into you. There's no happiness without you, Halusia."

I loved Artur so unreservedly and so wished his return to stability, to normalcy, that I took his speech as truth, as proof that his mind had cleared. What then followed was proof of how wrong I was. I tried to have a frank and open discussion with Artur, à la MRA, and confessed to him some of my own errors and faults, totally unaware that I was triggering a hideous flood of acrimony. For the only time in our years together I was terrified of my husband. I ran to some of our friends in the hotel and asked for help. A physician was called, and a sedative was injected, one which not only calmed Artur's body but also allowed him the respite of several hours deep sleep.

In that lull members of the Group and their leader, Buchman, discussed my situation. They decided Riki and I must be separated from Artur for our own good and safety. They, the Group, would bring Artur back to spiritual health. I was apprehensive at the thought of leaving Artur. He was very shortly to conduct at Salzburg, the scene of youthful triumphs. A successful appearance there would mitigate some of the disturbing talk about Artur's American debacles that was making the rounds of musical circles. His performance itself depended on many factors, not the least of which was my presence: a missing talisman in one of his frock-coat pockets, the lack of a kiss and a benediction, an insufficient pinch from the stage manager — all or one of these could affect Artur.

Nevertheless, despite my protests, Riki and I were literally kidnapped by the Group, bundled into a car with no extra clothing beyond what we were wearing, driven at breakneck speed to Geneva, and finally put on a plane for London. We would await passage to America there. The whole thing was done swiftly and expeditiously.

I was very near collapse, and cannot deny relief at being away from Artur's rage. But I did not quite believe the continuous assurances that my husband would be "all right," that MRA "knew what it was doing." I telephoned Caux sur Montreux to tell Artur what had happened and where I was going. That he was not allowed to take my calls did nothing to put me at ease. (Later, I heard that when he was told of my whereabouts, he took all the sleeping pills he could find. Luckily, a doctor found him in time.)

Artur set off for Salzburg, searching for us everywhere en route, calling all over Europe. Either he had not been told of our departure for

America, or the information never penetrated the dense fogs which shrouded his reason at that moment. Whichever the case, Artur arrived at Salzburg too late for all but his last scheduled rehearsal. Underprepared, and barely in control of himself, Artur conducted a Brahms Symphony at such breakneck speed that the orchestra nearly broke down and fell apart. The public and critics could not believe their ears. The reviews were catastrophic. The scene of his first major European triumph was the setting for his only artistic failure.

Artur never forgave the MRA Group for the irreparable consequences of their actions. He also never quite forgave me for — as he saw it — deserting him when I was most needed.

His professional image was now in serious disrepair. Indeed, some people thought he was finished. After he ascertained by a call to my sister Aniela that Riki and I were safe in Lake Placid, Artur moved along to the next leg of his summer's tour schedule, Italy. There, under the considerate guidance of Maestro Giulio Razzi, then musical director of *Radio-Televisione Italiana* (RAI), and Anna Venturini, the assistant in charge of operas and concerts, Artur was able to resume work. He went directly to the Italian capital where he rehearsed with Radio Roma for the Biennale di Venezia concert. The RAI di Roma's major contribution to the festival of contemporary music was Schoenberg's Violin Concerto, in those days a terribly difficult composition to cope with, although now people play and hear it easily. The soloist was Arrigo Pellicia. Both soloist and conductor had an immense success with the Venetian audiences which, for Artur, did much to undo the harm of the Salzburg fiasco. The concert certainly made Artur an instant reputation in Italy, and several invitations for appearances for the coming season were immediately extended.

A young Florentine music critic, Dottore Renato Mariani, wrote an enthusiastic review and after interviewing Artur did an even more enthusiastic feature article in which he referred to my husband as "*il grande* Rodzinski." Mariani's writings and his friendship were to profoundly affect our lives.

After his Venetian success, Artur telephoned me at Lake Placid, to say he was in better health and on his way home. When he arrived in the Adirondacks, his spirits were much improved, and he was as loving as he could be, all kisses and contrition as he gave me a peace offering, a gilded rosary of lovely workmanship which he had picked up in the Azores. "Pray for me with it," he asked.

The weather that late summer and fall was perfect, and Artur expended his surplus energies in making improvements around the house. With the help of a Polish gardener who lived in the area, he laid out flower beds and a windbreak of pines and spruces to protect the drive from the road to the house.

The new season began for Artur in mid-October — a season of guest appearances. On October 16, 1948, we drove to New York City, and the day after Artur left for Pittsburgh for a three-week engagement. He wrote a strange letter from there, one full of the most passionate love modified by reproaches for "deserting" him in Switzerland. He forgave me, he said, but could not immediately forget. "Only God and time will heal this wound," he wrote, then in the next breath, "I love you more than life itself." The letter wrenched my heart; I could not forgive myself for not having been at his side when he most needed me.

That following month, Artur was to leave for an extensive tour of Europe, conducting in seven countries. Since there would be too much travel for Riki, Artur urged us to remain at home, and I agreed — another decision I would regret.

My husband, who had shown no fear during a flight we once took through the mountain passes between Poland and Italy in a plane of only aluminized fabric, was now suddenly terrified at the thought of crossing the Atlantic in a modern plane. He was clearly agitated while he watched me pack his luggage the morning of his departure. He took two sedative capsules to calm his nerves and put several more in his pocket for the trip; then a supply went into his luggage.

At the airport we had a sentimental parting. Neither wanted to leave the other. Artur voiced these feelings emotionally, but I kept telling him it was for the best, that returning to work was what he needed.

Both Artur and the new heir to the British Throne arrived in London on the same day, November 14. At the time the city was wildly celebrating Prince Charles's birth, but Artur did not feel festive. He was sick. As soon as he had boarded the plane in New York he began to have severe cramping pains. The captain had offered to put down at Gander where Artur could receive medical attention, but he chose to go on.

Despite the pain, exhaustion from the trip, and a sleepless night, Artur attended the first rehearsal the next day. His sedatives had not eased the cramping sensations which spread from his abdomen to his back. He had also by now learned that if he took too much of the medication, he would be in no shape to conduct. As it was, he was not in condition. The soloist for the concert was Witold Malcuzynski, the pianist-nephew of one of my teachers at Two Jadwigas, then beginning to fulfill the promise his aunt had seen in him. Just when Artur and Witold prepared to walk on stage, my husband fainted. A doctor was called. Artur was taken to a private clinic outside London.

The place was operated by a Polish physician Malcuzynski knew, and it was from there that Artur called several days later, his husky voice weaker than the overseas cable would ordinarily have it. "Don't be scared," he began, and as he told me the facts I was aghast: the worst conceivable occurrence had indeed happened. "I've had a heart attack," he said. "I love you and miss you, Halusia." Then the doctor came on the line. "There is no need for you to come, Mrs. Rodzinska, he is in no danger. He only needs absolute bed rest, and in a month or so he'll come home to you."

I felt helpless at that great distance. All I could do for Artur was to send him a telegram every day in reply to one of his and not tell him about Riki's tonsillectomy. Artur had worried about that when it was just a possibility. The operation was a success, but the young patient was his father in miniature: he would not stay quietly in bed, and a few days later he was back in the hospital, hemorrhaging.

That same time I had a letter from Artur which went to my heart, both for what it said and my deceit about Riki's operation. He wrote:

My dearest Halusineczka, my treasure, I miss you so that I don't know how much longer I will be able to remain here without you. . . .

It is one of those rare sunny days, but I cannot enjoy it much without my very own sun at Park Avenue. This sounds like all my sentimental letters written from California in 1932, but it is every bit as sincere. Our love was a fresh wine then, but it has ripened in the years since, and I now begin to taste and appreciate our matrimonial tokay. . . .

I hope it all will last — but this is in God's hand. . . .

My electrocardiogram is lousy and there is not too much time left for me to enjoy that which I have ruined in the past. What an idiot I've been.

Millions of kisses from the stupid old fellow who intends to repair in the next year everything he destroyed in sixteen. . . .

Artur

On Thanksgiving Day soon after receiving that letter, I telephoned Artur and confessed Riki's operation, though I concealed the part about his hemorrhaging. Artur sounded strong and vigorous and was not at all resentful of my keeping the tonsillectomy secret — he was even grateful.

A few days later I had an appalling telegram from the Polish physician who supervised Artur's case in consultation with Sir John Parkinson, the famous British cardiologist. Artur, with the aid of his Polish nurse, had "escaped" and embarked for home.

It was on a grey December day that Riki and I met Artur at the ship. We had been standing for hours on the cold, windy dock when suddenly the boy began screaming delightedly. He had seen his father, walking very slowly, painfully down the gangway. I saw a man whose tread had lost all vitality. He was an old man — yet, the coming January, he would be only fifty-seven. If my face concealed what I saw in his, it was because he explained, "I could not rest apart from you."

Chapter 42

RIKI, Artur, and I wintered in Florida, leaving Babcia behind in New York with Susie Taylor. There was no thought of work now for my husband. He had enough to do domesticating those beasts of pain, boredom, and frustration. Getting in and out of bed, slowly dressing, taking a walk along the beach — initially, that was all the effort he could afford.

The heart attack was kept secret even from friends. "I would be ruined if word ever leaked," Artur reasoned. Accordingly, the fact was stubbornly concealed. Later, whenever overwork and exhaustion resulted in yet another heart attack, a variety of excuses had to be invented to camouflage the cancellation of a contract. The press used these excuses to create a picture of Rodzinski as a man of caprice, a man who would renege on an obligation for whatever eccentric justification a reporter's imagination could spin. Ultimately, the journalistic view of my husband as an irresponsible man was as damaging as the truth ever might have been. The press, for instance, linked Artur's Salzburg fiasco and the London attack unfavorably. Having been told that his illness was pneumonia, and that he had cancelled his European tour on physician's orders, journalists concluded that these were excuses, that my husband was a ruined man professionally. Physically Artur had run his course; artistically, however, there would be growth and achievement beyond even his own grandest expectations.

But first Artur had to be able to resume work, and in the winter of 1949 that time seemed awfully distant. Also, without some regular income, Artur's imaginary poorhouse appeared as proximate as an invalid's life. Then, happily, a letter from Goddard Lieberson of Columbia Records came bearing a gift and tidings of good things to come. The gift was a royalty check from reissued Rodzinski performances on the newly invented long-playing disks which were just being marketed. Sales had skyrocketed, and Goddard said the prospects were excellent. "If I were you, I would not worry about the future with this nice income," Lieberson wrote. "Just enjoy your rest." Goddard was not among those who knew the nature of Artur's enforced sabbatical.

By spring the doctors gave their qualified blessing to my husband's return to the podium. Some successful concerts in Los Angeles reassured Artur that he could still control an orchestra.

After he returned to Florida, he made a brief trip to Havana, Cuba, to hear Sascha Brailowsky with that city's orchestra. This led to an invitation to direct the Havana ensemble for the 1949–50 season that Artur accepted. "We will take Mother with us and spend a winter in the beautiful climate of Cuba." And so, after the summer in Lake Placid, we settled for the winter in Havana, in a splendid villa with a large garden, an ideal setting for all of us.

Artur's work was light — a concert every other week, with casual rehearsals. The orchestra was no prize, being far below the standard of any continental ensemble, but there were some good players, and some expertise. The only noteworthy achievement in that Havana season was Michael Rabin's debut with an orchestra. The violin prodigy, in whose career Artur had always taken interest, performed my granduncle Henryk Wieniawski's F-sharp Minor Concerto.

During his mid-season break, Artur conducted eight concerts at a special festival in San Francisco's War Memorial Opera House, the same building in which his son Richard would eventually have his first office. A trip down the coast took him again to Los Angeles and more concerts, then back to Havana. He looked amazingly well. When I asked how things had gone, he merely handed me a thick sheaf of newspaper reviews, saying, "Read them when I'm dead." But, of course, I read them immediately. Superb!

At the end of the Havana season, the orchestra's management asked Artur if he would consider the post of permanent director, commencing with 1950–51. He agreed, but only on the condition that the deadwood and dry rot be removed. The management agreed, but the musicians did not. Phhfffttt! And the Havana Symphony Orchestra was no more. The musicians disbanded, and Artur was once again at liberty. Never again would he have a regular podium, just a series of protracted guest engagements.

The first of these engagements was in Argentina where Artur conducted at the Teatro Colon. South America was filled with Polish emigrés and exiles and wherever we went we could find old friends and even relatives. The audiences were marvelous. After a performance of Tchaikovsky's Fifth, Artur was called back on stage for fifteen bows. But South America was not my husband's proper platform, though he would have considered residence in Uruguay and Brazil after conducting there.

Between our South American tours we received word that Artur's mother, eighty years old, was dying following an operation on a broken hip. We returned to Lake Placid in time to see her only briefly before she lost consciousness. The shock of her death was tremendous for Artur. He developed pneumonia. Riki, Susie Taylor, and I stood alone to watch the Babcia buried, in what has since become a piece of Poland among the Adirondacks, the graveyard of St. Agnes, our parish church.

Arthur Judson had still the power to keep Artur's American engagements to a minimum. Whenever a manager considered Artur, Judson would warn him: "The man's a trouble-maker. You'll regret getting mixed up with him." But some managers knew what lay behind Judson's charges and kept their faith in Artur.

The Quesada Agency which had engaged Artur for South America was interested in his conducting in Europe during the coming winter season. They wrote to Artur throughout the spring and summer, making offers he refused to consider. He had become deeply involved in another pursuit — the unraveling of the world's mysteries. Depositing himself in his studio's big armchair, he devoured books on philosophy, theology, metaphysics in an attempt logically to piece together the unknown.

Despite Artur's reluctance to commit himself, Quesada's European agent, Miss Keller, came to Riki Hill in the early fall. We sat on our front porch with the attractive young blond (whose good looks made Artur all the more attentive) and looked over the grand schemes she had drawn up. Concerts in Paris, Vienna, Brussels, Naples, Torino, and at La Scala, with an opera at Florence, and more. Artur said, "No. I stay right where I am." Miss Keller, however, persisted. She worked at Artur all that evening, and over breakfast the following morning. Tenacity paid off. "Here I was all set for a quiet winter with mountains, snow, and books, and now that's all upset," he said.

Miss Keller left, and Artur, who for so many months had looked on only Schopenhauer or Ouspensky as fit companions, now once again rummaged among his scores and played the piano. On October 14, 1951, he boarded the "Queen Mary" bound for Europe; Riki and I remained at Lake Placid.

"Cosi si deve dirigere" (that's the way one ought to conduct), a wildly enthusiastic voice shouted during the ovation which followed Artur's Teatro alla Scala debut in Milan. Other lusty voices shouted similar praises at concerts in Venice and Naples. Then Artur set up shop at the Teatro Communale in Florence, where he was to offer two pairs of programs, and prepare Moussorgsky's *Boris Godunov*. He had never done the opera, and spent days and days learning it in a studio the Communale's director, Maestro Francesco Siciliani, had put at his disposal.

In lieu of me as nurse, valet, benediction-giver, and guarantor of amulets, Artur found himself not one, but four surrogates. He told me of them when he returned in time for Riki's birthday. At home he unpacked a suitcase brimful of gifts for his son and wife, lest the latter dare suspect her husband of some infidelity. That I could not do, for his return brought a love that was nothing short of another honeymoon. Artur's successes in Europe had restored his confidence as an artist, and had revitalized him as a man.

Shortly afterward he went to Los Angeles to conduct the premiere of his friend George Antheil's Fifth Symphony. While there, he became interested in his friend's "friend," the same woman to whom Antheil had dedicated his Fifth. Although a cool letter that soon came mentioned no one, I knew there had to be a woman somewhere. Yet rather than feeling jealous, I was relaxed. Halina would skate and ski with her son while Artur's heart burned, and that is what Artur found us doing when he returned, unheralded. He had spent over an hour watching us with our friends and neighbors on the ice of Mirror Lake. Ray Lincoln who looked after the house and grounds of Riki Hill, had brought Artur home from the train station then dropped him by the side of the lake; there Artur studied us unobserved and thought his thoughts.

What his thoughts were, I cannot guess, but when we came home I was told of a "wonderful person" who would accompany him to South America instead of me. Moreover, he had invited this "marvelous creature" to the house to "learn how to take care" of him. Indeed! And yet, why not? I felt relieved of the burden of a trip just to play nurse, and I was having too much fun relearning how to ski and skate. "That's a wonderful idea, darling," was my only reply.

The young woman arrived two weeks later. She was attractive enough — but such a neurotic, quixotic fidget that she made Artur seem bovine by contrast. How, I wondered, will such a pair put up with each other, especially since Artur required non-stop, dawn-to-dawn petting, pacification, and medication. Artur was not in love, I could see. Flattery will go only so far, and I let it have its course. Among other things, I taught her how to administer a shot of camphoxil in my husband's derriere. When the lessons were over they left to rejoin each other somewhere on the southern side of the equator.

I had the satisfaction of knowing that Artur and his inamorata would not tolerate each other long, and so it was with light heart I flew with Riki to Cuba to retrieve some things from storage. I wound up our affairs in Havana and was preparing to return to Lake Placid when word came that toleration had reached an end. "MEET ME IN PANAMA WITH RIKI STOP LOVE YOUR ARTUR": ten words informed me, at international rates, that he had had a fiasco.

In the tropical heat a perspiring, haggard Artur met us at the plane. His thin summer suit fairly stuck to his skin as he smiled and took me into his arms to press me close. Reaching in his pocket, he made me put out my right hand, and on it he clasped three joined heavy chains of solid gold, a full pound's worth. Affixed to the bracelet was a little plate with my name. "I behaved like a fool. I am sorry," he said.

He completed that second triumphant South American tour with me as his nurse, valet, and loving wife.

In October of 1952, Artur decided that he would not be able to take the Lake Placid winter, and we returned to our apartment in New York City. There Maestro Francesco Siciliani, at Florence's Teatro Communale, cabled him an invitation — quickly accepted — to do Smetana's *Bartered Bride* and lead some concerts in January and Feburary of the coming year.

Artur's joy over the Florence engagement dissipated when he was hospitalized with severe chest pains. An embolism had formed in one of his lungs, and his physician Dr. Armistead Forkner prescribed bed rest, and lots of it. Dejection lurched over into the gloomiest of depressions and Artur just sat morosely in his hospital bed like a beached clamshell emptied of its former tenant. I tried to cheer him, this time with outside help. I brought friends to his bedside like other people bring flowers or baskets of fruit.

One friend, as it turned out, was a married woman — young, attractive, witty, and both accessible, and interested. At first I did not react. I had so far weathered enough flirtations to know how to take yet one more in stride. This one, alas, was the exception that proved all my confidence foolish. Artur went into ecstasies, wrote her long, passionate letters, and gave me his coldest shoulder. When he recovered enough to come home he was immersed in his hospital-bred romance to the exclusion of all else. I began to worry. Perhaps he was in love with this girl. Certainly, none of his prior peccadilloes had lasted so long. He seemed happy only when he was writing to "her." I told myself that all I had ever wanted was my husband's happiness — oh, blessed cliché! — and if she would make him happy, then let him go to her. But my anger was with myself. I felt discouraged that all my tricks for psychologically propping my husband's sagging ego were no longer of use, and I was hurt that whatever my allure might have been for Artur it could ever so suddenly be reduced to functions better filled by a live-in nurse.

After a week at home, Artur announced he was off to Dallas "on business," nothing more. I just happened to know that she was also in Dallas, lecturing. "All right," I said to myself, "he can have a divorce. I will keep Riki." A fair bargain, I thought.

But what wife who renounces the man she loves can resist one last tender gesture that would perhaps set aright all the wrongs he had suffered. My urge was to see Arthur Judson, and I did while my husband was in Texas.

A.J. received me cordially. Encouraged, I asked if he would at the very least shake hands with Artur, and, as the saying goes, "let bygones be bygones." I told him that even a token reconciliation could save Artur's health. Judson took my pathetic wife's plea and played with it. "I have always liked you," he began. "Yes, I've always had a warm spot for you, my dear, but I could never get along with your husband, and I don't intend to try now. I don't ever want to see him again." I returned home, feeling foolish and impotent.

My husband was not feeling so very potent himself. He called from Texas that night, dripping repentance. "Will you forgive me, darling? I made a dreadful mistake, but it's all over with." And much more of the same, ending, not unpredictably, with, "Will you forgive me? May I come home?"

"It's your home, Artur," I said. "Do as you wish." There would have to be some plea bargaining before clemency could be considered.

Chapter 43

IT was January 1952 and Artur had to leave for Italy and his engagement with the Teatro Communale in Florence. His fear of a transatlantic plane trip, without Riki and me, again had ugly consequences. These apprehensions, together with his usual pre-performance anxieties, made him incapable of action without the buttress of pills. He had managed to obtain strong sedatives from two different doctors, then dosed himself at his own discretion before the flight. To compound matters he had several drinks aloft. The combination literally knocked him out, and he had to be carried off the plane at Milan on a stretcher.

Poor Francesco Siciliani was actually nearer to a heart attack than Artur when Ada Finzi, my husband's Italian manager in Milan broke the news. Maestro Siciliani had expected to open his Teatro Communale winter season with a dynamic conductor named Rodzinski, not an invalid. Although Artur arrived in Florence a day later, he was in no condition for work. That, in any case, was the view of Professore Vincenzo Lapiccirella, a Florentine cardiologist. Indeed, Lapiccirella advised Siciliani to get another conductor. There was no cause for alarm, however. Once the potentiated effects of drugs and alcohol had worn off, my husband's blood pressure returned to normal, and he, a little limp but with no lesson learned, went to work. Rehearsals for Smetana's *Bartered Bride* commenced, and a performance followed in several weeks.

All of this I learned much later. In those same few days following Artur's departure, I enjoyed a psychic vacation of sorts. To be rid of his pathological ups and downs had become a necessity, even for a few days. The prospect of having done with them for a few months was pleasant. To meet my emotional needs I would not require lovers, as Artur did, but a renewal of the bonds with my sisters and old friends. Thus, with him away, our Park Avenue apartment immediately rang with the laughter of the Lilpop sisters, Marysia, Aniela, Felicia, and Halina. And there was New York's cultural life to take advantage of in a way that was rarely possible with Artur about, especially now that he needed or demanded continuous looking after.

The very night that saw Artur aboard a plane for Italy, I took Riki to a special performance at Carnegie Hall by Toscanini and his NBC ensemble. We sat to Maestro's left, in the first row, where we could watch his every gesture and facial expression. I wanted to impress on my son who it was that my generation considered its greatest orchestral conductor. The closing work on the program was Beethoven's Seventh, that same work in which Maestro's blood always ran a little ahead of his tempi. I will never forget his rapt look and movements when he reached the section of the score that he had once chided Artur for performing too rapidly. Maestro's right hand wildly churned the air as his left forefinger, extended toward his heart, trembled expressively.

I took the boy backstage, telling him, "You will meet a very great man tonight." But, unfortunately, we were met by Maestro's adolescent grandson, Walfredo, who said that *Babbo* would receive no one that night. I am sorry for Riki's sake as well as my own, for that proved to be the last time we ever would see Toscanini.

A few days later, Artur phoned. I had rather come to dread the ringing of the telephone, the protracted dialogues with long-distance operators, and then the news.

"Halina?" he queried over a bad connection.

"Yes, darling. Are you all right?"

"Fine. Work goes well. Tell me, how long would it take you to pack everything and come to Firenze?"

Stunned, I said, "Not long. But why?"

"I have the best imaginable prospects here. Siciliani understands me, and he wants me to move here and work in Florence. I think Italy is going to be our home from now on."

After a few expensive moments of silence *not* in which to gather my thoughts, but to get up enough breath to reply, I said, "I'll begin packing tonight."

"Very good. The 'Independence' sails for Genova in two days. Can you make that?"

"Yes, darling."

And two days later, Riki and I, and all of what constituted our *everything*, were on the winter-rough Atlantic, sailing east by southeast. It was hard, very, very hard to leave the United States. I now loved America for the experiences I had had, the people who remained behind, and for all the comforts of its familiarity.

Florence had done miracles for my husband. When he met us at the pier in Genova he was rejuvenated. The smile he had for his seven-year-old son and me was as fresh and warm as on that day I had first fallen in love with it in a Krakow hospital. But, then, Florence was my first city of miracles, the place where my sister Felicia so many years earlier had been given up for dead, only to live again. But where the intermediary in Fela's recovery had been *aquasanta* from Lourdes, it was Francesco Siciliani in Artur's. The young and musically-talented maestro had taken over the Communale and was determined to compete with Milan's La Scala. Rodzinski became his principal attraction versus La Scala's Herbert von Karajan, whose reputation since those distant Salzburg days had skyrocketed.

(*323*)

Finding Artur free, Siciliani wanted him to identify with the Communale and the spring festival, the Maggio Musicale Fiorentino, there to do "different" things, out-of-the-ordinary operas or new ones, with voices other than the same tired old celebrities. All of this bolstered Artur's ego and morale in a way that no number of love affairs ever did.

Before that 1952–53 Communale season would end, Artur became Florence's darling. And to keep things that way, my husband watched his health as never before. He avoided strain and overwork through careful and orderly scheduling, and always had at hand a nitroglycerine tablet against an angina pectoris spasm. The well-known immediate effect of the medication puzzled the orchestral players who could not comprehend why maestro would move his hand from his music stand to his lips, then turn brilliantly crimson. Except for Siciliani and Professore Lapiccirella, no one knew the exact reason.

In February we drove to Rome in our new Fiat. The RAI employee, Anna Venturini, was invaluable to us. She and I got along famously, being somewhat kindred types, even to the point of looking a bit like sisters. And as a manager she was a jewel. She understood the need for pampering and coddling any artist, and Artur in particular. Maestro Rodzinski wanted a big armchair in his *camerino?* He had one. Another electric heater? *Ecco!* Such treatment invariably won Artur's confidence instantly, completely.

Before a special performance of *Boris* which Artur was to give at Rome's Foro Italico auditorium for recording and broadcast by RAI, my husband became especially tense. Although he had successfully given his first performances of the piece the season before in Florence, he rehearsed the production with his usual perfectionism and had worked himself into a bad case of nerves. In his dressing room a tired and frightened Artur wavered about going on. He suddenly became pallid and perspired heavily. Anna asked him if there was anything she could do.

"Yes, there is, *cara*," Artur said. "Promise me something — that if anything happens to me, you will see after Halina and Riki."

"I promise, maestro," she replied with an affectionate smile that gave the lie to her own anxiety.

Those few words turned the trick. Artur became suddenly sprightly, relieved, and up to conducting a performance which easily could have killed anyone in his condition. The *Boris* reading with Boris Christoff was a stunning success, and its RAI recording is still aired in Italy. Even Artur was satisfied when, years later, recovering in bed from an attack, he heard it over the radio. As the last bars of the choral writing that closes the final act died away, a teary-eyed Artur mumbled to himself, "I didn't know I had done it so beautifully."

Important as the Moussorgsky production was, however, there was something far more important to be done in Rome. Important to me, anyway. On Monsignor Sheen's advice shortly before we had left New York, paper work and other formalities had made it possible for me to become Mrs. Artur Rodzinski in the eyes of the Church. On February 25, 1952, with our son as witness, Artur and I exchanged vows in Santa Susanna, the American Catholic Church on Via XX Settembre. Though far less reluctant to be married than the first time, he still went through the ceremony only for Riki and me, so that I could "be happy and at peace with the Church," which, up to now, had not allowed me the sacraments of Communion and Confession because I had been married in a Protestant Church.

Once again, and with better reason than before, we had no honeymoon. Artur deposited Riki and me in Florence while he conducted in Paris and Vienna. This time I did not mind, however. I was too busy. Riki was put into an English day school, Miss Barry's, on Via dei Bardi, while a Florentine friend and I went house-hunting.

As well as I knew Florence and its environs, mine was still the knowledge of a visitor. Had it not been for the help of Virginia Basso, the Rodzinskis probably would have kept house in some dark, dank *palazzo* along the Arno. Virginia steered me to what is everyone's fantasy of a Tuscan villa, the home of Dottore and Signora Giovanni Roatta. Located in San Domenico, on the way to Fiesole, it had the marvelous name of Il Frullino.

Artur fell in love with the place. It had grown in its charm and muted splendor from the tenth century, the dating of its tower, and the Renaissance villa and gardens that had evolved showed the unhurried consideration people gave to such things in those days. The Roattas occupied the tower and second floor of the villa. We moved into the ground level where views of the Florentine skyline, dominated by Brunelleschi's Duomo, and the villa's magnificent flower beds vied for the eye's attention.

A very special joy were the nightingales. We were enchanted by them. Neither Artur nor I had seen or heard one since we left Poland; and the American mockingbird, great virtuoso though it is, had never been a satisfactory substitute. We would stand for hours at night by the window, listening to their roulades and trills, watching the wind move among the tall and slender, moon-silhouetted cypresses, intoxicated by the perfume of the *gelsomino* that clambered up the villa's ancient walls.

Poles are Poles the world over, and where one is, three or four will congregate. We soon met a most extraordinary batch of them — "Mother" Niemiera, then a dowager of ninety years, her unmarried daughter, Miss Julia, and Mother's other daughter, Signora Zofia Peruzzi, the widow of an Italian admiral. In 1905 these ladies had come from Poland as tourists, and never could tear themselves away. The three women became our instant close friends, engulfing us with their exceptional warmth and culture. One of the things that endeared them to Artur was their intelligence, for no matter what abstruse subject he wanted to pursue however far, they could blithely follow along.

Offers of engagements came in from everywhere. The San Francisco Opera's director, Kurt Herbert Adler, made some tempting proposals. Another offer once again came from Japan, and this one was even more tempting. All travel and housing expenses were to be paid for the three of us, plus a generous fee for each concert, of which there would be four or five a week on tour. But the handsomest clause in the proffered contract covered any and all medical expenses. Artur was on the verge of accepting, but just at that moment rehearsals were to begin for another production at the Communale, and angina pains preceded them.

Professore Lapiccirella was consulted, and he gave Artur an electrocardiogram. "Signora," he said to me, "your husband's heart is so badly damaged he should not think of ever conducting, much less touring the Orient." Lapiccerella prescribed injections of Demerol, which my husband had developed a horrifying appetite for. Artur dreaded becoming an addict, yet he had a tendency to become one of necessity. Nothing except Demerol could ever ease the awful pain he would intermittently suffer.

In any case, Japan was not to hear Rodzinski, and the contract was returned along with a letter of regret.

There was an increasing number of such letters. Indeed, they sometimes were the bulk of Artur's correspondence, now handled by Signorina Camilla Roatta, our landlord's daughter. Camilla was bilingual, speaking perfect English which was her mother's native tongue, and could take dictation and type. Also she had other qualifications to be my husband's secretary: a sense of humor and much patience with Artur's fussiness. One day's dictation would invariably be revised the next, with additions. For Artur, letters required as many rehearsals as a piece of music. One was never put into the mail until absolutely imperative or when each sentence had its proper cadence and choice of words.

One pleasant afternoon when the weather was turning warm, gentle Miss Julia Niemiera stopped in to visit us with the nephew of one of her Florentine Polish friends. In his early twenties, he had just arrived from Poland, and like everyone who had lived under the Nazis, had a story to tell. His somewhat interested me, though he himself did not. I cannot even recall his face, much less his name. But whatever he talked about — and that, too, did not make much of an impression — called for sympathy and encouragement, which I gave. This infuriated Artur, and, within the limits of decent behavior, he showed his fury in the young man's presence. Alone with me, he was openly livid. I weathered the anger, knowing it would subside overnight.

A few days later a messenger brought a box of lovely fresh gardenias. Their perfume was almost stifling when I opened the box and found a card, addressed to Artur and me. It was from our young visitor, and merely said that the blossoms had been cut from his uncle's garden. This was too much for Artur. Having quite a heavy string of infidelities to his own credit, he knew a thing or two about such matters. He assuredly knew something about sending flowers to married women, and he thereupon vehemently charged me with having an affair with the young man.

I quickly took Riki by the arm, and ran from the house into a wheat field which bordered Il Frullino's gardens, and on the pretext of a game, hid there with the child among the ripe grain. A few moments passed before we heard Artur's car door slam, his motor race, and then recede in the distance. "Daddy's gone," Riki said anxiously, and we returned to the house.

Artur did not come back for dinner. I expected he needed time to let off steam. But ten o'clock came and he still was not at home. I became concerned, though not enough to lose any sleep. When I turned down my bed covers, my nose was assaulted by the aroma of the flowers which had set off the storm. Artur had systematically distributed the blossoms between the sheets, and left a scrap of paper on which were scrawled the words "Enjoy the perfume."

When I awoke the next morning, Artur had not yet returned. "He's teaching me a lesson," I said to myself, and went about my day "learning" it, breakfasting with Riki, and packing things Artur would want at the Communale where that morning at 11:00 he should have been rehearsing.

Toward noon, a call came from the theater to say that Artur was ill. I rushed into the city and found him stretched out on his dressing-room sofa. Professor Lapiccirella was with him. "Don't worry, Signora," the doctor said. "He was working and took ill, but it is nothing serious. It seems he spent the night in Vallombrosa."

Vallombrosa is at least 3,000 feet high and very cool after sundown. Florence, not too much above sea level, was at the time in the grip of one of its gummy heat spells. Artur's heart was not much affected — the attack was of heat prostration.

While concerned about him, I realized it was his temper tantrum that set aside the sense a cardiac needs to prevent trouble. Artur resented my coolness. At home that evening there was no peace, just a steady drum roll, crescendo of bad temper. After Riki was in bed, it exploded. I did not need him, Riki did not need him, no one needed him. . . . ergo, what use was life?

Artur raced to his room and returned brandishing the famous revolver he had purchased while a student in Lvov. I shouted to him to put the stupid thing down, and to come to me, but he was now outside in the garden. For what seemed an infinity there was no sound but that of a nightingale's song. I must have prayed to fill that dreadful wordless span of time — I cannot be sure, for the memory of the shot I then heard is greater than any other thought I can retrieve from those moments.

The nightingale was silent. I hoped Artur had not killed it, for intuitively I knew he had not shot himself. I rushed to where he was lying on the ground, face down, his right hand and the gun it held tucked into his left armpit. I fell to my knees, and took what I was supposed to believe was my husband's lifeless form into my arms, to stroke and kiss his brow, each cheek, his lips, and tell him over and over again how much I loved him, needed him. My words were genuine, and so were my tears. Finally, the farce was over: he opened his eyes.

I helped him to his feet, brushing away some leaves that clung to his trousers and, supporting him, walked with him to his room. He put the pistol in his pocket, wordlessly, then sagged into a chair. The foolishness, the anger, the jealousy, the infidelities, the innocent "suicide" — these were merely slight expressions of the man's need to extort by one twist or another each measure and drop of love from me and life itself.

Chapter 44

ARTUR'S first Florentine season ended with a concert in the courtyard of the Palazzo Pitti, then we fled the city. Florence and even our villa in San Domenico became a bake oven that June.

At the suggestion of our landlord and neighbor at Il Frullino, Dottore Roatta, we headed northward to the Casa di Cura of a certain Dr. Guggenberg in the Italian Alpine town of Bressanone. Artur underwent something called the *Kneip Kuhr*, a hydropathic, vegetarian regimen which depends more on the faith of its patients than on any scientific fact for its effectiveness: beet hamburgers and carrot filets in alternation with hot herbal baths and walks in cold mountain streams were supposed to cure a variety of nervous disorders. The results, good in my husband's case, largely came from the orderly life strictly adhered to by all of Dr. Guggenberg's clients — and heaven knows Artur needed some sort of discipline, no matter whether imposed from within or without.

In September of 1952, Artur opened the Biennale di Venezia season, fully relaxed by the *Kneip Kuhr's* spinach patés and rosemary soaks. He was naturally anxious about the event — indeed, if he had no nerves before a performance, there was really cause to worry. But he needed no sedatives or tranquilizers to sleep or to relax after rehearsals. We went by gondola to the Teatro Fenice, Artur in tails, and I in a dress of that exquisite shade Canaletto and Guardi used to depict the canals when seen by sunlight.

Soon after, he made another festival appearance, conducting the inaugural performance at Perugia's Sagra Umbra. This festival, created and directed by Artur's "boss" and colleague, Francesco Siciliani, was devoted to religious music, and the two men selected a stunning opener:

Berlioz's *Messe des Mortes*. The huge performance apparatus this piece calls for was available in entirety, and the augmented brass and percussion sections were distributed antiphonally in San Pietro, the Umbrian city's largest church. Somehow, the romantically imperial splendor of Berlioz's musical visions, originally composed for the interment of Napoleon at Les Invalides in Paris, seemed in scale with the much less monumental church, perhaps because the frescos and panels that decorate San Pietro's walls served as windows into the soul of the Requiem Mass's text. I was much affected by the piece which I had never previously heard. The opportunities are so rare, the performance costs so great.

The lack of a signed contract with the Ryerson board had been my husband's chief blunder in Chicago. A signed one was what now took Artur back to New York for several weeks, a confusion with a firm, now defunct, called Remington Records, an outfit that rather flew by night in those early days of long-playing recordings. In the meantime, I found and settled us into an apartment on Florence's Piazza Donatello for the winter. It seemed an ideal place with a view of the Cimitero dei Inglesi where so many famous Englishmen lie buried. Il Frullino had been rented since we left it. As it proved, we had exchanged the nuisance of driving to and from San Domenico for the racket of the trucks on Via degli Artisti which runs into Piazza Donatello — a bad bargain. But I had signed the lease and paid the customary advances before realizing the street is a main access route for commercial traffic. The noise could be horrendous, and I was concerned lest my insomniac, anxiety-prone husband fall back on one of his time-tested habits — pills or bad temper.

I discussed the problem with a friend in RAI's engineering section, and he designed a sound-proofing contraption which, when pulled along the street wall, decreased the exterior racket. It worked, but not well enough; and I was tormented with worry by the time Artur arrived. To my surprise, he did not mind the noise. Indeed, he was so patently glad to be back in Florence after a month in New York that complaints would have been the last thing to utter. He was sweet and loving, which could have been interpreted in a number of ways, neither least nor last being a concealed peccadillo. His affairs must have also gone well otherwise, for the poorhouse was temporarily forgotten when, on my birthday, he placed an emerald and diamond ring on my finger.

Artur began work on a production at the Teatro Communale of Tchaikovsky's *Pique Dame*. The first night was to be just after Christmas. He was delighted by the way things had proceeded in his absence. Siciliani, with his nearly infallible taste, had selected fine singers with a sense of the Slavic style and a scenic designer whose work was contemporary but appropriate. The stage director was a tough old bird, a Russian actress and pupil of Stanislavsky, Tatiana Pavlova. Heading the cast, at least in their parents' minds, were Riki and Maestro Siciliani's daughter Francesca. Both had small parts in the little troop of children in the first act.

On an afternoon free from rehearsals and school, Riki, Artur, and I set off on a walk out toward the football stadium. We had not gone far before Artur had to sit down. "I feel strange," he said. "What is it?" I asked. "I don't know," was his only reply.

That night, we found out. He became violently ill, vomiting fluid long after his stomach should have expelled everything. He appeared at the door of his bathroom to ask why he brought up so much red wine: "I only had a half glass with dinner," he said incredulously. I nearly fainted when I saw the "wine." I called Professore Lapiccirella. He came immediately and said Artur was hemorrhaging internally. "I don't know if I will be able to stop the bleeding," the physician told me. "*Cara,* pray. That and transfusions are all we can do for him."

Our maid Rosina, awakened by the commotion, had been listening, and rolled up the sleeve of her robe to expose an arm: *"Ecco, Dottore!* Take mine. I'm a universal type. You don't have to test. I gave during the war."

Rosina's generosity saved much precious time, of which there was none to spare. Artur's face had drained of color. He was so feeble that when Professore Lapiccirella released his wrist after taking his pulse it fell limply to his side. Lapiccirella and an assistant, Dottore Albioni, visited every few hours to administer stimulants to bolster Artur's heart. Throughout the day, it was touch and go. He rallied the next day, however.

A Polish friend came to give me a hand with the nursing. She had expected to find Artur depressed and despairing. On the contrary — though too weak to talk, he wrote jokes in a shaky hand on a scratch pad. One of his scrawls I still have was a quote from a song popular in Lvov when Artur was still a boy:

> *Is that my coffin you make, Mr. K.?*
> *Well, I don't mean to die today. . . .*

He also did not mean to cancel *Pique Dame.* Lapiccirella said it would be impossible for him to resume work. Siciliani preferred to drop the production rather than replace the conductor. Artur told both men not to be such crepe hangers. "I'll be in the pit, the curtain will go up. You'll see."

Artur stayed in bed for nearly two weeks, mustering strength from that fantastic hidden reservoir of his. To while away the hours, he had me dig out of our stored luggage a map of his beloved Lvov, a street plan our friend the novelist and poet Jozef Wittlin had given him when we first lived in New York City. Wittlin and Artur used to walk the streets of the place both men called home in their minds' eyes as their fingers traced the straight or winding colored lines that passed a university building, a favorite coffee house on the way to and from their respective residences, and the Opera House where Artur made his debut. To an exile or a wanderer, which is what some Poles are fated to be, home becomes ever so dear. At this point in his life, weakened by ill health and struggle, Artur's return in fantasy to the place of his youth was, I suppose, a sort of amble on the fringes of paradise. He may have been restoring himself by imagining himself young again.

It was hardly a boyish Artur who held a piano rehearsal with the principals as soon as he was fit. He was pale and had difficulty speaking. He merely sat in an armchair, his legs wrapped in a blanket, and quietly followed his score while his singers, Sena Jurinac, David Poleri and Gianna Pederzini, ran through their parts. They repaid Artur's determination to work by singing to their maestro's satisfaction.

The first orchestral rehearsal was two days later, but Artur was still too frail to conduct. Nonetheless he was present to hand his baton over to young Bruno Bartoletti who, as *maestro sostituto* had prepared the vocalists. Bruno, who later became musical director of Chicago's Lyric Opera, was very moved. He did not know, however, that it was in this very way that Artur chanced to rise from coach to conductor, a lifetime earlier in Lvov. Perhaps this thought was in Artur's mind along with all the others as his fingers traced the streets of that place.

Although he had to be helped into the pit the day of the final rehearsal, the sight of our son, cocksure and handsome in his costume when the curtain rose, was like an injection of adrenalin. His vigor returned in a flush of pride, and the rehearsal went beautifully, as did the premiere. Indeed, the three performances of *Pique Dame* were hits. The singers outdid themselves, the settings and staging were perfect, and the tense and beautifully nuanced whole had the audiences on their feet screaming with enthusiasm. Even today that production is cited as a model. One critic wrote that "if Rodzinski can make *Pique Dame* work on stage, he can make theatre of anything!"

This was not exactly Siciliani's view, unfortunately. He had rather limitedly thought of my husband as his man for the Slavic repertoire, either operatic or symphonic, and his clichéd conception rankled Artur.

This subject hung like a thin mist over the dinner table that St. Valentine's Day, 1953, when Siciliani and his wife were our guests. Siciliani talked about programming for his spring festival, the Maggio Musicale. Each season demanded a premiere of sufficient international significance to draw critics and audiences from all over the world. "I had hopes of Stokowski doing Prokofiev's *War and Peace*," he said, "but the old man needs another year."

"I can give it to you this May," Artur said.

"There's not enough time," Siciliani protested, "and I don't even know where to lay my hands on the music."

Artur smiled a bit as Siciliani continued, "La Scala is negotiating with the Russians for the rights."

"Could you get them?" Artur asked.

"There should be no trouble."

"*Allora*," Artur trumpeted. "You'll have your *Guerra e Pace* come May!"

Siciliani listened closely and with obviously mounting glee as Artur unfolded his scheme for pulling a coup on the most prestigious opera house in Italy. When Siciliani and his wife left, it was agreed Artur should proceed on his own and that the Communale's director would cooperate.

Artur knew that a full score and parts lay gathering dust in the Metropolitan Opera House's library in New York. There had been plans to do it in the United States, but finances decided the matter negatively. The production called for a cast of no less than forty soloists, some of whom could double in various parts, a large chorus, and an immense number of scene changes. Moreover, it had to be cut down to workable proportions. Prokofiev and his wife, in preparing the libretto from Tolstoy's epic historical novel, had been loath to omit a single incident. The uncut score takes almost as long to perform as a fast reader requires to finish the novel — at least two or three nights.

Money was no worry for the Communale and the Maggio Musicale. The Italian Government would see to the subsidies, and after Siciliani checked with the Ministry of Culture, they were in fact guaranteed. Artur then had me make contact over the phone with Leeds Music Corporation, the Russians' agents in New York. In the weeks it took to get the performance materials sent, Artur prepared and led a pair of concerts at the Communale, one an all-Gershwin program, the other topped off by Stravinsky's *Sacre du Printemps* which was sensational. A Milanese critic, writing in that city's *Corriere della Sera*, said that he had never really heard the piece before. I doubt that Stravinsky would have concurred in the critical enthusiasm, however, since Artur never failed to conduct the work with a heat the composer repeatedly disavowed.

When the packing cases stuffed with Prokofiev's score and parts arrived at Piazza Donatello, Siciliani and Artur tore them open. They went over the score nervously, and with some disappointment.

"The music's not very interesting," Siciliani said.

"Oh, I don't know," Artur said. "We can prune here, drop that scene altogether."

And then the two were off and running. Their biggest chore was to make Tolstoy's prose epic into theatrical poetry, something which the Prokofievs lost beneath a burden of words and music. The text was translated from Russian to Italian under Artur's supervision before composer Vito Frazzi was brought in to fit the new text to the vocal parts, and make some slight alterations in the lines for the sake of musical and prosodical sense. Then the whole vocal score, copied out anew, was subjected to scrutiny for cuts. Scenes were dropped or elided, but only where Artur and Siciliani believed that a character or a reference to an incident in the plot was sufficiently established in terms of the music and action. It was rather like making a *Reader's Digest* condensation, in itself, a barbaric act, but in the case of *War and Peace* a blessing. The end product, though long enough in performance, was theatrically effective and contained the best of Prokofiev's music.

Casting forty soloists was an immense job which Siciliani did in concert with Artur. Luckily, the Communale's *capo* knew just about every singer at work on Italian stages. Artur trusted his director's judgments, and, in any case, could not afford too much strain, either physically or emotionally. Professore Lapiccirella had made some X-rays of my husband's stomach which found that the ulcer Artur always feared had actually erupted into a volcano-like wound which threatened to recommence its bleeding if Artur neglected diet and other medical regimens.

Siciliani picked Rosanna Carteri, a young, attractive soprano, for the part of Natasha, and the other parts, save for Andrey and Pierre, rather fell in place. Andrey had to be handsome, youthful, and a musically-strong baritone — an unlikely combination under the best of circumstances. Yet a fellow who had sung a small part in the *Pique Dame* production just might do, Artur thought. But he doubted Ettore Bastianini could handle the acting. Since Tatiana Pavlova was to direct the action, perhaps she could coach him. Once that was resolved, Siciliani and my husband picked up the hunt for a Pierre, a truly full-throated tenor. The two men scouted everywhere, and they almost quarreled because rehearsals were coming up and no one was yet contracted. Siciliani had to go to Rome on business — and at that precise moment when Artur's nerves most needed to know who the tenor would be. But when the youthful opera producer returned he handed Artur an acceptable Pierre. "I found him in the dining car on the train," Siciliani said. "He's tall, too good-looking for the part, but with a wig and eyeglasses he might do."

"Can he sing?" Artur wanted to know.

"He has a lovely voice and could even develop into something great," was Siciliani's evaluation.

"I take your word," Artur answered, and the Pierre was put to work. Since Siciliani had "discovered" Maria Callas, Renata Tebaldi, and a host of equally great artists and voices, Artur believed the tenor Franco Corelli just possibly might work out.

The rest of the cast was then as famous as Bastianini, now lamentably gone, and Corelli, still handsomely among us, soon proved to be. Among the forty solo voices were those of Fedora Barbieri, Renato Capecchi, Fernando Corena, Mirto Picchi, Italo Tajo.

The cast was more than satisfactory, and scenery fine. Artur's only annoyance was Pavlova. The stage director, he thought, was erratic and difficult to work with. He, of all persons, should have had some tolerance for such things. What really piqued him was her lack of musicality. Still, Siciliani had faith in the woman, and Artur disguised his irritation, but only thinly.

Pavlova's and Artur's rising mutual annoyances apart, rehearsals progressed nicely into the spring, at which time we moved from Piazza Donatello to a stupendous villa near Piazza Bellosguardo, just above and outside Florence. It was Lo Strozzino, the summer residence of the same family that used to winter in the splendid Palazzo Strozzi in the heart of the old city. The villa was no less magnificent, only a bit smaller. Its gardens were a monument to the arts of landscape architects, a Boboli reduced but slightly in scale, with a maze of boxwood hedges, tall feathery cypresses, ancient marble statues (some dating back to Roman times), and beds of flowers all colors of the spectrum.

Our new home was the most magnificent setting in which I have ever lived. The garden was a thoroughly twentieth-century dream for Riki, who, together with a companion, played for hours at all sorts of imaginative games among the hedges and around the flower beds. And Artur no less enjoyed the idea of a make-believe life within the frame of a Renaissance picture. He chose as his room a truly palatial space, one as grandly removed from his tiny quarters in our first home in Cleveland as its little park is from the Giardino Le Cascine on which his window now looked, with the dusty, grey-green Tuscan hills beyond. "How glorious," he said. "Probably never again will we live in a place such as this."

"But," he continued, "why can't I do a masterpiece like this?" — and he waved the album cover of the recording of Wagner's *Parsifal* he had just listened to, a performance led by Hans Knappertsbusch at Bayreuth.

"Be patient, darling," I said.

"No, Siciliani thinks I'm only good enough to play Slavic music. Now if he would give me a *Parsifal* or a *Tristan*. . . ."

I began to insinuate that if he made the unwieldy and sometimes merely lugubrious score of *War and Peace* come alive, Siciliani would give him the sky. Heaven knows how Artur tried. To add to the strain of whipping the ensemble together, the weather turned muggy, and the Communale became an oven. Every now and then Artur would have to take a whiff of oxygen which, at Lapiccirella's suggestion, I now carried around concealed beneath a coat or sweater. The oxygen and stimulants kept him at work.

Artur's irritations with Pavlova added to the stress of rehearsals. She was as variable as the winds in her ideas, and though she worked very hard with soloists and choruses, she did so with little or no regard for the music. This drove Artur close to distraction. "Opera to that woman is a play with a lousy script," he cursed between sips of a cola beverage spiked with Coramine.

When the sets were built and in place, many other problems cropped up. Moscow did not burn just right. Kutuzov's entrance had to be on a real horse; Napoleon could not be allowed even to hint an allusion to Mussolini, or there might be a riot.

Meanwhile, publicity for the first production of *War and Peace* outside the Soviet Union was building up an impressive interest among critics and the public. The musical intelligentsia wanted to see if Rodzinski could pull off another *Lady Macbeth of Mzensk*, and American critics from everywhere were coming just for the purpose. The performances were all sold out weeks before the first curtain.

The dress rehearsal brought the niggling differences between Pavlova and Artur to a head. The stage director had the chorus in motion during one scene when it was imperative that the singers stand still to watch Artur's beat. "That's not the way we first worked it out," he shouted, stopping the orchestra. "You've changed things again, and now they can't see my cues!" He was furious. "I will not go on stage with her tomorrow night," he swore. Siciliani cajoled. "Nothing, nothing will make me stand near that woman, that ancient caviar can, that lunatic!" After the tirade, Siciliani, who knew something about artistic temperaments, was concerned about the bad impression his conductor and stage director would make before an audience that was attuned to such things.

"You know what they will say when he doesn't come on stage with her. What shall we do?" Siciliani said to me while Artur changed clothes.

"Something will come to us," I said, and the next night I had a stroke of genius: the thought of sending a bouquet of roses to Pavlova in Artur's name and a single rose to Artur with a note that read, "Wishing you a triumph . . . Pavlova."

When each reached the theater, they found the flowers awaiting them, and raced into each other's arms, their little war ending in a sentimental, Slavic kind of peace. I was terribly proud of my trick, which nobody ever discovered.

The performance went well. Napoleon walked through, almost unnoticed. Kutuzov's horse behaved. Moscow burned satisfactorily until the smoke got trapped in a sudden draft and nearly choked and blinded the players in the pit. The snow fell slowly at first; then a flake-filled bag suspended overhead broke, and an avalanche all but buried a troop of retreating French soldiers.

In spite of such gaffes, Michael Steinberg was able to write for *"The New York Times:*

What the performance had in sensitivity and power it owed to Artur Rodzinski's clear and intelligent understanding of the opera in all its musical and dramatic aspects and to his incomparable ability to pull all the elements together into the representation of the Tolstoy epic. It was the creative conducting of a great man of the musical theatre, and it was a happy thing to see how much the evening, next to the huge success of the opera itself, became a personal triumph for Rodzinski.

After this conquest at the Maggio Musicale, the Rodzinskis, like Bonaparte after Moscow, made a westward retreat for home. The reason in both instances was the same: Florence, like Moscow, had become a furnace.

Chapter 45

It was a very happy summer, in 1953, in our Lake Placid home, with lots of guests and social life.

In September, we sailed directly to Naples, where Artur had three months of work in Teatro San Carlo. Certainly, Naples was not much changed since I had previously visited her in 1935. Vesuvius stood in precisely the same spot when Artur, his mother, and I had summered at the Villa Cocumella in Sorrento. The only difference when we arrived was the angle of the view and the view itself. We lived at the Villa Rivalta in Posilippo which had once served as the British Prime Minister's base of operations during the war, and the volcano was now quiet, with not even a wisp of smoke coming from its cone. In fact, the only excitement was when Artur bathed in the big, black marble tub where Churchill had soaked for hours at a time. "Imagine," Artur would say, "the fate of the world was brooded upon here."

The instrumentalists of the Teatro San Carlo, whose season Artur was to open, were not easy to manage. Rehearsals were an exasperating experience; the musicians would not concentrate and chattered incessantly. When Artur was on the edge of erupting angrily, the concertmaster explained that the blue sky and warm sun were too seductive for the men to concentrate. Artur would not relent, however, and he gained close to total cooperation, thereby giving the lie to those who say Neapolitans are ungovernable.

Siciliani, knowing the Napolitani and the San Carlo well, had advised against Artur taking the engagements on grounds my husband soon enough discovered for himself to be valid. Not only were the musicians an unruly lot, but the management was a bit dense, and musically illiterate. The Superintendent was a dignified, if paunchy, *Commendatore* whose love for opera precluded any knowledge of the genre. When plans for the season had been discussed earlier, this gentleman replied to the suggestion that *Tristano ed Isotta* (Tristan and Isolde) be given: "We can't afford both. We'll do *Tristano* this season, *Isotta* the next!" When Alban Berg's *Lulu* came up in the talks, somebody objected to the work on the grounds that the Countess Geschwitz was "a Lesbian." The Superintendent cavalierly wiped away the stigma associated with this deviant taste by proposing to change her into "an Austrian."

Artur took all this with humor. Although the work was tiring because this orchestra needed more rehearsals than the one in Florence, he found it fair compensation to be able to do operas and concert programs which Siciliani regularly sequestered for other conductors. The concerts were successful with the audiences which demanded (and got) unprecedented encores. The first *Tristano* saw the conductor upstaging his *Isotta* who left the stage angrily because the public had more cheers and flowers for Rodzinski than for her.

During a slight break in the schedule we watched Roberto Rosselini stage Honegger's *Jeanne d'Arc* for his beautiful wife, Ingrid Bergman. Reciprocating the courtesy, Bergman attended Artur's rehearsals of *Carmen*. "How I would love to sing that part," the actress said, to which Artur replied, "How I wish you could!"

Artur's Carmen was another Scandinavian beauty, Inge Borgh, who neither knew the part, nor had arrived for rehearsals. By the time Borgh came with her personal Escamillo, my husband, young Franco Corelli (as Jose), and Sena Jurinac (the Michaela) were two rehearsals away from performance. Borgh's costumes were a shabby lot of rags, and she quite obviously had never sung the role. Her on (as well as off) stage Escamillo walked through his part, but only mouthed the phrases, never uttering a note above a sotto voce, not even in the torero's big Act Two aria. Artur was furious, and rushed his well-prepared orchestra through the piece. "If the baritone doesn't need a rehearsal, he can rest easy that the orchestra doesn't," was the way my husband reasoned.

During the intermission, the Escamillo suddenly found his voice. "If your husband takes that tempo tomorrow night I'll throw a chair at him," he shrieked at me. The man seemed fool enough to do it, and I went to the Superintendent and apprised him of the likelihood. The *Commendatore*, who had previously ignored Artur's expressed worries, suddenly decided to replace the Scandinavian Gypsy and her pet bull fighter. The thought of a scandal or a scene in the house forced the Superintendent's hand. Artur was initially in despair, but as luck would have it, Giuletta Simionato and Ugo Savarese were able to fill in, and even without rehearsals, everyone did a creditable job. Indeed, the audience and critics, not knowing of the behind-the-scenes happenings, were ecstatic. Maestro Vittorio Gui, himself a fine opera conductor, did know, and after the performance which he attended in my box said, "If I hadn't seen and heard for myself, I would never believe this was possible!"

In between concerts and operas in Naples, Artur returned to Florence to do his first Wagnerian opera for Siciliani, a *Tannhäuser*. It seemed ridiculous that my husband, who prided himself on his Wagner, should have to prove his ability to Siciliani in one of the German master's lesser works. But Artur did just that, and splendidly. Maestro Borelli, writing in *Nazione Sera*, stated that "Florence should build a monument to Rodzinski, because there never had been nor ever again will be a performance like his *Tannhäuser* here." This might sound dreadfully hyperbolic, but the words came from a perfect Wagnerite, a man who gave up Communism because the Party once anathematized the composer's work, one who, if he is to be believed, listened to *Parsifal* recordings on his knees.

Two more excellent performances of *Tannhäuser* followed, with Borelli in pious attendance at both. But having converted the critic to his views of Wagner was less meaningful to Artur than having effectively convinced Siciliani that this Polish conductor knew a thing or two about the composer.

Concert engagements at Brussels followed, and while Artur was away I moved our belongings from Naples back to Florence. Riki and I rejoined him in Milan where he made his La Scala operatic debut with a production of Gounod's *Faust,* starring Elizabeth Schwarzkopf as Marguerite and Boris Christoff as Mephistopheles. The critics praised everything, but one of them further noted that the opera was a waste of my husband's talents. La Scala's management was of the same opinion, and asked Artur to conduct several other productions. He refused out of exhaustion and the need to conserve some strength for other commitments that season. His manager, Ada Finzi, told Artur that it would be "unwise" to reject the La Scala offer. Riki decided the matter. "I won't let you force my father to work so hard," he said.

The eight-year-old Richard surely was in a position to back up his threat. Quite an intimacy had developed between father and son, each by now having matured enough to appreciate the other's opinions on such critical issues as how much work without time for rest and play would make a dull daddy. As long as Artur avoided overtiring himself or becoming the victim of an overburdened schedule, both his health and his temper remained in balance, and Artur was "fun" for his son to be with. Both missed one another equally when Artur went off on engagements now, though we were able to travel as a family for Artur's remaining conducting dates in Torino and Rome before settling down semi-permanently again in Florence.

Our new home in the Tuscan city was one more splendid Renaissance building, the Villa Mercede on Piazza Bellosguardo. We had a ground-floor apartment with access to a garden of cypresses, pines, and fruit trees, and the walls were overgrown with fragrant glicinia. It was a gem of a place, and my old house-hunting friend Virginia Basso and her husband Raymond were our neighbors in the apartment above. It was on the Bassos' piano that Richard practiced his lessons so that Artur, who, like most performers, detested the sounds of a beginner's efforts, would be spared any annoyance. But despite the old villa's thick walls and high ceilings, the father heard his son at his Czerny, and on more than one occasion asked Riki to stop. The least-pitched sound was especially bothersome to Artur whenever he was studying a score, and soon after we moved into the Villa Mercede he had begun work on a Communale program which he wanted to prepare for carefully.

The second half of the program was to consist of Wagner orchestral selections from various operas, including the "Good Friday Spell" from *Parsifal*. I attended the rehearsals regularly now, in contrast to earlier years; but I was in attendance less as a listener than a nurse, always clinging to a small valise packed with the various medications Artur might require plus a small oxygen tank. We tried to keep these precautions very, very secret.

I was drifting into a reverie as Artur took the orchestra through the poignant *Parsifal* excerpt when, suddenly, the exquisite music stopped. Before I quite realized what happened, Artur had left the stage for his dressing room, where I hurried. The manager was standing outside the door, looking very distressed. "Dear God," I prayed, "let it not be another attack." In the room I found Artur seated in his armchair, tears streaming down his cheeks.

"I can't go ahead, Halina," he sobbed. "The music . . . it is too, too beautiful."

Never before had I seen my husband lose control over his emotions while at work. Conducting Wagner's music was always an emotionally transcendent experience for Artur, but he had always been able to put what he felt *into* the reading.

The performance the next day came off splendidly, however. The music which had been "too beautiful" in rehearsal for the conductor's emotions to contain was a seraphic revelation in the concert hall. The critic for *Nuovo Corriere* wrote that "it was one of those concerts that will remain forever in the memory of those fortunate enough to have heard it."

This was increasingly the estimate of all Artur's performances in Italy. His artistry truly had begun to flower, again. And after this particular concert, Siciliani had a complete change of mind. "Nobody conducts Wagner better than you, maestro," he said, and then solemnly promised my husband that on the first possible date he would schedule a *Tristano*. This cheered Artur, but it was not enough of a boost to compensate for the cliché at La Scala that Rodzinski and the Slavic repertoire were as one. He was scheduled to do Tchaikovsky's *Eugene Onegin*, which he hardly considered his forte. "If you must do something Russian, do *Boris*," he had argued, but he could not persuade the Milanese theater's Superintendent. "There's nothing I can do with it," he complained to me over the phone. But, after a bout of psychosomatic glums, including low blood pressure, he got up to do a first-rate job of drawing what little drama there is from Tchaikovsky's opus.

The performances' success cost Artur much energy, as always happened when he did theater pieces. When he returned to Florence in time to conduct at the Maggio Musicale, he was tired, and his heart showed the strain. Professore Lapiccirella advised him to cancel his festival obligations, and this he did with pleasure. He had been scheduled to do yet one more Slavic opera, this time, Tchaikovsky's *Mazeppa*, a piece Rodzinski, if not the world, could well do without.

With no commitments at the festival, Artur was able to be a relaxed listener at the concerts which included a recital by our old friend Artur Rubinstein. The pianist arrived in Florence with Nela, and their two youngest children, Alina (named after Nela's sister, my old classmate at Two Jadwigas), and little John, who played the piano for my husband, whom I remember saying, "That boy is a born artist!" It was a sentimental reunion in Florence for everyone.

During the month of the festival, Artur had been "a good boy," so to say, and when the city's summer swelter began, he rewarded himself for taking care of his health: he bought an Alfa Romeo. Although the car was a prize for living sensibly, it was also a forecast of a new phase of restlessness, which began with a vacation trip through the Dolomites and Austrian Alps. My husband was like a child with his new toy. He could hardly resist showing how it cornered and braked at outrageous speeds along the steep, winding mountain roads. He also relished the admiring stares of people in all the little towns on our way to Vienna where Artur was contracted to tape some readings with the Vienna Symphony Orchestra for the Westminster Recording Company.

The Austrian capital was not much like the city of Artur's youth. Many familiar sights had been destroyed or were rebuilt and still had a jarring look of newness. Though reconstructed from the original plans down to the last door knob and hinge, the Wiener Staatsoper little resembled the house in which Mahler and his designer Alfred Roller had staged so many historic productions. Also disconcerting was the fact that the Viennese lived like foreigners in their own city. A shopping trip involved the crossing of American, French, and Russian "borders," the military checkpoints of the Allied Occupation Forces. Neither of us was displeased to be away as soon as the recordings had been made. They were accomplished so satisfactorily that Westminster asked Artur to do several more in London the coming fall.

On our way to Kitzbühel where we were to vacation, Artur made the mistake of passing through Salzburg. Driving through the town brought up all his ill-digested fears and resentments of the past, not just of the fiasco in 1948 which had ruined his name at the Festival, but all of the ugliness that had led to it — our quarrels, my "abduction" by the Moral Rearmament group, and the feuds and misunderstandings with Judson and Ryerson. Then, in an attempt to purge himself, he ran away to Bayreuth to attend a festival performance of *Parsifal*, that work which he had always wished to stage again and which had always been so emotionally cathartic for him. A friend saw him outside the Wagner theater during the intervals and later told me that Artur was actually crying.

On our way back to Florence Artur began a litany, slightly changed but very familiar: Florence was a dull city outside of the festival season; there was not enough work for him; the winter weather was gloomy; he needed life around him, stimulation. In sum, we were about to move. This time it was to Rome where he had been offered a series of concerts with the Accademia di Santa Cecilia Orchestra, plus concerts and operas for Radio Italiana di Roma.

In September, while Artur went to London to make more recordings for Westminster with its talented producer, Kurt List, my son and I set up house in the Italian capital in a beautifully furnished apartment on Viale di Villa Massimo. I enrolled Riki in the Notre Dame International School for boys, attended mostly by American children, then prepared for Artur's return.

In the middle of October, Riki and I went to meet him at Rome's Ciampino Airport, taking the lovely drive along the Via Appia, passing through that fabulous suburb of the ancient Roman dead which extends almost to the landing strip. I was rather hoping that, like some old Roman civil dignitary, I would return in a formal triumphal procession honoring my husband. Instead, I brought home an invalid.

Although his recordings in London had gone well, Artur had tired himself in contract bickerings with Westminster executives. He had become wary since the days of the difficulties with NBC and with Ryerson. Burned, too, by his ugly experiences with Arthur Judson, he would not trust this sort of business wrangling to an agent. All during the drive to the apartment he took nitroglycerine and had a hard time breathing. He did not even look at his new surroundings, but went directly to bed.

When morning came, he began to complain of severe chest pains. His color was dreadful, his pulse and breathing irregular. Lapiccirella had given us the names of his colleagues in Rome, but none of them was at home. It was Sunday, and everyone was away. Even a call to Salvatore Mundi, the American hospital, brought no response. All the while that I searched for a doctor, Artur's anxieties mounted, and with his apprehension the pain grew more severe. The nitroglycerine did not help, and I had no Demerol which I would gladly have given him, regardless of the consequences. All I could do was lie at his side, hold his hand, and wipe the perspiration from his pain-creased forehead.

Finally, in the late afternoon, a doctor did come, bringing an electrocardiograph machine and oxygen. He diagnosed a severe attack, and wanted to hospitalize Artur, but my husband would hear none of it. The fear of Rodzinski's health becoming public record was greater than pain or death. Consequently, nurses were brought in on round-the-clock service, and he was kept under heavy sedation. The effects, the possible revival of an unwanted addictive craving, would have to be borne along with the other ordeals of recuperation.

Professore Lapiccirella visited at the first possible moment. Artur was better, but terribly weak, and always in need of medication or oxygen. The Florentine physician told him that his EKG showed signs of

(341)

great recent damage. "This time, *caro Arturo*, you've had the real thing. You must follow orders. It's bed for you, and no conducting for at least three months." Artur was too weak to protest, and too sick to even think of it.

The next few months were dreadful for him. This ordinarily vigorous man, as good as dead without his music making, could not even sustain the effort of reading. He could do nothing but brood on the big unanswerables which had preoccupied him for years, thinking out once again all the routes he might have taken. He thought of conversations he had had in Florence the year before with a young Dominican nun, at the Villa Schifanoia, an American girl with as much spiritual wisdom as affinity for the arts. But Sister Ignacia could only explain faith as faith, that thing which Artur once had, lost, and could not recover through any force of intellect or of philosophical readings. All this former student of Nadia Boulanger could do for my husband was give him a black rosary, and urge him to pray. The chaplet became one of so many other talismans with which his pockets now fairly bulged when he conducted, but it had not bridged the chasm between fearful superstitions and the release of real belief.

Artur attempted to draw out Riki on these subjects. The boy's simple-hearted faith was something his father envied, and he thought perhaps Riki could communicate it to him, if not by words at least by physical propinquity as the two lay side by side, sometimes locked in a loving hug, in my husband's sickbed. Whatever joy there was for Artur came in those moments when the two were together, alone.

I had my hands full with the press, the American reporters in particular. Since Artur's engagements with Santa Cecilia had to be cancelled, stringers and overseas correspondents for major U.S. publications were after a story consistent with my husband's doings in Chicago and New York. They interrogated me — questioned would be imprecise — in the shrewdest way, for they hoped to discover that Rodzinski had once again quarreled with management and broken his contract. I rather think they heard the evasions I gave out as lies, but they printed them in lieu of anything truer. Artur once more had "pneumonia."

Day by day, week by week, Artur regained his strength. He began to receive visitors — Michael Rabin, his mother, and our Roman friend Anna Venturini were among the first — but any talk, especially of music, was taxing. Then he revived enough for drives into the Campagna Romana or to the deserted beaches of Ostia. Soon, talk of music and the future posed no effort at all, and he had me learn to type and take dictation. I was already burdened enough with the duties of wife, mother, housekeeper, valet, and nurse, and I fought the secretarial course as hard as I could; not surprisingly, I lost the struggle. Taking his letters down in longhand was a sort of punishment I would be reluctant to inflict even on an enemy.

Soon after Christmas, though not the three months after his attack that Lapiccirella advised, Artur returned to work, doing a pair of programs (Stravinsky's *Rite of Spring*) at the Teatro Argentina with the Santa Cecilia Orchestra. The first one went off very well, but rehearsals for the second proved too much. He developed a bad bronchitis and was forced to cancel. Another recuperation followed, and a recovery in time to do several concerts for Siciliani in Florence. More rest was forced on him before he could lead the RAI ensemble in the accompaniment to Karol Szymanowski's First Violin Concerto, with our Polish friend Henryk Szeryng as soloist. Both men were completely and emotionally enmeshed in Karol's composition and projected this to the audience. The response, as in Florence earlier, was stupendous.

Artur was growing and growing artistically. There seemed very few things he could not accomplish with the Italian players. And the enthusiasm of the public in Florence, in Rome, and then Torino where he next conducted, fed this growth. Determined to leave behind proof of his flourishing talent other than sheaves of press notices, Artur undertook two months of recording sessions in London for Westminster that spring. This time I joined him with Riki.

London had much changed since my last visit in 1948. There were still craters to be filled in, structures that dangerously tottered, but most of the major damage had been repaired or rebuilt.

We stayed in the home of a Russian emigré family, Mr. and Mrs. Voronin, who had a small apartment to let. Artur could not abide hotels unless absolutely necessary, and certainly never for long stays. The Voronin ménage was far from a hotel — and it was the home of another of Artur's pet hates: pervasive food smells. Our hosts kept numerous cats and fed them fresh fish. Fortunately our rooms were sprayed frequently with a pine deodorant, which kept the cat and fish smells to a tolerable minimum. In short order we even began to feel at home among the Turkish carpets, countless pillows, vases, and dim, fringed, or beaded lamps which reminded Artur of Sophie Braslau's old New York apartment in the Thirties.

The recording sessions were held in the town hall of the London suburb of Walthamstow. The acoustics were excellent, and the building was completely away from traffic. Each day, Westminster sent a very old Rolls-Royce limousine with an equally old driver (appropriately named Wheeler) to fetch my husband and me. He would bundle Artur beneath a blanket against the London spring damp and chill while I stowed my medical supplies on the seat beside him, along with the scores, fetishes, and whatever else had to be at hand. Sometimes Riki would go along for the pleasant, hour-long drive, but ordinarily he stayed at home in Mrs. Voronin's care to do lessons with a tutor. One day, when Riki insisted on going with us, his father said he must work with his teacher instead. The child disconsolately asked, "Isn't love more important than lessons?" Artur and I were deeply moved by a question for which there was no satisfactory answer.

Actually, the two had as many compensating free days in each other's company as days of study or recordings, and their favorite pastime was a long walk through nearby Kensington Gardens, often topped off with a lunch at restaurants run by former Polish Navy men or Ognisko (The Hearth), that had become a center for the many Polish intelligentsia who had taken up residence in England following the war.

There was nothing reduced in Artur's ability to work as long as his health held up. In those two months in Walthamstow's town hall Artur recorded a spate of major works, one after the other, seemingly without respite: the disks of Tchaikovsky's three great symphonies plus his *Nutcracker* in entirety, Wagner excerpts, an all-Richard Strauss album, Dvorak's *New World Symphony*, and a number of other items. The ensemble was Sir Thomas Beecham's Royal Philharmonic Orchestra.

The producer, Dr. Kurt List, himself a composer, knew how to make musical use of the new equipment then coming into use in the first years of high-fidelity disks. Artur and he had also done several disks for a special Westminster "Laboratory" Series which even today are, for monaural recordings of that day, amazingly crisp and well articulated in sound.

The players responded well to Artur's directions, and List was absolutely elated with each take. Artur's experiences with effecting tonal balances in the primitive days of 78-rpm disks, when only two carbon microphones picked up a limited frequency range, showed to excellent effect with the sophisticated equipment of the mid-1950's. Withal, Artur became fussier. With the possibility of repeated takes and editing offered by recording on tape, my husband's quest for the perfect result sometimes got out of hand. Even though the critical ears of Kurt List were completely satisfied, Artur's might not be.

Dr. List sat in the control booth, gauging balances through earphones as Artur conducted rehearsals. Periodically, he would ask Artur if a clarinet passage could be a bit softer, or if the celli could play a bit louder. My husband would mark these suggestions into his score, then play through the piece again, with all of List's suggestions taken into consideration. I was amazed at his patience, and his willingness to essay a passage or an entire piece several times over until it was just so. Nothing in a recording of Strauss's *Till Eulenspiegel* satisfied him, however, even after several complete takes. "The strings, the soul of the orchestra, sound thin — something's all wrong," he said, although List was satisfied with the sound and interpretation of one particular take.

"The balances are all wrong," Artur argued. "You'll have to adjust the microphones, Dr. List."

"But, Dr. Rodzinski, I don't think you are giving the recording a fair hearing," List countered.

"It isn't as clear or crisp as von Karajan's latest," Artur said, and List promised to bring it to the next day's work session for comparison.

The following morning, List waved the von Karajan *Eulenspiegel* disk through the control booth window, and said over the intercom, "Here's how your competition sounds." Artur nodded and smiled as he listened over the loudspeakers. "Now here is your last take," List said, and played another recording. Artur scowled. He interrupted the music with a wave of his hand and said, "Can't *you* hear the difference — the first was by far the superior."

List laughed. "Of course, because the first was yours."

The second recording was actually von Karajan and the Berlin Philharmonic, and Artur laughingly agreed that his own balances were, perhaps, a bit better.

Chapter 46

THE tale of 1955, 1956, and 1957 is all of a piece with that of the previous seven years, except in its intensity and compactness. It is an account of a man's physical degeneration compensated by a fantastic efflorescence of his talents, of possibilities arrived too late to become likelihoods.

Anyone who has borne with me this far has had his fill of sporadic ups and much more constant downs. Indeed, in looking over these pages even I am choked by their pall of sickness, of emotional distress, of failures on the brinks of success. And yet the one or two triumphant moments ever allotted to a lifetime, in an artist's instance, are what the rest was all about. Perhaps I am saying great artistic achievements are bought with the coin of suffering. Certainly, this is a Romantic notion consistent with the age in which Artur was born. But I also suggest something else: without the bad there is no true measurement of the good. The satisfaction of a release hinges on the intensity of the tension that precedes. Love is like this, and death, too. Surely a great love or an heroic end depends on how passionately and fully one has loved and lived.

My husband, in spite of all that seemed like self-defeating folly in him, was what he was because of an ardent involvement with life, and this on the grandest scale. In this sense he not only had a rage for living, but also an insatiable compulsion to wring from life each last drop of what, for him, it held. Such a man could thus hardly fail but to live on extremes. Surely he could never be satisfied to do things by halves.

In some respects I was not the wife for Artur. I could rarely match his intensity of interest or concern, if indeed such a matching was either possible or desirable. Yet this same quality also made me a good wife for him, for in my shallowness I could mirror his depths. I complemented rather than confronted or challenged him. These responses, among others, had been his first wife's errors. Her musicianship and forceful personality had been a gauntlet constantly flung at Artur's feet. Since I never knew or learned enough of music, the points of confrontation or challenge over this in our life together were at a minimum. I simply loved the man, for whatever reasons one loves, and accepted him as a phenomenon, one outside most human categories. But the cost of such love and nearly interminable acceptance is huge, and to this day I still pay it. It was, in large measure, the suppression or subversion of what constituted my self.

I have no regrets for this, and much to remember that is indeed greater than most people can even dream of, but in these days and years of which I write I earned the nickname in Italy of *schiava* (slave). Halina Lilpop had vanished into Mrs. Artur Rodzinski. In the early years of our marriage had I not occasionally asserted myself, I now realize that I might have dematerialized altogether. In the last three years of Artur's life, self-assertion was interdicted. Any quarrel, even difference of opinion, could have killed this man who was dying by shreds and atoms, or so I believed.

I assuredly could not doubt that he was dying, though often I hoped the evidence the doctors offered would be found false. But every performance my husband conducted proved them right. Artur had been told by his Florentine cardiologist, Professore Lapiccirella, to retire, that further conducting was suicide. The Italian conductor Vittorio De Sabata, also a cardiac, had retired, but he told Artur that it was preferable to be dead than to live without one's means of expression, an opinion in which Artur concurred. In June 1956, our friend the poet Jan Lechon jumped from a hotel window in New York City. We read the news in the Paris edition of the *Herald-Tribune*. We were shocked, of course, and knew that the reasons for the death of one of Poland's greatest lyric geniuses were complicated. Lechon's various imbroglios, the women, the men, the extortionist's threatening notes led him, in the words of the American poet Daniel Hoffman, to be

> . . . *found*
> *"Apparently fallen"*
> *From his high window,*
> *That voice*
> *Stilled now*
> *On New York's alien ground.* *

Had the poet still been able to sing he would not have chosen to die. For years his pen produced only an essay or two, some journalistic

* Daniel Hoffman, "The Translator's Party," from *The Center of Attention*, Vintage Books, N.Y. 1974.

pieces, and a diary, and even these few things solely through the encouragement of his psychiatrist and another of our friends, Dr. Gustav Bychowski.

"No," Artur said, reading the news account, "If I am to kill myself, it will be doing what I love, the only thing I know — making music."

And make music he did. From the beginning of the 1955 season, he played a number of religious works, Monteverdi's beautiful *Vespro della Beata Virgine* and Mozart's *Vespre Solemnes di Confessore* being among the oddities that caught his attention. The Mozart work brought him a young American soprano from Radnor, Pennsylvania, who had been trained at the Curtis Institute, Anna Moffo. She was studying in Italy as a Fulbright scholar, and was unknown to anyone except RAI's Anna Venturini. "Don't worry about her, maestro," Anna said to Artur, when she suggested her name. "Just listen to her and decide if she is good enough." Anna Moffo's voice turned out to be as beautiful as she, and my husband worked diligently and successfully with her. After the Mozart performance, Anna's career was launched. She told Artur that if she continued to work with him, she "could become a great singer," something that happened anyway.

Among other works done in Rome with RAI in 1955–56 was Szymanowski's ballet *Harnasie* for orchestra and chorus. Indeed, it was a season of large-scale choral works for Artur, ending with Beethoven's Ninth in Torino, with Teresa Stich-Randall, Ira Malaniuk, Nicolai Gedda, and Frederick Guthrie as soloists. After the performance, Teresa came to say good-bye to Artur, weeping. "I have never been so moved, so inspired in my life, maestro," she said. One critic pointedly disagreed with the soprano, however, and his review hurt Artur. Not that he was spoiled by enthusiastic press notices, but, as he put it, "When I play something in a way that satisfied *me*, they pan it. If I am bad and I know it, they rave."

There were other performances, equally fine and a fulfillment of Artur's talents, but fewer than in the season before. Increased bouts of angina, heart failure, and related illness accounted for the difference. In his enforced inactivity he returned to photography to pass the time. Also, some good things periodically relieved the tension. In fact, three of them occurred that year. One was a promise from Francesco Siciliani of a *Tristan und Isolde* at the coming year's Maggio Musicale. The others followed on the heels of this good news.

Artur had been invited by Maestro Fernando Previtali, the director of Santa Cecilia's orchestra, to serve on a jury for an international conducting competition. Ill health kept him from attending most of the preliminaries, but when he was informed that three Poles were among the finalists, Artur forced himself to go. He even invited the young conductors to our apartment on Viale di Villa Massimo and listened raptly to their views of Poland and its musical life.

In the days following, Artur attended the finalists' performances. He was in dreadful condition, having developed a badly ulcerated heel as a result of the edema which accompanies certain kinds of heart malfunctions. Nonetheless he took part in the jury's deliberations, which, like most such affairs, were terribly partisan and political. The Italian members wished to award the prize to a Santa Cecilia student. The non-Italians wanted one of the three Poles. Artur cast the deciding vote, less for partisan reasons than the fellow's indisputable gifts. The winner was Stanislaw Skrowaczewski, today the conductor of the Minnesota Symphony Orchestra.

At about this time, Dr. Paul Dudley White came to Rome for a cardiology convention. We knew of the physician's effective treatment of President Dwight Eisenhower, and after reading about his visit in the *Rome Daily American*, I arranged for Artur to meet with him. He examined my husband with our Roman doctor Professore Sibiglia present and agreed with his Italian colleague's findings. He prescribed nothing that Sibiglia had not used, concluding his consultation with the advice to eat less and exercise more. Artur, who ordinarily ate like a bird, was told to cut his food intake even further. "But the exercise is even more important," Dr. White stressed. "The car is modern man's undoing. Walk. I do every day. We were lucky with President Eisenhower — he likes to play golf."

Artur was not likely to go about swatting a tiny ball with a metal-headed stick, but the next day, despite his ulcerated foot, he began to take strolls. "He must have done something more for Eisenhower," Artur said. "Perhaps, if he took care of me directly, or used the kinds of medicine they must have in America. . . ." But Artur's speculations were rather little more than that. Before, he had had hopes for a miracle which would remove the scar tissue from his hopelessly damaged heart.

Artur was able to rouse himself to make some more recordings for Westminster in London, but there were several unpleasant contractual bickerings once more. He refused to sign with the company again, and instead made an agreement with E.M.I. (Electrical and Musical Industries, Ltd.), the British parent of American Capitol Records. While in England, Artur was approached with an offer to open the coming year's Covent Garden season, but even thought of it had to be put in abeyance.

A more immediate concern was an engagement with the Amsterdam Concertgebouw, the fine ensemble Willem Mengelberg had developed. Artur would be gone for eight days, which worried me, but it was impossible to go with him. When he returned, my misgivings had been justified. An incident of the sort I could have forestalled, had occurred. After fine rehearsals which promised an excellent performance, and an excellent first half of the program itself, a manager's agent came to Artur's dressing room during intermission to discuss some recording business that had fallen through. Artur became furious, and lost his mood for the music of the second half of the concert. "It was a failure," he said.

The concert's failure bought on his heart's failure. Instead of preparing the RAI di Roma orchestra for several scheduled concerts, Artur was confined to bed in the Clinica Valle Giulia where he was treated for a severe coronary. If there was anything good to come out of the painful, tiresome repetition of an accustomed and even predictable agony, it was a friendship with a young cardiologist, Dottore Gianfranco Scarlini, who took a very personal interest in my husband's case. Scarlini showered *Il Maestro* with the love and admiration of a music lover, specifics for an ailing heart few medical texts suggest. In two weeks, thanks to Dottore Scarlini, Artur was home, and rambling with Riki on Dr. White's prescribed walks around the Villa Borghese Park, close by our new apartment on Via Mangili.

Soon after his birthday in 1957, Artur took an engagement with Rome's RAI orchestra. Among the pieces to be rehearsed was Strauss's demanding and symbolically imperative *Ein Heldenleben*. Dottore Scarlini attended all the work sessions and the concert as well for medical and personal reasons. He did not want to lose either a patient or a maestro. Artur brought off the Strauss tone poem at the public performance in his most blazingly flamboyant style. When Scarlini and I met him in his *camerino* afterward, he was sunk deep in his armchair and seemed to be completely done in. The doctor took his pulse, and beamed, "It's rather fast, but regular!" My husband gave back Scarlini's smile with interest. He, indeed, repaid him for his renewed lease on life with the gleaming silver of a *Der Rosenkavalier* at Torino a short time later. The public's appreciative reactions to the performances, however, were less important to Artur than the fact that he was able to hold up under the rigors of rehearsing and conducting such a big work.

He now looked forward to the Maggio Musicale production of *Tristan* which seemed almost like a diploma or certificate of proficiency when Francesco Siciliani finally granted it to Artur. My husband, over the years, had rethought the work many times, which was his way. Something so large and as patently beautiful must also have as much beauty in each detail, he believed, and the whole must be a cumulative statement of its parts. "This music grows like a flower, petal by petal, and all from a seed," he said.

Another encouragement to undertake the *Tristan*, aside from showing what he could do with the non-Slavic repertoire and a chance to try out his most recent thinking on Wagner's *capolavoro*, was the cast which Siciliani had assembled. Tristan would be the redoubtable Wolfgang Windgassen, one of the finest *heldentenors* of his generation. Brangäne would be sung by the American mezzo, Grace Hoffman. And the sensational young Swedish soprano, Birgit Nilsson, had been cast as Isolde.

In April we moved into the Albergo Anglo-Americano, directly across the way from the Communale's stage entrance. Artur's reception by the hotel management was a bit regal and, for Florentines, effusive — flowers and many salutations of *"Carissimo Maestro"* and orders given to care for the wants of *"Il piu illustre musicista, Dottore Rodzinski."* In the jostling bustle of the greeting, Artur misstepped on entering the elevator, perhaps not. He experienced a sudden pain in his lower back and hip. He was frantic when the pain refused to subside and, indeed, grew acute. He could barely lie down. Professore Lapiccirella was out of town I was told when I called his office, but another physician was recommended. He prescribed hot compresses. Hot compresses I made with the help of an electric tea kettle.

"How can I begin rehearsals in two days," Artur asked, wincing as much from the steamy cloths I laid on his skin as the pain itself. He had a sleepless and uncomfortable night, torn between anxiety and discomfort, but, to his great credit, he took no pills. Even had he taken a sedative, and Seconal now was the stuff with which his craving for sleep's release was satisfied, it would have done no good. I had taken Dottore Scarlini into my confidence about this aspect of Artur's case when the young physician treated him in Rome, and he had shown me how to doctor the capsules into relative harmlessness. "They don't work on me like they used to," Artur would complain, not knowing that most of the pills he took were either all or partly sugar.

Professore Lapiccirella found a miserably sore and sleep-starved conductor when he came the following morning. The Florentine doctor had him cheerful in moments. Away with the compresses was his first order. "It's a typical sciatica. Large doses of B-12 and you'll be fit in forty-eight hours," he promised. I had a hard time finding a spot for the B-12 on Artur's skinny seat already sore from two daily injections of Canfoxil and Myocardin, his heart medications. But I found a tiny patch of skin less blue or green than the rest, and there the injection was administered. On the morrow, he was better and was, in fact, after forty-eight hours quite fit.

We walked to the Communale where the orchestra greeted Artur like an old friend. When the affections and applause were done with, the players worked like demons. Now that I attended rehearsals I could observe for myself Artur's amazing efficiency in rehearsal on which players had so often remarked. With a minimum of words, he was able to draw out the subtlest sorts of shadings from the instrumentalists. To a harpist he might say which part of the finger to pluck with. To an English horn he might suggest specific tonguing and dynamic to better articulate a passage. And all of this was said with the greatest respect and courtesy for the players. Even the singers, who, like Windgassen, had appeared in their roles many times, listened compliantly to Artur's wishes, and did things completely new to them. Windgassen had never before expired in the last act in just the manner Artur thought right. "You're mortally wounded. You're a dying man when you await Isolde's return. You have no strength. Much, much less voice, Herr Windgassen." The tenor performed the passage as Artur wanted, and to the satisfaction of tenor and conductor.

Nilsson was just then at the outset of her career, with a voice the color of gold. She had been favorably compared with Kirsten Flagstad, but, as Artur noted, she was clearly someone great in her own right. "She needs no comparisons," he said. "When the public hears this voice, only the fools will say she is like so-and-so. The people with sense will see there is only one Nilsson!"

Predictably, working on a piece he understood and knew so well, and with such fine artists, was salutary for my husband. He did not forget the good effects of exercise, and he walked a little, though he much preferred to take a carriage ride through Le Cascine, Florence's city park, so marvelously lush in the early spring.

He was his former self, as if the attrition of the years, the ravages of heartbreaks and heart attacks, had fallen away as does the withered casing of a bud to reveal a fresh blossom. When Riki and I walked from the Anglo-Americano to the Communale's stage door with him we both saw a bounce to his step and felt the electrical charges he was emitting. There would be a good performance.

And there was. The musical guest in my box — Gladys Swarthout — was stunned at the end of the first act. So was her husband, Frank Chapman, and Ambassador and Mrs. Zellerbach.

During intermission, Professore Lapiccirella came to check Artur and to rave about the performance. He gave him an injection of Canfoxil and a whiff of oxygen while I mounted guard over the door. Such ministrations could not become known.

Act Two reached even greater heights. The great Love Duet was filled with a sensual poetry of exactly the kind that all men yearn to grasp, if not to know. The blending and balance of Nilsson's and Windgassen's voices were more aurally concupiscent than even the sexual act which implicitly underlies the scene.

Backstage I could report to Artur that the audience was euphoric. Lapiccirella was, and so, too, was Artur, though he kept saying, "I can't make it without another injection." The physician tossed me a wink, my cue to prepare a placebo, an injection of sterile water, which he then administered. Lapiccirella had no love for overmedicating — he as well as Dottore Scarlini had shown me how to doctor Artur's pills and shots — and "reluctantly" gave Artur his Canfoxil, his cola beverage with Coramine, et cetera, et cetera. "His heart could not be stronger, Halina," he said to me in an aside.

In Act Three Windgassen died with all the unfulfilled longings of Gottfried von Strassburg's Sad Knight. But Nilsson's "*Liebestod.*" The ovation that followed could not even be compared with any I had previously witnessed in Florence.

When I reached Artur's dressing room, Maestro Siciliani was talking, his tone at once impressed, moved, apologetic. A Pole could understand Wagner as well as a German. "*Solamente Lei deve dirigere 'Parsifal' nella prossima stagione,*" he said to a smile-wreathed, fully-vindicated Artur: "You alone must do next season's *Parsifal!*"

The second and third performances of *Tristan* went as well as the first. The press notices were spectacular enough to draw Signora Giovanni Gronchi, the wife of Italy's President, from the precincts of the Quirinale in Rome to attend. *Time* in America wrote that "the star of the occasion was Rodzinski . . . ."

Luckily, the tired conductor, husband, and father was able to vacation directly after the last performance, in preparation for recording sessions with his new company E.M.I., in London. We took our leisure at Flims in Switzerland where, alas, the weather was cold, all gloomy skies and rain most of that summer. We left for London in early September.

Before the recording sessions began, we met Arnold Szyfman, the Polish Theater director who was responsible for the reconstruction of the Teatr Wielki in Warsaw. He had accomplished not just a stone-for-stone copy of the old jewel which the Nazis had reduced to cinders (with the exception of the facade), but a much grander facility that incorporated all the latest concepts of theater design. Szyfman, formerly the director of the Teatr Polski, wanted Artur to come back to Poland to open the new house as its artistic director. The offer appealed very much to my husband's sentimental side, particularly that part of him which wanted to return to his roots, the source of his present celebrity. When Szyfman stated the proposition, thirty-six years had passed since Artur made his debut in that same theater as Emil Mlynarski's assistant. But the idea, flattering and attractive though it seemed, could not be leaped at. "If I'm still alive next spring, we'll talk about it then," he said.

The recordings got underway with the Philharmonia men, England's best. The results were several disks: an all-Strauss record, a set of Spanish moderns, and some Russian pieces. Certainly, they were the most sonically lush disks Artur lived to produce, especially his recording of Strauss's *Death and Transfiguration.*.

The work went well, too well, perhaps. Good things now regularly demanded their dues. Riki and I caught influenza, and Artur also came down with it, or else had suffered heart failure. The young English physician who came in the middle of the night when I called could not be certain. All either of us knew was that Artur had slipped into a coma and was close to suffocation. Both lungs were filled with water. He was given an injection to resorb the fluid into the surrounding tissue.

"All we can do is wait and watch," the doctor said, and we kept watch most of the night with the help of the strong black tea the hotel's night porter made. The doctor was so tender with Artur, almost as if treating his own child. He constantly fluffed and adjusted the pillows beneath the unconscious man's head, wiped his perspiring forehead and the fluid that frothed about his lips. As he left, exhausted, he reassured me that in two hours my husband's lungs ought to clear and promised to return after "forty winks or so."

Riki, poor boy, still ailing himself, awoke alone in his room and was terrified when he found out his father was sick again. I kissed him and held him close, by which he understood so much. And yet, like the child he was, he went back to bed after I promised "nothing bad would happen to Daddy."

When the doctor returned, Artur seemed to have passed the crisis. He breathed more regularly, the foam ceased bubbling at the corners of his mouth. The nurse and I arranged him in an elevated position so that he might be more comfortable when consciousness returned. When it did, Artur dimly saw the face of a pink-cheeked, dark-eyed British beauty. He gave her a very careful once-over, somewhat astonished and disoriented by the change in the woman who was his customary nurse, and then pursed his lips as if to whistle or kiss, whichever may have been in his mind. At that instant he saw me, and he smiled broadly. I knew, then, how fully he had come back.

The bed recuperation in England was not the happiest either of us had experienced. Artur was depressed by having to cancel further recordings, at least for the time being, and also to drop a long-desired production of *Elektra* for RAI di Roma. Twenty years had elapsed since, against Arthur Judson's wishes, my husband presented the work in concert with the New York Philharmonic — and had scored such a triumph.

Once we returned to Rome, things picked up immeasurably. The stimulus was the care of Dottore Scarlini who, no matter how busy he was with private patients at the Clinica Valle Giulia, could find time to visit his *caro maestro*, and give him either a placebo or the much more real medicine of admiring love. Scarlini stayed with Artur until he made him smile, not always an easily accomplished goal, then whirred away on his Lambretta to see those who had more pressing needs.

By November, Artur was handing over program schedules to RAI's Anna Venturini. One composition he especially wanted to do was Mahler's *Das Lied von Der Erde* which he had performed last in 1944. Since it had been written by the composer in apprehension of his own end, Artur had an especially strong urge to play the piece. But it so happened that the composition had been assigned to the young American, Lorin Maazel, then working quite hard to put aside the impression of a prodigy in short pants. "Anna," Artur pleaded, "please get the piece back for me. I'm sure Maazel will return it if you tell him I had had it planned a year ago." Maazel would not relinquish the piece; but then he had no idea his colleague was an ailing man with sometimes awful intimations of death.

The season resumed with concerts for RAI spaced at reasonable intervals for sufficient rest between. Artur's recuperative powers were diminishing, though still amazing enough.

Artur was asked to conduct a special Vatican concert. When Anna Venturini placed the papal request and program before him, Artur immediately said yes. Moreover, Pope Pius XII had suggested two works which Artur loved: Beethoven's First Symphony and Wagner's last act of *Parsifal* with the "Good Friday Spell."

(353)

At about this time, a hysterectomy I had long postponed simply had to be performed. Artur, with his dread of surgery, could not be told. So, with the complicity of Gianfranco Scarlini, I told him I was being admitted to the Clinica Valle Giulia "for tests." The ruse worked, but not all that well. When I awoke from the anesthesia, there was Artur with a huge bouquet of roses.

During my hospital stay, Artur met several times with Carol Fox of Chicago's Lyric Opera Company. She offered him a chance to "come back" to his favorite American audience and an irresistible schedule: three *Tristans*, featuring his new ideal Isolde, Birgit Nilsson, and three performances of *Boris*, with Boris Christoff in the title role, all in October and November.

"Won't that be too much?" I asked.

"Not really. I held up for three *Tristans* in Florence," he replied.

"But the Moussorgsky — it's so big."

"Yes, but it isn't as emotionally demanding. Besides, Miss Fox has promised to augment the opera orchestra with players from the Chicago Symphony, and to give me an assistant."

He had already accepted, and was really enthusiastic about going back to America, even homesick.

As the Vatican concert's date drew closer, Artur became fussy. In addition to the Wagner and Beethoven, Pope Pius had asked for a work by a friend of his, a cantata by a composer named Perosi. Artur wanted only the best singers. Anna Venturini found them in Gustav Neidlinger and James Loomis. The bells in the *Parsifal* excerpt had to be just right. The ones she ordered from La Scala were sent back. Bayreuth's were the only ones that would do, and dear Anna, bless her, got them.

The rehearsal at the Vatican was on the day preceding the performance. The work was to be done in the *Aula della Benedizione*, that vast chamber on the upper floor directly above the vestibule of St. Peter's Basilica. While the musicians, the vocal soloists, and the boys' and men's choirs rehearsed, carpenters and upholsterers, silent as angels, fluttered about, setting up seats, risers, and draperies. Anna was fretful that these doings would annoy Artur, but he did not notice them. He wanted to make this a performance like none other the Pope had ever heard. We knew Pius was an extremely musical man, and that as a "prisoner" of the Vatican, self-imposed ever since the Concordat with Mussolini, he had not been able to attend the opera or concerts which had once been the sole sensual pleasure of his long life. Since his elevation, Pope Pius's only musical outlets were records and radio concerts, and it was through these he became aware of my husband's gifts. "Christ's Vicar shall have a performance to make him pleased," Artur said after he rehearsed for several hours, seated on a high stool as usual during rehearsals.

On the afternoon of April 12, 1958, a sunny, warm day, Riki, Artur, and I drove to the Vatican with a great sense of occasion. I was dressed in a specially-made, floor-length black gown, and wore a black lace veil. Riki looked like a slightly uncomfortable schoolboy in his best grey flannels, his dimples flashing out periodically from beneath the otherwise solemn face he put on.

It remained for his father to look the best, however. He was handsome enough in his frock coat with the button of his Order of Polonia Restituta in his lapel. But what really was beautiful was the glow on his face, especially as we were waved through the gate by the Swiss Guards, then still splendid and handsome in their Michelangelo-designed uniforms.

From an interior courtyard, we were passed along to the ceremonial *Scala Del Mareciallo,* ordinarily reserved for dignitaries and notables who come to see the Pope. From the head of the stairs we walked the length of the huge *Aula* down a wide aisle lined on either side with chairs. There were seated Vatican court functionaries and their wives, many of whom came from old Roman aristocracy, also diplomats, all of whom wore their decorations on full-dress suits. To the rear were ordinary priests and nuns. At the front, seated in elegant, gilded armchairs, were bishops and cardinals, the latter modestly attired in the *abito piano,* (a black cassock with scarlet trim and sashes and tiny purple capes called *fariuolas*). The Holy Father's throne awaited him on a dais, above which was suspended a canopy of scarlet velour and the papal coat of arms, all about twenty or so paces to the left of Artur's podium. Riki and I were led by Anna Venturini to a gallery directly across from where Pius would sit.

Artur was taken to a small enclosure to be used as his dressing room It had walls of scarlet tapestry — the place where the Pope would stop for a while before attending large audiences.

The concert was to begin exactly at five o'clock. Orchestra and chorus were in position when Artur came to the podium. Then, prompt to the second, the wide doors at the end of the hall opened wide, and the Pope entered, carried aloft by the Swiss Guard on his *sedia gestatoria,* garbed in a white cassock, small cape, and skullcap. Pius XII looked like an apparition in the bright television lights.

The *sedia* was lowered to the floor. The Pope stepped down, then mounted the three steps to his throne. The hall was silent. Artur bowed permission, then turned to begin the concert.

From where I sat, I could see His Holiness tapping his foot, smiling at Beethoven's jokes, wagging a finger as if he wanted to conduct in Artur's stead. He obviously knew every nuance of the score of the First Symphony which followed his friend Perosi's *Il Natale del Redentore.* At the brief interval, a Papal chamberlain went to Artur with a message that was whispered. My husband smiled, paused for a moment, then nodded, and a high chair was brought for him to sit on for the second half of the concert. He later told me the attendant whispered that *"Sua Santita* has heard you are not well, and wishes you to continue seated." Artur could not refuse so thoughtful a gesture on His Holiness's part.

The *Parsifal* excerpts which Artur next conducted took hold of him as I had never heard or seen before. He was quite literally transfigured.

"Mama, this is the grandest moment of my life," Riki whispered. I could barely raise the corners of my mouth to wince a smile so close was I to a flood of tears. It was, indeed, a truly grand moment, and I almost wished I could prolong it to an eternity.

Then the special bells from Bayreuth resounded through the hall. The Wagner was done, and there was absolute silence. Artur always wished it received that way. He felt the music's religious character, plus the Bayreuth tradition of silence after its performance, precluded such stuff as hand beating against hand. Besides, he was usually too emotionally stirred to take bows. Finished, he turned and walked off the platform, forgetting he was not to leave the Pontiff's presence. There was an instant of embarrassed silence in which the august eminences and excellencies in the front rows turned heads from one side to the next. Pope Pius, also embarrassed, tentatively began to applaud, but no Rodzinski was there to receive the favor.

After a bit, Artur came out in the company of a chamberlain who led him to Pius's throne. Riki and I were also brought forward and I could hear the Pope's compliments: "*Che stupenda esecuzione, che stupenda,*" "What a stupendous performance," he said, "How satisfying it must be to lead the men where you want them." Riki and I were then introduced and were each given rosaries in a small leather box with the Papal Seal. I really was overwhelmed when I knelt to kiss the man's hand, but it was Artur who most strongly reacted to the proximity of the Holy Father.

Oddly enough, it was precisely that faith which my husband thought he had forever lost that enabled him in the following days to become serene and contemplative. Pius was simply a man named Pacelli. But it was a belief in God that made Artur so venerate the person; for an act of faith is faith itself, however fleeting, inconsistent, or transient. Artur wanted thereafter very much to have a private audience with Pius, and this Kazimierz Papee, Poland's ambassador to the Vatican and a friend of ours, said it was possible to arrange. But nothing could be done since we had to go away. "There will be other opportunities," Papee said, and Artur agreed.

This extraordinary event at the Vatican led to several truly happy weeks, both for Artur as a person and his work. He led a special RAI di Torino concert at which once more a religious work figured, this time Karol Szymanowski's tender *Stabat Mater*. For a number of reasons this performance had special meaning for Artur but most important was that it was being transmitted to Poland. Later, he received many letters of thanks and congratulations from our homeland. These also spoke of the excitement in the press about Artur's expected arrival in June, perhaps to assume the direction of the Teatr Wielki, though this was hardly more than a thought at that moment. Rather more to the point was that Artur felt homesick, after twenty-one years' absence, for Poland — and almost as much so for America.

Before visiting either, however, there had to be one further trip to London to complete the Strauss disk he had begun for E.M.I. It was a final take of *Salome's Dance* and the voluptuousness of the recorded stereophonic sound had him enthralled. He now wanted to record much, much more, especially a *Tristan und Isolde*. The E.M.I. people were interested in Nilsson, but found the need for a tenor of equal greatness and stature to be a sticky problem. Windgassen was under contract to another company, John Vickers was not yet ready, and so on through a short list of likely *heldentenors*. In any case, E.M.I. said, Artur's Chicago performance would be "scouted."

On our way back to Rome we visited in Milan with Francesco Siciliani who had been appointed artistic director of La Scala. Over a lengthy luncheon at Savini's, Siciliani reviewed his forthcoming season's plans, which included "showing the theater and Rodzinski at their best."

"You have never done anything important here, maestro; now you will show the Milanese what *Parsifal* should be. That should be toward Easter. And somewhere in the middle of the season, you will premiere the revised score of Shostakovich's *Lady Macbeth* — he calls it now *Katerina Ismailova*.

Artur's face flushed with excitement, fairly exploded into a smile.

Elated and back in Rome, we saw the visiting Shostakovich and his wife. The two men greeted each other with hugs like two familiar, friendly bears. The Russian said his work progressed slowly, but that he would try to finish it as soon as he could. He was pleased that once again Artur would conduct its first non-Soviet performance as he had that of *Lady Macbeth* twenty-three years earlier. "You made that a lively production," Shostakovitch said. "Maybe you can do as well by *Katerina*." I thought to myself, "Yes, he will — if his health holds up."

In that same week in which we saw the Shostakovitches and later had them to dinner, an invitation came from George Szell to lead the Cleveland Orchestra in a pair of concerts at Severance Hall following Artur's Chicago engagements. "It will be fun to see all our friends and everyone there again," he mused. Then, after a while, he said, "perhaps such things come too late, Halina, perhaps I will not have the strength."

I assured him of the contrary, but in my heart I knew I lied.

In May our Polish visas had been obtained and a chauffeur found to drive our car and luggage to Vienna; from there we could fend for ourselves. Riki was graduated from Rome's Notre Dame School the same month, with a medal for scholastic excellence which made his father very happy. The investment in a professional microscope and a library of books on natural science, among other things, had yielded a bumper crop of paternal satisfaction. "Who knows, maybe he'll become a physician like his uncle?" Artur wondered. For a fact, Artur had not done much to encourage the boy's interests in music.

Before leaving for Poland, there was a production for RAI di Roma of Moussorgsky's last opera, *Khovantchina*, with a stellar cast led by Boris Christoff. The press, which by now had taken a proprietary interest in

Artur, thought the performance "superb," and continually referred to my husband as *our* admired conductor." Arthur was pleased with the favorable reactions and pleased with our imminent departure for Poland, but also fatigued.

When we saw Dottore Scarlini the night after *Khovantchina*, my husband told his friend, "Soon I will kiss Polish soil, but can I survive the excitement? I go back a sick and weakened fraction of myself."

"That's nonsense, maestro," Scarlini said. "You're fine — here, let's have a listen." And with that Scarlini took out his stethoscope and checked Artur's heart, then began to sound his chest, his back, and listen some more. "Let's take your temperature, maestro, something does not sound right."

The temperature was above normal.

Artur's expression was that of someone handed his own sentence to read. Then his eyes pleaded for a reprieve, probation, at least a stay.

"Maestro, it's another pneumonia and you've got to be hospitalized for a few days," was Dr. Scarlini's judgment.

The days in the Clinica Valle Giulia protracted into more than two weeks. The pneumonia lingered. Artur's ability to bounce back was fast diminishing. He knew this, as did his heart. His depression was awful. He was the child told that promises are made to be broken. He was the involuntary nomad perpetually damned to homesickness.

"Maestro cannot go to Poland," Scarlini told me. "The best we can hope for is to build him up for his return to America."

Artur took Scarlini's news with only a veneer of self-restraint. "I suppose this means I'll never see Poland again," he said, looking away to a corner of his room.

"*No, maestro, caro amico* — it doesn't mean anything of the sort. You will rest through the summer and be fit to conduct in October. Later, after America, you can consider Poland. Just now you're not as strong as you used to be."

"Yes . . . yes. . . ."

After his stay in the hospital, Artur was well enough to make the trip by train to Venice for a fortnight, from where we were to go on to Cortina d'Ampezzo and its clear mountain air. He and Riki went sightseeing by gondola several mornings, and then, over lunch in our rooms at the newly-opened Hotel Cipriani on the Giudecca, they talked of the wonderful buildings and of the pretty girls, the leather goods and glassware stalls.

At Cortina, Artur's spirits improved somewhat, enough at any rate to pursue his passion for photography.

One afternoon, driving through the mountains, we stopped at the roadside to take some photos of an unusual scene, a wooden cross of peculiar beauty standing in relief against the distant mountains and the ruins of a castle nearby. He took several shots, then leaned on the guard rail to study the view. The sun, though directly over my shoulder, was the right brightness for a good exposure on Artur's old bellows camera which I continued to use. I took a black and white photo of him, with the cross to his left. The only thing that marred the picture was my shadow, stretching toward, but not touching Artur's — the one in which I had so long lived.

"Look at this and remember it well," Artur told our son. "You will never see such beauty but here."

"But at home in America there are beautiful things, too, Daddy," the boy countered.

"Yes, you're right, Riki," Artur agreed sadly.

Chapter 47

We set sail from Genoa on September 2, aboard the "Cristoforo Colombo." She was spanking new then, and looked like an elegant piece of sea-going bone china, almost blue in her gleaming whiteness, almost too graceful, too delicate to carve a way across the Atlantic.

The weather could not have been better for a sailing. The air was clear, with just that tang of sea salt which Artur and I always found so stimulating. The harbor itself was especially lovely at that hour of sunset. Rising like faces in a crowded amphitheater from the water's edge to the hills high and beyond, the city's white buildings were tinged with the pinks and roses of the early evening sun as the pilot boat and tugs left us in the roadstead heading southward.

We were in excellent spirits, particularly Artur whose enthusiasm for the Chicago engagements was coupled, at least temporarily, with reasonably sound health. It was always a sure sign of a good mood when his Leica clicked and his Bell and Howell cranked records of the things he saw. He talked animatedly with Riki and me of our return to America. The prospect of "going home" after five years made me giddy. Soon I would see Riki Hill and the Adirondacks, mountains not nearly as dramatic as the Dolomites around Cortina d'Ampezzo, but far friendlier, and ours, since our home was among them. And there would soon be the faces of old friends in New York City, Lake Placid, and later in Chicago.

We arrived in Naples early the next morning to choruses of hoarsely tooting tugs and screaming gulls, and a vision of Vesuvius.

While we were still in our cabins, our names were also called out, to our surprise, by Dr. Gianfranco Scarlini and his wife, Loretta. They had come, complete with bouquet of roses, to pass the layover time in port with us. It was an affectionate gesture which I greatly appreciated, as did Artur. While I put the flowers in our rooms, the two men talked.

The doctor gave my husband a professional glance from head to toe as he clasped his hand, and said, "Maestro, you look as if sea air agrees with you."

Artur smiled and reached for his photographic equipment. "Come, *Dottore*, let's make pictures," he said. The NATO fleet was in port, and while the mists still lingered there were fine shots of ships to be had, of the port's handsome sprawl, and the majestic indifference of Vesuvius.

Artur and Riki started off for the deck, but Scarlini held back. He took me by my arm for a second, and said in a hurried, anxious whisper, "*Cara Signora*, I do not like his appearance at all. This *Tristano* may be too great a strain for him."

"Nonsense, *Dottore*," I said, laughing. "He has been in high spirits and good health for some time now, and certainly you know how both work hand in hand with him. And Chicago and *Tristano* will stimulate his heart more than any of your injections. You will see."

I do not know how convincing I sounded, or even if I was myself convinced. Scarlini clearly was not, and he shook his head like a worried son as he started off to catch up with Artur and Riki. He stopped in the cabin door for a moment and, without looking up, said, "I would advise him otherwise as a doctor, but perhaps you are right, that a success in Chicago is what he needs. Still, I will be concerned until his return."

That was the last mention Scarlini made of Artur's health for the remainder of the day which we made as pleasant and shared as fully as we could.

After Artur ran out of camera angles from the ship, we took a cab through the city, stopping here and there to photograph views that for some reason or other Artur felt he wanted to preserve.

In the vicinity of the San Carlo Opera House, Artur's stamina gave out. We went to the *galleria*, the glass-enclosed arcade nearby, and Artur sat down at a coffee-bar table to rest, insisting that the Scarlinis, Riki, and I continue our tour. After an hour or so, we rejoined Artur and took a cab back to the "Colombo" in time for lunch.

Artur's mood was distinctly muted. He made no attempt to tease poor Scarlini by pretending to take some of those things which his diet strictly forbade, and which he so enjoyed, from the endless succession of trays of delicacies that are prelude to an Italian Line luncheon. He said no to the heaped platters of tissue-thin slices of prosciutto rolled up like pink diplomas, the pieces of thickly-buttered bread on which stood slices of boiled egg dotted with eyes of anchovy paste which the waiters kept bringing by again and again. Instead, he docilely ate a clear vegetable broth, some *risotto*, and fruit; we, on the other hand, ate everything from antipasto to a rich custard, and coffee.

For the half hour or so before departure, Scarlini and Artur talked as Loretta and I looked over some of my dresses in the adjoining cabin. Their conversation, which I could not help overhearing, was affectionate, but it was also remote in an uncanny way, a sort of leave-taking that suggested permanence.

By the time the warning bell for visitors rang, we had moved ourselves and our talk to the deck where we all fell to hugging and kissing one another.

"Maestro, I hope to see you back here very soon, with a huge triumph in hand, and as fit as a fiddle," Scarlini said, giving Artur an affectionate embrace.

"Yes, *Dottore*, you will see, both a triumph and a fiddle without broken strings," was Artur's reply.

With three ear-splitting hoots, the hawsers that bound the "Colombo" to Naples were cast off. The tiny port tugs nudged us into the channel, and we were on our way.

Through the streams of colored paper and flights of confetti we still saw the Scarlinis and waved to them until their faces were no bigger than the dots of confetti flecking the ship's railing, somehow thinking we could hear their shouts of farewell and good wishes even above the thousands of other voices bidding our fellow passengers safe voyage and God's protection. From where we stood at the "Colombo's" stern as the shore receded, the view of the bay was truly magnificent. To our left we saw the Villa Rivalta high on the cliffs of Posilippo, our home for those three months in 1953 when Artur conducted operas at San Carlo and several orchestra concerts. To the right lay Sorrento, and we could see the Albergo Cocumella where Artur, his mother, and I spent several months in 1935. Artur seemed only to see those sights we knew so well through his cameras' viewfinders. He seemed bent on clutching at or capturing each last detail on film as if to possess it forever.

"After so many years," he said quietly, "it is almost like leaving home."

He took photos until he used up all the film. Then he put his arm around my shoulder and together we watched this vibrant piece of our Italian life retire behind us in a heavy haze colored splendidly with the reds and mauves of sunset. Vesuvius was almost completely wrapped in mist, save for her cone which gallantly and stubbornly stood out in firmness and dignity against the sky. The "Colombo" veered westward into the Mediterranean as we rounded the southerly horn of the harbor. "I am certain this is the last glimpse I will ever have of Italy," he murmured. The air was peaceful, except for the distant laugh of a solitary gull. Then we went to dress for dinner.

The following day brought with it not just good weather and the excitements known to any traveler of the Mediterranean, but good spirits to Artur. He was up and about earlier than usual and did not seem to have trouble with dressing. Certainly, he put up no struggle over injections, pills, and all the other medical rituals that he complained of when he was truly down. By the time we reached Gibraltar, he was already on deck, cameras at the ready for the fun of the bumboats and their smuggler merchants selling Hong Kong-made nylon scarves, American cigarettes, and plastic amber at ridiculous prices.

As we sailed near the Canary Islands, nature put on a show for us. A volcano had been born and was literally making a new island in the time it took for it to pass in and out of view. The eruptions caused a deafening roar, even at our distance, and we could see gigantic rocks hurled skyward through the smoke and flame. Artur was so stimulated by these pyrotechnics that he adopted a festive attitude about the whole trip.

"Why not truly enjoy ourselves," he said, and agreed to attend the Captain's cocktail party that night. We dressed formally, and as I straightened Artur's bow tie he gave me a loving squeeze and a kiss.

"Tonight, Halusia, I will have a good time. I'll eat Russian caviar when no Pole is looking, and drink all the French champagne the steward can pour." We attended that party like a pair of honeymooners, and did precisely what Artur had said, except that he did not stop with caviar and champagne. With reckless abandon, he ate every salty tidbit that passed his way, breaking his diet with no thought of the consequences. And I, wanting to see him happy, selfishly said none of the cautionary words which were truly in order. Perhaps I too much wanted to keep him in his near euphoria, even to the extent of being willing to pay the inevitable price.

And pay it we both did. When morning came Artur was ill.

"Call the doctor," he said, gasping for air.

Once again, heart failure; and on the eve of something he so desperately wanted and psychologically needed, the "comeback" in Chicago that would be a reaffirmation of himself as an artist in a city which unreservedly thought of him as its own.

Fortunately, the ship's doctor, a young man who served in this capacity in exchange for a vacation trip, had had Artur's attention at the party the night before. He was alert and intelligent, interested in music and respectful of Artur's work. Most important, he was sensitive to my husband as a man and to our need for discretion. The last thing wanted was for the press to discover the real nature of Artur's quasi-retirement. The little blurb on the husks of disks released by Westminster Recordings spoke of Rodzinski "preferring guest engagements to tenure." And although this was true in an artistic sense, the physical facts of the matter were that a steady situation would have killed him.

At any rate, the young doctor had those qualities and characteristics which made my husband follow his advice confidently. So Artur stayed in bed from the morning of the attack until it was time to put ashore in New York City. The doctor's visits were also therapeutic. The two daily spent several hours discussing a broad range of subjects, and Artur seemed much revived each time the younger man left. But in another respect the recovery was not as it should have been. While the enforced rest necessarily helped him hoard up energy for the ordeal ahead, Artur also kept to his bed for another reason: fear that he would not be able to keep his commitments. He only hinted about this dread, but it could be the only justification for his not being up and about as soon as he felt well enough.

This fear, and some other dark mood, also colored his dealings with the reporters and photographers who came aboard when the "Colombo" picked up the pilot. Artur's little jokes and whimsical poses were not at all convincing. Had the reporters assigned to cover such stories included the music critics who knew Artur personally, they would have seen through his act to the underlying issue he did not want ventilated as page-one copy. As it was, Rodzinski's return to conduct in America after an absence of eight years did make the front pages. The appearance of our friend Adlai Stevenson aboard ship to greet members of his family returning from Italy distracted the reporters, and none pursued the little slips Artur made. There were not even innuendos in print to give away our secret.

We went directly to the Carlyle Hotel rather than to Lake Placid. Artur had scheduled appointments with some members of the musical press. He also was involved with Arthur Percival, the laundromat millionaire who had purchased our home in Stockbridge, and who was still doggedly promoting the talents of his violinist wife.

Percival had been lavishing gifts on Arthur Judson, Bruno Zirato, and their various agencies in attempts to launch his wife's career, largely to no avail. The Diamond Concerto he had commissioned had yet to be premiered. (Indeed, as of this writing, the Concerto has disappeared, much to David's chagrin, for he has written and published two subsequent concertos, but is without even a copy of his first.)

Judson, while not taking Dorothea Percival's performing abilities seriously, had a characteristically avaricious interest in her husband's money, and so good relations existed between the two men at this time. And Percival, knowing how much Artur wanted to make up things with the Judson group, had suggested in his letters that he could bring my husband and at least Bruno Zirato together.

Preoccupied with Percival's schemes for an accord with Judson, Artur gave only half-hearted interviews to the reporters. Ordinarily, he delighted in outlining grandiose plans for the future, and in making outrageous statements which he knew to be good copy. This time, the reporters had to dig for their stories. Artur volunteered almost nothing, spoke with little enthusiasm about the forthcoming *Tristan* and Birgit Nilsson. He said nothing of the projected *Boris* in Chicago, let alone of signing contracts with La Scala to do Shostakovich's revised *Katerina Ismailova* and *Parsifal*. Most of what he did say sounded sarcastic and condescending, two attitudes that can inspire reporters to write stories of a kind Artur could hardly afford just then.

(*363*)

As soon as the press left, Artur grew irritable. "Why the hell doesn't Percival telephone?" he kept asking.

I obviously had no answer, and was not about to tell him all my efforts to track down the man had failed. Artur would simply not give up the idea of retrieving what he lost by the scandal of his Philharmonic resignation. He would even settle, at this eleventh hour, for an amicable relationship with Judson.

"There's no reason why we can't be civilized with each other," he said. "Zirato has always had a good word for me, and if Percival can bring about a meeting. . . ."

Artur's temper simmered all afternoon, and when Percival finally did arrive with Dorothea at five o'clock, I felt sure there would be a scene. There wasn't one — on Artur's part, at any rate. Percival appeared already much less than sober, and promptly insisted we take ourselves and our conversation down to the cocktail lounge where he proceeded to get drunker. He was completely unable to carry on a coherent conversation. Poor Artur kept trying to get some clue from him about his promised "plans" for a meeting with Zirato — to no avail. And all the while Dorothea sat by in bland composure.

When we left the Percivals, Artur was seething. The day had been squandered on a buffoon and a pipe dream, and an unnecessary revival of guilt feelings about the whole Judson-Zirato-Philharmonic debacle. That evening, after dinner, we went to visit my sister Marysia at her apartment on Madison Avenue. The reunion helped to cheer Artur, though Marysia was shocked by my husband's appearance.

"Good God, Halina," she said, "he looks terrible."

"Marysia," I replied, "you exaggerate. Wait until he gets to Riki Hill and some sunshine, and you will see how fit he will be."

We took the overnight train for Lake Placid and were met at the station by Ray Lincoln. In the few minutes' drive to Riki Hill, Artur's depression of the previous day vanished, dissipated by the bright sunlight and the thick green foliage of the birches, beeches, and evergreens that line the roads on the way to our home. The house had been rented that summer, with the help of Ray and his wife Lera who had planted the garden in the spring so that the place would look "lived in" when the agent brought prospective tenants.

There were pots of fiery red geraniums and boxes of red and purple petunias along the front porch railing, and in the flower beds Ray had seeded nasturtiums which still sent out their gold and coppery-red trumpets near my favorite phlox, delphiniums, and daisies. Artur was thrilled by the pines and spruces he had planted as a windbreak along the driveway. When last he saw them, they were only shoulder high. Now they had grown tall and strong, and were full of that gummy fragrance evergreens have at summer's end.

Artur set himself a strict regimen of exercise, rest, and food. He would take leisurely strolls on level ground, with either Riki or me for company, stopping at ten-minute intervals until his heart regained its natural rhythm, an exercise recommended by George Hart, the Lake Placid doctor who had treated Artur since 1950. Artur would take these walks, stopwatch in hand to time precisely his periods of movement and of rest, in the morning before lunch and in the evening before dinner. In the other hours, he stretched out on a chaise longue in the garden to tan. He wanted at least to look healthy for Chicago. Luckily, the weather throughout what remained of September was ideal, and his color improved.

Despite all the care he took with rest, exercise, diet, and the avoidance of emotional stress, Artur could not escape the fact that he was a very, very sick man, a reality which most painfully presented itself every morning. Getting out of bed was a miniature hell. He would first have to sit up to breakfast after an injection, then let his feet down over the side of the bed, pausing between each movement for his heart to regulate its beat to the new position. If he moved too fast, he would have immediate need for a nitroglycerine tablet to open the constricted blood vessels. Then came shaving, bathing, and dressing, every movement performed in slow motion. I stood nearby ready to assist whenever I saw him in difficulty; but, if I sensed he was edgy, I discreetly stayed out of his way. Even though he might need my help, an irritation could easily upset his heart. Whenever he was cheerful, he rather enjoyed my helping him tie his shoelaces or put on a jacket. He liked being treated like a child, though he hated being physically reduced to one.

Riki enrolled as a boarding student at Northwood School, no more than fifteen minutes' drive from the house.

One afternoon, after an overnight frost had helped to change the colors of the foliage, Artur and I walked across the meadow behind our house to admire the surrounding birches and beeches. The clover and alfalfa had been mown only a short time before and a fresh green smell still clung to the ground. Here and there, where the mowers' blades missed, an Indian paintbrush stood to wag its red-gold head. Artur had not had an easy time getting started for the day; he was upset by news from Cleveland the night before.

The pair of concerts he had expected to conduct in Severance Hall with "his boys" were dropped from the schedule. Artur, according to a letter from the board of directors, had asked an "exorbitant fee." Admittedly, it was a high sum for a conductor in those days, more like what top soloists were paid. But it was the amount the Lyric Opera had agreed to for each performance in Chicago. And Artur felt he was worth as much as any violinist or pianist to the orchestra he had built to a precision instrument in the ten years he directed it. Although the notice came from management, George Szell, then artistic director, was the man who must have made the decision. Artur took the cancellation as an artistic affront from Szell as well as a personal disappointment. He was the man whom Artur helped to start his New York career. It had been fifteen years since Artur conducted in Cleveland, and he yearned to see those players with whom he had shared so much musical growth. More than a handful of them had been cultivated by Artur while they were still students in the Curtis Institute training orchestra.

This unpleasantness shrouded his thoughts as we walked through the meadow, and when I made some passing remark about the sweet smell of a new-mown hayfield, he gripped my arm tightly and said, "You have no idea how I long to be under this grass, Halina. I am so terribly tired."

The words were not new — he had said that sort of thing in moments of dejection. But they pierced me through this particular time because of their tone of accepted defeat, and the look of utter bleakness which accompanied them.

"Artur," I said, "Cleveland will regret its actions, especially after *Tristan* in Chicago. They will be embarrassed."

"No," he replied. "It isn't Cleveland alone I think about. It is how exhausted I am with everything. But, then, you wouldn't understand — you are so healthy." And with that he gave my arm a loving squeeze and tried to be more cheerful as we walked toward the house and dinner.

Riki's going away to school depressed Artur, but the boy was home within a week with a throat infection. Although Artur would not permit himself to be exposed to his son's coughing and sneezing — any infection he contracted could have gotten far out of hand — he was cheered by Riki's presence in the house. Artur once again fell into a slump when Riki finally recovered and had to return to his dormitory. He went about his walks, with his Leica when I was not with him, taking still pictures of the rapidly changing fall colors. These slides were far different from any other autumnal portraits he had ever composed. These no longer sought to capture the fiery and dramatic displays of nature's final defiance to the approach of winter. Rather, he now learned to identify with nature's more subtle expressions of gentle resignation in facing the inevitability of slumber. The colors are soft shades of beige and grey and the subject matter delicate and fine; and the photographs are ultimately profoundly sad.

One afternoon while we were walking together slowly, Artur stopped to admire a sturdy old maple which grows by the side of the road to our house. It was in the full crimson fury of its autumn apparel. Several minutes passed, but he still stood looking at the tree, his head cocked to one side. It began to drizzle, and I suggested we start back, but he wanted to linger on regardless of the rain.

"I must remember this, Halina. The memory of it will have to serve me for a long, long time."

He had his camera with him, but he took no photograph that day, and on the days that followed he went for his walks with the camera left behind in its case in his room.

Except for the walks, and an occasional visit to or from Riki, Artur did little but rest through September and early October. He read the newspapers every day, and from time to time might pick up a book which struck his fancy, though he hardly read anything through.

George Hart invariably found some positive word for Artur which would lift his spirits, but he was not encouraging with me in private. After giving him an EKG one day, he said that there wasn't much to be done except make Artur comfortable, prevent stress, and so on — all the things that I had been doing for years. Still Artur insisted on being examined by physician after physician as if a laying on of the right doctor's hands would remove the fear of his heart attacks and eliminate the pain of angina.

On the evening of September 26 Artur and I were listening to the news when the telephone rang. It was Witold.

"Where are you calling from?" I asked.

"New York. I'm here with the Polish Delegation to the United Nations," was his reply. "I arrived just a while ago, and called Marysia. She told me you were up there — that Artur's not well." After a moment's hesitation, he asked, "Do you think he would speak with me?"

"I'll see," I replied as I put my hand over the telephone and whispered to Artur, "Witold. What shall I say?"

His face looked perplexed for a moment, then relaxed. "Let me talk to him. After all, he is my son."

I helped Artur from his bed, where he had been sitting propped with pillows, to the phone. Then I left the room for my own, next door. But I could hear what seemed like a cordial discussion. They kept referring to each other as "Old Man" in Polish, a warm sort of way they had when they sometimes spoke which I had not heard in many years. The call ended, and Artur informed me that Witold would arrive the following day for the weekend. He seemed very pleased with the idea, and equally pleased that he could put their differences aside. "After all, he *is* my son." He said the words with a pride that existed well apart from their political disagreements. Still, I was concerned. The two men could grate on each other's nerves. Both were determined to hold to their viewpoints. Both were as inflexible as evangelists. And both, from their respective stances, could make irritating good sense.

Instead of readying himself for bed, Artur sat down at the piano in his room and treated himself to an hour or so of Chopin, a mixture of the gayest waltzes, melancholy mazurkas, and one or two stirring Polonaises. His psychic barometer was up.

The next day, Witold and Artur greeted each other warmly. Handshakes became bearhugs with much patting of backs. Then they stood apart to take a long appraising look at each other. Witold could hardly conceal his surprise at Artur's appearance.

"You've grown a little older, Old Man," he said.

And Artur, amused, returned the compliment, for Witold, too, had aged. He was grey at the temples, not unlike Artur when he had proposed to me twenty-seven years before. But the changes in Witold's appearance bespoke some obvious strain in the four years since we had last seen him, when he came to Rome to visit with Artur following a heart attack.

The two stayed closeted away most of the time Witold was at Riki Hill, and I held my breath, waiting for the inevitable upsetting remark which could put them at each other's throats and lay Artur up for a week following another heart failure. But nothing of the kind was said. They talked over their political differences, the changes in their lives, their attitudes, and their views of the future with a composure that was rare. Indeed, it seemed as if Artur were the diplomat. Witold left that Sunday morning with an invitation to return the following weekend to celebrate his birthday with us.

When Witold was gone, Artur said, "We accept each other now for what we are. We're both older."

The next weekend I baked a cake which Riki, who was allowed home for a visit, and I secretly decorated while Witold and Artur once more were locked away talking. We surprised Witold with the cake after dinner. He was very moved, and we all believed him when he said, "This is my happiest birthday."

Riki and Witold got to know each other better. The two got on famously, establishing a closeness that, but for geographic separation, I believe would have grown stronger over the years. This sense of kinship between the two sons made their father happy. When it was time for Riki to return to Northwood on Sunday morning, the three drove off together in our blue Chevrolet. After dropping Riki off, Witold and Artur motored up Whiteface Mountain, the most imposing Adirondack peak, and accessible almost to the top by car and then he took Witold to the train station.

Artur remained indoors over the next few days, mostly propped up in bed with his scores of *Tristan* and *Boris,* singing to himself in a hoarse, croaking voice, and at every hour, interrupting himself to listen to the news. Pope Pius had fallen ill, and his condition was worsening with each report.

Ever since the Vatican concert, and the short audience that followed, Artur lived in hope of seeing Pius again. Just as he somehow believed that eventually he might find the physician who by his mere touch could release him from his physical pain, so he still sought a spiritual counselor who might do the same for his soul. As I remember the books that littered the table next to his bed, I can say that more than ever he was searching for some key to faith and peace of mind. I sometimes wonder if, had the chance presented itself, Pius might not have said just the right things to Artur, though Artur sought in Pius another Buchman.

In any event, the chance never came, for Pope Pius died on October 8. Artur was desolate, listening to the broadcast from the Vatican which announced his death. Tears streamed down his cheeks as he kept saying, more to himself than to me, "There was a strong bond between us." When the newscaster in the course of a background story on the days preceding the Pope's loss of consciousness, said Pius had asked to hear the recording of Beethoven's First Symphony which Artur had conducted for him that spring, Artur broke down completely.

We stayed up late into the night to hear the eulogies and homage paid to this great man, and when we eventually went to sleep, our hearts were in Rome.

Riki's absence from home was a loss that saddened Artur. But the loss of Pius deeply wounded him. Yet he preferred to be alone in his unhappiness, taking his exercise according to the doctor's program by himself. While I busied myself with chores about the house, I watched him through the windows as he ambled over the meadow or the front lawn, his brown leather jacket and corduroy slacks hanging from his drooping frame. He would stop periodically to rest, and stare down at the ground or fixedly on a cloud above, savoring each detail he observed with a quiet and loving intensity.

The afternoon before we were to leave for Chicago, we took one last drive through the countryside. A severe frost had finally struck, the trees along the Ausable gorge had turned their most brilliant and terminal hues, that one riotous statement which nature allows itself in the Adirondacks before the long, white sleep of winter.

At home, after dinner, Artur sat at the piano, and played for more than an hour before bed, singing in his hoarse voice from time to time. I recognized some of the music and words, but could not think of either their title or composer. I heard him very softly half sing, half speak, *"Still ist mein Herz und harret seiner Stünde! Die liebe Erde allüberall . . .,"* and then linger to caress the long-drawn phrases on the word *ewig* — ever.

The piano stopped, and I took that to be the cue to assist him into bed.

"What was that, Artur? I know it, but I can't recall."

"Mahler. *Das Lied von Der Erde,* he said quietly. "You know, that score was written fifty years ago this year — 1908. And he never lived to hear it, his farewell to earth."

Chapter 48

IF I had believed in omens, the events of the twenty-four hours before leaving from Lake Placid for Chicago could only have been read as a forecast of the worst. Artur created another of his nightmares about travel arrangements. We were to fly from nearby Saranac Lake to New York City where we would make connections for the Chicago plane. On the eve of our departure, Artur began to speak with increasing misgivings of travel in an unpressurized twin-engine plane, although he had flown in such planes many times in the past with no ill results.

I took most of this in stride. His keyed-up state before settling down with a new ensemble was understandably exacerbated by ill health. Knowing this, I was not unprepared for his announcement on arising the next morning. Artur had decided to travel by train.

There was still time to make new reservations, cancel old ones, and reconfirm those that could stand. There was time, that is, between packing clothing for several weeks, medicines, fetishes, books, scores, and all the other portable paraphernalia of an ailing conductor's establishment — and giving injections, preparing meals, and dealing with the telephone.

The phone service in the Adirondacks in those days was not the glory of the American communications industry. The only innovation since the time of Alexander Bell was that the subscriber no longer cranked for the operator's attention. To place a long-distance call was an interminable and confusing task, especially when pressed for time.

Between sessions with the telephone, I busied myself with my various jobs, one of which was sterilizing Artur's reusable plastic syringes (an English novelty that did not come to America until much, much later). I had just set an aluminum pan of them to boil on the electric stove when the telephone rang in Artur's room, at the opposite end of the house. The call and the wrangling over arrangements went on and on, and quite some time elapsed before I managed to get the last compartment on the night train from Lake Placid. When I hung up, Artur who was across the room propped in bed studying the *Tristan* score, asked if I noticed a peculiar odor. I looked to his doorway to see a reminder of the forgotten syringes, an opaque, blue cloud, moving down the hall. The smell was that acrid stench of melting and smoldering plastic and aluminum.

Artur was livid. He sprang out of bed, unassisted, charging me with trying to burn the house down. He also cursed me roundly for not having used the electric timer. All of this poured out of him as we stumbled into the kitchen through the blinding and choking smoke to turn on the exhaust fan and to open windows. I knew I had done nothing wrong, that nothing of the sort would have happened had it not been for the nonsense about changing our traveling arrangements, but I could not say a word — just choke on that thick, blue smoke and smell which hung hideously about the house until evening when Ray Lincoln came to drive us to the train. Although Artur was still furious he perked up on seeing Riki in the car. I had asked the Northwood School to allow the boy to come with us to the station. Like one of those mercury-weighted toys, Artur sprang back on his psychological feet the moment he saw his son, and the trip to New York was pleasant. Witold met us at La Guardia airport to pass an hour or so waiting for the plane with us. This, too, raised Artur's spirits, as did the reception in Chicago.

Byron Belt, a young assistant manager of the Lyric, met us at the airport along with a platoon of reporters and photographers. Belt was so sweet toward Artur, and the presence of the reporters so salutary for his ego, that he rose to the occasion. He struck the stance of the elder musical statesman returning to his homeland after a long and unjust exile. The air he conveyed was "as mellow as an autumn afternoon," to use the words of Donal Henahan, then on the *Chicago Daily News* staff.

Danny Newman had arranged our accommodations, and we found ourselves comfortably situated in the apartment of the Hotel Pearson's manager. This was a great convenience for me, since I could cook Artur's food without anyone questioning the nature of his diet. I had barely begun to unpack when the apartment was brimming with fresh flowers and friendly faces from a decade before. The phone rang constantly with good wishes to Artur, and each conversation with an old acquaintance was worth a shot of adrenalin.

When things quieted down, he set to work, all misgivings and fears forgotten. He conferred with the librarian about cuts in the score, made his wishes known to the chorus master, and had a reunion with his stage director from Cleveland's days of operatic glory, Wilhelm von Wymetal, who already had a fair idea of what was wanted in Chicago. Artur was so much like a field marshal engaged in battle that he even suffered questions from the Lyric's publicity staff with an unusual grace. Later in the day, Carol Fox and Lee Schaenen, the youthful conductor who had been selected (with Artur's approval) to assist at the rehearsals, came with bad news: the extra men from the Chicago Symphony which Artur had asked to have to fill the Lyric's ensemble to Wagnerian proportions were just simply not available.

When Miss Fox broke the news to him, Artur dropped the wreaths of smiles from his face, shed Don Henahan's "mellow afternoon in autumn" for something akin to the Ice Age.

(*371*)

"Why?" he demanded in a Caesarian sotto voce.

"Because Dr. Reiner has rescheduled rehearsals with the Chicago Symphony," was the terse and honest reply.

"I see," he said, turning on his heel to leave poor Miss Fox looking hurt and justifiably concerned.

When we were alone, he exploded. "How in God's name am I to make that bunch sound like a *Tristan* orchestra?"

The question was rhetorical. For purposes of balance he needed extra strings — if for nothing else, to cover the fullness of Wagner's brass writing.

The loss of the extra musicians, however, was another affront to Artur as an artist, one no less jealously motivated than Szell's cancellation of the pair of concerts in Cleveland (where, at least, the issue of Artur's fee demands served some justification).

Fritz Reiner was never friendly toward Artur. There was a period, at about the time of Artur's Philharmonic appointment, when Reiner aggressively courted Arthur Judson's favor. Certainly, there was no pleasure for Reiner in Artur's move to New York. But at the heart of the matter was the fact that after ten years' absence, my husband still had a strong hold on the popular imagination of Chicago's audiences. His year with the Symphony, though it ended in a disaster, was now a legend. Although Reiner had raised the orchestra to a technical level that made it peerless in some respects, he had none of Artur's panache or charm, or that sense of being excitingly in the center of things, including controversy. This *Tristan* especially concerned Reiner, for with the same work ten years before, Artur had sung his swan song so magnificently that the opera house still echoed the public's wild applause. It would do Reiner no particular good to advance another success for Rodzinski at his own expense, especially since conductors never really had a secure footing in that city. Artur would not have wanted the Chicago Symphony — even if made a lifetime gift of it with no strings attached. Walter Hendel, then Reiner's assistant and formerly Artur's at the Philharmonic, a man with whom we had had cordial, even close relations, was afraid to call Artur for old time's sake.

In the morning, Artur met with his assistant. After they discussed what was to be done with the score in general terms, Artur indicated very specifically what to rehearse carefully and gave Schaenen some advice on how to achieve the best results. I was not in the room while they talked, but I imagine young Schaenen must have said all the right things because Artur was cheered and his mood positive when the discussion ended.

Rehearsals with the orchestra went well — far better than Artur had imagined. Schaenen had the ensemble under control while Artur either sat behind the podium or paced the aisles nearby, only occasionally interrupting with suggestions. The piano rehearsals with the cast were another matter. Karl Liebl, the Tristan, had a good, sweet voice; he was not, however, a *heldentenor* to match the fullness of Birgit Nilsson's

Isolde. But Artur was kind and patient in a way that drew from Liebl the finest he could produce. Artur had an uncanny and peculiar genius with singers. It seemed he could give a frog the confidence to sing the Queen of Night. Grace Hoffman, the Brangäne, had a big voice with many warm and rich registers throughout her range, but her long Act Two monologue and duet with Isolde had Artur quite concerned. William Wilderman as King Marke and Walter Cassel as Kurwenal could be relied upon to turn in excellent performances. Artur's worry remained the crucial second act — how Hoffman and Liebl would come off against Nilsson.

Artur took the podium for the dress rehearsal two days before the performance, and a promise of success was in the wind. Everyone was pleased — everyone except Artur. More could be done with the second act, and on the day before the performance itself Artur wanted one more run-through. Nilsson said "no." She had much at stake. She was in Chicago for the first time, singing Isolde for an audience which still had Flagstad in its collective ear, and as Flagstad's "successor" she wanted to be in her best form. Artur, on the other hand, still had his old mania for rehearsals, and he was concerned with the performance's total effect. Although irritated, and not yet sure of a comfortable ensemble in the second act, Artur did not press the matter. He rehearsed the act without her, perhaps consoled by memories of how Nilsson's artistry had not failed him earlier in Florence. Moreover, he had other things to divert his attentions. One of his fetishes was missing — the rosary given him by our Florentine friend, Sister Ignacia.

"I cannot, I *will* not conduct without it," he said.

I cursed myself for not packing it, but in the idiotic travesty of the day we left Lake Placid, I forgot to make sure it was among the amulets I stowed in Artur's attaché case, along with the sweat-rusted pistol and a photo of Pius XII. We made a call to Northwood School to Riki who, in the company of a teacher, scoured the Lake Placid house for two hours, luckily coming across it in a briefcase of Artur's at the back of a closet. It arrived by plane and messenger in time for opening night, Saturday, November 1. All through the day, as 7:30 P.M. and the moment for his downbeat approached, Artur primed himself with the electricity he needed to carry off a good performance.

Some days before, in a conversation with "Wymie" von Wymetal, Artur had said: "There must be passion and fire, but one must be able to use an extinguisher if it gets out of hand." He continued, "There is an emotional pitch to which one must rise, but one cannot exceed it. The art is knowing when — and how — to pull back, to hold within bounds. Not every climax in making love can be the ultimate one."

We drove to the opera by cab, in silence. So high was Artur's pitch of emotional excitation he seemed to give off electrical sparks. One piece of the wrong sort of verbal tinder in his presence would have started a blaze.

When we got out of the car at the stage door, an attendant tried to relieve me of the frock coat I carried over my arm to conceal the sweater-wrapped oxygen tank clutched in my hand. It was a terrifying moment. The doorman's kindly gesture could have revealed to cameras and prying eyes that tell-tale apparatus. Artur coolly sailed ahead through photographers and Lyric management personnel to his Isolde's dressing room, as I mumbled something vague about superstitions and hurried after him.

At Nilsson's dressing room, Artur dropped off a suggestion or two, and complimented her on how handsome she looked in her costume. She was eager to be on stage, like a thoroughbred sure of her field and competition. When Artur reached his own dressing room, he called for his Tristan and Brangaene, and gave them also a few suggestions, plus a large dose of confidence which sent Miss Hoffman and Liebl away glowing. Somehow, Artur's electricity was contagious even before the music making actually began. These preliminaries over, I made sure the rosary, revolver, and picture of Riki and Pius were all in place. Artur was ready. Before I left him to the managers and performance, however, I made the Sign of the Cross on his forehead and over his heart, and kissed him for added good fortune. Then I made my way quickly to my seat in the front row, just behind the podium, where I could reach out and touch Artur had I wanted to.

The moment Artur's face was seen in the back of the pit by the audience in the highest parts of the gallery a roar of shouts and applause arose. I had often observed that semblance of transfiguration on his face as he looked up, to nowhere in particular, hands at his sides, to drink in the sounds of appreciation and approval, but I could not recall a time when he seemed too frail to confront it. He lifted his arms in a gesture of embrace to the house which further swelled its noise. Then he turned to begin. The silence which fell the moment his back was to the audience was as sure a sign of authority as that he then exercised over the orchestra and the singers on stage. From the first yearning, groping notes of the Prelude to the jubilant fanfares which bring King Marke and his retinue on stage, everyone in the performance (including the audience) was transcendent. The orchestra had never sounded so full, so rich, nor played so well in anyone's memory. Nilsson as before, took something from Artur which returned itself in the form of a dynamism that would carry him through the ordeal of the night. It was as though he had become Wagner's will and its executor.

Wagner once wrote to Mathilde von Wesendonck, his paramour at the time of the opera's composition, "This *Tristan* is becoming frightening. . . . I am scared that it will be forbidden . . . a bad performance might change it into a parody, but a perfect one might excite the audience to the point of insanity."

I am not a musician, and so I do not have the words that would technically explain what it was Artur did at each performance of *Tristan* which, increasingly over the years, had produced reactions of the sort

Wagner referred to; but whatever it might have been technically, spiritually it was in the realm of the mysterious or miraculous which laymen can sometimes understand. The applause at the end of Acts One and Two followed immediately and with an hysterical urgency. But when the curtain fell on those last soft chords of the final act, and Artur's barely noticeable baton fell gently to his side as he lowered his head into his sloping shoulders, there passed what seemed an infinity of rapt silence before once more a sea of applause welled up to engulf the house. Curtain call after curtain call was demanded by an audience that was on its feet to pay tribute to a creative act which had preternaturally occurred with them as witness. Nilsson was received by the Chicagoans as Flagstad once had been, and when Artur finally made his appearance on stage before the curtain with the principals, the ovation was deafening.

My sister Fela and her husband Kazik who had driven from their home in Oshkosh and I quickly made our way backstage while the artists took their bows. I saw Nilsson in the wings for a second, her face flushed with excitement and throbbing with life. She was waiting with Liebl and Hoffman to return to the stage for a bow with Artur who then stood alone before the great curtain, afloat in the adulation. "This was my greatest *Tristan*" she said, her breath coming in gulps, "It will never be the same again." Perhaps she exaggerated, perhaps not. She was still under the stress of the moment, filled with the emotions and the intensity of the performance itself. But years later, following her superb performance in *Tristan* in San Francisco (a production mounted by the company of which my son was by then artistic assistant) she cited the Isoldes she had sung with Artur as the greatest of her career.

The Krances and I threaded our way into Artur's dressing room past musicians packing up instruments, past stagehands dismantling and stowing scenery and costume trunks, and past those ranks of people who always are seen backstage but whose function no one knows. We arrived just a few moments before Miss Fox and Belt entered with Artur. He looked drained, pale to the point of transparency. He was terribly winded. He gave us a tired smile of greeting, then sat down to brace himself as the tide of well-wishers flowed in. Many of the people who came to pay their compliments were unashamedly crying.

Among the well-wishers were two artist-and-repertoire men from Capitol Records, the American affiliate of E.M.I. of London, with whom Artur had made his last recordings. They had been asked to fly in from California for the performance and prepare an estimate of the possibility of a recording. Both men were enthusiastic and raised our hopes that a Rodzinski *Tristan* would be made at last.

It was after midnight before Artur could change shirts and we all could leave for the Pearson, where Fela, Kazik, Artur, and I sat up until 3:00 A.M. The two musicians did a thorough postmortem on the performance and talked of music in general, while Fela and I spoke of our children and of the many small things that somehow were never included in our letters over the years since we were last together. Only when Artur felt wound down enough to sleep did we all say good night, the Krances to return to Oshkosh the next day.

In the morning Artur could hardly speak. He could not even raise his head from the pillow. I called Dr. Clifford Barborka, our musician-physician friend who had been the first to note an anomaly in Artur's electrocardiogram during the Chicago troubles nearly ten years earlier. He quickly came. After examining him, he said Artur's debilitation was understandable: "You are wrung out from yesterday's exertions, Maestro. You've got to stay in bed and conserve your strength."

That evening, after a day of dozing or drowsing, Artur was strong enough to talk. Our conversation quickly lapsed into the old, by now threadbare, game of agreeing while disagreeing, of trying to hold inevitable conclusions in abeyance. He spoke of his ill health, I reminded him of the doctor's advice about bed rest. Admittedly bed rest would see him through the next two *Tristans*, but he then would be utterly depleted. *Boris* would be impossible. I, countering with what I thought to be expected, spoke of the many times in the past when the same things had been said under similar circumstances and how, somehow, he nonetheless had found the stamina to pull through.

"It is different this time. You must call Miss Fox and cancel *Boris*. I will not be able to do it."

Secretly, I agreed with him. I had reservations about the Moussorgsky work from the outset, but still I recalled to him the many occasions when he had bounced back from ill health and fatigue with energy enough to fulfill cancelled commitments, only to destroy himself later with remorse and self-castigation.

"Artur, I am only thinking of how often this has happened in the past," I said.

"You can speak of the past all you wish. I have the present and the future to think about," he said curtly, and painfully reached into the drawer of the table beside his bed for a sheet of letter paper. He began writing. In a few minutes he handed me an envelope addressed to Riki.

"What is this about?" I asked.

"I want Richard's decision!" he came back at me acidly.

"For God's sake, Artur, must you drag in a child who is more than a thousand miles away?"

"Mail it!" he ordered, his voice at a whisper, and fighting for breath. I did, and the letter came back to dwell on my conscience later, though when I put it in the mail slot outside the apartment door, I thought only of Artur's suffering and Riki's likely confusion.

By the time Monday's papers arrived, Arthur was already up and around. A Sunday in bed had revived him, but the reviews were the restorative he truly needed. After reading them, he was almost in condition to conduct that same night.

Claudia Cassidy sang her usual hyperboles in the *Tribune* most of which read like promotional copy today. Artur, however, respected her musical sensibility, having attended concerts she covered, and often agreed with her estimates. Robert Marsh, whose opinion Artur valued, wrote equally enthusiastically in the *Sun Times*. The *Chicago American*'s Roger Dettmer matched the other two, praise for praise, but ended his review with a short paragraph which made Artur grin with pleasure:

> Maestro Rodzinski is back: we ought
> never again let him leave.

"I hope Reiner reads *that*," I said, with impish malice.

Rather than concur in the spitefulness of my remark, Artur said, "I hold nothing against him, really. We made it without his players. Besides, he doesn't have an easy time of it here."

In addition to the reviews, Monday brought Lee Schaenen and director Vladimir Rosing, with whom Artur had cleverly staged a *Faust* with the young Tucker and Hines in the Hollywood Bowl years before. They came to Artur to discuss *Boris*, still slated to premiere November 17. Although I dared not raise the subject, it appeared that Artur had deferred his decision to cancel that opera. Had he been in proper physical condition, however, he would already have been rehearsing the orchestra and chorus in this difficult work. With *Boris*, as with *Tristan*, he left all but a dress run-through to Schaenen whose skill he had come to appreciate. Indeed, Artur seemed so satisfied with the way things were progressing that the decision to drop the Moussorgsky seemed forgotten — at least, for the moment.

Dr. Barborka arrived to examine Artur soon after the men from the opera left. He found Artur's condition improving, but privately he expressed reservations about any immediate resumption of work. Certainly, he said, *Boris* was out of the question. As usual, I said that we should wait and see, even though deep within, I, too, knew there was little possibility of it. But I could not give voice to my fears and feelings. Living in public pretense from day to day, crisis after crisis, I could only say aloud that it was good the next *Tristan* was four days away. How much the pretense had begun to color my own sense of reality, I do not know; but I must have been buying myself hope, and time for Artur, when I told Dr. Barborka, "We will see how he is after the *Tristan*." The doctor, poor man, could merely shrug in agreement.

We passed those four days quietly. When Artur was not conferring with Schaenen or others from the Lyric, we watched television coverage of the events at the Vatican. Pius's successor had been elected, Giovanni Cardinal Roncalli, the Patriarch of Venice. Artur had been following the speculations in the press, on radio, and television like a member of the Papal Secretariat of State. When this wonderful man, so different from the stern and indomitable Pacelli, was chosen by the Consistory, Artur felt disappointed. We watched John XXIII's consecration as Pontiff on Tuesday, November 4. John's benign and aged appearance as he was carried into St. Peter's suggested none of the intellectual sharpness or strength with which he reinvigorated the Church in a way that would have been very much to my husband's liking.

As he watched John's hunched-over figure bless the applauding throng in the basilica's nave, Artur asked, "Why did they place so great a burden on the shoulders of such an old, tired man?" He might have been asking himself the same question.

The second *Tristan* was as splendid as the first in total effect. In its details, it was superior; that Friday night found the singers more tightly knit as an ensemble, and the orchestra playing and sounding better than ever. But the effort, as before, left Artur limp, and I wondered if there would be enough time before Monday, November 10, for him to recover the strength to carry off the intensified demands of a third performance. Given Artur's determined drive to draw the maximum from whatever resources he had, that second *Tristan* could only be considered yet another rehearsal. The last performance would represent what he had been striving for all along: he would scale expressive elevations with singers and orchestra to surprise even them, for the more they gave so Artur could give of himself.

The morning he was to conduct, he said, "I don't think I will be able to do it. I'm too weak."

I was frightened. This was out of character. I called Dr. Barborka, but he was not in town. His calls were being answered by a Dr. Keever who examined Artur and found his heart and blood pressure unchanged.

Though reassured by the doctor's words, he was listless throughout the day. That evening, in the cab to the opera house, he was still lower. He whipped up his fervor, however, and once in the dressing room, even before taking off his raincoat, he called Schaenen and the tenor, Liebl, to him, and sat at the piano to suggest some changes. He was particularly concerned with how Liebl should sing various phrases in his death monologue, particularly the words at the end of it, *"Das Schiff — säh'st du's noch micht?"* He wanted a decrescendo, almost to the point of a pitched whisper.

Liebl left, certain he could do what was asked. I then gave Artur his medications, blessed and kissed him, and went to my seat. The roar and applause which announced Artur's presence in the pit descended from the gallery — and were even louder and longer at the end of Act One.

But when Artur turned to accept the ovation at the end of the first act, Ellen Carpenter, who was sitting with me, was startled.

"Halina, I'm worried. He doesn't look as though he'll be able to finish," she said, pressing my hand in concern.

"Don't worry, Ellen," I replied. "He'll be all right, you'll see."

She joined me in Artur's dressing room while I helped him with a dry shirt, gave him some cola with several drops of coramine to sip, and injected him with camphoxil. He did not speak, though he acknowledged Ellen's presence with a warm smile.

(378)

The performance of Act Two was exalting beyond my ability to describe. Nilsson hit those three high C's Isolde sings before Tristan rushes into the garden as if she had been flown to them. When the curtain fell and the audience began to applaud wildly, Artur almost seemed reluctant to turn and accept his share of the ovation before leaving the pit. He looked at me and whispered hoarsely, "I won't be able to carry through to the end."

"Don't be afraid, darling," I said. "You'll find the power. You see how well it goes."

When Ellen and I entered Artur's room, he was stretched out on a sofa. "I can do no more," he said. "I can't."

There was nothing I could say. I knew how he felt, not just simply about the physical exertions on his worn body, but also his fear of reaching for those restrained climactic moments of the last act.

He returned to the pit to an aggressively enthusiastic audience. The applause was tumultuous. Yet Artur's sloping back and shock of thick white hair framed in a halo of light from his music stand brought instant silence. Then came the mournful, muted string chords of the Act Three introduction.

The poignancy of the timpani strokes, following Liebl's last phrases before his death, meant to represent the faltering and final beats of Tristan's heart, cut through me as they had rarely done before, or since. Then came Nilsson's *Liebestod*, not as the great set piece it often is in the hands of lesser artists, but as part of the flow of the work toward its inexorable end. With her velvety pianissimos, her expression of a love too great to survive the dead was that of both the Isolde of Wagner's fantasies and Artur's dreams.

The tumult which followed the few seconds' hush after the final curtain was almost as incredible as the performance. It seemed much like the response at a revival meeting — a blind, unreasoning outpouring of sentiment. Although the cheers and clapping were directed at the artists, they were equally a tribute to the audience's ability to be moved.

Artur was done for. Once back in his dressing room the last drops of physical strength and of will power drained away. His spirit, or Wagner's — even of that God he so wanted to believe in — had alone carried him through the rigors of the last act. His face was the color of beeswax, and his eyes had an unnatural glitter to them. He could barely breathe let alone respond to all the well-wishers who flooded in to see him.

Robert Marsh, of the *Sun Times*, in a burst of enthusiasm, came to congratulate Artur and deliver what he thought a piece of exciting news: Rudolph Bing, arch-enemy of Wagner at the Met was in the audience; the performance had decided him to mount *Tristan* the following season "with Nilsson, and Klemperer conducting!" The remark hurt — how much, Marsh never knew, for Artur just smiled sadly and nodded his head.

We left the theater in the company of von Wymetal and his wife,

Hilde, and took a cab for the Pearson. There the four of us critiqued the performance and Artur had a few drinks to relax and improve his circulation. Wymie was full of joy at working with Artur again. They talked of their prior *Tristans* and of *Lady Macbeth*, the opera which "put them on the map." Artur avoided speaking about his contract with Siciliani to do Shostakovitch's revised version, *Katerina Ismailova*, at La Scala the next season. "It would hurt his feelings not to be part of the crew," Artur later said as, once unwound, and with a few whiffs of oxygen, he felt he could sleep, at about 2:30 A.M.

After several hours, through a haze of sleep, I heard Artur call my name feebly, hoarsely.

"I cannot breathe . . . the doctor . . ."

His face was puffed, his eyes hurt, his legs were swollen and of poor color. His heart was not working as it should. I gave him the only aid I could, oxygen, before phoning the doctor. Dr. Keever came and found that Artur had experienced severe heart failure. He wanted to move him to a hospital immediately.

Artur adamantly refused. "If I am to die, it will be here. Nobody must know I am ill."

"But, Dr. Rodzinski, I simply cannot treat you here," the physician told him.

"No," was Artur's obdurate reply. "You can take me out of here in a coffin, but not an ambulance."

There was nothing further to say. Dr. Keever left in despair.

Later that morning, Dr. Barborka, back from his trip, joined his colleague in examining Artur. His diagnosis was the same, but he better understood Artur's mind and did not press for hospitalization.

"Of course, Artur, there is no thinking now about *Boris*," Dr. Barborka said. "Any work is beyond discussion for a long while to come." Artur seemed to take the news indifferently.

"Cancellations are nothing new these days," he said, "but we must find a way to conceal the cause."

"We could announce that you picked up an infection, a flu is going around," Dr. Barborka offered.

"Does that seem strong enough to you?" Artur asked. "You know how the press will insinuate something else. I do not have the best of reputations in some quarters."

The doctors left. Artur fell silent. After a few moments, he began thinking aloud: he really was not well . . . certainly not well enough to do an opera for some time to come . . . he should save himself for La Scala. Then, he made up his mind.

"Call the Lyric and tell Miss Fox I cannot conduct. Give her Barborka's story about the flu," he said.

I did just this, and what Artur all along had feared happened. When Miss Fox gave the story to the papers, a few writers with more malice than ink in their pens contrived copy which implied that Artur had fought with the Lyric's management. This greatly upset everyone there.

Far greater damage, however, was in the offing. *Time* magazine wanted "to do a story," ostensibly on the success of *Tristan*. What they were actually after was controversy, whether it existed or not. I offered the Chicago representative a telephone interview, and told him I had plenty of previously unpublished photographs. But the man insisted on talking with Artur and on bringing a photographer. Artur painfully got out of bed to play his part. "I cannot refuse them," he said, as I helped him into a dressing gown and ascot. "They like to needle and insinuate. We'll try and fool them."

When the reporter and his photographer came to the Pearson on Thursday, November 13, they found things which, had they been the least bit perceptive, would have told them the true story, not the piece of nonsense *Time* published. As it happened, the reporter saw the oxygen tank, but was innocent enough to accept my excuse: "He uses it to clear the congestion in his chest."

In the issue of November 24, they quoted Artur as saying that he "wouldn't accept a permanent job if . . . offered . . . on a golden plate" when asked if he would accept a post in Chicago. *Time* was inventing possibilities that denied facts. The magazine praised the performance of *Tristan*, but managed to convert Artur's cancellation of *Boris* into a "typical" Rodzinski stunt. When the reporter asked me why there were so many doctors in attendance if Artur had only the flu, I was quoted as replying that he needed them "to tell him . . . he's all right."

During the interview, the photographer urged Artur to assume a conducting pose. This sort of photo is always dreadfully false at best, and one might have thought the photographer, a fine craftsman, would have known this. Artur posed with great pain after a swallow of brandy to stimulate his heart. This led to two things — the worst series of pictures ever taken of Artur, and a parenthetical remark by Artur in the article, "I want to go out and get drunk!" I am quite sure at that moment he well may have wanted to. The physical and psychological strain of the interview was immense.

The photographer courteously sent me a set of the pictures later. To this day I cannot look at them without feelings of revulsion and pain. Yet there was an element of truth to them, too. The photo that appeared in the magazine, under the heading "Artur & The Dragons," caught the demonic side of his personality by inadvertence. Actually, it is a picture of a suffering man.

Despite his weakness and discomfort, Artur worked with Schaenen on *Boris*, discussing trouble spots and ways to handle them. In the eventuality a substitute conductor might not be found, young Schaenen would be obliged to direct a score that is difficult enough for the most experienced men. Miss Fox was fortunate, however. Georges Sebastian was available to take over at close to the last minute, and Artur and I were free to leave Chicago.

On November 18, my saddest birthday in more than a half century, Artur and I flew from Chicago to Boston once again in search of a miracle. Although Dr. Barborka had said Artur could recuperate in Lake Placid before embarking for Italy, Artur insisted we see Dr. Paul Dudley White. Artur was hopeful that in the two years since he had seen Dr. White in Rome research had yielded some new discoveries.

Since Artur would not use a wheelchair he had to use the walls to support himself as he walked the long corridors of the old O'Hare terminal to the flight gate. I could not assist him: my hands were full of luggage and coats. At one point I asked him to hold our tickets, and he could not.

Aboard the plane we were seated comfortably in a lounge area at the rear, and Artur, who, even ill, never missed a good-looking girl, enjoyed flirting with the charming and attractive stewardesses. He showed them his grotesque photo in *Time* — the issue covering *Tristan* was then on the newsstands — and asked the young women if he looked as old or mean as the picture. Their playful replies put him in such a good mood that, after days of almost no food, he agreed to eat a filet mignon. But he was too weak to cut the meat, yet too proud to appear so helpless. Somehow, one of the stewardesses sensed this and tactfully diverted him with a joke while I did the job almost unnoticed.

In Boston we went directly to Phillips House, the unit of Massachusetts General Hospital where Dr. White had his private clinic. Artur was admitted quickly and discreetly. A young assistant to Dr. White visited Artur within the hour to ask if he was satisfied with his room. He replied affirmatively, but inquired where I would stay. The doctor said there were hotel accommodations available nearby.

"If my wife can't be with me, I'll sign myself out," Artur snapped. His tone was so definite, the fuss he made so commanding that a Phillips House administrator swept a few rules into a closet and had a bed placed in Artur's room for my use. Artur slept well that night, better than I did. I was too anxious about Dr. White's visit.

The following morning that frail man, so small next to Artur, yet with more vigor in any two of his strides than my husband could summon to cross the entire room, gave him a thorough examination. Artur was like a child in Dr. White's presence, a very frightened, tired child. He submitted docilely to each of the physician's requests. When the cold metal of Dr. White's stethoscope touched his chest, Artur smiled as if his respite were finally at hand. The examination done, the doctor patted Artur on the shoulder and signaled with his eyes for me to follow him from the room. Artur was not the least bit suspicious.

In the corridor, Dr. White was candid: "It is serious, Mrs. Rodzinski — probably more serious than you realize."

His appraisal of my understanding was correct, for I recited in quick order all the times Artur had been knocked down by an attack only to recover and return to even more arduous tasks. He listened to my optimistic, faith-inspired recitation, which by now probably had the tone and style of a litany. And for a fact, I wanted to believe that the life

Artur had been living — a quasi-invalid's, really — could continue indefinitely. But there was a breach in my thinking between fact and fancy — between science and religious hope, to be precise.

"I shall do all I can," Dr. White said.

"Artur has faith in you, Doctor."

"You can see for yourself what I have prescribed," he said, showing me the chart on which he wrote as I talked. I was startled by what I read.

"But, Dr. White," I said in disbelief, "you *know* his entire medical history, you *know* what Demerol does to him."

"Mrs. Rodzinski, there's no reason to worry about an addiction this time," he said.

Artur was put under oxygen that day. His pulse rate had changed completely, which puzzled me, but when the once much-craved injection was administered by an assistant, with Dr. White in attendance, the look on Artur's face was one of peace and good cheer. The narcotic immediately dispelled his anxious fears along with his pain, and if there was an aspect of his expression which disturbed me, it was the look of separation.

"I am so happy, Halusia," he said. "I feel so secure in this man's hands." And he then drifted off to that nebulous world where the drug takes one, somewhere between what is real and a land where only pleasant fantasies are fulfilled.

In a few days Artur roused enough energy to study the scores of *Parsifal* and *Lady Macbeth* in piano reductions. He had received a letter from Siciliani, dated November 9, which said that Shostakovich had not too severely changed the work from the form in which Artur first knew it. Several scenes had been enlarged. A number of minor instrumental details, such as the trombone slides which once had shocked audiences, were eliminated altogether. And the vocal writing had been made more lyrical. Artur could refresh his memory and select a cast with the 1935 piano score.

He turned the pages of the heavy books slowly, painfully, every now and again stopping to concentrate with difficulty on some passage or other. The effort exhausted him.

Sick as he was, Artur continued to plan the coming season. I prepared his schedule, as I had for years, on large sheets of stiff paper so that he saw at a glance how his commitments for rehearsals and performances would fall. I was worried the calendar was becoming too crowded. There were concerts with RAI at Rome in January; February and March would be taken up at La Scala rehearsing for at least five demanding performances of *Lady Macbeth;* then *Parsifal,* with as many performances before Easter. There were to be concerts in April at Torino, and, once again, in May. In addition, the National Opera House in the Italian capital wanted Artur, and there were dozens of other invitations he had yet to accept. He had reached a peak of popularity in Italy

(383)

where he could have worked an entire season had his health permitted. And he was given carte blanche; with so little time or energy left, he was free to conduct whatever he wished.

"So many good things come to me now," he would say softly, dozing off for catnaps, exhausted by the efforts of figuring a schedule.

Witold was able to visit for a few hours. But Artur was under the oxygen tent and too sedated to say much of sense. The son quietly held the hand of his father silently.

On November 22, Riki came to pass his Thanksgiving recess with us.

The morning of November 25, Artur began to show new, unfavorable symptoms. His legs were swollen and had a blue cast. "There are blood clots," Dr. White explained, and recommended they be surgically removed. Artur would have nothing to do with the knife, still nurturing that fear of surgery which stemmed from his adolescence when an appendectomy had nearly killed him.

"I've suffered enough, Doctor," he said.

But the condition of his legs worsened, and the surgeon who examined them repeated White's advice. Artur held out still: "We'll talk about an operation some other time."

He was especially listless on Thanksgiving Day. "I feel strange today," he said, "something is different."

He was out of sorts, and oddly fretful. I stepped into the corridor for a moment, and he called, "Halina, don't leave me. Please don't go away."

Riki's visit cheered Artur a bit, but the boy had to leave early for a dinner party to which we both had been invited. Our hosts were people we knew in Cortina d'Ampezzo. They had two young daughters, and Riki, ever his father's son, was attracted to, or in love with, one or both of the girls.

I stayed with Artur. At one point, as I adjusted the oxygen tent for him, and when my back was turned, he said, "I love you."

I pretended the oxygen's hissing had kept me from hearing and asked him to repeat his words.

"You heard me," he whispered.

I tried to conceal my tears by fussing with his pajamas, but he brushed my attentions aside and told me to sit with him.

"You know, Halusia," he said, "that *Tristan*, I might not have done it as well as others have in my lifetime, but no one has ever loved it more than I have."

Toward the dinner hour, a young Polish nurse whom Artur liked came on duty on our floor. He urged me to go to the dining room and have a Thanksgiving dinner. I went, but I could barely swallow any food, and returned to Artur's room just as the nurse administered a Demerol injection. He asked if I ate well, when Riki might return. But the questions came from those dream-world shores along which the drug helped him to loiter.

"Where would I have been without you, Halusia?" he whispered. In moments, he was catnapping.

I kissed his hand and held it to my neck where he would not feel the tears that, try as I might, I could not hold back. I glanced at his face from the corner of my blurred eyes to see him whispering something, what, I cannot say. Then, with a quick, convulsive, deep breath, he rose up from his pillow to lurch over on his side, terribly calm, terribly still.

The doctors and nurses came at my call. They administered an injection directly into his heart, but Artur's body only responded in peace.

✑ *EPILOGUE* ✑

AFTER Artur's death, and for two long barren years, I lived only in an awareness of my physical loss. Although I paid lip service to the fact that he was free from the suffering which his body, his turbulent emotions, and circumstances inflicted on him, I was less conscious of his being at peace than of his absence from my life's routine. There were no longer the sounds of stirring in an adjacent bedroom to signal the start of another day, no freshly brewed coffee to bring to his room, no red and blue pencils to sharpen. Where once I had told the time of day by such chores I now watched clock faces as if they unfolded time without purpose. And there were also the silences to be reckoned with, those lengthy spans of daytime without a voice except that of an occasional caller on the telephone, an apartment house doorman, or the grocery clerk. There were no tensions, either. There was as much peace for me as at last there was for Artur. Our years of rages and quarreling were done with; but so, too, were the periods of tenderness and warmth which usually came with his reaffirmation of our love.

I seemed to live in a state of psychological, even physical vertigo. But I did have Riki to help me keep my balance. And soon enough, the mornings' sounds in a small New York apartment became attached to an altogether different round of duties and functions: the preparation of a boy's breakfast, the supervision of his toothbrush and washcloth, and hours he passed doing lessons.

After two years without music except from a radio or phonograph, I acquiesced when my sister Marysia insisted we attend a New York Philharmonic concert. I have no memory of the program, nor do I remember if I was able to listen. The hours in Carnegie Hall were too terrible, too emotionally intense for awarenesses beyond that of the experience itself. It was the first time I had heard the orchestra in that auditorium without the sight of my husband's shoulder line as the visual focus of my attentions. But the stage was a mass of familiar faces: Saul Goodman far to the rear at his kettles, William Lincer, the first viola, Harold Gomberg with his oboe, John Corigliano, and so many, many others. After the performance, Marysia urged me to go backstage with her to congratulate Lenny Bernstein. I was reluctant, not because of any bad feeling but it seemed such an awkward thing to do. Marysia prevailed, however, and we joined the queue of well-wishers in the Green Room. When Lenny greeted me with outstretched arms and that winning smile of his, another unpleasant hurdle back to reality, to a beginning again, had been leaped.

When still a girl, and mourning my mother's death, a family friend once said, "She did not die to rob her daughters of their youth." I now told myself the very same thing, that Artur had not died to take away my life, but rather to lead me to yet another life than the one we had once shared.

For one thing, he had left me the legacy of his name. The stature it had attracted countless charities who asked me to lend it time and again. I soon began to realize that my name had to be bestowed judiciously and with regard to the quality of the undertaking.

That I was a Pole and an American offered a number of likelihoods; and that my name was inseparable from things musical further expanded the choices. When still a girl I had been initiated in work for the blind and that interest was renewed when I joined the organization my brother-in-law Kazik Krance and Fela had begun in New York. My support brought me the title of president and I actively am working in behalf of the Committee for the Blind of Poland to support a training school for blind and crippled children at Laski, a suburb of Warsaw.

Where music is concerned, my charitable efforts involved the Harlem School for the Arts. Dorothy Maynor, her days of professional singing behind her, had begun the school. Through it she is bestowing upon the children of New York's ghettos a sense of dignity by providing them with the means to express themselves through music, painting, and theater. That was, and still is, a work too valuable for me to ignore. Both Dorothy's friendship and the Harlem School's accomplishments are among the treasures of my present life.

As east-west political tensions began to relax, I found myself a clearing house for visiting Polish musicians. A conductor one day, a composer the next, and then dozens of singers, pianists, violinists, cellists, and even a clarinet player made their way to my apartment door. From the vast assortment of talents that came to me for help, a few were of striking ability. But it was less my duty to assess their talents than to help them find financial assistance through the understanding offices of Dr. Eugene Kusielewicz of the Kosciuszko Foundation and to open the door for their artistry be it by arranging for auditions for sympathetic orchestra managers and conductors or by presenting them to the greatest teachers of our day. It is these dozens of adopted youngsters who give me a real joy as I watch them grow freely in a life of music.

The words *to grow freely in a life of music* have deep meaning for me because they contain much of what I learned from my years with Artur, and much of his bequest to others who stand on American podiums.

For Artur, the making of music was not simply the expedient expression of a talent — it was the spine of his existence, his way of life, a nonverbal philosophy which summed up his actuality. Although he was not a composer, his public art made the identical demands on him that a creative personality can exercise in private. He needed those same freedoms to pursue a composition in performance that the composer indulges in in the quiet of his study, the freedom to explore new depths and new horizons, and the freedom to encourage his audiences to follow.

This was what his quarrel with the New York Philharmonic was about. It was the essence of his dispute in Chicago.

His battle with the Philharmonic's management was that of the artist against a corporate structure which viewed his role as one of an expendable employee. His freedom to program, to develop audiences for a broad spectrum of music, was denied him because it ran counter to an obdurate business ethic. Artur's thrust for artistic independence also ran up against a corporate network of interlocking managements, agency-artist relationships, and personal power that, if not patently illegal, was surely unethical. All this has since changed.

Today, Pierre Boulez can look forward in the works he selects without the need to justify the artistic validity of his choices to an accounts-minded management. He can freely cultivate the audiences of tomorrow with music the young understand (and some of us older subscribers also enjoy the stimulation of the different sounds he generates).

Today, one can view Artur's gestures of defiance against the musical powers of his period as more than expressions of uncompromising idealism, as he himself often characterized them during his moments of regret and recrimination. True, his actions stemmed from turbulent forces within himself which, in the lives of other men, might have led to less-personally destructive and nearly as effective results. But though his battles initially appeared to the public, and even to Artur, as foolhardy acts, they now can be seen in the perspective of time as the price that had to be paid for the freedom his successors presently enjoy. As conductors' bequests to the future go, Artur's has proved not inconsiderable.

This new freedom, however, also comes at a price. As I reflect upon the era of the "giants" — the Toscaninis, Furtwänglers, Walters, Koussevitskys, de Sabatas, Reiners, Monteuxs, Beechams, Rodzinskis, and so forth — I am particularly reminded of what they all had in common: a profound awareness of and meticulous devotion to their craft. They were erudite craftsmen who would demand attention to each and every smallest detail with the absolute authority born of their wisdom and conviction. They were masters of a total concept. A Toscanini would leap out of the pit and dash on stage to correct an artist's slightest gesture which he might find to be inappropriate.

But in the giants' wake came a generation untempered by the conditions with which their predecessors had been faced. Furthermore, the transcontinental train and transoceanic ships were superseded by the airplane, and "jet set" idols were born more concerned with a brief appearance with an orchestra here and a short rehearsal period for an opera house there, and even the position of artistic director not of one but of two and perhaps even of three performing organizations simultaneously. What can these conductors give to an orchestra? Deprived of time and focus of commitment, they can simply not afford the indescribably painstaking task of caring about the maintenance of the most delicate and volatile of all instruments, the symphony orchestra.

With few exceptions, the orchestras have begun to enter a period of decline. In opera houses, non-performing administrators have taken the artistic helm, and in productions, stage directors have stepped into the conceptual void left by the sometime conductors.

But I have always been an optimist and in this instance believe that I have reason to remain one. My long life-span has witnessed many cycles. Practically born into the Warsaw opera at the turn of the century, I rode with Artur on the crest of a golden age as it unfolded in both American and European concert halls and opera houses. I witnessed many of the greatest artistic triumphs of our century; I then also observed many of its greatest losses.

Now, I am brought back to the opera house as Riki, who is an artistic administrator at the Metropolitan Opera, introduces me to the new wave of leadership. Although responsible to the Executive Director, his "boss" is the newly appointed Musical Director, James Levine. He is a brilliant conductor and is only thirty-two years old. In him, as in a few others of his generation, I once again see the emergence of the genuine craftsman. Among them there is an awareness of all the pitfalls; in their enthusiasm they are ultimately guided by a scrupulous dedication to their ideals which they pursue with unremitting artistic integrity.

It is a clear brisk autumn day in New York as I write the last lines of this Epilogue. I feel invigorated. It has all been most, most worthwhile.

ARTUR RODZINSKI ON RECORDS

Compiled by Michael Gray

Cleveland Orchestra/Columbia Records
1939–1942

Beethoven: Symphony No. 1
Berlioz: *Symphonie Fantastique*
Berg: Violin Concerto (L. Krasner)
Debussy: *La Mer*
Järnfelt: *Praeludium*
Kern: *Showboat* Scenario
Mendelssohn: Incidental Music for *A Midsummer Night's Dream*
Moussorgsky: Prelude to *Khovantchina*
Ravel: *Daphnis et Chloe*, Suite No. 2; *Rapsodie Espagnole; Alborada del Gracioso*
Rimsky-Korsakov: *Scheherazade*
Shostakovitch: Symphony No. 1; Symphony No. 5
Sibelius: Symphony No. 5
Strauss: *Till Eulenspiegel; Ein Heldenleben; Rosenkavalier* Waltzes; *Dance of the Seven Veils*
Tchaikovsky: *Marche Slav; Romeo and Juliet;* Symphony No. 5; 1812 Overture
Weber: Overture to *Der Freischütz*
Weinberger: *Under the Spreading Chestnut Tree*

NBC Symphony Orchestra/World's Greatest Music Records
1939

Franck: Symphony in D Minor
Tchaikovsky: Symphony No. 4

New York Philharmonic/Columbia Records
1944–1946

Bizet: Symphony in C
Brahms: Symphony No. 1; Symphony No. 2
Copland: *Lincoln Portrait* (Spencer)
Enesco: *Roumanian Rhapsody* No. 1
Gershwin: *An American in Paris*
Gould: *Spirituals*
Ibert: *Escales*
Moussorgsky: *Pictures at an Exhibition; Gopak*
Prokofiev: Symphony No. 5

(*389*)

Rachmaninoff: Piano Concerto No. 2 (Sandor); Symphony No. 2
Saint-Saëns: Piano Concerto No. 4 (Casadesus)
Tchaikovsky: *Nutcracker* Suite; Symphony No. 6
Wagner: Excerpts from *Lohengrin, Tristan und Isolde, Walküre;* "Siegfried Idyll"
Wolf-Ferrari: *Secret of Suzanne* Overture

Chicago Symphony Orchestra/RCA Victor
1947

Khatchaturian: Gayne Ballet Suite
Mendelssohn: Symphony No. 3
Strauss: *Also Sprach Zarathustra*
Wagner: Prelude and *Liebestod, Tristan und Isolde;* Prelude to Act III

Columbia Symphony Orchestra/Columbia Records
1950

Twilight Concert No. 1 (Works by Bizet, Liszt, Rossini, Tchaikovsky, Debussy, Mendelssohn, Rachmaninoff)
Twilight Concert No. 2 (Works by Dinicu, Franck, Debussy, Prokofiev, Gershwin, Offenbach, Rimsky-Korsakov)

Austrian Symphony/Remington Records
1952

Beethoven: Symphony No. 1; *Leonore* Overture No. 3

Volksoper Orchestra, Vienna/Westminster Records
1954

Chopin: Piano Concertos No. 1 and 2 (Badura-Skoda)
Franck: Symphony in D Minor; *Chasseur Maudit*
Mozart: Bassoon Concerto, K. 191 (Oehlberger); Clarinet Concerto, K. 622 (Wlach)
Schumann: Piano Concerto; *Konzertstück*, Op. 92; Introduction and Allegro, Op. 134 (Demus)
Tchaikovsky: *Swan Lake* and *Nutcracker* Suites

Royal Philharmonic Orchestra/Westminster Records
1954–1956

Beethoven: Symphony No. 5
Bizet: *Carmen* and *L'Arlesienne* Suites
Bloch: *Schelomo* (Janigro)
Borodin: Polovtsian Dances
Brahms: Violin Concerto (Morini)
Bruch: *Kol Nidrei; Canzone* (Janigro)
Dvorak: Symphony No. 9; Slavonic Dances, Op. 46 and 72
Franck: Symphonic Variations (Badura-Skoda)
Grieg: *Peer Gynt* Suites No. 1 and 2; Piano Concerto (Boukoff)
Ippolitov-Ivanov: *Caucasian Sketches*
Kodaly: "Galanta" Dances; "Marosszék" Dances; *Háry János* Suite

Moussorgsky: *Pictures at an Exhibition; Night on Bare Mountain*
Prokofiev: *Classical Symphony; Love for Three Oranges* Suite; *Peter and the Wolf*
    (Moore)
Rimsky-Korsakov: Piano Concerto (Badura-Skoda)
Schubert: Symphony No. 8 ("Unfinished")
Shostakovitch: Symphony No. 5
Strauss, Johann: Waltzes
Strauss: *Till Eulenspiegel; Don Juan; Rosenkavalier* Suite
Tchaikovsky: *Nutcracker* Ballet; Symphonies No. 4, No. 5, and No. 6; Violin
    Concerto (Morini)
Wagner: Orchestral excerpts

Royal Philharmonic and Philharmonia
Orchestras/EMI Records
1957–1958

Albeniz: Excerpts from *Iberia*
Falla: *Ritual Fire Dance;* Dances from *Three-Cornered Hat*
Glinka: *Ruslan and Ludmilla* Overture
Granados: Excerpts from *Danzas españolas*
Moussorgsky: Prelude to *Khovantchina*
Rimsky-Korsakov: *Russian Easter* Overture
Strauss: *Death and Transfiguration; Dance of the Seven Veils; Dance Suite after Cou-
    perin* (Philharmonia Orchestra)
Tchaikovsky: *Romeo and Juliet*

In addition to commercial records, broadcast tapes exist of Rodzinski performances of *Tristan und Isolde, Khovantchina, Der Rosenkavalier, Tann-häuser, War and Peace*, and *Pique Dame*.

Index

(*393*)

Bursitis, Rodzinski's, 83, 95
    treatment for, 74–78, 80–82, 99
Burton, Harold, 150

Café Ziemianska, 37
Caliet, Lucien, 109
California, attitude toward, 58
Camp Kilmer (New Jersey), concert at, 219
Capecchi, Renato, 333
Carmen (Bizet), 126, 127
    in Naples, 337
Carnegie Hall, 63, 95, 192
Carnegie Hall (film), 276
Carpenter, Ellen, 119, 295, 378
Carpenter, John Alden, 118–119, 295
Carraceni, 147
Carteri, Rosanna, 333
Cassidy, Claudia, 287, 295, 300, 305, 309, 376–377
    on *Tristan und Isolde*, 299
Caux sur Montreux (Switzerland), 312
CBS radio concerts, 152–153
Chairmen, sensitivity of, 137
Chapman, Frank, 351
Chicago (Illinois), 150
    Rodzinski's return to, 371–381
    See also Chicago Symphony Orchestra
Chicago City Council, 310
Chicago Symphony Orchestra, 184, 220, 222–223
    contract negotiations with, 301
    offer to Rodzinski, 287–288
    personnel changes in, 296
    Rodzinski's disengagement from, 303–310, 387
    Rodzinski's engagement by, 293
Children, Rodzinski's attitudes toward, 86, 132
Chotzinoff, Samuel, 121, 163, 183
Citizenship, Halina's, 196
Clark, W. C., Jr., 94
Cleveland (Ohio), 90–91, 123
    characterized, 115
    opera in, 114–115, 150
    Rodzinskis' arrival at, 105–106
    Rodzinski's invitation to, 59
    See also Cleveland Symphony Orchestra
Clevelanders, characterized, 90–91
Cleveland Plain Dealer, 105, 124, 136, 142
    on Rodzinski's departure, 224
Cleveland Symphony Orchestra, 91, 105
    board of directors of, 280

charity concert by, 218–219
and opera, 96–97, 103, 144–145
Rodzinski's departure from, 223–224, 227–228
Rodzinski's fourth season with, 150
Rodzinski's rejection by, 365–366
Rodzinski's second season with, 110–114
Rodzinski's sixth season with, 186–188
Rodzinski's third season with, 136–142, 144–145
tours of, 142
Colin, Ralph, 284, 285
Columbia Records, recording for, 202
Compliments, Rodzinski's attitude toward, 154
Conducting, Rodzinski's mannerisms of, 70, 109
Conductors, Rodzinski's advice to, 244
Contemporary music, controversy over, 244–246
Cooley, Carleton, 150
Copland, Aaron, 117
Corelli, Franco, 333
Corena, Fernando, 333
Countess, The (Moniuszko), 139
Courtship, Halina's and Rodzinski's, 47–50, 55
Craft, Robert, 261
Creston, Paul, 246
Critics
    evaluated, 347
    See also Reviews; *names of critics*
Curie-Sklodowska, Mme. Marie, 30
Curtis Institute of Music (Philadelphia), 35, 110
Czapski, Jozef, 40
Czapski, Marya, 40

Damnation of Faust (Berlioz), 220
Damrosch, Papa, 189
Daphnis et Chloe (Ravel), 166, 167, 236
Death and Transfiguration (Strauss), 7, 61
Death of Rodzinski, impact of, 8, 385–386
Defauw, Désiré, 287, 300
Der Rosenkavalier (Strauss), 133, 138, 349
De Sabata, Vittorio, 346
    Toscanini on, 79
Detroit Symphony Orchestra, 84
Dettmer, Roger, 377
Die Meistersinger (Wagner), 103
Die Walküre (Wagner), 103
Distin, William, 275
Divine Poem (Scriabin), 189–190

(*401*)